CONSEQUENCES OF IMPAIRED CONSENT TRANSFERS

Legal rules and principles do not exist in isolation, but form part of a system. In this structural comparison between English and German law, Birke Häcker explores the rules and principles governing impaired consent transfers of movable property and their reversal in two- and three-party situations.

This book is a re-publication of a work first published by Mohr Siebeck in Germany.

Consequences of Impaired Consent Transfers

A Structural Comparison of English and German Law

Birke Häcker

·HART·
PUBLISHING
OXFORD AND PORTLAND, OREGON
2013

HART PUBLISHING

Bloomsbury Publishing Plc

Kemp House, Chawley Park, Cumnor Hill, Oxford, OX2 9PH, UK

1385 Broadway, New York, NY 10018, USA

HART PUBLISHING, the Hart/Stag logo, BLOOMSBURY and the Diana logo are trademarks of Bloomsbury Publishing Plc

First printed by Mohr Siebeck Tübingen in 2009. Reissued in Hardback in 2013 by Hart Publishing Ltd.

A catalogue record for this book is available from the British Library.

Library of Congress Cataloging-in-Publication data

ISBN: 978-1-84946-565-6

Typeset by Compuscript Ltd, Shannon

Meinen Lehrern

Denn nur durch Vergleichung
unterscheidet man sich
und erfährt, was man ist,
*um ganz zu werden, der man sein soll.**

Preface to the Republication

This is a republication of a monograph first published in 2009 by Mohr Siebeck (Tübingen) as volume number 223 of the StudIPR series (*Studien zum ausländischen und internationalen Privatrecht*) edited by the Max Planck Institute for Comparative and International Private Law (Hamburg). The text is unaltered bar the correction of a few typographical errors.

Although case law and literature have – of course – not stood still since then, the basic structural observations proffered here are unaffected by recent developments. In particular, English law continues to adhere to the traditional 'unjust factor' approach to determine when a right of restitution for unjust enrichment arises. As Lord Sumption pointed out in the *FII* litigation, it still does not recognize a *condictio indebiti* along Civilian lines but instead requires the claimant to identify an established ground of restitution (*Test Claimants in the Franked Investment Income Group Litigation v Revenue & Customs Commissioners* [2012] UKSC 19, at [162]).

One debate in English law which has lately gained fresh impetus, however, is that relating to mistaken gifts. In *Pitt v Holt*, the Supreme Court ruled that a voluntary disposition could only be set aside where there had been a "causative mistake of sufficient gravity" such that it would be "unconscionable" to let the transaction stand (*Pitt v Holt, Futter v Futter* [2013] UKSC 26, at [122] ff). This makes the argument advanced here in favour of a pure causative mistake test (at pp 113–19) harder to sustain. It remains to be seen how the seriousness criterion will be applied in practice, in how far it can actually help distinguish between different types of (motivational) mistakes, and whether its implementation will in due course necessitate the development of a fully-blown English theory of gifts. For the time being, the reader should simply bear these issues in mind.

I am grateful to Richard Hart and the whole team at Hart Publishing for making the republication possible.

München, July 2013 *Birke Häcker*

* Thomas Mann, *Joseph und seine Brüder (Joseph in Ägypten).*

Original Acknowledgements

This book is an updated version of a thesis written at the University of Oxford between Michaelmas Term 2004 and Trinity Term 2007, during my time as a Prize Fellow of All Souls College. It was inspired and due to be supervised by the late Professor Peter Birks, who passed away shortly before I could begin working on it. I am extremely grateful to Mr William Swadling for taking over as my supervisor and providing invaluable guidance and advice throughout the project, and to Professor Andrew Burrows and Professor Reinhard Zimmermann for acting as my DPhil examiners. The *viva voce* examination took place on 5 November 2007.

All Souls College was a haven and a home: I owe a huge debt of gratitude to this wonderful institution and to the Warden and Fellows for all their support and kindness over the years. My thanks are further due to Professor Stephan Lorenz and his staff at Ludwig-Maximilians-Universität München for the hospitality extended on various occasions, as well as to Professor Andrew Ashworth, Associate Professor Elise Bant, Dr Paul Brand, Professor James Edelman, Dr Thomas Krebs, Mr Ben McFarlane, Professor Thomas Rüfner, Mr Andrew Scott, Professor Robert Stevens, Professor Hannes Unberath, and Professor Stefan Vogenauer for their open ears, good advice, and many lively discussions on matters great and small. I am particularly indebted to Professor Charles Mitchell for his numerous comments on an earlier draft of the manuscript, to Ms Beatrice Dafft for checking individual chapters, and to Dr Sebastian Lohsse for his kind help and meticulous eye at the proof stage.

The manuscript was finalized in the summer of 2008. I have sought to incorporate such case law and literature as was available to me before the end of June, though it was possible to take account of some later developments. All Souls College generously provided the funding for this publication. I am grateful to the Max Planck Institute for Comparative and International Private Law (Hamburg) and Mohr Siebeck for accepting the study into this series as well as to Ms Ilse König for her patient aid with the formatting.

Finally, and most importantly of all, I would like to thank my dear husband, Tobias Reker, and my dear parents, Otto and Heide Häcker, without whose love, encouragement and unfailing support this book would never have been written.

München, December 2008 *Birke Häcker*

Overview of Contents

Part Three: Three-Party Situations

Part Four: Summing Up

Table of Contents

Part Two:
Two-Party Situations

Part Three:
Three-Party Situations

Table of Abbreviations

ABGB	Allgemeines Bürgerliches Gesetzbuch (Austria)
AC	Appeal Cases (3rd series)
AcP	Archiv für die civilistische Praxis
Ad & El	Adolphus & Ellis' Queen's Bench Reports
aff'd	affirmed
AG	Aktiengesellschaft
Alberta L Rev	Alberta Law Review
All ER	All England Law Reports
All ER (Comm)	All England Law Reports (Commercial Cases)
ALR	Allgemeines Landrecht für die Preußischen Staaten (Prussia)
alt	alternative
Am J Comp L	American Journal of Comparative Law
App Cas	Appeal Cases (2nd series)
arg e	argument from (*argumentum e*)
Art	Article
Atk	Atkyns' Chancery Reports
B	Baron
BAGE	Entscheidungen des Bundesarbeitsgerichts
Barn & Ald	Barnewall & Alderson's King's Bench Reports
Barn & Ad	Barnewall & Adolphus' King's Bench Reports
Barn & Cress	Barnewall & Cresswell's King's Bench Reports
BC	Borough Council
Beav	Beavan's Rolls Court Reports
Begr	Begründer (founding author/editor)
Best & S	Best & Smith's Queen's Bench Reports
BGB	Bürgerliches Gesetzbuch
BGB-E	Entwurf eines bürgerlichen Gesetzbuches für das Deutsche Reich
BGH	Bundesgerichtshof
BGHZ	Entscheidungen des Bundesgerichtshofes in Zivilsachen
Bing NC	Bingham's New Cases, English Common Pleas
Bl H	Henry Blackstone's Common Plea Reports
BLR	Building Law Reports
Brod & Bing	Broderip and Bingham's Common Pleas Reports
Bros	Brothers
BS	Building Society
Burr	Burrow's King's Bench Reports tempore Mansfield
CA	Court of Appeal
CA in Ch	Court of Appeal in Chancery
Can Bar Rev	Canadian Bar Review
Can Bus LJ	Canadian Business Law Journal

CB	Common Bench Reports
CB NS	Common Bench Reports, New Series
CC	Code Civil (France)
CCR	Crown Cases Reserved
cf	compare (*confer*)
ch(s)	chapter(s) (abbreviation used when referring to a cited piece of work)
Ch	Law Reports, Chancery Division (3rd series)
ChD	Chancery Division
ChD Com Ct	Chancery Division, Companies Court
Ch App	Chancery Appeals
CJ	(Lord) Chief Justice
CLC	Commercial Law Cases
CLJ	Cambridge Law Journal
CLP	Current Legal Problems
CLR	Commonwealth Law Reports (Australia)
CLY	Current Law Year Book
Cmnd	Command Paper (abbreviation used for papers issued 1956–86)
Co	Company
Colum L Rev	Columbia Law Review
Com LR	Commercial Law Reports
Corp	Corporation
Cr & Ph	Craig and Phillips' Chancery Reports
Cromp M & R	Crompton, Meeson & Roscoe's Exchequer Reports
CUP	Cambridge University Press
DB	Der Betrieb
DC	Divisional Court
De G F & J	De Gex, Fisher and Jones' Chancery Reports
De G J & S	De Gex, Jones and Smith's Chancery Reports
DJZ	Deutsche Juristen-Zeitung
Doug	Douglas' King's Bench Reports
East	East's Term Reports, King's Bench
ed(s)	editor(s)
Edin L Rev	Edinburgh Law Review
edn	edition
eg	for example (*exempli gratia*)
El Bl & El	Ellis, Blackburn & Ellis' Queen's Bench Reports
ER	English Reports
ERPL	European Review of Private Law
esp	especially
et al	and others (*et alii*)
etc	and so forth (*et cetera*)
EWCA Civ	England and Wales Court of Appeal (Civil Division)
EWHC	England and Wales High Court
Ex	Law Reports, Exchequer Cases
ex p	on behalf of (*ex parte*)
Exch Ch	Exchequer Chamber
Exch Rep	Exchequer Reports
f/ff	next/following
fn	footnote (abbreviation used when referring to a cited piece of work)

gen ed	general editor
Harv Int LJ	Harvard International Law Journal
HC	High Court
HCA	High Court of Australia
HL	House of Lords
(LR) HL	Law Reports, English and Irish Appeals
(LR) HL Sc	Law Reports, Scotch and Divorce Appeals
HMSO	Her Majesty's Stationery Office
Hurl & C	Hurlstone & Coltman's Exchequer Reports
Hurl & N	Hurlstone & Norman's Exchequer Reports
ibid	in the same place (*ibidem*) (abbreviation also used to refer to another passage in the same case or in the same piece of work)
ie	that is (*id est*)
Inc	Incorporated
InsO	Insolvenzordnung
IR	Irish Reports
IRC	Inland Revenue Commissioners
J	Mr(s) Justice
JCL	Journal of Contract Law
JherJB	Jherings Jahrbücher für die Dogmatik des Bürgerlichen Rechts
JR	Juristische Rundschau
Jurid Rev	Juridical Review
JuS	Juristische Schulung
JW	Juristische Wochenschrift
JZ	Juristenzeitung
Kay & J	Kay & Johnson's Vice Chancellor's Reports
KB	Law Reports, King's Bench (3rd series)
KBD	King's Bench Division
KO	Konkursordnung
KTS	Konkurs, Treuhand, Sanierung: Zeitschrift für Insolvenzrecht
LBC	Lawbook Co
LC	Lord Chancellor
Ld Raym	Lord Raymond's King's Bench and Common Pleas Reports
LJ/LJJ	Lord Justice / Lord Justices
LJ Exch	Law Journal Reports, Exchequer New Series
Lloyd's Rep	Lloyd's (List) Law Reports
Lloyd's Rep Bank	Lloyd's Law Reports: Banking
LMCLQ	Lloyd's Maritime and Commercial Law Quarterly
Loy LA L Rev	Loyola of Los Angeles Law Review
LQR	Law Quarterly Review
LR	Law Reports (1st series: abbreviation dropped after 1875)
LS	Legal Studies
LT	Law Times Reports
Ltd	Limited
Mass	Massachusetts
Maul & Sel	Maule & Selwyn's King's Bench Reports
Mees & W	Meeson & Welsby's Exchequer Reports
Mer	Merivale's Chancery Reports
Mlle	Mademoiselle
MLR	Modern Law Review

MR	Master of the Rolls
n/nn	note/notes (abbreviations used when referring to a footnote in the current chapter, unless otherwise indicated)
NJW	Neue Juristische Wochenschrift
NJW-RR	Neue Juristische Wochenschrift: Rechtsprechungs-Report
No(s)	Number(s)
NSWSC	New South Wales Supreme Court
NSWSC Comm	New South Wales Supreme Court, Commercial Division
NZBLQ	New Zealand Business Law Quarterly
NZCA	Court of Appeal of New Zealand
NZHC	High Court of New Zealand
NZI	Neue Zeitschrift für das Recht der Insolvenz und Sanierung
NZLR	New Zealand Law Reports
NZ L Rev	New Zealand Law Review
OGH BrZ	Oberster Gerichtshof für die Britische Zone
OJLS	Oxford Journal of Legal Studies
OLG	Oberlandesgericht
OUP	Oxford University Press
p/pp	page/pages (abbreviation used when referring to the present book)
para(s)	paragraph(s)
PC	Privy Council
PCB	Private Client Business
plc	public limited company
Pty Ltd	Proprietary limited company
QB	Law Reports, Queen's Bench (3rd series)
QBD	Queen's Bench Division
QBD Comm	Queen's Bench Division, Commercial Court
QBD TCC	Queen's Bench Division, Technology and Construction Court
R	The King/Queen (*Rex/Regina*) = The Crown
RabelsZ	Rabels Zeitschrift für ausländisches und internationales Privatrecht
rev'd	reversed
RG	Reichsgericht
RGZ	Entscheidungen des Reichsgerichts in Zivilsachen
RheinZ	Rheinische Zeitschrift für Zivil- und Prozeßrecht des In- und Auslandes
RLR	Restitution Law Review
Rly	Railway
s/ss	section/sections
SA	Société anonyme
sic	as in the original
SpA	Società per Azioni
StBG	Strafgesetzbuch
Str	Strange's King's Bench Reports
Taunt	Taunton's Common Pleas Reports
TLR	Times Law Reports
tr	translator
TR	Dunford & East's Term Reports, King's Bench
TruLI	Trolley's Trust Law International
U Chi L Rev	University of Chicago Law Review
UK	United Kingdom

UKHL	United Kingdom House of Lords
UKPC	United Kingdom Privy Council
UWALR	University of Western Australia Law Review
v	against (*versus*)
Ves Jun	Vesey Junior's Chancery Reports
vol(s)	volume(s)
WLR	Weekly Law Reports
WM	Wertpapier-Mitteilungen
You	Younge's Exchequer in Equity Reports
ZEuP	Zeitschrift für Europäisches Privatrecht
ZHR	Zeitschrift für das gesamte Handels- und Konkursrecht
ZSS (RA)	Zeitschrift der Savigny-Stiftung für Rechtsgeschichte (Romanistische Abteilung)

Short Glossary of German Terminology

German	English (or Latin) equivalent
Abstraktionsprinzip	principle of abstraction
Anfechtung	~ rescission / avoidance
arglistige Täuschung	~ fraudulent misrepresentation
Aussonderung	segregation (in insolvency)
Besitz	possession
Besitzer	possessor
bösgläubig	~ *mala fide*
dinglicher Vertrag	real contract / real agreement
Eigenschaftsirrtum	mistake as to an essential characteristic
Eigentum	ownership
Eigentümer	owner
Eigentümer-Besitzer-Verhältnis	relationship between owner and illegitimate possessor
Eingriffskondiktion	infringement-based restitutionary claim
Erklärungsirrtum	mistake as to declaration (of intention)
Ersatzaussonderung	segregation of substitutes
Fehleridentität	identity of defect
gutgläubig	~ *bona fide*
Inhaltsirrtum	mistake as to content (of a declaration of intention)
Leistung	performance
Leistungskondiktion	performance-based restitutionary claim
Naturalrestitution	specific reinstatement
Nichtleistungskondiktion	non-performance-based restitutionary claim
Rechtsgeschäft	legal transaction
Rechtsgrund	legal basis / cause
redlicher Besitzer	~ *bona fide* possessor
Schuldvertrag	obligatory contract
Trennungsprinzip	principle of separation
Treuhand	~ trust
Treuhänder	~ trustee
Übergabe	delivery
ungerechtfertigte Bereicherung	unjustified enrichment
Verfügung	conveyance / disposition
Verfügungsgeschäft	dispository transaction
Verpflichtungsgeschäft	obligatory transaction
Vertrag	contract
Wegfall der Bereicherung	disenrichment / change of position
widerrechtliche Drohung	~ duress
Willenserklärung	declaration of intention

Part One:

Setting the Scene

Chapter I

Introduction

A. Aim of Project and Methodology

Although this book is based on a thesis, it does not contain a θέσις (*thesis*) in the sense of a single intellectual proposition which it sets out to prove. Instead, its aim is in some respects more modest, in others perhaps more ambitious. The book seeks to explore the fundamental structures pertaining to a core area of private law in comparative perspective. It analyses the English and German law on impaired consent transfers and their consequences, paying particular attention to the way in which the interplay of various legal rules and principles[1] determines the processes by which such transfers are unwound (both in terms of personal and property rights).

Take the following example: A sells and delivers or makes a gift of a painting to B, but he does so on the basis of some incorrect assumption or while under some form of pressure.[2] How do English and German law respond to this and similar situations? That depends on a large number of different parameters, such as the proper characterization of the factors inducing and influencing A's actions, the nature of the transaction(s) between A and B, whether or not B is still in possession of the painting and – where he has passed it on to a third party C, eg by way of sale or gift – the exact circumstances of B's dealing with C. In both legal systems, the outcome of the stipulated case and any variation on it is the product of a complex interaction between (primarily) the rules and principles of con-

[1] The terms 'rules' and 'principles' are not co-extensive. Principles are general legal maxims whose implementation requires concrete rules: cf K Larenz, *Methodenlehre der Rechtswissenschaft* (6th edn Springer, Berlin 1991) 437–90, esp 474–82. Yet the demarcation line between the two is fuzzy in practice, such that 'rules' and 'principles' often overlap, especially in a non-codified legal system like the English. Both terms are used here to indicate that we are concerned with general maxims as well as concrete norms of varying specificity. No attempt will be made in what follows to draw a clear boundary between abstract principles and concrete rules, and both terms will, moreover, be employed interchangeably for legal norms of a certain level of generality.

[2] For exposition purposes, the word 'pressure' is used in a very broad sense within the present chapter, encompassing both threats emanating from another party ('duress') and more subtle forms of inter-personal influence, typically resulting from a relationship of emotional or other dependency ('undue influence'): see below, text to n 36.

tract law, property law and the law relating to the reversal of 'unjust' or 'unjustified' enrichments. Metaphorically speaking, these rules and principles, though originating in different branches of the law, together constitute the component parts of an intricate machinery whose operation within each legal system is the subject-matter of this book. It is hoped that a comparison of the machinery's structures will not only contribute to the ongoing dialogue between English and German lawyers in the relevant fields, but will also enhance our understanding of each legal system as such. Knowledge of foreign solutions to similar problems often opens our eyes to the strengths and weaknesses of our own approach.

Given the aim of the current investigation, its methodology is to a large extent predetermined. At a fundamental level, it shares many of the features of traditional comparative law functionalism as espoused most prominently by Konrad Zweigert and Hein Kötz.[3] By asking how the German and English legal systems respond to the problem of impaired consent transfers, and in particular what rules and principles play a role in their reversal, the book focuses on the functions which these rules and principles perform in balancing all the competing interests at stake. Of course, as with most functionalist projects, it is virtually impossible to frame the research question in entirely neutral terms.[4] The very notion of an 'impaired consent transfer' imports certain legal connotations. What is 'consent', and when is it 'impaired'? What is meant by 'transfer', and how is a transfer effected within a given legal system? While the task of delineating these terms and thus the scope of our inquiry more precisely can be postponed until later,[5] it is worth stressing here that reference to certain (shared) legal concepts and categories will be inevitable. This is because, in view of its overarching structural concern, the present book is much more interested in the *legal* than in the *social* background and function of the rules and principles it investigates.

---

[3] T Weir (tr), K Zweigert and H Kötz, *An Introduction to Comparative Law* (3rd edn OUP, Oxford 1998) 32–47. On functionalism generally see eg M Graziadei, "The Functionalist Heritage" in P Legrand and R Munday (eds), *Comparative Legal Studies: Traditions and Transitions* (CUP, Cambridge 2003) 100; J Husa, "Farewell to Functionalism or Methodological Tolerance?" RabelsZ 67 (2003) 419, esp 422–34; R Hyland, "Comparative Law" in D Patterson (ed), *A Companion to Philosophy of Law and Legal Theory* (Blackwell, Oxford 1996) 184, 187–90; R Michaels, "The Functional Method of Comparative Law" in M Reimann and R Zimmermann (eds), *The Oxford Handbook of Comparative Law* (OUP, Oxford 2006) 339.

[4] Cf M van Hoecke, "Deep Level Comparative Law" in M van Hoecke (ed), *Epistemology and Methodology of Comparative Law* (Hart, Oxford 2004) 165, 169–70; Hyland in *Companion* (n 3) 189.

[5] See below, section B of the present chapter (pp 9–13).

The emphasis on exploring and comparing rules and principles as part of a larger *system of law* also accounts for a number of methodological departures from traditional functionalism. According to the orthodoxy, "the solutions we find in the different jurisdictions must be cut loose from their conceptual context and stripped of their national doctrinal overtones".[6] Kötz has thus likened the functionalist approach to that of a 'black box', into one side of which is fed the 'problem' and which spews out the 'solution' on the other.[7] However, he also notes that outcomes are often less interesting than the processes by which they are generated.[8] The aim of the present book is to explore the inside of the English and German 'black boxes' in order to highlight and compare their internal processes *as such*. To this end, it is necessary to jettison a basic distinction commonly drawn by comparative lawyers: that between a rule-based and a case-based approach.[9] The former proceeds by comparing and contrasting individual rules, principles and concepts in the abstract, while the latter looks at the outcome of actual (or hypothetical) cases. Yet in order fully to understand the solutions produced by a legal system in respect of a particular problem, it is essential to look at both rules and cases equally. Rules and principles do not operate in isolation, but in conjunction with other rules and principles, and on the basis of a certain conceptual framework.[10] The outcome of concrete cases is, in turn, determined by the interaction between such rules and principles when applied to a specific factual scenario. To see the whole picture, we must adopt an integrated approach which regards rules and principles as axioms whose combination gives shape to the legal system and yields solutions to cases. Only an awareness of the structural setup endows us with the ability to recognize when, how, and why a variation of the underlying facts, or the change of a particular rule, alters the outcome of a given case.

Connected with the focus on the internal operation of the 'black box' constituted by each legal system are a number of further departures from orthodox functionalism. First and foremost among them is the rejection of the famous – and equally notorious – *praesumptio similitudinis* (presump-

---

[6] *Zweigert & Kötz* (n 3) 44.

[7] H Kötz, "Abschied von der Rechtskreislehre?" ZEuP 1998, 493, 505.

[8] Ibid. M Rheinstein, "Teaching Comparative Law" (1937–38) 5 U Chi L Rev 615, 621, even claims that a "general morphology of law" can be developed "in no other way ... than on the basis of a structural, formalistic comparison".

[9] Cf eg van Hoecke in *Epistemology and Methodology* (n 4) 167–69.

[10] This is the reason why E Rabel, "Aufgabe und Notwendigkeit der Rechtsvergleichung" RheinZ 13 (1924) 279, 281, called for more *systematische Rechtsvergleichung* (system-oriented comparison). The essay is reprinted in HG Leser (ed), *Ernst Rabel: Gesammelte Aufsätze, vol 3: Arbeiten zur Rechtsvergleichung und zur Rechtsvereinheitlichung 1919–1954* (Mohr Siebeck, Tübingen 1967) 1.

tion of similarity) which has its roots in the observation that "as a general rule developed nations answer the needs of legal business in the same or in a very similar way".[11] Like its anti-functionalist counterpart, that deriving from the so-called 'difference theory',[12] the presumption of similarity is liable to restrict the comparative inquiry unduly by pre-empting its conclusions.[13] It is preferable to start off without any presumptions, either of similarity or of dissimilarity, and to be on the lookout for both phenomena. In fact, the comparison between two legal systems may be most rewarding where similar rules or principles, as a result of their interaction with other rules and principles, lead to different outcomes, or where the solutions of cases converge despite apparent discrepancies in the applicable rules and principles.[14]

Next is the question of perspective. Traditional functionalist doctrine maintains that the comparatist has to adopt "an outsider's non-normative view of different legal systems, which is opposite to that of legal dogmatics or practice oriented national legal study".[15] In so far as this approach protects a lawyer trained in one legal system from the dangers of assessing foreign rules as if they formed part of his own system and from false *déjà vu* experiences,[16] it has much to commend itself. However, as regards each legal system individually, the adoption of an internal point of view becomes inevitable if we are to appreciate the mechanisms operating within the 'black box'. Comparability is then reached not by means of an external epistemic perspective, but through the possibility of mapping different systems across one another using the various similarities and discrepancies between individual rules and principles as reference points. All this requires us to commit to is the perception and treatment of national law as a

---

[11] *Zweigert & Kötz* (n 3) 40. G Dannemann "Comparative Law: Study of Similarities or Differences?" in M Reimann and R Zimmermann (eds), *The Oxford Handbook of Comparative Law* (OUP, Oxford 2006) 383, 395, points out that, on closer inspection, the presumption applies only to *outcomes* of cases and "only to those areas of (a) substantive (b) private law which (c) are not culturally or politically sensitive".

[12] Advocated most prominently by G Frankenberg, "Critical Comparisons: Rethinking Comparative Law" (1985) 26 Harv Int LJ 411, and P Legrand, "The Same and the Different" in P Legrand and R Munday (eds), *Comparative Legal Studies: Traditions and Transitions* (CUP, Cambridge 2003) 240.

[13] Hyland in *Companion* (n 3) 190. Cf also Husa RabelsZ 67 (n 3) 424–25; Michaels in *Oxford Handbook* (n 3) 269–72.

[14] Cf Dannemann in *Oxford Handbook* (n 11) 406–8; van Hoecke in *Epistemology and Methodology* (n 4) 171.

[15] Husa RabelsZ 67 (n 3) 438. Similar also: R Sacco, "Legal Formants: A Dynamic Approach to Comparative Law" (1991) 39 Am J Comp L 1, 25, who describes the comparative method as "the opposite of the dogmatic".

[16] Cf O Kahn-Freund, "Comparative Law as an Academic Subject" (1966) 82 LQR 40, 52–54.

coherent 'system' rather than just an accumulation of rules. There can be no doubt that German law fulfils that postulate. Its Civil Code (*Bürgerliches Gesetzbuch*, abbreviated BGB), in particular, is the product of centuries of systematization. More difficulties are caused by English law, whose incremental development via forms of action[17] and non-academic practice in the Inns of Court long obscured the potential for system-building.[18] Yet even the Common law tradition is not beyond the reach of the Gaian institutional scheme, as already demonstrated by the works of Bracton and William Blackstone.[19] The cause has most recently been championed by the late Peter Birks. He was convinced that the Common law was at least as amenable to a classification in terms of events as Civilian legal systems.[20] Today, his writing on the subject provides something like a 'common frame of reference' for an ever increasing number of Common lawyers throughout the world.[21] This book avowedly adopts Birks' scheme as the basic framework of the 'system' of English private law. It is hence premised on the assumption that rights – whether personal or proprietary – are generated by events, the three nominate categories of events being 'consent', 'wrongs' and 'unjust enrichment'.[22]

Finally, a word on what the book is not intended to do. Traditional functionalism envisages an evaluative stage after the process of description and comparison has been completed. The comparative lawyer is encouraged to

---

[17] On the history of the forms of action see JH Baker, *An Introduction to English Legal History* (4th edn Butterworths, London 2002) 53–70.

[18] Cf eg T Weir, "The Common Law System" in R David (gen ed), *International Encyclopedia of Comparative Law, vol 2: The Legal Systems of the World, ch 2: Structure and Divisions of the Law* (Mohr Siebeck, Tübingen 1974) 77, 77–80 ([2–82]–[2–86]).

[19] G Woodbine (ed) and S Thorne (tr), *De Legibus et Consuetudinibus Angliae: Bracton on the Laws and Customs of England* (Harvard University Press, Cambridge/Mass 1968–77); W Blackstone, *Commentaries on the Laws of England: vols 1–4* (Clarendon Press, Oxford 1765–69), reprinted in facsimile by the University of Chicago Press (Chicago 1979).

[20] Esp P Birks, "Definition and Division: A Meditation on *Institutes* 3.13" in P Birks (ed), *The Classification of Obligations* (Clarendon Press, Oxford 1997) 1; P Birks, "Rights, Wrongs, and Remedies" (2000) 20 OJLS 1. On the advantages of having a taxonomy see also E McKendrick, "Taxonomy: Does It Matter?" in D Johnston and R Zimmermann (eds), *Unjustified Enrichment: Key Issues in Comparative Perspective* (CUP, Cambridge 2002) 627.

[21] See eg A Burrows (ed), *English Private Law* (2nd edn OUP, Oxford 2007) esp xxix–xxxiii (Burrows); J Edelman and E Bant, *Unjust Enrichment in Australia* (OUP, Sydney 2006) esp 1–14; M McInnes, "Taxonomic Lessons for the Supreme Court of Canada" in C Rickett and R Grantham (eds), *Structure and Justification in Private Law: Essays for Peter Birks* (Hart, Oxford 2008) 77, esp 79–91; and many of the contributions in A Burrows and A Rodger (eds), *Mapping the Law: Essays in Memory of Peter Birks* (OUP, Oxford 2006).

[22] A fourth, ragbag category encompasses 'miscellaneous other events'.

assess which legal system provides the 'best' solution to the problem under consideration.[23] Often, this has the purpose of furthering some project of harmonization or even unification of law.[24] No such goal is pursued here. Instead, the study exhausts itself in what has variously been described, perhaps in an allusion to Hans Kelsen's 'Pure Theory of Law',[25] as '*Reine Rechtsvergleichung*' (pure comparative law).[26] This is not to say that there will not be occasion to consider the appropriateness of one or the other actual or supposed rule within the national legal system. In fact, that is an almost inevitable by-product of the descriptive and the comparative stages. Depicting English or German law from an internal point of view entails, after all, an account of the issues which are unsettled or disputed, and may at times even require commitment to a certain position. Those questions which have a bearing on the further discussion will have to be resolved within the relevant system before any comparison starts, while other, less pertinent ones will be raised but left open. At the next stage, comparison itself may prompt us to rethink orthodoxies normally taken for granted – not because the other legal system adopts a different solution *per se*, but because the process of comparison exposes or highlights self-standing inadequacies of the system concerned.[27] Sometimes, therefore, the book will contain suggestions for how German or English law could or should be reformed. However, since any modification of a rule within the 'black box'

---

23 *Zweigert & Kötz* (n 3) 43–44, 46–47. But note that Rabel RheinZ 13 (n 10) 280, did not regard *Rechtskritik* (critical evaluation of law) as part of comparative law proper.

24 Sceptical about functionalism's suitability as a tool for unifying law: Michaels in *Oxford Handbook* (n 3) 376–78.

25 Cf H Kelsen, *Reine Rechtslehre: Einleitung in die rechtswissenschaftliche Problematik* (Deuticke, Leipzig 1934); H Kelsen, *Reine Rechtslehre. Mit einem Anhang: Das Problem der Gerechtigkeit* (2nd edn Deuticke, Wien 1960); M Knight (tr), H Kelsen, *Pure Theory of Law: Translation from the second (revised and enlarged) German edition* (University of California Press, Berkeley 1967).

26 Cf eg H Stoll, "Zur Legitimität und normativen Relevanz rechtsvergleichender Argumente im Zivilrecht" in H Koziol and P Rummel (eds), *Im Dienste der Gerechtigkeit: Festschrift für Franz Bydlinski* (Springer, Wien 2002) 429, 434. M Schmitthoff, "The Science of Comparative Law" (1939–41) 7 CLJ 94, 96, attributes the phrase *Reine Rechtsvergleichung* to Ernst Rabel without, however, giving a reference. Building on his earlier essay in RheinZ 13 (n 10), Rabel indeed uses the phrase in E Rabel, "Rechtsvergleichung und internationale Rechtsprechung" RabelsZ 1 (1927) 5, 6 fn 1, and again in E Rabel, "Die Fachgebiete des Kaiser-Wilhelm-Instituts für ausländisches und internationales Privatrecht (gegründet 1926) 1900–1935" in M Planck (ed), *25 Jahre Kaiser-Wilhelm-Gesellschaft zur Förderung der Wissenschaften, vol 3: Die Geisteswissenschaften* (Springer, Berlin 1937) 77, 81–82, reprinted in *Gesammelte Aufsätze: vol 3* (n 10) 180, 185–86. Note that Rabel was writing before the first edition of Kelsen's seminal work (n 25) had been published.

27 Dannemann in *Oxford Handbook* (n 11) 416; Michaels in *Oxford Handbook* (n 3) 379–80.

has potential repercussions for the entire machinery of the legal system, most of these suggestions must remain tentative. Their desirability and feasibility cannot usually be assessed by reference to impaired consent transfer cases alone. Reform proposals typically require a wider policy debate which this book does not seek to furnish. All it endeavours to do is identify areas worthy of (renewed) attention and indicate how a particular solution might best be implemented in light of the overall framework and pre-existing structures of the legal system.

Ultimately, therefore, the present study contains a number of major or minor theses on either English or German law, or on how they are best viewed in relation to one another, instead of a grand overarching argument. If the absence of a single θέσις needs to be accounted for, then it can be put down to the fact that the project is targeted first and foremost at a better understanding of the structures shaping the two legal systems in the area of impaired consent transfers. And if "[t]he primary object of comparative law, as of all sciences, is knowledge",[28] then the enhancement of understanding must be a legitimate primary aim of any comparative study.

B. Scope of Inquiry

On both the German and the English maps of the law, the envisaged research topic covers potentially vast areas. A complete analysis of *all* the consequences flowing from *any* type of transfer to which the transferor's consent is *somehow* impaired would far exceed the confines of this study. It is therefore necessary to refine the scope of inquiry in certain respects without losing sight of the 'big picture' which is central to the idea of a structural comparison. Let us look at each element of the book's title in turn.

First, what is meant by 'transfer'? The word is ambiguous. It is sometimes used generically to denote a shift of value or wealth from one person to another, but it can also refer – more specifically – to a change in the possession of an object, or to the passing of that all-embracing property right over the object which is usually termed 'ownership', but which is better described as 'title' as far as the English common law is concerned.[29] The act by which ownership or title is transferred from one person to another is commonly called a 'conveyance'. When this book speaks of the 'conveyance of an object', it means a 'transfer of ownership' for the purposes of German law and a 'transfer of title' for the purposes of English

---

28 *Zweigert & Kötz* (n 3) 15. Cf also Rabel RheinZ 13 (n 10) 285; Sacco (1991) 39 Am J Comp L (n 15) 1–6.

29 See below, Chapter II.D.1.a (pp 36–37).

law. Of course, the conveyance of an object usually entails a transfer of value to the transferee and will often be accompanied by a transfer of actual possession. The primary concern here is with 'transfers' as conveyances.[30] Since, however, most problems connected with defective conveyances arise in cases where the transferee has obtained possession of the object from the transferor, we will focus on conveyances that are brought about by, or are at least followed by, a transfer of actual possession (in the sense of a physical delivery of the object in question).[31]

The operation of those fundamental legal rules and principles which determine the validity and finality of a transfer are most clearly exposed where the transfer relates to a corporeal object[32] and when it is an informal one. Registration requirements and similar formalities tend to obscure the picture. The inquiry is therefore restricted to informal conveyances of tangible, movable property ('choses in possession'). Intangibles and estates in land are excluded from express consideration, as are any formal modes of conveyance applicable to movables (such as transfers of title by deed in English law). However, to the extent that cases involving intangible assets or formal transfers of tangibles illustrate a more general point or legal principle, they are nevertheless taken into account. Conversely, many of the observations and conclusions arrived at will, with appropriate modifications, also have a bearing on conveyances of interests in land and on transfers of intangibles (especially so-called 'choses in action').[33]

Second, when does a transferor's agreement to the transfer rest on 'impaired consent'? The book looks only at transferors who have the potential to give full and free consent. Its ambit does not extend to the special rules governing infancy and mental incapacity.[34] The typical impairments of consent which can affect a fully competent adult are mistake and pressure (in the widest sense of the word). A mistake is any erroneous belief con-

---

[30] This includes all transfers intended by the transferor to have conveyancing effect, whether or not the transfer of ownership/title is actually successful. To avoid confusion, transfers of value in the generic sense or transfers of (merely) possession will be explicitly referred to as such where appropriate.

[31] For present purposes, actual possession can be equated with *unmittelbarer Besitz* (cf § 854 I BGB).

[32] Only corporeal objects, defined in § 90 BGB as 'things', can be owned and possessed.

[33] On the English distinction between 'real' and 'personal property' as well as the sub-divisions of the latter into 'choses in action' and 'choses in possession' see eg *English Private Law* (2nd edn) (n 21) [4.13]–[4.20] (Swadling); ELG Tyler and NE Palmer, *Crossley Vaines on Personal Property* (5th edn Butterworths, London 1973) 11–14.

[34] On the rules governing transactions entered into by minors or by persons lacking the requisite mental capacity see overview in E Peel, *Treitel: The Law of Contract* (12th edn Sweet & Maxwell, London 2007) [12–001]–[12–063], and cf also the Minors' Contracts Act 1987 as well as the Mental Capacity Act 2005.

cerning an existing state of affairs. It is constituted by incorrect factual data in a person's mind.[35] It may be spontaneous or induced by some misrepresentation. The latter can be fraudulent, negligent, or wholly innocent. Inter-personal pressure broadly takes two forms.[36] One is direct compulsion, ie the threatening of a person with some (actual or perceived) evil unless he or she behaves in a specified way. In law, this compulsion may or may not be illegitimate and thus amount to 'duress'. The other form of pressure is the exercise, whether advertently or inadvertently, of emotional or other influence accompanying certain close relationships of trust and confidence ('undue influence'). With the exception of a special constellation relating to fundamental mistakes shared by both parties,[37] the present book will look at the entire spectrum of such impairments. Yet insofar as an impairment of the transferor's consent has an *external* cause, the focus is on the paradigm case in which it is referable to the transferee as the other party to the transaction. Mistakes induced by outsiders or pressure emanating from third parties will not be specifically considered.[38]

Describing the inquiry as concerned with 'impaired consent transfers' is, in the light of what has been said so far, potentially misleading, at least to German readers. They are accustomed to thinking of the conveyance as a separate and independent – 'abstract' – transaction from any (contractual) obligation underlying it.[39] Viewed from this perspective, the book title may suggest that only the conveyancing stage is at issue and that certain impairments, especially so-called 'motivational mistakes' inducing the transfer, are irrelevant. Yet that is not the case. Given the aim of sketching out the 'big picture' and the basic functionalist starting point, the notion of an 'impaired consent transfer' must be understood broadly to encompass all conveyances influenced and accompanied by an impairment of consent. These conveyances have to be appraised in conjunction with any obligatory transactions preceding them.

---

[35] Cf *Roles v Pascall & Sons* [1911] 1 KB 982 (CA) 987 (Buckley LJ); *Great Peace Shipping Ltd v Tsavliris Salvage (International) Ltd (The Great Peace)* [2002] EWCA Civ 1407, [2003] QB 679, [28] (Lord Phillips MR). There is a question about whether and when ignorance of a particular fact can also count as or entail a mistake: cf eg D Sheehan, "What is a Mistake?" (2000) 20 LS 538, 541–45. Usually, the relevant data will be actively on a person's mind.

[36] Pressure can also be purely circumstantial, resulting eg from extreme poverty. Such circumstantial pressure is rarely recognized and will not be specifically considered.

[37] See below, text to nn 40–44.

[38] For a historical and comparative analysis of third party involvement see S Martens, *Durch Dritte verursachte Willensmängel* (Mohr Siebeck, Tübingen 2007).

[39] On the so-called principles of separation and abstraction see below, Chapter II.D.3.b (pp 49–50) and Chapter III.B.1 (pp 58–59).

Third, why the emphasis on the 'consequences' of such transfers? This is because we are here more interested in the characteristic mechanisms pertaining to their reversal (where applicable) than in outlining the exact scope of all recognized impairments. Of course, the nature of a defect and its legal qualification have a bearing on the consequences that flow from it. To that extent, the defect itself as well as its larger context acquire central importance. We will therefore typify impairments of consent and the way they are brought about (eg fraudulently or negligently induced mistakes of various sorts, pressure amounting to duress, etc) without, however, asking whether – outside a core area – the relevant categories are completely co-extensive (eg whether the ambit of fraud by non-disclosure, or economic duress, is wider in English or in German law). It is hoped that once the fundamental structures of each legal system have been exposed, borderline cases can simply be slotted into their appropriate place.

The special constellation which, though squarely within the parameters outlined above, is excluded from the present inquiry relates to what English lawyers call 'common mistake' and what is familiar to German lawyers under the term *Fehlen der Geschäftsgrundlage*.[40] Where two parties enter into a contractual relationship on the basis of a shared misapprehension about some fundamental aspect, such that the performance of the contract becomes something "essentially different" from what the parties envisaged,[41] they may exceptionally be able to recover assets transferred in pursuance of the agreement. In English law, common mistake automatically renders a contract void *ab initio*,[42] and the transaction is reversed according to the normal rules and principles of unjust enrichment. German law, by contrast, regards adjustment of the contractual terms as the primary remedy and allows for termination only as a measure of last resort.[43] Common mistake and *Fehlen der Geschäftsgrundlage* are, in many respects, more closely aligned with the doctrine of frustration (*Wegfall der*

[40] Note that the match between common mistake and *Fehlen der Geschäftsgrundlage* is not exact, eg in relation to initial impossibility. Prime examples of common mistake cases under English law, such situations are governed by special rules on impossibility in German law (§ 275 BGB). For an account in English of the German position and a comparative discussion see B Markesinis, H Unberath and A Johnston, *The German Law of Contract: A Comparative Treatise* (2nd edn Hart, Oxford 2006) 319–48.

[41] Cf *Bell v Lever Bros Ltd* [1932] AC 161 (HL) 218 (Lord Atkin).

[42] The possibility of rescission in equity for less serious shared mistakes, as suggested in *Solle v Butcher* [1950] 1 KB 671 (CA), has since been forcefully rejected by the Court of Appeal in *The Great Peace* (n 35).

[43] The doctrine of the so-called 'transactional foundation' (*Geschäftsgrundlage*) is judicial in origin and has recently been codified in § 313 BGB.

Geschäftsgrundlage) than with the ordinary law governing mistake.[44] There is no particularly noteworthy interaction with the other rules, principles and concepts considered here. A comparative discussion, though undoubtedly rewarding in its own terms, would add little to the present analysis and has therefore been thought dispensable.

C. Structure of Book and Main Theses

Due to the absence from this book of a core argument in favour of a single proposition, any preliminary overview is bound to be cursory. It would be premature at this stage to pre-empt all the observations and suggestions which are prompted by the structural comparison of English and German law. Their relevance would not be obvious without the surrounding context. All the present section is intended to do is provide the reader with a 'map' of the book. What follows is therefore a brief outline of the book's basic structure as well as the theme and content of each chapter, including any main theses put forward in it.

Together with this introduction, Chapter II sets the scene for the ensuing body of six substantive chapters. By comparing and contrasting in the abstract some basic principles of English and German contract law, property law, and the law of unjust(ified) enrichment, it seeks to elucidate the conceptual background to the various rules which determine the practical outcome of cases and whose interplay will be explored later on. In this sense, Chapter II acts as a bridge between doctrinal premises and functional analysis.

The body of the book is then split into two main parts. The first (Part Two, encompassing Chapters III to V) deals with the consequences of impaired consent transfers in 'pure' two-party situations. These are constituted by the basic case in which no strangers to the transaction are involved at all. The second main part of the book (Part Three, encompassing Chapters VI to VIII) considers some of the special questions arising when the transferee has conveyed or purported to convey the object on to a third party before the transferor has had a chance to assert rights he may have in respect of it. Both legal systems will always be dealt with individually before comparative observations are made.

Chapter III accordingly contains an exposition of the fundamental parameters shaping the transferor's relationship with the transferee under the German BGB. In particular, it explains how the so-called 'principle of ab-

---

[44] Cf § 313 I, II BGB; *Bell v Lever Bros Ltd* [1931] 1 KB 557 (CA) 584–85 (Scrutton LJ); *The Great Peace* (n 35) esp [61]–[75], [85], [90], [156].

straction' leads to a two-track regime for the unwinding of impaired consent transfers. Where the impairment of the transferor's consent is relevant at all, it can either affect both the conveyance and the obligatory contract underlying it, or – more often – merely the latter. In the first case, the transaction is reversed according to the principles governing the relationship between an owner of a chattel and its (illegitimate) possessor, in the second according to the rules governing restitution of unjustified enrichments.

Chapter IV attempts to provide a similar basic framework for English law. After explaining the operation of the 'unjust factor' regime, especially its interaction with the law on rescission of contracts, and the different views on the possibility of 'alternative analysis' (concerning the relationship between personal claims to restitution for unjust enrichment and the existence of vested property rights in the object transferred), it turns to the controversial topic of 'proprietary restitution'. When, if ever, does the transferee's unjust enrichment at the transferor's expense generate a new proprietary interest in the transferor, and what form does this proprietary interest take? It will be argued that, as the law stands, a generalized power model of proprietary restitution best fits the picture in all impaired consent transfer situations.

Chapter V draws the strings of Chapters III and IV together. It begins with a basic comparison of the scope of recovery in both legal systems, before moving on to ask whether English law, like German law, boasts a 'principle of abstraction'. On the basis of what was said in Chapter IV about the different modes of conveyance and the availability and form of proprietary restitution, it concludes that transfers of title by delivery could well be described as 'abstract' in English law. However, given the structure of the English law on rescission and its interaction with the law of property and unjust enrichment, abstraction loses much of its gist. The chapter concludes with some comparative observations on the scope and relevance of proprietary relief and on the position of the transferor in the transferee's insolvency.

Chapter VI is the first to look at the special issues raised by three-party cases. Building on the structural foundations provided by Chapters III and IV, it explores the position of third parties to whom the transferee has conveyed or purported to convey the object he received from the transferor.[45] To the extent that the transferor had any sort of proprietary interest in it at the moment of the transferee's conveyance, this is primarily determined by the rules on *bona fide* purchase. To the extent that he did not, the question

---

[45] We will not specifically consider cases in which the third party acquires possession of the object as the transferee's bailee (ie where he becomes *unmittelbarer Fremdbesitzer*), eg under a contract of hire or by way of a gratuitous loan for use.

arises whether and under what circumstances he is or should be able to assert a personal claim in unjust(ified) enrichment against the third party recipient. It will be seen that while German law may offer too much third party protection, English law arguably offers too little in certain respects.

Chapter VII is the only chapter without direct comparative significance. This is because it deals with a problem which cannot – for structural reasons – arise in German law, but which has the potential to cause serious distortions in three-party cases under English law. The so-called 'third party rights bar to rescission' maintains that a contract can no longer be rescinded once an innocent third party purchaser for value has acquired a proprietary interest in the object conveyed under it. It will be argued that, given the existence of free-standing *bona fide* purchase rules, the third party rights bar to rescission ought to be abolished at the next opportunity.

Chapter VIII finally adverts to the conditions under which the transferor can claim substitute assets from the transferee (or remote recipients), such as the purchase price paid to the transferee by the acquirer of the original asset. In English law, this is the realm of 'tracing' and 'claiming'. If proprietary restitution is indeed as widely available as suggested in Chapter IV, then rights to the traceable substitute(s) of the object transferred will be equally common. Although German law is much more restrictive about granting proprietary relief and does not embrace a general principle of 'real subrogation', it can achieve remarkably similar results through its law of unjustified enrichment in conjunction with the rule which allows for the 'segregation of substitutes' in insolvency.

A short thematic summary is contained in Chapter IX. It concludes the book.

Chapter II

Basic Principles Compared and Contrasted

A. Introduction

This chapter is intended to set out, compare and contrast the basic rules and principles which determine the consequences of impaired consent transfers and the mechanisms of their reversal in two- and three-party situations. Analysing such situations is an exercise on the interface of contract law, property law and the law relating to unjust(ified) enrichments. It also touches on aspects of tort or delict. The interrelationship between these various areas within the English and the German legal systems is best understood by developing an awareness of how the applicable rules and principles differ on an abstract or conceptual level. It is, of course, impossible within the confines of this book to give a comprehensive comparative account of the entire spectrum of core private law. Nor would such an account be of much service to the reader in elucidating the chapters which follow. The aim here is merely to draw attention to the more salient features of those areas of the law which will become relevant later on and which will then be fleshed out in detail. Highlighting the main similarities and, perhaps more often, discrepancies between the two legal systems will ensure that the complex interplay of rules and principles embedded in different parts of the law can be related back to their proper doctrinal context.

The sections which follow contain a comparative account of some basic issues of contract law (section B), the fundamental structure of the law relating to unjust(ified) enrichments (section C), and the main features of German and English personal property law (section D). It will be immediately obvious that these categories do not neatly align. Contract law is primarily about consent-based rights, usually – but not necessarily – personal rights.[1] Unjust(ified) enrichment concerns a category of rights generated by operation of law. These rights can, in theory at least, also be either

[1] Of course, contract law – as conventionally understood – also encompasses aspects of the law of wrongs (eg liability for breach of contract), and it may even have an overlap with the law of unjust(ified) enrichment in respect of the event generating the right to rescind a contract: cf below, discussion in Chapter IV.B.2.b/c (pp 106–13) and in Chapter V.B.1.a.iii (pp 171–74).

personal (*in personam*) or proprietary (*in rem*).[2] Property law cuts across the events-based classificatory scheme. It comprises the rules and principles pertaining to rights or other interests *in rem*. As a response-based category, property law overlaps and interacts with the primarily events-oriented law of contract and unjust(ified) enrichment. Yet the fact that the different areas of law discussed below do not line up neatly does not make their individual treatment any less useful as a starting point. They represent the rubrics in which we have become accustomed to thinking. So long as we recognize the possibility of overlaps, there is no danger in continuing to adhere to the conventional divisions and nomenclature.

It will also not have escaped the reader's attention that something is missing from the above line-up. Unjust(ified) enrichment is not the only event capable of generating rights non-consensually. Rights also arise by operation of law where a wrong, characterized by the breach of a duty,[3] has been committed. Broadly speaking, wrongs are governed by the law of delict under the German Civil Code (§§ 823 ff BGB), and they appear as different 'torts' as far as the English common law is concerned. However, it should be noted that the law of wrongs is in fact wider than both delict and tort.[4] In the present context, wrongs are of twofold relevance only. On the one hand, they play a role in the protection of property rights. On the other hand, they may form part of the broader background picture of an impaired consent transfer (where the transfer is wrongfully induced). Given that the former aspect can conveniently be discussed in the section on property law and that the latter requires no abstract preliminaries, a separate section introducing and comparing the German law of delict with English tort law has been thought dispensable. Suffice it to point out up-front that the German law of delict tends to require the culpable infringement of one of a number of specified protected rights or interests (cf § 823 I BGB).[5] English tort law is historically built around a plethora of different forms of action similarly protecting specified rights or interests

[2] There is no logical reason why property rights cannot be generated by unjust(ified) enrichment, even if it should turn out that some legal systems only allow for a personal response: cf P Birks, *Unjust Enrichment* (2nd edn OUP, Oxford 2005) 32–33.

[3] Cf P Birks, "Rights, Wrongs, and Remedies" (2000) 20 OJLS 1, 31. Defining wrongdoing by reference to a breach of duty may be more palatable to English than to German lawyers, for whom 'wrongs' are intimately tied up with the response 'compensation' or 'reinstatement'. This, in turn, raises questions – which we cannot here pursue – about the appropriate classification of 'restitution for wrongs' and its relationship with the law of unjust(ified) enrichment (keyword: *Rechtswidrigkeitslehre*).

[4] It also encompasses, for example, breaches of contract (cf n 1), the quasi-contractual liability for *culpa in contrahendo* in German law (cf Chapter III.E.2, pp 94–97), and equitable wrongdoing in English law.

[5] But contrast § 823 II BGB and § 826 BGB.

(though often imposing strict liability), but it has now become dominated by the tort of negligence, which imposes liability for causing loss through the culpable breach of a 'duty of care' without apparently requiring the infringement of any particular right or interest.[6]

B. Basic Principles of Contract Law

1. Notion of a Contract

The term 'contract' is a dangerous one in any comparative study. Though a literal translation of the German word '*Vertrag*', the English word 'contract' carries very different connotations in the minds of Common lawyers from those in the minds of their German colleagues. And while it is difficult to provide a precise and comprehensive definition for either legal system, it is clear that the notion of a 'contract' is significantly wider in German than in English law.

In German law, a contract can be described as a legal transaction (*Rechtsgeschäft*) effected by the mutual expression of consent of two or more parties.[7] A contract is thus any agreement by means of which the parties intend to and do bring about specific legal consequences. English law, by contrast, associates the term with promises or agreements giving rise to legal obligations.[8] To be enforceable as a contract under English law, an informal agreement between two or more parties needs to be supported by consideration.[9]

---

[6] For a cogent criticism of these "two incompatible conceptions" of tort law and for a rights-based re-conceptualization of negligence liability see R Stevens, *Torts and Rights* (OUP, Oxford 2007).

[7] Cf eg O Palandt (Begr), *Bürgerliches Gesetzbuch* (67th edn Beck, München 2008) Einf v § 145 [1] (Heinrichs). The term *Vertrag* is not defined in the BGB, but is presupposed by it, eg in §§ 145 ff and § 311 BGB. A legal transaction (*Rechtsgeschäft*: cf §§ 104 ff BGB) consists of one or more declarations of intention (*Willenserklärungen*: cf §§ 116 ff BGB) which bring about a legally recognized effect. For an English account of this terminology see B Markesinis, H Unberath and A Johnston, *The German Law of Contract: A Comparative Treatise* (2nd edn Hart, Oxford 2006) 25–27.

[8] Cf eg J Beatson, *Anson's Law of Contract* (28th edn OUP, Oxford 2002) 1–2; SA Smith, *Atiyah's Introduction to the Law of Contract* (6th edn Clarendon Press, Oxford 2005) 28–29; E Peel, *Treitel: The Law of Contract* (12th edn Sweet & Maxwell, London 2007) [1–001]; A Burrows (ed), *English Private Law* (2nd edn OUP, Oxford 2007) [8.01] (Treitel). Critical of defining contracts in terms of agreements or promises: H Beale (gen ed), *Chitty on Contracts* (29th edn Sweet & Maxwell, London 2004) vol 1 [1–001]–[1–003] (Whittaker).

[9] Promises not supported by consideration are only binding if they are contained in a deed: cf Law of Property (Miscellaneous Provisions) Act 1989, s 1, on the appropriate

The English conception of contract is narrower than the German in two important respects. On the one hand, the common law doctrine of consideration places non-bargain transactions beyond the reach of contract law. On the other hand, contracts in English law have what may be described as a necessary obligatory element. Agreements which are not at least partly concerned with the creation, variation or discharge of personal rights and liabilities are not regarded as contractual. Let us examine each aspect in turn.

a) Gratuitous Transactions

The gratuitous conferral of a benefit by one party on another can be the subject-matter of a contract under German law, while it cannot under English law. Contractual relations in English law exist only where each party has given or promised to give something of value.[10] The core English notion of a contract thus roughly corresponds to what German lawyers would describe as a reciprocal or *synallagmatic* contract, under which each party's performance is promised and rendered in order to secure the other party's counter-performance (*do-ut-des* relationship).[11] In the present context, this discrepancy of understanding impacts primarily on the law relating to gratuitous transfers of chattels: German law regards gifts as contractual transactions, English law does not. The practical relevance of the distinction should not be overstated. Neither system enforces informal promises to make a gift, even if accepted by the intended donee.[12] Yet the

---

formality requirements. It is debatable whether such promises are properly classed as 'contractual'. Exceptionally, even an informal gratuitous promise may become enforceable under the so-called doctrine of 'promissory estoppel' if the promisee has detrimentally relied upon it: cf *Central London Property Trust Ltd v High Trees House Ltd* [1947] KB 130 (KBD). Yet this kind of estoppel acts only as a 'shield' and does not give rise to a new cause of action: cf *Combe v Combe* [1951] 2 KB 215 (CA).

[10] Insofar as promises contained in deeds are regarded as 'contractual' (cf n 9 immediately above), they constitute an exception to this principle.

[11] The language of 'reciprocity' is preferable to the description of *synallagmatic* contracts as being 'bilateral' in English law. This is because English lawyers use the term 'bilateral contracts' in a very specific sense, namely to distinguish contracts in which each party gives an enforceable promise of performance to the other from so-called 'unilateral contracts'. In a unilateral contract, one party can enforce the other's promise (often a promise to the world at large) upon performing some act requested by the other, without being under any prior obligation to perform the requested act. The classic example of a unilateral contract is to be found in the case of *Carlill v Carbolic Smoke Ball Co* [1893] 1 QB 256 (CA).

[12] Although German law does not boast a doctrine of consideration, § 518 I BGB stipulates a formality requirement (attestation by a notary) in default of which a promise to make a gift is not enforceable. According to § 518 II BGB, the lack of form is 'healed' by actual performance.

conceptual framework underpinning gift transactions has, as will be seen, some important repercussions where the donor's consent to the gift was impaired.

b) 'Real Agreements'

The second distinction between German and English law is connected to the first. A system like the English, which regards contracts as being about legally enforceable promises, necessarily focuses on their role in creating (or modifying)[13] obligations. Although some contractual agreements may incidentally also affect property rights, the bargain aspect of contracting dominates the Common law notion. German law is not so restricted. Its wider definition of contract allows for the application of the concept not merely within the realm of rights *in personam*, but also to agreements with (purely) *in rem* effects. A contract which concerns the creation of obligations is called 'obligatory contract' (*Schuldvertrag*).[14] One which transfers, varies or extinguishes property rights is called 'real contract' (*dinglicher Vertrag*).[15] To avoid confusion, the use of the term 'contract' will, unless indicated otherwise, be confined to its former, narrower meaning. A contract which serves to alter property rights will be referred to as 'real agreement'.

2. Rescission of Contract

Both English and German law recognize that there are circumstances in which a party ought not to be held to an otherwise binding contractual

---

[13] It is not entirely clear – and usually irrelevant – whether an agreement between the contracting parties to vary/discharge their original contract automatically entails the intended variation/discharge, or whether it constitutes a separate obligatory contract by which both parties bind themselves to specific conduct with regard to their previously incurred obligations (eg non-enforcement of the original contract).

[14] The obligatory transaction is commonly also referred to as *Verpflichtungsgeschäft*. The variation or discharge of existing obligations is properly classified as a *Verfügungsgeschäft* (cf n 15). As in English law (cf n 13), there is a question about the extent to which contracts of variation/discharge directly affect the parties' original obligations: cf eg the discussion in J von Staudinger (Begr), *J von Staudingers Kommentar zum Bürgerlichen Gesetzbuch: §§ 779–811* (Neubearbeitung 2002: Sellier de Gruyter, Berlin 2002) § 779 [40]–[48] (Marburger), for contracts of compromise.

[15] A legal transaction entailing a transfer, variation, encumbrance or extinction of an existing right, whether that right be *in rem* or *in personam*, is commonly referred to as *Verfügungsgeschäft* (dispository transaction). If the transaction is effected pursuant to and in discharge of a legal obligation, it is also called *Erfüllungsgeschäft* (transaction of fulfilment). Given that we are here concerned with conveyances of movable objects, we can – for exposition purposes – restrict our usage of the terms *Verfügungsgeschäft*, *Erfüllungsgeschäft* and 'real contract/agreement' to transfers of rights *in rem*, more specifically to transfers of 'ownership'.

agreement.[16] This will normally be warranted where his or her consent to the agreement is regarded as in some relevant way defective. Although the circumstances under which consent is considered to be sufficiently defective differ as between the two legal systems,[17] the mechanism by which the impairment is given legal recognition is similar. Only in very exceptional circumstances will defective consent be treated as completely non-existent. In most cases, the party in question is afforded the option of avoiding the contract retroactively[18] by a mechanism called 'rescission' (*Anfechtung*).[19] Rescission is a self-help remedy.[20] It involves evidencing an intention not to be bound by the agreement and (usually) communicating this to the other party.[21] Under both systems, the right to rescind may be lost by affirmation or lapse of time.[22]

---

[16] The term 'contractual agreement' here includes 'real agreements' for the purposes of German law.

[17] See below, text to nn 23–35.

[18] Cf § 142 I BGB. Rescission can be contrasted with 'termination' of a contract (eg for repudiatory breach), which operates only prospectively: cf Lord Wilberforce's comments in *Johnson v Agnew* [1980] AC 367 (HL) 392–93, and in *Photo Production Ltd v Securicor Transport Ltd* [1980] AC 827 (HL) 844–45, and see §§ 346 ff BGB (*Rücktritt*).

[19] Although lawyers in both legal systems generally talk about rescission or avoidance of a contract, what they actually mean is that the party entitled to rescind can revoke his or her defective consent to the agreement. German law is more explicit about this than English law. The rules on rescission are contained in the 'General Part' of the BGB. Where operative, an impairment of consent allows the party concerned to avoid his 'declaration of intention' (*Willenserklärung*): §§ 119, 120, 123 BGB. The avoidance of any legal transaction constituted by two or more corresponding declarations of intention (in the case of a contract) is the necessary consequence: § 142 I BGB.

[20] This is uncontroversial in German law and is widely thought to be the current English position: cf eg *Abram Steamship Co Ltd (In Liquidation) v Westville Shipping Co Ltd (In Liquidation)* [1923] AC 773 (HL) 781 (Lord Atkinson); *Anson's Law of Contract* (n 8) 253; *Atiyah's Law of Contract* (n 8) 375; J Cartwright, *Misrepresentation, Mistake and Non-Disclosure* (2nd edn Sweet & Maxwell, London 2007) [4.18]; M Furmston, *Cheshire, Fifoot & Furmston's Law of Contract* (15th edn OUP, Oxford 2007) 353; but contrast now *Islington London BC v Uckac* [2006] EWCA Civ 340, [2006] 1 WLR 1303, [26] (Dyson LJ). Critical, esp as far as rescission in equity is concerned: J O'Sullivan, "Rescission as a Self-Help Remedy: A Critical Analysis" (2000) 59 CLJ 509.

[21] Cf § 143 BGB. Note that, under English law, the communication requirement is dispensed with in cases of fraudulent misrepresentation: *Car & Universal Finance Co Ltd v Caldwell* [1965] 1 QB 525 (CA). Critical of the *Caldwell* ruling: Law Reform Committee, *Twelfth Report: Transfer of Title to Chattels* (Cmnd 2958, 1966) [16]. In German law, actual receipt of the rescinding party's communication may also be dispensable, but only if the other party deliberately prevents or evades it (*Zugangsverhinderung*): BGH NJW 1996, 1967.

[22] Affirmation: § 144 BGB; *Sharpley v Louth and East Coast Rly Co* (1876) 2 ChD 663 (CA); *Long v Lloyd* [1958] 1 WLR 753 (CA). Lapse of time: §§ 121, 124 BGB; *Leaf v International Galleries* [1950] 2 KB 86 (CA). In both legal systems, lapse of time does

The grounds for rescission recognized by English and German law are only partly co-extensive. This is because the two systems are in some respects asking different questions. When deciding what counts as an impairment of consent sufficient to warrant rescission, one can either examine the way in which the defect was brought about (the 'procedural' or 'process-oriented' approach) or look at the nature of the defect itself, ie what it relates to (the 'substantive' or 'content-oriented' approach). Broadly speaking, English law adopts the former approach, while the German BGB contains a mixture of 'content-oriented' and 'process-oriented' grounds for rescission.

a) Grounds for Rescission in English Law

For present purposes, there are two main categories of case in which English law allows a person to rescind a contract. The first is where his consent was given as a result of a misrepresentation made by the other party.[23] This scenario can be described as one of induced mistake. The second is where the consent, though untainted by mistake, was elicited by some form of improper pressure or undue influence.[24]

The generalization in the preceding paragraph must not obscure the fact that rescission is an area with historical roots in both common law and equitable jurisdiction.[25] This distinction has lost much of its practical relevance since the procedural fusion of both systems through the Judicature

---

not bar rescission in fraud cases so long as the victim remains ignorant of the fraud: cf § 124 II BGB; *Rolfe v Gregory* (1865) 4 De G J & S 576, 579; 46 ER 1042, 1044; *Armstrong v Jackson* [1917] 2 KB 822 (KBD) 830–31.

[23] See below, nn 27–28. Misrepresentations made by third parties are only operative if made on behalf of a contracting party or if the contracting party had at least notice of them: cf eg *Re Liverpool Borough Bank (Duranty's Case)* (1858) 26 Beav 268, 270–71; 53 ER 901, 902; *Lynde v Anglo-Italian Hemp Spinning Co* [1896] 1 Ch 178 (ChD) 182–83; *Barclays Bank plc v O'Brien* [1994] 1 AC 180 (HL). The latter aspect (knowledge or notice of a misrepresentation made by a third party giving rise to a right to rescind) sits somewhat uneasily with the rule that knowledge or notice of a *spontaneous* mistake made by the other party is usually irrelevant: cf *Smith v Hughes* (1871) LR 6 QB 597 (QB); Cartwright *Misrepresentation* (n 20) [4.78]; D O'Sullivan, S Elliott and R Zakrzewski, *The Law of Rescission* (OUP, Oxford 2008) [9.06].

[24] See below, nn 27–28. Where the pressure or influence emanates from a third party, the line of cases following *Barclays Bank v O'Brien* (n 23), itself a misrepresentation case, suggests that rescission will only be available if the other contracting party had sufficient notice: cf eg *CIBC Mortgages plc v Pitt* [1994] 1 AC 200 (HL); *Royal Bank of Scotland plc v Etridge (No 2)* [2001] UKHL 44, [2002] 2 AC 773.

[25] For a short overview of the history of rescission see eg Cartwright *Misrepresentation* (n 20) [4.01]–[4.04]; *Cheshire, Fifoot & Furmston* (n 20) 354–55; J O'Sullivan (2000) 59 CLJ (n 20) 516–25. A more detailed account is contained in D O'Sullivan et al *Law of Rescission* (n 23), esp [3.01]–[3.54].

Acts 1873–75.[26] It is nevertheless worth noting that the common law restricts its intervention to what might be described as the most serious type of case within each category outlined above. At law, a contract can only be rescinded for fraudulent misrepresentation and for duress.[27] Equity is more generous in granting relief, recognizing non-fraudulent (ie negligent or innocent) misrepresentation as well as undue influence as grounds for rescission.[28]

b) Grounds for Rescission in German Law

In contrast to English law, the primary focus of German law is on the 'substantive' nature of a particular defect. All contracts (including real agreements) can be rescinded by a party who, when declaring his intention to contract, was mistaken about the content of his declaration as interpreted from the other party's perspective[29] (§ 119 I alt 1 BGB: *Inhaltsirrtum*) or did not intend to make a declaration with such content at all (§ 119 I alt 2 BGB: *Erklärungsirrtum*).[30] The same is true where the party was mistaken about a quality or characteristic of the person or the object to whom/which the declaration relates, so long as this quality or characteristic is commonly considered to be essential (§ 119 II BGB: *Eigenschaftsirrtum*). It will be evident that these provisions cover some, but by no means all types of

---

[26] Supreme Court of Judicature Acts 1873 and 1875.

[27] Fraud: eg *Load v Green* (1846) 15 Mees & W 216, 153 ER 828; *Spence v Crawford* [1939] 3 All ER 271 (HL); *Car & Universal Finance Co Ltd v Caldwell* [1965] 1 QB 525 (CA). Duress: eg *Dimskal Shipping Co SA v International Transport Workers Federation (The Evia Luck) (No 2)* [1992] 2 AC 152 (HL); and cf also the *obiter dicta* in *Pao On v Lau Yiu Long* [1980] AC 614 (PC) 634; *Universe Tankships Inc of Monrovia v International Transport Workers Federation (The Universe Sentinel)* [1983] 1 AC 366 (HL) 383 (Lord Diplock), 400 (Lord Scarman). Contrast *Barton v Armstrong* [1976] AC 104 (PC), where certain deeds signed under extreme pressure (death threats) were said to be 'void' for duress.

[28] Non-fraudulent misrepresentation: eg *Redgrave v Hurd* (1881) 20 ChD 1 (CA); cf also the *obiter dicta* in *Derry v Peek* (1889) 14 App Cas 337 (HL) 347 (Lord Bramwell), 359 (Lord Hershell). Undue Influence: eg *Royal Bank of Scotland plc v Etridge (No 2)* [2001] UKHL 44, [2002] 2 AC 773. Rescission for non-fraudulent misrepresentation is subject to the courts' discretion to award damages *in lieu* of rescission under the Misrepresentation Act 1967, s 2(2). Note that the term 'innocent misrepresentation' is sometimes used to denote all instances of non-fraudulent misrepresentation, thus encompassing negligent misrepresentations as well as innocent misrepresentations in the narrower sense of the word.

[29] On the interpretation of declarations of intention see §§ 133, 157 BGB.

[30] There is a proviso relating to causation: rescission under § 119 BGB is only possible "if it is to be assumed that [the rescinding party] would not have made [the declaration of intention] in knowledge of all the relevant facts and on a rational appreciation of the case".

mistake which may be present in a party's mind when entering into the contract.[31] A party will not normally be allowed to avoid an agreement unless he was mistaken as to its content or effect as such. With the possible exception of cases falling under § 119 II BGB,[32] mere 'motivational mistakes' (*Motivirrtümer*), ie misapprehensions affecting a person's reasons for contracting which are external to the terms of the agreement itself, are irrelevant.

In some circumstances, however, the focus of the BGB shifts from the substantive quality of a party's consent to the way in which it was obtained. Like English law, German law recognizes fraudulent misrepresentation (*arglistige Täuschung*)[33] and duress (*widerrechtliche Drohung*)[34] as grounds for rescission (§ 123 I BGB). If a fraudulent misrepresentation made by the other party[35] induces a person to enter into a contract, that contract can be rescinded regardless of the nature of the mistake.

---

[31] The case where one contracting party's declaration of intention is miscommunicated to the other (cf § 120 BGB) will not be specifically addressed in this book.

[32] There is a debate over whether mistakes as to an essential quality or characteristic of an object or person (§ 119 II BGB) are properly regarded as 'motivational mistakes'. Contrast eg E Zitelmann, *Irrtum und Rechtsgeschäft: Eine psychologisch-juristische Untersuchung* (Duncker & Humblot, Leipzig 1879) esp 414–16, 433–61; A von Tuhr, *Der Allgemeine Teil des Deutschen Bürgerlichen Rechts: vol 2/1* (Duncker & Humblot, Berlin 1914) 577–78; K Larenz, *Allgemeiner Teil des deutschen Bürgerlichen Rechts* (7th edn Beck, München 1989) 378–82; K Larenz and M Wolf, *Allgemeiner Teil des Bürgerlichen Rechts* (9th edn Beck, München 2004) 660–65, with eg W Flume, *Eigenschaftsirrtum und Kauf* (Regensberg, Münster 1948) esp 13–21; W Flume, *Allgemeiner Teil des Bürgerlichen Rechts, vol 2: Das Rechtsgeschäft* (3rd edn Springer, Berlin 1979) 476–79; W Schmidt-Rimpler, "Eigenschaftsirrtum und Erklärungsirrtum" in HC Nipperdey (ed), *Das deutsche Privatrecht in der Mitte des 20. Jahrhunderts: Festschrift für Heinrich Lehmann zum 80. Geburtstag* (de Gruyter, Berlin 1956) vol 1, 213. Cf also summary of the debate with critical analysis in FJ Säcker and R Rixecker (eds), *Münchener Kommentar zum Bürgerlichen Gesetzbuch, vol 1/1: §§ 1–240* (5th edn Beck, München 2006) § 119 [107]–[112] (Kramer); M Schmoeckel, J Rückert and R Zimmermann (eds), *Historisch-kritischer Kommentar zum BGB, vol 1: §§ 1–240* (Mohr Siebeck, Tübingen 2003) §§ 116–124 [62]–[72] (Schermaier, who warns against mis- or over-interpreting Zitelmann's psychological will theory at [58]).

[33] The term *arglistige Täuschung* can also be translated as 'deception' or 'deceit', but it is here rendered as 'fraudulent misrepresentation' to emphasize the parallel with the English common law ground for rescission.

[34] The term *widerrechtliche Drohung* can also be translated as 'coercion', but it is here rendered as 'duress' to emphasize the parallel with the English common law ground for rescission.

[35] § 123 II BGB deals with the situation where the fraudulent misrepresentation is made by a third party. Rescission is only possible if the other contracting party knew or ought to have known of the deception. The German position is thus similar to that in English law: cf n 23.

C. Basic Principles of the Law Relating to Unjust(ified) Enrichment

1. Establishing a Claim

The law of unjust(ified) enrichment is concerned with a category of rights arising by operation of law. As the slight nuance in terminology (unjust/ unjustified) indicates, Civilian and Common law systems adopt a different view of the event they call 'unjust(ified) enrichment'.[36] This difference accounts for the main discrepancy between the German law of 'unjustified enrichment' (*ungerechtfertigte Bereicherung*), set out in §§ 812 ff BGB, and the English law on 'unjust enrichment' (often also referred to as the law of 'restitution'). In both legal systems, a claim to restitution for unjust(ified) enrichment rests on three core constituent elements.[37] The first two are the same in German and English law. The defendant must be enriched, and his enrichment must be at the claimant's expense. Only at the third and final stage of the inquiry does the difference of approach show up. German law, in the Civilian tradition, asks whether the defendant's enrichment is 'unjustified' in the sense of being without a sufficient legal basis or cause (*sine causa*). English law, by way of contrast, traditionally requires the identification of a specific factor which makes the defendant's enrichment 'unjust' as against the claimant and provides a positive reason for restitution.

a) German Law: Performance, Non-Performance, and Absence of Basis

§ 812 I 1 BGB provides that "[a] person who, without legal cause, obtains something by way of another person's performance or in some other way at another's expense, is obliged to surrender to that person what he has so obtained". This is the central provision around which the entire German law of unjustified enrichment revolves. After much debate during the first half of the 20th century, it is now widely accepted that § 812 I 1 BGB con-

---

[36] For an overview cf eg P Birks, "Comparative Unjust Enrichment" in P Birks and A Pretto (eds), *Themes in Comparative Law: In Honour of Bernard Rudden* (OUP, Oxford 2002) 137, 146–50.

[37] In *Woolwich Equitable Building Society v Inland Revenue Commissioners* [1993] AC 70 (HL) 196–97, Lord Browne-Wilkinson summed up the English position as follows: "Although as yet there is in English law no general rule giving the plaintiff a right of recovery from the defendant who has been unjustly enriched at the plaintiff's expense, the concept of unjust enrichment lies at the heart of all the individual instances in which the law does give a right of recovery". It is debatable whether English law has in fact not yet developed a general unjust enrichment claim, but in practice cases still tend to be pleaded and decided by reference to the traditional forms of action: cf n 66.

tains the bright line dividing the law on unjustified enrichment into two distinct categories, namely performance and non-performance cases.[38] If a claim is made for restitution of what the claimant has by 'performance' (*Leistung*) deliberately and purposefully bestowed upon the defendant (*Leistungskondiktion*), then the link between the parties is such that the defendant's enrichment is necessarily at the claimant's expense.[39] If, on the other hand, the defendant's enrichment cannot be accounted for by anybody's performance, but occurs "in some other way", the question arises under what circumstances it can be regarded as being at the claimant's expense.[40] One answer is that, in a non-performance-based claim to restitution (*Nichtleistungskondiktion*), the relevant connection is established whenever the defendant's enrichment results from his interference (*Eingriff*) with a wealth-allocating right of the claimant's, such as a property right.[41] Though contentious in its detail, the so-called *Eingriffskondiktion* is by far the most significant sub-category of *Nichtleistungskondiktion*.[42]

---

[38] Cf esp W Wilburg, *Die Lehre von der ungerechtfertigten Bereicherung nach österreichischem und deutschem Recht* (Leuschner & Lubensky, Graz 1934); and E von Caemmerer, "Bereicherung und unerlaubte Handlung" in H Dölle, M Rheinstein and K Zweigert (eds), *Festschrift für Ernst Rabel* (Mohr Siebeck, Tübingen 1954) vol 1, 333, reprinted in HG Leser (ed), *Ernst von Caemmerer: Gesammelte Schriften, vol 1: Rechtsvergleichung und Schuldrecht* (Mohr Siebeck, Tübingen 1968) 209; E von Caemmerer, "Grundprobleme des Bereicherungsrechts" in HG Leser (ed), *Ernst von Caemmerer: Gesammelte Schriften, vol 1: Rechtsvergleichung und Schuldrecht* (Mohr Siebeck, Tübingen 1968) 370, 376–90. For an account in English of this development see T Krebs, *Restitution at the Crossroads: A Comparative Study* (Cavendish, London 2001) 201–37; R Zimmermann and J du Plessis, "Basic Features of the German Law of Unjustified Enrichment" [1994] RLR 14, esp 24–30.

[39] Beside the *condictio indebiti* in § 812 I 1 alt 1 BGB, performance-based enrichment claims are also contained in § 812 I 2 alt 1 BGB (*condictio ob causam finitam*), § 812 I 2 alt 2 BGB (*condictio ob rem*, also known as the *condictio causa data causa non secuta*) and in § 817 1 BGB (*condictio ob turpem vel iniustam causam*).

[40] Where the enrichment at issue is obtained by way of a person's performance (whether it be the claimant's or a third party's), recourse to a non-performance-based claim is usually barred: so-called 'precedence' of performance relationships (*Vorrang der Leistungsbeziehung*).

[41] The theory about the attributive content of rights (*Lehre vom Zuweisungsgehalt*) was developed by Walter Wilburg and Ernst von Caemmerer: cf Wilburg *Lehre von der ungerechtfertigten Bereicherung* (n 38); von Caemmerer in *Festschrift Rabel* (n 38). A rival theory defines the interference primarily by reference to its unlawfulness (*Rechtswidrigkeitslehre*): eg HH Jakobs, *Eingriffserwerb und Vermögensverschiebung in der Lehre von der ungerechtfertigten Bereicherung* (Röhrscheid, Bonn 1964) 23–64. This theory goes back to the seminal work of F Schulz, "System der Rechte auf den Eingriffserwerb" AcP 105 (1909) 1.

[42] Special instances of the *Eingriffskondiktion* are contained in § 816 I 1 BGB and in § 951 BGB. Other non-performance-based claims are the *Verwendungskondiktion* (restitution for inadvertent expenditure on a thing belonging to another in cases not covered by

Once it is clear that the defendant's enrichment was, by performance or otherwise, at the claimant's expense, German law asks whether there is a valid legal basis or juristic reason (*Rechtsgrund* or *causa*) which justifies the enrichment. If not, it will have to be reversed. The operation of the *sine causa* approach can best be illustrated using the *Leistungskondiktion* contained in § 812 I 1 alt 1 BGB as an example.[43] A claimant who consciously enriches the defendant by way of performance usually does so in order to discharge an obligation, such as one generated by contract. That obligation constitutes the legal basis or *causa* justifying the transfer of wealth from the claimant to the defendant.[44] Should it later turn out to have been non-existent (eg because the contract was void from the outset or because it has subsequently been avoided retroactively), there is no explanatory basis for the defendant's enrichment. His enrichment is *unjustified.* The law imposes on him a duty to disgorge it to the claimant. In our example, the transferor-claimant would accordingly have a *condictio indebiti* (§ 812 I 1 alt 1 BGB) to recover what he has by performance bestowed upon the transferee-defendant.

The important point to note is that – structurally at least – the law of unjustified enrichment (§§ 812 ff BGB) is not concerned with the reason why an enrichment lacks a sufficient basis. Such questions are for other areas of

§§ 994 ff BGB) and the *Rückgriffskondiktion* (restitutionary recourse for discharge of another's debt in cases where the payment does not constitute a performance to that other and where there is no subrogation).

[43] For the *Eingriffskondiktion* in § 812 I 1 alt 2 BGB, the interference with a wealth-allocating right of the claimant's and the defendant's lack of entitlement will usually be two sides of the same coin. The *Rechtswidrigkeitslehre* (cf n 41) considers the entire question as part of the unlawfulness inquiry.

[44] The terms *Rechtsgrund* and *causa* are often used interchangeably, but there is another, more subjective sense of the *causa* concept. *Causa* in the subjective sense refers to the intended purpose in effecting a particular legal transaction. If the intention is, for example, to discharge a particular obligation, then the performance is made *solvendi causa*. The obligation to be discharged constitutes the legal basis (*Rechtsgrund*). Whether the parties are successful in fulfilling their subjective *causa* depends, in the case of the *causa solvendi*, on the objective existence or non-existence of the *Rechtsgrund.* The *causa solvendi* is the most common reason for rendering a performance (hence *condictio indebiti*). However, a performance may also be made to effect a gift without a prior promise of gift (*causa donandi* – cf § 516 I BGB: *Handschenkung*), to bring into existence a debt (*causa credendi* – but note that a loan agreement, now regulated by § 488 BGB, is no longer classified as *Realvertrag* coming into existence only upon delivery), or to bring about a particular state of affairs (*datio ob rem*). In the latter case, the appropriate enrichment claim is the *condictio ob rem* in § 812 I 2 alt 2 BGB. For an account of all the recognized types of *causae* in the subjective sense cf eg A von Tuhr, *Der Allgemeine Teil des Deutschen Bürgerlichen Rechts: vol 2/2* (Duncker & Humblot, Berlin 1918) 67–80. For a critical comparative perspective see H Scott, "Restitution of Extra-Contractual Transfers: Limits of the Absence of Legal Ground Analysis" [2006] RLR 93.

the law to decide. It will, for instance, be up to the general rules and principles of the BGB to determine when a contract is null and void (eg for illegality, § 134 BGB) or under what circumstances an agreement can be rescinded (eg for mistake, § 119 BGB). And while the implications of unwinding transactions will normally be borne in mind by the legislature and courts when framing and applying the general rules and principles on invalidity, §§ 812 ff BGB do not inquire behind this verdict on the absence of basis.

b) English Law: Unjust Factors and the New Birksian Model

The Common law has traditionally adopted a different approach. Rather than asking whether the defendant's enrichment at the claimant's expense can be justified by reference to some other part of the legal system, it looks to see whether there is a sufficient reason for ordering the defendant to make restitution to the claimant. Such reasons for restitution are called 'unjust factors'. They are internal to the law of unjust enrichment. Though varying in their exact scope and inevitably developing over time, the unjust factors most relevant to the present study represent in essence the legal acknowledgement of the fact that the claimant's consent to the defendant's enrichment was somehow defective.[45] The claimant may, for example, have been labouring under a mistake when he made the conveyance, or he may have acted under the impression of some improper pressure or undue influence. His intention to effect the transfer was imperfect. Mistake, duress and undue influence are reasons for restitution.[46] It is unsurprising that, despite the autonomy of the law of unjust enrichment from other parts of the law, its unjust factors resemble and to some extent duplicate the grounds for rescission of a contract outlined above.[47] They are also instances of impairments of consent being legally recognized. Yet the law of unjust enrichment is in certain respects more generous than contract law. The most significant deviation is that it regards all causative mistakes as

[45] We are not here concerned with cases in which the claimant's consent was qualified (unjust factor: failure of consideration) or where restitution is purely policy-motivated.

[46] For details cf P Birks, *An Introduction to the Law of Restitution* (Clarendon Press, Oxford 1985, paperback edn 1989) 146–85; A Burrows, *The Law of Restitution* (2nd edn Butterworths, London 2002) 128–81, 211–59; G Jones (ed), R Goff and G Jones, *The Law of Restitution* (7th edn Sweet & Maxwell, London 2007) [4–001]–[11–015]; G Virgo, *The Principles of the Law of Restitution* (2nd edn OUP, Oxford 2006) 137–215, 247–67. Necessity, legal compulsion and 'exploitation of weakness' fall outside the ambit of this book and will not be specifically considered.

[47] Yet note that the right to rescind a contract may itself be referable to a principle against unjust enrichment more broadly conceived. On the conceptual basis of the right to rescind a contract see below, Chapter IV.B.2.b (pp 106–9) and Chapter V.B.1.a.iii (pp 171–74).

prima facie relevant,[48] even those which are not induced by the other party and would not be sufficient to invalidate a contract.[49] A spontaneous mistake by the transferor usually makes the transfer unjust. So as not to undermine the restrictive contractual principles, a claim in unjust enrichment will, however, fail if a valid contract governs the parties' relationship and sanctions the transfer of wealth from the claimant to the defendant.[50]

Given that the English law of unjust enrichment focuses so strongly on the claimant's state of mind, it has some difficulty dealing with non-participatory enrichments, ie those not involving a voluntary transfer of wealth from the claimant to the defendant.[51] The defendant may, for example, simply have appropriated and used a chattel belonging to the claimant. What, if any,[52] is the reason for restitution in such a scenario? One advocated solution is that 'ignorance' and 'powerlessness' should be recognized as unjust factors on the basis that 'no consent' is an even stronger ground for restitution than impaired consent.[53] The problem with this *a fortiori* argument is that it is hard to sustain a claimant-sided analysis in cases where the claimant is in no way involved in the defendant's enrichment.[54] This might explain why the courts have never expressly endorsed the inclusion of 'ignorance' or 'powerlessness' in the list of unjust factors. Alternative suggestions for dealing with non-participatory enrichments usu-

---

[48] For an overview of the development of the unjust factor 'mistake' see below, Chapter IV.B.1 (at pp 102–3).

[49] On the difference between mistakes relevant in the contractual context and those relevant to the law of unjust enrichment see eg D Friedmann, "The Objective Principle and Mistake and Involuntariness in Contract and Restitution" (2003) 119 LQR 68.

[50] See below, Chapter IV.B.2.a (pp 105–6).

[51] Such cases tend to be caught by the principles governing 'restitution for wrongs', but these principles are widely thought not to form part of the law of unjust enrichment proper: cf Birks *Unjust Enrichment* (n 2) 277–81; P Birks, "Misnomer" in WR Cornish and others (eds), *Restitution Past, Present and Future: Essays in Honour of Gareth Jones* (Hart, Oxford 1998) 1; Virgo *Principles* (n 46) 8–11. More cautious: *Goff & Jones* (n 46) [1–095]. Critical: Burrows *Restitution* (n 46) 5–7; A Burrows, "Quadrating Restitution and Unjust Enrichment: A Matter of Principle?" [2000] RLR 257; M McInnes, "Restitution, Unjust Enrichment and the Perfect Quadration Thesis" [1999] RLR 118; A Tettenborn, "Misnomer – A Response to Professor Birks" in WR Cornish and others (eds), *Restitution Past, Present and Future: Essays in Honour of Gareth Jones* (Hart, Oxford 1998) 31.

[52] It is sometimes suggested, whether explicitly or by necessary implication, that the law of unjust enrichment has no relevance at all outside the context of participatory enrichments: eg W Swadling, "A Claim in Restitution?" [1996] LMCLQ 63; W Swadling, "Ignorance and Unjust Enrichment: The Problem of Title" (2008) 28 OJLS 627.

[53] Eg Birks *Introduction* (n 46) 140–46; Burrows *Restitution* (n 46) 182–210. Critical: Virgo *Principles* (n 46) 131–36.

[54] Cf now also R Chambers and J Penner, "Ignorance" in S Degeling and J Edelman (eds), *Unjust Enrichment in Commercial Law* (Thomson Reuters, Sydney 2008) 253, 255.

ally focus on whether the defendant has in some way interfered with the claimant's rights.[55] It is worth noting the similarity between this approach and that adopted by German law in non-performance cases under the category called *Eingriffskondiktion*.[56]

There is an ongoing debate in English law about the feasibility and desirability of moving towards a more Civilian understanding of unjust enrichment. Shortly before his death in 2004, Peter Birks argued that the time was ripe for changing direction and that the Common law should henceforth embrace 'absence of basis' as the only reason (outside the law of wrongs) for reversing an enrichment by operation of law.[57] Conceptually, the magnitude of this proposed re-orientation of unjust enrichment can hardly be exaggerated. In practical terms, however, the discrepancy between the different approaches is likely to be small.[58] Even under the new Birksian model, most of the traditional unjust factors remain relevant as reasons upon which the 'absence of basis' depends.[59] So far, the new

---

[55] Most authors advocating this approach believe that 'restitution for wrongs' (cf n 51) would then naturally merge into unjust enrichment law: J Beatson, "The Nature of Waiver of Tort" in J Beatson, *The Use and Abuse of Unjust Enrichment: Essays on the Law of Restitution* (Clarendon Press, Oxford 1991) 206; D Friedmann, "Restitution for Wrongs: The Basis of Liability" in WR Cornish and others (eds), *Restitution Past, Present and Future: Essays in Honour of Gareth Jones* (Hart, Oxford 1998) 133; T Krebs, "The Fallacy of 'Restitution for Wrongs'" in A Burrows and A Rodger (eds), *Mapping the Law: Essays in Memory of Peter Birks* (OUP, Oxford 2006) 379. Similar, but upholding the distinction between restitution for (autonomous) unjust enrichment and restitution for wrongs: L Smith, "Unjust Enrichment, Property, and the Structure of Trusts" (2000) 116 LQR 412, esp 416–24.

[56] Cf above, text to nn 40–42.

[57] P Birks, *Unjust Enrichment* (2nd edn OUP, Oxford 2005) esp 101–28. For background, see the preceding debate between S Meier, *Irrtum und Zweckverfehlung: Die Rolle der unjust-Gründe bei rechtsgrundlosen Leistungen im englischen Recht* (Mohr Siebeck, Tübingen 1999); S Meier, "Unjust Factors and Legal Grounds" in D Johnston and R Zimmermann (eds), *Unjustified Enrichment: Key Issues in Comparative Perspective* (CUP, Cambridge 2002) 37; and T Krebs, *Restitution at the Crossroads: A Comparative Study* (Cavendish, London 2001); T Krebs, "In Defence of Unjust Factors" in D Johnston and R Zimmermann (eds), *Unjustified Enrichment: Key Issues in Comparative Perspective* (CUP, Cambridge 2002) 76.

[58] One case which *may* well have been decided differently on an 'absence of basis' approach is *CTN Cash and Carry Ltd v Gallaher Ltd* [1994] 4 All ER 714 (CA): cf G Dannemann, "Unjust Enrichment as Absence of Basis: Can English Law Cope?" in A Burrows and A Rodger (eds), *Mapping the Law: Essays in Memory of Peter Birks* (OUP, Oxford 2006) 363, 373–75.

[59] Birks *Unjust Enrichment* (n 57) 116: "A pyramid can be constructed in which, at the base, the particular unjust factors such as mistake, pressure, and undue influence become reasons why, higher up, there is no basis for the defendant's acquisition, which is then the master reason why, higher up still, the enrichment is unjust and must be surrendered". A reconciliation between the two approaches is also envisaged by T Baloch,

scheme has met with reservation.[60] In *Deutsche Morgan Grenfell Group plc v Inland Revenue Commissioners*,[61] the House of Lords declined the opportunity to move English law over to an 'absence of basis' model. Only two of their Lordships mentioned the new Birksian scheme,[62] and although Lord Walker showed some sympathy towards it,[63] his reasoning is in fact more compatible with the orthodox unjust factor approach.[64] Under these circumstances, it seems appropriate to conduct the comparative analysis on the basis of the traditional model of restitution for unjust enrichment. It should, however, be noted that most – if not all – of the observations and conclusions put forward here could be re-conceptualized to fit the absence of basis model.[65]

2. Content of Claim and Disenrichment Defence

Once it has been established that the defendant is unjust(ified)ly enriched at the claimant's expense, two questions arise. First, how is this enrichment to be reversed? And second, to what extent does the defendant's subsequent disenrichment afford him a defence to the claimant's action?

"The Unjust Enrichment Pyramid" (2007) 123 LQR 636; R Stevens, "Is there a Law of Unjust Enrichment?" in S Degeling and J Edelman (eds), *Unjust Enrichment in Commercial Law* (Thomson Reuters, Sydney 2008) 11, esp 31–33.

60 Eg A Burrows, "Absence of Basis: The New Birksian Scheme" in A Burrows and A Rodger (eds), *Mapping the Law: Essays in Memory of Peter Birks* (OUP, Oxford 2006) 33; *Goff & Jones* (n 46) 16–17 fn 5; Scott [2006] RLR (n 44); Virgo *Principles* (n 46) 127–30. Similar: J Edelman, "The Meaning of 'Unjust' in the English Law of Unjust Enrichment" (2006) 14 ERPL 309, who prefers the traditional scheme of unjust factors to the 'absence of basis' approach while conceding that English law has not yet settled on either. Contrast: Stevens in *Unjust Enrichment in Commercial Law* (n 59), who sees 'absence of basis' as the indispensable common denominator holding the law of unjust enrichment together.

61 [2006] UKHL 49, [2007] 1 AC 558.

62 Ibid [21]–[22] (Lord Hoffmann) and [150]–[158] (Lord Walker).

63 Ibid [158]. Lord Hoffmann left the issue open: ibid [22]. In the Court of Appeal, the model had been rejected by Buxton LJ: [2005] EWCA Civ 78, [2006] Ch 243, [274].

64 Lord Walker adhered to a reading of s 32(1)(c) of the Limitation Act 1980 which required the claimant's mistake to have formed an "essential ingredient of the cause of action": cf B Häcker, "Still at the Crossroads" (2007) 123 LQR 177, esp 181–82.

65 In some areas, the unjust factor approach may be easier to apply than the absence of basis model, eg in the context of non-participatory enrichments and in explaining the conceptual foundation of the right to rescind a contract: cf A Burrows and others, "The New Birksian Approach to Unjust Enrichment" [2004] RLR 260, 272 (Stevens), 275–76 (Krebs), 288 (Tettenborn); Burrows in *Mapping the Law* (n 60) 39–40. Cf also the critical assessment of 'transfer' cases by Scott [2006] RLR (n 44), esp 98–104.

a) Effecting Restitution

The answers given by English and German law on the mode of effecting restitution differ significantly. Under the English common law, a personal claim based on unjust enrichment is for restitution of the *money value* of the defendant's enrichment.[66] It is quantified by assessing the amount by which the defendant's wealth, considered as an abstract fund, is swollen at the moment of receipt.[67] The defendant becomes indebted to the claimant for this amount, but he is not normally and without more under any duty to surrender a particular asset.[68] German law, by contrast, imposes on him in the first instance an obligation to disgorge the enrichment *in specie*.[69] In keeping with the general preference of German law for specific remedies,[70] § 812 I 1 BGB orders the defendant to surrender what he has obtained (*Herausgabe des Erlangten*). This duty extends to any benefits from the use of a chattel and its 'fruits' (collectively described as 'secondary benefits') as well as to surrogate assets (§ 818 I BGB).[71] Only where precise restitution *in specie* is for some reason impossible is the personal claim converted into one for value restitution (§ 818 II BGB).[72]

---

66 The main common law remedies are the action for money had and received (to the claimant's use), the action for money paid (to the defendant's use) as well as *quantum meruit* and *quantum valebat* claims. On the history of these forms of action see eg JH Baker, "The History of Quasi-Contract in English Law" in WR Cornish and others (eds), *Restitution Past, Present and Future: Essays in Honour of Gareth Jones* (Hart, Oxford 1998) 37.

67 This is what Birks *Introduction* (n 46) 75–98, describes as the 'first measure' (value received). It can be contrasted with the 'second measure' (value surviving), which has at most a gap-filling role as far as personal claims are concerned: cf ibid 85–87; L Smith, *The Law of Tracing* (Clarendon Press, Oxford 1997) 30–33.

68 Cf P Birks (ed), *English Private Law* (OUP, Oxford 2000) vol 2 [15.177]–[15.179] (Birks), followed by *English Private Law* (2nd edn) (n 8) [18.169]–[18.171] (C Mitchell); Birks *Unjust Enrichment* (n 57) 168–70, 171–72. See also Burrows *Restitution* (n 46) 52–53. Compare and contrast R Chambers "Resulting Trusts" in A Burrows and A Rodger (eds), *Mapping the Law: Essays in Memory of Peter Birks* (OUP, Oxford 2006) 247, 256–57.

69 For present purposes, this will be called a 'right *in personam ad rem (acquirendam)*', but it should not be confused with the historical concept of the *ius ad rem*, which denoted an embryonic property right. On the distinction see H Coing, *Europäisches Privatrecht: vol 1* (Beck, München 1985) 175–76.

70 The so-called principle of *Naturalrestitution* (specific reinstatement) applies throughout German private law, eg when a person is under an obligation to compensate another: § 249 BGB.

71 On the scope of a claimant's right to substitutes under § 818 I BGB, and in particular on the exclusion of so-called *commoda ex negotiatione*, see below, Chapter VIII.C.2.a (esp pp 305–6).

72 The fact that the primary remedy under §§ 812, 818 BGB is restitution *in specie* does not necessarily imply that the enrichment itself must be understood to consist of a

A proviso needs to be entered at this point, lest the aforementioned contrast should lead the reader to believe that English law never allows for restitution *in specie*. There is a debate in the Common law world about the possibility of so-called 'proprietary restitution'. Whether, and under what circumstances, proprietary restitution is the appropriate response to unjust enrichment is extremely contentious.[73] One aim of this book is to take stock of the case law and academic debate, and to suggest a systematically coherent solution to the question of when – and in what form – proprietary restitution is warranted in impaired consent transfer cases. Suffice it to note for the time being that, even if unjust enrichment were to generate a proprietary response, this would not automatically enable the claimant to recover a specific asset. Rights *in rem* have to be asserted according to the general rules of English property law. As will be seen below,[74] these may, but need not, allow for specific recovery.

b) Disenrichment

In both legal systems, the most important and most common defence to a claim in unjust(ified) enrichment is that the defendant is no longer enriched. English lawyers usually refer to this plea of subsequent disenrichment as 'change of position',[75] while German lawyers call it *Wegfall der Bereicherung* (literally: 'loss' or 'disappearance of the enrichment'). If made out, the disenrichment defence ensures that the defendant's obligation to make restitution is confined to the value of the enrichment still surviving in his hands.[76] It prevents the strict liability regime outlined above,

specific asset. W Flume, "Der Wegfall der Bereicherung vom römischen zum geltenden Recht" in Rechts- und Staatswissenschaftliche Fakultät Göttingen (ed), *Festschrift für Hans Niedermeyer zum 70. Geburtstag* (Schwartz & Co, Göttingen 1963) 103, esp 153–54, argues that German law differs from Roman law in defining a recipient's enrichment not by reference to the particular asset received, but by reference to his overall wealth measured in the abstract.

[73] The term 'proprietary restitution' denotes the reversal of an unjust enrichment via a right or other interest *in rem*. For a discussion of the issue see Chapter IV.D (pp 125–59).

[74] See section D.2.a of the present chapter (at pp 42–43).

[75] Subsequent disenrichment is the main field of application of the change of position defence. However, the latter plea may actually be wider than the former and prevent recovery even in cases where the defendant – though not disenriched – has otherwise irreversibly altered his position in reliance on the security of his receipt. The element of 'reliance', on the other hand, features more centrally in the notion of 'change of position' than in that of 'disenrichment': cf the discussion by J Edelman and E Bant, *Unjust Enrichment in Australia* (OUP, Sydney 2006) 320–22, 323–31.

[76] In German law, this is the defendant's 'abstractly' rather than his 'traceably surviving' enrichment: cf eg BGHZ 1, 75, 81; BGHZ 55, 128, 134; see also K Rebmann, FJ Säcker and R Rixecker (eds), *Münchener Kommentar zum Bürgerlichen Gesetzbuch, vol 5: §§ 705–853* (4th edn Beck, München 2004) § 818 [62]–[72] (Lieb); Zimmer-

under which even innocent defendants can be exposed to liability,[77] from operating too harshly. While every recipient of an unjust(ified) enrichment, irrespective of his state of mind or level of culpability, is required to give up extant gains, he is not to be left out-of-pocket without good reason. In effect, the disenrichment defence works as a (partial or complete) release from the obligation to make restitution. Only in so far as the enrichee is not deemed worthy of protection (eg because he knew of his liability) is he debarred from pleading the defence.

German law achieves this result by a rather convoluted route. According to § 818 III BGB, the obligation to make restitution of the asset obtained, to surrender secondary benefits and surrogates (§ 818 I BGB), or to disgorge the value of the enrichment (§ 818 II BGB) is excluded to the extent that the recipient is no longer enriched. It will be noted that the provision makes no reference to the defendant's state of mind. The disqualification of certain defendants is instead implicit in §§ 818 IV, 819, 820 BGB. Through an elaborate chain of references, these sections deprive enrichees who were aware of their restitutionary liability or deliberately closed their eyes to the obvious,[78] those who acted illegally or immorally in receiving a performance,[79] or who knew that their receipt was in some way conditional[80] of the opportunity to invoke the disenrichment defence by holding them liable according to the BGB's 'general provisions'.[81]

In English law, the change of position defence is of relatively recent pedigree. Only in 1991 did the House of Lords formally acknowledge its existence.[82] Unsurprisingly, its exact ramifications remain yet to be worked out.[83] One of the most contentious questions concerns the level of knowledge or fault which will disqualify a defendant from relying on his disenrichment. Suggestions range from 'bad faith'[84] over subjective or objective

---

mann/du Plessis [1994] RLR (n 38) 38–40. With regard to English law, the issue is still not finally settled. Birks in *English Private Law* (1st edn) (n 68) [15.250], favours the German approach, and this liberal interpretation can glean some support from the causal link test of disenrichment approved in *Scottish Equitable plc v Derby* [2001] EWCA Civ 369, [2001] 3 All ER 818, [31] (Robert Walker LJ): cf Virgo *Principles* (n 46) 694.

[77] See section C.1 of the present chapter (esp overview on p 25).

[78] § 819 I BGB, interpreted in accordance with BGHZ 133, 246.

[79] § 819 II BGB is specifically aimed at the *condictio ob turpem vel iniustam causam* in § 817 1 BGB (cf n 39).

[80] § 820 I BGB is specifically aimed at the *condictio ob rem* (*condictio causa data causa non secuta*) and the *condictio ob causam finitam* in § 812 I 2 BGB (cf n 39).

[81] For details see below, Chapter III.C.2.b (pp 68–71).

[82] *Lipkin Gorman (a firm) v Karpnale Ltd* [1991] 2 AC 548 (HL).

[83] For an overview of the various debates see A Burrows, "Change of Position: The View from England" (2003) 36 Loy LA L Rev 803. Cf also the forthcoming monograph by E Bant, *The Change of Position Defence* (Hart, Oxford 2009).

[84] *Lipkin Gorman v Karpnale* (n 82) 580 (Lord Goff).

'dishonesty'[85] to the unhelpful term 'unconscionability',[86] though it is clear that mere negligence does not suffice.[87] English courts will not therefore adopt a test of relative blameworthiness such as that favoured in New Zealand.[88] It seems possible that the requirements of 'bad faith', 'dishonesty' and 'unconscionability' will come to resemble §§ 819, 820 BGB and prevent only defendants who knew that they were not (unconditionally) entitled to keep an enrichment, or who deliberately shut their eyes to the obvious, from invoking the change of position defence.

D. Basic Principles of Property Law

1. Conception of 'Ownership'

It is in the area of property law that we encounter the greatest divergences between the Civilian and the Common law tradition. Their very idea of what it means to 'own' something is fundamentally different, as is their understanding of the relationship between 'property' and possession. German law, like Roman law, embraces an absolute notion of ownership, while the equivalent English concept can be described as non-absolute in at least two respects.[89] Firstly, in building its theory of 'ownership' around the right to possession, English law adopts a system of relative titles as opposed to absolute entitlements. Secondly, the recognition that equitable

---

[85] Cf *Niru Battery Manufacturing Co v Milestone Trading Ltd (No 1)* [2002] EWHC 1425 (QBD Comm), [2002] 2 All ER (Comm) 705, [122]–[135], where Moore-Bick J discussed the various standards of 'dishonesty' and ultimately concluded (at [135]) that 'good faith' was "a broad concept ... capable of embracing a failure to act in a commercially acceptable way and sharp practice of a kind that falls short of outright [subjective] dishonesty as well as [subjective] dishonesty itself". See also the discussion by P Birks, "Change of Position: The Two Central Questions" (2004) 120 LQR 373, 375–76, who suggests that this effectively amounts to criterion of 'objective dishonesty'.

[86] Cf *Niru Battery Manufacturing Co v Milestone Trading Ltd (No 1)* [2003] EWCA Civ 1446, [2004] QB 985, [148]–[162] (Clarke LJ), but note that Clarke LJ thought his standard to be the same as that applied by Moore-Bick J at first instance: ibid [164]. Compare the passage set out in n 85 immediately above, and see the critical comments by Birks (2004) 120 LQR (n 85) 376–77, and A Burrows, "Clouding the Issues on Change of Position" (2004) 63 CLJ 276, 277–78.

[87] *Dextra Bank & Trust Co Ltd v Bank of Jamaica* [2002] 1 All ER (Comm) 193 (PC) [40]–[46].

[88] *National Bank of New Zealand Ltd v Waitaki International Processing (NI) Ltd* [1999] 2 NZLR 211 (NZCA). Cf *Dextra Bank v Bank of Jamaica* (n 87) [45].

[89] In the context of immovables (realty), there is or was additionally the possibility of temporal slicing: cf eg FH Lawson and B Rudden, *The Law of Property* (3rd edn OUP, Oxford 2002) 97–100. Nowadays, such temporal slicing is no longer possible at common law and has become the exclusive realm of equity.

interests are in some sense 'proprietary' has led to the idea of ownership being 'split' into a bare legal title and an equitable (or beneficial) interest.

a) Absolute Notion of Ownership and Relativity of Title

In ordinary language, the word 'property' is ambiguous. It is sometimes used to refer to a thing and sometimes to a person's rights over a thing. Only the latter meaning is – strictly speaking – accurate in legal parlance.[90] The most extensive right a person can have over a thing may be called 'ownership'.

In German law, the notion is fairly straightforward. Ownership can be roughly equated with the Roman concept of *dominium*. The owner of a corporeal object is the person who is in principle entitled to "deal with the thing as he pleases and exclude others from any interference".[91] It belongs to him, and only him. Ownership is in theory absolute. A person owns an object to the exclusion of all others. The object can have only one owner (or group of co-owners)[92] at any one time. While ownership will often coincide with possession, there is no conceptual link between the two. The former is a question of legal entitlement, the latter primarily a question of the factual matrix.[93] Only when an evidential impasse prevents the issue of ownership from being resolved conclusively is the person in possession of a movable object deemed to be its owner (§ 1006 BGB).[94]

English law does not really accommodate the notion of 'ownership' as such. Although the language of 'owning' and 'belonging to' is commonly used, even in technical legal discourse, the central concept within English

---

[90] It will not always be possible within this book to avoid using the term 'property' to refer to an object: too engrained are some of the expressions, eg 'damage to property'.

[91] § 903 1 BGB. In Latin terminology: *ius utendi, fruendi, abutendi* (the right to use, to make a profit, and to exploit in any way).

[92] Co-ownership is possible in the form of ownership in common (*Miteigentum nach Bruchteilen*: § 1008 BGB) or joint ownership (*Gesamthandseigentum*).

[93] Actual possession requires sufficient physical control over an object (*corpus*) coupled with the intention to possess (*animus*). Whether a person has the requisite degree of control is determined by reference to the prevailing socio-legal standards: BGHZ 101, 186, 188.

[94] § 1006 I 1 BGB raises the rebuttable presumption that when the possessor of a movable object came into actual possession of it, he obtained 'proprietary possession' (*Eigenbesitz* or *possessio pro suo*) and at the same time acquired ownership unconditionally, which he has since retained throughout the time of his possession: cf eg *Palandt* (n 7) § 1006 [4] (Bassenge); BGH NJW 1967, 2008; BGH NJW 1975, 1269, 1270; BGHZ 64, 395, 396. Note that the BGB contains special provisions protecting a person's possession: §§ 861 ff BGB (*possessorische Besitzschutzansprüche*) protect possession as a factual state of affairs, while § 1007 BGB (*petitorische Besitzschutzansprüche*) protects a better right to possession of movables. The latter provision is of very little relevance beside §§ 861 ff and §§ 985 ff, 1006 BGB: *Palandt* (n 7) § 1007 [1] (Bassenge).

personal property law is that of 'title'. Title is a shorthand for the (theoretically perpetual) right to immediate and exclusive possession of a thing.[95] With the right to immediate and exclusive possession come all the benefits normally associated with 'ownership', such as the right to use and enjoy. Title thus connotes a generalized proprietary interest in an object which is protected against interference by third parties and can be alienated. However, in contradistinction to Civilian 'ownership', a common law 'title' does not have the characteristic of being absolute and unique. This is because possession itself is a root of title.[96] The mere fact of possession generates a right to possession (and thus a title to the object in question), irrespective of whether there already exists a person with a similar earlier right. Several people can thus have competing rights to possession of the same thing. In accordance with the maxim *qui prior est tempore potior est iure*, their titles are ranked in the order of their creation. An earlier title is stronger than a later one. This leads to the fundamental notion of 'relativity of title', around which English property law revolves. A person who has title to an object has a right *in rem* which is good against the whole world save any person with a better title to the same object. Hence, even a finder or a thief acquires *a* title to the thing found or stolen,[97] albeit one which is defeasible by the person who lost it or the victim of the theft (as well as by anybody else with a superior title). Only the holder of the first or best possible title to an object can be called its 'owner' in any meaningful sense. However, since English property law is solely concerned with the question of relative entitlements to possession, the language of ownership is best avoided for comparative purposes. It is worth noting that any presumption of the sort contained in § 1006 BGB seems unnecessary in a system which treats possession not merely as an *indicium*, but as a very root of title.[98]

---

[95] Cf eg *English Private Law* (2nd edn) (n 8) [4.131] (Swadling). To count as 'title', the right to immediate and exclusive possession has to be good against the whole world save any person with a better title (see text to nn 96–98). A mere contractual or other purely personal entitlement will not in itself suffice: *Jarvis v Williams* [1955] 1 WLR 71 (CA). Misleading in this regard: *International Factors Ltd v Rodriguez* [1979] QB 351 (CA); *Iran v Barakat Galleries Ltd* [2007] EWCA Civ 1374, [2008] 3 WLR 486.

[96] This was already noted by F Pollock and RS Wright, *An Essay on Possession in the Common Law* (Clarendon Press, Oxford 1888) 22, and it explains why English lawyers often refer to so-called 'possessory titles'.

[97] Finding: *Armory v Delamirie* (1722) 1 Str 505, 93 ER 664; *Parker v British Airways Board* [1982] QB 1004 (CA). Theft: *Costello v Chief Constable of Derbyshire Constabulary* [2001] EWCA Civ 381, [2001] 1 WLR 1437. Against the widespread misapprehension that thieves do not acquire any title: G Battersby, "Acquiring Title by Theft" (2002) 65 MLR 603.

[98] Only a legal system like the German, which conceives of ownership as absolute and conceptually independent of possession, requires an evidential presumption to bridge the gap between factual control and legal entitlement (bearing in mind the way property

b) Legal and Equitable Proprietary Interests

There is another sense in which English law adheres to a less absolute concept of 'property' and 'ownership' than German law. It derives from the peculiar historical division of the English Common law (in the broad sense) into the rules and principles of the common law (in the narrow sense) administered by the King's Courts, and those of equity developed by the more flexible jurisdiction of the Court of Chancery.[99] This division gave birth to the remarkable and distinctly English institution known as the 'trust'. The term describes a special way of holding rights. Rights, whether personal or proprietary, are usually held outright. Their holder is free to use them as he likes, subject only to the restrictions imposed on him by the common law. If, however, he holds those rights on trust, equity has something to say about the way he deals with them. The trust mechanism ensures that the holder of the rights in question (the trustee) uses them not for his own personal purposes, but for the benefit of a specified third party (the beneficiary).

The proprietary relevance of the trust stems from the fact that the rights held under it are often property rights, and that the Court of Chancery was willing to exercise its jurisdiction not only against the original trustee himself, but also against certain third parties. If a person agrees (or is compelled) to hold his title to an object on trust for somebody else, then an equitable interest is created and becomes engrafted on what is henceforth a 'bare' legal title.[100] This process is often described, albeit perhaps not entirely accurately, as a 'splitting up' of the formerly uniform interest into a 'legal' and an 'equitable title'. Should the trustee later dispose of the legal title in circumstances other than those authorized by the terms of the trust (ie in breach of trust), then the beneficiary will – subject to the rules on *bona fide* purchase[101] – be able to assert his equitable interest against third

is protected in both systems: cf below, text to nn 109–122). Yet in spite of this, some English authors treat possession as no more than *prima facie* proof of 'ownership': *Pollock & Wright on Possession* (n 96) 25; ELG Tyler and N Palmer, *Crossley Vaines on Personal Property* (5th edn London, Butterworths 1973) 45; D Fox, "Relativity of Title at Law and in Equity" (2006) 65 CLJ 330, esp 342–44. A Bell, *Modern Law of Personal Property in England and Ireland* (Butterworths, London 1989) 76–77, even asserts that the inadmissibility of the *ius tertii* defence is a consequence of regarding possession as *conclusive* evidence of ownership.

99 For an account of the development see eg JH Baker, *An Introduction to English Legal History* (4th edn Butterworths, London 2002) 37–52, 97–116; SFC Milsom, *Historical Foundations of the Common Law* (2nd edn Butterworths, London 1981) 37–96.

100 Before the trust is created, no equitable interest exists: *Westdeutsche Landesbank Girozentrale v Islington London BC* [1996] AC 669 (HL) 706 (Lord Browne-Wilkinson); J Hackney, *Understanding Equity and Trusts* (Fontana, London 1987) 25.

101 See below, section D.4 of the present chapter (esp text to nn 176–177 on p 52).

parties acquiring the title in question.[102] After much debate about the exact nature of a beneficiary's interest in trust property, the trust's ability to bind strangers to its creation eventually led to the recognition that the beneficiary has more than merely a bundle of rights *in personam* against the trustee. There is now a broad consensus in English law that the beneficiary's right in respect of the object held on trust for him is properly characterized as 'proprietary'.[103] Although it is important to bear in mind that equitable interests are, by their very nature, not fully comparable to common law property rights,[104] it will be convenient for present purposes to adhere to the conventional terminology and to refer to equitable interests as rights *in rem*.[105]

German law knows no equivalent 'division' of ownership. While it too recognizes that in some situations a person holds rights for the benefit of another, via a device described by the umbrella term *Treuhand*, it has failed to develop an overarching theory of the kind that English law boasts. A *Treuhand* arises only in a limited number of particular instances (scattered throughout the BGB and developed outside the statutory framework), each subject to its own specific rules and principles.[106] The common fea-

[102] It is unclear whether and to what extent such third parties come under similar fiduciary obligations as the consensual (express) trustee, but it seems practically inconceivable that a court would hold them subject to any management or investment duties.

[103] Eg *Tinsley v Milligan* [1994] 1 AC 340 (HL) 371 (Lord Browne- Wilkinson). Seminal: AW Scott, "The Nature of the Rights of the *Cestui Que Trust*" (1917) 17 Colum L Rev 269. For an overview of the debate see DWM Walters, "The Nature of the Trust Beneficiary's Interest" (1967) 45 Can Bar Rev 219; PH Pettit, *Equity and the Law of Trusts* (10th edn OUP, Oxford 2006) 81–84.

[104] Despite occasional suggestions to the contrary, an equitable interest is only ever exigible against the holder for the time being of the right or interest to which it relates. This leads B McFarlane, *The Structure of Property Law* (Hart, Oxford 2008) esp 66–79, to argue that equitable interests are neither purely personal nor fully proprietary, but *sui generis*. He distinguishes between genuine 'property rights' (rights against things which are *prima facie* binding on the whole world) and so-called 'persistent rights' (equitable interests, being 'rights against rights' which are *prima facie* binding on anyone acquiring a right affected by them).

[105] The terms 'property right', 'proprietary interest', and 'right/interest *in rem*' are therefore used to denote a right or interest which relates – whether directly or indirectly – to a physical object (with which we are here exclusively concerned) and which is *prima facie* binding on the whole world (at common law) or at least potentially binding on anyone acquiring the right affected by it (in equity). This choice of terminology is for simplicity of exposition only. It should not be understood to indicate any substantive disagreement with McFarlane's thesis about the nature of equitable interests (cf n 104).

[106] In some of these situations, the *Treuhand* is functionally equivalent to a trust. For a comparative analysis see eg H Kötz, *Trust und Treuhand: Eine rechtsvergleichende Darstellung des anglo-amerikanischen Trust und funktionsverwandter Institute des deutschen Rechts* (Vandenhoeck & Ruprecht, Göttingen 1963). For the broader historical and

ture of all *Treuhand* situations is that the external power of the 'trustee' (*Treuhänder*) in respect of the asset concerned exceeds the extent to which he is internally authorized to deal with it, ie as a matter of his relationship with the 'beneficiary'. This accounts for the fact that the German *Treuhand* does not normally bind third parties who have acquired *Treuhand* assets in breach of the 'trustee's' duties.[107] The effects of a *Treuhand* are personal, not proprietary.[108] Its existence therefore makes no inroad into the absolute notion of ownership under German law.

2. Assertion and Protection of Property Rights

Closely connected with the fundamentally different conceptions of 'ownership' are significant divergences between the ways in which property rights are asserted and protected in the German and English legal systems.

a) Direct and Indirect Assertion of Property Rights

The main remedy by which German law enables the owner of a thing to recover possession of it is the *vindicatio* (§ 985 BGB).[109] Like its Roman ancestor, the *vindicatio* contained in § 985 BGB represents a direct assertion of ownership. The claimant states his case simply by saying: "This thing is mine". If he can substantiate his assertion, where necessary with the help of presumptions,[110] and if the defendant cannot show a right to

---

comparative perspective cf R Helmholz and R Zimmermann (eds), *Itinera Fiduciae: Trust and Treuhand in Historical Perspective* (Duncker & Humblot, Berlin 1998); J Wolff, *Trust, Fiducia und fiduziarische Treuhand: Historisch-rechtsvergleichende Untersuchung mit einer Darstellung des Trust in Schottland sowie des römischen und österreichischen Fideikommiss* (Lang, Frankfurt/Main 2005).

[107] An exception is only made for cases in which the third party has fraudulently and thus immorally acted in concert with the *Treuhänder*: cf RGZ 153, 366, 370–71; BGH NJW 1968, 1471.

[108] Note, however, that *Treuhand* assets are treated as not belonging to the 'trustee's' estate as far as the 'trustee's' other creditors are concerned: cf BGHZ 11, 37, 41; BGH NJW 1959, 1223, 1224. For this reason, the *Treuhand* has variously been described as 'quasi-proprietary': eg W Siebert, *Das rechtsgeschäftliche Treuhandverhältnis: Ein dogmatischer und rechtsvergleichender Beitrag zum allgemeinen Treuhandproblem* (Elwert, Marburg 1933) esp 149–72, 195–200; CW Canaris, "Die Verdinglichung obligatorischer Rechte" in HH Jakobs and others (eds), *Festschrift für Werner Flume zum 70. Geburtstag* (Schmidt, Köln 1978) vol 1, 371, 410–19. For an account of the development in comparative perspective see S Grundmann, "The Evolution of Trust and Treuhand in the 20th Century" in R Helmholz and R Zimmermann (eds), *Itinera Fiduciae: Trust and Treuhand in Historical Perspective* (Duncker & Humblot, Berlin 1998) 469.

[109] There may be competing claims to possession under § 861 BGB and § 1007 BGB: see n 94 above.

[110] See above, n 94 and corresponding text.

possession which is good vis-à-vis the claimant,[111] the *vindicatio* will be successful and the claimant will obtain a court order enabling him to recover possession of the object in question.[112] Interferences not amounting to a deprivation or withholding of possession can be stayed and even forestalled in advance of their occurrence using the *actio negatoria* in § 1004 BGB. Like the *rei vindicatio*, this action constitutes a direct assertion of ownership.[113]

In England, there is no action at common law corresponding to the *vindicatio* or the *actio negatoria*.[114] Title to goods is asserted not directly, but indirectly via the law of wrongs. A claimant cannot say in court: "I have a title to this thing". He has to say: "The defendant has wrongfully interfered with my right to immediate and exclusive possession of such-and-such an object and has so committed a tort against me". To be wrongful, the interference need not necessarily be deliberate or even negligent. However, as a result of its incremental and haphazard development, English tort law has failed to establish a single, all-embracing tort of wrongful interference with another's right to possession. Instead, a number of different and in part overlapping torts came to provide the means for the indirect assertion of title. Conversion (also called 'trover'), trespass to goods and detinue were the principal actions relating to chattels, ie movable objects.[115] In 1977, the Torts (Interference with Goods) Act abolished the old action of detinue and, though not creating any new tort, subsumed conversion and trespass to goods – together with the tort of negligence in so far as it results in damage to goods or to an interest in goods – under a statutory regime streamlining certain remedial and procedural aspects of all 'wrongful interferences with goods'.[116] Conversion now dominates the scene. At its heart lies the idea of misappropriation, but this is understood in a broad

---

[111] Cf § 986 I BGB.

[112] In Roman law, by contrast, a defendant could not be forced to deliver up the object. He would be condemned to pay its estimated value (*condemnatio pecuniaria*) unless he returned it to the claimant: see eg F Schulz, *Classical Roman Law* (Clarendon Press, Oxford 1951) 369–72.

[113] Again, there may be a competing claim (based on the claimant's factual possession) under § 862 BGB: cf nn 94 and 109 above.

[114] Two possible exceptions are interpleader proceedings, as eg in *Trustee of the Property of FC Jones & Sons (a firm) v Jones* [1997] Ch 159 (CA), and – historically – the action of ejectment for the recovery of land: cf *English Private Law* (2nd edn) (n 8) [17.320] (Edelman/Davies).

[115] For an account of their scope and development, and for details on the special tort governing injury to a bailor's 'reversionary interest', see eg A Dugdale and M Jones (gen eds), *Clerk & Lindsell on Torts* (19th edn Sweet & Maxwell, London 2006) ch 17, esp [17–01]–[17–03] (Tettenborn).

[116] Torts (Interference with Goods) Act 1977, ss 1–2. Cf *Clerk & Lindsell* (n 115) [17–04]–[17–05] (Tettenborn).

sense. Whenever the claimant's grievance is that the defendant has dealt with a movable object in a way which calls into question or denies the claimant's (better) right to possession, the appropriate action is conversion. To make up for the lack of a *vindicatio* at common law, liability in conversion is strict.[117] The defendant's state of mind is irrelevant. It should be noted that the primary remedy for conversion is not specific recovery, but damages.[118] While the court adjudicating the dispute now has a discretion to order delivery up of the goods in question,[119] the normal mechanism is that damages are paid and that this extinguishes the claimant's title to the goods.[120] Damages are, at the claimant's option, calculated either by reference to his loss (usually, but not restricted to, the market value of the goods)[121] or by reference to the defendant's gain (which may exceed the claimant's loss).[122]

Unlike the common law, equity does have something approximating a *vindicatio*. A claimant with an equitable interest in an object can ask the court to make a declaration to the effect that the defendant holds the (legal) title on trust for him.[123] Under the rule in *Saunders v Vautier*,[124] he may also be able to 'execute the trust' and force the defendant to transfer the title to him (typically by delivery of the object).[125] Title can thereafter be

[117] Cf eg Law Reform Committee, *Eighteenth Report: Conversion and Detinue* (Cmnd 4774, 1971) [13]. In *Hollins v Fowler* (1872) LR 7 QB 616 (Exch Ch) 639, Cleasby B said: "The liability under [the action for trover] is founded upon what has been regarded as a salutary rule for the protection of property, namely, that persons deal with the property in chattels or exercise acts of ownership over them at their own peril".

[118] Prior to the 1977 Act, an award of damages was the only remedy for conversion. Delivery up was the realm of detinue. Cf *General and Finance Facilities v Cooks Cars (Romford)* [1963] 1 WLR 644 (CA) 648–51 (Diplock LJ).

[119] Torts (Interference with Goods) Act 1977, s 3.

[120] Torts (Interference with Goods) Act 1977, s 5. The process is often described as a 'forced judicial sale', but – given that the defendant already has (or had) a title to the goods by virtue of his possession – the extinction of the claimant's superior title is usually sufficient.

[121] *Kuwait Airways Corp v Iraqi Airways Co (Nos 4 & 5)* [2002] UKHL 19, [2002] 2 AC 883, [67] (Lord Nicholls). His Lordship questioned whether an innocent converter would ever be held liable for losses exceeding the amount of his gain: ibid [79].

[122] *Lamine v Dorrell* (1701) 2 Ld Raym 1216, 92 ER 303; *United Australia Ltd v Barclays Bank Ltd* [1941] AC 1 (HL). These gain-based damages constitute a form of 'restitution for wrongs' (cf n 51).

[123] Such a declaration seems to have been at issue in *Macmillan Inc v Bishopsgate Investment Trust plc (No 3)* [1996] 1 WLR 387 (CA).

[124] (1841) 4 Beav 115, 49 ER 282; aff'd (1841) Cr & Ph 240, 41 ER 482.

[125] The claimant needs to be a competent adult and the sole beneficiary absolutely entitled to the trust property. For a recent analysis of the rule and its scope see P Matthews, "The Comparative Importance of the Rule in *Saunders v Vautier*" (2006) 122 LQR 266.

asserted in the ordinary way.[126] It is worth adding that, unless he happens to be in possession of the trust assets,[127] a beneficiary *as such* cannot invoke the common law torts outlined above.[128]

b) The Protection of Property Rights in Context

Having considered the way in which ownership and title are asserted in German and English law, it is now necessary to examine briefly the broader context of the protection afforded to property rights in chattels.

(i) Protection through the law of wrongs

In both legal systems, much of the work is done by the law of wrongs. As far as the English common law is concerned, this is already evident from what was said above. Under the regime of the Torts (Interference with Goods) Act 1977, title to chattels is protected primarily via the torts of conversion and trespass to goods. They are supplemented by the tort of negligence. Although not specifically concerned with damage to property, the tort of negligence attains importance whenever goods are physically injured in circumstances not amounting to an interference with possession. To bring a successful action, the claimant needs to establish that the defendant caused the damage and, in doing so, breached a duty of care owed to the claimant. As the name 'negligence' suggests, liability is fault-based, not strict.[129] Equitable interests, too, are protected through wrongs-based claims. Breach of trust, 'knowing assistance' in a breach of trust, and (probably)[130] 'knowing receipt' of trust property are the appropriate heads of liability where the unauthorized disposition by a trustee over assets held

---

[126] Where the transfer of title is effected by delivery, it will not be necessary to bring a claim in conversion against the (former) trustee. In practice, a trust beneficiary who proceeds under *Saunders v Vautier* (n 124) would therefore appear to stand better chances of specific recovery than a claimant who relies on a pre-existing title and sues for conversion: cf text to nn 118–120.

[127] *Healey v Healey* [1915] 1 KB 938 (KBD).

[128] *MCC Proceeds Inc v Lehman Bros International (Europe)* [1998] 4 All ER 675 (CA).

[129] Damages are purely compensatory, measured by reference to the claimant's reasonably foreseeable loss.

[130] There is a debate about the exact nature and scope of liability for 'knowing receipt': cf (in chronological order) P Birks, "Misdirected Funds: Restitution from the Recipient" [1989] LMCLQ 296; W Swadling, "Some Lessons from the Law of Torts" in P Birks (ed), *The Frontiers of Liability* (OUP, Oxford 1994) vol 1, 41, 42–47; D Nicholls, "Knowing Receipt: The Need for a New Landmark" in WR Cornish and others (eds), *Restitution Past, Present and Future: Essays in Honour of Gareth Jones* (Hart, Oxford 1998) 231; Smith (2000) 116 LQR (n 55) 428–36; P Birks, "Receipt" in P Birks and A Pretto (eds), *Breach of Trust* (Hart, Oxford 2002) 213.

on trust is concerned.[131] Each involves the breach of a duty recognized in equity only.

In German law, § 823 I BGB is the main delictual provision dealing, *inter alia*, with damage to property. It imposes liability on "a person who, intentionally or negligently, unlawfully injures another's life, body, health, liberty, property, or other right".[132] Differently to English law, where damages – ie the payment of monetary compensation – are the primary remedy, the so-called principle of *Naturalrestitution* (specific reinstatement) in § 249 I BGB ensures that reparation is made *in specie* whenever possible.

(ii) Protection through the law of unjust(ified) enrichment

Unjust(ified) enrichment may also have a role in the protection of property rights. German law is explicit about this. Given that the delictual liability imposed by the BGB generally depends on fault (§§ 823 ff BGB) and aims only at putting the claimant into the position he would have been in had the delict not been committed (§§ 249 ff BGB), it is left to the provisions on unjustified enrichment (§§ 812 ff BGB) to ensure that the defendant, even if innocent, is stripped of extant gains. This is the realm of the *Eingriffskondiktion*, which constitutes, as has already been observed, the most important category of *Nichtleistungskondiktion*.[133] One way of obtaining a relevant enrichment at the claimant's expense, other than by way of his performance, is by making unauthorized use of an object belonging to him. Property rights are wealth-allocating rights. If they are infringed in a manner which enables the defendant to appropriate to himself value allocated to the claimant owner, the resulting shift of wealth is reversed by the law of unjustified enrichment (cf § 812 I 1 alt 2 BGB).[134] § 816 I 1 BGB con-

---

[131] Breach of trust is generally regarded as a strict liability wrong (cf *Booth v Booth* (1838) 1 Beav 125, 48 ER 886), but it probably requires the defendant to have been aware of his position as a trustee. 'Knowing assistance' depends on dishonesty: *Royal Brunei Airlines Sdn Bhd v Tan* [1995] 2 AC 378 (PC), *Twinsectra Ltd v Yardley* [2002] UKHL 12, [2002] 2 AC 164. 'Knowing receipt', in so far as it is a wrong (cf n 130), seems also to require fault of some sort (contra only: Swadling in *Frontiers of Liability* (n 130) esp 47), but the requisite level of culpability is unclear: contrast eg *Re Montagu's Settlement Trusts* [1987] Ch 264 (ChD) (dishonesty), with *Belmont Finance Corp v Williams Furniture Ltd (No 2)* [1980] 1 All ER 393 (CA) (negligence), and *Bank of Credit and Commerce International (Overseas) Ltd v Akindele* [2001] Ch 437 (CA) ('unconscionability'). Cf the discussion in Chapter VI.C.2.a below (at pp 235–37).

[132] § 823 II BGB, by imposing the same liability on anyone contravening a statute intended to protect others (such as the German Criminal Code, StGB) often produces a concurrent claim.

[133] See above, section C.1.a of the present chapter (esp text to nn 40–42 on p 26).

[134] Note, however, that §§ 987 ff BGB take precedence in certain situations: cf text to n 147 below.

tains a special case of the *Eingriffskondiktion*.[135] It provides for the situation in which the defendant has, without authorization, disposed of an asset belonging to the claimant.[136]

Whether and how far unjust enrichment claims play a part in the protection of proprietary interests under English law is unclear and extremely contentious. Those who regard 'ignorance' and 'powerlessness' as unjust factors perceive a large field of application, ranging from the defendant's unauthorized use or disposal to the receipt of goods to which the claimant has a better title.[137] The same is true if one discerns some sort of interference with property rights as decisive in cases of non-participatory enrichments.[138] Only authors who dispute that unjust enrichment has any relevance outside the context of consensual transfers of rights from one party to another deny its property-protecting function.[139] In view of the fact that English law recognizes strict liability wrongs much more widely than German law does, and that it often allows for a gain-based award of damages where they have been committed ('restitution for wrongs'), this latter view may yet win the day.[140]

(iii) Relationship between 'owner' and illegitimate possessor of an object

Whenever a defendant is in possession of the claimant's goods in circumstances which would allow the claimant directly or indirectly to assert his (superior) interest, several ancillary questions arise. They concern the extent to which the defendant is obliged to make restitution to the claimant for any use he has made of the object, when he will be liable for its loss, damage or destruction, or whether he can demand to be compensated for having expended money on it.[141] Under English law, all such issues are determined by the general rules of tort and (possibly) unjust enrichment law. For example, if the defendant uses the claimant's chattel, this will

---

[135] Another special case is dealt with in § 951 BGB, which refers to § 812 I 1 alt 2 BGB (*Rechtsgrundverweisung*).

[136] §§ 987 ff BGB never bar recourse to the law of unjustified enrichment (cf n 134) as far as the actual 'substance' of the object itself is concerned, as eg in the case of an unauthorized disposition.

[137] See above, n 53 and corresponding text. On receipt-based unjust enrichment liability in particular see Birks in *Breach of Trust* (n 130) 228–39.

[138] See above, n 55 and corresponding text.

[139] See references in n 52 above.

[140] Alternatively, restitution for wrongs could come to be reinterpreted as a part of the law of unjust enrichment: see references in n 55 above.

[141] For a historical and comparative study of the law relating to reimbursement for expenditure see D Verse, "Improvements and Enrichment: A Comparative Analysis" [1998] RLR 85; D Verse, *Verwendungen im Eigentümer-Besitzer-Verhältnis: Eine kritische Betrachtung aus historisch-rechtsvergleichender Sicht* (Mohr Siebeck, Tübingen 1999).

prima facie constitute a gain which has to be disgorged.[142] Since liability in conversion is strict, the defendant is in principle liable to the claimant even if the object in question is accidentally lost, damaged or destroyed.[143] Finally, the Torts (Interference with Goods) Act 1977 contains guidance on when the defendant's good faith improvements are to be taken into account in the claimant's action for 'wrongful interference'.[144]

German law adopts a different approach. In §§ 987–1003, the BGB contains special rules governing the relationship between an owner of a thing and its illegitimate possessor (*Eigentümer-Besitzer-Verhältnis*). These provisions are intended to privilege possessors who are unaware of their lack of a right to possess. Such *bona fide* possessors (*redliche Besitzer*) incur only a very limited liability to the owner with regard to their use of and even the destruction of the object in question.[145] They are, moreover, generously reimbursed for any expenditure they have incurred for its preservation or amelioration.[146] In order to prevent the rules of the *Eigentümer-Besitzer-Verhältnis* from being undermined, its existence is said to 'bar' recourse to the law of unjustified enrichment (§§ 812 ff BGB) and the law of delict (§§ 823 ff BGB) to the extent that a conflict could arise between them (*Sperrwirkung des Eigentümer-Besitzer-Verhältnisses*).[147]

3. Modes of Conveyance and their Relationship with Underlying (Contractual) Obligations

When ownership or title to a movable object is to be transferred from one person to another, two main questions arise. Firstly, what – if any – form does the conveyance have to take? Secondly, if the conveyance is made in

[142] It is unclear whether, beside the claim to gain-based damages for conversion (cf n 122 and corresponding text), the claimant also has a claim in unjust enrichment (cf text to nn 51–55 and to nn 137–140), and – if so – to what extent the change of position defence applies to the wrongs-based claim. In *Lipkin Gorman v Karpnale* (n 82) 580, Lord Goff stated that the defence "should not be open to a wrongdoer", but he did not specify how he wanted the term 'wrongdoer' to be understood.

[143] But query whether an innocent converter would nowadays be held liable beyond the measure of his (surviving?) enrichment: cf n 121 above. This question is closely connected to the one addressed in n 142.

[144] Torts (Interference with Goods) Act 1977, s 6. Cf also *Greenwood v Bennett* [1973] QB 195 (CA). On the problem of quantification see R Stevens, "Three Enrichment Issues" in A Burrows and A Rodger (eds), *Mapping the Law: Essays in Memory of Peter Birks* (OUP, Oxford 2006) 49, 50–54.

[145] Cf §§ 987–992 BGB and below, Chapter III.D.2.a (at pp 80–81).

[146] Cf §§ 994–996 BGB and below, Chapter III.D.2.a (at p 80).

[147] Cf §§ 992, 993 I BGB.

order to discharge a (contractual) obligation, does its validity depend on the validity of that obligation?

a) Effecting a Conveyance of Movables

Broadly speaking, a transfer of property rights can be broken down into a subjective or mental and an objective or physical element. Subjectively, the parties involved need to consent to the transaction.[148] They must want the conveyance, even if their intention is in some way defective.[149] However, the parties' subjective assent is typically not enough. Ownership or title cannot usually pass by intent alone. As a general rule, both German and English law require conveyances to be accompanied by an element of publicity. As far as movables are concerned, the requisite outward manifestation of the transfer is the delivery of the object in question by the transferor to the transferee (*traditio*).[150] The core case of delivery is a physical handing over (*Übergabe*). Actual possession passes from the transferor to the transferee. Exceptionally, the delivery may be very attenuated in its physical requirements, eg where the object is too unwieldy to be surrendered,[151] or delivery may even be purely constructive, eg where the intended transferee is already in possession of the object as a bailee or employee of the transferor's[152] or where the transferor retains actual possession of the object as the transferee's bailee.[153]

---

148 There is a question whether, in English law, a gratuitous transfer can be effected without the recipient's consent: cf *Standing v Bowring* (1886) 31 ChD 282 (CA); J Hill, "The Role of the Donee's Consent in the Law of Gift" (2001) 117 LQR 127.

149 Determining the relevance and consequences of such defects is the purpose of this book. Most defects of intention do not render the consent completely 'void' in law.

150 §§ 929 ff BGB; *Irons v Smallpiece* (1819) 2 Barn & Ald 551, 106 ER 467; *Cochrane v Moore* (1890) 25 QBD 57 (CA).

151 'Long-handed delivery' (*traditio longa manu*): §§ 929, 854 II BGB; *Chaplin v Rogers* (1800) 1 East 192, 194–95; 102 ER 75, 76 (Lord Kenyon CJ). Probably also *Rawlinson v Mort* (1905) 93 LT 555 (KBD); *Thomas v Times Book Co Ltd* [1966] 1 WLR 911 (ChD). Perhaps *Lock v Heath* (1892) 8 TLR 295 (QBD), usually described as a case of 'symbolic delivery'.

152 'Short-handed delivery' (*traditio brevi manu*): § 929 2 BGB; *Re Stoneham* [1919] 1 Ch 149 (ChD); *Pascoe v Turner* [1979] 1 WLR 431 (CA); *Winter v Winter* (1861) 4 LT 639 (QB).

153 The so-called *constitutum possessorium* is recognized as a substitute for actual delivery in § 930 BGB, but there may not be much place for it in English law (especially in the light of the *solo consensu* principle, which already dispenses with the delivery requirement in certain situations: see below, text to nn 156–158). In the gift context, at any rate, the common law insists that the transferor divest himself of actual possession: *Cochrane v Moore* (n 150). In equity, the delivery requirement can be 'circumvented' by the creation of an express trust, but 'equity will not perfect an imperfect gift': *Milroy v Lord* (1862) 4 De G F & J 264, 45 ER 1185. Cf also the discussion by L van Vliet,

While German law always insists on some form of *traditio*, whether actual or constructive, for the conveyance of a movable object to take effect, the English common law has developed other means of transferring title. For one, a formal written document known as a deed can be drawn up.[154] If properly executed and containing an unequivocal statement to this effect, the deed immediately and without more vests title in the transferee.[155] Conveyances by deed are, however, relatively rare in practice. Much more important is the possibility of effecting a conveyance without (actual or constructive) delivery within the English law of sale. This goes back to a development in the 15th century, when buyers of specific goods began to be allowed to sue their sellers in the tort of detinue for non-delivery. Since the action of detinue involved asserting a better right to possession, it came to be inferred that title to the goods had passed to the buyer without the need for any *traditio*.[156] In the context of sale, therefore, the parties' intention alone is capable of effecting a conveyance. This common law principle was first put on a statutory footing in 1893.[157] It is now contained in the Sale of Goods Act 1979, section 17(1) of which provides that "[w]here there is a contract for the sale of specific or ascertained goods the property in them is transferred to the buyer at such time as the parties to the contract intend it to be transferred".[158] If the contract of sale is unconditional and the goods are in a deliverable state, then, unless a different intention appears, "the property in the goods passes to the buyer when the contract is made, and it is immaterial whether the time of payment or the time of delivery, or both, be postponed".[159] As a consequence, sale transactions

---

Transfer of Movables in German, French, English and Dutch Law (Ars Aequi Libri, Nijmegen 2000) 127–28.

[154] Formality requirements: Law of Property (Miscellaneous Provisions) Act 1989, s 1. On the history of the deed as a mechanism of conveyance see eg W Holdsworth, *A History of English Law: vol 3* (4th edn Methuen & Co, London 1935) 357–58.

[155] Cf *Standing v Bowring* (1886) 31 ChD 282 (CA). For conveyances by deed to be effective against third parties and recognized in the transferor's insolvency, they need to be duly registered in accordance with the provisions of the Bills of Sale Act 1878. A deed which effects a conveyance must be distinguished from mere promises to convey made in deed (cf n 9).

[156] On the history of sale see Baker *Introduction* (n 99) 384–85; Holdworth *History: vol 3* (n 154) 356–57; Milsom *Historical Foundations* (n 99) 265–66.

[157] Sale of Goods Act 1893, s 17.

[158] The term 'property' can simply be read as 'title'. Slightly different: G Battersby and AD Preston, "The Concepts of 'Property', 'Title' and 'Owner' Used in the Sale of Goods Act 1893" (1972) 35 MLR 268, referring to "a title to the absolute legal interest in the goods sold".

[159] Sale of Goods Act 1979, s 18 rule 1. Note however, the observation by Diplock LJ in *Ward (RV) v Bignall* [1967] 1 QB 534 (CA) 545, that "in modern times very little is

constitute a major exception to the rule that English law, like German law, requires conveyances of personalty to be effected by delivery.

b) Causality and Abstraction

Where a conveyance is made in pursuance of a contractual obligation, it may be asked whether the transfer of ownership or title is a transaction separate from the underlying contract, and – if so – whether its validity in any way depends on the validity of that contract. German law is much more explicit than English law in formulating and answering these questions. It distinguishes sharply between, on the one hand, the obligatory contract establishing the parties' personal rights and liabilities (*Verpflichtungsgeschäft*), and the real agreement effecting the transfer of ownership (*Verfügungsgeschäft*) on the other.[160] Contract and conveyance are distinct legal transactions. This is known as the 'principle of separation' (*Trennungsprinzip*). Closely connected with, but going beyond the principle of separation, is the so-called 'principle of abstraction' (*Abstraktionsprinzip*). Developed by 19th century Historical/Pandectist jurisprudence and usually attributed to Friedrich Carl von Savigny,[161] the principle of abstraction leads to a virtually complete independence of the conveyance from the underlying obligatory contract. The latter may constitute the reason or legal basis (*causa* or *Rechtsgrund*) for the former,[162] but it is not a condition for the validity of the transfer. Every transaction has to be assessed on its own merits, by reference to the general rules of contract law. Two consequences follow. Firstly, the conclusion by the parties of an obligatory contract in no way impacts on their rights *in rem*.[163] Secondly, a *traditio*

---

needed to give rise to the inference that the property in specific goods is to pass only on delivery or payment".

[160] Although in our context the *Verfügungsgeschäft* necessarily concerns property rights, the term covers any dispository transaction, ie any legal transaction by which rights (whether *in rem* or *in personam*) are transferred, varied, encumbered or extinguished: cf n 15 above.

[161] FC von Savigny, *System des heutigen römischen Rechts: vol 3* (Veit & Co, Berlin 1840) esp 312–13, 354–58. Cf W Felgentraeger, *Friedrich Carl v. Savignys Einfluß auf die Übereignungslehre* (Deichert, Leipzig 1927); D Haag Molkenteller, *Die These vom dinglichen Vertrag* (Lang, Frankfurt/Main 1991) 86–102; A Stadler, *Gestaltungsfreiheit und Verkehrsschutz durch Abstraktion* (Mohr Siebeck, Tübingen 1996) 49–52. HH Jakobs, "Gibt es den dinglichen Vertrag?" ZSS (RA) 119 (2002) 269, 280–294, has drawn attention to the significant (and hitherto underrated) contribution made by Gustav Hugo towards Savigny's identification of a separate 'real agreement' in conveyances, and consequently towards the formulation of the principle of abstraction.

[162] See above, section C.1.a of the present chapter (at p 27).

[163] This is already evident from the fact that ownership will not pass unless there is an actual or constructive delivery of the object to be conveyed: see above, section D.3.a of the present chapter (at pp 47–48).

coupled with an appropriate real agreement effects a transfer of ownership irrespective of whether there exists a valid *causa* or *Rechtsgrund* for the transfer. It can therefore easily happen that a conveyance is unimpeachably valid although the underlying obligation is non-existent or voidable. This is the gist of abstraction.

When comparing the German abstract transfer system with the English modes of conveyance, it is often assumed and sometimes asserted that the BGB's insistence on an abstract conveyance can be contrasted with the common law's causal consensual approach.[164] Yet this is only partly correct. Title can pass by virtue of the parties' intent (*solo consensu*) only in sale cases.[165] To the extent that the existence of a contract of sale enables English law to dispense with the delivery requirement, it may indeed be said that title passes by contract. Does this necessarily lead to a causal consensual transfer system? Although the inference is *prima facie* plausible, we will see that it is open to some doubt.[166] In any event, it does not hold good outside the context in which the sale rule applies.[167] Quite the contrary. Where title cannot pass by intent alone, requiring an additional element such as delivery, there is a case to be made for the proposition that English law, like German law, adheres to a principle of separation, and possibly even to abstraction. The notable absence of English literature on the issue has been a cause of much puzzlement and even criticism for comparative lawyers looking at the Common law through continental eyes. One main purpose of the present book is to explore the background of this problem and to shed some light onto the mystery surrounding the English model of property transfers, especially their relationship with underlying (contractual) obligations.[168]

4. *Nemo dat* Principle and *bona fide* Purchase Rules

Every legal system has to strike a balance between two competing interests.[169] One is the sanctity of property rights. Such rights should not be lost involuntarily. The other is the security of transactions. It would greatly

---

[164] Eg U Mattei, *Basic Principles of Property Law: A Comparative Legal and Economic Introduction* (Greenwood, London 2000) 106; U Drobnig, "Transfer of Property" in A Hartkamp and others (eds), *Towards a European Civil Code* (3rd edn Kluwer Law International, New York 2004) 725, esp 735–38.

[165] It is unclear whether the sale rule extends to similar contracts such as barter, or even to all transactions for value: see below, Chapter IV.D.3.a (at pp 135–36).

[166] See below, Chapter IV.D.2 (at pp 133–34) and IV.D.3.a (at pp 136–37).

[167] On barter and other transactions for value see n 165 above.

[168] See esp Chapter V.C below (pp 191–202).

[169] Cf the classic statement by Denning LJ in *Bishopsgate Motor Finance Corp v Transport Brakes Ltd* [1949] 1 KB 332 (CA) 336–37.

impede trade if every person acquiring a chattel always had to investigate its history and provenance. English and German law approach the problem of balancing these aims from different angles. English law adheres to the Latin maxim *nemo dat quod non habet*.[170] No-one can transfer more or better rights than he himself has. Subject to a limited number of exceptions, superior titles to an object are unaffected by other parties' dealings with it. German law starts from the opposite premise. It recognizes a general principle of *bona fide* purchase which is only disapplied in specific situations.

The *nemo dat* rule is fundamental to English personal property law. A transferor can pass to a transferee no better title than his own.[171] Given that the mere fact of possession generates a right to possession,[172] a transferor will usually have *a* title to pass, but it may not be a very strong one. The common law is cautious about making 'exceptions' to the *nemo dat* principle.[173] A general defence of good faith purchase for value is available only in the case of money used as currency, bills of exchange and similar negotiable instruments.[174] After the abolition of the old 'market overt' rule in 1994,[175] the three most important situations in which an acquirer of title to goods may defeat a person with a potentially better right to possession are set out in sections 23–25 of the Sale of Goods Act 1979. They concern conveyances by a person with a voidable title to goods (section 23), by a seller who remains in possession of goods after having sold them (section 24), and by a buyer who is let into possession of goods with the seller's consent before he has acquired the seller's title to them (section 25). Equity

---

170 This was also the rule in Roman law. Digest 50.17.54 (Ulpian) reads: "*nemo plus iuris ad alium transferre potest, quam ipse haberet*".

171 For sale transactions, the *nemo dat* principle is expressed in the Sale of Goods Act 1979, s 21.

172 See above, text to n 96.

173 Although the rules on *bona fide* purchase are commonly described as *nemo dat* 'exceptions', it may be more accurate to say that – in at least some and perhaps all of the relevant instances – the claimant's superior title or other interest is simply extinguished where they apply.

174 *Miller v Race* (1758) 1 Burr 452, 97 ER 398; *Peacock v Rhodes* (1781) 2 Doug 633, 99 ER 402; *Wookey v Pole* (1820) 4 Barn & Ald 1, 106 ER 839. The *bona fide* purchaser of a bill of exchange is known as the 'holder in due course': cf Bills of Exchange Act 1882, s 29. *Bona fide* purchase will typically occur in the context of bearer instruments, but in *Peacock v Rhodes* (above), Lord Mansfield said that he saw "no difference between a note indorsed blank, and one payable to bearer", an observation supported by *Wookey v Pole* (above).

175 Previously contained in the Sale of Goods Act 1979, s 22, which read: "Where goods are sold in market overt, according to the usage of the market, the buyer acquires a good title to the goods, provided that he buys them in good faith and without notice of any defect or want of title on the part of the seller".

is more generous than the common law in allowing 'exceptions' to the *nemo dat* principle. Any *bona fide* purchaser of a legal estate for value without (actual or constructive) notice of an equitable interest affecting the estate will take free from it.[176] Such a purchaser is generally known as 'equity's darling'.[177] In our context this means that a person who, in good faith and without notice, acquires legal title to a movable object and gives valuable consideration in exchange, is not bound by a pre-existing equitable interest. However, the same is not true if he acquires only an equitable interest in the object. Here the application of the *nemo dat* principle is strict. As between two competing equitable interests, the first in time prevails.[178] Although a *bona fide* purchaser of an equitable interest takes free from so-called 'mere equities' (ie lesser equitable interests, such as equitable powers *in rem* or rights to rectify a deed),[179] he can never defeat a pre-existing vested equitable interest.

It has already been pointed out that the German Civil Code contains a much more general principle of *bona fide* purchase. The basic rule is that a person taking a conveyance of a movable object from a non-owner acquires ownership unless he knows, or would and should – but for his own gross negligence – be aware, that it does not belong to the transferor (§ 932 BGB). Underlying is the idea that the transferor's possession clothes him with the appearance of ownership (*Rechtsschein des Besitzes*).[180] Since the object's true owner will usually have consented to the transferor's possession, he ought to be the one suffering the consequences of its abuse.[181] This element of risk allocation accounts for the one major exception to the general principle of *bona fide* purchase. If the object in question has been lost or stolen, so that the owner has parted with possession involuntarily, *bona fide* purchase is not possible (§ 935 I BGB). A counter-exception is made only for money, bearer instruments, and things transferred at public

---

[176] Eg *Pilcher v Rawlins* (1872) LR 7 Ch App 259 (CA in Ch); *Cave v Cave* (1880) 15 ChD 639 (ChD) in respect of the legal mortgagee; *Macmillan Inc v Bishopsgate Investment Trust plc (No 3)* [1996] 1 WLR 387 (CA).

[177] Historically, Courts of Equity had no jurisdiction over such a person: *Pilcher v Rawlings* (n 176) 268–69 (James LJ). Hackney *Understanding Equity and Trusts* (n 100) 24–25, points out that "[i]t is ... quite misleading to describe the purchaser ... as 'Equity's darling'. Equity shows him no affection at all, he has simply shown himself to belong to that large class of common law owners with whom Equity has nothing to do".

[178] Eg *Cave v Cave* (n 176) in respect of the equitable mortgagees.

[179] Cf *Phillips v Phillips* (1861) 4 De G F & J 208, 45 ER 1164.

[180] Cf § 1006 BGB. Special rules apply where the transferor remains in possession as the transferee's bailee (*constitutum possessorium*), or where he has bailed the object to a third party: §§ 933, 934 BGB.

[181] The principle is expressed in the maxim "Wo Du Deinen Glauben gelassen hast, mußt Du ihn suchen". ("Go and look for your confidence where you have reposed it").

auction (§ 935 II BGB). As in English law, the special treatment of money and bearer instruments is a concession to the overwhelming commercial importance of currency.

E. No Conclusion

There can be no conclusion to this chapter. It merely sets the scene for the analysis of impaired consent transfers and their unwinding which follows in Parts Two and Three of this book. The relevance of all the rules and principles which have been discussed, compared and contrasted here may not be immediately evident. It need not be at this stage. The cornerstones have been laid, the field remains yet to be mapped out.

Part Two:

Two-Party Situations

Chapter III

German Law and the Consequences of Abstraction

A. Introduction

Imagine the following scenario. The owner of a painting, A, agrees – under a particular arrangement – to convey that painting to a second party, B, and he hands it over. It later transpires that A's consent to the transaction[1] was in some respect defective. If the law recognizes the defect as one sufficient to 'vitiate' A's consent, how does it unwind the transfer? This chapter is the first in a series of three dealing with this question in two-party relationships, ie in cases where B is either still in possession of the painting or, though out of possession, has at any rate not passed it on to a third party purchaser.[2] The concern of the current chapter is to describe the position in German law. It seeks to illustrate how the interaction between contract law and property law leads to a two-track system of unwinding impaired consent transfers. Depending on the nature of the defect and all the surrounding circumstances, the relationship between A and B is either governed exclusively by the law of unjustified enrichment (§§ 812 ff BGB) or is subject to the special rules applying between an owner of a thing and its illegitimate possessor (§§ 985 ff BGB).

The chapter begins with an account of how German law, through the operation of the principle of abstraction, arrives at the decisive junction leading down one or the other track (section B). It then analyses both the unjustified enrichment regime in cases where the conveyance itself is unimpeachable (section C) and the rules applying between owner and illegitimate possessor where it is not (section D). In the course of this analysis, discrepancies between the two regimes are highlighted and suggestions for their resolution discussed. Finally, the question of wrongs-based claims connected with the culpable inducement of the impaired consent transfer is briefly addressed to complete the picture (section E).

---

[1] The word 'transaction' must here be understood in an untechnical, wide sense.

[2] Three-party situations are the subject-matter of Part Three of this book (Chapters VI to VIII). In 'pure' two-party situations, A may be out of possession because the painting has been destroyed, lost or stolen.

B. Relationship between Contract and Conveyance

1. The Principles of Separation and Abstraction in Operation

The principles of separation (*Trennungsprinzip*) and abstraction (*Abstraktionsprinzip*) have already been introduced.[3] They are, in a sense, a by-product of the wide German notion of contract as any legal transaction effected by the mutual expression of consent of at least two parties. A contract may determine the parties' personal rights and liabilities, but a contractual agreement is also necessary to transfer property rights in pursuance of such personal obligations. In the latter case, it is called a 'real contract' or 'real agreement' (*dinglicher Vertrag*).[4] The principle of separation maintains that the obligatory contract (*Verpflichtungsgeschäft*) and the subsequent disposition by way of conveyance (*Verfügungsgeschäft*) are distinct legal transactions, while the principle of abstraction ensures that the validity of the latter does not depend on the existence or validity of the former. The *causa traditionis*, ie the reason or legal basis for the transfer, is external to the transfer itself.[5] This is what a German lawyer means when he insists that a *Verfügungsgeschäft* is abstract rather than causal.[6]

In our example, if A and B are agreed that ownership of the painting shall pass to B and the requisite *traditio* (here an actual physical delivery) has occurred, B becomes the new owner of the painting (§ 929 1 BGB). The reason why A is making the conveyance is irrelevant. It may be in pursuance of a previously negotiated contract of sale (§ 433 BGB) or barter (§§ 480, 433 BGB), a formal or informal promise of a gift (§ 518 BGB),[7] or even in pursuance of an obligation otherwise imposed on him (eg the obligation of an heir to carry a testamentary legacy into execution: §§ 1939, 2147, 2174 BGB). In practice, of course, the parties' real agreement concerning the passing of ownership will often coincide with an agreement about an underlying causal contract. Imagine A handing the

---

[3] See above, Chapter II.D.3.b (pp 49–50).

[4] See above, Chapter II.B.1.b (p 20).

[5] Cf *Motive zu dem Entwurfe eines Bürgerlichen Gesetzbuches für das Deutsche Reich* (2nd edn Guttentag, Berlin 1896) vol 1, 127.

[6] Obligatory contracts usually carry their *causa* within themselves. Exceptionally, however, a *Verpflichtungsgeschäft* can be characterized as 'abstract' and a *Verfügungsgeschäft* as 'causal': A Stadler, *Gestaltungsfreiheit und Verkehrsschutz durch Abstraktion* (Mohr Siebeck, Tübingen 1996) 15–18. For a critical re-analysis of the issue see C Tu, *Abstrakte Verfügungen und kausale Verpflichtungen? Über die Bedeutungslosigkeit der Einordnung eines Rechtsgeschäftes als Verfügungs- oder Verpflichtungsgeschäft für die Frage nach seiner Abstraktion oder Kausalität* (Nomos, Baden-Baden 2007).

[7] A conveyance by way of gift need not necessarily be preceded by any promise: § 516 I BGB (*Handschenkung*).

painting to B with words of gift and B uttering his thanks,[8] or B buying the painting from A at a flea market and immediately taking it away. To the ordinary observer, the *Verpflichtungs-* and the *Verfügungsgeschäft* will look like one single transaction. Only a (German?!) lawyer would muse over the fact that two or more[9] separate contracts have been concluded. However, the distinctness of the transfer from its *Rechtsgrund* or *causa* acquires great practical relevance where something is amiss with the parties' intentions. The principle of abstraction (based on that of separation) then requires a careful assessment of each contract individually.

It has already been pointed out that the law's general approach to the situation in which a fully competent adult is labouring under some relevant defect of consent when entering into a contractual agreement is not to invalidate the agreement automatically, but to afford the person concerned a choice whether or not to uphold it.[10] The person is given the right to avoid his or her declaration of intention (*Willenserklärung*), thereby revoking his or her consent to the legal transaction (*Rechtsgeschäft*). Where this right is exercised, the contract is rescinded and set aside *ab initio* (cf § 142 I BGB). It will be recalled that defects recognized by German law are mistakes about the content of one's declaration of intention or the lack of intent to make such a declaration at all (§ 119 I BGB), mistakes about an essential quality or characteristic of a person or an object to which the declaration relates (§ 119 II BGB), and finally fraud and duress (§ 123 I BGB).[11] Given that the principle abstraction calls for the real agreement effecting a conveyance to be scrutinized independently of the obligatory contract, and given that the essential content of the real agreement differs from that of the underlying contract, it can – and often does – happen that the *Verpflichtungsgeschäft* is rescindable for some impairment of the transferor's intention, while the *Verfügungsgeschäft* stands unimpeachable.[12] The crucial question is therefore which impairments impact only on the obligatory contract, and under what circumstances the real agreement is also infected. Outlining the answer to this question is the concern of the remainder of the present section.

---

[8] In the case of a *Handschenkung* (cf n 7), the conveyance is made *donandi causa*, not *solvendi causa*.

[9] If and when B pays for the painting, each note or coin is conveyed by virtue of a separate real agreement.

[10] See above, Chapter II.B.2 (at p 21).

[11] The special case in which one contracting party's declaration of intention is miscommunicated to the other (cf § 120 BGB) does not fall to be considered within the parameters of this book.

[12] The reverse is theoretically conceivable, but extremely rare in practice. The *Verpflichtungsgeschäft* is much more likely to be affected by a relevant defect than the *Verfügungsgeschäft*.

2. Impairments Affecting only the Obligatory Contract

Many impairments of consent, when they are relevant at all, will affect only the obligatory contract underlying a transfer. Take the example of a spontaneous mistake by the seller of a painting, A, about the contract price. A may have made a typing error in his letter to B, offering to sell the painting for € 450, even though he actually intended to ask € 540. B replies "price agreed – will pay by bank transfer" and comes to pick up the painting. Or A may be a flea market seller in Berlin who accepts the £ 20 note which B, a British tourist, is tendering for an old watercolour of the Brandenburg Gate (thereby offering to pay this amount for it), in the mistaken belief that it is a £ 50 note. We have seen that German law, unlike English law, does not in principle exclude rescission of a contract for a party's spontaneous mistake. All depends on whether the mistake is one falling within the BGB's recognized grounds for rescission. Here A was, in both cases, mistaken about the terms of the bargain he has struck with B. He can revoke his declaration of intention to sell at the objectively agreed price under § 119 I BGB (*Erklärungs-* or *Inhaltsirrtum* respectively) and thereby set aside the obligatory contract of sale. However, A was not mistaken about the content of the real agreement which he has entered into. His intention, when handing the painting to B, was to pass ownership to B, and that intention has been carried into effect. A's conveyance is not flawed in any legally relevant way. The fact that he wrongly believed the underlying contract of sale to have been concluded at the price he subjectively envisaged is a mere 'motivational mistake' as far as the real agreement is concerned. Property has therefore unavoidably passed to B, irrespective of whether the causal contract which constitutes the legal basis for the transfer is later (retroactively) destroyed by A's rescission.

3. Impairments Affecting both Contract and Conveyance

Although the operation of the principle of abstraction means that the impairment of the transferor's consent will often impact only on the obligatory contract underlying a conveyance, there are some circumstances in which the real agreement is also affected. Both contract and conveyance are then invalid or voidable, and our transferor A retains – or, as the case may be, retroactively regains – ownership of the painting. If such situations can be described as constituting 'exceptions' to the principle of abstraction, we must divide them into two categories, the first encompassing real, the second merely apparent exceptions.

a) Real Exceptions to the Principle of Abstraction

Sometimes the fate of the transferor's conveyance is inextricably linked to the fate of the obligatory contract. This is always the case where the real agreement is expressly[13] made subject to the condition that the underlying obligatory transaction is – and remains – valid. The imposition of this sort of condition, though extremely rare in practice, is regarded as a legitimate circumvention of abstraction.[14] Unless otherwise provided, any contract can be conditionally concluded (§ 158 BGB).

A second mechanism by which the invalidity (or avoidance) of the legal basis is automatically carried over to the conveyance is commonly thought to lie in § 139 BGB.[15] This section provides that where one part of a single legal transaction is void, the whole transaction is void unless it can be assumed that it would have been entered into even in the absence of the void part. In our context, this means that *if*, in an appropriate case, we were able to classify the obligatory contract and the real agreement as a 'single legal transaction' (*einheitliches Rechtsgeschäft*), rescission of the former would *ipso iure* also avoid the latter. However, so as not to undermine the principle of abstraction, there is a broad consensus that § 139 BGB must be applied extremely restrictively to the relationship between obligatory contract and conveyance,[16] and much is to be said for the view which denies that the provision can be invoked at all.[17]

---

[13] The condition cannot usually be implied since to do so would completely undermine the principle of abstraction: cf H Grigoleit, "Abstraktion und Willensmängel: Die Anfechtbarkeit des Verfügungsgeschäfts" AcP 199 (1999) 379, 411–12.

[14] Eg RGZ 54, 340, 341; RGZ 57, 95, 96; Grigoleit AcP 199 (n 13) 410–11; O Jauernig, "Trennungsprinzip und Abstraktionsprinzip" JuS 1994, 721, 723–24; O Palandt (Begr), *Bürgerliches Gesetzbuch* (67th edn Beck, München 2008) Überbl v § 104 [24] (Heinrichs/Ellenberger), who are more amenable than Grigoleit (n 13) to the implication of an appropriate condition; FJ Säcker and R Rixecker (eds), *Münchener Kommentar zum Bürgerlichen Gesetzbuch, vol 1/1: §§ 1–240* (5th edn Beck, München 2006) § 158 [26] (Westermann). Critical for cases where the obligatory contract is void rather than voidable (on the basis that the condition is then not a genuine one because is does not relate to an uncertain future event): Stadler *Gestaltungsfreiheit* (n 6) 84–90.

[15] Eg BGHZ 31, 321, 323; BGHZ 112, 376, 378; BGH NJW 1992, 3237, 3238; U Eisenhardt, "Die Einheitlichkeit des Rechtsgeschäfts und die Überwindung des Abstraktionsprinzips" JZ 1991, 271; W Kaufmann, "Wirkt die Anfechtung des Kausalgeschäfts wegen Willensmangels auch auf die dingliche Einigung?" JW 33 (1904) 349.

[16] Cf esp BGH NJW 1952, 60, 60–61; BGH NJW-RR 1989, 519.

[17] W Flume, *Allgemeiner Teil des Bürgerlichen Rechts, vol 2: Das Rechtsgeschäft* (3rd edn Springer, Berlin 1979) 177–78, 571; Grigoleit AcP 199 (n 13) 413–16; Jauernig JuS 1994 (n 14) 724; Stadler *Gestaltungsfreiheit* (n 6) 92–95.

b) Apparent Exceptions to the Principle of Abstraction

Only an apparent exception to the principle of abstraction exists in a case where the defect in the transferor's consent is such that it affects the real agreement as well as the underlying contract. Imagine that B is an art expert to whom A takes his painting to be valued. B recognizes the painting as one by John Constable, but tells A that it is by a little-known 19th century artist in order to acquire it cheaply for himself. If the plot is successful, B's fraudulent misrepresentation will have induced A to consent not only to the obligatory contract of sale, but also to the real agreement. Both can be rescinded for B's fraud (§ 123 I BGB). The reason why the real agreement is voidable is not the voidability of the underlying bargain, but because the conveyance suffers from the same legally relevant defect as the sale contract. Fraud (*arglistige Täuschung*) and duress (*widerrechtliche Drohung*) are prime examples of impairments which typically affect both contract and conveyance.[18] This constellation is referred to as one of *Fehleridentität* (identity of defect). Other examples where the same defect usually allows a transferor to revoke his consent to both contract and conveyance are where he is mistaken about the identity of the object he is transferring (*error in obiecto/corpore*) or about the identity of his contract partner (*error in persona*).[19] Both types of identity mistake constitute a kind of *Inhaltsirrtum* and are therefore caught by § 119 I BGB.

There is a dispute over the question whether and in what circumstances a mistake about an essential quality of the object transferred or about a characteristic of the other contracting party (*Eigenschaftsirrtum*) warrants rescission of the real agreement as well as the obligatory contract. For the purposes of § 119 II BGB, an *Eigenschaftsirrtum* is any misapprehension about a factual or legal characteristic of a person or a thing which is re-

---

[18] RGZ 69, 13, 16; RGZ 70, 55, 57–58; RGZ 70, 88, 89; RGZ 138, 45, 46–47, 48; BGHZ 58, 257, 258; Grigoleit AcP 199 (n 13) 404–6; *Palandt* (n 14) Überbl v § 104 [23] (Heinrichs); Stadler *Gestaltungsfreiheit* (n 6) 181–83; J von Staudinger (Begr), *J von Staudingers Kommentar zum Bürgerlichen Gesetzbuch: §§ 854–882* (Neubearbeitung 2007: Sellier de Gruyter, Berlin 2007) § 873 [136] (Gursky): "Bei Anfechtung nach § 123 müssen besondere Umstände vorliegen, um annehmen zu können, die Täuschung oder Drohung sei für das Verfügungsgeschäft nicht in gleicher Weise ursächlich gewesen wie für das Grundgeschäft". ("In the case of rescission under § 123 [BGB], special circumstances have to be present before it is possible to assume that the fraudulent misrepresentation or the duress were not causative in the same way for the conveyance as for the obligatory contract").

[19] Grigoleit AcP 199 (n 13) 393–96; Stadler *Gestaltungsfreiheit* (n 6) 175–77, who rightly points out that an *error in obiecto* will in practice often be discovered before the conveyance is made (ibid 176).

garded as commercially relevant.[20] Assume that A, having inherited a small collection of paintings, had unilaterally formed the view that one of the pictures was by an undistinguished artist, when in fact it was a Constable.[21] Can he, after selling and delivering the painting to a friend, B, retroactively revest ownership in himself by rescinding the conveyance in accordance with § 119 II BGB? According to one view, this should be possible, since the real agreement is as tainted by A's mistake as the contract underlying it,[22] at least if contract and conveyance constituted an economic unit and were effected at the same time.[23] Proponents of the contrary opinion maintain that a particular characteristic of an object or person can never be considered 'essential' within an abstract conveyance, where only the fact of transfer, the identity of the object and that of the parties need to be agreed upon.[24]

4. A Word on 'Undue Influence' as 'Immoral Exploitation'

While it is true that German law, like English law, normally approaches impairments of consent of competent adults via the mechanism of rescission, it is worth pointing out that there is one situation in which it adopts a different strategy. This concerns what English lawyers would think of as typical 'undue influence' cases. Where a close personal relationship of trust and confidence exists between two parties and one enters into an economically disadvantageous transaction in favour of the other, a presump-

---

[20] With respect to objects, every characteristic is essential which is of such nature and duration that it affects the object's usability and value: cf RGZ 61, 84, 86; BGHZ 34, 32, 41. This does not, however, include the value as such: RGZ 64, 266, 269.

[21] Cf BGH NJW 1988, 2597, where the seller of a painting believed it to be by Frank Duveneck, when in fact it was a work of the more famous Wilhelm Leibl.

[22] Eg Flume *Rechtsgeschäft* (n 17) 479, 489 (but note Flume's view on the proper qualification and scope of § 119 II BGB: ibid 476–79); S Grundmann, "Zur Anfechtbarkeit des Verfügungsgeschäfts" JA 1985, 80, 81 (only for mistakes on the part of the transferor); R Singer, *Selbstbestimmung und Verkehrsschutz im Recht der Willenserklärungen* (Beck, München 1995) 50; *Staudinger* (n 18) § 873 [136] (Gursky).

[23] Cf RGZ 66, 385, 389–90, where a person's creditworthiness was regarded as an essential characteristic. Critical of applying § 119 II BGB to this type of mistake: Flume *Rechtsgeschäft* (n 17) 487. Query whether the *Reichsgericht* was not in fact treating the case primarily as one of § 139 BGB (cf text to nn 15–17) rather than as one of *Fehleridentität* (which is how the decision has come to be understood). This latter view would seem to be supported by Kaufmann JW 33 (n 15) 350, who argues that a mistake about the transferee's creditworthiness can only ever affect the real agreement via § 139 BGB.

[24] Eg Grigoleit AcP 199 (n 13) 396–403; S Schloßmann, *Der Irrtum über wesentliche Eigenschaften der Person oder der Sache nach dem BGB* (Fischer, Jena 1903) 16–19; Stadler *Gestaltungsfreiheit* (n 6) 177–80. Critical of this approach: *Staudinger* (n 18) § 873 [136] (Gursky).

tion is raised that this party's consent to the transaction was impaired by reason of his or her emotional dependency on the other party.[25] The BGB does not recognize 'undue influence' as a ground for rescission, but its general clause on immoral contracts contained in § 138 is capable of encompassing some of the situations in question.[26] Contracts which contravene the standard of good morals are void (§ 138 I BGB). Hence, if A's sale to B is at a noticeable undervalue in circumstances where B is taking advantage of A's emotional attachment, the transaction may be invalidated under § 138 BGB.[27] However, unless the transaction is so disadvantageous that it technically amounts to usury (*Wucher*) and thus falls under § 138 II BGB,[28] only the obligatory contract will normally be regarded as tainted by the immorality.[29]

C. Contract Void, but Conveyance Valid

This section is concerned with the rules applying to the reversal of transfers which are, as a result of the principle of abstraction, unimpeachable from the perspective of property law, but which are made without a valid legal basis. It may be that no legal basis existed in the first place (eg the testament granting a legacy has been superseded by a more recent will),

---

[25] For a recent restatement of the English position see *Royal Bank of Scotland plc v Etridge (No 2)* [2001] UKHL 44, [2002] 2 AC 773.

[26] The match is not exact. § 138 BGB applies to contracts which have nothing to do with defects in a party's consent (eg contracts contravening sexual *mores* or those facilitating criminal acts). On the other hand, § 138 BGB does not extend to all of the situations which would be caught by the English doctrine of 'undue influence': see below, Chapter V.B.1.iii (pp 183–84).

[27] Cf the discussion by S Lorenz, *Der Schutz vor dem unerwünschten Vertrag: Eine Untersuchung von Möglichkeiten und Grenzen der Abschlußkontrolle im geltenden Recht* (Beck, München 1997) 248–59, who makes clear that § 138 I BGB will not be lightly invoked in two-party cases. This is because the sanction (automatic invalidity) does not allow the party 'protected' by it to affirm the contract, as would be possible in a rescission case.

[28] It is widely assumed, by reference to the wording of § 138 II BGB ("*sich ... gewähren läßt*"), that the conveyance *to* the usurer is void: RGZ 57, 95, 97; BGH NJW 1982, 2767; BGH NJW 1994, 1275; Flume *Rechtsgeschäft* (n 17) 382. Yet this interpretation is incorrect from a historical point of view: cf R Zimmermann, "Sittenwidrigkeit und Abstraktion" JR 1985, 48.

[29] Due to the principle of abstraction, the conveyance is commonly said to be 'morally neutral'. However, in the light of the transferor's plight, there may be situations where the real agreement itself is 'immoral' within the meaning of § 138 I BGB (contrast n 28), so that *Fehleridentität* becomes a possibility: see Flume *Rechtsgeschäft* (n 17) 382–88. Stadler *Gestaltungsfreiheit* (n 6) 146–47, and Zimmermann JR 1985 (n 28) 51–52, do not think that this will often be the case.

that an underlying contract is invalidated by some public policy provision (eg §§ 134, 138 BGB), or that it is subsequently avoided *ab initio* by the transferor's rescission (eg for mistake according to § 119 I BGB).[30] When the transferor effects the conveyance, he is labouring under a mere motivational liability mistake. He cannot revest ownership in himself, but he can bring a claim to recover the transferee's unjustified enrichment.[31] The first part of this section describes the nature and content of the transferor's personal claim to restitution. The second part analyses the transferee's position as regards any loss or damage to the object received, and as regards any expenses incurred as a result of its acquisition. Much depends on whether he is a *bona fide* or a *mala fide* enrichee. Finally, the third part considers the special problems which arise when reciprocal (*synallagmatic*) contracts are to be unwound.

1. The Personal Claim to Restitution *in specie*

The basic structure of the German law on unjustified enrichment (§§ 812 ff BGB) has already been outlined.[32] A person who transfers ownership of a chattel to another in pursuance of a non-existent obligation enriches that other by his performance without an explanatory basis. This gives rise to a claim under § 812 I 1 alt 1 BGB (*Leistungskondiktion*).[33] The transferee comes under an obligation to surrender what he has obtained. In our example, B has, without a sufficient legal basis, obtained both ownership and possession of the painting through A's performance. A is entitled to have that ownership and possession retransferred to him.[34] By his *condictio indebiti*, A asserts a personal claim for specific recovery, ie a right *in personam ad rem acquirendam*. Like most other rights *in personam*, the *condictio* claim is not protected in the transferee's insolvency.[35] An enrichment creditor is an ordinary general creditor.

---

[30] See above, section B.2 of the present chapter (p 60).

[31] If the transferor is not mistaken, but knows of the absence of basis, recovery is usually barred: § 814 BGB.

[32] See above, Chapter II.C.1.a and II.C.2 (at pp 25–28, 32, 33–34).

[33] A concurrent claim under § 817 1 BGB (*condictio ob turpem vel iniustam causam*) typically exists where the transferee's receipt of the chattel was *contra bonos mores*, eg if the contract was void under § 138 I BGB for immoral exploitation. The claim under § 817 1 BGB will, however, only be of importance where the *condictio indebiti* under § 812 I 1 alt 1 BGB is barred by § 814 BGB: cf n 31 above.

[34] B has to re-convey the painting to A in accordance with § 929 BGB.

[35] On the policy debate connected with this question see below, in Chapter V.D.3 (at pp 207–8).

2. The Regime of the Law on Unjustified Enrichment

The personal claim to restitution *in specie* discussed above is only a starting point. It reflects the scope of the enrichment creditor's (transferor A's) entitlement vis-à-vis the enrichment debtor (transferee B) directly after the transfer in question. Since A will often not be immediately aware of his right to restitution, he may not assert it at once. Until he does, much can happen. B will have had the use and enjoyment of a work of art, but he may also have incurred expenditure as a result of its receipt. Moreover, the painting may have been damaged, destroyed or lost before A seeks to recover it. Whether and how such situations affect A's claim in unjustified enrichment is primarily determined by § 818 BGB. Since the operation of this provision depends on the interaction between its sub-sections, it will be convenient to remind ourselves of their content before assessing how they impact on the position of different classes of enrichees.

According to § 818 I BGB, the enrichee's obligation to surrender *in specie* what he has obtained extends to any 'secondary benefits' (*Nutzungen*), ie advantages derived from the use of a thing and its fruits,[36] as well as to certain surrogate assets of the object received, eg an insurance payout for its destruction.[37] Where and in so far as specific restitution cannot be made, § 818 II BGB substitutes a claim for value restitution. At the same time, § 818 III BGB excludes the obligation to make restitution to the extent that the recipient is no longer enriched. Finally, § 818 IV BGB rather ominously provides that the recipient becomes liable under the BGB's 'general provisions' once proceedings have been commenced against him, and § 819 I BGB stipulates that the same applies if the recipient knows of the lack of legal basis at the time of his receipt or if he later becomes aware of it.

As a result of § 819 I BGB, there exists a bright dividing line between enrichees who knew of the invalidity or voidability[38] of the obligatory contract at the time of the conveyance or who subsequently learnt the relevant

---

[36] Cf § 100 BGB.

[37] It is generally assumed that § 818 I BGB does not refer to surrogate assets obtained by way of contractual exchange (*rechtsgeschäftliche Surrogate* or *commoda ex negotiatione*): eg RGZ 86, 343, 347; RGZ 101, 389, 391. The issue is discussed in Chapter VIII.C.2.a below (pp 305–8).

[38] § 142 II BGB provides that a person who knew (or ought to have known) of the voidability of a legal transaction is, when avoidance later occurs, to be treated as if he had known (or as if he ought to have known) of its invalidity. Only positive knowledge is at issue in the context of § 819 I BGB. Note, however, the impact of the maxim that *falsa demonstratio non nocet*: cf Chapter V.B.1.b.ii below (at pp 180–81).

facts, and those who did not. We will call the former *mala fide* and the latter *bona fide* enrichees.[39]

a) Position of *bona fide* Enrichees

Bona fide enrichees are in a favourable position. As a result of § 818 III BGB, their liability will never exceed the abstractly surviving value of their enrichment.[40] Their duty to make restitution *in specie* of what they have obtained or, where this is not possible, value restitution, is limited to the amount by which their overall wealth is still swollen as a result of the receipt.[41] Secondary benefits, for example, need only be disgorged to the extent that they have not been 'used up'.[42]

If the object itself is damaged, lost or destroyed, the enrichee is merely liable to surrender any surrogate asset (eg insurance payout). Otherwise he is freed from liability.[43] Subject to the special rules concerning fully executed reciprocal contracts which will be considered below,[44] the principle that the owner of a thing bears the risk of accidents (*res perit domino* or *casum sentit dominus*) is practically inverted. This even applies where the enrichee himself disposes of the object, so that the relevant 'loss' is not accidental. Assume that our transferee B received the painting from A either as a gift or in discharge of a supposed legacy and, because he loathes art, subsequently burns it or donates it to an art gallery.[45] If the *bona fide* enrichee no longer has what he obtained, then (provided, of course, that he has not saved expenditure he would otherwise have incurred and retains no

---

[39] Note that the terms *bona fide(s)* and *mala fide(s)* are here used for exposition purposes only. They are not fully co-extensive with the legal definition of 'good faith' contained in § 932 II BGB.

[40] Cf eg RGZ 118, 185, 187; BGHZ 1, 75, 81; BGHZ 55, 128, 134; BGHZ 118, 383, 386; W Flume, "Der Wegfall der Bereicherung in der Entwicklung vom römischen zum geltenden Recht" in Rechts- und Staatswissenschaftliche Fakultät Göttingen (ed), *Festschrift für Hans Niedermeyer zum 70. Geburtstag* (Schwartz & Co, Göttingen 1953) 103, 153–54; *Palandt* (n 14) § 818 [27] (Sprau).

[41] Many details are contentious: cf overview in K Rebmann, FJ Säcker and R Rixecker (eds), *Münchener Kommentar zum Bürgerlichen Gesetzbuch, vol 5: §§ 705–853* (4th edn Beck, München 2004) § 818 [62]–[78] (Lieb).

[42] The use value of an object is typically transitory. Only if the enrichee has saved expenditure which he would otherwise have incurred can his wealth still be regarded as swollen by the use.

[43] Since any notional obligation to make value restitution (cf § 818 II BGB) is immediately cancelled out by the defendant's corresponding disenrichment, it may be better to say that such an obligation never arises.

[44] See section C.3 of the present chapter (pp 71–77).

[45] Three-party situations will be considered in detail in Part Three of this book (in Chapters VI to VIII).

similar financial benefits)[46] he is completely disenriched and his liability to make restitution comes to an end.

The possibility of invoking § 818 III BGB goes beyond the scenario just considered. It also extends to cases where the disenrichment occurs in relation to something other than the precise object which the enrichee acquired. Imagine that our donee B – this time an art lover – incurs expenditure which he would not otherwise have had as a result of relying on his receipt of the painting. He may send a taxi to collect it from A's house, expend money on having it professionally restored, or simply take his wife out to an expensive restaurant to celebrate the acquisition (where they would not normally have gone). Although he could return the painting, he need only do so if A agrees to pay these expenses.[47] As a general rule, the *bona fide* enrichee is allowed to 'subtract' from his liability to make restitution any disenriching expenditure occasioned by the enriching receipt.[48]

b) Position of *mala fide* Enrichees

It has already been noted that, according to §§ 819 I, 818 IV BGB, an enrichee who is or becomes aware of his (potential) liability to make restitution is answerable under the BGB's 'general provisions'.[49] Much debate

[46] The special case in which the enrichee uses the object received to acquire substitute assets which he still retains is discussed in Chapter VIII.C.2.a below (pp 305–8).

[47] Since B's disenrichment cannot simply be offset against A's claim (as in pure money cases), A has to offer the relevant amount in simultaneous exchange for the painting (*Zug-um-Zug*): cf BGH NJW 1980, 1789, 1790; K Larenz and CW Canaris, *Lehrbuch des Schuldrechts: vol 2/2* (13th edn Beck, München 1994) 301–2; *Münchener Kommentar: vol 5* (n 41) § 818 [69]–[70] (Lieb).

[48] This is entirely uncontentious as far as acquisition costs (eg taxi fare) and expenditure on the object itself (eg restoration) are concerned: cf *Palandt* (n 14) § 818 [41]–[42] (Sprau). Yet it would be wrong to conclude that other causally connected disenrichments (eg cost of dinner) do not count. While certain restrictions may be appropriate in the context of unwinding reciprocal contracts (see below, section C.3 of the present chapter, esp pp 73–77) none of them apply where the recipient has incurred financial detriment in reliance on the security of a *gratuitous* receipt. A generous application of § 818 III BGB would, moreover, also seem warranted where the object gratuitously acquired causes consequential loss to the enrichee (eg a dog received as a birthday present rips up one of the donee's expensive carpets). The distinction between gratuitous and other transactions should therefore be borne in mind when considering the contentious question concerning the extent to which losses resulting from simply 'having' an object count as relevant disenrichments: contrast *Motive* (n 5) vol 2, 837–38; *Palandt* (n 14) § 818 [44] (Sprau); with Flume in *Festschrift Niedermeyer* (n 40) 155–56; Larenz/Canaris *Schuldrecht 2/2* (n 47) 300; J von Staudinger (Begr), *J von Staudingers Kommentar zum Bürgerlichen Gesetzbuch: §§ 812–822* (Neubearbeitung 2007: Sellier de Gruyter, Berlin 2007) § 818 [40] (S Lorenz).

[49] § 819 II BGB contains a similar reference for the *condictio ob turpem vel iniustam causam* in § 817 1 BGB (cf n 33).

surrounds the exact meaning of this phrase and its consequences. The most widely held view is that the reference must be understood as leading via § 292 BGB to §§ 987 ff BGB, ie to the special rules governing the relationship between an owner of an object and its illegitimate possessor.[50] §§ 987 ff BGB regulate in great detail the allocation of secondary benefits, reimbursement for expenditure on the object, and the possessor's liability for loss or damage. All of this will be considered in section D below. For present purposes, it suffices to note the practical effects for the *mala fide* enrichee. Such a defendant will be liable to disgorge not merely any secondary benefits actually obtained as a result of the receipt, but will also have to pay for those which he culpably failed to reap contrary to the principles of good husbandry (§§ 987, 990 BGB). He can recover money he has expended on improving the object only according to the stringent conditions of *negotiorum gestio* (§§ 994 II, 677 ff BGB).[51] Finally, and most importantly, he is liable to compensate the transferor for any loss, damage or deterioration to the object transferred if he culpably brought about that loss, damage or deterioration, or if it occurred while he was technically *in mora* (*Verzug*), ie late in fulfilling his obligation to make restitution (§§ 989, 990 BGB).[52] Once, therefore, our art ignoramus B learns of his

---

[50] A point of controversy is whether and to what extent §§ 275 ff BGB are applicable as well: cf discussion by HG Koppensteiner and E Kramer, *Ungerechtfertigte Bereicherung* (2nd edn de Gruyter, Berlin 1988) 148–50; Larenz/Canaris *Schuldrecht 2/2* (n 47) 314–16; D Reuter and M Martinek, *Ungerechtfertigte Bereicherung* (Mohr Siebeck, Tübingen 1983) 631–42; and contrast RGZ 99, 161, 168, with RGZ 151, 361, 373–74. The Federal Supreme Court (*Bundesgerichtshof*) regards § 279 BGB (now repealed) and § 285 BGB (formerly contained in § 281 BGB) as encompassed: BGHZ 83, 293; BGHZ 75, 203. On the application of § 285 BGB see below, Chapter VIII.C.2.b (pp 308–9).

[51] In particular: the enrichee can demand to be reimbursed only where the improvement was in the transferor's interest (§§ 994 II, 683 1, 670 BGB), in the public interest (§§ 994 II, 683 2, 679, 670 BGB), or if the transferor subsequently ratifies it (§§ 994 II, 684 2, 683 1, 670 BGB). There is a dispute over whether § 684 2 BGB is also caught by the reference: see below, text to nn 106–108.

[52] It has been suggested that a *mala fide* enrichee will almost inevitably be *in mora* since his position is the same as that of a debtor against whom proceedings are pending (§§ 819 I, 818 IV BGB): HP Westermann (ed), *Erman: Bürgerliches Gesetzbuch* (12th edn Schmidt, Köln 2008) vol 2, § 819 [9] (Westermann/Buck-Heeb). Similar: *Staudinger* (n 48) § 819 [16] (S Lorenz). The enrichee would then be strictly liable for all losses under § 287 2 BGB. However, this understanding of §§ 819 I, 818 IV BGB reads too much into the reference: *Koppensteiner/Kramer* (n 50) 150; Larenz/Canaris *Schuldrecht 2/2* (n 47) 317–18. Similar: *Münchener Kommentar: vol 5* (n 41) § 818 [159] (Lieb). On the interpretation of the reference cf also OGH BrZ NJW 1950, 641, 642; H Lange, "Verzugshaftung des Bereicherungsschuldners und des Besitzers" JZ 1964, 640. *Motive* (n 5) vol 2, 841, deals with the point in relation to *mala fides superveniens*. Initial bad faith was thought always to entail the delict of *furtum* and thus *mora*: see n 56 below.

duty to re-convey the painting to A, he can no longer get away with burning it. If he does, he will be required to make good A's loss.

What about the disenrichment defence? It is often said that § 818 III BGB does not apply to *mala fide* enrichees.[53] Yet this assertion is, at best, imprecise, and misleading at the worst.[54] Clearly, a *mala fide* enrichee can no longer claim to have detrimentally changed his position in reliance on the security of his receipt. In that sense, subsequent dispositions do not relieve him of liability. Whether, however, he is also disqualified as far as accidental disenrichments are concerned, is very doubtful. Imagine that, in the gift/legacy example, the destruction of the painting was a result not of B's conduct, but an act of God (eg lightning striking B's house). Should B nevertheless have to make value restitution to A? That depends on our view of the relationship between §§ 819 I, 818 IV BGB and § 818 I, II and III BGB. Were one blindly to follow the orthodox assertion that a *mala fide* enrichee cannot invoke § 818 III BGB, one might be driven to the apparently straightforward conclusion that B is saddled with the obligation to make value restitution (§ 818 II BGB) without being able to bring into account the disenrichment suffered through the accidental loss.[55] This view, however, has no support in the wording or structure of § 818 BGB and directly contravenes the intentions of the historical legislator.[56] There

---

53 RGZ 99, 161, 168; RGZ 170, 65, 68; BGHZ 55, 128, 132; BGHZ 72, 252, 254–55.

54 Cf also *Staudinger* (n 48) § 818 [52] (S Lorenz).

55 See the cautioning comments by D Medicus, "Die verschärfte Haftung des Bereicherungsschuldners" JuS 1993, 705, 710. Misleading: GC Schwarz and M Wandt, *Gesetzliche Schuldverhältnisse* (2nd edn Vahlen, München 2006) 242–45. Also slightly misleading: Larenz/Canaris *Schuldrecht 2/2* (n 47), who on the one hand (at 260, 319) suggest the existence of a liability to make value restitution independent of the enrichment (*bereicherungsunabhängige Wertersatzhaftung*) where the enrichee is *mala fide*, but on the other (ibid 327) recognize that the *mala fide* enrichee does not usually bear the risk of accidental loss. W Flume, "Die Saldotheorie und die Rechtsfigur der ungerechtfertigten Bereicherung" AcP 194 (1994) 427, 445–46, makes the availability of the disenrichment defence dependent only on whether the *mala fide* enrichee has voluntarily chosen to accept the financial risks connected with 'having' the object (which is typically the case in reciprocal contracts, but not in gift cases): see further below, text to nn 79–80.

56 *Motive* (n 5) vol 2, 841, makes this clear for cases where the recipient's bad faith supervenes after receipt. It was assumed that any person who accepts a performance in the knowledge that it is not due would necessarily commit a delict: ibid 840. (According to D.13.1.18, citing Scaevola, it was *furtum* or theft to accept coins in the knowledge that they were not owing). Such an enrichee would – in the eyes of the historical legislator – always be strictly liable for the loss or destruction of the object received: cf § 848 BGB, a provision which is descended from the maxim *fur semper in mora*. Although it can no longer be said that a delict is necessarily committed in *all* cases of initial bad faith, § 848 BGB would still seem to apply where the defendant enrichee has defrauded or unlawfully coerced the claimant into making the transfer (cf section E.1 of the present chapter). On the operation and scope of § 848 BGB see below, nn 111–112 and corresponding text.

are two better ways of dealing with the problem.[57] We could understand the reference to the BGB's 'general provisions' as conclusive, so that there is no room for the operation of either § 818 II or III BGB.[58] A's enrichment claim for surrender of the painting is then treated as if it had been a *vindicatio* claim under § 985 BGB. Liability for damage or destruction arises only if B was at fault or *in mora* (cf §§ 989, 990 BGB). Alternatively, we could continue to apply both § 818 II BGB and a last vestige of § 818 III BGB for accidental disenrichments alongside the 'general provisions'.[59] Whichever approach we adopt, the outcome must be that the accidental loss or destruction of the object received can relieve even a *mala fide* enrichee like B – so long as he is not technically *in mora* – from his liability in unjustified enrichment.[60]

In summary: although a *mala fide* enrichee's position is not nearly as favourable as that of a *bona fide* enrichee in respect of secondary benefits and changes of position, even an enrichee who is aware of his restitutionary liability is not without more required to 'disgorge' an enrichment which has evaporated through no fault of his own.

3. Unwinding Reciprocal Contracts

A particular problem arises where the transfer is made pursuant to a reciprocal (*synallagmatic*) contract and the transferor has already received the agreed counter-performance. If he is unable to restore what he has obtained in accordance with the contract, can he nevertheless reclaim the subject-matter of his own performance? Imagine that, in our example, A and B had agreed on a barter whereby A's Constable (this time correctly identified as such) was to be exchanged for a painting by Jean-Baptiste-Camille Corot owned by B. After both conveyances have been effected,

---

[57] See the discussion in *Staudinger* (n 48) § 818 [52] (S Lorenz).

[58] Eg *Koppensteiner/Kramer* (n 50) 150–51; probably also the previous edition of *Staudinger*: J von Staudinger (Begr), *J von Staudingers Kommentar zum Bürgerlichen Gesetzbuch:§§ 812–822* (Neubearbeitung 1999: Sellier de Gruyter, Berlin 1999) § 818 [52] (W Lorenz).

[59] "*Restfunktion des § 818 III*": cf OGH BrZ NJW 1950, 641, 642; Medicus JuS 1993 (n 55) 709–10; *Münchener Kommentar: vol 5* (n 41) § 819 [155] (Lieb); *Palandt* (n 14) § 819 [9] (Sprau). This view appears to be supported by the current edition of *Staudinger* (n 48) § 818 [52] (S Lorenz).

[60] Note the special position of those *mala fide* enrichees who have committed a delict in obtaining the painting: cf n 56 above. They will incur a wrongs-based liability to pay compensation (cf section E.1 of the present chapter, pp 93–94), and they should – in respect of the victim's claim for recovery of the painting – always be treated as if they were *in mora*: see below, nn 111–112 and corresponding text. In accordance with § 848 BGB, they would then be strictly liable even for accidental loss, damage or destruction.

the Corot is destroyed as a result of A's negligence. A later discovers a ground for rescission, avoids the obligatory contract and asks B to return the Constable.[61] Can B refuse to do so on the basis that A is no longer in a position to return B's counter-performance? And would it make a difference if the Corot had been stolen from A's house (without any fault of his own)?

a) Two-Claims Theory

The so-called 'two-claims theory' (*Zweikondiktionenlehre*) treats the parties' mutual claims as in principle independent.[62] A has a *Leistungskondiktion* (§ 812 I 1 alt 1 BGB) against B, and B has one against A. The fate of one claim does not impact on the other. A's right to have the Constable reconveyed is thus unaffected by B's inability to reclaim the Corot as a result of A's disenrichment (§ 818 III BGB). Under the two-claims theory, each party bears the risk of the other's disenrichment. [63]

This model is widely criticized as inappropriate for the unwinding of reciprocal contracts which have been performed on both sides and thus fully executed.[64] The *synallagmatic* connection between the parties' performances, ie the fact that each conveyance was effected in consideration of the other (*do-ut-des* relationship), ought – it is argued – to find some recognition in the unwinding process. For our example, this means that since the disenrichment has occurred in A's sphere, B ought not (or not necessarily) to lose out by having to return the Constable without receiving back the Corot. Two main approaches have been developed in an attempt to remedy the perceived defects of the two-claims theory. One is called the

---

[61] Alternatively, A may discover that the contract was for some reason void from the outset, so that the mutual obligations to perform never existed in the first place.

[62] Eg P Oertmann, "Bereicherungsansprüche bei nichtigen Geschäften" DJZ 20 (1915) 1063; K Schneider, "Zur Bestimmung des Umfangs der Bereicherung nach Erfüllung eines nichtigen Vertrages" JherJB 61 (1912) 179; A v Tuhr, "Zur Lehre von der ungerechtfertigten Bereicherung" in *Aus Römischem und Bürgerlichem Recht: Ernst Immanuel Bekker zum 16. August 1907* (Hof-Buchdruckerei, Weimar 1907) 291, 307–9; recently again D Kaiser, *Die Rückabwicklung gegenseitiger Verträge wegen Nicht- und Schlechterfüllung nach BGB* (Mohr Siebeck, Tübingen 2000) esp 318–34. On this view, the parties' mutual claims are connected only via an ordinary right of retention (*Zurückbehaltungsrecht*) under § 273 BGB.

[63] As Kaiser *Rückabwicklung* (n 62) 334, rightly points out, this risk-allocation is partially reversed through claims for recovery of reliance losses, eg a rescinding party's duty to pay damages under § 122 BGB. Cf also below, text to n 165.

[64] A summary of all the criticisms levelled against the two-claims theory (with further references) is to be found eg in P Hellwege, *Die Rückabwicklung gegenseitiger Verträge als einheitliches Problem* (Mohr Siebeck, Tübingen 2004) 101–4. Cf also E Horst, *Die Beschränkung der Bereicherungshaftung* (Doctoral Thesis, Köln 1961) 141–51.

Saldotheorie, the other can be described as a modified version of the two-claims theory.

b) *Saldotheorie*

According to the *Saldotheorie*, it is wrong to start from the proposition – as does the two-claims theory – that each party to an executed reciprocal contract has an independent *condictio indebiti* against the other in the event of this contract later turning out to be void. Instead, the value of each party's performance has to be automatically offset against that of the other, so that there is notionally only ever a one-sided restitutionary claim constituted by the difference in value between the mutual enrichments (*Saldo*).[65] Developed by the jurisprudence of the Imperial Supreme Court (*Reichsgericht*) and still applied by the Federal Supreme Court (*Bundesgerichtshof*), the balance-sheet approach rests, in its inception, on a two-fold application of § 818 III BGB. The party who has performed in accordance with the contract (here B), but whose claim to restitution is diminished by the other party's (here A's) disenrichment, is regarded as being himself disenriched, at least to the extent to which his own claim is diminished.[66] Nowadays, the preferred justification for the *Saldotheorie* is that it reflects the 'factual reciprocity' (*faktisches Synallagma*) between the parties' mutual performances.[67] Imagine that the Constable had been worth € 900,000 and the Corot € 700,000. According to the *Saldotheorie*, B is enriched to the tune of € 200,000. This is the maximum scope of his liability to A under § 812 I 1 alt 1 BGB.[68] The fact that the Corot has been

[65] In practice, this nevertheless means mutual restitution by simultaneous exchange (*Abwicklung Zug-um-Zug*) while both parties' performances can still be surrendered *in specie*: BGH NJW 1963, 1870; BGH NJW 1988, 3011. For an account in English of the *Saldotheorie* see eg R Zimmermann and J du Plessis, "Basic Features of the German Law of Unjustified Enrichment" [1994] RLR 14, 40–42.

[66] Cf eg RGZ 54, 137, 141; BGHZ 57, 137, 150; BGHZ 72, 252, 255–56. The relevant disenrichment on B's part can either be understood to consist in the mere rendering of the promised counter-performance *to* A, or alternatively in B's subsequent inability to reclaim the (full) counter-performance *from* A. The former view would appear to underlie esp RGZ 139, 208, 213, while the latter is preferred by BGHZ 57, 137, 150; BGHZ 72, 252, 255. On the consequences of these different approaches see below, text to nn 73–75.

[67] Cf BGHZ 57, 137, 150; BGHZ 72, 252, 256; BGHZ 126, 105, 108; E von Caemmerer, "Bereicherung und unerlaubte Handlung" in H Dölle, M Rheinstein and K Zweigert (eds), *Festschrift für Ernst Rabel* (Mohr Siebeck, Tübingen 1954) vol 1, 333, 386–87, reprinted in HG Leser (ed), *Ernst von Caemmerer: Gesammelte Schriften, vol 1: Rechtsvergleichung und Schuldrecht* (Mohr Siebeck, Tübingen 1968) 209, 262–64; HG Leser, *Von der Saldotheorie zum faktischen Synallagma: Ein Beitrag zur Lehre vom Wegfall der Bereicherung* (Doctoral Thesis, Freiburg/Breisgau 1956).

[68] If, in the converse case, the Corot had been worth € 900,000 and the Constable € 700,000, A would have been the party enriched to the tune of € 200,000. The loss of

destroyed or stolen is irrelevant. From the moment the paintings are exchanged, A bears the risk of such an incident. In order to recover the Constable, he would have to pay B € 700,000.[69]

There are, however, situations in which the balance-sheet approach is regarded as inappropriate. Exceptions to the *Saldotheorie* are made for cases where the party who is no longer able to return what he or she has received was the victim of fraud[70] or immoral exploitation under § 138 BGB.[71] Yet it could be argued that these exceptions are either too broad or too narrow, on any explanation of the *Saldotheorie*. Under its more modern justification, that of 'factual reciprocity', there is no absolutely compelling reason to relieve a fully competent adult of the normal risk allocation in the unwinding of *synallagmatic* contracts as exemplified by the *Saldotheorie*.[72] If, by way of contrast, the *Saldotheorie* is founded on a twofold application of § 818 III BGB, all depends on how exactly the relevant disenrichment (on the part of the party who would still be in a position to make specific restitution) is defined.[73] On the one hand, we could regard the mere rendering of performance *as such* as a form of (anticipatory) disenrichment. In that case, the above-mentioned exceptions to the *Saldotheorie* would appear to be too narrow. The balance-sheet approach ought then to be disapplied whenever it would operate in favour of a party who was aware of the invalidity or voidability of the underlying legal basis when performing his or her side of the bargain (and not merely in fraud

---

the Corot would have constituted a complete disenrichment on A's part. Although B's *condictio indebiti* under § 812 I 1 alt 1 BGB would therefore have evaporated (§ 818 III BGB), he would at least not have had to return the Constable to A.

[69] This can be seen as the value of the Corot, or alternatively as the difference between the value of the Constable (€ 900,000) and the value of A's *condictio indebiti* (€ 200,000). In the converse scenario (cf n 68 immediately above), A would also have to pay B € 700,000 in order to recover the Constable.

[70] BGHZ 53, 144; BGHZ 57, 137, 146–51. Contra still: RGZ 54, 137. Although a victim of fraud would normally be allowed to rescind both the obligatory contract and the conveyance under § 123 I BGB (cf n 18 and corresponding text), he may well choose to avoid only the former.

[71] BGHZ 146, 298, 307–9 (*wucherähnliches Geschäft*). Contra still: RGZ 139, 208, 213. The same would probably be true in a duress case.

[72] E von Caemmerer, " 'Mortuus Redhibetur': Bemerkungen zu den Urteilen BGHZ 53, 144 und 57, 137" in G Paulus, U Diederichsen and CW Canaris (eds), *Festschrift für Karl Larenz zum 70. Geburtstag* (Beck, München 1973) 621, esp 636–38, reprinted in HG Leser (ed), *Ernst von Caemmerer: Gesammelte Schriften, vol 3: 1968–1982* (Mohr Siebeck, Tübingen 1983) 167, esp 182–84. Cf also the discussion by U Büdenbender, "Die Berücksichtigung der Gegenleistung bei der Rückabwicklung gegenseitiger Verträge" AcP 200 (2000) 627, 661–62.

[73] Cf comment in n 66 above.

cases). A person who is *mala fide*[74] as regards the existence of a valid *Rechtsgrund* should be unable to invoke § 818 III BGB as far as his own performance is concerned. Where B knows that A will be able to rescind the contract of barter and nevertheless conveys the Corot to him in exchange for the Constable, he cannot claim to have changed his position in reliance on the permanence of his own acquisition. On the other hand, however, the exceptions to the *Saldotheorie* could also be seen as too broad. If one regards not B's performance of the contract *per se* as the relevant disenrichment, but A's supervening inability to make counter-restitution, then B's so-conceived disenrichment might well be classified as 'accidental', and he should – in accordance with what was said above – be freed from his own liability to make restitution to A.[75]

Be that as it may, the *Saldotheorie* ensures at the very least that parties who were unaware of their (potential) restitutionary liability do not have to bear the full risk of the other party's disenrichment once the reciprocal contract has been executed.

c) Modified Two-Claims Theory

One weakness of the *Saldotheorie* is that the balance-sheet approach is insensitive to the exact circumstances which prevent one party from making restitution to the other. For example, it cannot distinguish between cases where the disenrichment is accidental (eg where the painting is stolen from A's house) from those in which it is in some way self-induced (eg where the painting is destroyed as a result of A's negligence). Nor does the *Saldotheorie* adequately deal with situations in which one party's performance is still outstanding (eg if A has not yet transferred the Constable to B when the Corot perishes in his hands).[76] This has led leading academics back to the two-claims theory, but in a modified form. Though the suggested modifications differ in their detail, all proponents of the modified

---

[74] On the present use of the term *mala fide(s)* see above, n 39 and corresponding text.

[75] See above, text to nn 53–60. BGHZ 72, 252, may have been wrongly reasoned on this count. The decision is nevertheless defensible on the basis that the defendant vendor was *in mora* in accepting the claimant purchaser's offer of re-conveyance: cf K Tiedtke, "Der Wegfall der Bereicherung nach Rechtshängigkeit des Rückgewähranspruchs" DB 1979, 1261. Another aspect worth bearing in mind is the following. It will be recalled that, in 'ordinary' cases of disenrichment, § 848 BGB ensures that the fraudster is strictly liable for an object perishing in his own hands: cf n 60. This provision cannot, however, be used to impose on B the risk of 'accidental' disenrichment resulting from A's inability to make counter-restitution. A general disqualification of delictual enrichees could only be achieved by 'transposing' the risk distribution inherent in § 848 onto the *Saldotheorie*.

[76] In that case, there is nothing to offset. Until A performs, B bears the full risk of A's disenrichment. § 818 III BGB applies in the ordinary way, and B's claim to restitution is completely destroyed by A's loss of the painting.

approach seek to restrict the application of § 818 III BGB so as to make reliance on it more difficult for the party who is no longer able to make restitution. Two theories are worth mentioning in particular. Both proceed from considerations of risk allocation.

Claus-Wilhelm Canaris argues that, in the case of reciprocal contracts, § 818 III BGB does not normally encompass disenrichments which can be ascribed to the recipient's own dealing with the object he has acquired.[77] § 818 III BGB primarily protects an enrichee's reliance on the permanence of his receipt. In a *synallagmatic* contract, such reliance will necessarily be coupled with the belief that his own performance is irretrievably lost. The disenriched party cannot therefore, via § 818 III BGB, avoid having to make restitution to the other party for what he has received, while at the same time demanding the return of his counter-performance (*Lehre von der Gegenleistungskondiktion*). According to Canaris' approach, A could invoke the disenrichment defence where the Corot is stolen, but not where it perishes as a result of his own carelessness.[78]

Werner Flume goes even further in restricting the scope of § 818 III BGB.[79] He suggests that only disenrichments that are directly attributable to the acquisition itself or its (supposed) cause should relieve an enrichee of liability. Those which can instead be ascribed to the recipient's autonomous economic decision to structure his wealth in a particular way, namely by substituting one asset for another, are to be borne by him. They should be excluded from the ambit of § 818 III BGB (*Lehre von der vermögensmäßigen Entscheidung*). Unless A's agreement to the exchange has been secured in a way which does not allow us to attribute to him the relevant economic decision (eg by fraud, duress, or undue influence amounting to immoral exploitation),[80] the risks connected with 'having' the Corot, a

---

[77] CW Canaris, "Die Gegenleistungskondiktion" in B Pfister and M Will (eds), *Festschrift für Werner Lorenz zum siebzigsten Geburtstag* (Mohr Siebeck, Tübingen 1991) 19; Larenz/Canaris *Schuldrecht 2/2* (n 47) 321–38.

[78] Canaris is willing to make an exception only where the suggested restriction of § 818 III BGB would undermine the purpose of the provision rendering the obligatory contract void or voidable, eg in certain – but by no means all – cases of fraud/duress (§ 123 BGB) and immoral exploitation (§ 138 BGB): Canaris in *Festschrift Lorenz* (n 77) 40–42; Larenz/Canaris *Schuldrecht 2/2* (n 47) 329–31.

[79] W Flume, "Der Wegfall der Bereicherung in der Entwicklung vom römischen zum geltenden Recht" in Rechts- und Staatswissenschaftliche Fakultät Göttingen (ed), *Festschrift für Hans Niedermeyer zum 70. Geburtstag* (Schwartz & Co, Göttingen 1953) 103, 148–76, esp 151–69; W Flume, "Die Saldotheorie und die Rechtsfigur der ungerechtfertigten Bereicherung" AcP 194 (1994) 427, esp 439–50.

[80] Flume in *Festschrift Niedermeyer* (n 79) 172–74; Flume AcP 194 (n 79) 441. According to Flume, even a rescinding party's *spontaneous* mistake may prevent the economic decision to substitute one asset for another from being attributable to him, provided only that the mistake affected the 'if' rather than merely the 'how' of the con-

painting which may be particularly attractive to burglars or susceptible to physical damage, must be allocated to him rather than B.[81] The disenrichment defence can then be invoked in neither our theft nor our destruction scenario.[82]

D. Invalidity of both Contract and Conveyance

While the previous section was concerned with cases where a conveyance is valid but lacks a legal basis or *causa*, the present section analyses the reversal of impaired consent transfers in situations where the real agreement is also void or voidable. We have seen that this may be because it is expressly made conditional on the existence and validity of the legal basis or because the identical defect allows the transferor to rescind both the obligatory contract and the conveyance (eg under § 123 I BGB).[83] Since rescission operates retroactively (§ 142 I BGB), a rescinding transferor is

---

tract. Yet it may be asked whether a (non-induced) mistake actually calls into question the factual 'reality' of the decision to make the substitution any more than it is called into question by factors rendering the contract void *ipso iure*: cf also Hellwege *Rückabwicklung* (n 64) 131–32; Horst *Beschränkung der Bereicherungshaftung* (n 64) 157, 160–61. Flume himself notes that the party rescinding a contract for spontaneous mistake will, as a result of § 122 BGB, usually bear the risk of his/her own disenrichment in any event (query in passing whether § 122 BGB can be regarded as a variant disenrichment defence: cf Chapter V.B.1.a.iii, at pp 173–74). If we nevertheless accept Flume's stipulated exception for spontaneous (§ 119 BGB) as well as fraudulently induced mistakes (§ 123 BGB), then his theory would appear to have only very limited relevance for our core case, in which A's conveyance to B is made pursuant to a contract which A later avoids. However, Flume's version of the modified two-claims theory would still be fully applicable where A renders performance in the mistaken belief that a contract he has entered into (without any impairment of consent) is valid, when it is in fact void, eg for B's lack of capacity: cf n 61 above.

81 The ordinary risks connected with owning any work of art (eg the risk of theft or fire) should *a fortiori* be borne by A since they would have materialized in any event. If he had not exchanged the Constable for the Corot, he would also have suffered the loss (the Constable would then have perished in the flames or been stolen).

82 In his later work, Flume suggests that the disenriched party (A) should be exempt from bearing the risk of accidental loss or damage (theft or destruction of the Corot) to the extent that the same loss or damage would also have occurred had the object remained in the hands of the other party (B): AcP 194 (n 79) 441–42. Critical: Hellwege *Rückabwicklung* (n 64) 134; *Staudinger* (n 48) § 818 [43] (S Lorenz).

83 See above, text to nn 13–14 (conditional conveyances) and text to nn 18–24 (*Fehleridentität*: the identical defect affects both obligatory contract and conveyance). It will be recalled that, very exceptionally, a real agreement may be invalidated by the same 'immorality' (§ 138 BGB) which also invalidates the underlying contract: see above, nn 28–29 and corresponding text.

treated as though he had never lost ownership of the object in question. Yet given that the conveyance involved not only a real agreement about the passing of property, but also a delivery (§ 929 1 BGB), the transferor's rescission often results in a split of ownership and possession. The first part of this section outlines the nature of the transferor-owner's claims against the transferee-possessor with regard to the restoration of possession. In the second, the special rules governing ancillary questions in the relationship between an owner and a *bona fide* or *mala fide* possessor are set out. It will become evident that there are some incongruities with the regime of the law of unjustified enrichment described in section C above. These incongruities are the subject-matter of the third part of the current section.

1. *Vindicatio* and *condictio possessionis*

It will be recalled that the primary remedy by which the owner of an object can demand its surrender from a possessor who has no right to possession as against him is the *vindicatio* (§ 985 BGB).[84] The *vindicatio* constitutes a direct assertion of ownership and provides for specific recovery. If, in our example, A has rescinded both the obligatory contract and the real agreement, thereby retroactively invalidating the transfer of ownership, B is – and was from the moment of delivery – a possessor of the painting without any right to possess it. § 985 BGB requires him to give up possession to the owner A. The *vindicatio* claimant is in a very favourable position. Since the object he is claiming belongs to him, it does not form part of the defendant's estate in the case of the defendant's insolvency. The owner has a right to segregate and retrieve it outside insolvency proceedings (*Aussonderungsrecht*: § 47 InsO). Thus, even if B has become insolvent by the time A exercises his rights to rescind, the painting will be taken from amongst B's assets before the distribution to his general creditors begins.

For the sake of completeness, it should be pointed out that there exists, beside the *vindicatio*, a claim in unjustified enrichment. It is, once again, again a *Leistungskondiktion* in the form of a *condictio indebiti* (§ 812 I 1 alt 1 BGB). B has, by virtue of A's performance, but without legal cause, obtained possession – though not ownership – of the painting. This gives rise to a *condictio possessionis*. The *condictio possessionis* freely competes with the *vindicatio*. As its name indicates, it too is directed at a re-transfer of possession.

---

[84] See above, Chapter II.D.2.a (at pp 40–41).

2. The Special Provisions of the *Eigentümer-Besitzer-Verhältnis*

We have already seen that §§ 987 ff BGB contain special provisions regulating the relationship between an owner of a thing and its illegitimate possessor (*Eigentümer-Besitzer-Verhältnis*).[85] They concern the allocation of secondary benefits (*Nutzungen*), the possessor's liability in damages for loss, destruction or deterioration of the object (*Schadensersatz*), and the extent to which the owner has to reimburse him for any expenditure on it (*Verwendungsersatz*). In so far as these provisions apply, they bar recourse to the general law of delict and unjustified enrichment (*Sperrwirkung des Eigentümer-Besitzer-Verhältnisses*).[86]

Within §§ 987 ff BGB, we must again distinguish between the position of *bona fide* and *mala fide* possessors.[87] According to § 990 BGB, a *mala fide* possessor is one who was not in 'good faith' when he acquired possession, or who subsequently learnt of his lack of a right to possess (or of the relevant ground for rescission)[88]. He is treated in the same way as a possessor against whom legal proceedings are pending.[89] The reference to 'good faith' in § 990 BGB implies that not only positive knowledge at the time of the acquisition counts as *mala fides*, but even grossly negligent ignorance (cf § 932 II BGB). The notion of the *mala fide* possessor is hence slightly broader than that of the *mala fide* enrichee in § 819 I BGB.[90] If B would, but for his own gross negligence, have known of A's ground for rescission (in respect of the conveyance) at the time when he received the painting,[91] he is in 'bad faith'.

---

[85] See above, Chapter II.D.2.b.iii (at p 46). Note that §§ 987 ff BGB will apply retroactively where a possessor's ownership and/or his right to possession are divested with retroactive effect, eg through rescission: *Palandt* (n 14) Vorb v § 987 [7] (Bassenge); K Rebmann, FJ Säcker and R Rixecker (eds), *Münchener Kommentar zum Bürgerlichen Gesetzbuch, vol 6: §§ 854–1296* (4th edn Beck, München 2004) Vorbemerkungen zu §§ 987–1003 [18] (Medicus).

[86] This can be inferred from §§ 992, 993 I BGB, which allow competing claims under §§ 812 ff BGB and §§ 823 ff BGB only in exceptional circumstances.

[87] The terms *bona fide(s)* and *mala fide(s)* are used for the purposes of exposition only (cf also n 39 above). Their exact meaning in the context of §§ 987 ff BGB is explained in the text to nn 88–91. In the terminology of § 993 BGB, a *bona fide* possessor is called '*redlicher Besitzer*'.

[88] Cf § 142 II BGB.

[89] Reference in § 990 I BGB to § 987 BGB and § 989 BGB.

[90] Cf text to nn 38–39 above.

[91] After receipt, only positive knowledge will lead to supervening '*Unredlichkeit*' (*mala fides* for present purposes): cf § 990 I 2 BGB.

a) Position of *bona fide* Possessors

As explained in Chapter II, the rules of the *Eigentümer-Besitzer-Verhältnis* are aimed at privileging the *bona fide* possessor of an object belonging to another.[92] Such a person is in principle entitled to keep any secondary benefits which the object regularly yields, even if they are still amongst his assets (*arg e* § 993 I BGB).[93] Only where the *bona fide* possessor's acquisition of the object was gratuitous does he have to disgorge secondary benefits according to the principles of unjustified enrichment (§ 988 BGB). If B had bought the Constable from A and, upon receiving it, had hired it out to an art gallery for a couple of months, then – subject to the *caveat* to be discussed below[94] – it looks as though he need not pay over the collected rent (a 'civil fruit') when A vindicates the painting.

Since our *bona fide* possessor will, *ex hypothesi*, believe the object acquired to be his, he may well expend money on it. Such expenditure is generally recoverable if it is 'necessary' (*notwendig*) or 'useful' (*nützlich*). Necessary expenditure encompasses all costs reasonably incurred for the maintenance and preservation of the object in question, eg urgent repair expenses.[95] The owner has to reimburse a *bona fide* possessor for all necessary expenditure apart from those costs which constitute the regular maintenance costs of an object the secondary benefits of which the possessor is entitled to keep (§ 994 I BGB). Expenditure which is not 'necessary' in the above sense is recoverable as 'useful expenditure' to the extent that it has enhanced the object's value and the enhancement still subsists at the moment when the owner recovers possession (§ 996 BGB). To enforce his claims, the *bona fide* possessor has a right to retain the object until reimbursed by the owner (§ 1000 BGB).[96] Assuming that B incurred costs in preserving the painting or having it professionally restored, A's *vindicatio* will only be successful if he indemnifies B in accordance with §§ 994 I, 996 BGB.

The *bona fide* possessor is not liable to compensate the owner for any loss, damage or deterioration sustained by the object while in his posses-

---

92 See above, Chapter II.D.2.b.iii (at p 46).

93 Secondary benefits which exceed the object's ordinary yield (*Übermaßfrüchte*) have to be disgorged according to the principles of unjustified enrichment: § 993 I BGB.

94 See below, section D.3.b of the present chapter (pp 86–87, esp text to nn 125–130).

95 Cf RGZ 117, 112, 115; RGZ 139, 353, 357; BGHZ 131, 220, 222–23; *Palandt* (n 14) § 994 [5] (Bassenge); J von Staudinger (Begr), *J von Staudingers Kommentar zum Bürgerlichen Gesetzbuch: §§ 985–1011* (Neubearbeitung 2006: Sellier de Gruyter, Berlin 2006) § 994 [1]–[7] (Gursky). Whether expenditure which qualifies as 'necessary' was actually successful (in the sense of achieving its intended purpose) is irrelevant.

96 If the owner has already recovered possession, claims for necessary and useful expenditure can be asserted via a separate action: cf § 1001 BGB.

sion (*arg e* §§ 989, 990 I, 992 BGB). A therefore bears the risk that B is no longer able to return the painting (eg because it has been stolen from his house) or that he can only return it in a poor condition (eg because he has negligently dropped it), provided only that the loss or damage occurred while B was still in good faith. Where, however, the *bona fide* possessor remains enriched despite the destruction, that enrichment has to be disgorged. Assume, for example, that the object in question was a fungible which has been consumed by B, or that it has, through accession or specification, become part of B's assets (cf §§ 946 ff BGB). In both cases, A's ownership is lost.[97] Although B, as a *bona fide* possessor, will not be liable to compensate A for this loss, his consumption of the fungible or his 'acquisition'[98] of the object by operation of law under §§ 946 ff BGB constitutes an interference with A's right of ownership. This gives rise to an *Eingriffskondiktion* under § 812 I 1 alt 2 BGB in the case of consumption, and under §§ 951 I 1, 812 I 1 alt 2 BGB in the case of accession or specification.[99] To the extent that B is still enriched (eg by not having had to consume his own fungibles), he has to disgorge this surplus in money.[100]

b) Position of *mala fide* Possessors

Mala fide possessors are subject to a much stricter regime. They cannot legitimately treat the object they possess as their own and are expected to show a certain amount of care in dealing with it. We have already briefly encountered the rules applicable to *mala fide* possessors when discussing the position of *mala fide* enrichees.[101] As far as secondary benefits are concerned, *mala fide* possessors not only need to disgorge all the benefits they have actually drawn from the object, but are also required to compensate the owner for any which they have culpably failed to reap contrary to the rules of good husbandry (§§ 987, 990 I BGB).

---

[97] The special case in which A's ownership is lost by virtue of the rules on *bona fide* purchase by a third party (§§ 932 ff BGB) will be considered in Part Three of this book (Chapters VI and VIII).

[98] It is better to speak of a destruction of the original object as a separate legal entity, given that B does not actually acquire any new rights.

[99] Note that recourse to the law of unjustified enrichment is, despite what was said above (n 86 and corresponding text), not barred by §§ 987 ff BGB as far as the 'substance' of the object itself is concerned: cf eg BGHZ 14, 7, 8; BGHZ 55, 176, 178–79; *Münchener Kommentar: vol 6* (n 85) § 993 [10] (Medicus); *Staudinger* (n 95) Vorbemerkungen zu §§ 987–993 [43] (Gursky).

[100] As a *bona fide* enrichee, B can – of course – rely on any relevant subsequent disenrichment (§ 818 III BGB).

[101] See above, section C.2.b of the present chapter (text to nn 50–52 on p 69).

Recovery of expenditure on the object is very limited. *Mala fide* possessors are not entitled to claim for 'useful' expenditure (*arg e* § 996 BGB),[102] and they are to be reimbursed for 'necessary' expenditure only in accordance with the stringent rules of *negotiorum gestio* (§§ 994 II, 677 ff BGB). This means that the cost of any maintenance or preservation measure will be imposed on the owner in three situations. First, if the measure was objectively in his interest and corresponded to his (actual or presumed) wishes.[103] Second, if – though against the owner's wishes – it discharged a duty of the owner's which was in the public interest.[104] Or third, if the owner subsequently ratifies the measure.[105] It is not entirely clear whether 'necessary' expenditure not qualifying under one of these provisions can ever be recovered.[106] If it can, as the courts and most academic lawyers hold,[107] then only according to the principles of unjustified enrichment, ie to the extent that the owner benefits from them (cf §§ 684 1, 818 BGB).[108]

A *mala fide* possessor who intentionally or negligently causes the object in question to deteriorate or perish, or who culpably puts it out of his power to return it to the owner, is liable to compensate the owner for any loss resulting therefrom (§§ 989, 990 I BGB).[109] If he was technically *in mora*, ie had wrongfully delayed returning the object despite the owner's demand, his liability is strict (§§ 990 II, 287 2 BGB).[110] In that case, he is

---

[102] But cf C Wendehorst, *Ausgleich und Anspruch: Theorie einer Vorteils- und Nachteilsausgleichung im Schuldrecht* (Mohr Siebeck, Tübingen 1999) 344, 349–57, who does not regard this position as wholly satisfactory and discusses means of allowing at least partial recovery.

[103] Cf §§ 994 II, 683 1, 670 BGB.

[104] Cf §§ 994 II, 683 2, 679, 670 BGB.

[105] Cf §§ 994 II, 684 2, 683 1, 670 BGB.

[106] This depends on whether § 684 1 BGB is also caught by the reference in § 994 II BGB: contrast *Münchener Kommentar: vol 6* (n 85) § 994 [19] (Medicus), with *Staudinger* (n 95) § 994 [27] (Gursky).

[107] Eg RGZ 117, 112, 114–16; BGH NJW 1955, 340, 341; BGH NJW 1975, 1553, 1556; BGH JZ 1991, 986, 990; *Erman* (n 52) vol 2, § 994 [32] (Ebbing); *Münchener Kommentar: vol 6* (n 85) § 994 [19] (Medicus); *Palandt* (n 14) § 994 [8] (Bassenge). Contra: *Staudinger* (n 95) § 994 [27] (Gursky).

[108] On this reading, the conditions under which a *mala fide* possessor can recover 'necessary expenditure' (§§ 994 II, 684 1, 818 BGB) are the same as those under which a *bona fide* possessor can recover 'useful expenditure' (§ 996 BGB).

[109] 'Fault' in § 989 BGB encompasses intention and negligence: § 276 BGB. Note that there may be a concurrent claim in unjustified enrichment: cf text to nn 97–100 above.

[110] A (potentially) competing strict liability claim to pay compensation will exist under the rules of 'false' *negotiorum gestio* (§§ 687 II 1, 678 BGB) if the possessor, in handling the object as he did, deliberately treated the owner's business as if it were his own. This requires the possessor to have positive knowledge of his lack of right to possess. The relationship between §§ 987 ff BGB and § 687 II BGB is not entirely settled. Some authors argue that the owner has to decide whether to proceed under § 687 II BGB

made to pay damages even if he was in no way to blame for the object's deterioration, destruction or loss. Since a person who has committed a delict in obtaining an object is treated as being automatically in delay ("*fur semper in mora*"), it seems that a fraudster will always be strictly liable to the transferor who has rescinded the real agreement under § 123 I BGB, unless the loss would also have occurred if the delict had not been committed (cf § 848 BGB).[111] The same may be true of a person exercising duress.[112] As an exception to the general rule, §§ 987 ff BGB do not bar recourse to the law of delict in such a situation (cf § 992 BGB).[113]

3. Incongruities with the Law on Unjustified Enrichment

Despite the frequent cross-references between the rules and principles of the *Eigentümer-Besitzer-Verhältnis* and those of unjustified enrichment,[114] there are some significant differences between the regimes of §§ 985 ff BGB and §§ 812 ff BGB. In the context of unwinding impaired consent

---

or §§ 987 ff BGB: K Rebmann, FJ Säcker and R Rixecker (eds), *Münchener Kommentar zum Bürgerlichen Gesetzbuch, vol 4: §§ 611–704* (4th edn Beck, München 2005) Vorbemerkungen §§ 677 ff [18] (Seiler); J von Staudinger (Begr), *J von Staudingers Kommentar zum Bürgerlichen Gesetzbuch: §§ 657–704* (Neubearbeitung 2006: Sellier de Gruyter, Berlin 2006) § 687 [59] (Bergmann). There is otherwise indeed a danger of undermining the requirements of §§ 987 ff BGB (esp the liability threshold in § 990 BGB) by selective recourse to § 687 II BGB. In BGH WM 1956, 1279, 1281, where a claim under §§ 687 II 1, 678 BGB was found to have been established, the Federal Supreme Court left open whether there could have been a parallel liability under §§ 989, 990 BGB.

111 Fraud is a delict under §§ 823 II BGB, 263 StGB: see below, section E.1 of the present chapter. It is not entirely clear whether § 848 BGB, which is primarily intended to capture cases of unlawful interferences with possession (§ 858 I alt 1 BGB: *verbotene Eigenmacht*) such as theft, also applies where the owner has voluntarily parted with possession; yet the history of the provision suggests a wide reading. Even though the scope of § 848 BGB may no longer be as broad as it was once thought to be (cf n 56 above), it should still be possible to invoke the provision in all cases covered by § 992 BGB and/or § 823 II BGB: cf also *Münchener Kommentar: vol 6* (n 85) § 992 [11] (Medicus); J von Staudinger (Begr), *J von Staudingers Kommentar zum Bürgerlichen Gesetzbuch: §§ 840–853* (Neubearbeitung 2007: Sellier de Gruyter, Berlin 2007) § 848 [6] (Vieweg).

112 Duress may amount to a delict under §§ 823 II BGB, 240/253 StGB: see below, section E.1 of the present chapter (pp 93–94). Although it is debatable whether § 240 StGB (coercion), being primarily concerned with the protection of liberty rather than property, is caught by the reference in § 992 BGB, the aggravated crime in § 253 StGB (blackmail/extortion) clearly is encompassed.

113 If the fraudster himself is responsible for the loss, damage or destruction (in the sense of causing it), he will therefore also incur liability under § 823 I BGB (for wrongful infringement of the victim's retroactively revested right of ownership) besides being exposed to the claim under §§ 989, 990 I BGB and that under §§ 823 II BGB, 263 StGB.

114 Eg in §§ 993 I, 818 BGB; §§ 988, 818 BGB; §§ 994 II, 684 1, (812), 818 BGB; §§ 819 I, 818 IV, 292, 987 ff BGB.

transfers, these differences lead to incongruities which ultimately have their root in the operation of the principle of abstraction. The purpose of this last part of section D is to draw attention to the most salient inconsistencies and to outline some suggestions of how they might be mitigated or overcome.

a) The Nature of the Primary Claim

If the impairment of the transferor's consent allows him to avoid both the obligatory contract and the real agreement, his primary claim for recovery of the object is a *vindicatio* (§ 985 BGB). If only the obligatory transaction can be rescinded, the transferor's claim is a *condictio indebiti* (§ 812 I 1 alt 1 BGB) aimed at re-conveyance of the object. We have seen that the *vindicatio* claimant, being owner, can segregate his chattel from an insolvent's estate (§ 47 InsO). An enrichment creditor, by contrast, has no such right. His claim in unjustified enrichment is a personal one, and it is not privileged in insolvency proceedings.[115] The different treatment of the *vindicatio* and the *condictio indebiti* reflects the distinction between a right *in rem* and a right *in personam ad rem acquirendam*.

In view of the similarities in the underlying factual matrix, the discrepancy between cases where the transferor retains or retroactively regains ownership and those where the conveyance is unimpeachable from the perspective of property law has variously been thought inappropriate. There are two principal routes by which we could – if we wished – assimilate the treatment of all transferors in insolvency. One is to deny transferor-owners the favourable treatment in the transferee-possessor's insolvency, the other is to enhance the position of enrichment creditors.

A radical suggestion is that whenever there has been a 'performance' (*Leistung*) by one party to the other, the rules on performance-based unjustified enrichment claims ought to be accorded precedence over those governing the relationship between the owner of an object and its illegitimate possessor.[116] On this view, it could be argued that where the convey-

---

[115] HP Kirchhof, HJ Lwowski and R Stürner (eds), *Münchener Kommentar zur Insolvenzordnung, vol 1: §§ 1–102* (2nd edn Beck, München 2007) § 47 [374] (Ganter). It is interesting to note that the courts disapply the *Saldotheorie* (cf text to nn 65–69 above) where its operation would privilege an enrichment creditor in his debtor's insolvency: BGHZ 161, 241.

[116] Eg E von Caemmerer, "Leistungsrückgewähr bei gutgläubigem Erwerb" in *Festschrift für Gustav Boehmer* (Röhrscheid, Bonn 1954) 145, 154–55 fn 42, reprinted in HG Leser (ed), *Ernst von Caemmerer: Gesammelte Schriften, vol 1: Rechtsvergleichung und Schuldrecht* (Mohr Siebeck, Tübingen 1968) 295, 308–9 fn 42; G Hager, "Grundfälle zur Systematik des Eigentümer-Besitzer-Verhältnisses und der bereicherungsrechtlichen Kondiktionen" JuS 1987, 877, 879–880; *Reuter/Martinek* (n 50) 681–86; H Siber, "Eigentumsanspruch und schuldrechtliche Herausgabeansprüche vom Standpunkte der

ance is invalid, the transferor-owner should be forced to proceed by the *condictio (possessionis)* rather than by the *vindicatio*.[117] Yet even of those authors who plead for a primacy of the enrichment regime in principle, the vast majority would not extend this reasoning to the primary claim.[118] § 985 BGB, the quintessential hub of ownership as an absolute concept, would otherwise be reduced to a provision protecting owners from involuntary losses of possession.[119]

Going down the second route, we could treat the *condictio indebiti* preferentially in a transferee's insolvency. An argument for according priority to such a right *in personam* might be that an enrichment creditor has enlarged the insolvent enrichee's estate without wanting to extend credit to him and without the opportunity to bargain for security.[120] This aspect was indeed considered by the compilers of the BGB, but the enrichment creditor's fate was in the end regarded as an acceptable (and indeed desirable)

Rechtsneuordnung" JherJB 89 (1941) 1, 90–94; D Waltjen, "Das Eigentümer-Besitzer-Verhältnis und Ansprüche aus ungerechtfertigter Bereicherung" AcP 175 (1975) 109, esp 119–120. Similar, but with exceptions, eg for cases of fraud and duress: U Köbl, *Das Eigentümer-Besitzer-Verhältnis im Anspruchssystem des BGB* (Duncker & Humblot, Berlin 1971) 250–65. See also A Flessner, *Wegfall der Bereicherung: Rechtsvergleichung und Kritik* (de Gruyter and Mohr Siebeck, Berlin and Tübingen 1970) 144–45, 147–49.

[117] This seems to be the position of Siber JherJB 89 (n 116) 91, and that of Waltjen AcP 175 (n 116) 119–20. How such a *condictio (possessionis)* would – and is intended to – be treated in the transferee's insolvency is, unfortunately, not discussed. On the one hand, it might be said that the envisaged primacy of the *condictio* is purely formal (and without relevance) as far as the insolvency context is concerned, in which case a right of segregation under § 47 InsO should not be excluded. Certain personal claims for recovery of possession, eg in the relationship between lessor and lessee or bailor and bailee, are indeed recognized as entailing a right to segregate: cf *Münchener Kommentar InsO: vol 1* (n 115) § 47 [340]–[345], esp [341] (Ganter). On the other hand, however, it would be strange if the deliberate decision to refer the transferor to the *condictio indebiti* were subsequently 'undermined' by granting him the privileges normally associated with a *vindicatio*. If, therefore, the precedence of § 812 I 1 alt 1 BGB over § 985 BGB is to be taken wholly seriously, it needs to entail the exclusion of § 47 InsO in the relationship between transferor-owner and transferee-possessor. *Münchener Kommentar InsO: vol 1* (n 115) § 47 [327] (Ganter), also denies that the *condictio possessionis* can support a right to segregate (though the passage does not specifically deal with our question – it probably envisages the case where the transferee does not acquire ownership because the transferor was not in a position to give it).

[118] The precedence of the *Leistungskondiktion* is only intended as one of § 818 BGB over §§ 987 ff BGB: von Caemmerer in *Festschrift Boehmer* (n 116) fn 42; Köbl *Eigentümer-Besitzer-Verhältnis* (n 116) 211–12. *Reuter/Martinek* (n 50) 669–71, 681

[119] § 985 BGB would become practically co-extensive with § 1007 II BGB and thus be rendered redundant: cf *Reuter/Martinek* (n 50) 668–70, for further discussion of this and other arguments.

[120] See already A von Tuhr, *Der Allgemeine Teil des Deutschen Bürgerlichen Rechts: vol 2/2* (Duncker & Humblot, Berlin 1918) 111–12.

corollary of abstraction.[121] Any attempt to elevate him above the enrichee's general creditors is therefore unlikely to succeed as the law stands.[122]

b) The Problem of Restitution for Secondary Benefits

Given the reference in §§ 819 I, 818 IV BGB to §§ 987 ff BGB, the *mala fide* enrichee is under the same liability with regard to secondary benefits as the *mala fide* possessor. However, the position of a *bona fide* possessor differs significantly from that of a *bona fide* enrichee. While the former is normally allowed to retain all secondary benefits reaped in accordance with the rules of good husbandry,[123] the latter (despite being owner of the object in question!) has to disgorge them to the extent that he is still enriched.[124]

Since § 988 BGB provides for restitution of secondary benefits in accordance with §§ 812 ff BGB where possession has been acquired gratuitously, this will not matter much in the case of a donee. In gratuitous transactions, the *bona fide* possessor is no better off than a *bona fide* enrichee. But even where the acquisition was not gratuitous, it is widely agreed that an assimilation of the claimant owner's unfavourable position to the favourable position of an enrichment creditor is necessary and possible.[125] Those who support a general primacy of enrichment law over the rules of the *Eigentümer-Besitzer-Verhältnis* where the parties are in a performance relationship would simply hold the *bona fide* possessor liable under § 818 I–III BGB.[126] Most academic writers, however, prefer to give the owner a choice whether to claim secondary benefits via the *Leistungskondiktion* (§§ 812 I 1 alt 1, 818 BGB) or via §§ 987 ff BGB, arguing that

[121] A Achilles, H Gebhard and P Spahn (eds), *Protokolle der Kommission für die zweite Lesung des Entwurfs des Bürgerlichen Gesetzbuchs: vol 2* (Guttentag, Berlin 1898) 721–24. The fact that the Bankruptcy Code (*Konkursordnung*) had recently been reformed to do away with many of the old privileges and preferences also played a role: ibid 724.

[122] Note, however, the argument that it might be possible to treat the enrichment creditor's claim like one by the beneficiary under a 'trust' (*Treuhand*) against his trustee, and thus afford him a right of segregation *de lege lata*: Stadler *Gestaltungsfreiheit* (n 6) 449–65, drawing on D Assfalg, *Die Behandlung von Treugut im Konkurse des Treuhänders* (de Gruyter, Berlin 1960) esp 151, 164–65. More critical, but with a similar concern: V Behr, *Wertverfolgung: Rechtsvergleichende Überlegungen zur Abgrenzung kollidierender Gläubigerinteressen* (Metzner, Frankfurt/Main 1986) 607–9, 613–15. On the position *de lege ferenda* see below, discussion in Chapter V.D.3 (at pp 207–8).

[123] See above, text to nn 93–94.

[124] See above, text to n 42.

[125] For a reverse assimilation only: HJ Wieling, "Die Nutzungen des gutgläubigen Besitzers, insbesondere in fehlgeschlagenen Vertragsverhältnissen" AcP 169 (1969) 137, esp 144–56, who argues that, in failed reciprocal contracts, even a *bona fide* enrichee should be allowed to retain secondary benefits as if he were a *bona fide* possessor.

[126] Of the references contained in n 116 cf esp Waltjen AcP 175 (n 116) 120, 122.

§ 993 I BGB does not bar recourse to the law of unjustified enrichment where both contract and conveyance are ineffective.[127] The courts, decidedly rejecting the direct applicability of §§ 812, 818 BGB and instead insisting on a general precedence of §§ 987 ff BGB over enrichment law,[128] have sought to solve the problem through an analogous application of § 988 BGB.[129] By treating a *bona fide* possessor who possesses *sine causa* in the same way as one who possesses gratuitously, they ensure that a 'transferee' who has acquired *only* possession from the 'transferor' is not better off than one who has *also* acquired ownership.[130]

c) The Problem of Disenriching Expenditure by the Transferee

There is no provision corresponding to § 818 III BGB in §§ 987 ff BGB. This is of little consequence for *mala fide* possessors. Most cannot legitimately claim to have relied on the security of their receipt.[131] However, the absence of a disenrichment clause applying in the relationship between the owner of an object and its *bona fide* possessor puts the latter in a markedly weaker position than a *bona fide* enrichee. While the enrichee can typically deduct from his liability to make restitution any expenditure causally connected with the acquisition,[132] the possessor will only be reimbursed for 'necessary' (§ 994 BGB) and 'useful' (§ 996 BGB) expenditure on the object in question.[133] Imagine that, in our example, B is a *bona fide* donee of the painting.[134] If ownership passes *sine causa* but unavoidably, A has to bear all costs incurred by B for the benefit of the painting (whether or not necessary for its preservation and maintenance, and whether or not still enhancing the painting's value) as well as those otherwise incurred by him in reliance on the permanence of his receipt (eg for a celebratory dinner).

---

[127] Eg Larenz/Canaris *Schuldrecht 2/2* (n 47) 340; *Münchener Kommentar: vol 6* (n 85) § 988 [9], § 993 [7] (Medicus); *Palandt* (n 14) § 988 [8], § 993 [3] (Bassenge); W Pinger, *Funktion und dogmatische Einordnung des Eigentümer-Besitzer-Verhältnisses* (Beck, München 1973) 49; *Staudinger* (n 95) Vorbemerkungen zu §§ 987–993 [49] (Gursky); *Erman* (n 52) vol 2, Vor §§ 987–993 [85] (Ebbing). Critical: Wieling AcP 169 (n 125) esp 139–42. Also critical: *Reuter/Martinek* (n 50) 679–81.

[128] So-called 'exclusivity theory' (*Ausschließlichkeitstheorie*): RGZ 163, 348, esp 351–52; and see already RGZ 137, 206, 208–11.

[129] RGZ 163, 348, esp 353–57. Cf also BGHZ 10, 350, 357; BGHZ 32, 76, 94.

[130] The analogy is very problematic in three-party cases: cf eg *Münchener Kommentar: vol 6* (n 85) § 988 [8] (Medicus); *Staudinger* (n 95) Vorbemerkungen zu §§ 987–993 [48] (Gursky); Pinger *Funktion* (n 127) 50.

[131] Yet recall that a *mala fide* possessor will not necessarily have positive knowledge of his own position, as is the case with a *mala fide* enrichee: see text to nn 90–91 above.

[132] See above, section C.2.a of the present chapter (pp 67–68).

[133] See above, section D.2.a of the present chapter (text to nn 95–96 on p 80).

[134] Reciprocal transactions will be specifically considered below, text to nn 141–148.

Such expenses reduce the amount of B's abstractly surviving enrichment under § 818 III BGB. If, by contrast, the conveyance can be avoided, so that B has not acquired ownership, A is only liable to reimburse him for costs which qualify as 'necessary' or 'useful' expenditure on the painting.[135] Under the regime of §§ 987 ff BGB, all other expenses (eg the cost of an unnecessary and unsuccessful restoration attempt, or those for the dinner) have to be borne by B himself.

Again, any adjustment which may be thought desirable can be made from two angles. Either the *bona fide* possessor's position is improved, or the *bona fide* enrichee's ability to rely on § 818 III BGB restricted. Let us first look at the former alternative. In so far as a general precedence of enrichment law over §§ 987 ff BGB in performance situations finds favour,[136] the application of § 818 III BGB to the *bona fide* possessor should follow as a matter of course. Yet it has been pointed out that this approach contradicts the BGB's basic legislative framework and may only be defensible where the invalidity of the conveyance reflects a special policy designed to protect the transferee-possessor, rather than being concerned with the protection of the transferor-owner's interests (as would tend to be the case in our impaired consent transfer scenarios).[137] There is indeed nothing inherently inconsistent about holding that a donee who has at least acquired ownership, even if *sine causa*, should be better off than one who has obtained no more than possession.[138] However, it will be recalled that many academics afford the owner a free choice between proceeding via the *condictio indebiti* (§§ 812 I 1 alt 1, 818 BGB) or the *vindicatio* (§§ 985, 987 ff BGB) where both contract and conveyance are ineffective.[139] The defence in § 818 III BGB then applies to the former,[140] but not the latter claim, and all depends on which the owner decides to pursue.

This leads us to consider the special problems raised by invalid reciprocal contracts, where the transferee-possessor, B, has given value in ex-

---

[135] To the extent that B is required to disgorge secondary benefits under § 988 BGB, this includes regular maintenance costs: *arg e* § 994 I 2 BGB.

[136] See above, nn 116–118 and corresponding text.

[137] Larenz/Canaris *Schuldrecht 2/2* (n 47) 341–43. Similar: Köbl *Eigentümer-Besitzer-Verhältnis* (n 116) 259–60, for whom the outright precedence of §§ 812, 818 ff BGB over §§ 987 ff BGB is not warranted in the case of fraud and duress (§ 123 BGB), though she insists that it does apply in spontaneous mistakes cases (§ 119 BGB).

[138] Compare and contrast the argument used to justify the analogous application of § 988 BGB to possessors under an invalid reciprocal contract: text to n 130 above.

[139] See above, n 127 and corresponding text.

[140] It is not entirely clear why some authors suggest that only disenriching expenditure on the object itself counts for the purposes of § 818 III BGB, even where the defendant's receipt was gratuitous: see eg *Staudinger* (n 95) Vorbemerkungen zu §§ 994–1003 [47] (Gursky), and cf comment in n 48 above.

change for the painting. The main reason why the owner, A, may want to choose the *condictio* over the *vindicatio* is, after all, because it enables him to take advantage of the more generous enrichment rules governing the recovery of secondary benefits in the context of transactions for value (§ 818 I instead of § 993 I BGB).[141] It could be argued that if A avails himself of this option, he should – as a corrollary – bear the disadvantages of the wide disenrichment clause in § 818 III.[142] On the approach of the courts, who achieve the recovery of secondary benefits via the analogy with § 988 BGB,[143] B's disenrichment as such is never relevant to the primary claim. Application of § 818 III BGB to the *vindicatio* would offend the judicial doctrine about the 'exclusivity' of §§ 987 ff BGB (so-called '*Ausschließlichkeitstheorie*')[144] and would, more importantly, constitute an unacceptable inroad into the law's recognition and protection of ownership. The only concession the courts can make (on the property law side) to narrow the gap between § 818 III BGB on the one hand and §§ 994, 996 BGB on the other, is to acknowledge that a *bona fide* possessor who, despite having given value, is liable to disgorge secondary benefits in accordance with § 988 BGB, may reclaim the regular maintenance costs of the object as 'necessary expenditure' (cf § 994 I 2 BGB).[145]

Yet this restrictive approach need not be appropriate, given that the problem of disenriching expenditure can also be tackled from the opposite angle. A number of authors have argued that § 818 III BGB ought indeed to be assimilated to §§ 994, 996 BGB whenever the transferee has obtained ownership in pursuance of an invalid reciprocal contract.[146] This restriction

---

[141] In gratuitous transactions, the *bona fide* possessor has to disgorge secondary benefits in accordance with §§ 988, 818 I BGB: cf text after n 124 above.

[142] Cf Larenz/Canaris *Schuldrecht 2/2* (n 47) 344; *Reuter/Martinek* (n 50) 675 (but see also 679–81); M Wolf, "Die Verwendungsersatzansprüche des Besitzers im Anspruchssystem" AcP 166 (1966) 188, 197–99 (discussion restricted to expenditure on the object itself). *Staudinger* (n 95) Vorbemerkungen zu §§ 994–1003 [47] (Gursky), is more critical of this argument. Although he agrees in principle that A's claim under §§ 812 I 1 alt 1, 818 I BGB must be subject to § 818 III BGB, he points out that the special context of reciprocal contracts may impact on the availability and scope of the disenrichment defence (keyword: *Saldotheorie*). One such restriction of § 818 III BGB, based on Flume's version of the 'modified two-claims theory' (cf text to nn 79–81), is discussed below, in the text to nn 146–148. Contrast Canaris in *Festschrift Lorenz* (n 77) 46–47, whose own version of the 'modified two-claims theory' does not necessarily prevent the recognition of disenriching expenditure under § 818 III BGB.

[143] See above, text to n 129.

[144] See n 128 above. § 818 III does, of course, apply to the claim under § 988 BGB.

[145] On the possibility of a reverse assimilation (by an appropriate restriction of § 818 III BGB) see immediately below, text to nn 146–148, and esp case reference in n 147.

[146] Eg W Flume, "Aufwendungen und Erträge bei der Rückabwicklung nichtiger gegenseitiger Verträge als Problematik der Rechtsfigur der ungerechtfertigten Bereicherung"

of the disenrichment defence can be justified by reference to Flume's doctrine of asset-structuring decisions (*Lehre von der vermögensmäßigen Entscheidung*), which was outlined above.[147] If B bought the painting from A and expended money on having it re-framed (without thereby achieving any enhancement of its value) before A rescinded the contract of sale, then B's 'disenrichment' must – according to this theory – be ascribed to his own investment decision rather than to his *indebite* receipt.[148]

Although it may ultimately be impossible to streamline § 818 BGB and §§ 987 ff BGB completely, at any rate as far as a *bona fide* donee's disenriching expenditure is concerned, it should be noted that in our scenario the discrepancies would in practice not appear to be as large as in theory. This is because many impaired consent transfers which are unwound according to §§ 985 ff BGB will depend on a rescission by the transferor.[149] Ownership will have retroactively revested in A either because the identical defect allowed him to avoid both the obligatory contract and the real agreement (*Fehleridentität*) or because the latter was expressly made conditional on the validity of the former.[150] Within its rules on rescission, the BGB contains a clause requiring the party rescinding an agreement for

---

in W Schön (ed), *Gedächtnisschrift für Brigitte Knobbe-Keuk* (Schmidt, Köln 1997) 111, 117–21; Wieling AcP 169 (n 125) 150–52. Cf also M Diesselhorst, *Die Natur der Sache als außergesetzliche Rechtsquelle verfolgt an der Rechtsprechung zur Saldotheorie* (Mohr Siebeck, Tübingen 1968) 118, 122–23. Similar, but not confined to reciprocal contracts: V Emmerich, *Das Verhältnis der Nebenfolgen der Vindikation zu anderen Ansprüchen* (Doctoral Thesis, Universität des Saarlandes 1966) 149–50. J Kohler, *Die gestörte Rückabwicklung gescheiterter Austauschverträge* (Heymanns, Köln 1989) 462–91, wants to disapply § 818 III BGB and allow a separate *condictio* for recovery of expenditure (*Aufwendungskondiktion*). Critical of restricting § 818 III BGB as far as expenditure on the object itself is concerned: Canaris in *Festschrift Lorenz* (n 77) 46–47; Larenz/Canaris *Schuldrecht 2/2* (n 47) 333–34; Kaiser *Rückabwicklung* (n 62) 412.

[147] See above, text to nn 79–81. The Federal Supreme Court has effectively moved in this direction by maintaining that, in reciprocal contracts, the judicial *Saldotheorie* sometimes requires the 'risk' of disenrichment constituted by reliance expenditure connected with the acquisition to be borne by the party incurring it (without – however – specifying any precise criteria): BGHZ 116, 251. Critical of the court's reasoning: CW Canaris, "Der Vorrang außerbereicherungsrechtlicher, insbesondere dinglicher Wertungen gegenüber der Saldotheorie und dem Subsidiaritätsdogma" JZ 1992, 1114; J Kohler, "Erforderliche und klare Worte zum Entreicherungseinwand" NJW 1992, 3145; *Münchener Kommentar: vol 5* (n 41) § 818 [72], [77] (Lieb).

[148] Flume in *Gedenkschrift Knobbe-Keuk* (n 146) 120–21, esp 121: "Die nicht werterhöhende Verwendung geht zu Lasten des Verwenders". ("Expenditure on the object which does not enhance its value is to be borne by the person incurring it"). Flume expressly states that this would be otherwise in the case of a gift: ibid 121 fn 34.

[149] Automatic invalidity of A's conveyance to B (eg under § 138 BGB) will be extremely rare in cases of the type considered in this book.

[150] See above, section B.3 of the present chapter (pp 60–63).

spontaneous mistake to compensate the other for any loss suffered as a result of relying on its validity, up to the amount of the other's performance interest (§ 122 I BGB). Most *bona fide* transferees will thus be able to recover expenditure they have incurred in reliance on the permanence of their receipt under § 122 I BGB, even if this expenditure qualifies as neither 'necessary' nor 'useful' for the purposes of §§ 994, 996 BGB.[151] If our donor A successfully avoids his conveyance to B under § 119 BGB,[152] and B neither knew nor ought to have known of A's mistake when he invited his wife to dinner, the cost of the dinner is a relevant reliance loss.[153]

d) The Problem of the Transferor's Disenrichment in Reciprocal Contracts

Finally, a question arises about the unwinding of reciprocal contracts in circumstances where the transferor retains ownership, but cannot return the transferee's counter-performance. Let us recall the barter case.[154] This time, A exchanges one of his oil paintings ascribed to a little-known 19th century artist for one of B's small Turner watercolours (with both works thought to be of roughly equal value). Unbeknown to either A or B, the oil painting is in fact a priceless Constable. As in the example considered above, the watercolour is stolen from A's house or destroyed as a result of his negligence. When A discovers the true state of affairs, he asks B to return the Constable. Assuming that § 119 II BGB allows A to rescind both the contract of barter and the conveyance to B (on the basis of his mistake about the painting's authorship),[155] how does German law deal with the fact that he is unable to give back the Turner watercolour?

The difference between this scenario and the one considered above is that A's claim against B is now not a *condictio indebiti* (§ 812 I 1 alt 1

---

151 § 122 BGB thus to some extent undermines the argument restricting a *bona fide* enrichee's reliance on § 818 III BGB in reciprocal contracts: cf above, text to nn 76–82 and esp text to nn 146–148. Flume recognizes this: Flume in *Festschrift Niedermeyer* (n 79) 173; Flume AcP 194 (n 79) 441.

152 It will be recalled that cases of *Fehleridentität* are rare in the context of § 119 BGB: see text to nn 19–24. Identity of defect typically occurs where fraud and duress are in play (§ 123 BGB). In such cases, the transferee will usually (though not inevitably: cf n 153) be *mala fide*, either because he himself has exercised the fraud/duress or because he is aware of a third party's misconduct.

153 Some gaps will, however, remain. If B was ignorant of A's ground for rescission due to his own (simple) negligence, he is disqualified from recovering his reliance loss (§ 122 II BGB), even though he is technically a *bona fide* possessor. And since § 122 BGB does not apply to rescission under § 123 BGB, there may be the odd case in which B has no claim under § 122 BGB despite being *bona fide*, eg if A rescinds for duress exercised by a third party.

154 See above, section C.3 of the present chapter (esp at pp 71–72).

155 The question is contentious: see above, text to nn 20–24.

BGB), but a *vindicatio* (§ 985 BGB). Looking at each party's claim separately, the result is very similar to that of the traditional two-claims theory.[156] A can rely on the loss of the Turner to fend off B's claim in unjustified enrichment (§ 818 III BGB),[157] while he himself can vindicate the Constable. We have seen that this outcome is widely regarded as inappropriate in view of the factual reciprocity in the parties' relationship (esp when combined with B's *bona fides*).[158] B should not – or at any rate not necessarily – be made to bear the risk of A's disenrichment. Yet of the two solutions developed to overcome the weaknesses of the two-claims theory, only one can satisfactorily deal with the present scenario. This is the modified two-claims theory as espoused by Canaris and Flume.[159] It will be recalled that both authors impose restrictions on A's ability to invoke § 818 III BGB. To the extent that these restrictions apply,[160] the loss of the watercolour does not provide A with a defence to B's *condictio indebiti*. He will be liable to pay over the value of the lost Turner watercolour (§ 818 II BGB) before recovering the Constable painting. Under the modified two-claims theory, the nature of A's claim against B is completely irrelevant when considering the scope of B's enrichment claim against A.[161]

The *Saldotheorie*, on the other hand, fails in the present scenario. Its balance-sheet approach cannot work unless both parties' claims are in unjustified enrichment. Property rights do not lend themselves to set-off. No proponent of the *Saldotheorie* has as yet provided a fully satisfactory solution to the conundrum.[162] However, for the specific case of rescission at

---

[156] Cf section C.3.a of the present chapter (at p 72).

[157] Due to the principle of abstraction, B's conveyance of the Turner watercolour to A is unaffected by A's retroactive rescission of the contract of exchange. Only the real agreement in respect of the Constable painting can be rescinded (on an appropriate interpretation of § 119 II BGB).

[158] See above, text to n 64 and to nn 72–74.

[159] See above, section C.3.c of the present chapter (pp 75–77).

[160] Canaris' restrictions apply only in the negligent destruction scenario, not in the theft example. Flume's theory would in principle appear to cover both cases, but note that he doubts the possibility of holding a party like A (whose spontaneous mistake is such that it entitles him to rescind the contract under § 119 BGB) to his or her 'asset-structuring decision': cf n 80 above.

[161] On the more difficult case where both conveyances are invalid: cf Flume in *Festschrift Niedermeyer* (n 79) 169–72; Wendehorst *Ausgleich und Anspruch* (n 102) 387–93.

[162] See the discussion in Hellwege *Rückabwicklung* (n 64) 170–71; Wendehorst *Ausgleich und Anspruch* (n 102) 392 (considering the parallel case in which A is exposed to a *vindicatio* rather than a *condictio*). The only viable suggestion would appear to be the recognition of an extended right of retention on B's part: cf Diesselhorst *Natur der Sache* (n 146) 77; Leser *Saldotheorie* (n 67) 61–67 (slightly more cautious); Stadler *Gestaltungsfreiheit* (n 6) 340–42; Wieling AcP 169 (n 125) 154.

issue here,[163] it is submitted that an answer again lies in § 122 BGB. Whether or not we take seriously the foundation of the *Saldotheorie* on a double application of § 818 III BGB,[164] we must recognize that B's conveyance of the watercolour to A in discharge of a contractual obligation which – as a result of A's rescission under § 119 II BGB – later turns out to have been non-existent all along, constitutes an (anticipatory) reliance loss. As such, it should be recoverable in accordance with § 122 I BGB.[165]

E. Competing Wrongs-Based Claims

We have so far been considering the consequences of an impairment in the transferor's consent leading to the invalidity of the obligatory contract and sometimes the real agreement. The focus on the enrichment regime (§§ 812 ff BGB) when contrasted with that governing the relationship between owner and illegitimate possessor (§§ 985 ff BGB), and on the relevance of a transferee's *bona* or *mala fides* under both sets of rules, should not obscure from view the other ways in which a transferee's state of mind and behaviour impact on the overall scheme of mutual claims and liabilities. Sometimes the defect in the transferor's consent is simply the flip-side of the transferee's wrongful conduct in inducing it. A short examination of such 'inducement wrongs' is necessary to complete our picture, even though they are not strictly a 'consequence' of, but rather a precursor to the impairment.

1. Fraud and Duress

If the reason why a transferor can rescind an obligatory contract and – if he wishes – also the conveyance is that the transferee has induced both transactions by a fraudulent misrepresentation or coercion amounting to duress, the transferee will not only be treated as a *mala fide* enrichee or possessor (as the case may be),[166] but will typically also be subject to competing claims under § 823 BGB and § 826 BGB.[167] § 823 II BGB imposes a

---

[163] It was assumed that A's mistake about the authorship of the oil painting afforded him a right to rescind both the obligatory contract of barter and the subsequent conveyance: see text to n 155 above.

[164] See above, text to nn 65–66.

[165] Again, some gaps will inevitably remain due to the disqualification threshold (negligence) in § 122 II BGB: cf n 153 above.

[166] See above, sections C.2.b and D.2.b of the present chapter (pp 68–71, 81–83).

[167] Note that a 'delictual' possessor (cf § 992 BGB) will usually be strictly liable for any loss/damage to the object he has obtained: see text to nn 111–112 and cf § 848 BGB. The same would appear to be true where a *mala fide* enrichee has committed a delict at

delictual liability on anybody who culpably infringes a statute that is intended for the protection of others. One such statute is the German Criminal Code (*Strafgesetzbuch*, StGB). Where an intentional misrepresentation made with a view to a gain causes the victim to effect an economically disadvantageous disposition, the misrepresentor's conduct amounts to fraud (*Betrug*), punishable under § 263 StGB. A person exercising duress on another may be criminally liable for coercion (*Nötigung*) under § 240 StGB or blackmail/extortion (*Erpressung*) under § 253 StGB. According to § 826 BGB, moreover, anybody who intentionally and with an awareness of all the relevant circumstances causes loss to another in a manner which is considered to be 'immoral' (*contra bonos mores*) has to make good that loss. In practice, the relevance of delictual claims under §§ 823 II, 826 BGB lies primarily in the transferor's ability to claim compensation for consequential losses not otherwise recoverable[168] and to obtain relief after the time limit for rescission has expired (cf § 124 BGB).[169]

2. Negligent Misrepresentation as *culpa in contrahendo*

What if the transferee's misrepresentation was not fraudulent, but merely negligent (*fahrlässige Täuschung*)? Assume that B is the owner of a gallery who offers to value and buy paintings brought in by the public. If B

the inducement/receipt stage: see n 60 above. Note, moreover, that fraud and duress will typically also give rise to a competing liability for *culpa in contrahendo*: see below, section E.2 of the present chapter (esp text to nn 172–179 on pp 95–97).

[168] Losses resulting from not being able to dispose of the object while it is in the transferee's possession (*Vorenthaltungsschäden*) are generally thought to be irrecoverable under §§ 989, 990 I BGB: cf BGH NJW-RR 1993, 626, 628; O Jauernig (ed), *Bürgerliches Gesetzbuch: Kommentar* (12th edn Beck, München 2007) § 989 [2], 990 [6] (Jauernig); *Münchener Kommentar: vol 6* (n 85) § 989 [11] (Medicus); *Palandt* (n 14) § 989 [6] (Bassenge).

[169] It is disputed whether a wrongs-based claim for cancellation of the contract (cf § 249 I BGB) should still be allowed after the expiry of the one-year time limit for rescission laid down in § 124 BGB. The courts regularly hold that it is available: eg RGZ 84, 131, 134; BGH NJW 1962, 1196, 1198–99; BGHZ 42, 37, 42; BGH NJW 1979, 1983; BGH NJW 1984, 2814, 2815; BGH NJW 1997, 254; BGH NJW-RR 2002, 308. Critical: OLG Hamm NJW-RR 1995, 205. The historical legislator saw the potential for conflict and specifically approved the more generous limitation regime applicable to delictual claims: *Motive* (n 5) vol 1, 208, and vol 2, 20–21. This leads some authors to distinguish between the delictual liability under §§ 823, 826 BGB on the one hand and the liability for *culpa in contrahendo* (cf n 167) on the other: eg J von Staudinger (Begr), *J von Staudingers Kommentar zum Bürgerlichen Gesetzbuch: §§ 90–133* (Neubearbeitung 2004: Sellier de Gruyter, Berlin 2004) § 123 [95]–[96] (Singer/von Finckenstein); probably also *Münchener Kommentar: vol 1/1* (n 14) § 123 [35a] (Kramer). The courts do not generally draw this distinction. For a detailed discussion of the entire issue see Lorenz *Schutz vor dem unerwünschten Vertrag* (n 27) 332–37.

negligently fails to identify A's painting as a Constable and informs him that it is by a little-known 19th century artist, he will have negligently induced a mistake in A about an essential quality of the painting. Should this mistake lead A to sell and convey the Constable to B, he can rescind the contract of sale (and possibly even the conveyance)[170] under § 119 II BGB. However, B's negligent misrepresentation will often induce in A what is seen as a mere 'motivational mistake'. If B is correct in ascribing A's painting to the little-known artist, but negligently quotes too low a market price for it (forgetting that a similar work by the same artist has just been sold at auction for several times the amount),[171] A cannot avoid the subsequent transaction(s) under any head of § 119 BGB. Hence, a negligent misrepresentation by one contracting party may – but need not – induce an operative mistake in the other. Unless the mistake is one which happens to fall under § 119 BGB, no ground for rescission avails the transferor.

Yet it should not be assumed that he has no remedy in such a case. Making a negligent misrepresentation in pre-contractual negotiations counts as *culpa in contrahendo* (fault in contracting) which itself gives rise to a claim for compensation.[172] A brainchild of Rudolph von Jhering,[173] the doctrine of *culpa in contrahendo* was seized on by the Imperial Supreme Court (*Reichsgericht*) to circumvent – *praeter legem* – certain perceived lacunae within the law of delict.[174] It was finally put onto a statutory footing in 2002 and is now contained in § 311 II BGB. The essence of the doctrine is that a pre-contractual duty of care arises as soon as two parties come into contact with a view to contracting.[175] A party who culpably fails to comply with this duty of care is liable to compensate the other for any

---

170 See above, text to nn 20–24.

171 Note that a (false) statement about the value or market price of an object will not without more amount to a (mis)representation, especially in the context of arm's length bargaining. Here, however, B has held himself out as an art expert, offered his valuation services, and based his assessment of A's painting on specific factual criteria (namely recent auction results).

172 Cf eg RGZ 103, 47, 50; BGH NJW 1962, 1196; BGH NJW 1998, 302, 303–4.

173 R von Jhering, "Culpa in Contrahendo oder Schadensersatz bei nichtigen oder nicht zur Perfection gelangten Verträgen" JherJB 4 (1861) 1. As the title suggests, the doctrine was initially intended to cover cases where no valid contract comes into existence at all. Note, however, that the doctrine has a broader precursor in the Prussian *Allgemeines Landrecht* of 1794: Part I, Title 5, §§ 284 ff ALR.

174 RGZ 78, 239; RGZ 95, 58, 60; RGZ 107, 357, 362. The lacunae consisted in the lack of a remedy for pure economic loss (see text to n 176) and in the availability of the exculpation defence in § 831 BGB (which does not exist in contractual or quasi-contractual relationships: cf § 278 BGB).

175 For a general account of *culpa in contrahendo* in English see B Markesinis, H Unberath and A Johnston, *The German Law of Contract: A Comparative Treatise* (Hart, Oxford 2006) 91–108.

loss suffered as a result thereof (cf §§ 280 I, 241 II, 311 II BGB). Though based on a breach of duty and thus on a form of 'wrongdoing', liability for *culpa in contrahendo* is not technically classified as delictual, but as quasi-contractual (*vertragsähnlich*). This is important. In our scenario, B has negligently caused A pure economic loss, and loss unconnected with any damage to one of the rights or interests listed in § 823 I BGB (life, bodily integrity, liberty, property, etc) is generally not recoverable under the German law of delict.[176]

Culpa in contrahendo can thus provide a remedy for negligently induced impaired consent transfers in situations which the fathers of the BGB envisaged would be covered neither by the principles of rescission nor the rules of delict.[177] The only condition is said to be that the representee must have suffered some economic detriment (*Vermögensschaden*) through contracting.[178] It will be recalled that the primary form which compensation takes under §§ 249 ff BGB is specific reinstatement (*Naturalrestitution*) rather than monetary damages. A transferee whose negligent misrepresentation has caused the transferor to enter into the obligatory

---

[176] The *intentional* infliction of pure economic loss is caught by § 826 BGB if it contravenes 'good morals'. § 823 II BGB in conjunction with the German Criminal Code (StGB) encompasses further special situations: see text to nn 167–169 above.

[177] It is widely agreed that the existence of § 123 BGB does not militate against the recognition of a claim under the *culpa in contrahendo* doctrine: eg BGH NJW 1962, 1196, 1198–99; NJW 1968, 986, 987; NJW 1969, 1625, 1626; H Fleischer, "Konkurrenzprobleme um die culpa in contrahendo: Fahrlässige Irreführung versus arglistige Täuschung" AcP 200 (2000) 91, 93–108; *Palandt* (n 14) § 123 [27] (Heinrichs/Ellenberger), § 311 [13] (Grüneberg). On the problem of the appropriate limitation period see references in n 169 above.

[178] Cf BGH NJW 1998, 302; OLG Celle NJW-RR 2006, 1283; W Krüger, "Vertragsrückabwicklung im Wege des Schadensersatzes" in R Bork, T Hoeren and P Pohlmann (eds), *Recht und Risiko: Festschrift für Helmut Kollhosser zum 70. Geburtstag* (VVW, Karlsruhe 2004) vol 2, 329, esp 331–36; M Lieb, "Vertragsaufhebung oder Geldersatz? Überlegungen über die Rechtsfolgen von culpa in contrahendo" in *Festschrift der Rechtswissenschaftlichen Fakultät zur 600-Jahr-Feier der Universität zu Köln* (Heymanns, Köln 1988) 251, 258–61. The test has recently become increasingly subjective: cf BGH NJW 1998, 302, 304; BGHZ 160, 149, 153; BGHZ 162, 306, 310 (the latter two cases concerned delictual claims proper). A significant number of authors want to dispense with the loss requirement altogether, arguing that the impairment of the mistaken party's contractual autonomy alone should be sufficient for a *culpa in contrahendo* claim: eg Fleischer AcP 200 (n 177) 108–18; HC Grigoleit, "Neuere Tendenzen zur schadensrechtlichen Vertragsaufhebung" NJW 1999, 900, 901–2; Lorenz *Schutz vor dem unerwünschten Vertrag* (n 27) esp 388–90; *Palandt* (n 14) § 311 [13] (Grüneberg); J von Staudinger (Begr), *J von Staudingers Kommentar zum Bürgerlichen Gesetzbuch: §§ 311–312f* (Neubearbeitung 2005: Sellier de Gruyter, Berlin 2005) § 311 [143] (Löwisch). In view of the wording of the new §§ 241 II, 311 II BGB ("interests"), the latter interpretation may ultimately win the day: cf *Erman* (n 52) vol 1, § 311 [17], [43] (Kindl).

contract, and subsequently to effect the conveyance, is under a duty to put the latter into the position he would have been in had he not become involved in these transactions.[179] The transferee-representor has to agree to the dissolution of the contract, retransfer the object in question, and make good any consequential loss. Of course, the wrongs-based personal claim for *culpa in contrahendo* is not protected in the wrongdoer's insolvency. The entire transaction is unwound according to §§ 249 ff BGB. This regime differs significantly from both §§ 812 ff BGB and §§ 985 ff BGB. The transferor's contributory negligence, for example, can be taken into account to reduce the amount of the transferee's liability (§ 254 BGB). On the other hand, that liability extends to lost profits (§ 252 BGB), whether or not the transferee was *mala fide*.[180] There are no special provisions governing recovery of secondary benefits.[181] Since the focus of §§ 249 ff BGB is on the transferor's loss rather than on the transferee's gain, the transferee will always be liable to pay the value of the object in question if he can no longer return it (§ 251 I BGB). Disenrichment is no defence.

The upshot is that the doctrine of *culpa in contrahendo* caters for situations in which a defect of the transferor's consent can be ascribed to the transferee's negligence, but which may not be covered by any ground for avoidance of legal transactions. The remedial consequences of the doctrine, however, are out of line with those entailed by rescission.

3. Immoral Exploitation of Emotional Attachment

It was pointed out above that contracts entered into as a result of the transferee's 'undue influence' over the transferor may sometimes be void for the contravention of 'good morals' under § 138 BGB.[182] The corresponding inducement wrong is the intentional infliction of loss *contra bonos mores* (§ 826 BGB).[183] Although the morality standards of § 138 BGB and

179 If the transferor can prove that the parties would have entered into the obligatory contract on terms other than those actually agreed (eg sale for a higher price), then the transferee's duty is to make good the discrepancy between the actual and the hypothetical terms of the contract (eg by paying the difference in value between the two prices): see BGHZ 69, 53; BGH NJW 1988, 2234; BGH NJW 1989, 1793; BGH NJW 1998, 2900; BGH NJW 2001, 2875; BGHZ 168, 135. Cf the English decision of *Clef Aquitaine Sarl v Laporte Materials (Barrow) Ltd* [2001] QB 488 (CA).

180 Note that simple negligence (which does not count as *mala fides* for the purposes of §§ 987 ff BGB and, *a fortiori*, § 819 I BGB) is sufficient to trigger liability for *culpa in contrahendo*.

181 The claimant's inability to reap such benefits himself may, of course, count as a relevant 'loss' in appropriate circumstances.

182 See above, section B.4 of the present chapter (pp 63–64).

183 § 826 BGB has already been mentioned in section E.1 of the present chapter.

§ 826 BGB are in principle independent,[184] there will be a good deal of overlap. If the transferee deliberately exploits the transferor's emotional attachment in order to make a profit for himself, knowing that this requires the infliction of a loss upon the transferor and being aware of all the circumstances which attract the stigma of 'immorality', he should be liable to make good that loss.[185] In practice, a claim under § 826 BGB will again only be of significance for financial detriments not covered by §§ 812 ff BGB or (where applicable) §§ 985 ff BGB.[186]

F. Summary

German law has different ways of dealing with situations which might generically be described as 'impaired consent transfers' of movable objects. This chapter has attempted to outline the basic patterns that emerge in the simplest scenario, namely pure two-party cases. The main focus has been on those impairments of consent which generate a right in the affected party to avoid his or her defective agreement. These were fraud, duress and certain types of spontaneous mistake. However, mention was also made of other possible responses, namely automatic invalidity of the transaction (in certain cases of 'undue influence') or its reversal according to the principles of specific reinstatement after the commission of a wrong (particularly relevant in cases of a motivational mistake induced by negligent misrepresentation: doctrine of *culpa in contrahendo*).

Where German law provides for the invalidity or avoidance of the affected legal transaction(s), the operation of the principles of separation and abstraction leads to a crossroads. The transfer in question will be unwound in one of two ways. A relevant impairment will affect either the obligatory contract underlying a transfer (ie its legal basis) alone, or also the real agreement effecting the conveyance. In the former case, the transaction is reversed purely according to the principles of unjustified enrichment (§§ 812 ff BGB). In the latter, the transferor's *vindicatio* (§ 985 BGB) competes with a *condictio possessionis*, but the special provisions of the *Eigentümer-Besitzer-Verhältnis* (§§ 987 ff BGB) are widely thought to bar recourse to the law of unjustified enrichment more generally (esp to the

[184] Cf BGHZ 10, 228, 232; BGH NJW 1970, 657, 658; *Münchener Kommentar: vol 5* (n 41) § 826 [9], [40] (Wagner); J von Staudinger (Begr), *J von Staudingers Kommentar zum Bürgerlichen Gesetzbuch*: *§§ 826–829* (Neubearbeitung 2003: Sellier de Gruyter, Berlin 2003) § 826 [44] (Oechsler).

[185] Cf RGZ 143, 48, 50–52.

[186] On the question whether and when § 138 BGB renders the conveyance void see above, nn 28–29 and corresponding text.

liability regime of § 818 BGB). A comparison between §§ 812 ff BGB and §§ 985 ff BGB highlights a number of incongruities between the two systems of unwinding impaired consent transfers. In some respects, these can be and have been bridged. The most important remaining discrepancy relates to the treatment of the transferor's primary claim in the event of the transferee's insolvency. Only the *vindicatio* claimant can segregate the object transferred from the insolvent's estate and thus avoid having to join the queue of the latter's unsecured general creditors.

Chapter IV

Personal and Proprietary Restitution under English Law

A. Introduction

Having examined in the previous chapter how German law deals with impaired consent transfers and their consequences in two-party cases, we must now do the same for English law. This is a much more difficult task. Given the incremental development of the Common law and the relatively late emancipation of a separate 'law of restitution' or 'unjust enrichment',[1] many questions which have a direct bearing on the issues here under consideration are still unsettled. At the interface of contract, unjust enrichment and property law, the waters are distinctly murky. If any one difficulty can be identified as paramount for the purposes of the present inquiry, it concerns the existence and form of what is generally referred to as 'proprietary restitution'. The problem is this. Assume that A has sold and delivered or made a gift of a painting to B under circumstances which give rise to a claim in unjust enrichment. Does A now have merely a personal right against B, or can he (additionally or alternatively) assert some sort of proprietary interest in respect of the painting? One main aim of this chapter is to provide an account of the current state of English law and to suggest a conceptually sound and systematically coherent view of the nature and basis of proprietary restitution.

The discussion begins with a general outline of how the unjust factor regime operates, especially in contract and gift cases (section B). It then turns to the intricate relationship between a personal restitutionary claim and property rights, focusing initially on situations in which the purported conveyance is invalid so that the transferor never loses his title (section C). The largest part of the chapter is devoted to examining the availability and form of proprietary restitution in cases where title passes to the transferee

[1] In England, the first textbook on the subject was published in 1966: R Goff and G Jones, *The Law of Restitution* (Sweet & Maxwell, London 1966). The subject gained explicit and final judicial recognition only in *Lipkin Gorman (a firm) v Karpnale Ltd* [1991] 2 AC 548 (HL). One reason is that, historically, much of the area was shrouded in the language of 'implied' or 'quasi-contract'. A brief historical overview is contained in the current edition of *Goff & Jones*: G Jones (ed), R Goff and G Jones, *The Law of Restitution* (7th edn Sweet & Maxwell, London 2007) [1–001]–[1–016].

despite the impairment of the transferor's consent (section D). Finally, competing wrongs-based claims are again considered to complete the picture (section E).

B. Operation of the Unjust Factor Regime

1. General Principles

Let us briefly recall the basic structure of the English law of unjust enrichment. A claim in unjust enrichment rests on three pillars.[2] First, the defendant must be enriched. Second, his enrichment must be at the claimant's expense. And third, the enrichment must qualify as 'unjust' by virtue of some recognized 'unjust factor'. *Prima facie*, this orthodox scheme seems simple enough. On closer analysis, however, all three requirements are fraught with difficulties. Lack of space forbids a comprehensive discussion, but mention must be made of the more salient problems relevant to the present context, so as to provide a framework for the discussion which follows.

The first problem concerns the identification and determination of the defendant's enrichment. Here the main point of controversy – 'subjective devaluation'[3] aside – is whether to approach this question factually or normatively. Take, for example, a case in which the painting is delivered by A to B, but title never passes. To what extent, if any, can B be regarded as enriched? The answer depends, at least in part, on the relationship between a personal claim to restitution and persisting property rights, discussed in section C below.

Once established, the defendant's enrichment has to be shown to be at the claimant's expense. It must somehow be derived from the claimant's wealth. This second requirement raises the issue whether the claimant needs to have suffered an impoverishment which corresponds to the defendant's gain. The point is disputed.[4] It has certain repercussions for situations

---

[2] See above, Chapter II.C.1 (p 25), and cf the observation by Lord Browne-Wilkinson in *Woolwich Equitable BS v Inland Revenue Commissioners* [1993] AC 70 (HL) 196–97.

[3] On 'subjective devaluation' see eg P Birks, *An Introduction to the Law of Restitution* (Clarendon Press, Oxford 1985, paperback edn 1989) 109–28; A Burrows, *The Law of Restitution* (2nd edn Butterworths, London 2002) 18–25; G Virgo, *The Principles of the Law of Restitution* (2nd edn OUP, Oxford 2006) 66–69. German lawyers would speak of an enrichment being 'imposed' on the defendant (*aufgedrängte Bereicherung*).

[4] Contrast eg P Birks, *Unjust Enrichment* (2nd edn OUP, Oxford 2005) 78–86, with M McInnes, "Interceptive Subtraction, Unjust Enrichment and Wrongs – A Reply to Professor Birks" (2003) 62 CLJ 697. The debate is related to the one about the appro-

where the transferor retains his title despite the delivery as well as for three-party cases.[5] However, in most of the two-party transfer scenarios considered here, the defendant's enrichment is participatory and referable to the claimant's performance (conveyance), so that there will be a sufficient impoverishment on any view.

The third requirement is that there must be some factor making the defendant's enrichment at the claimant's expense 'unjust'. Contrasting the orthodox unjust factor approach with the Civilian notion of 'absence of basis', we saw that English law (still) prefers to identify positive reasons for reversing an enrichment rather than invoking the absence of a justification for its retention by the defendant.[6] In the context of the present study, the relevant unjust factors are mistake (whether spontaneous or induced), duress and undue influence. These constitute recognized defects of the transferor's consent impairing his decision-making process. A word must be said on mistake. In contrast to mere (legally irrelevant) mispredictions, a mistake is made out whenever the claimant acts on false data about an *existing* state of affairs.[7] Historically, not every mistake provided a sufficient ground for restitution. For a long time, it was thought that only liability mistakes counted,[8] and then only if they were premised on a misapprehension of fact rather than law.[9] However, both restrictions have now been abandoned. In *Barclays Bank Ltd v WJ Simms Son & Cooke (Southern)*

---

priate approach towards non-performance cases and the proper taxonomical classification of 'restitution for wrongs': see n 42 below as well as n 51 on p 29 and n 55 on p 30.

[5] See below, section C of the present chapter (pp 119–25) and Chapter VI.C.2.b (at pp 238–40).

[6] See above, Chapter II.C.1.b (pp 28–31).

[7] On the distinction between mistakes and mispredictions and the relationship between the two see Birks *Introduction* (n 3) 147–48; W Seah, "Mispredictions, Mistakes and the Law of Unjust Enrichment" [2007] RLR 93; D Sheehan, "What is a Mistake?" (2000) 20 LS 538, 551–52; *Dextra Bank & Trust Co Ltd v Bank of Jamaica* [2002] 1 All ER (Comm) 193 (PC) [28]–[32]. The line can be very narrow, as the case of *Ogden v Trustees of the RHS Griffiths 2003 Settlement* [2008] EWHC 118 (ChD), [2008] 2 All ER 655, illustrates: see below, n 90 and text to nn 85–87.

[8] *Kelly v Solari* (1841) 9 Mees & W 54, 58; 152 ER 24, 26 (Parke B); *Aiken v Short* (1856) 1 Hurl & N 210, 215; 156 ER 1180, 1182 (Bramwell B); *Baylis v Bishop of London* [1913] 1 Ch 127 (CA). The requirement of a liability mistake took English law remarkably close to the Civilian *condictio indebiti*, since the parties' subjective *causa solvendi* necessarily fails if the obligation which the performance purports to discharge (the legal basis of the transfer) is non-existent: cf S Meier, *Irrtum und Zweckverfehlung: Die Rolle der unjust-Gründe bei rechtsgrundlosen Leistungen im englischen Recht* (Mohr Siebeck, Tübingen 1999) 31–34.

[9] *Bilbie v Lumley* (1802) 2 East 469, 102 ER 448; *Rogers v Ingham* (1876) 3 ChD 351 (CA); *Henderson v Folkestone Waterworks Co* (1885) 1 TLR 329 (QBD); *Re Hatch* [1919] 1 Ch 351 (ChD); *Sawyer v Window Brace Ltd* [1943] 1 KB 32 (KBD).

Ltd,[10] Robert Goff J (as he then was)[11] reviewed the preceding case law and concluded that it did not unequivocally support the 'supposed liability' test. He held that a claim for restitution could in principle be founded on *any* causative mistake, provided only that it was a mistake of fact (and not of law). This latter hurdle, much criticized, continued in existence until the House of Lords finally abolished the so-called 'mistake of law bar' in *Kleinwort Benson Ltd v Lincoln City Council*.[12] A generalized causative mistake test has since been approved on various occasions.[13]

In liberalizing the preconditions of liability, the courts realized that any extension of the types of mistake upon which a claim to restitution for unjust enrichment can be founded (a development in the claimant's interest) would have to be counter-balanced by a change of position or disenrichment defence (protecting the defendant's interest in the security of his receipt).[14] Such a defence was explicitly recognized as part of English law in the landmark case of *Lipkin Gorman (a firm) v Karpnale Ltd*.[15] It ensures that the claimant's right to demand restitution is normally limited to the enrichment still surviving in the defendant's hands. Two crucial issues remain to be resolved in relation to the disenrichment defence.[16] The first has already been mentioned and concerns the circumstances under which the defendant will be disqualified from invoking it.[17] The second is closely connected. How broadly does the defence operate? Is it confined to cases where the defendant has detrimentally relied on his receipt, as the terminology of 'change of position' indicates, or can it be applied to any disenrichment caused by the enriching receipt, including in particular accidental

---

[10] [1980] QB 677 (QBD Comm).

[11] Robert Goff J later became Lord Goff of Chieveley.

[12] [1999] 2 AC 349 (HL).

[13] Eg *Nurdin & Peacock plc v DB Ramsden & Co Ltd* [1999] 1 WLR 1249 (ChD); *Lloyds Bank plc v Independent Insurance Co Ltd* [2000] QB 110 (CA); *Deutsche Morgan Grenfell Group plc v Inland Revenue Commissioners* [2006] UKHL 49, [2007] 1 AC 558, [60] (Lord Hope), [143] (Lord Walker). For Australia, the causative mistake test was authoritatively adopted in *David Securities Pty Ltd v Commonwealth Bank of Australia* (1992) 175 CLR 353 (HCA).

[14] Cf *Barclays Bank v Simms* (n 10) 695 (Robert Goff J); *Kleinwort Benson v Lincoln City Council* (n 12) 372–73 (Lord Goff), 412 (Lord Hope).

[15] [1991] 2 AC 548 (HL).

[16] A further question, which cannot be addressed here, is the extent to which non-disenriching, but irreversible, changes of position also provide a defence: cf the discussion in J Edelman and E Bant, *Unjust Enrichment in Australia* (OUP, Sydney 2006) 319–21. In *Commerzbank AG v Price-Jones* [2003] EWCA Civ 1663, the Court of Appeal indicated that it would, in an appropriate case, be willing to recognize non-pecuniary changes of position.

[17] See above, Chapter II.C.2.b (at pp 34–35).

loss of (or damage to) the object received?[18] The wider view has been accepted in New Zealand,[19] and there are *dicta* in English cases which point in the same direction.[20] A generous handling of the defence does indeed seem to fit best with the liberalization of the unjust factor regime. However, it is submitted that the inclusion of disenrichments which are not reliance-based may require an adjustment to the disqualifying factors. While the enrichee's state of mind – whatever the threshold of disqualification will eventually turn out to be – is rightly essential to self-induced changes of position, it should arguably be irrelevant where the disenrichment is purely accidental. As in German law,[21] there is a case to be made for the proposition that even bad faith enrichees ought to be relieved of liability to the extent that they are disenriched through no fault of their own (and perhaps to the extent that they have not deliberately or at least culpably delayed making restitution).[22]

When looking at the nature of the claimant's remedy, we noted that the primary response within the English law of unjust enrichment was not restitution *in specie*, but a monetary claim to the value of the defendant's enrichment.[23] However, two immediate *caveats* are warranted. One is the possibility of proprietary restitution, which has already been mentioned and which will be discussed in section D below. The other is the supposed rule that in English law a contract cannot be rescinded unless the parties can be restored to their precise pre-contractual positions (requirement of

---

[18] Andrew Burrows refers to these options as the 'wide' and the 'narrow' version of the defence: Burrows *Restitution* (n 3) 512–17; A Burrows, "Change of Position: The View from England" (2003) 36 Loy LA Law Rev 803, 804–9.

[19] *National Bank of New Zealand Ltd v Waitaki International Processing (NI) Ltd* [1999] 2 NZLR 211 (NZCA).

[20] *Scottish Equitable plc v Derby* [2001] EWCA Civ 369, [2001] 3 All ER 818, [30]–[31] (Robert Walker LJ); *Rose v AIB Group (UK) plc* [2003] EWHC 1737 (ChD Com Ct), [2003] 1 WLR 2791, [49] (Warren QC); *Commerzbank v Price-Jones* (n 16) [54] (Munby J).

[21] See above, Chapter III.C.2.b (at pp 70–71).

[22] As in German law, restrictions may also be appropriate for reciprocal contracts, where the defendant has – irrespective of his good or bad faith – deliberately made the decision to substitute one asset for another and thus consciously incurred the risks connected with the 'having' of a particular object: cf above, Chapter III.C.3.c (pp 75–77). Such reasoning is already apparent as far as the unjust factor 'failure of consideration' is concerned: *Goss v Chilcott* [1996] AC 778 (PC) 799. Note, however, that the issue is probably not as critical in English law as under the BGB: the requirement of *restitutio in integrum* or counter-restitution as a pre-condition of rescission will solve the problem in many cases of impaired consent transfers: see below, section B.2.c of the present chapter (pp 109–13).

[23] See above, Chapter II.C.2.a (esp p 32).

restitutio in integrum).[24] It is to the relationship between unjust enrichment and rescission of contract that we now turn.

2. Unjust Enrichment and Rescission of Contract

Of the many questions which arise at the interface between contract law and unjust enrichment, three are of particular relevance in the present context. First, how does the unjust factor regime operate in a contractual setting? Second, what – if any – event generates the right to rescind a contract? Third, what are we to make of the so-called *restitutio in integrum* requirement? We will consider each question in turn.

a) The Contractual Bar to Restitution for Unjust Enrichment

When Robert Goff J relieved English law of the restrictive 'supposed liability' test in *Barclays Bank v Simms*,[25] he acknowledged that certain exceptions to recovery for mistake were necessary to make a regime based purely on causation workable. Besides good faith changes of position by the enrichee, the discharge of a valid obligation was a compelling reason to deny restitution despite the existence of a causative mistake for a particular transfer.[26]

Though occasioned by the abolition of the liability mistake rule, Robert Goff J's statement contains a more fundamental observation about the law of unjust enrichment. No unjust factor can be allowed to found a claim to restitution where its operation would undermine other, more specific, rules governing the parties' relationship. If, in our example, A is under a contractual obligation to convey and deliver an object to B and effects the transfer in accordance with this obligation,[27] the fact that his consent was impaired will not automatically make B's enrichment 'unjust'. Contractual principles supersede and trump the law of unjust enrichment at this point. B is, at any rate, not under any *immediate* obligation to make restitution to

[24] See below, section B.2.c of the present chapter (pp 109–13).

[25] See above, n 10 and corresponding text.

[26] Robert Goff J said (at [1980] QB 677, 695): "(1) If a person pays money to another under a mistake of fact which causes him to make the payment, he is prima facie entitled to recover it as money paid under a mistake of fact. (2) His claim may however fail if (a) the payer intends that the payee shall have the money at all events ...; or (b) the payment is made for good consideration, *in particular if the money is paid to discharge, and does discharge, a debt owed to the payee* ...; or (c) the payee has changed his position in good faith ..." (emphasis added).

[27] Note that, as a result of the *solo consensu* principle, this scenario will be rarer in English than in German law: see above, Chapter II.D.3.a (esp pp 48–49), and below, section D.3.a of the present chapter (esp pp 135–36).

A. The existence of the contract as a valid reason for the transfer justifies the allocation of wealth to B. One might say that, under the unjust factor approach, the presence of a legal basis precludes a claim in unjust enrichment, rather than its absence justifying the claim.[28]

This is, of course, not the end of the matter. Under certain circumstances, a contract can be rescinded and the legal basis for the transfer retroactively destroyed. If A manages to avoid his contract with B, the unjust factors can again operate freely. And since the English grounds for rescission (misrepresentation, duress and undue influence)[29] mirror the unjust factors in all but spontaneous mistake cases, the practical relevance of the contractual bar to restitution for unjust enrichment is largely confined to the latter.[30]

b) The Basis of the Right to Rescind a Contract

The close resemblance between the grounds for rescission and the unjust factors may be no coincidence. It has been suggested that the right to rescind a contract not only helps free the way for the assertion of a restitutionary claim, but is itself a product of the law of unjust enrichment.[31] The right to rescind is generated in favour of one party to a contract whenever that contract bestows a benefit on the other in circumstances which the legal system regards as 'unjust'. The exercise of the right avoids the contract and thus restores the pre-contractual position.

---

[28] Cf *Steam Saw Mills Co Ltd v Baring Bros & Co Ltd* [1922] 1 Ch 244 (CA) 250–51 (Lord Sterndale MR), 254 (Warrington LJ); *David Securities v Commonwealth Bank of Australia* (n 13) 392 (Brennan J). This leads Meier *Irrtum und Zweckverfehlung* (n 8) 101–3, to conclude that the Common law to an extent already adopts the legal basis approach. Unsurprisingly, the reverse pattern can be observed in German law, where the absence of a liability mistake usually precludes a *condictio indebiti*: § 814 BGB (albeit that the provision does not apply where the claimant expressly reserves the right to recover his performance: cf BGHZ 83, 278, 282).

[29] It will be recalled that fraud and duress are grounds for rescission at common law, while non-fraudulent (negligent and innocent) misrepresentation and undue influence are recognized only in equity: see above, Chapter II.B.2.a (pp 22–23). Note that, under section 2(2) of the Misrepresentation Act 1967, a court may deny rescission for non-fraudulent misrepresentation, declare the contract subsisting, and award damages *in lieu* of rescission.

[30] In cases of induced mistake, duress or undue influence, the contractual bar to restitution for unjust enrichment plays a role only where rescission of the contract is itself barred, eg on the ground of affirmation or delay.

[31] Eg E Bant, "*Restitutio in Integrum* and the Change of Position Defence: Lessons from Rescission" [2007] RLR 13, 15–16; Birks *Introduction* (n 3) 163, 171–72; *Edelman & Bant* (n 16), 23, 102; NY Nahan, "Rescission: A Case for Rejecting the Classical Model?" (1997) 26 UWALR 66, 72–73. Probably also G Jones (ed), R Goff and G Jones, *The Law of Restitution* (7th edn Sweet & Maxwell, London 2007) [9–001]–[9–053].

Sometimes a distinction is drawn in this context between executed and executory contracts. Rescission is said to be a 'restitutionary remedy' in the case of the former, but not the latter.[32] Yet it is difficult to understand why the characterization of the remedy should turn on whether or not performance has already been rendered. For one, it is – as we shall see – by no means clear whether and to what extent rescission of the contract *per se* reverses transfers that have occurred in pursuance of it.[33] Moreover, there is good reason to think that a personal contractual claim, though still unperformed, constitutes a sufficient enrichment in its own right.[34] By entering into the contract, each party confers a valuable right *in personam* on the other to demand performance or, failing this, at least damages for breach of contract. Where one party obtains this right *in personam* 'unjustly', eg because he has induced the other to contract by means of some misrepresentation,[35] his enrichment is not secure. The other party has the option of divesting it unilaterally. Viewed in this light, the right to rescind an executory contract is best described as a power *in personam* retroactively to cancel out mutual contractual claims. By revoking his consent to the transaction which generated them, the rescinding party is effecting restitution of the misrepresentor's unjust enrichment at his (the representee's) expense, while at the same time giving up what he himself obtained at the misrepresentor's expense.

It may be asked how we can be so sure that we are dealing with restitution for unjust enrichment rather than restitution for wrongs?[36] After all, the circumstances giving rise to the transferor's right to rescind will often constitute a breach of duty by the transferee.[37] There are two possible answers. Both involve the observation that not all rescission cases involve actionable wrongs. This is most evident when considering innocent misrepresentation and undue influence. There is no tort of misrepresentation

---

[32] Burrows *Restitution* (n 3) 57–58; Virgo *Principles* (n 3) 28–29.

[33] See below, section D.2 and D.3.b of the present chapter (pp 130–34, 138–42).

[34] Bant [2007] RLR (n 31) 16; Nahan (1997) 26 UWALR (n 31) 72–73; *Edelman & Bant* (n 16) 102. Cf already W Blackstone, *Commentaries on the Laws of England: vol 2* (Clarendon Press, Oxford 1766) 443 (ch 30.IX), who observes that "a contract *executed* ... conveys a *chose in possession*; a contract *executory* conveys only a *chose in action*" (emphasis in the original). In *Adam v Newbigging* (1886) 34 ChD 582 (CA), Bowen LJ stated (at 595): "There ought ... to be a giving back and a taking back on both sides, *including the giving back and the taking back of the obligations which the contract has created,* as well as the giving back and the taking back of the advantages" (emphasis added), but note that this was an executed contract case with obligations to third parties.

[35] On the meaning of 'unjust' in this context see discussion in text to nn 36–43.

[36] The word 'restitution for wrongs' is here used in the traditional sense of a claimant choosing to assert a gain-based (as opposed to a loss-based) remedy for a tort or recognized equitable wrong. Compare, however, the comments in nn 42 and 43 below.

[37] See below, section E of the present chapter (pp 159–62).

per se,[38] and while undue influence is often described as a form of 'equitable wrongdoing',[39] Mummery LJ in *Pesticcio v Huet* recently emphasized that the basis for the court's intervention was not any wrongful act on the part of the transferee, but the transferor's impaired autonomy.[40] The orthodox approach therefore maintains that the right to rescind is simply generated by the defect tainting the transferor's contractual consent.[41] Yet there is another possibility. If those authors who propose an infringement analysis of non-participatory enrichments are right,[42] their reasoning could be

---

38 A misrepresentation is actionable as a wrong only if it amounts to the tort of deceit, the tort of negligence, or to a negligent misrepresentation under the Misrepresentation Act 1967, s 2(1): see below, section E.1 and E.2 of the present chapter (pp 160–61). In *Derry v Peek* (1889) 14 App Cas 337 (HL) 362, Lord Herschell emphasized that there was no 'right' to have only correct information imparted, and hence no breach of duty where an innocent misrepresentation is made. Cf also *Hulton v Hulton* [1917] 1 KB 813 (CA), where it was held that a wife's claim to rescission of a deed for her husband's fraudulent misrepresentation was not an "action for a tort" under the Married Women's Property Act 1882, s 12.

39 Eg *Barclays Bank plc v O'Brien* [1994] 1 AC 180 (HL) 189–91 (Lord Browne-Wilkinson); *CIBC Mortgages plc v Pitt* [1994] 1 AC 200 (HL) 209–10 (Lord Browne-Wilkinson); *Mahoney v Purnell* [1996] 3 All ER 61 (QBD) esp 82 (May J); *Royal Bank of Scotland plc v Etridge (No 2)* [2001] UKHL 44, [2002] 2 AC 773, [103]–[108] (Lord Hobhouse); *National Commercial Bank (Jamaica) Ltd v Hew's Executors* [2003] UKPC 51, [28]–[33] (Lord Millett); *Yorkshire Bank plc v Tinsley* [2004] EWCA Civ 816, [2004] 1 WLR 2380, [32], [35] (Peter Gibson LJ).

40 [2004] EWCA Civ 372 (CA) [20], approved in *Macklin v Dowsett* [2004] EWCA Civ 904, [10] (Auld LJ). See also *Allcard v Skinner* (1887) 36 ChD 145 (CA) 171 (Cotton LJ); *Hammond v Osborn* [2002] EWCA Civ 885, [1] (Sir Martin Nourse), [46] (Ward LJ); *Jennings v Cairns* [2003] EWCA Civ 1935, [40] (Arden LJ). This is not to say that undue influence cannot overlap with certain forms of equitable wrongdoing: see below, section E.3 of the present chapter (p 162).

41 Cf P Birks and NY Chin, "On the Nature of Undue Influence" in J Beatson and D Friedmann (eds), *Good Faith and Fault in Contract Law* (Clarendon Press, Oxford 1995) 57; P Birks, "Undue Influence as Wrongful Exploitation" (2004) 120 LQR 34. Critical of the claimant-sided analysis: R Bigwood, "Undue Influence: 'Impaired Consent' or 'Wicked Exploitation'?" (1996) 16 OJLS 503; D Capper, "Undue Influence and Unconscionability: A Rationalisation" (1998) 114 LQR 479, 492–99.

42 See above, Chapter II.C.1.b. (text to n 55 on pp 29–30). Many of these authors regard 'restitution for wrongs' as part of the law of unjust enrichment proper: J Beatson, "The Nature of Waiver of Tort" in J Beatson, *The Use and Abuse of Unjust Enrichment: Essays on the Law of Restitution* (Clarendon Press, Oxford 1991) 206; D Friedmann, "Restitution for Wrongs: The Basis of Liability" in WR Cornish and others (eds), *Restitution Past, Present and Future: Essays in Honour of Gareth Jones* (Hart, Oxford 1998) 133; T Krebs, "Eingriffskondiktion und Restitution for Wrongs im englischen Recht" in R Zimmermann (ed), *Grundstrukturen eines europäischen Bereicherungsrechts* (Mohr Siebeck, Tübingen 2005) 141; T Krebs, "The Fallacy of 'Restitution for Wrongs'" in A Burrows and A Rodger (eds), *Mapping the Law: Essays in Memory of Peter Birks* (OUP, Oxford 2006) 379.

extended to explain rescission of contract. Although the transferee's enrichment itself is participatory in such a case (namely the acquisition of rights by virtue of the contractual agreement), and although the transferor's lack of autonomy does indeed impact on the quality of his consent to the agreement, what ultimately accounts for this lack of autonomy is the transferee's misrepresentation, duress or undue influence. The mere fact that the mistake was induced by the transferee, or that the duress or undue influence emanated from him, however innocently, could be seen as an interference with the transferor's autonomy in decision-making. It is not necessary to regard the interference as a breach of duty amounting to an actionable 'wrong' (in the sense of a recognized tort or equitable equivalent). This construct may seem unduly complicated at first sight,[43] but it has the merit of explaining conceptually why spontaneous mistakes are insufficient to generate a right of rescission.

c) The Requirement of *restitutio in integrum*

Conceiving of the right to rescind a contract as generated by unjust enrichment goes some way towards elucidating the much-discussed requirement of *restitutio in integrum*. This requirement becomes relevant where the contract in question has been wholly or partly executed on both sides before one party seeks to rescind. Traditionally, it was thought to be a precondition for rescission that both parties can be restored to their precise pre-contractual positions (*status quo ante*).[44] As a result, a situation could arise in which a transferor was denied the right to avoid the contract under which the transfer took place, although he had at all times been suffering from a relevant defect of consent. Recall and vary our barter case from the previous chapter:[45] A agrees to exchange his Constable painting for a painting belonging to B, which B tells him is by Corot. After the paintings have been exchanged, the 'Corot' is damaged or destroyed. A later discovers that the painting he acquired was a forgery and not by Corot at all. He pur-

[43] The greatest difficulty lies in explaining how there can ever be a non-wrongful interference with a right, given that 'wrongs' are defined in terms of 'breaches of duty', and 'duties' correlate with 'rights'. A person's autonomy, of course, is not a 'right' as such (but more akin to an 'interest'), yet this alone is not a satisfactory answer. It may therefore be that the solution will ultimately have to be found by severing the link between 'wrongdoing' and a defendant's liability to pay compensation, which is the approach suggested or implied by the authors mentioned in n 42. We could then give up the traditional 'parasitic' theory of restitution for wrongs: cf n 36 above.

[44] Cf eg *Clarke v Dickson* (1858) El Bl & El 148, 120 ER 463; *Western Bank of Scotland v Addie* (1867) LR 1 HL Sc 145 (HL) 164–65 (Lord Cranworth); recently again *Halpern v Halpern (No 2)* [2006] EWHC 1728 (QBD Comm), [2007] QB 88, but rev'd [2007] EWCA Civ 291, [2008] QB 195, [56]–[77].

[45] See above, Chapter III.C.3 (at pp 71–72).

ports to rescind the contract on the basis of B's misrepresentation and asks for the return of his performance.[46] The traditional requirement of exact *restitutio in integrum* prevents A recovering the Constable because he cannot restore the would-be-Corot to B in substantially the same condition in which he received it.

What drives the *restitutio in integrum* requirement? Given that there may be a considerable difference in value between the parties' mutual performances, it is perhaps surprising that the party otherwise entitled to rescind should be held to the bargain merely because precise restitution *in specie* has become impossible. A closer examination of the *restitutio in integrum* bar shows that it is less rigid than first meets the eye. For money paid under a contract, it has never been a requirement that the exact notes and coins be restored.[47] Nor was the defendant necessarily able to resist rescission solely because he would thereby suffer a loss exceeding that which could be made good by the reversal of his performance.[48] In equity, courts have, moreover, long been willing to make monetary allowances for benefits in kind which the rescinding party cannot physically return, so long as 'practical' or 'substantial' justice is done.[49] There are indications that the common law may now be willing to follow equity's flexible lead.[50] In the light of these concessions, the real concern underlying the require-

---

[46] It used to be thought that contracts could not be rescinded for non-fraudulent misrepresentation after they had been fully executed: *Seddon v North Eastern Salt Co Ltd* [1905] 1 Ch 326 (ChD), but this rule – which was often simply ignored – was finally abolished by the Misrepresentation Act 1967, s 1.

[47] Cf *Westdeutsche Landesbank Girozentrale v Islington London BC* [1996] AC 669 (HL) 681–82 (Lord Goff), considering the case of a void contract.

[48] *Armstrong v Jackson* [1917] 2 KB 822 (KBD) esp 829 (McCardie J): "Deterioration of the subject-matter does not ... destroy the right to rescind nor prevent a restitutio in integrum" (the 'deterioration' in this case was due to an external cause, and not a result of the rescinding party's conduct); *Adam v Newbigging* (1886) 34 ChD 582 (CA), aff'd (1888) 13 App Cas 308 (HL); *Mackenzie v Royal Bank of Canada* [1934] AC 468 (PC) esp 476 (Lord Atkin): "There is no difficulty as to restitutio in integrum. The mere fact that the party making the representation has treated the contract as binding and has acted on it does not preclude relief. Nor can it be said that the plaintiff received anything under the contract which she is unable to restore". To the extent that the latter case involved a consequential reliance loss sustained by an innocent misrepresentor, it may – but need not – have been wrongly decided: see discussion in n 59 below.

[49] *Erlanger v New Sombrero Phosphate Co* (1878) 3 App Cas 1218 (HL) 1278–79 (Lord Blackburn); *Lagunas Nitrate Co v Lagunas Syndicate* [1899] 2 Ch 392 (CA) 456–57 (Rigby LJ); *Alati v Kruger* (1955) 94 CLR 216 (HCA) 223–24 (Dixon CJ); *O'Sullivan v Management Agency and Music Ltd* [1985] QB 428 (CA).

[50] *Smith New Court Securities Ltd v Scrimgeour Vickers (Asset Management) Ltd* [1997] AC 254 (HL) 262 (Lord Browne-Wilkinson); *Halpern v Halpern (No 2)* [2007] EWCA Civ 291, [2008] QB 195, [56]–[77], esp [70]–[76] (Carnwath LJ).

ment of *restitutio in integrum* can perhaps be gleaned from a statement made by Lord Wright in *Spence v Crawford*:

"To take the simplest case, if a plaintiff who has been defrauded seeks to have the contract annulled and his money or property restored to him, it would be inequitable if he did not also restore what he had got under the contract from the defendant. Though the defendant has been fraudulent, he must not be robbed, nor must the plaintiff be unjustly enriched, as he would be if he both got back what he had parted with and kept what he had received in return".[51]

Making *restitutio in integrum* a precondition for rescission thus appears to have been a crude way of ensuring the mutuality of restitution in the days before the emergence of a distinct doctrine of unjust enrichment. It provides a rough-and-ready solution to the problems which German courts have attempted to address by means of the *Saldotheorie*.[52] And if, as was suggested above, the right to rescind a contract is itself generated by the defendant's enrichment at the claimant's expense, then the *restitutio in integrum* requirement may be no more than an embryonic disenrichment defence against the exercise of the claimant's power to avoid the contract (and to annul any proprietary effects which the contract may have had).[53]

With the gradual emancipation of unjust enrichment law from its historical entanglement in different forms of action, the *restitutio in integrum* bar has become ripe for re-assessment. Insisting on precise restitution *in specie* looks distinctly odd in a system which is on the whole content to

[51] [1939] 3 All ER 271 (HL) 288–89. Note that *Spence v Crawford* was a Scottish case, but the relevant principles were thought to be the same as under English law. Cf also *Adam v Newbigging* (1886) 34 ChD 582 (CA) 595 (Bowen LJ): "There ought ... to be a giving back and a taking back on both sides" (already cited in n 34 above).

[52] See above, Chapter III.C.3.b (esp pp 73–74), and cf Birks *Unjust Enrichment* (n 4) 226.

[53] Similar: E Bant, "*Restitutio in Integrum* and the Change of Position Defence: Lessons from Rescission" [2007] RLR 13, who helpfully distinguishes between 'change in exchange' (the defendant's rendering of the agreed counter-performance) and 'defendant-instigated changes of position' (his further consequential reliance). The *restitutio in integrum* bar does not normally cater for the latter. Whether it should is a matter of debate: cf n 59 and corresponding text. D Friedmann, "Reversible Transfers – The Two Categories" [2003] RLR 1, 5, observes "that the doctrine [of change of position] cannot be applied in the contractual context without being substantially qualified." It may be that the requirement of *restitutio in integrum* is precisely such a qualification. More sceptical about the similarity between the two defences: P Hellwege, "Unwinding Mutual Contracts: *Restitutio in Integrum* v. the Defence of Change of Position" in D Johnston and R Zimmermann (eds), *Unjustified Enrichment: Key Issues in Comparative Perspective* (CUP, Cambridge 2002) 243, esp 282–84; D O'Sullivan, S Elliott and R Zakrzewski, *The Law of Rescission* (OUP, Oxford 2008) [18.07].

have recourse to monetary remedies wherever possible.[54] The modern approach is therefore to dissolve the *restitutio in integrum* requirement into an obligation imposed on the rescinding party to make counter-restitution to the other.[55] Where it is impossible to return a benefit in kind, the benefit can usually be valued and restored at least in economic terms. 'Pecuniary rescission' is the useful metaphor which has been coined to illustrate the process.[56] On this interpretation of *restitutio in integrum*, our example no longer causes any difficulties. A can be allowed to rescind his contract with B and recover the Constable, provided only that he restores the economic value of the would-be-Corot to B.[57] There is another advantage to this approach. Once the *restitutio in integrum* requirement is viewed as part of the general law of unjust enrichment, it becomes possible to fine-tune the parties' mutual claims. We acquire a yardstick by which we can assess the existing case law and justify departures from individual decisions where appropriate. It may be that where B's misrepresentation was fraudulent, A should be relieved of the liability to make counter-restitution to the extent that he is no longer enriched, but not where B was merely negligent or completely innocent.[58] And perhaps a transferee-defendant who acted in good faith ought to be able to recover for changes of position which cannot be made up by the mere return of his performance.[59]

---

[54] This is true of most unjust enrichment 'remedies' at common law (see above, Chapter II.C.2.a, n 66 and corresponding text on p 32) and also of all wrongs-based claims to compensation for loss sustained (contrast §§ 249 ff BGB).

[55] Eg Birks *Introduction* (n 3) 415–24; Burrows *Restitution* (n 3) 176–79, 541–42; M Chen-Wishart, "Unjust Factors and the Restitutionary Response" (2000) 20 OJLS 557, 566–68; *Goff & Jones* (n 31) [9–025]; Virgo *Principles* (n 3) 31–33.

[56] P Birks, "Unjust Factors and Wrongs: Pecuniary Rescission for Undue Influence" [1997] RLR 72; Nahan (1997) 27 UWALR (n 31) esp 66–67, 82–85; S Worthington, "The Proprietary Consequences of Rescission" [2002] RLR 28, 65–67.

[57] From the perspective which regards A's power to rescind as generated by B's unjust enrichment at his expense (cf section B.2.b of the present chapter), the exercise of the power is simply conditional on making good B's otherwise permanent disenrichment.

[58] Traditionally, the *restitutio in integrum* bar has been applied strictly, even against victims of fraud: cf *Clarke v Dickson* (1858) El Bl & El 148, 120 ER 463, where Crompton J explained in argument (El Bl & El 152, 120 ER 465): "If you are fraudulently induced to buy a cake you may return it and get back the price; but you cannot both eat your cake and return your cake". However, his Lordship confined the proposition to cases where the rescinding party has, "*by his own act*", put it out of his power to make counter-restitution (El Bl & El 155, 120 ER 466, emphasis added). This leaves open the possibility of relieving the defrauded party of at least the risk of accidental disenrichments. It is interesting to note that the German *Saldotheorie* (cf text to n 52) was initially also applied against victims of fraud (RGZ 54, 137), but that fraud is nowadays considered to warrant an exception from it: BGHZ 53, 144; BGHZ 57, 137.

[59] The reliance losses incurred by the innocent misrepresentor in *Mackenzie v Royal Bank of Canada* (n 48) should thus arguably have been taken into account: cf G Jones,

The upshot is that impossibility of exact *restitutio in integrum* need not and should not constitute a bar to rescission of contract, even if the right to rescind is itself enrichment-based. All issues at stake can be understood as ordinary aspects of mutual restitution for unjust enrichment. It will usually be sufficient if the exercise of the right to rescind is treated as conditional on the rescinding party's willingness and ability to make counter-restitution to the other (whether *in specie* or in value terms) and perhaps on his reimbursing the other party for any further reliance losses (if and where appropriate).

3. Unjust Enrichment and Restitution for Mistaken Gifts

In the light of the above observations on restitution after impaired consent transfers in the contractual context, it might be thought that gifts could pose no great challenge to the unjust factor regime. Gifts are, after all, non-contractual transactions under English law.[60] They are gratuitous transfers of property rights (usually title) by one party to another and as such unsupported by consideration. Any unjust factor should, without more, be able to operate in a gift scenario.[61] However, the position is not as clear-cut. Although recovery will typically be allowed where the impairment of the donor's consent can be characterized as induced mistake, duress or undue influence,[62] spontaneous mistakes still cause great difficulty in both

"Some Thoughts on Change of Position" in A Burrows and A Rodger (eds), *Mapping the Law: Essays in Memory of Peter Birks* (OUP, Oxford 2006) 65, 74–75, 81; *Goff & Jones* (n 31) [40–007], [40–015]; and see also Bant [2007] RLR (n 53) 26–30. All three contributions advert to the tension between, on the one hand, the innocent misrepresentor's good faith, and on the other his role in inducing the contract. It is interesting to note that, in German law, a claim for reliance losses under § 122 BGB has been held to be excluded where the rescinding party's mistake was innocently induced by the other: RGZ 81, 395, 398–99 (*exceptio doli*). If this is anything to go by, it supports – rather than undermines – the *Mackenzie* case.

[60] See above, Chapter II.B.1.a (pp 19–20).

[61] Cf *David Securities v Commonwealth Bank of Australia* (n 13) 392–93, where Brennan J observed, albeit *obiter*: "Apart from cases where a payment is made by mistake to satisfy a defendant's supposed right to receive it, a plaintiff may mistakenly make a payment by way of gift, not intending to acquire a benefit or discharge a liability. If the payer would not have paid the money had the payer known all the relevant circumstances, both legal and factual, the defendant is unjustly enriched by the receipt. In principle, there seems to be no reason ... why the donor should not be entitled to restitution in such a case". Critical: P Watts, "Mistaken Payments and the Law of Restitution" [1993] LMCLQ 145, esp 147–48.

[62] Misrepresentation (ie induced mistake): eg *Re Glubb* [1900] 1 Ch 354 (CA). Undue influence: eg *Allcard v Skinner* (1887) 36 ChD 145 (CA); *Hammond v Osborn* [2002] EWCA Civ 885; *Pesticcio v Huet* [2004] EWCA Civ 372. There seem to be no relevant cases of 'gifts' induced by duress.

theory and practice.[63] Imagine that A makes a birthday present of an early Andy Warhol painting together with a substantial sum of money to his nephew B (who is a fan of pop-art), believing him to be an impoverished bachelor, when in fact B has just married a rich lady whom A despises.[64] A would not have made the gifts had he been aware of this. Can he, when the truth later emerges, ask B to return the painting (or its value) and to repay the money on the basis that B has been unjustly enriched at his, A's, expense?

The case law on mistaken gifts is sparse and very often intertwined with the (supposedly) special rules applying to deeds.[65] A number of decisions, however, suggest that not every mistake warrants restitution. In *Ogilvie v Littleboy*,[66] Lindley LJ stated:

> "Gifts cannot be revoked, nor can deeds of gift be set aside, simply because the donors wish they had not made them and would like to have back the property given. Where there is no fraud, no undue influence, no fiduciary relation between donor and donee, no mistake induced by those who derive any benefit by it, a gift, whether by mere delivery or by deed, is binding on the donor. [...] In the absence of all such circumstances of suspicion a donor can only obtain back property which he has given away by showing that he was under some mistake of so serious a character as to render it unjust on the part of the donee to retain the property given to him".[67]

To say that, in order to found a claim in unjust enrichment, the claimant's mistake has to render the defendant's enrichment 'unjust' is – with all due respect – circular, at least from a modern perspective. Yet Lindley LJ's statement nevertheless reflects the two main grounds on which judges have sought to restrict recovery. On the one hand, a parallel is often drawn between gifts and contracts. Just as the latter are voidable only for induced mistakes, so gifts cannot on this approach be avoided (or 'rescinded') unless the donee is in some way responsible for the donor's misappre-

---

63 See only the heated debate in the academic literature (in chronological order): Meier *Irrtum und Zweckverfehlung* (n 8) 49–50, 86–91, 103–8; T Krebs, *Restitution at the Crossroads: A Comparative Study* (Cavendish, London 2001) 43, 70, 76–81; S Meier, "Unjust Factors and Legal Grounds" in D Johnston and R Zimmermann (eds), *Unjustified Enrichment: Key Issues in Comparative Perspective* (CUP, Cambridge 2002) 37, esp 40–54; HW Tang "Restitution for Mistaken Gifts" (2004) 20 JCL 1; J Hilliard, "Gibbon v Mitchell Reconsidered: Mistakes as to Effects and Mistakes as to Consequences" [2004] PCB 357 (part 1), [2005] PCB 31 (part 2); O'Sullivan et al *Law of Rescission* (n 53) [29.15]–[29.49].

64 Variation of an example given by A Tettenborn, *The Law of Restitution in England and Ireland* (3rd edn Cavendish, London 2002) 76.

65 On the rules governing rescission of deeds see n 80 below.

66 (1897) 13 TLR 399 (CA).

67 Ibid 400.

hension.[68] Thus, Lord Scott recently remarked *obiter* in *Deutsche Morgan Grenfell Group plc v Inland Revenue Commissioners*:

> "There are, I think, some problems about voluntary payments made as gifts but that would not have been made but for some causative mistake, whether of fact or law, eg a gift of £ 1000 by A to B where B is believed by A to be impecunious but is in fact a person of substantial wealth and where A would not have made the gift if he had known that to be so. My present opinion is that unless there were some other reason, such as a misrepresentation by B, to enable the gift to be set aside, the mistake made by A would not suffice, notwithstanding that the payment had not been made pursuant to any legal obligation and that but for the mistake it would not have been made".[69]

On the other hand, mistakes are sometimes distinguished according to their seriousness and nature. In *Morgan v Ashcroft*,[70] for example, where the erroneous double settlement of a bookmaker's debt was at issue, Sir Wilfrid Greene MR observed that only a "mistake of fact which can be described as fundamental or basic" would entitle a person who knowingly made a voluntary payment to recover it. He implied that 'non-fundamental' mistakes were to be treated as irrelevant 'motives'.[71]

What are we to make of these restrictions? On closer analysis, it is possible to call their validity into question. The analogy between gifts and contracts may well be helpful in describing the mechanism by which the transferor can recover a proprietary interest in the object transferred ('rescission' of a gratuitous conveyance).[72] It does not, however, necessitate the conclusion that recovery must be as closely circumscribed in the gift scenario as in a contract case. Donees have, after all, much less of a legitimate interest in the security of their receipt than purchasers for

---

[68] Implicit in *Re Glubb* (n 62) esp 361–62 (Lord Lindley MR). Similarly, in *Wilson v Thornbury* (1875) LR 10 Ch App 239 (CA in Ch) 248–49, James LJ held that in the absence of a "misrepresentation amounting to deception", a mistaken gift could not be recovered.

[69] [2006] UKHL 49, [2007] 1 AC 558, [87]. He expressly left the issue to be decided on another occasion.

[70] [1938] 1 KB 49 (CA).

[71] Ibid 66: "It appears to me that a person who intends to make a voluntary payment and thinks that he is making one kind of voluntary payment whereas upon the true facts he is making another kind of voluntary payment, does not make the payment under a mistake of fact which can be described as fundamental or basic. The essential quality of the payment, namely its voluntary character, is the same in each case. If a father, believing that his son has suffered a financial loss, gives him a sum of money, he surely could not claim repayment if he afterwards discovered that no such loss had occurred; and (to take the analogous case of contract) if instead of giving him money, he entered into a contract with his son, he surely could not claim that the contract was void. To hold the contrary would almost amount to saying that motive and not mistake was the decisive matter".

[72] See below, section D.3.c.ii of the present chapter (pp 146–51).

value.[73] When assessing Sir Wilfrid Greene MR's statement in *Morgan v Ashcroft*, it is crucial to note that his Lordship was thinking of situations in which the transferor's mistake prevents title passing to the transferee.[74] Yet a claim in unjust enrichment does not depend on a retention of title. On the contrary: it is first and foremost concerned with cases in which a conveyance is *prima facie* valid.[75] As Robert Goff J said in *Barclays Bank Ltd v WJ Simms Son & Cooke (Southern) Ltd*, "the kind of mistake that will ground recovery [in unjust enrichment] is ... far wider than the kind of mistake which will vitiate an intention to transfer property".[76] Moreover, we must not forget that Sir Wilfrid Greene MR was speaking at a time when the 'supposed liability' test and the 'mistake of law bar' were still in place.[77] And while the existence of a liability mistake can, *ex hypothesi*, never have been a precondition for the recovery of a mistaken gift, the restrictive approach pervading the old case law generally may explain a certain reluctance to order restitution where a gift was induced by a spontaneous 'motivational' mistake on the donor's part.[78]

This reluctance was, it should further be noted, by no means universally shared. A second, separate line of cases has been much more liberal in allowing recovery. In *Lady Hood of Avalon v Mackinnon*,[79] Eve J approved the rescission of a voluntary deed poll (executed by way of appointment under a marriage settlement) on the basis that when the settlor executed it, she had forgotten that she had already provided for the beneficiary.[80] In

[73] Cf also Chapter VI.D.2 (p 257).

[74] Following on from the passage set out in n 71, where the analogy with 'void' contracts is already drawn, his Lordship stated (at [1938] 1 KB 49, 66–67): "For example, if A makes a voluntary payment of money to B under the mistaken belief that he is C, it may well be that he can recover it. [...] If we are to be guided by the analogous case of contract, the mistake which I have mentioned [*error in persona*] ought to be held to negative the intention to pay the money and the money should be recoverable." On identity mistakes preventing a passing of title see text to nn 97–104 below.

[75] There are, indeed, authors who deny that unjust enrichment has *any* role to play where title does not pass to the defendant: see below, section C.1 of the present chapter (pp 121–22).

[76] [1980] QB 677 (QBD Comm) 689.

[77] Cf above, nn 8–9 and corresponding text.

[78] In *Morgan v Ashcroft* (n 70), for example, Sir Wilfrid Greene MR expressly drew on the principles laid down by Bramwell B in *Aiken v Short* (n 8).

[79] [1909] 1 Ch 476 (ChD).

[80] More recently, a voluntary deed was set aside for spontaneous mistake in *Gibbon v Mitchell* [1990] 1 WLR 1304 (ChD), but the test applied by the trial judge, Millett J, was a relatively narrow one. His Lordship stated (at 1309): "[W]herever there is a voluntary transaction by which one party intends to confer a bounty on another, the deed will be set aside if the court is satisfied that the disponor did not intend the transaction to have the effect which it did. It will be set aside for mistake whether the mistake is a mistake of law or of fact, so long as the mistake is as to the effect of the transaction itself and not

Ellis v Ellis,[81] a husband successfully reclaimed a gift of stock and shares he had made to his wife not realizing that it would be caught by an after-acquired property clause in their marriage settlement. Warrington J emphasized that the requirements for setting aside a gift were not as stringent as those for setting aside a transaction for value.[82] The New Zealand case of *University of Canterbury v Attorney-General*[83] is in a similar vein. The claimant had given shares to a charitable trust, acting under the impression that the trust needed money to implement its scholarship programme. In fact, the trust did not suffer from a lack of funds. Williamson J ordered the return of the shares. Although he described the mistake as "fundamental or basic" in order to satisfy Sir Wilfrid Greene MR's test, he was in essence allowing recovery for what the latter would have described as a pure motivational mistake.[84] A spontaneous mistake was recently again at issue in *Ogden v Trustees of the RHS Griffiths 2003 Settlement*.[85] The deceased grantor had assigned a reversionary interest in some shares to trustees. At the time, he thought that he was – by and large – of good health and therefore had a reasonable chance of surviving for seven years, after which the transfer would be exempt from inheritance tax upon his death.[86] In fact, however, he was already terminally ill with lung cancer and died just over a year later. Lewison J agreed with the executors that the deceased had

merely as to its consequences or the advantages to be gained by entering into it". This would seem to exclude not only mispredictions, but also motivational mistakes. However, Millett J's effects/consequences distinction is unsatisfactory in three respects. First, it has proved extremely difficult to apply in practice. Second, it fails to take account of *Lady Hood of Avalon v Mackinnon* (n 79), although the case was cited in argument. Thirdly and most importantly, it seems to transpose a criterion which is germane to the context of rectification (ie correction of deeds) into the very different context of rescission: see B Häcker, "Mistakes in the Execution of Documents: Recent Cases on Rectification and Related Doctrines" (2008) 19 KLJ 293, 322–25. For further criticisms see Hilliard [2004]/[2005] PCB (n 63). *Gibbon v Mitchell* was not followed in the recent case of *Ogden v Trustees of the RHS Griffiths 2003 Settlement* [2008] EWHC 118 (ChD), [2008] 2 All ER 655: cf n 87 below.

[81] (1909) 26 TLR 166 (ChD).

[82] Ibid 167. His Lordship expressly followed the decision in *Lady Hood of Avalon v Mackinnon* (n 79).

[83] [1995] 1 NZLR 78 (NZHC).

[84] Williamson J said (ibid 86): "Words such as fundamental, basic, material, causative are descriptive of a mistake which is of such a nature and importance in the context of the transaction that it is just to order a recipient to return the property". Critical: P Watts, "A Philanthropist Recovers His Gift" (1996) 2 NZBLQ 5, 6, who suggests that the outcome of the case can only "be supported on the basis that the donee ought to have perceived the donor's error".

[85] [2008] EWHC 118 (ChD), [2008] 2 All ER 655.

[86] The transaction qualified as a 'potentially exempt transfer' under the Inheritance Tax Act 1984, s 3A.

made a mistake about the state of his health which was sufficient to warrant equity's intervention. The transfer was set aside.[87]

It is submitted that the supposed restrictions on restitution for mistaken gifts – if ever they existed – have at any rate not survived the advent of the causative mistake test in *Barclays Bank v Simms*.[88] No sensible line can be drawn between 'mistake' and 'motive' within the English law of unjust enrichment.[89] Instead, the crucial distinction is between mistakes and mere mispredictions in the sense of disappointed expectations.[90] Provided that the donor was acting on false data when effecting the gift, he ought *prima facie* to be able to recover it. The only question we might ask is whether the relevant piece of data has to be actively on the donor's mind,[91] or whether it is sufficient to show that he would not have made the gift had he known about a particular state of affairs.[92] If the latter, then the uncle in our example should be able to recover both the painting and the money. If the former, his claim should arguably fail as far as the painting is concerned (assuming that he never gave any thought to the nephew's marital status or financial position when deciding that the Warhol would be a

[87] [2008] EWHC 118, [2008] 2 All ER 655, [30]–[31]. With regard to two earlier transfers which the executors also sought to impeach, Lewison J held that these were not made under an operative mistake since the deceased was not suffering from the cancer at the time: ibid [28]–[29]. About the effects/consequences distinction drawn in *Gibbon v Mitchell* (n 80) he said ([2008] EWHC 118, [2008] 2 All ER 655, [25]): "If and to the extent that Millett J intended to restrict the scope of the equitable jurisdiction to a mistake about the effects of a transaction, I respectfully disagree".

[88] See above, n 10 and corresponding text. Cf also *David Securities v Commonwealth Bank of Australia* (n 13) 392–93 (Brennan J); Birks *Unjust Enrichment* (n 4) 149–50; Burrows *Restitution* (n 3) 134–36, 142–45.

[89] This is how the different 'categories' of case are conventionally described: see, for example, the last sentence of Sir Wilfrid Greene MR's statement set out in n 71. More accurately, the reference should be to mistakes which relate to the reasons for effecting a transfer (motivational mistakes) and those which do not (eg mistakes about the nature of the transaction itself). *Goff & Jones* (n 31) [4–021], admit that "[t]he line between mistake and motive is a thin one" and then proceed to apply what looks like a pure causative mistake test. Note that, in other areas of English law (especially in contract and property law), the distinction between motivational and other mistakes has a certain relevance: cf eg D Friedmann, "The Objective Principle and Mistake and Involuntariness in Contract and Restitution" (2003) 119 LQR 68; Häcker (2008) 19 KLJ (n 80) esp 294–303.

[90] It is true that the facts of *Ogden v Trustees of the RHS Griffiths 2003 Settlement* (text to nn 85–86) vividly illustrate how thin the line between operative mistakes and irrelevant mispredictions can be. This is because most predictions rest on an assessment of certain current (factual) data. Lewison J nevertheless thought that the distinction was good in principle: cf [2008] EWHC 118, [2008] 2 All ER 655, [23].

[91] This is the approach preferred by Birks *Unjust Enrichment* (n 4) 149–50.

[92] This is the approach preferred by Krebs *Restitution at the Crossroads* (n 63) 79.

suitable present for a pop-art fanatic).[93] It is hard to see how either of these solutions is too harsh on the gratuitous recipient.[94] Outside the bargaining context, there is no danger of disturbing any deliberate risk allocation between the parties. The donee's interest in the security of his receipt is sufficiently protected by ensuring that he is not left out-of-pocket. This task can nowadays safely be left to the well-established change of position defence.[95]

C. Relationship between Personal Claims to Restitution for Unjust Enrichment and (Vested) Property Rights

Before we can turn to the debate about the availability and form of proprietary restitution, a few preliminary observations about the relationship between personal claims to restitution for unjust enrichment (rights *in personam*) and the existence of property rights (rights *in rem*) are warranted. In our example, how does the existence of a proprietary interest of A's, whether pre-existing or newly created, affect the personal rights and liabilities between A and B?

It will be convenient to consider this question primarily by reference to situations in which A's title to the painting survives the purported 'transfer' to B. If the impairment of A's consent is sufficiently serious to prevent title passing, only possession is transferred to B when the painting is handed over.[96] This typically happens where A is under a so-called 'fundamental' mistake about B's identity (*error in persona*).[97] An operative

---

93 On the relationship between 'mistake', 'ignorance', 'lack of belief', and the failure to think about an issue see eg Seah [2007] RLR (n 7) 96–99, esp 99; Sheehan (2000) 20 LS (n 7) 541–45. Watts [1993] LMCLQ (n 61) 147, sees the problem as lying not so much in the definition of 'mistake', but as one of causation: "It is true that, where the donor did not advert to the relevant fact, it cannot actually be said that his or her inadvertence *caused* the payment" (emphasis in the original).

94 Tang (2004) 20 JCL (n 63) reaches the opposite conclusion by invoking the anthropological and sociological context of gift-giving.

95 One of the concerns voiced by Tang (2004) 20 JCL (n 63) esp 24–25, relates to non-disenriching acts of reliance, yet most of these could be catered for by a generous application of the defence: cf n 16 above.

96 The acquisition of possession – of course – generates a new (weaker) title to the painting in B, but this title is original; it is not derived from A.

97 Eg *Cundy v Lindsay* (1878) 3 App Cas 459 (HL); *Ingram v Little* [1961] 1 QB 31 (CA): see below, text to nn 101–104. Similarly where the transferor's mistake is as to the identity of the object conveyed (*error in obiecto*): *R v Ashwell* (1885) 16 QBD 190 (CCR) esp 201 (Cave J). There may be severe forms of duress which have the same effect: cf *Duke de Cadaval v Collins* (1836) 4 Ad & El 858, 111 ER 1006; *Grainger v Hill* (1838) 4 Bing NC 212, 132 ER 769.

identity mistake, as opposed to a mere mistake about a person's attributes,[98] not only hinders the formation of a valid contract and thus precludes any conveyancing effect that the contract may have (in sale cases); it also prevents title passing by a subsequent delivery.[99] And though fundamental mistakes of this kind will be extremely rare, especially in face-to-face dealings,[100] they nevertheless occur. *Cundy v Lindsay*[101] and *Ingram v Little*[102] are the most prominent examples.[103] In both cases, the 'seller' of goods was held not to have lost title to them despite their delivery to a fraudulent 'purchaser' who had misrepresented his identity.[104] The question arises whether, instead of asserting his subsisting title via the tort of conversion,[105] the 'seller' could have chosen to bring a personal claim in unjust enrichment against the 'purchaser'.[106]

Whether or not such 'alternative analysis' is possible is usually only discussed in connection with the existence of an unjust factor called 'ig-

---

[98] *King's Norton Metal Co Ltd v Edridge, Merrett, & Co Ltd* (1897) 14 TLR 98 (CA); *Phillips v Brooks Ltd* [1919] 2 KB 243 (KBD); *Lewis v Averay* [1972] 1 QB 198 (CA).

[99] W Swadling, "Unjust Delivery" in A Burrows and A Rodger (eds), *Mapping the Law: Essays in Memory of Peter Birks* (OUP, Oxford 2006) 277, describes this situation – perhaps misleadingly – as one of 'unjust delivery'. The choice of terminology is slightly misleading because the allusion to the law of unjust enrichment suggests that we are dealing with conveyances which, though reversible, are *prima facie* valid. Yet voidable conveyances are precisely not Swadling's concern.

[100] Cf *Shogun Finance Ltd v Hudson* [2003] UKHL 62, [2004] 1 AC 919, esp [170] (Lord Phillips), [185]–[187] (Lord Walker). Lord Nicholls and Lord Millett (dissenting) wanted to go even further and do away with the special treatment of identity mistakes: ibid [18]–[35], [71]–[109]. See further below, Chapter V.B.1.b.i (at pp 175–77).

[101] (1878) 3 App Cas 459 (HL).

[102] [1961] 1 QB 31 (CA). As a face-to-face case, *Ingram v Little* may no longer be good law after *Shogun Finance v Hudson* (n 100). Lord Walker there thought that the case had been wrongly decided: [2003] UKHL 62, [2004] 1 AC 919, [185]. It is likely that courts will in the future require the parties to have been dealing at a distance (by correspondence) before finding an operative identity mistake.

[103] For a critical historical account cf C Macmillan, "Rogues, Swindlers and Cheats: The Development of Mistake of Identity in English Contract Law" (2005) 64 CLJ 711.

[104] We will see below that, on closer analysis, the recipient's knowledge of the identity mistake is crucial: Chapter V.B.1.b.i (esp pp 176–77). It explains why the sale contracts in *Cundy v Lindsay* (n 101) and *Ingram v Little* (n 102) were not validly concluded. Although it is not entirely clear whether such knowledge on the part of the recipient is also required to prevent a valid conveyance by delivery, the case of *R v Middleton* (1873) LR 2 CCR 38 suggests as much.

[105] In *Cundy v Lindsay* (n 101) and *Ingram v Little* (n 102) the defendants were actually innocent third parties, but there is no doubt that the fraudulent transferee, too, would have been liable in conversion.

[106] There is also a question whether and when a claim in unjust enrichment is available against *third party* purchasers from the fraudulent 'transferee': see below, Chapter VI.C.2.b (at pp 238–40).

norance' or 'powerlessness' (eg where B steals A's painting).[107] However, the debate is equally relevant to the fundamental mistake scenario considered here. Moreover, it reflects on certain basic assumptions about the proper relationship between rights and interests *in rem* and personal unjust enrichment claims. These assumptions – though they are rarely made express – have certain repercussions for the extent to which personal and proprietary restitution can co-exist. Most mistakes that a transferor like A makes are not so fundamental as to prevent title passing to B. Yet, as will be demonstrated in section D, it may be that B's unjust enrichment at A's expense generates a new property right, either in the form of a vested equitable interest under a trust or in the form of a (legal or equitable) power *in rem*. Without pre-empting the outcome of section D, and although the present section focuses primarily on the relationship between personal claims to restitution for unjust enrichment and the retention of pre-existing property rights in identity mistake cases, it is worth bearing in mind its potentially wider relevance. Three different approaches can be identified in the academic writing on the subject (judges do not generally advert to the issue).

1. Complete Exclusivity of Personal Claims and Property Rights

On one view, rights *in personam* generated by unjust enrichment and rights *in rem* are mutually exclusive. The subsistence of property rights is seen as precluding any personal claim to restitution for unjust enrichment.[108] If A retains his title to the painting despite its delivery to B, there is simply no unjust enrichment situation. While an unjust factor may well be present, the other two elements of the restitutionary claim are not. Title not having passed, B is not enriched, or at any rate not at A's expense. The title which B acquires by virtue of his possession is an original, not a derivative one. And even if A's property right is subsequently extinguished (eg through

[107] On the unjust factors 'ignorance' and 'powerlessness' see eg Birks *Introduction* (n 3) 140–46; Burrows *Restitution* (n 3) 182–210, esp 185–86; Virgo *Principles* (n 3) 131–34.

[108] W Swadling, "A Claim in Restitution?" [1996] LMCLQ 63, esp 65; W Swadling, "Ignorance and Unjust Enrichment: The Problem of Title" (2008) 28 OJLS 627. Similar: *Ilich v R* (1987) 162 CLR 110 (HCA) 140–41 (Brennan J). Cf also R Grantham and C Rickett, "Restitution, Property and Mistaken Payments" [1997] RLR 83, 87–88; R Grantham and C Rickett, "Property Rights as a Legally Significant Event" (2003) 62 CLJ 717, 741–44; but note that Grantham's and Rickett's approach actually differs from Swadling's: see below, n 118 and corresponding text.

bona fide purchase), there has at no point been a sufficiently direct 'transfer' which accounts for B's enrichment.[109]

This is an extremely normative approach to unjust enrichment, asking only whether there has been a transfer *of rights* from one party to the other. If not, the situation is governed exclusively by the rules of property law on the recovery of misappropriated assets (eg via a claim in the tort of conversion). Unjust enrichment has no role to play. However, given that the 'exclusionary view' is first and foremost geared towards the struggle against the recognition of 'ignorance' and 'powerlessness' as unjust factors (and thus ultimately against the recognition of non-participatory enrichments), this may not be the whole picture. Proponents of the view should perhaps be willing to make a small concession in fundamental mistake cases of the *Ingram v Little* and *Cundy v Lindsay* type. In these cases, there is (arguably) a voluntary transfer from A to B, albeit only one of possession. It would not be inconsistent with the 'exclusionary view' to allow a lesser personal unjust enrichment claim, similar to the *condictio possessionis* in German law.[110] But even if this possibility were accepted, the normative focus of the 'exclusionary view' would still require B's possession to be valued at less than the full market price of the painting.

2. Full Concurrence of Personal Claims and Property Rights

At the other end of the spectrum lies a more factually-oriented approach to what constitutes an enrichment at another's expense. It looks for a 'transfer of value' in the sense of a shift of realizable wealth. Under this approach, a personal claim in unjust enrichment is always available against B, whether or not A's consent is sufficiently impaired to prevent title passing, and

---

[109] Swadling [1996] LMCLQ (n 108) 65, sums up the argument: "In short, there is no claim in unjust enrichment because there is no 'transfer' from plaintiff to defendant".

[110] On the *condictio possessionis* and its competition with the *vindicatio* see above, Chapter III.D.1 (p 78). Although Virgo *Principles* (n 4) 131–36, 569–655, also regards claims based on unjust enrichment and claims based on the 'vindication of property rights' (which he classifies as restitutionary) as in principle mutually exclusive, his view seems compatible with recognizing 'lesser' unjust enrichment claims similar to the *condictio possessionis*. In his discussion of 'ignorance', he states (ibid 135): "If it is possible to show that the defendant has received an enrichment, even though the claimant has retained title to the property received by the defendant, and it can be shown that the defendant has obtained this benefit directly from the claimant, it should be possible to bring a restitutionary claim founded on the reversal of the defendant's unjust enrichment so long as it can be shown that the claimant was ignorant of the transfer. It is no bar to a restitutionary claim founded on unjust enrichment that the claimant could have brought a claim founded on the commission of a wrong, and neither should it matter that the claim could alternatively have been founded on the vindication of property rights". In our case, where ignorance is not at issue, the claimant's mistake would provide the unjust factor.

even in 'ignorance' cases.[111] When determining the extent of B's enrichment, the full market value of the painting (in the sense of the value of a good title to it) is taken into account. In order to meet the objection that the defendant's factual enrichment is less than the full market price so long as the claimant retains a better title to the object, it has been suggested that the claimant can choose not to rely on his superior title.[112] He may thus disregard or even 'renounce' his proprietary interest in the painting.[113] Yet not everybody regards such a normative concession within the factual approach as necessary or appropriate.[114] Another suggestion relies on an analogy with the tort of conversion: A's title is extinguished as soon as B pays up, just as when A chooses to proceed via the alternative route in the law of wrongs.[115] Whatever the construction, both results neatly fit with the basic principle of relativity of title within English property law.[116]

---

[111] Birks *Unjust Enrichment* (n 4) 63, 66–68; A Burrows, "Proprietary Restitution: Unmasking Unjust Enrichment" (2001) 117 LQR 412, 419; Burrows *Restitution* (n 3) 75–76, 185–86; A Burrows, "The Relationship between Unjust Enrichment and Property: Some Unresolved Issues" in S Degeling and J Edelman (eds), *Unjust Enrichment in Commercial Law* (Thomson Reuters, Sydney 2008) 333, 334–38; *Edelman & Bant* (n 16) 99, 102. Cf also P Birks, "Property and Unjust Enrichment: Categorical Truths" [1997] NZ L Rev 623, esp 642–50; P Birks, "Receipt" in P Birks and A Pretto (eds), *Breach of Trust* (Hart, Oxford 2002) 213, 231–33.

[112] Birks in *Breach of Trust* (n 111) 232: "The enrichment of the defendant is established with the aid of an election. The claimant elects not to insist on his pre-existing title. To insist on that title would be to assert that the asset was never added to the defendant's wealth. By contrast in treating it as having indeed enriched the defendant he accepts the fact of its having passed to him and abandons the contrary technicality".

[113] Birks *Unjust Enrichment* (n 4) 66: "[The claimant's] election to assert that [the defendant] has been unjustly enriched at his expense supposes a renunciation [ie extinction] of his title. Asserting his title or complaining of a wrongful interference he [the claimant] denies the enrichment but in claiming the value of the asset as an enrichment of the defendant at his expense he is renouncing his title".

[114] Critical of 'elective relinquishment': L Smith, "Tracing" in A Burrows and A Rodger (eds), *Mapping the Law: Essays in Memory of Peter Birks* (OUP, Oxford 2006) 119, 120–24, esp 121, who asks how the claimant can both freely relinquish his title and at the same time argue that the defendant has thereby been unjustly enriched at his expense. Similar: Swadling (2008) 28 OJLS (n 108) 651–53. Burrows in *Unjust Enrichment in Commercial Law* (n 111) 337–38, finds Birks' concession unnecessary and maintains a wholly factual stance: cf immediately below, n 115 and corresponding text.

[115] Cf Burrows *Restitution* (n 3) 76; Burrows in *Unjust Enrichment in Commercial Law* (n 111) 337–38, esp 338: "It is not the bringing of the claim in unjust enrichment but its satisfaction that results in the transfer of title; and this explanation of what happens to title is not critical to establishing the claim in unjust enrichment because the enrichment ... is a factual matter." Although Burrows uses the language of 'transfer of title', it will usually be sufficient if the claimant's superior title is extinguished upon satisfaction of his claim: cf Torts (Interference with Goods) Act 1977, s 5.

[116] See above, Chapter II.D.1.a (at pp 36–37).

When A's title falls away, B's is strengthened. Though not itself derived from A, B's title is henceforth the best possible right to possession and thus worth the full market value commonly ascribed to 'ownership'.[117]

3. Intermediate View

Between these two approaches, an intermediate third view can be identified. It rejects the idea that a claimant may choose between asserting a property right and treating the defendant as enriched at his expense, but at the same time accepts that a personal claim in unjust enrichment may be available as soon as a property right is lost. The intermediate view therefore addresses the criticisms levelled against both of the approaches outlined above. On the one hand, the claimant cannot simply 'wish away' a vested right *in rem* or disregard the fact that he retains his pre-existing title. On the other, it is sometimes possible for the claimant to establish the defendant's enrichment at his expense without demonstrating a voluntary transfer of any sort.

Two slightly different versions of the intermediate view can be distinguished. According to the first, a personal right to restitution lies latent beneath a claimant's vested right *in rem*. Since, however, the law of unjust enrichment is understood as 'subsidiary' to the rules of property law, this personal restitutionary claim comes to the surface only when the claimant loses his vested property right non-consensually (eg through consumption, *bona fide* purchase, or accession/specification).[118] It then ensures that the defendant has to disgorge any consequential enrichment. The second version of the intermediate approach is to some extent entailed by the arguments of those who believe that the unjust factor in non-participatory enrichment cases is not 'ignorance' or 'powerlessness', but the interference with or infringement of a wealth-allocating right.[119] Even if one rejected the subsidiarity argument, a personal claim in unjust enrichment could still be acknowledged to arise as soon as the claimant's vested property right (a wealth-allocating right *par excellence*) is lost, provided

---

[117] This assumes that there are no titles superior to A's.

[118] R Grantham and C Rickett, "Restitution, Property and Ignorance – A Reply to Mr Swadling" [1996] LMCLQ 463; R Grantham and C Rickett, "Property and Unjust Enrichment: Categorical Truths or Unnecessary Complexity?" [1997] NZ L Rev 668, esp 678–84. Grantham and Rickett ([1996] LMCLQ 463, 465) refer to *bona fide* purchase and 'mixing', but it is unclear what the proprietary effects of granular mixtures actually are in English law: see n 210 below.

[119] See above, authors cited in n 42. The view is also compatible with that of Smith in *Mapping the Law* (n 114) 120–24, who – it will be recalled – rejects the idea of 'elective relinquishment'.

only that this leaves the defendant's assets swollen.[120] In a fundamental mistake case, A would then be confined to the tort of conversion while his title to the painting survives, but he could switch to an unjust enrichment claim as soon as it is destroyed.

It is neither necessary nor possible within the confines of this book to decide definitively between the three approaches just outlined. However, in the light of the identity mistake scenario considered here, and in the light of what will be said later about proprietary restitution,[121] the second version of the intermediate view seems to be the most promising. It reconciles, as far as is possible, the 'exclusionary view' with the view that allows for a fully blown 'alternative analysis', while avoiding the most glaring weaknesses of both. As such, it comprises the best of both worlds.

D. Availability and Form of Proprietary Restitution

Let us now turn to the issue of proprietary restitution. As the term indicates, 'proprietary restitution' concerns newly generated rights or interests *in rem* arising as a response to unjust enrichment. While other legal systems (like the German) may return an empty box at the intersection of the event 'unjust enrichment' and the response 'rights *in rem*',[122] there is no logical or conceptual impossibility about proprietary restitution.[123] Two questions arise. First, does English law ever respond to unjust enrichment by the creation of a new property right? Second, what form does this right take? Though theoretically distinct, both questions are in practice closely interlinked and are therefore best treated together. Both questions are, moreover, not yet definitively settled.

Given that the law is still in a state of flux, how ought we to approach the issue of proprietary restitution? In the ongoing debate, policy arguments tend to play a significant role. It is asked whether English law should ever afford 'preferential treatment' to an unjust enrichment claimant by 'granting' him a new property right and thus allow him to segregate certain assets from the defendant's estate in the event of his insolvency.

---

120 Such an unjust enrichment claim would structurally resemble the instances of the *Eingriffskondiktion* contained in §§ 812 I 1 alt 2, 816 I 1, 951 BGB.

121 See below, section D.1.c of the present chapter (esp text to nn 146–147 on p 130).

122 The conclusion that German law has no form of 'proprietary restitution' may not be as secure as it appears on first sight. It rests on the assumption that the outer limits of enrichment law are conclusively defined by §§ 812 ff BGB (and the provisions referring to §§ 812 ff BGB). On the confines of enrichment law in comparative perspective see the discussion below, in Chapter V.B.1.a.iii and V.D.2 (pp 171–74, 204–6).

123 Birks [1997] NZ L Rev (n 111) 625–31; Birks *Unjust Enrichment* (n 4) 32–33.

Arguments put forward in favour of proprietary restitution are that an enrichment creditor has swollen the defendant's wealth, and that – unless the unjust factor is 'failure of consideration' – he has never consciously taken the risk of the defendant's insolvency.[124] Arguments against proprietary restitution are that there is no reason why an enrichment creditor should be in a better position than, for example, the victim of a tort, and that other creditors will also have swollen the defendant's wealth without being afforded 'priority' in his insolvency.[125] However, to ask whether a personal creditor deserves priority in his debtor's insolvency, and to 'impose' property rights accordingly, is putting the cart before the horse. The existence of property rights has potential repercussions far beyond the scope of insolvency law,[126] and policy decisions are, in any event, better left to Parliament.[127]

The aim here is to approach the matter by looking at the existing cases against the backdrop of the relevant areas of law. Property law, in conjunction with contract law, tells us how and when title passes to the transferee. It is primarily for property law, operating in conjunction with contract and unjust enrichment principles, to decide whether and to what extent the passing of title should be reversed. If this yields a result which is considered undesirable from a policy point of view, it is open to Parliament to remedy the defect through specific insolvency legislation.[128] We

---

[124] Eg Burrows *Restitution* (n 3) 69–72; Burrows (2001) 117 LQR (n 111) 423–28; G Jones, Comment on *Chase Manhattan Bank v Israel-British Bank* (1980) 39 CLJ 275, 276. Cf also R Goode, "Proprietary Restitutionary Claims" in WR Cornish and others (eds), *Restitution Past, Present and Future: Essays in Honour of Gareth Jones* (Hart, Oxford 1998) 63, 64–68. For a detailed and critical assessment of the policy arguments advanced in favour of proprietary restitution see W Swadling, "Policy Arguments for Proprietary Restitution" in S Degeling and J Edelman (eds), *Unjust Enrichment in Commercial Law* (Thomson Reuters, Sydney 2008) 359, 375–83.

[125] Cf eg W Swadling, "Property and Unjust Enrichment" in JW Harris (ed), *Property Problems: From Genes to Pension Funds* (Kluwer, London 1997) 130, 142–45; W Swadling, "Rescission, Property, and the Common Law" (2005) 121 LQR 123, 137–38; A Tettenborn, "Remedies for the Recovery of Money Paid by Mistake" (1980) 39 CLJ 272, 274–75. Also critical of proprietary restitution on the grounds of policy considerations: AJ Oakley, "Proprietary Claims and their Priority in Insolvency" (1995) 54 CLJ 376, esp 381–82, 397–404.

[126] Third party purchasers from the transferee, for example, are bound by the claimant-transferor's rights or other interests *in rem* unless a *nemo dat* 'exception' applies: see below, Chapter VI.C.1 (pp 226–33).

[127] Policy arguments (as a basis for the debate about 'proprietary restitution') are therefore expressly rejected by Birks *Unjust Enrichment* (n 4) 181, and by Swadling in *Unjust Enrichment in Commercial Law* (n 124) esp 372–75.

[128] A personal restitutionary claim could be afforded priority in the defendant's insolvency, or the assertion of a proprietary interest could be prevented in the insolvency context: see below, Chapter V.D.3 (esp p 209).

will begin by depicting the three main lines of thought on proprietary restitution before examining which best fits the cases and the basic principles of English contract, property and unjust enrichment law.[129] To structure the latter part of our enquiry, it will be convenient to distinguish according to the method of conveyance used, ie whether title has passed under a contract of sale or by delivery.

1. Three Models

a) No Proprietary Restitution

According to one view, proprietary restitution does not or should not exist.[130] If, in our example, A's consent is not so severely impaired as to prevent the conveyance occurring in the first place, he has no more than a personal claim to recover B's unjust enrichment at his expense. Title passes either irretrievably or not at all. This view can be understood as an extension of the 'exclusionary view' outlined above.[131] Not only does the retention of the relevant property right prevent a personal claim in unjust enrichment arising, but there is no remedy other than a personal unjust enrichment claim where the transfer of the property right is effective.

b) Immediately Vested Equitable Interest

Another view maintains that the event 'unjust enrichment' is capable of generating a proprietary response and holds that proprietary restitution takes the form of an immediately vested equitable interest under a trust.[132] As soon as A's title to the painting is transferred to B in circumstances which make B's receipt 'unjust', B holds it on trust for A.[133] Since the

---

[129] The present discussion will be confined to examining proprietary restitution in the specific context of *impaired consent transfer* cases. It should not be understood to make any broader claims about proprietary restitution more generally.

[130] Most prominently: Swadling in *Property Problems* (n 125). Cf also Swadling's contribution to A Burrows and others, "The New Birksian Approach to Unjust Enrichment" [2004] RLR 260, at 279–83.

[131] See above, section C.1 of the present chapter (pp 121–22).

[132] Most prominently: P Birks, "Restitution and Resulting Trusts" in S Goldstein (ed), *Equity and Contemporary Legal Developments* (Hebrew University, Jerusalem 1992) 335, reprinted in P Birks and F Rose (eds), *Restitution and Equity, vol 1: Resulting Trusts and Equitable Compensation* (Mansfield Press, London 2000) 265; R Chambers, *Resulting Trusts* (Clarendon Press, Oxford 1997).

[133] B McFarlane, *The Structure of Property Law* (Hart, Oxford 2008) 299–322, esp 305–12, has recently put forward a variation of the immediate interest model. As part of a broader argument about the nature of equitable interests, he suggests that a trust arises only when the recipient learns (or ought to become aware) of his obligation to make restitution. Since McFarlane's approach, though wedded to the conceptual premises of

equitable interest 'jumps back' to A, the trust can be described as a 'resulting trust'. And since the trust is created non-consensually, by operation of law, it can also be described as 'constructive'. Two justifications are generally advanced for the creation of a trust to reverse unjust enrichments. The first is the maxim that 'equity regards as done that which ought to be done'.[134] The second has recourse to the case law on so-called 'presumed resulting trusts'. These are trusts which arise when a gratuitous transfer is made outside a relationship of advancement.[135] Peter Birks and Robert Chambers have argued that what is being presumed in such cases is that the transferor did not intend to benefit the transferee.[136] A gratuitous transfer, they say, is an 'apparent gift', and 'equity is suspicious of gifts'.[137] They then reason that if equity imposes a resulting trust where a non-beneficial transfer is merely presumed, such a trust must *a fortiori* arise where it is positively proven, eg because the transferor's consent was 'vitiated' by mistake, illegitimate pressure or undue influence.[138] Hence, Birks and Chambers conclude, an immediately vested equitable interest can be regarded as a generalized proprietary response to unjust enrichment in all cases of impaired consent transfers.

---

the immediate interest model, shares many of the features of the power model (cf section D.1.c below, pp 129–30) as far as practical outcomes are concerned, it will not be separately considered in the body of the text. Footnote references to it will, however, be made in appropriate places.

[134] See esp R Chambers, "Resulting Trusts in Canada" (2002) 16 TruLI 104 and 138, 146–47, reprinted from (2000) 38 Alberta L Rev 378, 409–10; R Calnan, "Imposing Proprietary Rights" [2004] RLR 1, 12. For similar reasoning in the context of restitution for wrongs cf *Attorney-General of Hong Kong v Reid* [1994] 1 AC 324 (PC).

[135] The evidential 'presumption of advancement' applies between parent and child as well as between husband and wife, but not vice versa. Its application between spouses is anachronistic and likely to be reformed in the near future: see eg the failed Family Law (Property and Maintenance) Bill 2005/06, s 2. The presumption of advancement is usually thought of in terms of a presumption of gift-giving, but it may amount to no more than the absence of any reason for assuming that a trust was intended: *Martin v Martin* (1959) 110 CLR 297 (HCA) 303.

[136] Birks in *Equity and Contemporary Legal Developments* (n 132) esp 346; Chambers *Resulting Trusts* (n 132) esp 19–27. Chambers states (ibid 2) that "[a]ll resulting trusts come into being because the provider of property did not intend to benefit the recipient". On the other 'category' of resulting trusts ('automatic resulting trusts') see n 138 below.

[137] Birks in *Equity and Contemporary Legal Developments* (n 132) 343–46; Chambers *Resulting Trusts* (n 132) 11–39.

[138] Birks in *Equity and Contemporary Legal Developments* (n 132) 346–47; Chambers *Resulting Trusts* (n 132) 111–42, esp 111–15, 125–37. Another instance in which the intention not to benefit the recipient is proven and a resulting trust arises is where an express trust fails, eg for lack of certainty or non-exhaustion (so-called 'automatic resulting trust').

This model of proprietary restitution seems to be most closely related to the view which accepts the possibility of a co-existence between personal claims to restitution for unjust enrichment and vested property rights.[139] If, in a fundamental mistake case, A can simply choose not to rely on or to 'waive' his surviving title in order to establish B's enrichment at his expense,[140] then there is no problem about saying that, where title has passed, A has the choice between treating B as an ordinary debtor of a personal claim to the value of his enrichment or alternatively as a trustee of the painting.[141] Rights *in rem* generated by unjust enrichment are thus understood as additional remedies, effectively enhancing existing rights *in personam*.

c) Legal or Equitable Power *in rem*

The third approach to impaired consent transfer cases – albeit one which has not yet been formulated as succinctly as the other two – is to accept the possibility of proprietary restitution in principle, but to confine it to a power *in rem*.[142] Unlike an immediately vested interest, a power *in rem* is a merely potential or embryonic right *in rem*. It will be recalled that a 'power' entails the ability unilaterally to effect changes in respect of vested rights.[143] A power is '*in rem*' if it relates to a particular object or asset and is (in principle) exigible against third parties.[144] Powers *in rem* are hence lesser proprietary interests capable of modifying or re-allocating

---

139 See above, section C.2 of the present chapter (pp 122–24).

140 Cf text to nn 112–113 above. On a purely factual approach to what constitutes an 'enrichment', A does not even need to do this: cf text to nn 114–115.

141 Birks [1997] NZ L Rev (n 111) esp 655; Birks *Unjust Enrichment* (n 4) 68–69. Cf also *Westdeutsche Landesbank Girozentrale v Islington London BC* [1996] AC 669 (HL) 683–84 (Lord Goff). Note that R Chambers, "Resulting Trusts" in A Burrows and A Rodger (eds), *Mapping the Law: Essays in Memory of Peter Birks* (OUP, Oxford 2006) 247, 256–59, is markedly more cautious about the concurrence of a personal claim with a vested property right. He speaks of "two [different and possibly incompatible] kinds of restitution".

142 In his later work, Birks came close to defending a generalized power model for all impaired consent transfer cases: P Birks (ed), *English Private Law* (OUP, Oxford 2000) vol 2, [15–216]–[15–220]; Birks *Unjust Enrichment* (n 4) 184, 188–89, 192. Lord Millett, too, has shown some sympathy towards the idea of regarding impaired consent transfers as 'voidable': P Millett, "Restitution and Constructive Trusts" (1998) 114 LQR 399, 416. However, he qualified his endorsement of the power model by restricting it to chattels of 'special value' (see text to n 269 below) and has since been won over by Swadling's argument against proprietary restitution (cf text to n 130): P Millett, "Proprietary Restitution" in S Degeling and J Edelman (eds), *Equity in Commercial Law* (Thomson LBC, Sydney 2005) 309, 320 fn 31.

143 See above, text after n 35.

144 On the present use of the term '*in rem*' see above, n 105 on p 39.

vested rights *in rem*. They can be characterized as either legal or equitable, depending on whether they are effective at common law or only in equity. Under the power model of proprietary restitution, an enrichment creditor has the option of vesting a (legal or equitable) proprietary interest in himself, but he is normally free to decide whether or not to exercise this option.[145]

In many ways, the power model of proprietary restitution fits best with what was described above as the 'intermediate view' of the relationship between personal claims to restitution for unjust enrichment and vested rights *in rem*.[146] As soon as title to the painting passes from A to B, a personal unjust enrichment claim comes into existence. It is measured by the full market value of the object conveyed. The fact that A has a power to revest title or to bring a trust into existence does not affect this claim, so long as the power remains unexercised. However, as soon as A chooses to exercise it, the enrichment is reversed on the proprietary level, and he is thereafter bound to assert his right *in rem* in the ordinary way.[147]

2. Proprietary Restitution where Title Passes by Way of Sale

Let us first look at the availability and form of proprietary restitution in sale cases.[148] A is induced by a misrepresentation on B's part to sell and deliver a painting to him. Unless A is suffering from a fundamental mistake of the kind in *Cundy v Lindsay* or *Ingram v Little*,[149] the contract of sale is validly concluded. Assuming that it contains no retention of title clause or a similar postponement of conveyance, title passes immediately and without more (*solo consensu*).[150] However, as a result of B's misrepresentation, A has a right – or better: a power – to rescind and thereby avoid the contract. Given that the contract was the vehicle which effected the transfer of title, one would expect its rescission to have proprietary as well as personal consequences.

This is indeed the position in English law, at least since the seminal judgment of Parke B in *Load v Green*.[151] A rogue had fraudulently induced

---

[145] In cases of sale, the exercise of a power *in rem* may be inextricably tied to the exercise of a power *in personam*: see below, nn 160, 172, and corresponding text.

[146] See above, section C.3 of the present chapter (pp 124–25).

[147] Of course, under this model, a personal claim in unjust enrichment could again arise if A's revested property right was subsequently destroyed: cf text to nn 118, 120.

[148] On the scope of application of the 'sale' rule see below, text to nn 173–177.

[149] See above, nn 101–102 and corresponding text.

[150] Sale of Goods Act 1979, ss 17 and 18 rule 1.

[151] (1846) Mees & W 216, 153 ER 828. W Swadling, "Rescission, Property, and the Common Law" (2005) 121 LQR 123, demonstrates that most earlier cases adopted a different approach, either denying the transfer of title altogether, or holding it to have

the claimants to sell and deliver to him certain goods without paying for them. Soon afterwards, he became bankrupt. The claimants sought to recover the goods in question from his assignees in bankruptcy and, failing this, brought an action in trover (conversion) against them. They succeeded on the basis that they were free to annul the contract and thereby resume their property, ie revest title to the goods in themselves.[152] *Load v Green* has been followed and applied on numerous occasions, most prominently in *Car & Universal Finance Co Ltd v Caldwell*.[153] As the law stands, it is therefore beyond doubt that the common law right to rescind a contract of sale is (normally)[154] coupled with a power *in rem* to revest title.

What about rescission in equity? It will be recalled that the equitable grounds for rescission are broader than those recognized by the common law, extending beyond fraud and duress to non-fraudulent (negligent and innocent) misrepresentation and undue influence.[155] *Load v Green* was a case of fraud. The claimants had a common law power *in rem* which allowed them to 'pull back' full legal title.[156] Occasionally, it is assumed that title revests in the same way where the claimant's right to rescind exists only in equity.[157] Yet it is difficult to see how this should be possible. Equity has nothing to say about the position at law. Historically, the Chancery jurisdiction could supplement and to some extent correct, but it could never alter the common law. The procedural merger effected by the Judicature Acts 1873–75 did not change this. If, therefore, A rescinds the sale

---

passed irretrievably (ibid 142–52). However, it is worth noting that, prior to *Load v Green*, Parke J – as he then was – had already voiced his views on the proprietary effects of rescission in *Ferguson v Carrington* (1829) 9 Barn & Cress 57, 109 ER 22, and again in *Strutt v Smith* (1834) 1 Cromp M & R 312, 149 ER 1099.

[152] The 'reputed ownership clause' (Bankruptcy Act 1825, s 72) did not avail the defendants because the claimants had never consented to any 'apparent ownership' on the rogue's part and were – in any event – not the 'real owners' of the goods when the act of bankruptcy was committed: (1846) Mees & W 216, 223; 153 ER 828, 831.

[153] [1965] 1 QB 525 (CA), discussed in Chapter VI.C.1.b below (at pp 230–31). Cf also *Clough v London and North Western Rly Co* (1871) LR 7 Ex 26 (Exch Ch); *Re Eastgate, ex p Ward* [1905] 1 KB 465 (KBD); *Tilley v Bowman Ltd* [1910] 1 KB 745 (KBD); *Thomas v Heelas* [1988] CLY 3175 (CA).

[154] The power *in rem* may be lost by *bona fide* purchase: see below, Chapter VI.C.1.a (at pp 228–29). Yet this should not affect the transferor's right to rescind the contract, as the supposed 'third party rights bar to rescission' would seem to suggest: see below, Chapter VII (pp 259–74).

[155] See above, Chapter II.B.2.a (pp 22–23).

[156] Fraud was also made out in all of the other cases listed in n 153.

[157] Eg R Goode, *Commercial Law* (3rd edn LexisNexis, London 2004) 109 fn 314, citing *Car & Universal Finance Co Ltd v Caldwell* (n 153) 532 (Lord Denning MR) and *Newtons of Wembley Ltd v Williams* [1965] 1 QB 560 (CA) 571 (Sellers LJ) in support of this proposition, but neither of these judgments was concerned with or, indeed, contains any reference to rescission in equity.

contract with B on the ground that B, an art expert, negligently misidentified the painting's provenance, this does not affect B's common law right to possession, ie his (legal) title. The only thing equity can do is force B henceforth to hold the rights acquired under the contract on trust for A. A thereby obtains an equitable proprietary interest in the painting (often described as a 'revested equitable title').[158] As was pointed out in the Australian case of *Alati v Kruger*:

> "Of course, a rescission which the common law courts would not accept as valid cannot of its own force revest the legal title to property which had passed, but if a court of equity would treat it as effectual the equitable title to such property revests upon rescission".[159]

The position must therefore be that a legal right to rescind a contract of sale entails a legal power *in rem*, while an equitable right to rescind entails an equitable power *in rem*.[160]

Before we can safely conclude from the foregoing that the power model of proprietary restitution prevails in sale cases, it is worth briefly examining two challenges to this proposition. The first comes from Chambers. In his book on resulting trusts, he argues that, concurrently with the power *in rem* to revest title (which he calls a 'mere equity', irrespective of whether the right to rescind is legal or equitable), there arises an immediately vested equitable interest in favour of the transferor.[161] However, Chambers himself has since acknowledged that such a trust interest would be manifestly inconsistent with the idea underlying rescission, which is to give the transferor a choice whether or not to let the bargain stand.[162] The imme-

[158] Though widely adhered to, this terminology is misleading is two respects. First, the use of the word 'title' may suggest that the equitable proprietary interest carries with it a right to possession, which it does not (see below, text to n 302). Second, since A – as a person who held title to the painting outright prior to the transfer – did not start out with both a legal and an equitable interest in it (see n 230 below), the equitable interest is newly created. It does not, strictly speaking, '*re*vest' in A.

[159] (1955) 94 CLR 216 (HCA) 224 (Dixon CJ), endorsed in *O'Sullivan v Management Agency and Music Ltd* [1985] QB 428 (CA) 457 (Dunn LJ).

[160] This is the generally accepted view: eg Birks *Unjust Enrichment* (n 4) 183–84; J Cartwright, *Misrepresentation, Mistake and Non-Disclosure* (2nd edn Sweet & Maxwell, London 2007) [4.11]; Virgo *Principles* (n 3) 30–31; Worthington [2002] RLR (n 56) 37. Similar: O'Sullivan et al *Law of Rescission* (n 53) [16.01]–[16.09], [16.23]–[16.58]. Two questions remain: First, is rescission of the contract of sale ever possible without the concurrent exercise of the power *in rem*? Second, would rescission have the same proprietary effects if the *buyer* rescinded the contract? The answer to these questions partly depends on whether English law operates a theory of 'double effect': see below, text to nn 170–172, and esp the discussion in n 172.

[161] Chambers *Resulting Trusts* (n 132) 171–84.

[162] R Chambers, "Resulting Trusts and Equitable Compensation" (2001) 15 TruLI 2, 7; Chambers (2002) 16 TruLI (n 134) 145–47, esp 147 fn 31; Chambers in *Mapping the*

diate interest model has therefore been rightly rejected in the contractual context.[163]

The second challenge to the power model of proprietary restitution in sale cases comes from the opposite angle. William Swadling has questioned whether *Load v Green* was correctly decided.[164] He confines his criticism to the common law, but it is clear that he disapproves equally of proprietary consequences of rescission in equity. The gist of his argument is that if, subsequent to the conclusion of the contract, the seller has delivered the object sold to the buyer, rescission of the contract should no longer entail a revesting of title. This is because title will then have passed – unavoidably – by delivery.[165] From a conceptual point of view, Swadling's argument rests on two basic assumptions. One is that title can pass twice over: first *solo consensu* under the contract, and then again by delivery. The other is that where title does pass by delivery, it cannot be revested for the transferee's fraud. We will consider (and reject) the latter proposition below, when dealing with conveyances by delivery.[166] The difficulty with the former argument is that contract and delivery are alternative, not cumulative methods of conveyance. If title passes at the moment when the contract of sale is concluded, then the relationship between seller and buyer thereafter is one of bailment. A is in possession of B's painting with B's consent.[167] When A hands it over, this amounts to no more than an

---

Law (n 141), 257, 261. Note that McFarlane *Structure of Property Law* (n 133) esp 301–2, nevertheless believes in the concurrence. This is because he regards a common law power *in rem* as being essentially the same as a vested equitable interest under a trust: ibid 150–52, 224, 299–303.

163 *Guinness plc v Saunders* [1990] 2 AC 663 (HL) 698 (Lord Goff); *Lonrho plc v Al-Fayed (No 2)* [1992] 1 WLR 1 (ChD) 12–13 (Millett J); *Bristol and West Building Society v Mothew* [1998] Ch 1 (CA) 22 (Millett LJ); *Twinsectra Ltd v Yardley* [1999] Lloyd's Rep Bank 438 (CA) 461–62 (Potter LJ); *Shalson v Russo (Tracing Claims)* [2003] EWHC 1637 (ChD), [2005] Ch 281, [108] (Rimer J). Contra only: *Collings v Lee* [2001] 2 All ER 332 (CA); *Halley v Law Society* [2003] EWCA Civ 97. The former is a case of identity fraud in a contract for the sale of registered land and may be better explained on the basis that the conveyance to the 'transferee' would have been void at common law if personalty had been involved. On the latter case see the critical note by HW Tang, "Proprietary Relief without Rescission" (2004) 63 CLJ 30.

164 W Swadling, "Rescission, Property, and the Common Law" (2005) 121 LQR 123. Contrast: B Häcker, "Rescission of Contract and Revesting of Title: A Reply to Mr Swadling" [2006] RLR 106.

165 Swadling (2005) 121 LQR (n 164) esp 126, 152. Swadling refers to this as the 'principle of abstraction': ibid 139–41.

166 See below, section D.3 of the present chapter (at pp 138–42, esp text to n 218).

167 Cf *Worcester Works Finance Ltd v Cooden Engineering Co Ltd* [1972] 1 QB 210 (CA). A special characteristic of this bailment relationship is that the seller has a lien over the goods to secure his claims against the buyer (for payment of the purchase price): Sale of Goods Act 1979, ss 39(1)(a), 41.

ordinary delivery from a bailee to his bailor.[168] Even if A's intention to effect the conveyance were so generic as to survive until the moment of delivery, title (or at least the relevant title) is no longer his to give.[169] However, from a comparative perspective there is an interesting parallel between Swadling's argument and the so-called doctrine of 'double effect' (*Doppelwirkungslehre*) advanced by Theodor Kipp at the beginning of the 20th century.[170] Focusing on the question whether it was ever possible to rescind a void contract, Kipp contended that two sets of events, whether or not concurrent, could both be effective independently of one another to yield the same legal consequence. Yet although Kipp illustrated his theory, *inter alia*, by reference to the acquisition of ownership, he expressly denied its application where the later mode of acquisition was derivative rather than original.[171] Still, even if English law did (or ought to)[172] embrace the doctrine of 'double effect' and applied it to the scenario here under consideration, this would not entail the consequences advocated by Swadling *unless* he is right to assert that a transfer of title by delivery can never be avoided. To delivery cases let us now turn.

---

[168] The unpaid seller's lien (cf n 167) is thereby extinguished: Sale of Goods Act 1979, s 43(1).

[169] This is where voidable contract cases differ from cases in which the contract is completely void and delivery therefore capable of effecting a conveyance: Häcker [2006] RLR 106 (n 164) 109. Cf also section D.3.a of the present chapter (at pp 136–37, esp text to nn 181–185).

[170] T Kipp, "Über Doppelwirkungen im Recht, insbesondere über die Konkurrenz von Nichtigkeit und Anfechtbarkeit" in *Festschrift der Berliner Juristischen Fakultät für Ferdinand von Martitz zum fünfzigjährigen Doktorjubiläum* (Liebmann, Berlin 1911) 211. Agreeing: K Peter, "Die Möglichkeit mehrerer Gründe derselben Rechtsfolge und mehrerer gleicher Rechtsfolgen" AcP 132 (1930) 1; G Hubernagel, "Doppelwirkungen und Konkurrenzen" AcP 137 (1933) 205. Critical: HA Fischer, "Fiktionen und Bilder in der Rechtswissenschaft" AcP 117 (1919) 143, 183–88; WC Kersting, *Probleme der sog. Doppelwirkungen im Recht* (Doctoral Thesis, Hamburg 1964); G Husserl, *Recht und Welt* (Klostermann, Frankfurt/Main 1964) 217–48; B Oellers, "Doppelwirkungen im Recht?" AcP 169 (1969) 67.

[171] Kipp in *Festschrift v Martitz* (n 170) 221. Yet for 'double effect' in this case: Hubernagel AcP 137 (n 170) 233.

[172] The doctrine of double effect might be useful in two respects (cf n 160 above). First, it would enable the seller who has already delivered the goods to the buyer – if he so wishes – to rescind the contract of sale without thereby exercising a power *in rem* (and thus solve the problem of the supposed 'third party rights bar to rescission': cf Chapter VII, esp n 8 on p 261). Second, it could prevent a revesting of title in the seller where the *buyer* rescinds the sale contract for the *seller's* fraud, provided only that the seller has already delivered the goods to the buyer. Title would not revest in the fraudulent seller in such a case because his consent to the conveyance (at the moment of delivery) was in no way impaired.

3. Proprietary Restitution where Title Passes by Delivery

In order to examine the availability and form of proprietary restitution in delivery cases, we must first have a clear idea of when delivery becomes relevant as a means of conveyance. The short answer is: whenever the *solo consensu* principle does not apply and the transferor, A, passes possession to the transferee, B, in circumstances where both agree that title shall pass. This needs fleshing out.

a) The Ambit of Conveyances by Delivery

For present purposes, three situations are at issue. First, informal gifts from A to B (ie gifts made in the absence of a deed or a declaration of trust). Given that gifts are non-contractual transactions in English law, the delivery requirement in such cases is wholly uncontentious. Second, conveyances made in pursuance of a contractual obligation to which the *solo consensu* principle does not apply. Although it has been suggested that the *solo consensu* principle might extend beyond sale to contracts of barter, or perhaps to all cases where chattels are promised in exchange for valuable consideration,[173] there is no unambiguous English authority for this proposition.[174] In Ireland, the Supreme Court has held that title to a bartered chattel cannot pass without delivery.[175] On any view, money always requires a delivery. Title to notes and coins cannot be transferred through consent alone, even if the cash has been specifically set aside for a particu-

---

[173] Eg A Bell, *Modern Law of Personal Property in England and Ireland* (Butterworths, London 1989) 323–25; RH Kersley, *Goodeve's Modern Law of Personal Property* (9th edn Sweet & Maxwell, London 1949) 92, 144. More cautious: AG Guest (gen ed), *Benjamin's Sale of Goods* (7th edn Sweet & Maxwell, London 2006) [1–036] (Sealy). Many books do not advert to the question at all, treating the issue as if all outright conveyances of movables were either sale or gift transactions.

[174] In *Cochrane v Moore* (1890) 25 QBD 57 (CA), Lord Esher MR seemed to think that any "contract for good consideration" could pass title (ibid 74–75), while Fry and Bowen LJJ spoke only of "contracts of sale" (ibid 73). In *Koppel v Koppel* [1966] 1 WLR 802 (CA) 811 (Harman LJ), it was assumed that every transaction for "money or moneysworth" was caught by the Sale of Goods legislation. Critical of this assumption: EMC Canton, "Sale of Goods and Barter" (1976) 39 MLR 589, 592; cf also Goode *Commercial Law* (n 157) 202.

[175] *Flynn v Mackin* [1974] IR 101 (Irish SC) esp 111–12 (Walsh J). Cf also *O'Regan v White* [1919] 2 IR 346 (Irish CA), where Ronan LJ stated (at 362–63) that the sale of goods "is, as far as I know, the only case in which a contract passes the legal estate in property ... at common law".

lar creditor.[176] The same would appear to be true when a (gratuitous) loan of fungibles other than money is made.[177]

The third situation in which delivery may operate as a means of conveyance is slightly more problematic. It concerns the case where title would normally have passed *solo consensu*, but failed to do so because the parties' contractual agreement was invalid.[178] In *Cundy v Lindsay*, where a rogue had fraudulently induced the claimant to 'sell' and deliver handkerchiefs to him, but where the contract of sale was void as a result of the claimant's identity mistake, Lord Cairns LC stated that "if the property in the goods in question passed, it could only pass by way of contract. There is nothing else which could have passed the property".[179] However, this statement is inaccurate in so far as it suggests that delivery has been completely ousted as a method of conveyance by the development of the *solo consensu* principle in sale.[180] While a delivery may have no proprietary relevance where title has already passed by way of contract,[181] it retains a role where the invalidity of the sale contract prevents title passing *solo consensu*. The point is best illustrated by the well-known case of *Singh v Ali*.[182] A lorry was sold and delivered by the defendant to the claimant, but since the claimant could not obtain the haulage permit necessary to operate it, the lorry remained formally registered in the defendant's name.[183] When the parties later fell out, the defendant took the lorry away without the claimant's consent. The claimant's action in detinue and trespass was successful. Although the contract of sale was void for illegality (it contra-

---

[176] This would be different only if the money (eg a collectors' coin) was 'sold'.

[177] Such a transaction, in which the transferee promises to re-convey to the transferor an equivalent amount (*mutuum*), is best conceived of as a type of 'unilateral contract' in English law. Since the transferee does not provide any 'interest', the parties' agreement becomes binding only at the moment of delivery. The transferor is under no prior obligation to make the conveyance, whether or not he has promised to do so, and the *solo consensu* principle should not apply (even on the very widest view of its scope of operation: cf n 173 and corresponding text).

[178] For this scenario, we must assume that the transferor's intention to convey survives until the moment of delivery: cf n 169 and corresponding text and text to n 185.

[179] (1878) 3 App Cas 459 (HL) 464.

[180] Cf the discussion by Swadling (2005) 121 LQR (n 164) 126–27.

[181] Except for extinguishing the unpaid seller's lien: cf n 168 above. On the possibility of 'double effect' see text to nn 169–172 above.

[182] [1960] AC 167 (PC). Similar: *Stocks v Wilson* [1913] 2 KB 235 (KBD), where goods were delivered under a contract of sale void for infancy; *Belvoir Finance Co Ltd v Stapleton* [1971] 1 QB 210 (CA), where the delivery under an illegal sale contract was to a third party on the buyer's instructions.

[183] The fact that the defendant remained registered as the 'owner' of the lorry was irrelevant to the question of title since the register was not a document of title: [1960] AC 167, 177.

vened the relevant Road Transport legislation), title passed to the claimant when the lorry was handed over to him.[184] This must be because, at the time of delivery, both parties intended to put their illegal scheme into effect and wanted title to pass to the claimant as though the sale had been valid.[185] The discrepancy between this result and that in *Cundy v Lindsay*, where the claimant retained his title despite the delivery, is explained by the fact that the claimant's identity mistake in *Cundy v Lindsay* was such that his intention to pass title at the moment of delivery was altogether discounted.[186]

Given that conveyances by delivery can thus occur whenever the *solo consensu* principle does not apply, the final issue to address is whether a liability mistake on the part of the transferor prevents the effectiveness of the delivery. What if a person paid money under a contract void for lack of some formality? Or if the defendant in *Singh v Ali* had not been aware of the statutory illegality when making the delivery?[187] Does the question of proprietary restitution not arise in such a case because title never passes to the recipient in the first place? A *dictum* of Lord Wright's in *Norwich Union Fire Insurance Society Ltd v William Price Ltd*[188] suggests as much. Holding an insurance company which had made a payment in the mistaken belief that an insured event had occurred entitled to recover the amount, he described the claimant's liability mistake as "fundamental to the transaction" and said that it "prevented there being that intention which the common law regards as essential to the making of an agreement or the transfer of money or property".[189] This statement by Lord Wright was, incidentally, what inspired Sir Wilfrid Greene MR's restrictive approach

[184] [1960] AC 167, 176–77 (Lord Denning): "Although the transaction between the plaintiff and the defendant was illegal, nevertheless it was fully executed and carried out: and on that account it was effective to pass the property in the lorry to the plaintiff. [...] The title passed by the sale and delivery of the lorry to the plaintiff".

[185] Cf Swadling (2005) 121 LQR (n 164) 141. Two alternative explanations for the result have been advanced. One is that the contract was not void, but merely unenforceable: L van Vliet, *Transfer of Movables in German, French, English and Dutch Law* (Ars Aequi Libri, Nijmegen 2000) 114. The other is that no title passed, but that a claim in conversion was precluded by the *in pari delicto* principle: M Higgins, "The Transfer of Property under Illegal Transactions" (1962) 25 MLR 149. These alternative explanations are discussed below, in Chapter V.C.1.a (at pp 194–96).

[186] As Lord Hatherley observed in *Cundy v Lindsay* (1878) 3 App Cas 459, 467, "no goods had been delivered to anybody except for the purpose of transferring the property to *Blenkiron* (not *Blenkarn*)" (emphasis in the original). 'Blenkarn' was the name of the rogue, 'Blenkiron' the respectable company he impersonated.

[187] This is hard to imagine on the actual facts of the case, but the basic constellation is readily conceivable.

[188] [1934] AC 455 (PC).

[189] Ibid 461–62.

towards restitution of voluntary payments in *Morgan v Ashcroft*,[190] and it can be criticized on essentially the same grounds. The equation of mistakes which prevent title passing with those that justify a restitutionary claim is unwarranted.[191] A liability mistake is not as fundamental as an identity mistake. Like a mistake as to the transferee's attributes, it is insufficiently serious to justify treating the transferor's intention to convey as completely non-existent.[192]

Having established the ambit of conveyances by delivery, we can now move on to examine the availability and form of proprietary restitution in such cases. It is convenient to distinguish between situations in which the delivery is preceded by the conclusion of a valid contract (other than sale)[193] that has to be rescinded before recovery is allowed and cases where the transferor's right to restitution arises without more.

b) Where Title Passes Pursuant to a Valid Contract

Where there is a conveyance by delivery which discharges a valid (but rescindable) contractual obligation,[194] the immediate interest model of proprietary restitution can be ruled out at once. This is because a vested interest under a trust is, as we have seen, incompatible with the nature of the parties' relationship prior to rescission.[195] Although the 'right' (better: power) to rescind the contract may be based on unjust enrichment,[196] the parties' bargain – while it exists – justifies the allocation of wealth to the transferee and thus precludes both a personal claim to restitution for unjust enrichment and the creation of a fully-fleged right *in rem*.[197] In the

---

190 [1938] 1 KB 49 (CA) 65. See text to nn 70–71 above.

191 See above, text to nn 74–76.

192 Cf *Chambers v Miller* (1862) 13 CB NS 125, 143 ER 50; *R v Prince* (1868) LR 1 CCR 150. *R v Middleton* (n 104) and *R v Ashwell* (n 97) are not necessarily inconsistent with this, given that both involved an identity mistake of sorts. Discussing the issue with particular regard to the law of theft: Swadling in *Mapping the Law* (n 99), who is critical of the latter two decisions and queries whether any mistake should ever be regarded as sufficiently fundamental to make a delivery 'unjust'; G Williams, "Mistake in the Law of Theft" (1977) 36 CLJ 62.

193 More accurately: 'other than one under which title passes'. Depending on how broadly the *solo consensu* principle is understood to operate (cf text to nn 173–175), the exclusion extends to certain other contracts, eg barter, as well.

194 On the view taken here, this will also encompass cases where the parties' agreement about a gratuitous loan of fungibles becomes binding upon delivery: cf n 177 above.

195 See above, nn 162–163 and corresponding text.

196 See above, section B.2.b of the present chapter (pp 106–9).

197 Although the conveyance by delivery is now notionally independent of the contract in pursuance of which it is made, the law of unjust enrichment cannot be allowed to stultify contractual principles by giving the transferor a remedy which goes beyond that envisaged by (and compatible with) those contractual principles.

contractual context, the contest is therefore only between the view which rejects proprietary restitution and the power model.

Unfortunately, the case law is not wholly conclusive. Almost all cases are (of course) concerned with money, and we know or must assume that the payments were made through bank transfers rather than in cash. However, since judges seem to be treating such payments as analogous to cash transactions, we may nevertheless obtain some guidance from them for our scenario. The strongest case against proprietary restitution is *Re Goldcorp Exchange Ltd (In Receivership)*.[198] A company had defrauded some of its customers into purchasing gold bullion for future delivery on a non-allocated basis. When the company was wound up, the Privy Council held that the customers did not have any proprietary entitlement to the company's assets such as would have afforded them priority over a bank's crystallized floating charge. They had neither acquired rights in the bullion held by the company,[199] nor could they assert a proprietary interest in the money paid as purchase price. Lord Mustill stated that "[u]pon payment by the customers the purchase moneys became, and rescission or no rescission remained, the unencumbered property of the company".[200] *Prima facie*, this would seem to militate against proprietary restitution. Yet the decision in *Re Goldcorp* is not actually inconsistent with the power *in rem* model. For one, it was unclear whether the customers, in their eagerness to establish rights in respect of the unallocated bullion, had delayed too long before exercising their right to rescind the contract.[201] Even if not, their rescission occurred only after the bank's floating charge had crystallized.[202]

---

198 [1995] 1 AC 74 (PC).

199 If the metal had been allocated, the claimants would have acquired title: cf Sale of Goods Act 1979, s 18 rule 5 (for English law). In *Re Goldcorp*, this would appear to have been the position of the so-called "Walker & Hall claimants", who were able to assert a proprietary interest in the bullion still held by the company (subject to the so-called 'lowest intermediate balance' rule): see [1995] 1 AC 74, 107–10.

200 [1995] 1 AC 74, 102.

201 Ibid (Lord Mustill): "The customers have never rescinded the contracts of sale, but have throughout the proceedings asserted various forms of proprietary interest in the bullion, all of them derived in one way or another from the contracts of sale. This stance is wholly inconsistent with the notion that the contracts were and are so ineffectual that the customers are entitled to get their money back. As a last resort the non-allocated claimants invited the Board to treat the contracts as rescinded if their claims for a proprietary interest in bullion were rejected. There is however no mechanism which would permit the claimants to pause, as it were, half way through the delivery of the present judgment and elect at last to rescind".

202 Ibid (Lord Mustill): "[E]ven if such a course [cf end of quote in n 201 immediately above] were open, the remedies arising on rescission would come too late to affect the secured rights of the bank under its previously crystallised floating charge".

Re Goldcorp may therefore decide no more than that an unexercised power *in rem* is defeated by a vested security interest.[203]

The latter interpretation of *Re Goldcorp* becomes plausible in the light of a whole series of cases in which it was expressly or impliedly assumed that a proprietary interest in money revests in the payer when he rescinds the underlying contract.[204] In *El Ajou v Dollar Land Holdings plc*, Millett J – as he then was – opined that claimants who had been fraudulently induced to purchase shares were "entitled to rescind the transaction and revest the equitable title to the purchase money in themselves at least to the extent necessary to support an equitable tracing claim".[205] He had already voiced a similar view in *Lonrho plc v Al-Fayed (No 2)*,[206] and later repeated it in *Bristol and West Building Society v Mothew*.[207] The suggestion was recently taken up by Rimer J in *Shalson v Russo (Tracing Claims)*.[208] After a careful review of all the authorities, Rimer J concluded that *Re Goldcorp* did not stand in the way of 'title' revesting after rescission.[209]

We may ask ourselves why all these cases advert only to rescission in equity despite the fact that most of the payers were victims of fraud and should thus have been able to rescind their contracts (and conveyances) at common law. The answer is simple. By the time the frauds were discovered, the proceeds of the moneys paid had already become mixed with the fraudsters' general assets, raising a problem of identification.[210] Given

---

203 P Birks, "Establishing a Proprietary Base" [1995] RLR 83, 88; *Shalson v Russo (Tracing Claims)* [2003] EWHC 1637 (ChD), [2005] Ch 281, [126] (Rimer J). Cf also D Hayton, "Ascertainability in Transfer and Tracing of Title" [1994] LMCLQ 449, 452, who points out that any power *in rem* would have been lost when the purchase moneys were paid into an overdrawn bank account.

204 The conceptual explanation for this revesting of title (or the creation of an equitable interest) will differ as between those who are proponents of the immediate interest model, but accept the power model in the contractual context (cf Chambers in n 162), and proponents of the fully-blown power model. For the former, the title revests *because* rescission wipes away the contract. For the latter, rescission of the contract is a pre-condition for the exercise of a (notionally separate) power *in rem*: cf n 219 below.

205 [1993] 3 All ER 717 (ChD) 734, rev'd on different grounds [1994] 2 All ER 685 (CA). On 'tracing' and 'claiming' see below, text to nn 210–213 and Chapter VIII.B.1 (esp pp 276–77).

206 [1992] 1 WLR 1 (ChD) 12–13.

207 [1998] Ch 1 (CA) 22–23.

208 [2003] EWHC 1637 (ChD), [2005] Ch 281, [121]–[127].

209 Ibid [126]. He also expressed doubts whether the exercise of a power *in rem* would ever allow a rescinding party to 'sidestep' the statutory winding-up regime after a company has gone into compulsory liquidation: cf *Ayerst (Inspector of Taxes) v C & K (Construction) Ltd* [1976] AC 167 (HL), and n 222 on p 209.

210 There is a question, which cannot here be addressed, about the legal effects of mixing *as far as the original object* (eg a bank note paid by A to B) is concerned. A's common law power *in rem* to revest title to the original object can survive no longer than

that the common law, unlike equity, is said not to be able to trace through mixed funds,[211] any common law power could not have 'survived' until the moment of rescission.[212] In money cases, it will therefore be extremely rare for a conveyance (by delivery) to be voidable at law.[213] However, assuming that the *solo consensu* rule does not apply to barter,[214] the Irish case of *Anderson v Ryan*[215] would seem to illustrate the basic common law position. Henchy J there held that the fraudulently induced transfer of title to a motorcar under a voidable contract of exchange was voidable at the victim's instance so as to revest (legal) title in him unless and until a *bona fide* purchaser intervenes.[216] As Lord Goddard CJ stated – *obiter*, but not confined to any particular mode of conveyance – in *Moynes v Coopper*: "Where a transfer of property is obtained by fraud, there is no doubt but that the property does pass, subject ... to the right of the defrauded party on discovering the fraud to disaffirm the transaction and resume his property".[217] If this is right, then Swadling must be wrong to suggest that

---

title itself *would have survived* if A had managed to exercise the power prior to the mixing. The issue therefore turns on the rules applying to (non-consensual) granular mixtures. It is uncertain whether these follow the rule applicable to fluid mixtures (co-ownership as under § 948 BGB), or whether they do not result in any change of 'ownership' whatsoever (as was the case with *commixtio* in classical Roman law): cf eg P Birks, "Mixtures" in N Palmer and E McKendrick (eds), *Interests in Goods* (2nd edn LLP, London 1998) 227, esp 238–46; L Smith, *The Law of Tracing* (Clarendon Press, Oxford 1997) 70–104, esp 70–77. In *Lipkin Gorman v Karpnale Ltd* [1991] 2 AC 548 (HL) 572, Lord Goff stated that "at common law, property in money, like other fungibles, is lost as such when it is mixed with other money".

[211] See below, Chapter VIII.B.1.a.i (at pp 278–80). Millett J and Rimer J were acutely aware of these supposed differences between equity and the common law: cf *El Ajou v Dollar Land Holdings* [1993] 3 All ER 717, 733–34; *Shalson v Russo* (n 208) [110].

[212] Whether it is correct to speak of the 'survival' of a proprietary interest where a claimant's rights to traceable substitutes are concerned is itself contentious: cf Chapter VIII.B.1.a.iii below (pp 286–89).

[213] The money would either still have to be identifiable in the transferee's hands, or its value would have to be traceable through 'clean' substitutions.

[214] See above, n 175 and corresponding text.

[215] [1967] IR 34 (Irish HC).

[216] On the relevant principles of *bona fide* purchase see below, Chapter VI.C.1.a (at pp 228–29). Note that the dispute in *Anderson v Ryan* was between the *bona fide* purchaser and a fourth party purchaser from him. The original transferor was not involved in the proceedings.

[217] [1956] 1 QB 439 (DC) 445. Similarly, F Pollock and RS Wright, *An Essay on Possession in the Common Law* (Clarendon Press, Oxford 1888) 101, having discussed the case where the person delivering a chattel does not intend to pass title to the transferee, continue: "Where the giver *does* intend to pass property to the receiver, being induced thereto by some false representation of the receiver not affecting the substance of the transaction itself, there is a real though not finally valid consent; the agreement is voidable on the ground of fraud, but not void" (emphasis added).

title passes either irretrievably or not at all where a conveyance is effected by delivery.[218]

Although the case law is not yet finally settled, it is submitted that the power *in rem* model best reflects the assumptions underlying judicial *dicta* and at the same time provides a coherent explanation for proprietary restitution in the contractual context, bringing delivery cases into line with sale cases. Where title passes by delivery in pursuance of a voidable contract, it usually passes only voidably. Provided that the transferor's consent to the conveyance was still impaired in the relevant sense at the time of delivery, and provided that he rescinds the contract at least contemporaneously, he is also able to avoid the transfer of title.[219] If fraud or duress were in play, the common law will allow him to 'pull back' the legal right to possession. The 'lesser' impairments of consent recognized only in equity, ie non-fraudulently induced mistake and undue influence, generate an equitable power *in rem* which, when exercised, leads to the creation of a trust in the transferor's favour.

c) Where the Right to Restitution Arises without More

Let us now look at cases where the transferor's right to restitution arises without more, ie where no contract stands in the way of impeaching the delivery. Going back to our core example, assume that A, an old and frail artist, makes a gift of a valuable painting to his carer B, being induced thereto by B's undue influence. Or that he pays money to B in the mistaken belief that it is owing. What, if any, rights or interests *in rem* does A have after the transfer?

(i) Four main cases

As in the contractual scenario, the case law is sparse and often concerned with payments which have not been made in cash. However, since the relevant judgments again appear to treat payments by way of cheque or bank transfer on the same footing as cash transactions, we can once more obtain guidance from them for our conveyance-by-delivery scenario. There are four main cases to consider.

---

[218] Cf above, text to nn 164–166 on p 133.

[219] In delivery cases, rescission of the underlying contract should not effect an automatic revesting of title, given that the validity of the conveyance did not depend on the existence of a valid obligation to convey. However, communication of the intention to rescind the contract will, in the absence of evidence to the contrary, often have to be understood to include the exercise of the power *in rem*.

The first is *Chase Manhattan Bank NA v Israel-British Bank (London) Ltd*.[220] The claimant bank had, due to a clerical error, made a double payment of US $ 2 million to the defendant bank. When the latter became insolvent, the question arose whether the claimant could assert any proprietary interest in the traceable proceeds of the second payment. Goulding J held that, as a matter of New York law (by reference to which the substantive dispute fell to be decided), a mistaken payer 'retained' an equitable proprietary interest in the overpaid amount and that the recipient held the money on 'constructive trust' for him. *Obiter* he added that the position would be the same in English law.[221]

Doubt was cast on Goulding J's *dictum* by the House of Lords in *Westdeutsche Landesbank Girozentrale v Islington London BC*.[222] The defendant local authority had entered into an interest rate swap agreement with the claimant bank. Agreements of this kind were later held to be *ultra vires* and void.[223] It had already been decided that the council was under an obligation to repay to the bank the net balance between the (fixed-rate) payment it had received up front and its own (floating-rate) 'interest' payments.[224] Their Lordships were only asked to consider whether this restitutionary liability attracted simple or compound interest. As the law then stood,[225] compound interest was available under the courts' equitable jurisdiction, but not for common law claims. Counsel for the claimant bank argued that the bank's liability mistake had initially prevented any property right in the money paid up front passing to the council,[226] and that when the bank's legal title was destroyed through payment into a mixed bank account, it 'retained' an equitable interest, thus creating a trust in its favour.[227] The House of Lords unanimously rejected this argument. Judgment was given for the defendant authority.[228] A liability mistake did not

---

220 [1981] Ch 105 (ChD).

221 Ibid 118–20.

222 [1996] AC 669 (HL).

223 *Hazell v Hammersmith and Fulham London BC* [1992] 2 AC 1 (HL).

224 *Westdeutsche Landesbank Girozentrale v Islington London BC* [1994] 4 All ER 890 (QBD Comm), aff'd [1994] 1 WLR 938 (CA).

225 The legal position has since changed: see n 228 below.

226 Reliance was placed, *inter alia*, on the misleading statements by Lord Cairns LC in *Cundy v Lindsay* (cf text to n 179) and by Lord Wright in *Norwich Union Fire Insurance Society Ltd v William Price Ltd* (cf text to n 189): [1996] AC 669, 676–77.

227 Reliance was placed, *inter alia*, on *Sinclair v Brougham* [1914] AC 398 (HL), an old case concerning a buidling society's *ultra vires* banking business, and *Chase Manhattan v Israel-British Bank* (cf text to nn 220–221): [1996] AC 669, 676–77.

228 Lords Goff and Woolf dissented on the basis that compound interest should be made available for personal restitutionary claims: [1996] AC 669, esp 684, 690–98, 719–37. This step has now been taken by *Sempra Metals Ltd (formerly Metallgesellschaft Ltd) v Inland Revenue Commissioners* [2007] UKHL 34, [2008] 1 AC 561.

negative the intention to pass title, nor did the mere receipt of money paid under a void contract turn the recipient into a trustee for the payer.[229] The suggestion that the latter could 'retain' an equitable interest in the money after paying it away by mistake was based on a misunderstanding of the relationship between law and equity and therefore fallacious.[230] And in so far as a newly created equitable interest was at issue, an extension of the traditional categories of case in which a resulting trust arose was not warranted.[231] Lord Browne-Wilkinson gave the only speech explicitly dealing with *Chase Manhattan v Israel-British Bank*. He suggested that the decision could be justified on the basis that the defendant bank there *knew* of the claimant bank's mistake within two days of receiving the payment. Emphasizing that equity would not impose a trust unless the recipient's 'conscience' was sufficiently affected,[232] he said that "[a]lthough the mere receipt of the moneys, in ignorance of the mistake, gives rise to no trust, the retention of the moneys after the recipient bank learned of the mistake may well have given rise to a constructive trust".[233]

The third case to consider is *Banque Belge pour l'Etranger v Hambrouck*.[234] A rogue named Hambrouck had tortiously obtained a number of cheques purportedly drawn by his employer on the claimant bank, Banque Belge. He paid these into his account at Farrow's Bank and thereby defrauded Banque Belge into parting with a sum of about £ 6,000. Hambrouck subsequently gave part of this money to his mistress, a certain Mlle Spanoghe, for no or immoral consideration. She deposited it in her account at the London Joint City and Midland Bank. When Hambrouck's frauds were discovered, Mlle Spanoghe's account was still £ 315 in credit. In interpleader proceedings, the Court of Appeal held that Banque Belge was

---

229 [1996] AC 669, 683–90 (Lord Goff), 703–16 (Lord Browne-Wilkinson). Similar: *Sempra Metals v IRC* (n 228) [117] (Lord Nicholls): "Sempra retained no proprietary interest in the money it paid to the Inland Revenue, and it has no interest in the 'fruits' of that money".

230 [1996] AC 669, 706 (Lord Browne-Wilkinson): "A person solely entitled to the beneficial ownership of money or property, both at law and in equity, does not enjoy an equitable interest in that property. The legal title carries with it all rights. Unless and until there is a separation of the legal and equitable estates, there is no separate equitable title". In other words, equity simply has no jurisdiction over such a person.

231 Ibid 689–90 (Lord Goff), 708–9 (Lord Browne-Wilkinson).

232 Ibid 705: "Since the equitable jurisdiction to enforce trusts depends on the conscience of the holder of the legal interest being affected, he cannot be a trustee of the property if and so long as he is ignorant of the facts alleged to affect his conscience". A similar view is now taken by McFarlane *Structure of Property Law* (n 133) esp 306–7, 308–12, 315–16, 319–22, who also believes that no trust can arise before the recipient of a mistaken payment becomes aware of the fact making his receipt 'unjust'.

233 [1996] AC 669, 715.

234 [1921] 1 KB 321 (CA).

entitled to recover this amount. The credit on Mlle Spanoghe's account represented the traceable proceeds of Hambrouck's fraud, and Mlle Spanoghe was not a *bona fide* purchaser for value. Two of the three judges expressly premised their conclusion on the assumption that Hambrouck had obtained a 'voidable title' to the proceeds of his fraud.[235] Since there were (unusually) no mixed bank accounts in *Banque Belge*, the claimants did not need to invoke the equitable tracing rules and were free to reclaim the remaining £ 315 at common law.[236]

Finally, we need to take account of the decision in *Allcard v Skinner*.[237] It is the most prominent of a number of cases dealing with 'rescission' of gifts.[238] A young woman had made substantial gifts of money and railway stock to the Sisters of the Poor, a religious order, when entering the Sisterhood. Five years after leaving it, she sought to recover these gifts on the basis that they had been made under the undue influence of the Mother Superior. The Court of Appeal held that she could indeed have revoked them upon leaving the Sisterhood, but by a majority found that she had since delayed too long. Drawing an analogy with contract law, Lindley LJ said that undue influence made a gift voidable in equity, but that if the donor did not call it into question within a reasonable time after the influence under which it was made ceased, this would be treated as a kind of affirmation or ratification.[239] He also stated *obiter* that the gifts in question

---

[235] [1921] 1 KB 321, 325 (Bankes LJ), 332 (Atkin LJ). Only Scrutton LJ thought that Hambrouck had 'no title' as against the claimant bank: ibid 329. Atkin LJ explained the majority's approach as follows (at 332): "It does not appear to be necessary for this case to determine whether Hambrouck stole the money or obtained it by false pretences. At present it appears to me that the plaintiff Bank intended to pass the property in and the possession of the cash which under the operations of the clearing house they must be taken to have paid to the collecting bank. I will assume therefore that this is a case not of a void but of a voidable transaction by which Hambrouck obtained a title to the money until the plaintiffs elected to avoid his title, which they did when they made their claim in this action. The title would then revest in the plaintiffs subject to any title acquired in the meantime by any transferee for value without notice of the fraud".

[236] Ibid 327–28 (Bankes LJ), 333–36 (Atkin LJ). Scrutton LJ apparently preferred to trace in equity: ibid 330. The action was one for money had and received, yet this should not be taken to indicate that Banque Belge had only a right *in personam* against Mlle Spanoghe. Instead, Banque Belge was asserting a right *in rem*: cf the quotation in n 235 immediately above.

[237] (1887) 36 ChD 145 (CA).

[238] Cf also eg *Mitchell v Homfray* (1881) 8 QBD 587 (CA); *Re Glubb* [1900] 1 Ch 354 (CA); *Hammond v Osborn* [2002] EWCA Civ 885; *Pesticcio v Huet* [2004] EWCA Civ 372.

[239] (1887) 36 ChD 145, 181, 186–87. A similar result had previously been reached in *Mitchell v Homfray* (n 238).

would have been voidable at common law had fraud or duress been in play.[240]

(ii) Immediate interest instead of or in addition to a power in rem?

Where the transferor's right to restitution does not depend on the prior rescission of a contract underlying the delivery, the objection to the immediate interest model of proprietary restitution which prevailed in the contractual context disappears.[241] There is nothing inconsistent about reversing an unjust enrichment by means of a resulting trust in such a situation. Depending on one's view of the proper relationship between personal restitutionary claims and vested rights *in rem*, one could either allow the transferor's equitable interest to compete freely with his right *in personam* or – on the 'intermediate view' – confine him to asserting the equitable interest while it subsists.[242] The question arises whether such an approach is borne out by the cases, and whether the conceptual arguments used to justify it are convincing.

Of the four decisions outlined above, *Chase Manhattan Bank NA v Israel-British Bank (London) Ltd*[243] lends considerable support to the immediate interest model of proprietary restitution, albeit on the fallacious basis that the transferor 'retains' rather than 'obtains' an equitable interest in the asset transferred.[244] *Banque Belge pour l'Etranger v Hambrouck*[245] is at least not incompatible with this analysis. Although the case was decided at common law on the assumption that Hambrouck's title was 'voidable' as a result of his fraud, there is nothing to suggest that a concurrent trust would not have been found if the court's equitable jurisdiction had been invoked. Apart from the issue of redundancy (eg in relation to third party purchasers),[246] a legal power *in rem* could theoretically be supplanted by a vested equitable interest.[247] Yet the decidedly cool reception of *Chase*

---

240 (1887) 36 ChD 145, 181. Cf also *Re Glubb* (n 238) 361–62 (Lord Lindley MR).

241 Cf above, text to nn 162–163, 195.

242 See above, section C.2 and C.3 of the present chapter (pp 122–25).

243 [1981] Ch 105 (ChD), discussed above, text after n 220.

244 Cf above, n 230 and corresponding text.

245 [1921] 1 KB 321 (CA), discussed above, text after n 234.

246 The *bona fide* purchase rules are the same for legal powers *in rem* and vested equitable interests: see below, Chapter VI.C.1 (at pp 228–29, 233). This is one reason which leads McFarlane *Structure of Property Law* (n 133) 224, 299–303, to argue that legal powers *in rem* are essentially the same as vested equitable interests (which McFarlane calls 'persistent rights'): cf n 162 above.

247 Problems would, however, arise from the concurrence of equitable powers and vested equitable interests, since the former are more easily defeated by *bona fide* purchase than the latter: see below, chapter VI.C.1 (at pp 229, 233). McFarlane *Structure of Property Law* (n 133) esp 306–7, 309–10, avoids this problem by defining an equitable

Manhattan in *Westdeutsche Landesbank Girozentrale v Islington London BC*,[248] coupled with the overruling of *Sinclair v Brougham*,[249] an old case favouring the trust approach on which Goulding J in *Chase Manhattan* had relied, suggests that English law (unlike American law)[250] is reluctant automatically to impose a trust whenever property is transferred in circumstances giving rise to restitutionary liability. Moreover, the decision in *Allcard v Skinner*[251] highlights the difficulties of operating an immediate interest model of proprietary restitution alongside a power model and indicates that the latter alone prevails in England. It will be recalled that opinion in the Court of Appeal was divided over whether Miss Allcard could recover the gifts made to the Sisterhood. Lindley LJ, with whom Bowen LJ agreed in principle, treated Miss Allcard as having a right in equity to "avoid", "revoke" or "set aside" the gift in consequence of the Mother Superior's undue influence.[252] The fact that she had delayed too long before doing so amounted to a "ratification" or "confirmation" of it.[253] Cotton LJ, by way of contrast, thought that Miss Allcard had "never effectually parted" with the beneficial interest in the property and treated it "as being held by the Defendant in trust for her".[254] He found that her delay in seeking restitution did not deprive her of "her right to the fund

'power' as the transferor's *factual* ability to inform an innocent transferee of his obligation to make restitution and thus to bring about the awareness which is, in McFarlane's view (cf nn 133, 232), necessary for the creation of a trust. For McFarlane, there can therefore never be a concurrence between the two kinds of equitable interest.

[248] [1996] AC 669 (HL), discussed above, text after n 222.

[249] [1914] AC 398 (HL). Cf n 227 above.

[250] Under US law, by reference to which *Chase Manhattan v Israel-British Bank* (n 243) fell to be decided, Goulding J's conclusion would indeed appear to have been correct. The 'constructive trust' there does much of the work which in England is left to the law of rescission and restitution more generally.

[251] (1887) 36 ChD 145 (CA), discussed above, text after n 237.

[252] (1887) 36 ChD 145, 180–87.

[253] Ibid 187. Lindley LJ drew an express analogy with voidable contracts, citing *Clough v London and North Western Rly Co* (n 153). We find very similar reasoning in *Mitchell v Homfray* (n 238) 591, where Lord Selborne LC said: "It must be held that whether she [the donor] knew or not that she had *power to retract the gift*, she was determined to abide by her acts; this is not a case of mere acquiescence; she determined that she *would not undo what she had done*" (emphasis added).

[254] (1887) 36 ChD 145, 172–75. Note that he, too, spoke of 'setting aside' the transfer, but immediately added (ibid 173) that "[t]he case is not like that of a contract voidable for fraud. There the party defrauded must elect, and within a reasonable time, for till he does so he retains the right or the benefits, however inadequate, secured to him by the contract. It is to such a case that the judgment of the Court in *Clough* v. *London and North Western Railway Company* [(n 153)] applies, and not to a case of voluntary gift like the present, where the person seeking to set aside the transfer never received any benefit whatever from the transaction".

now in the Defendant's hands".[255] Ultimately, the discrepancy between his view and that of the majority reflects the distinction between a vested equitable interest and an equitable power *in rem*.

Taken as a whole, the English case law seems to be more consistent with the power model of proprietary restitution than with the immediate interest model, even where this is not dictated by the contractual context. Despite its anti-proprietary flavour, *Westdeutsche Landesbank Girozentrale v Islington London BC* is not incompatible with the power model.[256] Their Lordships' reluctance to follow the Birks/Chambers line of argument and the critical stance towards *Chase Manhattan v Israel-British Bank* were partly motivated by the desire to avoid imposing on a *bona fide* transferee the (supposedly onerous)[257] duties of a trustee.[258] There is no danger of this happening if the transferor has no more than a power *in rem*.[259] Since the exercise of the power will (in non-fraud cases, at any rate)[260] involve communication with the transferee, the 'conscience' of the latter will – to use Lord Browne-Wilkinson's terminology – necessarily be affected as soon as the trust arises.[261] It is worth noting that any power *in rem* which might have existed in *Westdeutsche Landesbank Girozentrale v Islington London BC* must have been destroyed long before the bank's liability mis-

---

[255] (1887) 36 ChD 145, 174.

[256] On a formal level, it should not be overlooked that *Westdeutsche* was decided at a time when the 'mistake of law' bar was still in place (cf n 12 and corresponding text), so that greater emphasis had to be placed on the unjust factor 'failure of consideration' than on 'mistake': cf esp [1996] AC 669, 689–90 (Lord Goff). Viewed from this angle, the scepticism shown towards proprietary restitution is readily comprehensible: cf Burrows *Restitution* (n 3) 71 fn 13.

[257] In fact, we know very little about the duties of non-consensual trustees: see below, nn 320–321 and corresponding text.

[258] [1996] AC 669, 689–90 (Lord Goff), 705–9 (Lord Browne-Wilkinson). The concerns are most clearly voiced in Lord Browne-Wilkinson's speech. Apart from not wishing to hold innocent recipients liable as trustees, his Lordship was also worried about the position of third party purchasers from the transferee. He gave the example of a person who advances a loan secured by an equitable charge over the transferee's assets (at 704). Such a purchaser would be defeated by the transferor if the latter had a vested equitable interest in the assets mistakenly transferred.

[259] The variant intermediate interest model suggested by McFarlane *Structure of Property Law* (n 133) avoids the difficulty by requiring the transferee to have knowledge or notice of his obligation to make restitution before imposing on him the duties of trusteeship. This closely resembles Lord Browne-Wilkinson's view (cf text to n 233).

[260] Rescission without notice seems to be possible in fraud cases: *Car & Universal Finance Co Ltd v Caldwell* [1965] 1 QB 525 (CA).

[261] The power model also caters for Lord Browne-Wilkinson's second concern (cf n 258 above). Unlike vested equitable interests, equitable powers *in rem* are defeated by *bona fide* purchasers of equitable interests, such as the equitable chargee in his Lordship's example: cf below, Chapter VI.C.1.a (at p 229).

take came to light. The defendant council had not only paid the money received from the claimant bank into a mixed bank account, but had overdrawn this account on several occasions, a circumstance which Lord Browne-Wilkinson considered to be of "central importance".[262] No traceable proceeds of the original payment this remained in the local authority's hands when the action for restitution was brought.[263]

What about the conceptual arguments in favour of an immediately vested equitable interest? It is submitted that neither of the two above-mentioned justifications for the creation of a trust is convincing. The maxim that 'equity regards as done that which ought to be done'[264] may well lead to the creation of a trust whenever a contractual promise to convey a particular estate (usually in realty) is specifically enforceable,[265] but its invocation causes great difficulties in connection with restitutionary claims, especially those concerning personal property.[266] It is far from clear that the transferee is under any obligation to re-convey the exact chattel he has received from the transferor.[267] Under the English common law, his primary duty is to surrender the value of his enrichment.[268] Writing extra-judicially, Lord Millett has suggested that proprietary restitution should be regarded as a form of 'specific unperformance' and should therefore be confined to "land or other property of special value to the transferor".[269] But even if judges had discretion to order delivery up of particular objects and made generous use of it, application of the maxim could not yield a trust in every impaired consent transfer situation. There is

---

[262] [1996] AC 669, 700.

[263] On claims to traceable substitute assets see below, Chapter VIII.B.1 (pp 276–94).

[264] See above, text to n 134.

[265] Eg *Lysaght v Edwards* (1876) 2 ChD 499 (ChD) 506 (Jessel MR); *Walsh v Lonsdale* (1882) 21 ChD 9 (CA). Critical: W Swadling, "The Vendor-Purchaser Constructive Trust" in S Degeling and J Edelman (eds), *Equity in Commercial Law* (Thomson LBC, Sydney 2005) 463. As far as the sale of goods goes, title will normally pass *solo consensu*. Specific performance (of the seller's obligation to deliver the object sold) can be ordered at the court's discretion, but will usually be confined to cases of unique chattels: cf Sale of Goods Act 1979, s 52.

[266] It will be recalled that even a claim in the tort of conversion, by which the claimant asserts a better title to goods, sounds in damages and allows for delivery up only in exceptional circumstances: Torts (Interference with Goods) Act 1977, s 3 (cf pp 41–42).

[267] Such an obligation is, at any rate, not immediate. Once a trust has been constituted, the beneficiary can 'collapse' it and call for a transfer of title: see below, text to nn 301–304. McFarlane *Structure of Property Law* (n 133) 305, who *does* envisage an immediate trust arising under certain circumstances, therefore defines the transferee-trustee's duty more cautiously, namely as an obligation not to use the right acquired (here title to a chattel) for his own benefit.

[268] See above, Chapter II.C.2.a (at p 32).

[269] Millett (1998) 114 LQR (n 142) 416.

simply no general enrichment-based right *in personam ad rem acquirendam* upon which an immediately constituted trust could be founded (and it would be circular to infer such a personal claim from the alleged existence of a restitutionary equitable interest).

Although the Birks/Chambers *a fortiori* argument from the case law on 'presumed resulting trusts' is more promising,[270] it also runs into difficulties. Historically, the presumption was not one of 'non-beneficial' transfer, but of a transfer on (express) trust for the transferor.[271] In *Westdeutsche Landesbank Girozentrale v Islington London BC*, the House of Lords rejected any suggestion that this had changed.[272] Presumptions are inferences of fact made to fill evidential gaps. When a gratuitous transfer occurs outside a relationship of advancement, the inference that a trust was declared is at least as likely as that it was an imperfectly intended gift. To describe it as an 'apparent gift' is therefore misleading.[273] Moreover, the mere fact that equity will not perfect an imperfect gift[274] does not necessarily support the proposition that it is generally 'suspicious of gifts'.[275] As the case law on so-called 'presumed undue influence' shows, equity's suspicion is aroused not by gifts amongst strangers, but instead by excessive generosity within close personal relationships of trust and confidence.[276] It would also be strange if a donor who established (whether or not with the help of presumptions) that a gift was induced through undue influence on the part of the donee were confined to 'rescinding' the gift,[277] while a transferor who is presumed to have made an 'apparent gift' non-beneficially were to acquire an immediately vested equitable interest.[278]

---

[270] Cf above, text to nn 135–138.

[271] See W Swadling, "A New Role for Resulting Trusts?" (1996) 16 LS 110. The historical starting point is not disputed by Birks and Chambers.

[272] [1996] AC 669, 689 (Lord Goff), 703, 708 (Lord Browne-Wilkinson).

[273] W Swadling, "Explaining Resulting Trusts" (2008) 124 LQR 72, 86.

[274] *Milroy v Lord* (1862) 4 De G F & J 264, 45 ER 1185.

[275] Swadling (2008) 124 LQR (n 273) 86–88.

[276] Eg *Wright v Vanderplank* (1855) 2 Kay & J 1, 69 ER 669; *Allcard v Skinner* (n 237); *Zamet v Hyman* [1961] 1 WLR 1442 (CA); *Hammond v Osborn* (n 238); *Pesticcio v Huet* (n 238). Cf *Royal Bank of Scotland plc v Etridge (No 2)* (n 39) for the most recent comprehensive restatement concerning the role played by presumptions in the law of undue influence.

[277] As in *Allcard v Skinner* (n 237); *Hammond v Osborn* (n 238); *Pesticcio v Huet* (n 238). All these cases involved an equitable power *in rem*.

[278] These propositions could only be reconciled by saying that gift cases differ from mistaken payment cases in so far as the donor's right to restitution (for mistake, undue influence, etc) does *not* follow without more. Transfers by way of gift would then have to be regarded as giving rise to a 'legal basis' (analogous to a contractual entitlement), which prevents the transferor asserting *any* kind of restitutionary claim before the 'gift' is formally 'rescinded'. This would appear to be the position now adopted by Chambers

Finally, and most importantly, it is hard to understand what is actually meant by a 'non-beneficial transfer'. The term merely denotes the absence of an intention to benefit in a very general sense. Yet there is a fundamental difference between a transferor's positive intention to transfer an asset on trust (ie to bestow a bare legal title on the transferee) and a transfer intended – albeit imperfectly – to be outright (ie unencumbered by an equitable interest). In the latter case, the transferor *does* want to benefit the transferee. So long as the impairment of his consent is not fundamental enough to deprive the conveyance of any effect whatsoever,[279] the legal system takes his intentions at face value, at least until he asserts a right to revoke his consent. The very plea of an imperfectly intended outright transfer not only rebuts the presumption of it being made to set up a trust,[280] but also precludes any suggestion that it was somehow meant to be 'non-beneficial'.[281] Ultimately, the loose umbrella term 'non-beneficial transfer' obscures a doubtful equation of situations where there is genuinely 'no intention to benefit' with cases of 'vitiated' (or better: 'impaired')[282] intention. While the former scenario may well warrant the immediate creation of a resulting trust where an intended trust fails (eg for lack of certainty),[283] it is preferable to afford the transferor no more than a power *in rem* to avoid his conveyance in the second.

(iii) Power in rem *where the transferor's mistake is spontaneous?*

Under a power *in rem* model of proprietary restitution, the most difficult question to answer is whether the power arises whenever an impaired consent transfer takes place, or whether it depends on a misrepresentation,

in *Mapping the Law* (n 141) 261, who states that there is no immediately vested interest "where the claimant must first rescind a contract *or other transaction* to recover ownership of an asset" (emphasis added). Chambers must here be referring to gifts. We can infer that he does not think of *conveyances as such* as 'other transactions' from his statement that the recipient's unjust enrichment in a mistaken payment case is "not part of a contract or other transaction", so that "rescission is not involved" in its reversal: R Chambers, *An Introduction to Property Law in Australia* (2nd edn Thomson LBC, Sydney 2008) [24.140].

[279] See above, text to nn 96–103.

[280] Cf Millett (1998) 114 LQR (n 142) 402; Swadling (1996) 16 LS (n 271) esp 111–12, 116–17, 131; Swadling (2008) 124 LQR (n 273) 92–93; *Westdeutsche Landesbank Girozentrale v Islington London BC* (n 222) 708 (Lord Browne-Wilkinson).

[281] In a mistaken payment case, for example, only a 'beneficial' transfer would fulfil the payer's objective of discharging his (supposed) liability.

[282] Robert Goff LJ's critical observations on the language of 'vitiated consent' in *Whittaker v Campbell* [1984] QB 318 (DC) 326–28, highlight the dangerous ambiguity inherent in the term 'vitiation'. 'Impaired consent' better reflects the idea that a party's intention, though defective, may be recognized by the legal system as *prima facie* valid.

[283] Cf n 138 above on so-called 'automatic resulting trusts'.

improper pressure or undue influence emanating from the transferee. If the latter, then a spontaneous mistake made by the transferor will not entitle him to revoke his consent to the transfer, either at law or in equity, and he will be confined to a personal restitutionary claim. Assume that the old and frail artist in our earlier example had made the gift to his carer, B, not as a result of B's undue influence, but motivated by the assumption that he, A, was terminally ill, when in fact he was – despite his frailty – in reasonably good health. He would be precluded from asserting any proprietary interest in the painting unless his misapprehension had actually been brought about by the carer. Equally, a self-induced liability mistake, such as the one in *Chase Manhattan v Israel-British Bank*,[284] would then not enable the payer to lay hands on the money transferred (or its traceable proceeds) in priority to the recipient's general creditors.

While the immediate interest model of proprietary restitution does not distinguish between different unjust factors here at stake, there are indications in the case law that the power model might. In *Allcard v Skinner*, for example, Lindley LJ's analogy between gifts and contracts suggests that Miss Allcard could not have avoided her transfer to the Sisterhood had it been based on a spontaneous mistake.[285] Indeed, in *Re Glubb*,[286] where the question concerned the circumstances under which donations made by charitable subscription could be revoked, it was regarded as crucial that the donations had been induced by an 'innocent' misrepresentation in one of the charity's circulars. It could thus be inferred that no power *in rem* exists below the misrepresentation threshold.

Before jumping to such a conclusion, however, we should consider that the case law on gifts may not be our best guide for the law relating to spontaneous mistakes more generally. It will be recalled that there was – and still is – a great deal of uncertainty over restitution for mistaken gifts.[287] Given that decisions like *Allcard v Skinner* and *Re Glubb* appear to be premised on the assumption that a gift cannot be recovered *at all* unless it rests on a 'fundamental' mistake or has been procured by some form of pressure, undue influence or misrepresentation,[288] we should not be surprised at their tenor. We are thus thrown back onto the case law on liability mistakes, and here the power model of proprietary restitution is, as we have seen, at least not precluded by the House of Lords decision in *Westdeutsche Landesbank Girozentrale v Islington London BC*.[289]

---

284 See above, n 220 and corresponding text.
285 See quotation set out in n 253 above.
286 [1900] 1 Ch 354 (CA).
287 See above, section B.3 of the present chapter (pp 113–19).
288 See above, text to nn 65–71.
289 See above, text to nn 257–263.

Conceptually, there is no great problem about generalizing the power model to encompass spontaneous as well as induced mistakes. Like the right to rescind a contract (which is best seen as a power *in personam* occasionally coupled with a power *in rem* to revest title), the power *in rem* that exists where a conveyance is effected by delivery does not depend on any actionable wrong having been committed.[290] It would otherwise not have availed the donors in *Re Glubb*.[291] Of the two possible explanations outlined above for the right to rescind a contract,[292] only one provides some support for the exclusion of spontaneous mistake cases. If, as the orthodoxy maintains, the focus is on the transferor's defective consent throughout,[293] then all mistakes must count. If, on the other hand, the right to rescind a contract depends on some interference by the transferee with the transferor's autonomous decision-making process,[294] then we have the beginnings of an argument against recognizing powers *in rem* where the transferor's mistake is spontaneous. It could be reasoned that the transferor A ought not to be able unilaterally to deprive the transferee B of a right validly bestowed upon him, unless B is in some way 'responsible' for the defect in A's consent (inducement by misrepresentation, duress or undue influence). In other words, spontaneous mistakes would act as 'unjust factors' for the purposes of *personal* restitutionary claims, but not for the purposes of *proprietary* restitution.

However, while the infringement analysis might usefully explain the absence of a right to rescind a contract for self-induced mistake,[295] it should not supersede the normal unjust factors where there is no issue of holding parties to their bargain. The interference with the transferor's autonomy and its impairment are, after all, two sides of the same coin. A distinction between innocently induced and spontaneous mistakes can hardly be justified outside the contractual sphere. Given that the power *in rem* is a product of the law of unjust enrichment on any view, it should in principle be generated whenever an unjust enrichment occurs. It is therefore submitted that proprietary restitution ought to be available even where the transferor's mistake was spontaneous. A generalized power *in rem* model of proprietary restitution in all impaired consent transfer cases is the result.[296]

---

290 See above, text to nn 36–40.

291 See above, n 286 and corresponding text. Although Lord Lindley MR described the error ('innocent' misrepresentation) in the charity's circular as a "blunder", no wrongs-based liability for negligent misstatement existed at the time of the decision.

292 See above, section B.2.b of the present chapter (at pp 108–9).

293 Cf text to n 41 above.

294 Cf text to n 42 above.

295 Cf text to n 43 above.

296 Under the generalized power model, proprietary restitution would be available in most situations which Birks and Chambers now describe as cases of 'initial failure of

4. Further Implications of the Power Model as between the Parties

If – as is suggested here – proprietary restitution is founded on the transferor's ability to revoke his defective consent to a conveyance either at common law or in equity, questions arise as to the further implications of this model as between the parties.[297] Three are particularly pertinent. First, after exercising his power *in rem*, how does the transferor assert his (re)vested property right? Second, how does the disenrichment defence operate in the context of proprietary restitution? Third, under what circumstances is the transferee liable if the object in question is destroyed, damaged or lost, and when can he demand to be remunerated for improvements he has made to it?

a) Asserting the Revested Property Right

In analysing how the transferor can assert his (re)vested proprietary interest, we have to distinguish two scenarios. Take the example in which A is induced by B's misrepresentation to make a conveyance of the painting. If B's misrepresentation was fraudulent and A has exercised his common law power *in rem*, he has thereby successfully 'pulled back' his former title (ie the right to immediate and exclusive possession of the painting). However, since the common law knows no direct assertion of title,[298] A cannot simply sue B for the return of the painting. Instead, he has to have recourse to tort law. B's failure to deliver the painting to A, being the person with the better right to possession, will constitute an act of conversion.[299] Under section 3 of the Torts (Interference with Goods) Act 1977, A may be able to obtain an order for specific delivery of the painting, but otherwise the remedy is purely monetary. Payment of damages will extinguish A's title.[300]

---

basis': cf Birks *Unjust Enrichment* (n 4) 185–94; Chambers in *Mapping the Law* (n 141) 261. However, it would not necessarily apply where restitution is purely policy-motivated and the transferor's consent in no way impaired, as eg in *Woolwich Equitable BS v Inland Revenue Commissioners* [1993] AC 70 (HL). In such cases, the transferor should be confined to a personal claim unless the policy in question specifically requires the creation of a power *in rem*.

[297] We are here concerned with 'pure' two-party situations. The implications of the power model for three-party situations will be considered in Part Three of this book. As will become evident from Chapter VI.C.1 (pp 226–33), the power model of proprietary restitution has important repercussions for the position of third party purchasers from the transferee: cf also nn 258, 261, above.

[298] See above, Chapter II.D.2.a (at pp 41–42).

[299] This is how A obtains 'priority' in the event of B's insolvency. B's trustee in bankruptcy will be personally liable in conversion unless he surrenders the object to A: see below, Chapter V.D.3 (esp text to n 205 on p 206).

[300] Torts (Interference with Goods) Act 1977, s 5.

If the misrepresentation which induced A to make the transfer was not fraudulent, A's revocation of consent will have brought an equitable interest into existence. B now holds title to the painting on trust for A. It will be recalled that, unlike the common law, equity does have a type of *vindicatio*.[301] The transferor-beneficiary A can ask the court to make a declaration confirming the existence of the trust. However, this may not be enough. As beneficiary, A has no right to possession of the trust assets.[302] He first has to 'execute' (collapse) the trust. Under the rule in *Saunders v Vautier*,[303] he can demand transfer of title to himself. In this way, he will usually be able to insist on a delivery of the painting.[304]

b) Disenrichment Defence to Proprietary Restitution

How does the power model of proprietary restitution deal with the situation where the transferee is disenriched subsequent to the transfer, but before the transferor has revoked his consent to it? A number of cases are unproblematic. Sometimes the transferor's power *in rem* is simply destroyed by the disenriching event. If the painting goes up in flames, A loses his ability to avoid the transfer.[305] No power *in rem* can exist without a *res* (thing) to attach to.[306] At other times, the transferee will be disqualified from the defence. A fraudster or a person exercising duress can hardly be heard to say that he has changed his position in reliance on the security of his receipt.[307] Finally, in the contractual context, the *restitutio in integrum* requirement ensures that the transferor cannot normally rescind his contract with the transferee without returning the transferee's counter-performance or its value.[308]

---

[301] See above, Chapter II.D.2.a (at p 42).

[302] This emerges most clearly from *MCC Proceeds Inc v Lehman Bros International (Europe)* [1998] 4 All ER 675 (CA).

[303] (1841) 4 Beav 115, 49 ER 282; aff'd (1841) Cr & Ph 240, 41 ER 482.

[304] It seems, therefore, that the exercise of an equitable power *in rem* will typically lead to specific recovery, while the exercise of a legal power *in rem* may not.

[305] Note that A's (legal or equitable) power *in rem* may be able to 'survive' a *bona fide* purchase of the painting in the sense of enabling A to claim the painting's traceable proceeds from B: see below, Chapter VIII.B.1.b (pp 289–94).

[306] As far as equitable powers *in rem* are concerned, their loss is explained by the destruction of the legal title to which they relate.

[307] There is a question about the extent to which non-fraudulent misrepresentors (or transferees who exert undue influence wholly inadvertently) should be able to invoke the defence: cf discussion in n 59 above.

[308] See above, section B.2.c of the present chapter (pp 109–13).

We are left with cases where an 'innocent' transferee, as a result of the transfer, has incurred costs which he would not otherwise have had.[309] Imagine that B, the lucky carer, takes his wife to dinner to celebrate A's gift, or that he expends money on insuring the painting. If A later wants to avoid the gift for a (spontaneous) mistake about the state of his health, B's disenrichment must somehow be taken into account. A's power *in rem* to bring a trust into existence is, after all, based on B's unjust enrichment. Tying the fate of a specific proprietary interest to the development over time of the transferee's abstractly surviving enrichment is a fiendishly difficult task.[310] Yet, as a result of the inchoate nature of powers *in rem*, the power model of proprietary restitution has less difficulty accommodating the defence than the immediate interest model.[311] If powers *in rem* are the proprietary equivalent of powers *in personam* to rescind contracts, then their exercise by the transferor can be made conditional upon indemnifying the other party for any relevant disenrichment, just as the exercise of a right to rescind a contract is conditional upon effecting counter-restitution.[312] Our mistaken donor A should therefore not be able to acquire a vested equitable interest in the painting without paying the dinner bill or reimbursing B for the cost of the insurance.[313]

c) Liability for Loss and Remuneration for Improvements

Imagine that B damages or destroys the painting while it is in his possession. To what extent can A demand financial redress for the loss thus occasioned to him? We must again distinguish between the position at common law and in equity, and additionally between cases in which A has already exercised his power *in rem* and ones where he has not yet done so.

If (legal) title has revested in A, then any act inconsistent with his better right to possession will make B liable in the tort of conversion. B comes

309 This may or may not include non-fraudulent misrepresentors or persons who inadvertently exercise undue influence: cf n 307 above.

310 Cf eg A Burrows (ed), *English Private Law* (2nd edn OUP, Oxford 2007) [18.224] (C Mitchell); A Burrows and others, "The New Birksian Approach to Unjust Enrichment" [2004] RLR 260, 278 (Virgo).

311 The immediate interest model has to resort to the discretion of the courts in order to operate the disenrichment defence: Birks *Unjust Enrichment* (n 4) 210; Burrows *Restitution* (n 3) 528; Burrows in *Unjust Enrichment in Commercial Law* (n 111) 356–57; *English Private Law* (2nd edn) (n 310) [18.226] (C Mitchell).

312 Also drawing on the parallel with rescission in the context of powers *in rem*: Birks *Unjust Enrichment* (n 4) 210; Burrows in *Unjust Enrichment in Commercial Law* (n 111) 357 fn 84.

313 Alternatively, B could be afforded a personal counter-claim against A and allowed a lien over the painting to secure it. For most practical purposes, the result would be the same.

under an obligation to pay damages to A. The damages will be measured by the value of the painting and will also extend to any consequential losses A may suffer.[314] If, however, the act in question occurs before A has had a chance to 'pull back' title, it seems that B will not be similarly liable.[315] Conversion is a wrongful interference with another's better right to possession of a chattel. In the scenario under consideration, B's conduct takes place at a time when he (still) has title to the painting, albeit one voidable at A's instance. A's power *in rem* to revest title does not carry with it any right to possession.[316] Nor does title revest retroactively, at least as far as the law of wrongs is concerned.[317] An act which is not wrongful at the time of its commission cannot later become wrongful by virtue of the fact that the allocation of property rights subsequently changes (even where this has retrospective effect for other purposes).[318]

We encounter a roughly similar pattern in equity. Let us first look at the scenario in which B damages or destroys the painting after A has exercised his equitable power *in rem*. Although B's conduct does not amount to the common law wrong of conversion,[319] he will probably be liable in equity for breach of trust.[320] Unfortunately, we cannot be absolutely sure of this.

---

[314] In *Kuwait Airways Corp v Iraqi Airways Co (Nos 4 & 5)* [2002] UKHL 19, [2002] 2 AC 883, Lord Nicholls suggested that innocent converters may not be liable to make good consequential losses (at [79]), but in our example of A exercising a common law power *in rem* B will typically be a fraudster or duressor and will, in any event, know of A's better right to possession.

[315] Note that B may have committed other torts (eg deceit) which do not depend on the exercise of A's power *in rem*: see below, section E.1 of the present chapter (p 160).

[316] This is implicit in *Stocks v Wilson* [1913] 2 KB 235 (KBD); *Lipkin Gorman v Karpnale Ltd* [1991] 2 AC 548 (HL) 572–74 (Lord Goff).

[317] We will see in Part Three of this book that the law of *bona fide* purchase adopts a similar approach (Chapter VI.C.1, esp pp 228–33), but that retroactive revesting may be recognized for the purposes of establishing rights based on unjust enrichment (Chapter VI.C.2.b, at pp 242–43, and Chapter VIII.B.1.b, at p 292).

[318] As Cotton LJ stated in *Bolton Partners v Lambert* (1889) 41 ChD 295 (CA) 307: "[A]n act lawful at the time of its performance [cannot] be rendered unlawful ... by the application of the doctrine of [retroactive] ratification". The controversial Australian doctrine of 'conversion by relation back', introduced in *Hunter BNZ Finance Ltd v CG Maloney Pty Ltd* (1988) 18 NSWLR 420 (NSWSC Comm), is not generally thought to apply in England, but cf the *dictum* in *Hounslow London BC v Jenkins* [2004] EWHC 315 (QBD) [15] (Pitchford J). See also O'Sullivan et al *Law of Rescission* (n 53) [14.15]–[14.16]. On the avoidance of fraudulent preferences in bankruptcy proceedings and trover (conversion) cf *Nixon v Jenkins* (1793) 2 Bl H 135, 126 ER 471; *Stevenson v Newnham* (1853) 13 CB 285, esp 302–4; 138 ER 1208, esp 1215–16 (Parke B); *Marks v Feldman* (1870) LR 5 QB 275 (Exch Ch); *Re Goldburg (No 2)* [1912] 1 KB 606 (KBD).

[319] See above, n 302 and corresponding text.

[320] There would be a lacuna in the law if a 'bare trustee' who puts it out of his power to comply with the beneficiary's request under *Saunders v Vautier* (n 303) for a retrans-

We simply do not know enough about the nature and extent of the duties of non-consensual trustees to decide whether a transferee like B, who knows (as a result of A's communication) that he no longer holds a chattel outright, comes under similar obligations as a person who has expressly agreed to become a trustee.[321] What is, at any rate, reasonably certain is that a liability for breach of trust is out of the question if the relevant act takes place *before* A revokes his consent to the transfer. In *Bristol and West Building Society v Mothew*, Millett LJ said: "[I]t is clear that on rescission the equitable title does not revest retrospectively so as to cause an application of trust money which was properly authorised when made to be afterwards treated as a breach of trust".[322] Like the common law, equity adheres to the principle that B's conduct cannot retroactively become wrongful.

Having established the circumstances under which B is liable to A for damage to or loss of the painting, we must conversely ask when, if ever, he can recover money he has spent on improving it. Imagine that he has had the painting professionally restored and, though happy to return it to A, would like to be reimbursed for this expenditure. If B has incurred such expenses prior to A's exercising his power *in rem*, then they constitute a

---

fer of title were never liable for an equitable wrong (which – for want of a better name – we may call 'breach of trust'). The only question is whether this liability is better conceived of as fault-based or strict. In other words, does the equitable wrong require the 'bare trustee' to be aware of holding title on trust for another (as in our case B will be), and does it require him to act culpably? *Re Montagu's Settlement Trusts* [1987] Ch 264 (ChD), where Sir Robert Megarry VC considered at some length the personal liability of a person who receives trust property in breach of trust, suggests that there can be no wrongs-based liability without the appropriate knowledge of the trust. (Note that his Lordship was using the language of 'constructive trusteeship' in a slightly different sense from the one employed here: his focus was on a trustee's *personal* rights and obligations, not on the mere fact of a title-holder being bound by an equitable interest).

[321] In *Lonrho plc v Al-Fayed (No 2)* [1992] 1 WLR 1 (ChD) 13, Millett J said: "It is a mistake to suppose that in every situation in which a constructive trust arises the legal owner is necessarily subject to all the fiduciary obligations and disabilities of an express trustee. Even after the representee has elected to avoid the contract and reclaim the property, the obligations of the representor would in my judgment be analogous to those of a vendor of property contracted to be sold, and would not extend beyond the property actually obtained by the contract and liable to be returned". This suggests that an equitable wrong of the type outlined in n 320 does indeed exist, even though a 'bare trustee' may not (otherwise) be under any fiduciary obligations towards the beneficiary, especially under no management and investment duties.

[322] [1998] Ch 1 (CA) 23. In *Lonrho plc v Al-Fayed (No 2)* (n 321) 12–13, he had already stated that "[a] contract obtained by fraudulent misrepresentation is voidable, not void, even in equity. The representee may elect to avoid it, but until he does so the representor is not a constructive trustee of the property transferred pursuant to the contract, *and no fiduciary relationship exists between him and the representee*" (emphasis added).

simple change of position and should be treated accordingly.[323] If, on the other hand, common law title or an equitable interest has already revested in A, then the disenrichment defence will not avail B. It is, moreover, unlikely that he has any other means of recovery. Although section 6 of the Torts (Interference with Goods) Act 1977 provides that, in proceedings for wrongful interference with goods, an allowance can be made for value-enhancing improvements, this depends on the improver having acted "in the mistaken but honest belief that he had a good title to them". This situation cannot arise in our example. B will either know that title has revested in A, or – if he is a fraudster – will at least have to expect this possibility.[324] Where the exercise of A's power *in rem* has created a trust, B will be similarly aware (even if only in a lay sense) that he no longer holds title outright. As a 'bare trustee', he is under no management obligations in respect of the painting and can therefore not expect to be indemnified for expenditure on it.[325]

E. Competing Wrongs-Based Claims

Before concluding, brief mention must again be made of those wrongs-based claims which – though concerned with a precursor rather than a consequence of impaired consent transfers – are so closely connected that any account of the law would be incomplete without them. We have seen that the 'unjust factors' giving rise to personal restitutionary claims and proprietary restitutionary interests reflect a defect in the transferor's intention. Often, the defect is induced by the transferee's conduct. If this conduct amounts to a breach of duty, a wrongs-based personal claim will compete

---

323 On the practical operation of the change of position defence in the context of proprietary restitution see above, text to nn 310–313. B will recover his expenditure if he was unaware of A's right to avoid the transaction, and possibly only if he was not 'responsible' for the defect in A's consent (cf n 307). In *Cheese v Thomas* [1994] 1 WLR 129 (CA) 137, Sir Donald Nicholls VC adverted to the question of improvements, albeit as an aspect of equity's great flexibility when ordering rescission: "As with the jurisdiction to grant relief, so with the precise form of the relief to be granted, equity as a court of conscience will look at all the circumstances and do what fairness requires. [...] If the defendant has improved the property he is ordered to return, the plaintiff may be required to compensate him".

324 If rescission is effected without notice to B under the so-called *Caldwell* doctrine (cf n 260 above).

325 Unless, perhaps, such expenditure was absolutely essential for the preservation of the painting (but only if we assume that a 'bare trustee' who knows that he does not hold title outright would be liable to the beneficiary for failing to ensure its safety and preservation, ie only if the equitable liability referred to in n 320 extended to omissions).

with the transferor's rights generated by unjust enrichment. Of course, the rule against double recovery always applies.

1. Fraud and Duress

Where B defrauds A into transferring title to him by making a deliberate misrepresentation and intending A to act upon it, he commits the tort of deceit.[326] Liability in deceit extends to all consequential losses, irrespective of whether or not they were foreseeable.[327] Hence, although a fraudulent defendant who damages or destroys the chattel in question before the claimant transferor has exercised his common law power *in rem* to revest title will not be liable in the tort of conversion,[328] the transferor can nevertheless recover damages for the entire loss flowing from the transaction via the tort of deceit.[329]

It is unclear whether all instances of duress are tortious. In *Universe Tankships Inc of Monrovia v International Transport Workers Federation (The Universe Sentinel)*,[330] Lord Scarman suggested as much. He said that "duress ... not only renders voidable a transaction into which a person has entered under its compulsion but is actionable as a tort, if it causes damage or loss".[331] Lord Diplock, on the other hand, stated in the same case: "The use of economic duress to induce another person to part with property or money is not a tort per se; the form that the duress takes may, or may not, be tortious".[332] Since there is no tort of duress as such, this view seems preferable. Many types of duress, especially outside the realm of economic duress, will undoubtedly amount to one of a number of different torts. The relevant heads of liability are wrongful interference with goods (ie trespass to goods and conversion), trespass to the person (assault and battery), and possibly intimidation.[333]

---

[326] The defendant must either know that his statement is untrue, or not believe in its truth, or must make it recklessly, not caring whether it is true or false: *Derry v Peek* (1889) 14 App Cas 337 (HL), esp 374 (Lord Hershell).

[327] *Doyle v Olby (Ironmongers) Ltd* [1969] 2 QB 158 (CA); *Smith New Court Securities Ltd v Scimgeour Vickers (Asset Management) Ltd* [1997] AC 254 (HL).

[328] See above, text to n 315.

[329] In practice, bringing a claim under the Misrepresentation Act 1967, s 2(1), will often be easier for the claimant: cf below, text to n 337.

[330] [1983] 1 AC 366 (HL).

[331] Ibid 400.

[332] Ibid 385.

[333] Although the tort of intimidation usually involves three parties, there are suggestions in *Rookes v Barnard* [1964] AC 1129 (HL) 1183 (Lord Evershed), 1205 (Lord Devlin), that two-party intimidation is also tortious. In the recent case of *OBG Ltd v Allan* [2007] UKHL 21, [2008] 1 AC 1, [61], Lord Hoffmann left the question open.

2. Negligent Misrepresentation

There are two possible wrongs-based claims where a negligent misrepresentation on B's part has induced A to make the transfer. They overlap, but are not co-extensive. Firstly, B's misstatement may be actionable in the tort of negligence under the principle enunciated in *Hedley Byrne & Co Ltd v Heller & Partners Ltd.*[334] This liability depends on B having breached a pre-existing duty of care towards A. It applies to all transactions, irrespective of their nature, ie to transfers by way of gift as much as to contracts. Damages in the tort of negligence extend to all reasonably foreseeable losses.[335]

Secondly, liability for a negligent misrepresentation may arise under section 2(1) of the Misrepresentation Act 1967, which reads:

> "Where a person has entered into a contract after a misrepresentation has been made to him by another party thereto and as a result thereof he has suffered loss, then, if the person making the misrepresentation would be liable to damages in respect thereof had the misrepresentation been made fraudulently, that person shall be so liable notwithstanding that the misrepresentation was not made fraudulently, unless he proves that he had reasonable ground to believe and did believe up to the time the contract was made that the facts represented were true."

On the one hand, this section is narrower than negligence liability under *Hedley Byrne v Heller*. It applies only in the contractual context.[336] On the other hand, however, it is wider than the *Hedley Byrne* principle. Claimants do not have to establish the existence of a prior duty of care, nor the defendant's breach of it. Instead, it is up to the latter to prove that the misrepresentation was made innocently. In our example, A would be well-advised to proceed under section 2(1) if this is possible, particularly if trying to recover consequential losses. As a result of the way the provision is worded (fiction of fraud), it has been held that the remoteness rules for a section 2(1) claim are the same as for the tort of deceit.[337]

---

[334] [1964] AC 465 (HL). The *Hedley Byrne* principle was first applied in the context of pre-contractual negotiations leading to the conclusion of a contract in *Esso Petroleum Co Ltd v Mardon* [1976] QB 801 (CA).

[335] *Overseas Tankship (UK) Ltd v Morts Dock & Engineering Co (The Wagon Mound)* [1961] AC 388 (PC).

[336] And, it seems, only to the extent that a valid contract has in fact been concluded.

[337] *Royscot Trust Ltd v Rogerson* [1991] 2 QB 297 (CA). Critical: R Hooley, "Damages and the Misrepresentation Act 1967" (1991) 107 LQR 547. In *Smith New Court v Scrimgeour Vickers* (n 327), Lord Browne-Wilkinson (at 267) and Lord Steyn (at 283) noted the difficulties with the interpretation adopted in *Royscot v Rogerson*, but declined to express an opinion on the issue. Note, however, that contributory negligence is available as a defence against a claim under section 2(1) of the Misrepresentation Act 1967 (which it is not in fraud cases): *Gran Gelato Ltd v Richcliff (Group) Ltd* [1992] Ch 560 (ChD) 572–75.

3. Undue Influence

We have already seen that undue influence is often described as a form of 'equitable wrongdoing', but that it is not (yet?) actionable *per se*.[338] Undue influence is primarily concerned with the impaired autonomy of one party to a transaction.[339] It is compatible with the utmost propriety of conduct on the part of the transferee. The behaviour of the Mother Superior in *Allcard v Skinner*, for instance, was entirely beyond reproach.[340] Although a strict liability wrong is theoretically conceivable, English courts have never held a purely innocent 'influencer' liable beyond the measure of his own enrichment. As Lord Millett said in *Agnew v Länsforsäkringsbolagens AB*:

> "There is no 'obligation' not to exercise undue influence in order to persuade a party to enter into a contract. The party exercising influence incurs no liability. It is merely that the party whose consent was obtained by the exercise of undue influence is entitled to have the contract set aside".[341]

Under aggravating circumstances, however, undue influence may well begin to overlap with certain forms of wrongdoing, entailing a duty to pay compensation. Active exploitation of another person's emotional attachment or other dependency typically crosses the line.[342] Similarly, if B stands in a fiduciary position towards A, buying the painting from him at an undervalue will usually amount to a breach of fiduciary duty.[343]

---

[338] See above, nn 39–40 and corresponding text on p 108.

[339] We can here leave open whether the analysis should be primarily claimant-sided or defendant-sided: cf text to nn 41–43 above.

[340] (1887) 36 ChD 145 (CA) 171–172, 179, 183–184, 185–186, 190–191.

[341] [2001] 1 AC 223 (HL) 265. His Lordship made this observation in connection with a conflict of laws question (on which he ultimately disagreed with the majority in the House of Lords).

[342] Cf P Birks, "Undue Influence as Wrongful Exploitation" (2004) 120 LQR 34, 37. This could explain the award of 'equitable compensation' in *Mahoney v Purnell* [1996] 3 All ER 61 (QBD). May J there said (at 91): "[a]lthough Mr Mahoney's claim is not conventionally framed in the language of breach of duty, his ground for equitable relief is founded on abuse of trust". Query what the appropriate equitable wrong is called.

[343] Fiduciaries owe a duty of loyalty to their principal. In particular, they are not allowed to put themselves into a position where their duty and their personal interests may conflict (no-conflict rule), and they are not allowed to use their position to make a profit for themselves (no-profit rule). See also the discussion by Millett LJ in *Bristol and West BS v Mothew* (n 322) 16–22.

F. Summary

This chapter has attempted a systematic description of how English law reverses impaired consent transfers of movables in two-party situations. It has outlined the operation of the unjust factor regime, focusing in particular on the contractual context and on the scope of restitution for mistaken gifts. The largest part of the chapter was devoted to the questions and problems which arise at the interface of unjust enrichment and property law. One of these is defining the proper relationship between a personal claim to restitution and pre-existing or newly created proprietary interests. Closely related is the debate about the availability and form of so-called 'proprietary restitution'. Three views on proprietary restitution currently compete in the case law and in academic writing: no proprietary restitution, the immediate interest (resulting trust) model, and the power model. Since policy considerations, ie whether or not a claimant in unjust enrichment deserves 'priority' in the defendant's insolvency, are primarily a matter for Parliament, this chapter has sought to approach the issue from a perspective internal to property law itself. It was argued that, taking account of the different modes of conveyance, proprietary restitution is best understood as the transferor's ability to revoke his defective consent to a transfer of title. Depending on the circumstances and the way in which the impairment was caused, his revocation of consent will take effect either at common law or in equity. This analysis leads to a generalized power *in rem* model of proprietary restitution. A transferor can revest (legal) title in himself if he has been defrauded or coerced by duress into making the conveyance. All other defects, including spontaneous mistakes outside the contractual context, are relevant in equity and allow for the creation of a trust in the transferor's favour. After exploring the further consequences flowing from such a generalized power model of proprietary restitution in the two-party relationship, the chapter concluded with a brief overview of the wrongs-based claims which compete with the transferor's personal and proprietary rights/interests generated by unjust enrichment.

Chapter V

Comparative Observations on Two-Party Cases

A. Introduction

The previous two chapters on the treatment by German and English law of impaired consent transfers in two-party situations painted two separate and largely isolated pictures. Each legal system works on its own conceptual premises and has accordingly developed its own structure of inquiry. As a consequence, each faces its own peculiar problems. It is now time to draw the strings together. If comparative law is to deepen our understanding of one legal system by reference to another, then the two pictures must not only be mapped out side by side, but across one another. 'Pegs' will have to be found to help us stabilize the comparative framework and pin down similarities and differences before their details can be properly appreciated. To provide some such pegs and to attempt a first impressionistic sketch of the resulting pattern is the purpose of this chapter.

At the outset, we will compare and contrast the basic scope of recovery under English and German law, looking in particular at the types of impairments which attract the law's intervention in bargaining situations and in the context of gifts (section B). Then follows a discussion of the vexed question whether English law, like German law, adheres to the so-called principles of separation and abstraction, and – if so – to what extent this matters (section C). Finally, we will turn to the related question about the nature and extent of proprietary relief, examining in particular the foundation of 'proprietary restitution' in enrichment law as well as the issue of the transferor's position in the transferee's insolvency (section D).

B. Scope of Recovery

1. Operative Impairments in the Contractual Context

When thinking comparatively about the circumstances under which a transferor who has effected a conveyance in pursuance or by virtue of a contract can require the transferee to make restitution, it is important to bear in mind that the very notion of what constitutes a 'contract' is much broader in German than in English law.[1] The basic co-ordinates of the exercise therefore require some clarification. What follows is an endeavour to delineate and compare the boundaries between relevant and irrelevant defects of consent within each legal system. It is primarily about when – not how – 'restitution' (in the widest sense of the word) follows an impaired consent transfer in the contractual context. Questions about the availability, form and incidents of proprietary relief are left until later. The focus here is on what German lawyers would call 'obligatory contracts' and what English law defines more narrowly as 'bargains'. While the following discussion thus pertains to agreements supported by consideration (especially reciprocal contracts such as sale or barter) in both legal systems, gratuitous transactions are only encompassed as far as German law is concerned.

a) Grounds for Rescission Compared

(i) 'Procedural' and 'substantive' grounds for rescission

Let us first look again at the grounds for rescinding a contract.[2] Rescission, ie avoidance of the contractual obligation *ab initio*, is a precondition for recovery in both German and English law.[3] A distinct parallel can be made out regarding fraud and duress, which afford grounds for rescission both at common law and under § 123 BGB. Fraudulently induced mistakes and the exertion of illegitimate pressure severely impinge on a contracting party's autonomy. They amount to a deliberate manipulation or purposive deflection of his or her will.[4] Autonomy is restored by affording the party concerned the option of treating the contract as non-existent. Where the transferee is thus responsible for the impairment of the transferor's consent, he is made to bear the consequences of rescission.[5]

---

[1] See above, Chapter II.B.1 (pp 18–20).

[2] See already above, Chapter II.B.2 (pp 20–24).

[3] In German law, the legal basis (*Rechtsgrund*) for the transfer is retroactively destroyed by rescission: see above, Chapter III.B.2 and III.C (at pp 60, 64–65). In English law, rescission removes the contractual bar to (fully-fledged) unjust enrichment claims: see above, Chapter IV.B.2.a (pp 105–6).

[4] Although it is sometimes said that duress 'vitiates' consent, eg in *Pao On v Lau Yiu Long* [1980] AC 614 (PC), it is better to regard consent as merely 'deflected': see eg PS Atiyah, "Economic Duress and the 'Overborne Will'" (1982) 98 LQR 197. A similar observation is already made by FC von Savigny, *System des heutigen römischen Rechts: vol 3* (Veit & Co, Berlin 1840) 102.

[5] The present book deals only with cases where the fraud or duress is perpetrated by the transferee. To the extent that rescission is allowed for fraudulent misrepresentations made by, or duress emanating from, third parties, the transferee is made to bear the 'risk' of the impairment without actually being 'responsible' for it.

It will be recalled that, below the threshold of fraud and duress, the grounds for rescission in English and German law diverge.[6] While it is fair to say that both legal systems strive to protect the contracting parties' autonomy in decision-making, they go about this task in very different ways. English law adopts what one might regard as the logical continuation of the 'procedural' or 'process-oriented' approach exemplified by the fraud and duress scenarios. It asks whether there is any reason why – contrary to the generally prevailing *caveat emptor/venditor* principle – the transferee should exceptionally bear the risk of a defect in the formation of the transferor's consent, even in the absence of deliberate manipulation. This is the realm of equity. Equity intervenes where the transferee has negligently or indeed wholly innocently induced a mistake in the transferor's mind which subsequently caused the latter to enter into the contract (non-fraudulent misrepresentation),[7] and where the transferor's autonomy was impaired by reason of his strong emotional or other dependency on the transferee (undue influence). Although no actionable wrongdoing may be in play, these circumstances warrant denying to the transferee the advantages he would otherwise derive from the bargain.[8]

German law proceeds differently. Outside the sphere of fraud and duress it does not look at the nature of the parties' interaction,[9] but instead considers 'substantively' the transferor's state of mind and the quality of his consent when (apparently) agreeing to the terms of a contract. The right to rescind under § 119 I BGB, in cases where a party is mistaken about the content of his declaration of intention or does not want to make such a declaration at all (*Inhalts-* or *Erklärungsirrtum*), is rooted in a pragmatic compromise between the 'will theory' and the 'declaratory theory' of contracting and depends on a lack of correspondence between what the transferor subjectively intended and what he objectively declared.[10] Since only

---

[6] See above, Chapter II.B.2 (at pp 22–24).

[7] Although old equity cases frequently refer to the need for establishing 'fraud' on the defendant's part, this should not be taken to imply that an intentional misstatement was required. Instead, it was regarded as 'fraudulent' for him to insist on a contract induced by his own (non-fraudulent) misrepresentation: cf J Cartwright, *Misrepresentation, Mistake and Non-Disclosure* (2nd edn Sweet & Maxwell, London 2007) [4.03]–[4.04].

[8] This can sometimes cause great hardship to the transferee, especially in the case of wholly innocent misrepresentations about minor matters. To avoid a grossly disproportionate response to relatively trivial misstatements, section 2(2) of the Misrepresentation Act 1967 gives courts a discretion to refuse rescission and to award damages *in lieu*.

[9] In fact, even in fraud cases, there is nothing to stop a victim having recourse to § 119 BGB where appropriate (esp § 119 II BGB). However, rescission under § 123 BGB will be preferable from a limitation point of view: compare § 121 BGB with § 124 BGB.

[10] On the historical development see eg W Flume, *Allgemeiner Teil des Bürgerlichen Rechts, vol 2: Das Rechtsgeschäft* (3rd edn Springer, Berlin 1979) 435–49; M Schmoeckel, J Rückert and R Zimmermann (eds), *Historisch-kritischer Kommentar zum BGB, vol 1:*

mismatches between external appearance and internal assent are relevant, mistakes made in the process of forming an intention to contract on particular terms, so-called 'motivational mistakes' (*Motivirrtümer*), do not count.[11] § 119 II BGB, whether or not correctly regarded as an exception to the principle that motivational mistakes are irrelevant,[12] also looks to the nature of the misapprehension. A remnant of the Roman category of *error in substantia*,[13] it provides a right to rescind whenever a party to a contract is mistaken about an essential quality or characteristic of a person or object to whom or which his declaration relates (*Eigenschaftsirrtum*). In a well-known German case, the seller of a painting believed to be by Frank Duveneck was able to rescind the contract and recover the work of art when it later turned out to be by the more famous Wilhelm Leibl.[14]

---

§§ 1–240 (Mohr Siebeck, Tübingen 2003) §§ 116–124 [1]–[29], [51]–[79] (Schermaier); R Zimmermann, *The Law of Obligations: Roman Foundations of the Civilian Tradition* (Clarendon Press, Oxford 1996) 583–620, esp 614–16.

[11] German courts have occasionally recognized a right to rescind, through an extended application of § 119 I alt 1 BGB (so-called '*erweiterter Inhaltsirrtum*'), where one party has made an apparent error in a calculation disclosed to the other party (*offener Kalkulationsirrtum*): RGZ 64, 266, 268; RGZ 101, 107; RGZ 105, 406. This approach has been widely criticized on the basis that a (genuine) calculation error amounts to a pure motivational mistake: cf Flume *Rechtsgeschäft* (n 10) 469–71; S Lorenz, *Der Schutz vor dem unerwünschten Vertrag: Eine Untersuchung von Möglichkeiten und Grenzen der Abschlußkontrolle im geltenden Recht* (Beck, München 1997) 271–75. The Federal Supreme Court has distanced itself from the solution: eg BGHZ 139, 177, esp 180–81.

[12] See above, n 32 on p 24. Summary of the debate in FJ Säcker and R Rixecker (eds), *Münchener Kommentar zum Bürgerlichen Gesetzbuch, vol 1/1: §§ 1–240* (5th edn Beck, München 2006) § 119 [107]–[112] (Kramer).

[13] Cf Zimmermann *Law of Obligations* (n 10) 592–96, 614–17.

[14] BGH NJW 1988, 2597. There was an interesting dispute in the litigation over whether Leibl was in fact more famous than Duveneck. The buyer argued that, in the United States, Duveneck's paintings were at least as valuable as Leibl's. (The parties' contract had been concluded in Munich). The Federal Supreme Court thought that none of this mattered: even if Duveneck had been more highly regarded than Leibl, this would not have affected the seller's right to rescind. The *Duveneck/Leibl* case can be contrasted with RGZ 135, 339, where the Imperial Supreme Court had previously reaffirmed that the rules governing the scheme of remedies for breach of contract (especially the short limitation periods) could not be circumvented by recourse to § 119 BGB. It was therefore not possible for the *buyer* of a painting mistakenly ascribed to Jakob Isaakssohn van Ruisdael to rescind the contract of sale when it emerged that Jakob Salomonssohn van Ruysdael was the artist. Note the distinct parallel here between the *Ruisdael* case and *Leaf v International Galleries* [1950] 2 KB 86 (CA). In *Leaf*, the Court of Appeal held that the buyer of a painting innocently misrepresented as being by Constable was precluded from rescinding the sale five years after making the purchase. The fact that he was deemed to have 'accepted' the painting meant that he had lost his remedies for breach of contract, and the right to rescind for innocent misrepresentation was "barred ... for the self-same reason": ibid 91 (Denning LJ).

(ii) Overlaps between the English and German grounds for rescission

Having noted the divergences between the 'procedural' or 'process-oriented' and the 'substantive' or 'content-oriented' approach to rescission outside the context of fraud and duress, we must now establish whether and to what extent the grounds for rescission in English and German law overlap. It is tempting to conclude that they are at least partially co-extensive, yet caution is in order.

Of course, some impairments will by their very nature only be recognized in one legal system. Take the case of a party spontaneously mistaken as to a term of the contract and thus about the content of his declaration of intention: the seller of a painting, subjectively intending to ask $ 32,000 for it, makes a typing error and objectively agrees to a price of $ 23,000. Here German law entitles him to rescind the contract of sale under § 119 I BGB,[15] while English law would (normally) hold him to his bargain.[16] Similarly, in the example given above, the vendor who sold a Leibl painting believing it to be by Duveneck was able to rely on § 119 II BGB, whereas in English law he would have come up against the *caveat venditor* principle.[17] On the other hand, it seems that a non-fraudulently induced motivational mistake affords a ground for rescission in English, but not usually in German law. A gallery owner who, on the basis of false information in an auction catalogue, tells one of his customers that a large collection of Matisse lithographs has just been thrown onto the market and thereby leads the customer to swap one of his own Matisse lithographs for a (supposedly rarer) one by Picasso, is an innocent misrepresentor.[18] One who fails to check current auction results before offering his valuation of the lithograph may be a negligent misrepresentor if the estimate turns out

---

[15] The distinction between *Inhalts-* and *Erklärungsirrtum* (§ 119 I alt 1 and 2 BGB) does not matter for present purposes. Note that the seller may be liable to pay damages for any reliance loss that the buyer suffers: § 122 BGB. See also below, text to nn 37–43.

[16] Cf *Centrovincial Estates plc v Merchant Investors Assurance Co Ltd* [1983] Com LR 158 (CA). The result would be different only if the buyer was or ought to have been aware of the seller's mistake and deliberately exploited it in order to 'snap up' a bargain: *Hartog v Colin & Shields* [1939] 3 All ER 566 (KBD). See discussion below, text to nn 68–74, 84–92 on pp 178–79, 181–83.

[17] Cf *Tamplin v James* (1880) 15 ChD 215 (CA), where the buyer was the mistaken party and the applicable principle accordingly that of *caveat emptor*.

[18] It is not easy to think of – or indeed find in the English case law – an example of an innocently induced motivational mistake which does not concern a particular quality or characteristic of the subject-matter to which the contract relates. This should not surprise us. Statements made during pre-contractual negotiations will often be classified as mere 'opinions' or 'puffs', and reliance (causation) is harder to prove the more remotely the representation pertains to the subject-matter of the contract. Moreover, an old case suggested that not all non-fraudulent misrepresentations counted: cf n 21 below.

to be wide of the mark.[19] Although mistaken, the customer has no remedy under § 119 BGB.[20] English law, by contrast, allows him to rescind the contract of sale in equity.[21]

The question arises when, if ever, a non-fraudulent misrepresentation leads to a mistake recognized by § 119 BGB. Such a case is hard to imagine for mistakes dealt with in § 119 I BGB. Any misapprehension about the terms of the agreement (as understood by an objective outsider) will typically be shared if induced by one party's non-fraudulent misrepresentation.[22] This either entails an interpretation of the agreement in line with what both parties subjectively intended (*falsa demonstratio non nocet*),[23]

---

[19] Note, however, that a false statement about the value or market price of an object will not without more amount to a misrepresentation, especially in the context of arm's length bargaining.

[20] In appropriate circumstances, he may, however, be able to have recourse to the principles governing *Fehlen der Geschäftsgrundlage* (roughly equivalent to common mistake), now codified in § 313 BGB, or – where negligence can be established – to the doctrine of *culpa in contrahendo*, now contained in §§ 280 I, 241 II, 311 II BGB. Cf also the suggestion in *Münchener Kommentar: vol 1/1* (n 12) § 119 [113]–[122] (Kramer), outlined in n 103 (on p 186) below.

[21] Although Blackburn J in *Kennedy v Panama, New Zealand & Australian Royal Mail Co Ltd* (1867) LR 2 QB 580 (QB) 587–88, said that an innocent misrepresentation would, as in Civilian legal systems, only entitle the representee to rescind the contract if "there is a complete difference in substance ... so as to constitute a failure of consideration", ie only if it induced an *error in substantia*, his Lordship is now generally understood to have been exploring the boundaries of so-called 'common mistake' rather than delineating the scope of rescission for misrepresentation: cf the treatment of Blackburn J's *dictum* in *Bell v Lever Bros Ltd* [1932] AC 161 (HL); *Great Peace Shipping Ltd v Tsavliris Salvage (Internationa)l Ltd (The Great Peace)* [2002] EWCA Civ 1407, [2003] QB 679; see also Cartwright *Misrepresentation* (n 7) [4.37] esp fn 62. Rescission should in principle be available for any type of misrepresentation, subject only to establishing causation (cf n 18 above), and subject to the courts' discretion to award damages *in lieu* of rescission under the Misrepresentation Act 1967, s 2(2) (cf n 8 above). This is reinforced if one considers that, after *Kleinwort Benson Ltd v Lincoln City Council* [1999] 2 AC 394 (HL), representations of law will, in all likelihood, be treated no differently to representations of fact: cf Cartwright *Misrepresentation* (n 7) [3.13], [3.34]–[3.37]; D O'Sullivan, S Elliott and R Zakrzewski, *The Law of Rescission* (OUP, Oxford 2008) [4.16]–[4.18].

[22] It must not be overlooked that all cases of non-fraudulent misrepresentation are, in a sense, also common mistake cases (albeit that the mistake may not be fundamental).

[23] Cf eg RGZ 99, 147; BGH NJW 1984, 721; Cartwright *Misrepresentation* (n 7) [13.10]. The maxim is more readily applied in German than in English law. This is because of the notionally separate remedy of rectification (cf n 24 immediately below). It is currently unclear to what extent the modern principles of interpretation, outlined by Lord Hoffmann in *Investors Compensation Scheme Ltd v West Bromwich BS* [1998] 1 WLR 896 (HL) 912–13, have made the remedy of rectification redundant: cf B Häcker, "Mistakes in the Execution of Documents: Recent Cases on Rectification and Related Doctrines" (2008) 19 KLJ 293, 304–20.

or at least warrants rectification of a written document for common mistake as far as English law is concerned.[24] A significant overlap between the English law on rescission for misrepresentation and § 119 I BGB does not therefore seem to exist. However, the negligent or innocent inducement of a mistake relevant under § 119 II BGB is readily conceivable. Imagine a gallery owner who incorrectly, but in good faith, ascribes the seller's Constable to a little-known 19th century artist and thus manages to buy it at an undervalue. Assuming that this kind of shared misapprehension about a characteristic of the object sold does not already constitute a fundamental common mistake in itself sufficient to impeach the contract of sale,[25] the transferor is at any rate entitled to avoid the bargain in both legal systems.

---

[24] The most recent authoritative restatement of the requirements for 'common mistake rectification' (often also called rectification for 'mutual' mistake) was provided by Peter Gibson LJ in *Swainland Builders Ltd v Freehold Properties Ltd* [2002] EWCA Civ 560, [33]. His Lordship summarized the law as follows: "The party seeking rectification must show that: (1) the parties had a common continuing intention, whether or not amounting to an agreement, in respect of a particular matter in the instrument to be rectified; (2) there was an outward expression of accord; (3) the intention continued at the time of the execution of the instrument sought to be rectified; (4) by mistake the instrument did not reflect that common intention". Older expositions of the relevant principles are to be found in *Frederick E Rose (London) Ltd v William H Pim Junior & Co Ltd* [1953] 2 QB 450 (CA) 461–62 (Denning LJ), and in *Agip SpA v Navigazione Alta Italia SpA (The Nai Genova and The Nai Superba)* [1984] 1 Lloyd's Rep 353 (CA) 359 (Slade LJ). In German law, documents can simply be interpreted to mean what the parties subjectively intended them to mean. The maxim *falsa demonstratio non nocet* does all the work. A separate act of rectification is not required.

[25] In German law, the special rules governing *Fehlen der Geschäftsgrundlage* (lack of transactional foundation), now contained in § 313 BGB, are regarded as subsidiary to the rules on rescission, and – in any event – they do not automatically render the affected contract void. In English law, by contrast, an operative common mistake *does* render the contract void without more. However, it must be doubted whether a shared mistake as to the authorship of a painting would ever be held sufficiently fundamental. In *Bell v Lever Bros* (n 21) 224, Lord Atkin gave the following example: "A buys a picture from B; both A and B believe it to be the work of an old master, and a high price is paid. It turns out to be a modern copy. A has no remedy in the absence of representation or warranty". In *Leaf v International Galleries* (n 14) 89, Denning LJ stated: "There was a mistake about the quality of the subject-matter, because both parties believed the picture to be a Constable; and that mistake was in one sense essential or fundamental. But such a mistake does not avoid the contract: there was no mistake at all about the subject-matter of the sale". If this were correct, then Blackburn J's comments in *Kennedy v Panama, New Zealand & Australian Royal Mail Co Ltd* (cf n 21 above) could be said to represent neither the current law relating to misrepresentation, nor the law governing common mistake post *The Great Peace* (n 21). Contrast, however, *Nicholson and Venn v Smith Marriott* (1947) 177 LT 189 (KBD) 192, where Hallett J, considering a sale of table linen incorrectly (but innocently) described as having been the "authentic property" of Charles I, observed: "I think that the absence of the crest and arms of Charles I – the absence of

(iii) Conceptual basis of rescission

A final comparative observation on the grounds for rescission relates to the conceptual basis of the right to rescind a contract. For English law, with its starting point in the 'objective theory' of contracting and its commitment to the sanctity of bargains, rescission constitutes a remedy[26] exceptionally available to a person who has entered into a contract labouring under some defect of consent. It enables that person – here the transferor – to destroy the bargain and its legal effects. We have seen that the right to rescind can be described as a power *in personam* (sometimes coupled with a power *in rem*) unilaterally to divest the other party – here the transferee – of rights acquired by virtue of the contract.[27] Within the scheme classifying rights according to their causative event, the right to rescind a contract is generated by the transferee's unjust enrichment at the transferor's expense in circumstances where there is sufficient reason to disregard the maxim *pacta sunt servanda* (because the defect emanated from the transferee's sphere of responsibility). On this view of rescission, there is potentially room for a disenrichment defence. We may, for example, want to prevent the transferor from exercising his right to rescind until he makes good the transferee's reliance losses.[28] It was suggested above that, beside ensuring counter-restitution, English law's *restitutio in integrum* requirement can be fine-tuned to cater for such situations.[29]

As far as German law is concerned, it is much harder to argue for the foundation of §§ 119 ff BGB in enrichment law. This is not merely because German lawyers conceive of their law of unjustified enrichment as technically confined to §§ 812 ff BGB, but as a result of the development

---

anything attesting or appearing to attest a connection between this table linen and that monarch ... – did make the goods obtained different in substance from those which the plaintiffs sought to buy and believed that they had bought. I should be disposed therefore, though recognising the great difficulties of the point and without any undue confidence in the correctness of my judgment, to hold if necessary that there was a mutual [ie common] mistake of the kind or category calculated to vitiate the assent of the parties and therefore to enable the plaintiffs to treat themselves as not bound by the contract".

[26] Cf *Dunbar Bank plc v Nadeem* [1998] 3 All ER 876 (CA) 884 (Millett LJ).

[27] See above, Chapter IV.B.2.b (at p 107).

[28] Of course, the transferee's state of mind may be such that he is disqualified from invoking the defence, eg if he is a fraudster. *Mackenzie v Royal Bank of Canada* [1934] AC 468 (PC) suggests that even innocent misrepresentors cannot recover reliance losses beyond the return of their counter-performance. There is a question whether this case was correctly decided: see discussion in n 59 on pp 112–13. On the one hand, the defendant bank acted in good faith; on the other, its innocent misrepresentation was what induced the contract in the first place. Note that the German courts have arrived at a position which is strikingly similar to that in *Mackenzie*: see n 39 below.

[29] See above, Chapter IV.B.2.c (at pp 111–13).

of the law on rescission. In his highly influential 19th century exposition of the law of mistake, Friedrich Carl von Savigny showed a clear commitment to the 'will theory' of contract.[30] As in Roman law, a relevant *error* was to render a contract automatically void on the basis that the mistaken party's apparent agreement was not backed by his genuine volition.[31] The theoretical construction was different only for cases of fraud and duress where the defect related to the factors motivating consent (deliberate deception and improper pressure) rather than to the quality of consent.[32] The compilers of the BGB initially followed Savigny in distinguishing between the invalidity of declarations of intention affected by *error* (situations now caught by § 119 BGB) and rescission for fraud and duress (now contained in § 123 BGB).[33] However, they later decided to settle for retroactive voidability in both scenarios (cf § 142 I BGB), presumably as a concession to the 'declaratory theory' of contract.[34] Yet this conceptual alignment can hardly be understood to have completely shifted the foundation of the law on *error*. To the extent that the will theory latently survives in § 119 BGB, the exercise of the right to rescind entails not a reversal of any unjustified enrichment, but constitutes the assertion by one party that the other has – properly speaking – never obtained any contractual rights at all. The apparent declaration of intention was a mere chimera, a nullity from the outset. Only by inferring from the statutory time limit within which the nullity of a declaration of intention has to be asserted (§ 121 BGB) some legal reality of the apparent declaration can we hope to connect up § 119 BGB with the

---

[30] FC von Savigny, *System des heutigen römischen Rechts: vol 3* (Veit & Co, Berlin 1840) esp 263–307, 323–473 (Beylage VIII). Cf also the later work by E Zitelmann, *Irrtum und Rechtsgeschäft: Eine psychologisch-juristische Untersuchung* (Duncker & Humblot, Leipzig 1879).

[31] Savigny *System: vol 3* (n 30) 263–64. Savigny's theory differed slightly from that of Roman law. In Roman law, the invalidity of the contract rested on a lack of *consensus* between the parties. For Savigny, the absence of a valid 'declaration of intention' by the mistaken party was crucial: cf Flume *Rechtsgeschäft* (n 10) 440–41.

[32] Savigny *System: vol 3* (n 30) 98–120, esp 102–4, 115–17. In Roman law, fraud and duress did not render a contract void, but would afford the victim a defence (*exceptio doli/metus*) or could be asserted by means of a separate action (*actio de dolo* or *actio quod metus causa*) for damages or *restitutio in integrum*: see eg Zimmermann *Law of Obligations* (n 10) 651–58.

[33] *Entwurf eines bürgerlichen Gesetzbuches für das Deutsche Reich: Erste Lesung* (Guttentag, Berlin 1888): compare §§ 97–99 BGB-E I (mistake) with §§ 103, 112, 113 BGB-E I (fraud/duress).

[34] For an overview of the legislative history see *Historisch-kritischer Kommentar: vol 1* (n 10) §§ 142–144 [1]–[7] (Schermaier), esp [6]. A survey of the broader historical background is provided by M Harder, "Die historische Entwicklung der Anfechtbarkeit von Willenserklärungen" AcP 173 (1973) 209; P Hellwege, *Die Rückabwicklung gegenseitiger Verträge als einheitliches Problem* (Mohr Siebeck, Tübingen 2004) 435–69.

principles of unjustified enrichment.[35] In any event, § 123 BGB is the more promising point of departure for such an endeavour. Fraud inducing a 'motivational mistake' and pressure amounting to duress do not prevent a valid declaration of intention from coming into existence. Instead, they constitute unlawful infringements of a contracting party's autonomy.[36] The right to revoke a declaration of intention under § 123 BGB could therefore be described as a self-help version of the *Eingriffskondiktion*.

Whether or not the historical pedigree of § 119 BGB ultimately allows for a conceptualization in enrichment terms, it is worth noting that there are certain parallels between its 'appendix' in § 122 BGB and the disen-

[35] From the perspective of a will theorist, § 119 BGB provides for a special kind of invalidity, namely 'nullity in suspense'. At the time of the drafting of the BGB, a contemporary writer described the mechanism of rescission envisaged by the draftsmen as the exercise of a private individual's 'power' to declare a legal transaction null and void: L Jacobi, "Die fehlerhaften Rechtsgeschäfte: Ein Beitrag zur Begriffslehre des deutschen bürgerlichen Rechts" AcP 86 (1896) 51, 118 ("Die Anfechtbarkeit ist nach dem Entwurf sachlich nichts anderes als die Befugnis zu einer privaten Nichtigkeitserklärung"). If one wanted to see this 'power' as a product of the law of unjustified enrichment, then one would have to say that a declaration of intention which is not supported by the genuine volition of the party making it, though *prima facie* binding under the BGB, lacks a valid *causa* and can therefore be impeached. This would, however, be a very unusual use of the *causa* concept. Normally, the term *causa* is reserved for either the legal basis to which a transaction relates (objective sense) or the parties' purpose in effecting the transaction (subjective sense): see above, n 44 on p 27. Interestingly, Jacobi AcP 86 (above) 74–76, was already critical of the idea of 'suspended nullity', and he saw the implications for the law of unjustified enrichment: "Man hat die Anfechtbarkeit klassificiren wollen als eine Unterart der Ungültigkeit oder der Nichtigkeit, suspensiv bedingte Ungültigkeit (Nichtigkeit), resolutiv bedingte Gültigkeit; nämlich diejenige Ungültigkeit (Nichtigkeit), welche abhängig ist von einer Willenserklärung, als einem Akte der Privatautonomie. Dadurch würde aber gerade dasjenige Unterscheidungsmerkmal verwischt werden, auf welches es hier ankommt. [...] Wird ein gewisses Moment, – z.B. ein auf Irrthum beruhender Fehler im Erklärungswillen, – rechtlich nicht als Nichtigkeit oder als Ungültigkeitsgrund behandelt, sondern als Anfechtungsgrund, so ist damit anerkannt, daß dieses Moment nicht einen Thatbestandsmangel darstellt, sondern nur als außerhalb des Thatbestandes liegender Restitutionsgrund (*ex aequitate*) in Betracht kommt". ("The voidability [of a transaction] has been classified as a species of invalidity or nullity, invalidity (nullity) subject to a suspensive condition, validity subject to a resolutive condition; namely that invalidity (nullity) which is dependent on a declaration of intention as an act of private autonomy. But this [way of looking at the matter] would obscure the very distinguishing criterion which is at issue here. [...] If a particular factor – eg a defect in the declarative intent resulting from mistake – is not treated in law as a nullity or as a reason for invalidity, but instead as a ground for rescission, then this involves the recognition that this factor does not constitute a defect in the declaration itself, but [that it] can only be relevant as a ground for restitution (*ex aequitate*) external to the declaration").

[36] Cf *Motive zu dem Entwurfe eines bürgerlichen Gesetzbuches für das Deutsche Reich* (2nd edn Guttentag, Berlin 1896) vol 1, 204.

richment clause in § 818 III BGB.[37] § 122 I BGB stipulates – as another concession to the concerns of the declaratory theory – that a party avoiding a contract under § 119 BGB is liable to the extent of the other party's reliance loss.[38] Liability is strict, but limited by the other's expectation interest (§ 122 I BGB), and it is altogether excluded if the other party knew or ought to have known of the mistake (§ 122 II BGB).[39] In practice, therefore, expenditure incurred by an innocent transferee in reliance on the validity of the contract, ie before he learns of the transferor's right to rescind, can be recovered in German as well as perhaps in English law.[40] However, despite the similar objectives of § 122 BGB and § 818 III BGB, the fact that the former provision is widely regarded as related to the doctrine of *culpa in contrahendo* or as imposing strict liability for risk-creation,[41] coupled with its negligence threshold of disqualification,[42] is evidence that the provision is not quite the same as the ordinary disenrichment defence.[43]

b) The Broader Picture

Confining the discussion on the scope of recovery in the contractual context to a comparison of the grounds for rescission and their theoretical

---

[37] The resemblance between § 122 and § 818 III BGB was already noted by A v Tuhr, "Zur Lehre von der ungerechtfertigten Bereicherung" in *Aus Römischem und Bürgerlichem Recht: Ernst Immanuel Bekker zum 16. August 1907* (Hof-Buchdruckerei, Weimar 1907) 291, 293–97, 313–20. More recently: B Rengier, "Wegfall der Bereicherung" AcP 177 (1977) 418, 430–36. Cf also T Krebs, *Restitution at the Crossroads: A Comparative Study* (Cavendish, London 2001) 42.

[38] § 122 BGB does not apply to rescission for fraud or duress under § 123 BGB, though an analogous application is discussed for cases where the illegitimate pressure is exerted by a third party: cf *Münchener Kommentar: vol 1/1* (n 12) § 123 [48] (Kramer).

[39] Interestingly, the fact that the mistake (under § 119 II BGB: cf text to nn 22–25) was induced, even if innocently, by the party suffering the reliance loss can also lead to a disqualification: RGZ 81, 395, 398–99. This is best explained on the basis of the parties' respective spheres of risk: cf n 41 below.

[40] On the position in English law see above, n 28 and corresponding text.

[41] Cf *Motive* (n 36) vol 1, 195. On the doctrine of *culpa in contrahendo* see above, Chapter III.E.2 (at pp 95–96). The justification and scope of liability for reliance losses changed during the drafting of the BGB. While the focus was initially on the rescinding party's fault ('*Deliktsprinzip*'), it later shifted to the mere causation of loss ('*Veranlassungsprinzip*'). Subsequently, an analysis in terms of spheres of risk ('*Sphärentheorie*') has found favour: eg CW Canaris, *Die Vertrauenshaftung im deutschen Privatrecht* (Beck, München 1971) 479–90, 532–39; Flume *Rechtsgeschäft* (n 10) 422–24. For a recent defence of the *culpa in contrahendo* approach see T Lobinger, *Rechtsgeschäftliche Verpflichtung und autonome Bindung* (Mohr Siebeck, Tübingen 1999) 207–18.

[42] Compare § 122 II BGB with §§ 819 I, 818 IV BGB.

[43] Note, moreover, that the effect of rescission, ie the actual avoidance of the contract in pursuance of which any performances will have been rendered, is not *conditional* on the payment of reliance damages, though a right of retention will often exist.

foundation would leave the picture incomplete. Some defects of consent or the situations in which they arise may be recognized as relevant by both legal systems, with only one using the rescission mechanism to deal with them. The question is where such 'hidden' overlaps occur. To answer it, we will have to explore four main areas: the category of identity mistakes, cases where there is a mistake as to the terms of a contractual agreement known to the other party, undue influence scenarios, and cases of motivational mistakes induced by negligent misrepresentation.

(i) Mistakes as to the identity of the other party

As a starting point, we can tentatively observe that a mistake about the identity of the other contracting party (*error in persona*) furnishes a ground for rescission in German law (under § 119 I BGB), while in English law it can prevent a contract from coming into existence in the first place.[44]

Before, however, making an assessment of 'hidden overlaps' between the two legal systems, it will be convenient to explore the boundaries of the English doctrine. *Cundy v Lindsay*,[45] *Ingram v Little*,[46] and – most recently – *Shogun Finance Ltd v Hudson*,[47] are the leading cases. They tread a notoriously fine line between operative identity mistakes and irrelevant mistakes about a person's attributes (especially his creditworthiness). Contrasting the outcome in *Ingram v Little*, where the claimant vendors' mistake about the purchaser's identity was regarded as sufficiently fundamental to render the contract of sale null and void, with that in cases like *Lewis v Averay*,[48] where it was not, highlights this. Unlike in German law, where the exact nature of the mistake usually determines no more than its qualification as *error in persona* under § 119 I BGB or as *Eigenschaftsirrtum* under § 119 II BGB,[49] it can turn out to be crucial in English law, especially in relation to third party purchasers for value.[50]

---

[44] Since mistakes about the identity of the object to which the contract relates (category of *error in obiecto/corpore*) are essentially no different from other mistakes about the (main) terms of an agreement, they will not be specifically considered here. The reader is referred to the discussion in section B.1.b.ii of the present chapter (pp 178–83).

[45] (1878) 3 App Cas 459 (HL). See pp 120, 136–37 above.

[46] [1961] 1 QB 31 (CA). See p 120 above.

[47] [2003] UKHL 62, [2004] 1 AC 919.

[48] [1972] 1 QB 198 (CA). Similar: *Phillips v Brooks Ltd* [1919] 2 KB 243 (KBD).

[49] A person's creditworthiness is generally regarded as an essential characteristic in all but cash transactions: RGZ 66, 385, 387–89; W Lindacher, "Rechte des vorleistungspflichtigen Verkäufers bei anfänglicher Kreditunwürdigkeit des Käufers" MDR 1977, 797–98; *Münchener Kommentar: vol 1/1* (n 12) [129] (Kramer). Critical: Flume *Rechtsgeschäft* (n 10) 486–87, arguing *e contrario* from § 321 BGB.

[50] Contrast the outcome of *Ingram v Little* (n 46) with that in *Lewis v Averay* (n 48), and see below, Chapter VI.C.1 (at pp 228–33). In German law, the protection of third

Unsurprisingly, the distinction between identity mistakes and mistakes as to attributes has come under attack.[51] Given the forceful dissenting speeches in *Shogun Finance Ltd v Hudson*,[52] its survival to this day was a close call. The majority of their Lordships upheld *Cundy v Lindsay* only on the basis that, in written communications, an identity mistake normally leads to a lack of correspondence between offer and acceptance.[53] *Ingram v Little* was doubted.[54] At least in face-to-face dealings, therefore, mistakes as to the identity of the other contracting party seem to be a thing of the past. A person must be taken to contract with the individual physically present in all but the most exceptional circumstances.

The majority's reasoning in *Shogun Finance v Hudson* exposes the true rationale behind the case law on identity mistakes. Where such a mistake is made out, it is not its existence *as such* which prevents the contract being validly concluded, but the fact that the other party is aware of it.[55] Indeed, all of the leading precedents involved deliberate deception. In each case, the fraudster knew that his victim was intending to deal with somebody else. Under these circumstances, the 'objective principle', by which we normally determine whether offer and acceptance correspond,[56] is modified to take account of his special knowledge. The reason why the identity

---

party purchasers is provided for by the principle of abstraction, or – in the last resort – by the rules on *bona fide* purchase: see below, Chapter VI.B.1 (pp 216–19).

[51] Eg Law Reform Committee, *Twelfth Report: Transfer of Title to Chattels* (Cmnd 2958, 1966) [13], [15]; *Lewis v Averay* (n 48) 206 (Lord Denning MR): "Again it has been suggested that a mistake as to the identity of a person is one thing; and a mistake as to his attributes is another. A mistake as to identity, it is said, avoids a contract; whereas a mistake as to attributes does not. But this is a distinction without a difference. A man's very name is one of his attributes. It is also a key to his identity. If then, he gives a false name, is it a mistake as to his identity? or a mistake as to his attributes? These fine distinctions do no good to the law".

[52] [2003] UKHL 62, [2004] 1 AC 919, [1]–[41] (Lord Nicholls), [56]–[110] (Lord Millett).

[53] Ibid [47], [50], [55] (Lord Hobhouse); [170] (Lord Phillips); [183], [188] (Lord Walker). For a powerful defence of the majority's reasoning see R Stevens, "Objectivity, Mistake and the Parol Evidence Rule" in A Burrows and E Peel (eds), *Contract Terms* (OUP, Oxford 2007) 101.

[54] Cf esp [2003] UKHL 62, [2004] 1 AC 919, [185], where Lord Walker (one of the majority) stated: "I consider that *Ingram v Little* was wrongly decided".

[55] Unfortunately, this is not always spelt out as clearly as it should be. Cartwright *Misrepresentation* (n 7) [14.15]–[14.16], explains how the influence of Continental jurisprudence (especially the writings of Pothier) may account for too subjective an approach within the English law on identity mistakes.

[56] On the 'objective principle' generally see the debate between Howarth and Vorster: W Howarth, "The Meaning of Objectivity in Contract" (1984) 100 LQR 265; JP Vorster, "A Comment on the Meaning of Objectivity in Contract" (1987) 103 LQR 274; W Howarth, "A Note on the Objective of Objectivity in Contract" (1987) 103 LQR 527.

mistake in cases like *Cundy v Lindsay* and *Ingram v Little* rendered the contract 'void' was because, from the fraudster's perspective, the victim's communication could not be understood as being addressed to him. We must therefore conclude that purely spontaneous identity mistakes which are unknown to the other party (and which are not evident on the face of any relevant document)[57] never prevent a valid contract from coming into existence under English law.[58] In neither case is there any room for rescission.[59] Nor is there a compelling reason why identity mistakes should be treated like mistakes as to attributes.[60] The question of third party protection is best solved via a reform of the rules on *bona fide* purchase,[61] and since a fraudster cannot set up his own fraud as a defence to an action, the victim always has the option of holding him to the otherwise void contract if this seems advantageous.[62]

In the light of what has just been said about the treatment of identity mistakes in English law, it will become evident that 'hidden overlaps' with rescission for *error in persona* under § 119 I BGB are practically impossible. Not only is the English doctrine much narrower than first meets the eye, but one must additionally bear in mind that § 119 I BGB is of little or no relevance as far as cases of identity fraud are concerned.[63] Where a person contracts under the pretence of being a specific third party, German law has recourse to the principles governing 'actions under the name of

---

57 Under the so-called 'parol evidence rule', extrinsic evidence cannot be used to vary, add to, or contradict the terms of a written instrument (the rule may no longer be an evidential one, but should now better be regarded as a principle of interpretation). Stevens in *Contract Terms* (n 53) esp 110–13, explains *Cundy v Lindsay* (n 45) and *Shogun Finance v Hudson* (n 47), where the relevant parties had only corresponded by writing, as applications of the rule.

58 See Cartwright *Misrepresentation* (n 7) [14.17]; AL Goodhart, "Mistake as to Identity in the Law of Contract" (1941) 57 LQR 228, 235–38; E Peel, *Treitel: The Law of Contract* (12th edn Sweet & Maxwell, London 2007) [8–050]; G Williams, "Mistake as to Party in the Law of Contract" (1945) 23 Can Bar Rev 271, 380–81. Stevens in *Contract Terms* (n 53) 119–21, distinguishes between identity mistakes in the contractual context (operative only when known to the other party) and in the context of conveyances by delivery (always operative according to Stevens).

59 In identity mistake cases, the contract is either void for lack of correspondence between offer and acceptance (if the mistake is known to the other party), or it is fully valid (if the mistake is not known: it is hard to conceive of an identity mistake being induced by the other party's non-fraudulent misrepresentation).

60 Equation of the two was the preferred solution of the minority in *Shogun Finance v Hudson*: cf n 52 above.

61 See below, Chapter VI.D.1.b (pp 255–56).

62 Stevens in *Contract Terms* (n 53) 117; Williams (1945) 23 Can Bar Rev (n 58) 396.

63 Indeed, like English law, German law might struggle to explain how A's declaration of intention, which B knows is not directed to him, can ever be validly 'accepted' by B (*as B*) so as to bring a contract between A and B into existence: but cf n 66 below.

another' (*Handeln unter fremdem Namen*), to which the rules of 'unauthorized agency' (*Vertretung ohne Vertretungsmacht*) in §§ 177 ff BGB apply by analogy.[64] If B, by letter, orders a painting from art dealer A, pretending to be a well-known and reputable lawyer C, C has the option of ratifying the transaction and adopting it as his own.[65] A case like *Cundy v Lindsay* would thus not be decided under § 119 I BGB (nor indeed under § 123 I BGB), and our enquiry into 'hidden overlaps' between this provision and the English law on mistakes as to the identity of the other party ultimately returns an empty set.[66]

(ii) Mistakes as to the terms of a contractual agreement known to the other party

The preceding discussion about identity mistakes leads to a more general question about the treatment of situations in which one party knows that the other is mistaken about the terms of an envisaged contract (without having induced that mistake).[67] How much scope – if any – is there for 'hidden overlaps' between § 119 I BGB and cases where, on a proper interpretation of offer and acceptance, no contract is concluded under English law?

The leading case is *Smith v Hughes*.[68] The defendant racehorse trainer had agreed to buy oats from the claimant farmer in the erroneous belief that they were old oats (which he needed to feed the horses), when in fact they were new. He refused to pay the purchase price upon discovering this. Remitting the case for a retrial, the Court of Queen's Bench drew a distinction between two situations. If the defendant's mistake concerned no more than a characteristic of the oats he was buying, without making their age a

---

64 Cf Flume *Rechtsgeschäft* (n 10) 459.

65 Cf §§ 177 I, 184 I BGB. Only if C refuses to ratify the transaction can A demand performance or, at his option, claim damages from the imposter B: § 179 I BGB.

66 §§ 177 ff BGB would not seem to apply where B knows that a declaration of intention is (contrary to objective appearances) not addressed to him, but where he does not know with whom A actually wishes to contract. In such a case of *error in persona*, there is no relevant 'impersonation', either actively or by acquiescence. Although it is arguable that no agreement at all is reached in this scenario (cf n 63 above), the preferable solution for practical purposes may lie in regarding the contract as concluded and giving A the option to avoid it under § 119 I BGB (without liability under § 122 BGB). This provides a straightforward means of allowing A to hold B to the contract if he so chooses. If this latter approach were adopted, there would be a small area of 'hidden overlaps'.

67 Induced mistakes about the terms of an agreement have already been addressed. They lead to the application of the maxim *falsa demonstratio non nocet* or rectification (in English law): see above, text to nn 22–24, where this is spelt out in relation to non-fraudulent misrepresentation.

68 (1871) LR 6 QB 597 (QB).

term of the contract, his incorrect assumption was a mere 'motive'[69] and not relevant unless actively induced by the other party's misrepresentation.[70] If, on the other hand, the defendant's error lay in believing that the claimant was warranting the oats to be old (ie that the offer contained a term to this effect), and if the claimant was aware of this,[71] then – according to the conventional understanding of *Smith v Hughes* – there would not have been a contract.[72] This is because the claimant could then not have insisted on a strictly objective interpretation of the defendant's apparent agreement.[73] Where one party's offer and the other party's purported acceptance of it (each as interpreted from the perspective of the reasonable person in the parties' positions and imbued with their knowledge) do not match, English law regards them as simply not being *ad idem* about the terms and conditions of their bargain.[74]

---

[69] (1871) LR 6 QB 597, 606 (Cockburn CJ).

[70] As Blackburn J explained (ibid 606–7): "I agree that even if the vendor was aware that the purchaser thought that the article possessed [a particular] quality, and would not have entered into the contract unless he had so thought, still the purchaser is bound, unless the vendor was guilty of some fraud or deceit upon him, and that a mere abstinence from disabusing the purchaser of that impression is not fraud or deceit; for, whatever may be the case in a court of morals, there is no legal obligation on the vendor to inform the purchaser that he is under a mistake, not induced by the act of the vendor".

[71] Subsequent cases have suggested that the rationale of *Smith v Hughes* extends beyond actual knowledge. It seems to be sufficient that one party ought reasonably to have known of the other's mistake about the terms of the contract: cf the *obiter dicta* in *Centrovincial Estates plc v Merchant Investors Assurance Co Ltd* [1983] Com LR 158 (CA). See also *Scriven Bros & Co v Hindley & Co* [1913] 3 KB 564 (KBD), where the conduct of the auctioneer acting for the claimant contributed to the defendant's mistake.

[72] Cf (1871) LR 6 QB 597, 611 (Hannen J): "In order to relieve the defendant it was necessary that the jury should find not merely that the plaintiff believed the defendant to believe that he was buying old oats, but that he believed the defendant to believe that he, the plaintiff, was contracting to sell old oats". Although the parties' contract is, in such a case, commonly assumed to be 'void', it is worth noting that Hannen J in *Smith v Hughes* did not actually say this: cf the passage from his judgment set out in n 86 below.

[73] In *Hartog v Colin & Shields* [1939] 3 All ER 566 (KBD), the defendant sellers of hare skins mistakenly offered them at a price *per pound* instead of *per piece* (there being approximately three pieces to the pound). Singleton J found that the claimant purchaser, who was also in the trade and knew that hare skins were customarily sold by the piece, must have realized the sellers' mistake, and held that he was not entitled to 'snap up' the bargain under these circumstances.

[74] (1871) LR 6 QB 597, 607 (Blackburn J): "I apprehend that if one of the parties intends to make a contract on one set of terms, and the other intends to make a contract on another set of terms, or, as it is sometimes expressed, the parties are not ad idem, there is no contract, unless the circumstances are such as to preclude one of the parties from denying that he has agreed to the terms of the other". On the latter qualification see below, text to n 86. The classic example of a case where lack of *consensus ad idem* prevented the conclusion of a valid contract, an example to which Hannen J in *Smith v*

Prima facie, one might assume that there must be cases which English law solves by means of this principle, while German law can be content to have recourse to its law on rescission under § 119 I BGB. After all, § 122 II BGB expressly envisages the possibility of one party recognizing the other's mistake. It provides that the rescinding party's liability to compensate the other for his or her reliance losses (§ 122 I BGB) does not arise if the party suffering the loss knew or ought to have known of the ground for rescission. Yet the impression that there may be significant 'hidden overlaps' between the *Smith v Hughes* principle and § 119 I BGB once again turns out to be fallacious. Recall our example in which the seller of a painting, A, mistypes his offer (asking $ 23,000 instead of $ 32,000 for it),[75] and assume that the buyer, B, realizes this. Neither legal system will allow B to 'snap up' the bargain and insist on delivery for only $ 23,000 (or to refuse appropriate restitution after delivery), but the reason is *not* that German law affords A a right to rescind while English law holds the contract void.

Let us look at German law first. Although our case could be solved via §§ 119 I, 122 II BGB, German law tends to deal with the issue as one of contractual interpretation.[76] Interpretation is logically prior to rescission,[77] and it is generally thought to go a long way. Where B knows on what terms A intends to contract ($ 32,000),[78] the doctrine of *falsa demonstratio non nocet* ensures that the agreement is concluded on A's intended terms, even if B's intention accords with the terms as they would appear to an outsider ($ 23,000), and even if B has in no way contributed to A's mistake.[79] The existence of § 122 II BGB, it is argued, does not necessarily militate against this approach, given that the disqualification envisaged by the provision can still operate where the other party's knowledge super-

Hughes expressly referred (ibid at 609), is *Raffles v Wichelhaus* (1864) 2 Hurl & C 906, 159 ER 375. Compare the German rules on *Dissens* in §§ 154, 155 BGB.

[75] See above, text to nn 15–16.

[76] The interpretation of contracts is governed by §§ 133, 157 BGB.

[77] See eg RGZ 85, 322, 324; Flume *Rechtsgeschäft* (n 10) 417–18.

[78] On the case where the buyer does not know what the seller's true intention is see below, n 81 and corresponding text.

[79] See eg RGZ 66, 427; BGH NJW 1959, 1363; BGH NJW 1984, 721; BGH NJW-RR 1995, 859; J von Staudinger (Begr), *J von Staudingers Kommentar zum Bürgerlichen Gesetzbuch: §§ 90–133* (Neubearbeitung 2004: Sellier de Guyter, Berlin 2004) § 133 [13] (Singer); Flume *Rechtsgeschäft* (n 10) 301. More restrictive: K Larenz and M Wolf, *Allgemeiner Teil des Bürgerlichen Rechts* (9th edn Beck, München 2004) 518, who would apply the *falsa demonstratio* doctrine only where B's conduct can be interpreted as indicating his subjective agreement and who would otherwise refer A to rescission under § 119 I BGB .

venes *after* the contract has been concluded.[80] Such a contract has to be rescinded. One might add that there is scope for the application of §§ 119 I, 122 II BGB in two further scenarios. First, where B is aware that A does not intend to contract for $ 23,000, but does not know what figure A actually has in mind.[81] Second, where B ought to realize that A is mistaken, but does not in fact realize it.[82]

In English law, there is markedly more scepticism about imposing on a contracting party a bargain which he neither objectively agreed to (at least from a 'fly on the wall' perspective) nor subjectively intended.[83] The fact that B cannot enforce the contract of sale at a price of $ 23,000 does not mean that A can enforce it at a price of $ 32,000, even where B recognized A's mistake. As the traditional understanding of *Smith v Hughes* indicates, there may simply be no contract at all. However, it is not entirely clear that English law never employs the maxim *falsa demonstratio non nocet*.[84] The guidance given by the Court of Queen's Bench in *Smith v Hughes* is consistent with the argument that the claimant farmer would have been bound by a warranty had he known that the defendant racehorse trainer had misunderstood his offer to contain one.[85] Indeed, Blackburn J observed that "if the parties are not ad idem, there is no contract, *unless the circumstances are such as to preclude one of the parties from denying that he has agreed*

---

[80] Cf A Trupp, "Die Bedeutung des § 133 BGB für die Auslegung von Willenserklärungen" NJW 1990, 1346, 1347.

[81] Affording A a right to rescind under § 119 I BGB would appear to be preferable to either (1) holding B to A's intended price of $ 32,000, of which B knew nothing, or (2) treating the contract as not having been concluded at all. On the parallel case in the context of A's *error in persona* cf above, comment in n 66.

[82] BGH NJW 1959, 1363; Flume *Rechtsgeschäft* (n 10) 302. This solution is preferable to the application of the *falsa demonstratio* maxim, which is what the approach advocated by Trupp NJW 1990 (n 80) entails. B's negligence in not spotting A's (probably negligent!) typing error would otherwise have disproportionately harsh consequences.

[83] Cf eg *Byrnlea Property Investments Ltd v Ramsay* [1969] 2 QB 253 (CA) 265 (Lord Denning MR): "A mistake made by one party to the knowledge of the other is a ground for avoiding a contract, but not for making one".

[84] Cf the discussion by Cartwright *Misrepresentation* (n 7) [13.04]–[13.19].

[85] *Treitel on Contract* (n 58) [8–051]. J Beatson, *Anson's Law of Contract* (28th edn OUP, Oxford 2002) 326, applies this reasoning to *Hartog v Colin & Shields* (n 73) and suggests that the defendant sellers could have enforced the contract on the basis of a price per piece of hare skins. Similar: H Beale (gen ed), *Chitty on Contracts* (29th edn Sweet & Maxwell, London 2004) vol 1, [5–068] (Beale). This view is not shared by Cartwright *Misrepresentation* (n 7) [13.28] fn 80 ("[T]he defendant could not have shown that there was in fact a contract at prices 'per piece', because there was no offer and acceptance on those terms"); SA Smith, *Atiyah's Introduction to the Law of Contract* (6th edn OUP, Oxford 2006) 78 fn 94 ("It cannot be assumed that the claimant would have been willing to contract on the terms the defendant had intended to offer").

to the terms of the other".[86] Yet the authority he cited in support of this proposition was a case of 'estoppel by representation',[87] for which mere acquiescence in another party's self-deception is not ordinarily enough.[88] The only other indication we have of an increasing willingness to enforce the contract on the mistaken party's terms is the recent spate of cases on so-called 'unilateral mistake rectification'.[89] These suggest that if B signs his name to A's written offer (stated to be for $ 23,000) in the knowledge that A intended the purchase price to be $ 32,000, then the document may later be rectified to read $ 32,000.[90] What is, at any rate, reasonably clear is that neither interpretation nor rectification will avail A where B did not

---

[86] (1871) LR 6 QB 597, 607 (emphasis added). His Lordship continued (ibid): "If, whatever a man's real intention may be, he so conducts himself that a reasonable man would believe that he was assenting to the terms proposed by the other party, and that other party upon that belief enters into the contract with him, the man thus conducting himself would be equally bound as if he had intended to agree with the other party's terms". Cf also Hannen J's statement to the same effect (ibid at 610): "If ... the plaintiff knew that the defendant, in dealing with him for oats, did so on the assumption that the plaintiff was contracting to sell him old oats, he was aware that the defendant apprehended the contract in a different sense to that in which he meant it, and he is thereby *deprived of the right to insist that the defendant shall be bound by that which was only the apparent, and not the real bargain*" (emphasis added).

[87] *Freeman v Cooke* (1848) 2 Exch Rep 654, 154 ER 652.

[88] There are two further problems with invoking the doctrine of estoppel. First, estoppel does not normally give rise to a cause of action, but provides merely a defence (and so cannot cater for all cases). Second, an estoppel will not normally be raised in the absence of detrimental reliance by the other party: cf Cartwright *Misrepresentation* (n 7) [13.11], who does not find the analogy helpful for these reasons.

[89] The doctrine was only developed during the second half of the 20th century. Its classic exposition is contained in Buckley LJ's judgment in *Thomas Bates & Son Ltd v Wyndham's (Lingerie) Ltd* [1981] 1 WLR 505 (CA) 515–16: "For this doctrine ... to apply I think it must be shown: first, that one party A erroneously believed that the document sought to be rectified contained a particular term or provision, or possibly did not contain a particular term or provision which, mistakenly, it did contain; secondly, that the other party B was aware of the omission or inclusion and that it was due to a mistake on the part of A; thirdly, that B has omitted to draw the mistake to the notice of A. And I think that there must be a fourth element involved, namely, that the mistake must be one calculated to benefit B. If these requirements are satisfied, the court may regard it as inequitable to allow B to resist rectification to give effect to A's intention on the ground that the mistake was not, at the time of execution of the document, a mutual [ie common] mistake." On the much older doctrine of 'common mistake rectification' see n 24 above.

[90] Note the more restrictive approach adopted by D McLauchlan, "The 'Drastic' Remedy of Rectification for Unilateral Mistake" (2008) 124 LQR 608, 617–21, who argues (at 620) that "where there is no such conduct [ie misleading conduct before or at the time of the signing of the contract giving rise to an estoppel] and the situation involves mere awareness of the mistake, the non-mistaken party ought not to be held to a contract that he did not intend to make. The most that the mistaken party can seek is avoidance of the agreement on the basis that no contract was formed".

know what price A had in mind,[91] or where B ought to have spotted A's error, but negligently failed to do so.[92] In these very limited categories of case, there will probably be 'hidden overlaps' between § 119 I BGB and contracts void for lack of correspondence between offer and acceptance in English law.[93]

(iii) Undue influence and immoral exploitation

The third scenario displays what could be described as the reverse pattern of the 'hidden overlaps' considered so far. Here English law furnishes a ground for rescission, while German law may hold the contract void without more. Recall our example of the transferor entering into a contract with the transferee in circumstances where a close relationship of trust and confidence exists between the parties and leads to the transferor's will being overborne by some form of emotional or other attachment. This situation, a typical example of undue influence as far as English law is concerned, can in certain circumstances be classified by German law as one of immoral exploitation under § 138 BGB.[94]

The match is by no means exact. Not all instances of undue influence are caught by § 138 BGB. On the one hand, it is improbable that a transferee such as the Mother Superior in *Allcard v Skinner*,[95] whose complete lack of moral blameworthiness was expressly noted by the court, would be regarded as having exploited the transferor *contra bonos mores*.[96] On the other hand, § 138 BGB generally requires the contract in question to be economically disadvantageous for the transferor, whereas undue influence in English law is in principle capable of encompassing even economically

---

[91] Cf McLaughlan (2008) 124 LQR (n 90) 619, but contrast *Chitty on Contracts* (n 85) vol 1, [5–072] (Beale).

[92] In *Centrovincial Estates plc v Merchant Investors Assurance Co Ltd* [1983] Com LR 159 (CA), it was suggested, albeit *obiter*, that a contract would not be validly concluded where one party ought reasonably to have known of the other's mistake about the contract price: cf n 71 above. The question whether B should be held to A's terms despite not having positive knowledge of A's mistake is considered in *Chitty on Contracts* (n 85) vol 1, [5–074] (Beale). On balance, the better view is that the contract is void.

[93] On the relevant German law see above, nn 81–82 and corresponding text.

[94] See above, Chapter III.B.4 (pp 63–64).

[95] (1887) 36 ChD 145 (CA), discussed in the text after n 237 on pp 145–46 above. Note that this was a case of gift, not one of 'contract' under English law.

[96] Although § 138 BGB can apply even in the absence of any reprehensible intention on the part of the transferee, the provision does not protect the transferor's contractual autonomy as such: cf S Lorenz, *Der Schutz vor dem unerwünschten Vertrag: Eine Untersuchung von Möglichkeiten und Grenzen der Abschlußkontrolle im geltenden Recht* (Beck, München 1997) 245–59.

neutral transactions.[97] The more restrictive German approach should not surprise us: where the invalidity of a transaction follows *ipso iure*, a legal system has to be much more careful about impeaching it than where the affected party is afforded a choice whether or not to let it stand (ie a right to rescind).[98]

(iv) Negligent misrepresentation and culpa in contrahendo

Finally, we must turn to negligent misrepresentation. A ground for rescission in English law, the negligent inducement by the transferee of a 'motivational' mistake in the transferor's mind which causes the latter to contract will usually only be relevant under the doctrine of *culpa in contrahendo* in German law.[99] While technically classified as quasi-contractual, *culpa in contrahendo* constitutes in essence a (non-delictual) wrongs-based liability, requiring the representor to put the representee into the position he would have been in had the negligent misstatement not been made in pre-contractual negotiations. Specific reinstatement being the primary remedy (cf § 249 I BGB), the transferor has a personal claim to annulment of the contract if he would not have entered into it but for the transferee's negligent misrepresentation. *Culpa in contrahendo* therefore to a degree fills what is sometimes perceived as a lacuna in German law between § 123 I alt 1 BGB (fraud: *arglistige Täuschung*) and § 119 BGB (mistake: *Irrtum*).[100] However, it does so only incompletely. It is widely assumed not to be able to cater for situations in which the representee has

---

[97] Lorenz *Schutz vor dem unerwünschten Vertrag* (n 96) 387–510, esp 445–53, argues that German law should use the doctrine of *culpa in contrahendo* to protect a party's autonomy from exploitation even in the absence of any disproportionality between performance and counter-performance (*Überrumpelungsschutz*). He uses English undue influence cases to support his view: ibid 453–87. In *Royal Bank of Scotland plc v Etridge (No 2)* [2001] UKHL 44, [2002] 2 AC 773, which contains the most recent authoritative restatement of the principles governing undue influence, Lord Nicholls explained the relevance of a financial disadvantage as follows (at [12]): "In *CIBC Mortgages plc v Pitt* [1994] 1 AC 200 your Lordships' House decided that in cases of undue influence disadvantage is not a necessary ingredient of the cause of action. It is not essential that the transaction should be disadvantageous to the pressurised or influenced person, either in financial terms or in any other way. However, in the nature of things, questions of undue influence will not usually arise, and the exercise of undue influence is unlikely to occur, where the transaction is innocuous. The issue is likely to arise only when, in some respect, the transaction was disadvantageous either from the outset or as matters turned out".

[98] Cf Lorenz *Schutz vor dem unerwünschten Vertrag* (n 96) 251.

[99] See above, Chapter III.E.2 (pp 94–97). Induced mistakes which fall under § 119 II BGB are discussed in the present chapter: cf text after n 24. They may, of course, also give rise to a claim for *culpa in contrahendo*, as is made clear by BGH NJW 1998, 898.

[100] Cf *Münchener Kommentar: vol 1/1* (n 12) § 119 [121] (Kramer).

suffered no economic detriment through contracting.[101] Moreover, we have seen that the remedial consequences of *culpa in contrahendo* (§§ 249 ff BGB) deviate from those entailed by rescission (§§ 812 ff BGB or §§ 985 ff BGB) in a number of important respects.[102]

This circumstance has prompted some authors to suggest that there is a better way of covering the middle ground between rescission for fraud (§ 123 BGB) and for mistake (§ 119 BGB). Most notably among them, Hans Christoph Grigoleit argues for an analogous application of § 123 I alt 1 BGB to instances of negligent misrepresentation (*fahrlässige Täuschung*).[103] He contends that the gradual erosion of the BGB's com-

---

[101] BGH NJW 1998, 302; BGH NJW 1998, 898; OLG Celle NJW-RR 2006, 1283. The requirement of an economic detriment has recently been attenuated through an increasing subjectivization: cf BGH NJW 1998, 302, 304: "Wird jemand durch ein haftungsbegründendes Verhalten zum Abschluß eines Vertrages gebracht, den er sonst nicht geschlossen hätte, kann er auch bei objektiver Werthaltigkeit von Leistung und Gegenleistung dadurch einen Vermögensschaden erleiden, daß die Leistung für seine Zwecke nicht voll brauchbar ist [...] Die Bejahung eines Vermögensschadens unter diesem Aspekt setzt allerdings voraus, daß die durch den unerwünschten Vertrag erlangte Leistung nicht nur aus rein subjektiver willkürlicher Sicht als Schaden angesehen wird, sondern daß auch die Verkehrsanschauung bei Berücksichtigung der obwaltenden Umstände den Vertragsschluß als unvernünftig, den konkreten Vermögensinteressen nicht angemessen und damit als nachteilig ansieht". ("If a person is induced by means of actionable wrongdoing to enter into a contract which he would not otherwise have entered into, it is possible for him to suffer an economic detriment by virtue of the fact that the performance is not wholly of use for his purposes, even if it is objectively worth its price. [...] However, the finding of an economic detriment on this approach requires the performance obtained by virtue of the unwanted contract not only to be regarded as detrimental from a purely subjective and individual point of view. Instead, the conclusion of the contract has to be regarded as irrational, as unsuitable for the individual's specific financial interests and thus as detrimental from the perspective of a reasonable person taking account of all the circumstances of the case"). This principle has since been endorsed in the context of delictual claims by BGHZ 160, 149, 153; BGHZ 162, 306, 310. Lorenz *Schutz vor dem unerwünschten Vertrag* (n 96) esp 388–90, wants to dispense with the requirement of an economic detriment altogether, arguing that the unwanted contract is in itself sufficiently detrimental. A number of authors share his point of view (see the references in n 178 on p 96), which can now draw some support from the wording of the new § 311 II BGB, requiring parties to have regard to one another's 'interests' (*Interessen*) during precontractual negotiations. Critical: W Krüger, "Vertragsrückabwicklung im Wege des Schadensersatzes" in R Bork, T Hoeren and P Pohlmann (eds), *Recht und Risiko: Festschrift für Helmut Kollhosser zum 70. Geburtstag* (VVW, Karlsruhe 2004) vol 2, 329, esp 334–40; M Lieb, "Culpa in contrahendo und rechtsgeschäftliche Entscheidungsfreiheit" in V Beuthien, M Fuchs and others (eds), *Festschrift für Dieter Medicus: Zum 70. Geburtstag* (Heymanns, Köln 1999) 337, 343–47.

[102] See above, Chapter III.E.2 (at pp 96–97).

[103] HC Grigoleit, *Vorvertragliche Informationshaftung: Vorsatzdogma, Rechtsfolgen, Schranken* (Beck, München 1997) 137–52; HC Grigoleit, "Abstraktion und Willensmängel: Die Anfechtbarkeit des Verfügungsgeschäfts" AcP 199 (1999) 379, 406–7;

mitment to the principle that liability – for what is, after all, pure economic loss – will only be imposed where one party intentionally misleads another ('*informationelles Vorsatzdogma*') warrants such an extension.[104] From a comparative perspective, Grigoleit's proposal represents a move towards the 'procedural' or 'process-oriented' approach espoused so distinctly by English law.[105] He justifies the right to rescind by how the mistake came about, namely inducement by the other party, not the 'substantive' quality of the mistake. Yet two important restrictions remain. They highlight that Grigoleit does not adopt the 'process-oriented' approach wholesale. Firstly, his insistence on a negligent inducement of the contract excludes purely innocent misrepresentations.[106] This can be explained by reference to the unity of the legal system: while the BGB may have overcome its earlier insistence on intentional conduct,[107] it does not dispense with a breach of duty.[108] Secondly, he expressly rejects the possibility of rescinding the *Verfügungsgeschäft*, which in our example is the conveyance of the

HC Grigoleit, "Neuere Tendenzen zur schadensrechtlichen Vertragsaufhebung" NJW 1999, 900, 902–4; HC Grigoleit, "Reformperspektiven der vorvertraglichen Informationshaftung" in R Schulze and H Schulte-Nölke (eds), *Die Schuldrechtsreform vor dem Hintergrund des Gemeinschaftsrechts* (Mohr Siebeck, Tübingen 2001) 269, esp 281–85. Similar: P Mankowski, *Beseitigungsrechte: Anfechtung, Widerruf und verwandte Institute* (Mohr Siebeck, Tübingen 2003) 209–10, 213–14, 221, and esp 342–46; S Martens, *Durch Dritte verursachte Willensmängel* (Mohr Siebeck, Tübingen 2007) 368–70. More critical: Lieb in *Festschrift Medicus* (n 101) 347–51. *Münchener Kommentar: vol 1/1* (n 12) § 119 [113]–[122] (Kramer), prefers to allow rescission on an extended reading of § 119 II BGB for all mistakes caused by the other party's conduct. On this suggestion see Grigoleit *Vorvertragliche Informationshaftung* (above) 149–51; Lorenz *Schutz vor dem unerwünschten Vertrag* (n 96) 284–94.

[104] Grigoleit *Vorvertragliche Informationshaftung* (n 103) 16–40, 137–40; Grigoleit in *Schuldrechtsreform vor dem Hintergrund des Gemeinschaftsrechts* (n 103) 271–74, 282–84. Cf also H Fleischer, "Konkurrenzprobleme um die culpa in contrahendo: Fahrlässige Irreführung versus arglistige Täuschung" AcP 200 (2000) 91, 97–100.

[105] See above, section B.1.a.i of the present chapter (at pp 165–66).

[106] By contrast, the approach suggested by Kramer in *Münchener Kommentar: vol 1/1* (cf n 103) encompasses innocent misrepresentations.

[107] See text to n 104 above.

[108] Cf Grigoleit *Vorvertragliche Informationshaftung* (n 103) 138: "Eine fahrlässige Informationspflichtverletzung ist nach heutigem Verständnis eine widerrechtliche Beeinträchtigung der freien Selbstbestimmung auf rechtsgeschäftlichem Gebiet, auch wenn sie von den Gesetzesverfassern noch nicht als solche anerkannt wurde". ("The negligent breach of a duty of information is, on today's understanding, a wrongful interference with [a person's] free self-determination in contractual matters, even if it was not recognized as such by the compilers of the BGB"). Grigoleit emphasizes that an *objective* breach of the duty to take care in making pre-contractual statements is enough, even in the absence of individual *subjective* culpability (such as would give rise to a claim for compensation): ibid 142–44.

painting, for negligent misrepresentation.[109] It will be recalled that a fraudulent misrepresentation usually entitles the transferor to rescind both the obligatory contract (*Verpflichtungsgeschäft*) and a consequential 'real agreement' under § 123 I BGB because both are 'infected' by the identical defect (*Fehleridentität*).[110] Given that the real agreement is normally no less a consequence of the negligently induced mistake than the underlying contract, in other words, that the relevant 'pattern' is the same as in fraud cases, this exclusion is perhaps surprising. Grigoleit sees the objection, but argues that the denial of rescission in respect of purely dispository transactions is nevertheless warranted in the light of the principles of separation and abstraction. The distinctness of *Verpflichtungs-* and *Verfügungsgeschäft*, he reasons, means that the duty to take care when making pre-contractual statements typically extends only to the former, the latter being predetermined by the obligations which the representee has incurred.[111] Furthermore, the legislator's deliberate decision to decouple the validity of the *Verfügungsgeschäft* from that of the underlying *Verpflichtungsgeschäft* in his view requires that the *de facto* exception to the principle of abstraction entailed by *Fehleridentität* be confined to the more serious case of fraud.[112]

2. Mistaken Gifts

It was noted at the beginning of this chapter that an analysis of relevant impairments of consent in the contractual context encompasses gift transactions in German, but not in English law.[113] As a result, the comparative vista changes when we turn our attention to gratuitous transfers. While the conceptualization of gifts in German law as executed non-bargain contracts prevents their recovery for any defect of consent which is not operative in relation to contracts generally,[114] English law is subject to no such constraints. Of course, the unjust factors as reasons for restitution of a gift largely mirror the grounds for rescission of a contractual agreement supported by consideration. We therefore find little deviation between the comparative picture painted above and the gift scenario as far as fraud, duress, undue influence, and negligent misrepresentation are concerned. However, when it comes to spontaneous and innocently induced mistakes,

---

[109] Grigoleit *Vorvertragliche Informationshaftung* (n 103) 140–41; Grigoleit AcP 199 (n 103) 407–8.

[110] See above, Chapter III.B.3.b (at p 62).

[111] Grigoleit *Vorvertragliche Informationshaftung* (n 103) 141; Grigoleit AcP 199 (n 103) 407.

[112] Grigoleit *Vorvertragliche Informationshaftung* (n 103) 141; Grigoleit AcP 199 (n 103) 407–8.

[113] See above, text after n 1.

[114] Cf *Motive* (n 36) vol 2, 288–89.

a rift appears. If German law, with its provisions on avoidance for mistake (§ 119 BGB), is often more generous towards transferors than English law in the context of bargains, the converse seems to be true in respect of mistaken gifts. Unless the donor can establish that he was defrauded (§ 123 I alt 1 BGB) or negligently induced to make the gift in breach of the donee's pre-transactional duty not to misinform (*culpa in contrahendo*), that he was under a misapprehension about what he was doing when executing it (*Inhalts*- or *Erklärungsirrtum* under § 119 I BGB), or that he was mistaken about some essential characteristic of the chattel in question or of the donee (*Eigenschaftsirrtum* under § 119 II BGB), he cannot recover in German law. Mistakes made in the process of forming the intention gratuitously to bestow a particular benefit on the transferee are generally irrelevant. By contrast, English law – it was argued above – has now developed so as to allow restitution for all mistaken gifts, including those resulting from spontaneous 'motivational' mistakes. As long as there is a genuine 'mistake', ie a mismatch between existing facts and the data in the donor's head, and not a mere misprediction of future events, restitution will or should follow.[115]

The denial of recovery in German law for all spontaneous and innocently induced mistakes not falling under § 119 BGB has, as the above discussion shows, sound conceptual reasons. Where contract law is *not* all about bargains, gift-givers and people who obtain a *quid pro quo* can be treated very much alike. However, this was not nearly as evident at the inception of the BGB as it appears to German lawyers today.[116] Only the practical difficulties of distinguishing bargains from gratuitous transactions and the need for maximum legal certainty persuaded the compilers of the BGB to apply the same rules of rescission across the board.[117] A

[115] See above, Chapter IV.B.3 (esp pp 116–19). It was there left open whether it is sufficient to show that the donor would not have made the gift but for his misapprehension about, or ignorance of, a certain state of affairs, or whether a genuine 'mistake' can only be established where a set of false data is actively on the donor's mind and 'feeds into' the decision-making process (cf text to nn 91–92 on p 118).

[116] This aspect is also highlighted by Krebs *Restitution at the Crossroads* (n 37) 60–64, to whose account of the contributions by Lenel, Lippmann and Schloßmann (all cited in n 118 below) the English-speaking reader may be referred.

[117] Cf *Motive* (n 36) vol 1, 201: "Es spricht zwar bei Rechtsgeschäften, durch welche einem Anderen ohne Entgelt Etwas versprochen oder übertragen wird, Manches für eine mildere Behandlung des Erklärenden. Allein die Scheidung zwischen entgeltlichen und unentgeltlichen Rechtsgeschäften ist, so einfach sie an sich zu sein scheint, schwer durchführbar. Die Feststellung, ob bzw. inwieweit ein Rechtsgeschäft ein unentgeltliches ist, begegnet vielfach, namentlich bei den sog. gemischten Geschäften, erheblichen Schwierigkeiten. Mit der Scheidung würde eine Unsicherheit in die Anwendbarkeit der Bestimmungen gebracht werden, welche deren praktischen Wert wesentlich beschränken müßte". ("It is true that there is something to be said for a more lenient treatment of the

number of academics writing at the beginning of the 20th century were seriously worried about the restrictions imposed by § 119 BGB on rescission in the gift context.[118] If one were today again to launch the beginnings of an attack on the German position, one might point out that the BGB itself contains some evidence for a lower threshold of recovery in the case of gratuitous acquisitions. Testamentary gifts, for example, can be rescinded not only for all motivational mistakes,[119] but even where the testator's expectations have been disappointed, ie for mere mispredictions (§ 2078 II BGB).[120] Although this possibility does not exist for *inter vivos* gifts, such gifts are recoverable if the donor subsequently falls into poverty (§ 528 I BGB) and for the donee's gross ingratitude (§§ 530 I, 531 BGB).[121] Finally, we will see in the next chapter that the law of unjustified enrichment also contains provisions which impose restitutionary liability on a

---

person making a declaration [of intention] in cases of legal transactions by means of which something is promised or transferred to another without consideration. Yet the distinction between transactions for value and gratuitous transactions is hard to operate in practice, however simple it may appear to be. Establishing whether or to what extent a transaction is gratuitous often gives rise to considerable difficulties, in particular where so-called 'mixed' transactions are concerned. The distinction would introduce into the application of the provisions an uncertainty which would inevitably have to reduce their practical value").

[118] Eg O Lenel, "Der Irrtum über wesentliche Eigenschaften" JherJB 44 (1902) 1, 24–26; L Lippmann, "Studien zu § 119 Abs. 2 BGB" AcP 102 (1907) 283, 377–87; S Schloßmann, *Der Irrtum über wesentliche Eigenschaften der Person und der Sache nach dem Bürgerlichen Gesetzbuch* (Fischer, Jena 1903) 67–71.

[119] Note that rescission for a mistake about the content of a testamentary disposition (§ 2078 I BGB: *Inhalts-* or *Erklärungsirrtum*, equivalent to § 119 I BGB) is also possible, but will often not be necessary. Testamentary documents are construed strictly in accordance with the testator's "true intention" (§ 133 BGB), not according to the more objective standard applicable to declarations of intention communicated to the other party (§§ 133, 157 BGB).

[120] § 2078 II BGB provides for a right to rescind "where the testator was induced to make the disposition by the erroneous assumption of a particular circumstance, *or by the [erroneous] expectation of its materialization or non-materialization*" (emphasis added). As is English law (cf n 115), there is a question about the extent to which the relevant 'circumstance' has to be actively on the testator's mind: for an overview of the debate see eg K Rebmann, FJ Säcker and R Rixecker (eds), *Münchener Kommentar zum Bürgerlichen Gesetzbuch, vol 9: §§ 1922–2385* (4th edn Beck, München 2004) § 2078 [25]–[29] (Leipold); J von Staudinger (Begr), *J von Staudingers Kommentar zum Bürgerlichen Gesetzbuch: §§ 2064–2196* (Neubearbeitung 2003: Sellier de Gruyter, Berlin 2003) § 2078 [17]–[24] (Otte). With regard to mispredictions, Leipold in *Münchener Kommentar: vol 9* (above) § 2078 [35]–[36], argues that developments which occur only *after* the testator's death should not normally be taken into account.

[121] It seems that § 530 I BGB is not applicable, whether directly or by analogy, where the donee's misconduct towards the donor precedes the gift (a case of 'motivational mistake').

donee in circumstances where a purchaser for value would not be so liable (§§ 816 I 2, 822 BGB).[122] It may be added that if a broader scope of recovery for mistaken gifts were to be introduced into German law,[123] this would best be done via the law of rescission, by an analogous application of – or through a new provision modelled on – §§ 119 II, 2078 II BGB.[124] The donee's reliance interest would then be adequately protected by his claim for compensation under § 122 BGB as well as by the disenrichment defence in § 818 III BGB.[125] With regard to the question of *Fehleridentität*, one feels tempted to adopt and adapt Grigoleit's argument set out above.[126] Desirable as restitution for mistaken gifts might be, the coherence of the legal system (most notably with a view to the existing grounds for rescission, especially § 119 I BGB) and the basic legislative decision in favour of abstraction, require us to prevent avoidance of the real agreement for a mere motivational mistake. If a donor's motive can justifiably be regarded as forming part of the *causa donandi*,[127] then a motivational mistake warrants restitution of an unjustified enrichment in the shape of a

---

[122] See below, Chapter VI.B.2.b (pp 221–26).

[123] Lenel JherJB 44 (n 118) 25–26, and Schloßmann *Irrtum über wesentliche Eigenschaften* (n 118) 69–71, accepting the restrictions of the existing legislative framework, argued for a liberal interpretation of § 119 II BGB in the context of gifts so as to take account of the donor's idiosyncrasies.

[124] The analogy with § 119 II BGB works only if a mistake about an essential quality can properly be regarded as a 'motivational mistake': cf n 12 and corresponding text. Lippmann AcP 102 (n 118) esp 379–82, 387–91, 399, who denies that § 119 II BGB has any application to gifts (on the basis that gifts are not *Verkehrsgeschäfte*, ie commercial transactions), draws the direct analogy with § 2078 BGB. Flume *Rechtsgeschäft* (n 10) 426, also invokes § 2078 BGB, but at the same time wants to impose liability under § 122 BGB on the donor rescinding an *inter vivos* gift. Note that, according to Flume's view, rescission is only necessary for undisclosed motives. Where disclosed, he maintains, a mistaken motive automatically invalidates the gift (contract).

[125] It may be asked whether a claim under § 122 BGB would actually add much to the protection which § 818 III BGB (properly understood) provides for the recipient of an executed gift.

[126] See text to nn 109–112 on pp 186–87.

[127] Cf Flume *Rechtsgeschäft* (n 10) 171–73, 426, drawing on J Domat, *Les Lois Civiles dans leur Ordre Naturel*, book 1, title 1, section 1 [VI]: "Dans les donations ... l'engagement de celui qui donne, a son fondement sur quelque motif raisonnable & juste, comme un service rendu, ou quelque'autre mérite du donataire, ou le seul plaisir de faire du bien. Et *ce motif tient lieu de cause* de la part de celui qui reçoit & ne donne rien" (emphasis added), cited after J Domat, *Les Loix Civiles dans leur Ordre Naturel, le Droit Public, et Legum Delectus* (nouvelle édition Durand, Paris 1777, revue par M de Héricourt) vol 1, 16. ("In gift transactions ... the commitment of the donor has as its basis some reasonable and just motive, such as some service rendered [by the donee], or some other merit of the donee, or the mere pleasure of doing good. And *this motive takes the place of the cause* on the part of the person who receives and gives nothing"). On the subjective and the objective notion of *causa* in German law see above, n 44 on p 27.

mistaken gift, but it does not call the validity of the conveyance as such into question.

C. Separation and Abstraction in English Law

When looking across the Channel, Civilian lawyers are often puzzled by the question whether and to what extent English law adheres to the principles of separation and abstraction.[128] It has been seen that these principles are fundamental to the German law of property, and that they play a pivotal role in determining whether an impaired consent transfer is to be unwound according to the rules on reversing unjustified enrichments (§§ 812 ff BGB) or in accordance with the rules governing the relationship between owner and illegitimate possessor of an object (§§ 985 ff BGB). While the principle of separation (*Trennungsprinzip*) asserts the distinctness of contract and conveyance, the principle of abstraction (*Abstraktionsprinzip*) maintains that the validity of the latter is independent of the existence and validity of the former. The aim here is to identify the relevance – or irrelevance – of these principles for English law in relation to impaired consent transfers of movables.

1. Relationship between Contract and Conveyance in English Law

a) The Principle of Separation

The first thing to note is that the scope of inquiry into the principle of separation is narrower in English than in German law. Transfers by way of gift can be left to one side because they do not rest on a notional contract between the donor and the donee. Our focus is on transfers in the contractual context, ie on bargains. Here one hallmark of the principle of separation is that the conclusion of an obligatory agreement does not, in and of itself, have proprietary consequences. A separate act of conveyance is necessary to transfer rights *in rem*. How does English law fare on this count?

As far as sale is concerned, we immediately encounter the rule that title to specific goods in a deliverable state is capable of passing (and by default does pass) as soon as an unconditional contract for their sale is

[128] L van Vliet, *Transfer of Movables in German, French, English and Dutch Law* (Ars Aequi Libri, Nijmegen 2000) 111–14, 130–32, is one of the few authors to tackle the question directly. He comes to the conclusion that English law operates a fully causal transfer system for movables. Cf now also L van Vliet, "The Transfer of Moveables in Scotland and England" (2008) 12 Edin L Rev 173.

concluded.[129] While it might be possible to construe this as the conclusion of an obligatory contract coupled with a simultaneous but *notionally separate* 'real' agreement to convey, such an interpretation seems highly artificial and meets the objection that the contract *as such* is generally regarded as the vehicle of conveyance.[130] And even where, in accordance with the parties' intentions, title to the goods in question passes at a later point (eg when payment is made), it is still the contractual intent which effects the conveyance.[131] We can glean this from the fact that the seller is not in a position unilaterally to prevent title passing when the event envisaged in the contract occurs.[132] Given that contracts of sale do therefore have direct proprietary consequences, we could say that – in this respect at least – the principle of separation has no application within English law. If one believes that sale principles apply, *mutatis mutandis*, to contracts for the exchange of goods or to all agreements supported by consideration, the same is true of barter and other bilateral contracts.[133]

In other situations, however, a different picture appears. Some contracts are incapable of passing title to the goods in question. If the Irish Supreme

---

[129] Sale of Goods Act 1979, ss 17, 18 rule 1. Before title passes, the contract is not a 'sale', but merely an 'agreement to sell': cf Sale of Goods Act 1979, s 2(4)–(6).

[130] Cf eg Sale of Goods Act 1979, s 2(1); P Atiyah, JN Adams and H MacQueen, *The Sale of Goods* (11th edn Pearson Longman, Harlow 2005) 34; *Chitty on Contracts* (n 85) vol 2, [43–009] (Guest/Reynolds/Harris); R Goode, *Commercial Law* (3rd edn LexisNexis, London 2004) 133, who says that "where goods are sold under a contract of sale by which the property is to pass immediately to the buyer, the agreement for sale is both a contract and a conveyance"; AG Guest (gen ed), *Benjamin's Sale of Goods* (7th edn Sweet & Maxwell, London 2006) [1–027] (Sealy), [5–018] (Guest).

[131] This is not to say that we cannot or should not conceive of the contract as *encompassing* an appropriate 'real agreement'. Indeed, there is much to be said for such a view, which avoids the difficulties connected with recognizing self-executing obligations. Yet, as van Vliet *Transfer of Movables* (n 128) 110, rightly points out, the retention of title scenario (cf also n 132) allows no firm conclusion one way or the other. The observation in *Benjamin's Sale of Goods* (n 130) [1–027] (Sealy), to the effect that "the sale involves not only a contract, but also a conveyance of the property in the goods", suggests that it is possible to distinguish between obligatory and 'real' aspects of the parties' agreement (without thereby implying the existence of two notionally *separate* transactions).

[132] A reservation or retention of title clause, for example, is a term *of the contract* making the passing of title conditional upon full payment of the purchase price: cf *Aluminium Industrie Vaassen BV v Romalpa Aluminium* [1976] 1 WLR 676 (CA). It is best understood as bestowing on the purchaser a power *in rem* to obtain title prospectively by fulfilling the condition (namely by paying the purchase price), and is thus comparable to the German *Anwartschaftsrecht*.

[133] See above, Chapter IV.D.3.a (at p 135). It will be recalled that bilateral contracts are ones where the parties make enforceable promises to one another. In a unilateral contract, one party's promise becomes binding only upon performance by the other of a requested act (without that other being under any obligation to perform).

Court in *Flynn v Mackin*[134] is right, then barter does not follow the sale model and falls into this category, which also contains (at least gratuitous) loans of fungibles.[135] Moreover, a contractual obligation to pay money does not execute itself. A debtor may have just the requisite amount of cash in his pocket and promise to pay up immediately (so that there is no problem of specificity), and still title to the notes and coins does not pass to his creditor without more. Outside the context of sale (as well as possibly barter and similar exchange transactions), a conveyance cannot be effected contractually, *solo consensu*, and transferors have to have recourse to one of the two older modes of conveyance, typically to the delivery of the object in question.

In this respect, it is worth noting that the requirements in English law for a conveyance by delivery are remarkably similar to those in German law (cf § 929 BGB). Not only does a transfer of actual physical possession have to take place unless the transferee is already in possession as the transferor's bailee,[136] but the parties need to agree on the proprietary significance of the delivery. They have to intend ownership or title to pass.[137] Although German law classifies their agreement as contractual ('*dinglicher Vertrag*') and English law does not, both cannot do without it.[138] The existence of some sort of a 'real agreement' between transferor and transferee might indeed be described as a conceptual necessity for any legal system prepared to accept conveyances that are truly distinct from their underlying contract (as opposed to being merely temporally delayed, eg due to an additional 'bare' delivery requirement).[139] We hence find what could be called a fully-blown principle of separation in English law.

The matter does not end here. Despite the ability of sale contracts to pass title *solo consensu* and thus to act as vehicles of conveyance, even they sometimes display features reminiscent of the principle of separation. For one, it is unclear how we are to analyse cases in which the parties agree that title to the object in question shall pass upon delivery to the

---

134 [1974] IR 101 (Irish SC), esp 111–12.

135 It was argued above (in n 177 on p 136) that a gratuitous loan of fungibles is best regarded as a type of unilateral contract in English law: the 'lender' is under no obligation to effect the transfer.

136 It is unclear whether English law, like German law (cf § 930 BGB), allows for conveyances by means of a *constitutum possessorium*: see above, n 153 on p 47.

137 Otherwise the 'transferee' will hold the chattel as the 'transferor's' bailee.

138 Cf F Pollock, *Principles of Contract at Law and in Equity* (Stevens & Sons, London 1876) 3: "[E]very conveyance includes an agreement".

139 Cf above, Chapter IV.D.2 and IV.D.3.a (at pp 133–38). HH Jakobs, "Gibt es den dinglichen Vertrag?" ZSS (RA) 119 (2002) 269, 300, goes so far as to describe the real agreement (including its abstract nature in German law) as "no more than the product of precise thinking" ("*nichts als das Produkt genauen Denkens*").

buyer. Is this a contractual conveyance intended to take effect when the seller physically hands over the object to the buyer (no separate real agreement), or is it a purely obligatory arrangement envisaging later delivery as a means of conveyance (including a real agreement)?[140] Moreover, we have seen that delivery plays a crucial role where a contract of sale is for some reason void, as in *Singh v Ali*.[141] It seems that the buyer will then obtain title by delivery under three conditions. First, the parties must still intend the conveyance at the moment of delivery, even if only in a layman's generic way.[142] Second, the seller must not be labouring under a fundamental mistake (eg as to the buyer's identity) rendering the conveyance by delivery just as ineffectual as the contract.[143] Finally, the policy underlying the nullity of the contract, eg its illegality, must not also warrant non-recognition of the conveyance, as eg where the legal system prohibits all dealing with the goods in question.[144]

Attempts have been made to explain away the supposed 'oddity' inherent in *Singh v Ali* by insisting that the contract for the sale of the lorry was not void, but merely unenforceable.[145] A distinction is drawn between situations where a statute expressly (or by necessary implication) provides for the nullity of an illegal contact and where it does not.[146] Yet even if this distinction existed so as to divide illegal contracts into two categories, it would still leave open the possibility of conveyances by delivery in cases of contracts falling into the 'nullity' group. In a parallel situation, Lush J

---

[140] The test applied above (whether the seller can unilaterally prevent the conveyance: text to n 132) does not work here. It is similar with cases in which generic or future goods have to be appropriated to the contract of sale before title can pass. Van Vliet *Transfer of Movables* (n 128) 105–7, argues that the parties' consent to the act of appropriation should be regarded as a kind of 'real agreement' in such a scenario.

[141] [1960] AC 167 (PC). See above, Chapter IV.D.3.a. (at pp 136–37). To an extent, the ensuing discussion will inevitably overlap with the discussion of the principle of abstraction in section C.1.b of the present chapter, further below (pp 196–98). The two principles are closely connected (abstraction pre-supposes a principle of separation). For exposition purposes, it has been thought convenient to consider cases of the type exemplified by *Singh v Ali* in conjunction with other sale cases.

[142] Their intention to pass title must survive the conclusion of the (void) contract, as it typically will where they do not appreciate the subtleties of the Sale of Goods legislation and/or are keen to put an illegal scheme into effect.

[143] Cf *Cundy v Lindsay* (n 45); *Ingram v Little* (n 46). It is unclear whether, as far as the conveyance is concerned, the mistake needs to be known to the other party. This appears to be denied by Stevens in *Contract Terms* (n 53) 119–21: see n 58 above.

[144] Cf *Bowmakers Ltd v Barnet Instruments Ltd* [1945] KB 65 (CA) 72, where du Parcq LJ gave the (then relevant) example of obscene books.

[145] Goode *Commercial Law* (n 130) 78–79, 133; van Vliet *Transfer of Movables* (n 128) 114.

[146] Goode *Commercial Law* (n 130) 133.

held that title to goods delivered to an infant could pass although the relevant contract of sale was unambiguously void under the Infants Relief Act 1874.[147] A second, entirely different line of argument approaches the issue from the opposite angle. It maintains that title does *not* actually pass (by delivery or otherwise) where the underlying contract of sale is illegal, but that the *in pari delicto* principle[148] prevents the 'seller' from asserting his right to immediate possession of the goods.[149] However, since the *in pari delicto* principle operates only *inter partes*, this explanation has to construct a novel *bona fide* purchase defence in order to ensure that those claiming through the 'transferor' do not succeed in an action for conversion against a party whose title is derived from the 'transferee'.[150] Moreover, the explanation has to dismiss as *obiter* various statements in the relevant cases that '*property*' passes when an illegal contract is executed (by delivery).[151] The suspicion arises that both alternative interpretations of *Singh v Ali* are partly motivated by the desire to maintain compatibility with Lord Cairns LC's misleading assertion in *Cundy v Lindsay*, that "if the property in the goods in question passed, it could only pass by way of contract".[152] Once this myth is dispelled, it becomes possible to admit that

---

[147] *Stocks v Wilson* [1913] 2 KB 235 (KBD) esp 246–47.

[148] The full maxim runs: *in pari delicto potior est conditio defendentis.*

[149] MJ Higgins, "The Transfer of Property under Illegal Contracts" (1962) 25 MLR 149.

[150] Ibid 161. Even on the broad interpretation of section 25(1) of the Sale of Goods Act 1979 subsequently adopted in *Newtons of Wembley Ltd v Williams* [1965] 1 QB 560 (CA) (cf pp 231–33), the provision does not apply where the person making the transfer never was a 'buyer in possession'. In Chapter VI.D.1.b below (pp 255–56), it will be argued that English law might indeed benefit from the introduction of a general principle of *bona fide* purchase, yet with entirely different cases in mind. On the view advocated here, the rules on *bona fide* purchase do not need to be invoked at all in the situations envisaged by Higgins (where the transferor knows of the illegality and is not mistaken).

[151] *Singh v Ali* (n 141) 176–77 (Lord Denning); Similar: *Belvoir Finance Co Ltd v Stapleton* [1971] 1 QB 210 (CA) 218 (Lord Denning MR), 220 (Sachs LJ), where delivery was made by the seller to the buyer's nominee, who subsequently became the buyer's bailee; *Scarfe v Morgan* (1838) 4 Mees & W 270, 282; 150 ER 1430, 1435–56, concerning the 'special property' constituted by a lien. Goode *Commercial Law* (n 130) 133 fn 454, cites *Belvoir Finance Co v Stapleton* (above) as authority for the proposition that the passing of title under an illegal contract is *not* dependent on delivery, presumably because the delivery was not directly to the buyer.

[152] (1878) 3 App Cas 459 (HL) 464 (cf text to n 179 on p 136). Goode *Commercial Law* (n 130) 79 fn 90, actually concludes that illegality usually renders a sale contract unenforceable rather than void "from the fact that illegality does not as a rule vitiate ... transfers of property made under the contract"; cf also ibid 133. For van Vliet *Transfer of Movables* (n 128) 114, the chosen explanation of *Singh v Ali* is part of a wider argument in favour of a causal transfer system in English law. Though van Vliet's theory can accommodate a 'real agreement' and thus the principle of separation, his discussion

delivery sometimes acts as a substitute conveyance where the *solo consensu* principle fails.

b) The Principle of Abstraction

This leads us to the question of abstraction. To what extent does English law adhere to the principle of abstraction *à la* BGB? Subject to what will be said below about the 'gist' of abstraction, the short answer seems to be as follows. To the extent that the principle of separation forms part of English law, conveyances by delivery appear to be abstract at law as well as in equity.[153] The effectiveness of a transfer by delivery does not depend on the existence or validity of any legal basis or *causa* for it.[154] Of course, the parties will usually have the discharge of a (contractual) obligation in mind when agreeing on a particular transfer, but their real agreement is not invalidated if the obligation envisaged does not in fact exist.

For the common law side of things, this emerges in relation to goods from the void sale contract scenario just considered,[155] and in relation to currency from the cases discussed in the previous chapter which show that – in spite of a few *dicta* to the contrary – a mere liability mistake on the

about causality and abstraction relies heavily on identity mistake cases like *Cundy v Lindsay*: ibid 111–12, esp 112 fn 84. It seems that Goode, too, subscribes to the causal approach beyond the context of sale. He suggests that the 'unenforceability' theory of an illegal contract is indispensable to explaining why conveyances *of money* paid in pursuance of it are valid: *Commercial Law* (n 130) 79 fn 90, 133. Higgins (1962) 25 MLR (n 149) 151, argues that "any deed or delivery executed in pursuance of an illegal contract is as ineffective to pass title as the contract itself". His basic starting point is therefore similar to van Vliet's, with the only relevant difference between their respective approaches concerning the effects properly ascribed to illegality.

[153] If one accepts the 'theory of double effect' (cf Chapter IV.D.2, esp text to nn 170–172 on p 134), then abstraction becomes a general feature of English property law, irrespective of the existence of the *solo consensu* rule.

[154] As far as a subjective understanding of the *causa* requirement goes (cf comment in n 44 on p 27), the case of *Dewar v Dewar* [1975] 1 WLR 1532 (ChD), where a mother paid money to her son as a gift, but he accepted it only as a loan, suggests that a lack of agreement about the *causa traditionis* will not invalidate the conveyance. However, the decision can alternatively be explained on the ground that the donee acquiesced in the mother's *causa donandi* by not repudiating the gift: cf ibid 1538–39; van Vliet *Transfer of Movables* (n 128) 131.

[155] See above, text to nn 141–152. T Weir, "Taking for Granted – The Ramifications of *nemo dat*" (1996) 49 CLP 325, 340–43, accepts this explanation of *Singh v Ali* (n 141), but maintains that *Ingram v Little* (n 46) was "a case where the delivery was invalidated because the *causa* was void". He finds this (supposed) discrepancy between contracts void for illegality and those void for *error in persona* puzzling and laments that "[t]he legal archaeologist of the future will have some difficulty in deducing the position of the common law in the mid-twentieth century". The argument here is that both decisions are perfectly reconcilable: cf text to nn 141–144 on p 194.

payer's part does not prevent title to notes and coins passing to the payee.[156] A valid conveyance by delivery requires no more than a change of possession and the parties' assent to the conveyance. Bar the existence of an operative *error in persona vel obiecto* or extreme duress amounting to *vis absoluta*,[157] no impairment of consent (including and especially a liability mistake) can prevent title passing. Indeed, if it were otherwise, there would be very little independent room for the law of unjust enrichment beside the transferor's wrongs-based claim in the tort of conversion.[158]

In equity, the position is slightly more difficult. The reasoning in *Chase Manhattan Bank NA v Israel-British Bank (London) Ltd*[159] might well suggest that equity adheres to a causal instead of an abstract transfer system. It will be recalled that Goulding J there talked of the payer 'retaining' a beneficial interest in the second (the mistaken) payment of US $ 2 million. However, as was pointed out in *Westdeutsche Landesbank Girozentrale v Islington London BC*,[160] this sort of 'proprietary arithmetic' is misconceived. A person who holds an asset outright does not have both legal title and an equitable interest in it.[161] There is therefore nothing to stay behind if money is paid although it is not owing. Any equitable right *in rem* which the transferor may have after the transfer is a new right, generated by the transferee's unjust enrichment at his expense. The case is entirely different from a scenario like *Cundy v Lindsay*,[162] where the defrauded vendor retained his common law title despite the apparent sale and delivery of the goods to the fraudster.

Yet even if equity is not committed to the causal principle in the form suggested by Goulding J in *Chase Manhattan*, we have to consider the possibility that it is anti-abstractionist in another sense. If proponents of the immediate interest model of proprietary restitution are right, then a resulting (or constructive) trust arises in favour of the transferor from the moment he acts on his liability mistake. His legally valid conveyance

---

156 Cf above, Chapter IV.D.3.a. (at pp 137–38), and see esp *Chambers v Miller* (1862) 13 CB NS 125, 143 ER 50; *R v Prince* (1868) LR 1 CCR 150; *Barclays Bank Ltd v WJ Simms Son & Cooke (Southern) Ltd* [1980] QB 677 (QBD Comm) 689.

157 This is probably what prevented title passing in *R v Middleton* (1873) LR 2 CCR 38, *R v Ashwell* (1885) 16 QBD 190 (CCR), and in *Duke de Cadaval v Collins* (1836) 4 Ad & El 858, 111 ER 1006, but cf the criticism by W Swadling, "Unjust Delivery" in A Burrows and A Rodger (eds), *Mapping the Law: Essays in Memory of Peter Birks* (OUP, Oxford 2006) 277, 292–96.

158 On the relationship in English law between personal rights to restitution for unjust enrichment and pre-existing property rights see above, Chapter IV.C (pp 119–25).

159 [1981] Ch 105 (ChD).

160 [1996] AC 669 (HL).

161 Ibid 706 (Lord Browne-Wilkinson).

162 (1878) 3 App Cas 459 (HL).

would thus be automatically reversed in equity. Such a mechanism closely resembles 'causality'. However, the immediate interest model of proprietary restitution is – for the reasons already outlined – ultimately not convincing in our impaired consent transfer scenario.[163] The ambiguous notion of 'non-beneficial transfer', which is used by its proponents to equate what they describe as 'vitiated' consent to a conveyance with the positive intention to benefit someone other than the transferee, is dangerously misleading. Equity may be more generous than the common law about the scope of relevant impairments (in recognizing non-fraudulently induced and even spontaneous mistakes), yet it too gives the party concerned a choice whether or not to uphold the transaction. It was argued here that, even though a personal right to restitution follows without more where a party attempts to discharge a non-existent debt, the transferor does not acquire an equitable interest in the money paid (or in its traceable proceeds) unless and until he exercises his equitable power *in rem*. This solution makes conveyances, in so far as they are separate from the underlying contract,[164] abstract in equity as well as at common law.

2. The Gist of Abstraction

If the relationship between contract and conveyance of movables in English law is such that we can, in places, make out the principles of separation and abstraction, why is this nevertheless not widely recognized? Why is English law often thought to be causal throughout, and why do we find suggestions that rescission of *any* contract (not just sale or barter) leads to an automatic proprietary reversal of transfers made in pursuance of it?[165] It is submitted that the answer lies in the structure of the English

---

[163] See above, Chapter IV.D.3.c.ii (esp pp 149–51). The argument was expressly confined to impaired consent transfer cases. It did not call into question the validity or appropriateness of the immediate interest model of proprietary restitution in other contexts, eg for 'automatic resulting trusts'.

[164] On the question of 'double effect' in cases where a transfer of title by virtue of a contract of sale is followed by a delivery see n 153 above.

[165] Automatic unilateral reversal (unless the other party is also mistaken) seems to be envisaged by eg P Birks, *An Introduction to the Law of Restitution* (Clarendon Press, Oxford 1985, paperback edn 1989) 171; *El Ajou v Dollar Land Holdings plc* [1993] 3 All ER 717 (ChD) 734 (Millett J); *Shalson v Russo (Tracing Claims)* [2003] EWHC 1637 (ChD), [2005] Ch 281, [121]–[127] (Rimer J). Automatic bilateral reversal is advocated by eg Goode *Commercial Law* (n 130) 109; S Worthington, "The Proprietary Consequences of Rescission" [2002] RLR 28, esp 37; probably also A Burrows, *The Law of Restitution* (2nd edn Butterworths, London 2002) 58–59. The exact nature of the transferee's right to recovery (personal claim or proprietary interest) will often not matter, given that the exercise of the transferor's right to rescind the contract is normally conditional upon making – or being able to make – counter-restitution (*restitutio in integrum*).

law on rescission, or – more precisely – the principles governing the avoidance of transactions generally. On the power model of proprietary restitution espoused here, the basis of the right to rescind a contract and the right to avoid a conveyance is essentially the same. One party is unjustly enriched at the other's expense, and that other is in consequence given the option of revoking his consent to both the contract and the conveyance. He has a power *in personam* to rescind the bargain and a power *in rem* to avoid the transfer of title.[166] Depending on the unjust factor involved, these powers can be either legal or equitable. Pressure amounting to duress and fraudulent misrepresentation will afford grounds for avoidance at common law; all other relevant impairments generate powers only in equity.

When looking at the relationship between contract and conveyance in German law, we saw that the gist of the principle of abstraction lies in the fact that an obligatory contract (the *Verpflichtungsgeschäft*) can be void or voidable, while at the same time the conveyance (the *Verfügungsgeschäft*) made in pursuance of it stands unimpeachable.[167] This was because the impairment affecting the former does not usually also infect the latter. Recall our example of A, as the result of a typing error, mistakenly agreeing to sell his picture to B for € 450 instead of € 540 (or for $ 23,000 instead of $ 32,000).[168] He can rescind the obligatory contract of sale under § 119 I BGB, but not the subsequent conveyance. A is under no relevant misapprehension about what he is doing when he transfers ownership to B. Or consider the case of a mistaken payment. The fact that A believes himself to be indebted to B is a mere motivational mistake as far as the real agreement is concerned. Under German law, A cannot recover ownership of the painting or any cash unilaterally. All he has is a personal claim against B for retransfer according to the law of unjustified enrichment (§ 812 I 1 alt 1 BGB).

In English law, the pattern is very different. Taking law and equity into account, it is hard to think of a situation in which the transfer of title from A to B cannot be impeached on the generalized power model of proprietary restitution advocated here. The proprietary response to unjust enrichment is virtually universal.[169] In the case of a fraudulent or negligent misrepre-

[166] In sale and any other bilateral contracts to which the *solo consensu* rule applies, the power *in rem* is probably (but cf n 153 above) coupled with the power *in personam*. In all other transactions, especially where money is paid in pursuance of a contract, the two powers are notionally separate.

[167] See above, Chapter III.B.1–2 (pp 58–60).

[168] Cf above, pp 60, 168. We will assume that B is unaware of A's mistake to avoid the operation of the maxim that *falsa demonstratio non nocet* (on which see pp 180–81).

[169] This is, of course, true only for *impaired* consent transfer cases. It does not hold good for the typical case of a *qualified* transfer, where the unjust factor is 'failure of consideration'.

sentation as to the painting's authorship or value,[170] for example, both the contract and the conveyance are infected by the same unjust factor. Both can be avoided. Cases of duress, undue influence or innocent misrepresentation work on the same pattern. Structurally, this corresponds to what would be called *Fehleridentität* in German law. Contract (*Verpflichtungs-*) and conveyance (*Verfügungsgeschäft*) are beset by the identical defect. We have seen that fraud and duress are the prime examples in which German law allows rescission of both transactions (under § 123 I BGB).[171] It is only because the BGB adopts – below the fraud/duress threshold – a 'substantive' or 'content-oriented' rather than a 'procedural' or 'process-oriented' approach to rescission that instances of *Fehleridentität* are relatively rare in German law.[172] In a system such as the English, however, which adopts the 'process-oriented' approach wholesale (lining up non-fraudulent misrepresentations beneath the fraud threshold, and undue influence beneath duress),[173] *Fehleridentität* is the almost inevitable consequence.[174] Of course, *Fehleridentität* is only an apparent exception to the principle of abstraction. But it explains why English law need not worry too much about distinguishing between the proprietary effects of rescinding different types of contract. In the sale scenario, title (or an equitable interest) will typically revest automatically.[175] In other cases, avoidance of the contract and the real agreement, though in theory separate acts, will in practice often both be contained in the transferor's communication of his decision to rescind.[176] Given the virtual emasculation of the principle of abstraction by 'process-oriented' grounds for avoidance, it is no coincidence that Grigoleit, when suggesting the analogous application of § 123 I alt 1 BGB to instances of negligent misrepresentation, felt compelled to argue against

[170] On representations as to value see comment in n 19 on p 169 above.

[171] See above, Chapter III.B.3.b (esp text to n 18 on p 62).

[172] Only an *error in persona vel obiecto* (§ 119 I BGB) and possibly a mistake as to an essential quality of the object (§ 119 II BGB) will do: cf esp text to nn 19–24 on pp 62–63 above.

[173] On the relevance of non-fraudulent misrepresentation and undue influence being *equitable* (as opposed to common law) grounds for rescission see below, text after n 184.

[174] If the transferor's defect of consent disappears between the conclusion of the contract and a subsequent conveyance by delivery, then the fact that he nevertheless makes the conveyance will have to be understood as an affirmation of the contract.

[175] As eg in *Load v Green* (1846) 15 Mees & W 216, 153 ER 828; *Car & Universal Finance Co Ltd v Caldwell* [1965] 1 QB 525 (CA). This is subject to any formalities which may prevent an automatic revesting of title (such as registration requirements), and it depends on not recognizing the doctrine of 'double effect' for English law (cf n 153 above).

[176] This probably explains why title to or an equitable interest in money paid pursuant to a contractual obligation is thought automatically to revest in the payer when he rescinds the contract: cf case references in n 165 above.

allowing rescission of the dispository transaction (*Verfügungsgeschäft*).[177] He saw that there was a danger of undermining the BGB's deliberate commitment to abstraction.[178] No similar constraints exist in English law. In the bargaining context, English law has decided to look exclusively at how consent is procured rather than the substantive nature of any mistake.[179] We should therefore not be surprised to find that there is little room for the effects of abstraction.

What about the mistaken payment case? Here there can be no issue of *Fehleridentität* since no contractual obligation needs setting aside. We have seen that, while there is little doubt that a conveyance by delivery can be avoided for induced mistake, the issue of proprietary restitution is still largely unresolved where the transferor's mistake is spontaneous. The argument here was that the power model should extend to this situation.[180] If the power *in rem* is generated by the transferee's unjust enrichment at the transferor's expense, then any causative mistake – even if purely motivational – counts, provided only that it does not undermine a bargain between the parties. On the generalized power model of proprietary restitution, the gist of abstraction is lost whenever mistake operates as unjust factor, whether or not it is spontaneous.

Before concluding, however, that the question of abstraction is meaningless in English law, a *caveat* is warranted. In four important respects, the concept has much explanatory value. First, in respect of conveyances made in pursuance of a contract which the parties know to be void, as in *Singh v Ali*.[181] Here the title which passes to the transferee is unimpeachable both at law and in equity. The validity of the transfer is neither directly nor indirectly affected by the absence of a legal basis. A second point is closely connected. Unless both parties to a contract were suffering from a relevant defect of consent, proprietary restitution is unilateral.[182] The buyer who defrauds the vendor into selling a painting does not regain any proprietary interest in the money he has paid over (or its traceable proceeds) when the vendor later rescinds the contract of sale.[183] Thirdly, the principle

---

[177] See above, text to nn 109–110.

[178] See above, text to nn 111–112.

[179] On the distinction between law and equity see below, text after n 184.

[180] See above, Chapter IV.D.3.c.iii (pp 151–53).

[181] [1960] AC 167 (PC). Cf text to nn 141–144 above.

[182] It is submitted that Goode *Commercial Law* (n 130) 109, and Worthington [2002] RLR (n 165) 37, are wrong to assert that property *necessarily* revests both ways upon rescission of contract. Note, however, that rescission will not usually be possible without *restitutio in integrum* or counter-restitution: cf n 165 above.

[183] Query whether a defrauded *buyer's* rescission of a contract of sale always revests title to the object sold in the *seller*, as Goode *Commercial Law* (n 130) 361, suggests. It

of abstraction prevents 'proprietary overkill'. It ensures that a mistaken payer acquires a (weak) power *in rem* instead of retaining or obtaining a (strong) vested interest.[184] Fourthly and finally, abstraction is helpful in appreciating the distinction between common law and equitable grounds for avoiding a transaction. Only fraud and duress generate a legal power *in rem* by means of which the transferor can revest title in himself and thus 'pull back' his former right to possession. Equity's power *in rem* is in many ways a less forceful weapon. It cannot be used to divest the transferee of his right to immediate possession. This has certain repercussions for the relationship between the parties,[185] and – as we shall see – also for the position of third party purchasers from the transferee.[186] A faint echo of genuine abstraction *à la* BGB thus lies buried in English law.

D. Reflections on 'Proprietary Restitution'

1. Form and Scope of Proprietary Relief

In light of the preceding discussion about the principles of separation and abstraction, our comparative analysis of the form and scope of proprietary relief can be fairly brief. On a generalized power model of proprietary restitution, English law resembles[187] German law in making proprietary relief dependent on the transferor revoking his consent to the conveyance and thus avoiding it. Indeed, where the same scenario yields a common law power *in rem* and also a right to rescind the 'real agreement' under the BGB regime, both legal systems produce parallel results. Fraud and duress cases are the relevant examples. For defects other than fraudulently induced mistakes and coercion by means of duress, German and English law diverge. Not only may one system deny recovery altogether where the other allows it,[188] but as a result of the interplay between the principle of abstraction and the grounds for rescission, the availability of proprietary relief is more

is submitted that a limited acceptance of the 'theory of double effect' could – and indeed should – prevent this: cf n 160 on p 132 and n 172 on p 134.

[184] This has important repercussions for the position of third party purchasers from the transferee: see below, Chapter VI.C.1 (at pp 228–33).

[185] Most importantly, a transferor who exercises an equitable power *in rem* cannot sue the transferee in the tort of conversion. Instead, he has to exercise his rights under *Saunders v Vautier* (1841) 4 Beav 115, 49 ER 282; aff'd (1841) Cr & Ph 240, 41 ER 482, and can then demand a retransfer of title: see above, Chapter IV.D.4.a (at p 155).

[186] See below, Chapter VI.C.1 (at pp 228–33).

[187] The two approaches are not identical: cf observations on retroactivity immediately below, text to 193–196.

[188] See above, esp section B.1.a.ii of the present chapter (esp at pp 168–69).

restricted in German than in English law. In the latter, the transferor's personal right to restitution is, as we have seen, virtually always backed up by an equitable power *in rem* to 'recover' a trust interest in the chattel transferred.[189] In the former, by contrast, *Fehleridentität* is a relatively rare constellation. Most transferors will have to content themselves with a personal claim to restitution of the transferee's enrichment under § 812 I 1 alt 1 BGB. Equity thus provides proprietary relief in English law where German law cannot do so.

Looking at the broader picture, the 'generosity' of English law towards the transferor conveniently makes up for certain discrepancies between German and English law as far as the nature of a personal claim in unjust(ified) enrichment is concerned. While § 812 I 1 alt 1 BGB imposes on the transferee an obligation to surrender *in specie* what he has obtained (ie ownership and possession of the chattel), the common law only requires him to disgorge the value of his enrichment.[190] If the transferor is to have any chance of specific recovery in English law, this is best achieved through affording him a proprietary interest in the chattel.[191]

Finally, an observation on the retroactivity of proprietary relief is warranted. In line with the principle that rescission avoids contracts *ex tunc* (§ 142 I BGB), German law regards ownership as never having passed where the real agreement is avoided. It can accordingly hold transferees liable for damaging, destroying or losing the object transferred in the period between conveyance and rescission (cf §§ 989, 990 I, 142 II BGB).[192] As with most wrongs-based claims in German law, liability depends on the defendant's fault. He needs to have acted negligently in causing the loss or damage (§ 989 I BGB). Moreover, to avoid undermining the privileged position of *bona fide* possessors,[193] he is also required to have been *mala fide* (§ 990 I). But since the transferee will still have been owner of the object at the relevant point in time, his bad faith is established not by reference to the absence of a right to possess another's chattel, but by reference to the voidability of the real agreement (§ 142 II BGB). English law takes a different stance. Although rescission normally also avoids contracts *ab initio*, it seems that the exercise of powers *in rem* has – at least as

---

[189] On the relationship between a personal right to restitution and a vested right *in rem* in English law see above, Chapter IV.C (pp 119–25).

[190] See above, Chapter II.C.2.a (at p 32).

[191] It has even been suggested that specific recoverability is or should be the main aim of proprietary restitution: P Millett, "Restitution and Constructive Trusts" (1998) 114 LQR 399, 416; repeated in P Millett, "Proprietary Restitution" in S Degeling and J Edelman (eds), *Equity in Commercial Law* (Thomson LBC, Sydney 2005) 309, 320–21.

[192] It will be recalled that §§ 987 ff BGB normally bar recourse to the ordinary law of delict (§§ 823 ff BGB): *arg e* § 992 BGB.

[193] Cf § 993 I BGB.

far as the law of wrongs is concerned – prospective effect only.[194] This is eminently sensible if one considers that English law neither links wrongdoing (necessarily) to fault nor provides special protection for *bona fide* possessors. Conversion and – in so far as is applicable – breach of trust are strict liability wrongs.[195] If the conveyance could be avoided with retroactive effect, then the transferee and his successors in title might be liable to the transferor for exercising a (supposed) right over the chattel which they had no reason to suspect would later be divested *ab initio*.[196] A system that makes wide use of strict liability wrongs has good reason to insist that an act which is lawful when committed cannot retroactively be classed as a breach of duty.

2. Proprietary Relief and the Confines of Enrichment Law

We have seen that, on the approach contended for here, English and German law resemble one another to the extent that they allow for the avoidance of conveyances by revocation of the transferor's consent to the real agreement. Yet one potentially significant difference between the two legal systems must nevertheless not be overlooked. Like the right to rescind a contract, the English power model of proprietary restitution rests on the transferee's unjust enrichment at the transferor's expense. In German law, by way of contrast, rescission of any contract, including the real agreement, is not generally seen as a part of the law of unjustified enrichment. Instead, it is predominantly understood as the assertion of the agreement's invalidity (which is in suspense until the mistaken party relies on the absence of consent).[197] This subtle conceptual distinction accounts for one great advantage of English over German law.

[194] See above, Chapter IV.D.4.c. (at pp 157–58). In this respect, the power *in rem* resembles what German lawyers would call an *Anwartschaftsrecht*. Even O'Sullivan et al *Law of Rescission* (n 21) [16.12]–[16.40], who assume that 'rescission' is fully retroactive in principle, emphasize that "[r]etrospective title creates no retrospective liability" under English law: ibid [16.41]. Cf also ibid [14.15].

[195] There is a question about whether non-consensual 'bare' trustees can at all be liable for breach of trust, and – if so – to what extent the traditional assumption that liability for breach of trust is strict has to be modified to take account of their special position: see n 320 on pp 157–58.

[196] The transferee's innocence is, of course, much harder to imagine in the case of rescission and revesting of title at common law (for fraud or duress) than in equity (for non-fraudulent misrepresentation or undue influence). In the scenarios we have been considering, he will typically be an intentional wrongdoer and will as such incur liability for the 'inducement wrongs' of deceit or trespass (though there may be a lacuna in economic duress cases): see above, Chapter IV.E.1 (p 160).

[197] See above, section B.1.a.iii of the present chapter (esp pp 171–73).

It will be recalled that the operation of the principle of abstraction leads to a bifurcated system of unwinding impaired consent transfers in German law. If the transferor is able to avoid only the obligatory contract justifying the transfer, the rules on the reversal of an unjustified enrichment determine the parties' mutual claims and liabilities (§§ 812 ff BGB). Where, however, the conveyance is also successfully impeached, the provisions governing the relationship between an owner of an object and its illegitimate possessor apply (§§ 985 ff BGB). We have seen that there exist a number of undesirable incongruities between these two regimes.[198] They derive from the fact that the rules applying between owner and possessor are primarily tailored to what might be described as 'ignorance' cases. Most notable among §§ 987 ff BGB is the lack of a disenrichment defence and the absence of a claim for secondary benefits against any *bona fide* possessor whose possession is not gratuitous. Imagine that the transferor-seller of a painting, A, has for some reason been able to avoid his conveyance to the innocent transferee-buyer, B. Under the 'exclusivity theory' (according to which §§ 812 ff BGB are ousted by §§ 987 ff BGB), only an analogous application of § 988 BGB ensures that B surrenders to A any surviving secondary benefits he has reaped from its possession (eg profits from renting it out).[199] On the other hand, A's ability to recover the painting by means of a *vindicatio* (§ 985 BGB) is in no way affected by what would otherwise be a relevant disenrichment on B's part, eg if B was a donee who has taken his wife out to a celebratory dinner in reliance on his receipt. True that the harshness of this latter lacuna is in practice mitigated through the imposition on A of liability for B's reliance losses (§ 122 BGB),[200] but this remains notionally an extraneous instrument.

English law presents a more integrated picture. With regard to the disenrichment defence, this is the product of understanding the transferor's power *in rem* to revest title as based on the transferee's unjust enrichment at his expense. B's change of position has automatic repercussions on A's ability to revest a proprietary interest in himself. He cannot do so without making good B's disenrichment, ie his reliance loss.[201] It does not make a difference whether the power in question is legal or equitable.[202] And

---

[198] See above, Chapter III.D.3 (pp 83–93).

[199] See above, Chapter III.D.3.b (at p 87, nn 128–129 and corresponding text).

[200] See above, Chapter III.D.3.c (at pp 90–91). On the similarities and differences between § 122 BGB and § 818 III BGB see text to nn 37–43 in the present chapter.

[201] See above, Chapter IV.D.4.b (at p 156). But recall that there is a question about the extent to which reliance losses incurred by a transferee who is in some way 'responsible' for the defect in the transferor's consent count as relevant disenrichments: cf n 28.

[202] But cf comments in nn 196, 201, above. In the case of fraud or duress, the only relevant (disenriching) 'reliance loss' will usually be the rendering of counter-performance by the transferee-defendant.

while the distinction between a revesting of title at common law and the creation of an equitable interest could be described as in some sense also entailing a two-track system of unwinding, the crevasse between the tracks is comparatively small. Expenditure for improvements simply becomes a relevant disenrichment. As far as the transferee's liability for secondary benefits is concerned, the decisive integrating factor is that personal rights to restitution for unjust enrichment are on no view entirely excluded by proprietary restitution. At least to the extent that there is no concurrence between A's right *in personam* against B and his revested right *in rem*,[203] any personal claim which may be available to recover an enrichment over and above the mere receipt of the asset survives the exercise of the power *in rem*. Whatever value remains of secondary benefits should therefore have to be disgorged.[204] Being an integral part of enrichment law, proprietary restitution fits seamlessly into the basic regime governing the reversal of *all* impaired consent transfers in English law.

3. Issues in Insolvency

In two-party situations, one main advantage of proprietary relief lies in the transferor's ability to obtain 'priority' in the transferee's insolvency, or – more precisely – to prevent the object conveyed falling into the latter's estate. Procedurally, the revested property right is asserted via a right of segregation in German law (§ 47 InsO). In English law, a trustee in bankruptcy who interferes with the transferor's better right to possession of a chattel is (personally) liable in conversion,[205] and he may be liable for breach

---

[203] See above, Chapter IV.C (esp pp 121–22 and pp 124–25).

[204] Unfortunately, there is still a lot of uncertainty in English law about the extent to which claims for the 'use value' of an object or other asset are available in unjust enrichment generally. This is no doubt due to the fact that it is often extremely difficult to measure such 'use value', especially if the particular characteristics and preferences of the individual recipient are taken into account. In *Sempra Metals Ltd (formerly Metallgesellschaft Ltd) v Inland Revenue Commissioners* [2007] UKHL 34, [2008] 1 AC 561, the House of Lords recently considered the issue in connection with prematurely levied tax and awarded compound interest at the 'conventional' rate (which was the below-market rate applicable to Government borrowing) as the relevant 'use value' of money.

[205] Cf *Tooke v Hollingworth* (1793) 5 TR 215, 101 ER 121; aff'd (1795) 2 Bl H 501, 126 ER 670; *Re Goldburg (No 2)* [1912] 1 KB 606 (KBD); *Clough Mill Ltd v Martin* [1985] 1 WLR 111 (CA). Note that, in modification of the basic common law position, the liability in conversion of an administrative receiver or company liquidator depends on fault: Insolvency Act 1986, s 234(3) and (4)(a). Cf also D Fox, "Common Law Claims to Substituted Assets" [1999] RLR 55, 72–73; R Goode, *Principles of Corporate Insolvency Law* (2nd edn Sweet & Maxwell, London 2005) [9–62], [10–90]; G Lightman, G Moss and others, *The Law of Administrators and Receivers of Companies* (Sweet & Maxwell, London 2007) [1–011], [7–20], [8–004], [10–057].

of trust if he fails to respect an equitable interest of the transferor's.[206] In any event, a beneficiary's right to execute the trust under the rule in *Saunders v Vautier*[207] will have the same effect as 'segregation'.[208] We have seen that proprietary relief appears to be more widely available in English than in German law. Under the generalized power model of proprietary restitution espoused here, virtually every defective transfer can be reversed *in rem* either at law or in equity. German law, by contrast, is very restrictive. The principle of abstraction ensures that the transferor will rarely have more than a personal restitutionary claim.

Not surprisingly, the position has been questioned on both sides of the Channel. In Germany, the matter appears to be settled *de lege lata*,[209] but it remains an occasional topic of discussion *de lege ferenda*. Critics of the principle of abstraction have long argued that the enrichment creditor's weak position is difficult to justify in policy terms, especially when contrasted with the strong position of a *vindicatio* claimant.[210] On the other

---

[206] A bankrupt's estate does not comprise assets held on trust by him for third parties: cf Insolvency Act 1986, s 283(1) and (3)(a). The circumstances under which a non-consensual trustee can be liable for 'breach of trust' are, however, not entirely clear: see above, pp 157–58, esp n 320.

[207] (1841) 4 Beav 115, 49 ER 282; aff'd (1841) Cr & Ph 240, 41 ER 482.

[208] Transfer of title to the beneficiary will typically require a delivery.

[209] From a comparative point of view, it is interesting to note that the attempts which have been made to elevate the enrichment creditor's claim above those of the transferee's general creditors *de lege lata* have relied heavily on the German equivalent of the trust, the *Treuhand*. Although the interest of a *Treuhand* beneficiary is not generally conceived of as 'proprietary', the beneficiary does enjoy a recognized right of segregation in the 'trustee's' insolvency: n 108 on p 40. This has been seized on (mainly – and perhaps unsurprisingly – by lawyers with a comparative background) to argue that the relationship between the parties to an enrichment claim is analogous to that between 'trustee' and 'beneficiary' and that it should therefore also afford the creditor a right of segregation: D Assfalg, *Die Behandlung von Treugut im Konkurse des Treuhänders* (de Gruyter, Berlin 1960) esp 151, 164–65; A Stadler, *Gestaltungsfreiheit und Verkehrsschutz durch Abstraktion* (Mohr Siebeck, Tübingen 1996) esp 453–61. More critical of the trust construction, but similar in terms of practical outcome: V Behr, *Wertverfolgung: Rechtsvergleichende Überlegungen zur Abgrenzung kollidierender Gläubigerinteressen* (Metzner, Frankfurt/Main 1986) 607–9, 613–15.

[210] Eg F Beyerle, "Der dingliche Vertrag" in *Festschrift für Gustav Boehmer* (Röhrscheid, Bonn 1954) 164, 172; G Kegel, "Verpflichtung und Verfügung: Sollen Verfügungen abstrakt oder kausal sein?" in W Flume and others (eds), *Internationales Recht und Wirtschaftsordnung: Festschrift für FA Mann* (Beck, München 1977) 57, 78–81; E May, *Die Möglichkeit der Beseitigung des Abstraktionsprinzips bei den Verfügungsgeschäften des Fahrnisrechts* (Möller, Rendsburg 1952) 36–37. Criticism of the supposedly 'ungermanic' principle of abstraction was particularly strong during the Third Reich: eg P Heck, *Das abstrakte dingliche Rechtsgeschäft* (Mohr Siebeck, Tübingen 1937); H Lange, "Rechtsgrundabhängigkeit der Verfügung im Boden- und Fahrnisrecht" AcP 146 (1941) 28; J Streier, *Eigentumsübergang und Kausalgeschäft* (Ludolph & Co, Bochum 1938).

hand, its supporters defend the discrepancy, upholding the diverging treatment of the *condictio* and the *vindicatio* in the defendant's insolvency as the very essence of Savigny's doctrine. This seems indeed also to have been the view of the historical legislator.[211] Others do not ascribe as much teleological content to the principle of abstraction. While insisting on the conceptual necessity of the doctrine and thus on the distinction between *condictio* and *vindicatio*, they would be happy to afford a right of segregation to a party who conveys a chattel to another in pursuance of a non-existent obligation.[212] On this view, the principle of abstraction is perfectly compatible with the preferential treatment of a *condictio* claimant.

In England, the law is less settled. If a trend is to be made out at all, it seems to be moving towards – and going even beyond – the current German position. Courts have recently begun to indicate unease about treating claimants in unjust enrichment as anything other than general creditors in the enrichee's insolvency. *Re Goldcorp Exchange Ltd (In Receivership)*[213] and *Westdeutsche Landesbank Girozentrale v Islington London BC*[214] are the most prominent examples of this development. They contain *dicta* to the effect that it would be inappropriate to let mistaken payers (including victims of fraud!) simply 'jump the queue' by affording them a proprietary interest in assets which would otherwise form part of the insolvent's estate.[215] Although both cases can still be squared with the power model of proprietary restitution endorsed in this book,[216] there is a possibility that the judiciary will at some future point deal the death-blow to the idea of proprietary interests generated by unjust enrichment. However, to do so would come at a price. Since the personal claim to restitution is purely value-oriented in English law, ie not a right *in personam ad rem* as under § 812 I 1 BGB, the corollary of denying proprietary restitution would be to

---

For a historical overview see eg Behr *Wertverfolgung* (n 209) 178–83; Stadler *Gestaltungsfreiheit* (n 209) 76–80.

[211] The fathers of the BGB expressly rejected the proposal of according enrichment creditors a right of segregation in the debtor's insolvency, *inter alia* because they were worried about 'undermining' the principle of abstraction: cf A Achilles, H Gebhard and P Spahn (eds), *Protokolle der Kommission für die zweite Lesung des Entwurfs des Bürgerlichen Gesetzbuchs: vol 2* (Guttentag, Berlin 1898) 721–24.

[212] Stadler *Gestaltungsfreiheit* (n 209) 442–65, esp 455–61 (*de lege lata*); Jakobs ZSS (RA) 119 (n 139) 324. Cf already A von Tuhr, *Der Allgemeine Teil des Deutschen Bürgerlichen Rechts: vol 2/2* (Duncker & Humblot, Berlin 1918) 111–12 (*de lege ferenda*).

[213] [1995] 1 AC 74 (PC). Cf text after n 198 on p 139.

[214] [1996] AC 669 (HL). Cf text after n 222 on p 143.

[215] *Re Goldcorp Exchange* (n 213) 102–3 (Lord Mustill); *Westdeutsche Landesbank Girozentrale v Islington London BC* (n 214) 684 (Lord Goff), 703 (Lord Browne-Wilkinson).

[216] See above, Chapter IV.D.3 (esp pp 139–40 and 148–49).

drastically diminish the transferor's chances of specific recovery.[217] Moreover, as will become evident from the following chapters, it would also have significant repercussions for three-party situations.[218] The position of third party purchasers from the transferee would be enhanced (arguably too far),[219] and the transferor's remedies in respect of traceable substitute assets dramatically curtailed.[220] The 'priority' issue is therefore better left to the legislature and tackled as a problem of insolvency law alone.[221] A statute could, for example, stipulate that powers *in rem* are lost as soon as the special regime governing the distribution of an insolvent's assets sets in,[222] or it could prevent the assertion of (re)vested proprietary interests by a provision similar to the 'reputed ownership' clause formerly contained in various Bankruptcy Acts.[223]

---

217 Due to the maxim that 'equity regards as done that which ought to be done', personal rights to specific assets (rights *in personam ad rem*) cannot be divorced from vested equitable interests under English law.

218 Cf below, esp Chapter VI.C (pp 226–49 on the position of third parties) and Chapter VIII.B.1 (pp 276–94 on the transferor's claim to traceable substitute assets).

219 The transferor would – unless 'leapfrogging' was recognized (cf pp 243–49) – no longer have a claim against *mala fide* purchasers and donees, as he does under both the immediate interest and the power model.

220 A claim to traceable substitutes would no longer be available.

221 A forceful argument against taking insolvency policy into account when deciding on the question of proprietary restitution (albeit one coming from the opposite angle of the debate) has recently been made by W Swadling, "Policy Arguments for Proprietary Restitution" in S Degeling and J Edelman (eds), *Unjust Enrichment in Commercial Law* (Thomson Reuters, Sydney 2008) 359.

222 This seems to have been envisaged by Rimer J in *Shalson v Russo* (n 165) [126]. Sympathetic towards the approach: P Watts, "Birks and Proprietary Claims, with Special Reference to Misrepresentation and to Ultra Vires Contracts" in C Rickett and R Grantham (eds), *Structure and Justification in Private Law: Essays for Peter Birks* (Hart, Oxford 2008) 361, 372–76, who argues that the existing section 127(1) of the Insolvency Act 1986 could already be read to have this effect for company liquidations.

223 Eg Bankruptcy Act 1825, s 72. Under the doctrine of 'reputed ownership', assignees in bankruptcy were under certain circumstances authorized to sell goods not belonging to the bankrupt for the benefit of his creditors. The doctrine applied where, at the moment of bankruptcy, the bankrupt had in his possession goods of which he was the 'apparent' or 'reputed owner' with the consent and permission of their 'true owner'. Underlying it was the idea that the 'true owner' had consciously cloaked the bankrupt with a false air of prosperity. This explains why the doctrine could not actually be invoked where the 'true owner' had been fraudulently induced to make a conveyance to the bankrupt. He had then not consented in the relevant way to the bankrupt's 'apparent ownership' and was always able to assert his (revested) title vis-à-vis the assignees: *Load v Green* (1846) 15 Mees & W 216, 153 ER 828; *Smith v Hudson* (1865) 6 Best & S 431, 122 ER 1254. Any new statutory provision dealing with 'proprietary restitution' would therefore have to go beyond the scope of the old doctrine. Interestingly, one of the arguments used to dismiss the suggestion of affording enrichment creditors a right of segregation in German

The policy arguments for and against affording the transferor preferential treatment in the transferee's insolvency need not be rehearsed here. They are finely balanced in both legal systems. From a systematic point of view, what needs to be emphasized is that there is often more than one way of implementing a policy decision. The measure which is least disruptive to the system as a whole is usually preferable. German law would be badly advised to sacrifice the principle of abstraction in order to ensure the equal treatment of *condictio* and *vindicatio* claims in a transferee's insolvency. Conversely, English lawyers should not resolve the dispute over the availability and form of proprietary restitution solely on the basis of its implications for the transferee's general creditors. If the transferor's preferential treatment seems unwarranted, the solution lies not in making English law more 'abstract' than German law, but in adjusting the insolvency regime.

E. Summary

The aim of this chapter has been to compare and contrast the unwinding of impaired consent transfers under English and German law in 'pure' two-party cases. It began in section B with an analysis of the scope of recovery in bargain- and gift-situations, taking into account not only the different grounds for rescission of contract but also functionally equivalent or similar mechanisms. English law was shown to be less willing than German law to let a spontaneously mistaken party escape from a bad bargain, but proved to be more generous (or at least more capable of generosity) in allowing restitution for mistaken gifts. Section C made an attempt to answer the question whether and to what extent English law adheres to the principles of separation and abstraction. It concluded that both played a role in the context of conveyances by delivery (where the *solo consensu*

law (cf n 211 and corresponding text) was precisely the apparent ownership of the enrichee: *Protokolle: vol 2* (n 211) 723: "Es werde nicht selten vorkommen, daß Jemand ein Grundstück oder auch werthvolle Mobilien Jahre lang ohne Rechtsgrund besitze und gerade wegen dieser Gegenstände, die allgemein als sein Eigentum betrachtet werden, Kredit erhalte". ("It would [indirect speech] not be rare for someone to possess a plot of land or even valuable movables for years without a legal basis, and for him to obtain credit precisely because of these items which are generally regarded as belonging to him"). It is an ironic twist of comparative legal history that opponents of a causal transfer system should later have sought to justify the existing consequences of abstraction by invoking the English doctrine of reputed ownership: cf discussion by E von Caemmerer, "Rechtsvergleichung und Reform der Fahrnisübereignung" RabelsZ 12 (1938/39) 675, 699–700, reprinted in HG Leser (ed), *Ernst von Caemmerer: Gesammelte Schriften, vol 1: Rechtsvergleichung und Schuldrecht* (Mohr Siebeck, Tübingen 1968) 146, 171–72, who explained why the comparison was misconceived.

principle does not apply), but that much of the 'gist' of abstraction was lacking in English law. As a result of the structure of the rules on rescission and their interplay with the power model of proprietary restitution, the identical impairment was liable to infect both contract and conveyance. *Fehleridentität*, far from constituting a rare 'exception' to the principle of abstraction, thus describes an almost inevitable pattern. Despite the fact that proprietary relief appears to be much more widely available in English than in German law, section D showed that English law does not encounter the problems German law comes up against when substituting an unwinding regime based on revested property rights (§§ 985 ff BGB) for one based on the transferee's unjust(ified) enrichment (§§ 812 ff BGB). This is because 'proprietary restitution' is a fully integrated part of English enrichment law. The main concern caused by its existence relates to the transferor's treatment in the transferee's insolvency. It was suggested that both legal systems ought to address policy issues of this kind via specific insolvency legislation rather than through an artificial extension or wholesale abolition of the principle of abstraction.

Part Three:

Three-Party Situations

Chapter VI

The Position of Third Party Purchasers

A. Introduction

This chapter is the first in a set of three dealing with impaired consent transfers in three-party situations. It constitutes an extension of the scenario considered in Part Two of the book. We there looked at how a transfer from A to B was properly unwound in English and German law where B was either still in possession of the object transferred, or – if out of possession – where he had lost or destroyed it. Part Three concerns the situation in which the reason for B's inability to return the object to A is the fact that he has conveyed (or purported to convey) it on to a third party purchaser C.[1] A plethora of different constellations can arise from this simple variation of the two-party scenario. B may have effected the transfer to C gratuitously or for valuable consideration,[2] he may have done so before or after A purports to exercise and assert his rights in respect of the object, and C may or may not have been aware of the circumstances under which B obtained the object from A.

The issue addressed by the present chapter relates to the position of a third party purchaser such as C. When does A have any claims against him, and what sort of claims? This depends, in the first instance, on whether the transfer from B to C was effective to pass to C a right *in rem* (in our case ownership or title) which A cannot impeach. If so, then the question arises, on a secondary level, whether C is ever subject to a personal claim by A despite the lack of any proprietary connection between them. We will see that German law affords third parties a high degree of protection on the first count, but that it sometimes counteracts the effects of abstraction and *bona fide* purchase on the second (section B). In English law, by contrast, the position of third party purchasers is more precarious at the proprietary

[1] We will not specifically consider cases where B purports to pass to C only possession, eg under a gratuitous bailment or a contract of hire, or where he transfers (or purports to transfer) to C a right *in rem* less than good title or ownership, eg by way of pledge (but cf comment in n 62 below). As far as English law is concerned, cases where C is the purchaser of an equitable interest will only be mentioned in passing.

[2] In spite of its colloquial meaning, the word 'purchaser' is not to be equated with 'buyer'. It does not even imply the giving of value.

level (section C). The chapter concludes with comparative observations on third party protection through abstraction and *bona fide* purchase as well as on the general weakness of gratuitous acquisitions (section D).

B. Extensive Proprietary Protection of Third Parties in German Law

1. The Effects of Abstraction and a General Principle of *bona fide* Purchase

The German BGB treats third parties taking conveyance of a chattel from a person to whom it has been transferred under the influence of some relevant defect of consent very favourably. In most cases, they will obtain ownership. It is irrelevant for this purpose whether they acquire the chattel for valuable consideration or gratuitously, and even their bad faith as regards the relationship between the original transferor, A, and the transferee, B, will not necessarily disqualify them. We need to distinguish between two situations. On the one hand, the third party purchaser, C, will be protected by the principle of abstraction if the conveyance from A to B is unimpeachable (though it lacks a valid legal basis or *causa*). On the other hand, C has a general principle of *bona fide* purchase to fall back on where the conveyance from A to B is void or voidable at A's behest.

a) Third Party Protection through Abstraction

It is often said that the most important function of the principle of abstraction concerns not two-, but three-party situations. Here its operation prevents the infection of the transaction between B and C (ie transferee and third party) with defects rooted in the relationship between A and B (ie original transferor and transferee).[3] Suppose that A sells and delivers a painting to B who subsequently conveys it on to C. We have seen that most impairments of A's consent will only affect the obligatory contract, giving rise to a *condictio indebiti* for re-conveyance of the painting. The transfer from A to B is unwound purely according to the law of unjustified enrichment (§§ 812 ff BGB).[4] A's (potential)[5] personal claim against B is a right

[3] Cf only the title of A Stadler, *Gestaltungsfreiheit und Verkehrsschutz durch Abstraktion* (Mohr Siebeck, Tübingen 1996) (a rough translation would be "*Freedom of Disposition and Commercial Security through Abstraction*"). The aspect of third party protection is already emphasized in *Motive zu dem Entwurfe eines Bürgerlichen Gesetzbuches für das Deutsche Reich* (2nd edn Guttentag, Berlin 1896) vol 3, 7: "Sicherheit im Rechtsverkehre" ("security in commercial transactions").

[4] See above, Chapter III.B.2 and III.C (pp 60, 64–77).

in personam ad rem acquirendam which in no way distracts from B's absolute proprietary interest in the painting. B has become its owner. As such, he is fully capable of making a valid conveyance to someone other than A. If he agrees to transfer his right *in rem* to C and delivers the painting accordingly, ownership passes (§ 929 1 BGB). It matters not that this is in breach of B's (potential) obligation to A. Indeed, it does not even matter that C is aware of B's (potential) restitutionary liability.[6] He acquires ownership simply by virtue of the fact that he receives the painting in the manner prescribed by the BGB from the person to whom it belongs.

b) Third Party Protection through *bona fide* Purchase

Now assume that the defect of A's consent is such that the conveyance to B as well as the underlying contract of sale is void or voidable (eg for fraud or duress under § 123 BGB). In this case, A retains – or retroactively regains – ownership of the painting. The relationship between A and B is governed by the rules applying between the owner of a thing and its illegitimate possessor (§§ 985 ff BGB).[7] When B purports to make the transfer to C, he does so as a non-owner. Here C is not protected by the effects of the principle of abstraction. However, he may instead be able to rely on the BGB's broad rules on *bona fide* purchase contained in §§ 932 ff.

§ 932 I 1 BGB provides that a purchaser[8] of a movable object acquires ownership of it by virtue of a transfer under § 929 BGB (ie through an appropriate real agreement coupled with a delivery)[9] even if the object does not belong to the person effecting the conveyance, unless the purchaser is in 'bad faith' (lacks 'good faith') at the moment when he would acquire such ownership (ie when the real agreement is concluded or delivery made)[10]. § 932 II BGB defines a lack of good faith as the purchaser's awareness that the object does not belong to the transferor,[11] or his grossly

[5] A may not yet have rescinded his contract of sale with B when B conveys the painting on to C. If and when he does, however, the contract is avoided with retroactive effect (§ 142 I BGB).

[6] Note that, in exceptional circumstances, C may be exposed to a delictual claim by A under § 826 BGB: cf text to n 189 below.

[7] See above, Chapter III.B.3 and III.D (pp 60–63, 77–93).

[8] On the meaning of the word 'purchaser' see n 2 above.

[9] We will not be considering the special rules (and problems!) of *bona fide* purchase in cases where delivery to the third party is constructive: cf §§ 929, 930, 933 BGB; §§ 929, 931, 934 BGB.

[10] Whichever is the later. Note that where the purchaser is already in possession of the object (cf § 929 2 BGB), his possession needs to have been obtained from the person purporting to effect the conveyance (§ 932 I 2 BGB).

[11] In our case, the relevant 'transferor' is the first transferee (B), not the original transferor (A).

negligent ignorance of this fact. The provision needs to be read in conjunction with § 142 II BGB, which equates knowledge of the right to rescind a transaction with knowledge of its invalidity.[12] The upshot is that our third party purchaser C is in bad faith (*mala fide*) if he knows, or as a result of his own gross negligence fails to notice, that A's conveyance of the painting to B is void or voidable. Simple negligence, by way of contrast, does not disqualify C.[13] As between two innocent parties, § 932 BGB prefers C's interest in the security of his receipt over A's interest in the security of his rights as owner. A justification for this choice can be gleaned from § 935 BGB. *Bona fide* purchase of lost or stolen things is not normally possible.[14] So long as A can be said to have voluntarily parted with possession of the painting, he has created an appearance of ownership in B's favour upon which C has relied.[15] In our scenario, A's loss of possession will almost inevitably be consensual. Neither mistake nor fraud negative the relevant 'natural' intention required to give up possession.[16] Even duress does not necessarily entail an involuntary loss for the purposes of § 935 BGB, except where the pressure brought to bear on A is so overwhelming that it is completely irresistible.[17]

---

[12] § 142 II BGB further equates negligent ignorance of the right to rescind with negligent ignorance of the invalidity. Note that the equation only applies where the right to rescind is in fact exercised.

[13] C will not be liable in delict (§ 823 I BGB) for infringing A's right of ownership in the case of simple negligence since that would undermine the scheme of §§ 932 ff BGB: cf RGZ 85, 61, 64; RGZ 90, 395, 397–98; BGH JZ 1956, 490; BGH WM 1967, 564, 566.

[14] Exceptions are made for money (cash), bearer instruments and things transferred at public auction: § 935 II BGB.

[15] Cf § 1006 BGB (*Rechtsschein des Besitzes*). We can here detect a remote parallel to the reasoning behind the old English doctrine of 'reputed ownership', although this applied in a different context (insolvency) and required the transferor to have *consciously* cloaked the transferee with a false air of prosperity: cf n 223 on pp 209–10, and see also Bramwell B's *dictum* in *Higgons v Burton* (1857) 26 LJ Exch 342, 344, set out in n 55 on p 227 below.

[16] RGZ 101, 224, 225–26; BGHZ 4, 10, 34–37; BGH NJW 1953, 1506, 1507; K Rebmann, FJ Säcker and R Rixecker (eds), *Münchener Kommentar zum Bürgerlichen Gesetzbuch, vol 6: §§ 854–1296* (4th edn Beck, München 2004) § 935 [9] (Quack); O Palandt (Begr), *Bürgerliches Gesetzbuch* (67th edn Beck, München 2008) § 935 [5] (Bassenge); J von Staudinger (Begr), *J von Staudingers Kommentar zum Bürgerlichen Gesetzbuch: §§ 925–984* (Neubearbeitung 2004: Sellier de Gruyter, Berlin 2004) § 935 [11] (Wiegand).

[17] BGHZ 4, 10, 38–39; BGH NJW 1953, 1506, 1507. Agreeing: O Jauernig (ed), *Bürgerliches Gesetzbuch: Kommentar* (12th edn Beck, München 2007) § 935 [4] (Jauernig); HT Soergel (Begr), *Bürgerliches Gesetzbuch, vol 14: §§ 854–984* (13th edn Kohlhammer, Stuttgart 2002) § 935 [5] (Henssler). Parts of the academic literature are critical of the case law, arguing that the loss of possession under the influence of threats is typically involuntary and ought therefore to preclude *bona fide* purchase: cf *Münchener Kommen-*

To sum up: German law's general principle of *bona fide* purchase acts as a sort of 'safety net' for those third parties whose acquisition is not already secured on a proprietary level by the operation of the principle of abstraction. In circumstances allowing for a *vindicatio* in the relationship between A and B, § 932 I 1 BGB steps in to protect C. Underlying this is the idea that A has clothed B with the appearance of ownership. Unless there is a reason why C cannot rely on this appearance (cf §§ 932 II, 142 II BGB), A bears the risk of losing his right *in rem* through B's unauthorized disposition.

2. Remaining Liability of Third Party Recipients

Where does this leave C in relation to A? Here we must distinguish cases where C has slipped through the double-layered net of proprietary protection constituted by abstraction and §§ 932 ff BGB, from those where a personal liability in unjustified enrichment exceptionally arises *despite* the acquisition of ownership by C.

a) Receipt of an Item Belonging to the Transferor

If the transfer from A to B is void or rescinded and C does not qualify as a *bona fide* purchaser, he obtains only possession when B purports to effect the conveyance to him. Ownership remains with A. Since there is no contractual arrangement between C and A conferring on the former a right to possession as against the latter (cf § 986 I BGB), their relationship is governed by §§ 985 ff BGB. So long as C remains in possession, A can recover the painting by means of a *vindicatio* (§ 985 BGB). All further rights and liabilities are determined by the rules of the owner-possessor-relationship (*Eigentümer-Besitzer-Verhältnis*) in §§ 987 ff BGB. Not having qualified for *bona fide* purchase, C is almost inevitably a *mala fide* possessor in our scenario.[18] He will therefore be liable to A for all secondary benefits he has reaped (§§ 987, 990 I BGB),[19] for any culpable damage,

---

tar: vol 6 (n 16) § 935 [9] (Quack); *Palandt* (n 16) § 935 [5] (Bassenge); *Staudinger* (n 16) § 935 [11] (Wiegand).

[18] Except in cases where A's loss of possession is classified as 'involuntary' as a result of his being exposed to (extreme) duress (cf n 17 and corresponding text), the reason why C does not qualify as a *bona fide* purchaser will be his knowledge or grossly negligent ignorance of the invalidity or voidability of A's conveyance to B (cf §§ 932 II, 142 II BGB). This state of mind also disqualifies C from the privileges accorded to *bona fide* possessors (cf § 990 I 1 BGB).

[19] If C were, exceptionally, a *bona fide* possessor (cf n 18) who had acquired possession gratuitously, he would be liable to disgorge secondary benefits in accordance with § 988 BGB.

loss or destruction of the painting (§§ 989, 990 I BGB),[20] and he is only entitled to reimbursement for 'necessary' expenditure (§ 994 BGB).[21]

Whether §§ 985 ff BGB determine C's position conclusively, or to what extent recourse can be had to the law of unjustified enrichment, is a matter of some interest. It will be recalled that §§ 987 ff BGB take precedence over §§ 812 ff BGB within their (limited) field of concern, but that they do not purport to exclude enrichment claims as far as the enrichment is derived from the 'substance' of the object itself.[22] Yet there is another principle to consider. According to this principle, the law of unjustified enrichment accords precedence to performance relationships over non-performance relationships (so-called *Vorrang der Leistungsbeziehung*).[23] To the extent that C's enrichment is accounted for by B's performance, a claim by A is excluded. This explains why A's *vindicatio* does not here compete with a *condictio possessionis* (as in two-party situations).[24] Although C has acquired possession of the painting, and although possession counts as a relevant enrichment under § 812 I 1 BGB, C's possession is derived from the previous possessor B (who bestowed it upon him by an act of performance) and was thus obtained at B's, not at A's expense.[25] But what about the case in which A's ownership is subsequently lost, leaving C enriched?[26] Are enrichment claims based on the infringement of A's right

---

[20] Delictual claims for infringement of A's right of ownership (§§ 823 ff BGB) will usually be excluded: cf §§ 992, 993 I BGB. However, where C has committed the crime of 'dealing in stolen goods' (§ 259 StGB: *Hehlerei*), which encompasses also the intentional dealing in goods obtained by fraud, he will be strictly liable for all consequential losses under § 823 II and under §§ 989, 990 BGB (cf § 848 BGB and see above, p 83).

[21] For details on the position of *mala fide* possessors see above, Chapter III.D.2.b (pp 81–83).

[22] See above, text to nn 97–100 on p 81.

[23] Also known as *Vorrang der Leistungskondiktion* (precedence of performance-based enrichment claims) or alternatively as *Subsidiarität der Eingriffskondiktion* (subsidiarity of infringement-based enrichment claims).

[24] Cf above, Chapter III.D.1 (p 78).

[25] A *caveat* is warranted here. If the suggestion advanced below (text to nn 190–204), namely that A's performance-based enrichment claim against B (*Leistungskondiktion* under § 812 I 1 alt 1 BGB) ought to be 'extended' to encompass the remote recipient C in cases where C is *mala fide* with respect to the legal basis between A and B, were accepted, then one would have to think about similarly 'extending' A's *condictio possessionis* against B to encompass the *mala fide* possessor C. Yet it will be seen that 'leap-frogging' B can only be justified in so far as it prevents what can be regarded as a lacuna in the relationship between A and C. The *mala fide* recipient from an enrichee-owner should (sometimes) be forced to surrender the object received to the enrichment creditor. No such lacuna exists where C is the *mala fide* recipient from a mere possessor. The proposed analogy with § 822 BGB is therefore not required in the latter scenario.

[26] This will become relevant where C disposes of the painting to a fourth party in circumstances where the *bona fide* purchase rules apply, leaving C with traceable substitute

of ownership (category *Eingriffskondiktion*) barred by C's performance relationship with B? The answer is that they are not.[27] This can be accounted for in two ways.[28] First, B's performance to C encompassed only possession, not ownership, so there is simply no precedence to observe in this respect. Second, the conflict of interest between the owner of the object disposed of without authorization (here A) and its third party purchaser (here C) is conclusively regulated by §§ 932 ff BGB. Where the rules of *bona fide* purchase do not avail C, the legal system has resolved this conflict against him, and C's dealings with B cannot then be used to justify an enrichment which is ultimately at A's expense.[29]

b) Gratuitous Acquisition of Ownership

In certain circumstances, C is exposed to claims by A despite the fact that he has become owner of the painting. The law of unjustified enrichment here counteracts the protection afforded to third party purchasers on the proprietary level. We have seen that the rules on the acquisition of ownership – whether as a result of abstraction or by virtue of the rules on *bona fide* purchase – do not distinguish between purchasers for value and those

---

assets. And it will also play a role where the object is a fungible which C consumes (thereby saving money), or where A's ownership of the object is lost by operation of law, eg under the rules of accession or specification (cf §§ 946 ff BGB).

[27] This is wholly uncontentious for the special case of the *Eingriffskondiktion* contained in § 816 I 1 BGB, which caters for the *bona fide* purchase scenario (outlined in n 26 above): cf BGHZ 9, 333. § 816 I 1 BGB is generally understood to found a claim to the traceable substitute assets of the object: see below, Chapter VIII.C.1.b.ii (pp 298–305). It is also well-settled that, in the consumption scenario (cf n 26), the 'ordinary' *Eingriffskondiktion* contained in § 812 I 1 alt 2 BGB can apply beside §§ 987 ff BGB and despite the fact that possession was obtained through the performance of an intermediary: cf BGHZ 14, 7. The specification/accession scenario (cf n 26) was long thought to be more problematic, but in the famous case of BGHZ 55, 176 (*Jungbullenfall*), the Federal Supreme Court held that a claim under §§ 951 I 1, 812 I 1 alt 2 BGB (another special case of the *Eingriffskondiktion*) would lie. It is clear that in all three scenarios, any purchase price which C may have paid to B does not count as a relevant disenrichment, even if C were to have acted in good faith: BGHZ 9, 333, 335–36; BGHZ 14, 7, 9–10; BGHZ 55, 176, 179–80; BGH NJW 1970, 2059.

[28] The two explanations which follow are closely connected and, in our scenario, no more than two sides of the same coin. However, the second explanation has a potentially broader reach. It can deal with cases where C's enrichment is referable to *both* A's loss of ownership and at the same time to a performance on B's part, eg where B – as part of his contract with C – effects the accession which results in C's enrichment at A's expense (without a prior delivery – a variation of the third example given in n 26 above).

[29] Cf BGHZ 55, 176, 177–78. The Federal Supreme Court suggested that while the acquisition of ownership under §§ 932 ff BGB provided a 'legal basis' in the relationship between former owner and *bona fide* purchaser (but cf comment in n 34 below), this was different where ownership was 'acquired' by virtue of §§ 946 ff BGB.

who receive an object gratuitously.[30] On a secondary, personal level, however, the position of the latter is markedly weaker than that of the former. § 816 I 2 BGB and § 822 BGB make such purchasers vulnerable to claims in unjustified enrichment. Both provisions ensure that a person who has acquired ownership gratuitously (here C) cannot retain this enrichment if the original transferor (here A) is thereby deprived of a claim he would otherwise have had against the original transferee (here B). § 816 I 2 BGB applies to cases where C is a *bona fide* purchaser under §§ 932 ff BGB, while § 822 BGB concerns the situation where B was, in consequence of the principle of abstraction, owner when making the conveyance to C.

(i) Personal liability under § 816 I 2 BGB

§ 816 I 1 BGB provides: "If an unauthorized person [here B] disposes of an object in such a way that the disposition is effective vis-à-vis the person entitled [here A], he is obliged to surrender to the person entitled what he has obtained by virtue of the disposition". As will be seen below, this passage concerns what English lawyers would call 'tracing' and 'claiming'.[31] It establishes A's personal claim to substitute assets where B has disposed of an item belonging to A in an unauthorized manner. But what if B has received no substitute? A's rights under § 816 I 1 BGB would appear to be worthless where the transfer from B to C was gratuitous.[32] This is why the section continues in § 816 I 2 BGB: "If the disposition is made gratuitously, the same obligation applies to the person who obtains an immediate legal advantage through the disposition [here C]". C is therefore under an obligation to surrender to A what he has gratuitously received from B, in our example ownership and possession of the painting.[33] Thus § 816 I 2

---

30 See above, section B.1.a–b of the present chapter (pp 216–19).

31 See below, Chapter VIII.C.1.b.ii (pp 298–305).

32 Depending on the exact interpretation of the provision (cf text to nn 126–128 on pp 299–300), it is possible to come to the conclusion that B is liable under § 816 I 1 BGB even where his transfer to C is gratuitous. And if he is *mala fide* (eg a fraudster), he will typically be disqualified from raising the disenrichment defence in § 818 III BGB. In this sense only, A's rights against B may not be worthless. Critical of the resulting concurrence of claims under § 816 I 1 BGB and § 816 I 2 BGB (and therefore favouring an interpretation of § 816 I 1 BGB which avoids the concurrence): K Rebmann, FJ Säcker and R Rixecker (eds), *Münchener Kommentar zum Bürgerlichen Gesetzbuch, vol 5: §§ 705–853* (4th edn Beck, München 2004) § 816 [4], [8], [42] (Lieb).

33 § 816 I 2 BGB can be regarded as an exception to the principle that a *Nichtleistungskondiktion* between A and C is barred where there is a valid performance relationship between B and C (*Vorrang der Leistungsbeziehung*): cf text to n 23 above. Yet although C obtains ownership by virtue of B's performance, he obtains it at A's, not at B's expense. There is a debate whether – as in the context of § 988 BGB – an acquisition *sine causa* should be equated with a gratuitous acquisition, ie whether § 816 I 2 BGB

BGB to some extent reverses the effects of §§ 932 ff BGB.[34] Although a gratuitous recipient can be a *bona fide* purchaser, his acquisition of ownership may not be permanent.

One could ask why the BGB goes to the trouble of 'correcting' the proprietary position via its law on unjustified enrichment instead of simply stating – as English law does – that only purchasers for value can take advantage of the *bona fide* purchase rules.[35] Three closely related reasons come to mind, one theoretical, the other two practical. Conceptually, any attempt to make the provision of valuable consideration a condition of *bona fide* purchase would come up against the principles of separation and abstraction.[36] The validity of the conveyance from B to C is entirely independent of the nature of the underlying obligatory contract. § 929 1 BGB requires only a delivery and a real agreement between the purchaser and a person entitled to make the transfer (ie either the owner or someone authorized by him). In setting out when a purchaser may reasonably rely on the appearance of ownership created by possession, the rules on *bona fide*

applies by analogy where the obligatory contract between B and C is void or rescinded: cf BGHZ 37, 363, and overview in *Palandt* (n 16) § 816 [16]–[19] (Sprau); *Münchener Kommentar: vol 5* (n 32) § 816 [40]–[41] (Lieb); J von Staudinger (Begr), *J von Staudingers Kommentar zum Bürgerlichen Gesetzbuch: §§ 812–822* (Neubearbeitung 2007: Sellier de Gruyter, Berlin 2007) § 816 [16]–[22] (S Lorenz). If such an equation is accepted, then A has a direct claim against C (so-called *Lehre von der Einheitskondiktion*). If it is rejected, then A is confined to a claim against B, who in turn has a claim against C which he will have to assign to A (so-called Lehre von der *Doppelkondiktion*). For an English account see C Zülch, "*Bona fide* Purchase, Property and Restitution: *Lipkin Gorman v Karpnale* in German Law" in W Swadling (ed), *The Limits of Restitutionary Claims: A Comparative Analysis* (UKNCCL, London 1997) 106, 125–36.

34 See above, section B.1.b of the present chapter (pp 217–19). The generality of the proposition that §§ 932 ff BGB entail a 'legal basis' for the *bona fide* purchaser's enrichment at the former owner's expense (cf n 29 above) must be doubted or at least qualified in the light of § 816 I 2 BGB. *Jauernig* (n 17) § 816 [19] (Stadler), sees § 816 I 2 BGB as an 'exception' to the general proposition, but it may be better to say that only *bona fide* purchase *for value* provides the requisite 'legal basis' or justification.

35 Although §§ 932 ff BGB apply only to so-called 'market transactions' (*Verkehrsgeschäfte*), this means no more than that transferor and transferee must not be substantially identical legal entities. It does not import a need for value to be given in exchange for the conveyance. It is nevertheless interesting to note that the question of whether *bona fide* purchase should depend on the provision of consideration had actually been considered by the draftsmen of the BGB, albeit only in the context of immovables: see A Achilles, H Gebhard and P Spahn (eds), *Protokolle der Kommission für die zweite Lesung des Entwurfs des Bürgerlichen Gesetzbuchs: vol 3* (Guttentag, Berlin 1899) 82–84, and cf the discussion by D Rothoeft, "Vermögensverlust und Bereicherungsausgleich" AcP 163 (1963) 215, 220.

36 This is what ultimately persuaded the BGB legislator not to introduce a consideration requirement as far as *bona fide* purchase of realty was concerned: cf *Protokolle: vol 3* (n 35) 82.

purchase merely help overcome the transferor's lack of entitlement. It is hard to see how the fact that the recipient is or is not a purchaser for value could be made relevant in this context.[37] From a practical point of view, there is also much to be said for protecting even gratuitous acquisitions under §§ 932 ff BGB and allowing the former owner no more than a personal claim against the recipient. First, liability under § 816 I 2 BGB is capped by the third party purchaser's abstractly surviving enrichment. C can invoke § 818 III BGB if he has expended money on restoring the painting or taking his wife to dinner in order to celebrate B's gift. Disenrichment would provide no defence to a *vindicatio*.[38] Secondly, the existing construction ensures that transfers effected by C (eg a conveyance to a fourth party D) are fully valid without further recourse to the *bona fide* purchase rules. C is owner of the painting when making the conveyance. Defects which ultimately originate in the relationship between A and B are thus not in danger of indefinite perpetuation down a chain of transactions.[39] Commercial certainty is increased. Of course, A pays the price for C's ability to rely on § 818 III BGB and the increase in commercial certainty. Given, however, that he enabled B to make the gratuitous trans-

---

[37] It was argued earlier that the English law on conveyances by delivery shares many features of the German abstract transfer system, even if English law ultimately lacks the 'gist' of abstraction *à la* BGB: see above, Chapter V.C (pp 191–202). If this is correct, then the question arises how the English *bona fide* purchase principles can sustain a requirement of consideration, especially in so far as the *solo consensu* rule does not apply (money cases in particular). The answer probably lies in the fact that English law does not think of *bona fide* purchase as acquisitive, but as normally extinctive (at least in money cases): cf n 51 below. B does not pass A's title on to C. Instead, he transfers his own (possessory) title, and the *bona fide* purchase rules then provide C with a *defence* against the assertion by A of his (previously superior) title in the notes and coins. Restricting this defence to purchasers for value is a legitimate choice for English law to make. Indeed, we will see below that it is possible, in certain situations (in which C does actually acquire A's former title, A thereby losing his *power in rem*), to conceive of *bona fide* purchase as a kind of conclusive change of position defence (one which does not inquire into the adequacy of the consideration): cf text to nn 175–178 below. Looking at it from this angle, the need for C to have given *some* value in exchange for the object before being allowed to invoke the *bona fide* purchase defence is self-explanatory.

[38] Under the regime of the *Eigentümer-Besitzer-Verhältnis*, C would be confined to claims for necessary (§ 994 BGB) and useful (§ 996 BGB) expenditure. Note that, unlike in the two-party scenario (cf Chapter III.D.3.c, esp pp 90–91), a third party possessor has no claim for recovery of reliance losses against the rescinding transferor under § 122 I BGB. This is because he was not the recipient of the declaration of intention which the transferor later avoids. In the three-party scenario, there is thus nothing to make up for the lack of a disenrichment defence in §§ 987 ff BGB.

[39] Note, however, that if the fourth party, D, is – in turn – a gratuitous recipient, then D may be liable to A under § 822 BGB: cf immediately below, section B.2.b.ii of the present chapter (pp 225–26).

fer to C in the first place, this fully accords with the idea underlying the German *bona fide* purchase rules.

(ii) Personal liability under § 822 BGB

§ 822 BGB in some sense mirrors § 816 I 2 BGB, but it is brought to bear in a different situation. The provision applies where A, as a result of the principle of abstraction, had lost ownership of the painting even before B made the gratuitous transfer to C. A was therefore confined to a *condictio* from the outset.[40] § 822 BGB provides:

> "If the recipient [here B] gratuitously bestows what he has obtained upon a third party [here C], then, to the extent that the recipient's liability to make restitution is in consequence excluded, the third party is obliged to surrender what he has received as if he had, without legal cause, received it from the creditor [here A]."

Although C acquired the painting from its owner, he is liable to surrender his enrichment to A in so far as B's enrichment liability towards A is thus excluded by § 818 III BGB.[41] Assume that, after effecting the transfer to B, A finds that there was no legal basis for it (eg because a supposed testamentary legacy turns out to be void)[42]. Before A has a chance to reclaim the painting, B makes a gift of it to C. If B does so not knowing of his restitutionary liability, he is now completely disenriched and A's claim under § 812 I 1 alt 1 BGB is destroyed.[43] In these circumstances, § 822 BGB provides that C comes under an obligation to surrender the painting to A as though he had, *sine causa*, received it directly from A.[44] It is sub-

[40] See above, section B.1.a of the present chapter (pp 216–17).

[41] There is a dispute whether § 822 BGB should also be applied – either directly or by analogy – where the reason why A cannot recover from B is that B is insolvent (rather than disenriched). Pro: eg V Behr, *Wertverfolgung: Rechtsvergleichende Überlegungen zur Abgrenzung kollidierender Gläubigerinteressen* (Metzner, Frankfurt/Main 1986) 278–81; HG Koppensteiner and E Kramer, *Ungerechtfertigte Bereicherung* (2nd edn de Gruyter, Berlin 1988) 23; R Knütel, "§ 822 BGB und die Schwächen unentgeltlichen Erwerbs" NJW 1989, 2504, 2508–9; *Münchener Kommentar: vol 5* (n 32) § 822 [6] (Lieb). Contra: eg BGH NJW 1969, 605; BGH NJW 1999, 1026, 1028; BGHZ 154, 88, 92; F Bockholdt, *Die Haftung des unentgeltlichen Erwerbers gemäß § 822 BGB* (Lang, Frankfurt/Main 2004) 256–64; U Kornblum, "Das Geschenk der Defraudantin" JuS 1970, 437, 441–42; D Reuter and M Martinek, *Ungerechtfertigte Bereicherung* (Mohr Siebeck, Tübingen 1983) 366–67; *Staudinger* (n 33) § 822 [11] (S Lorenz).

[42] Cf §§ 1939, 2147, 2174 BGB.

[43] Note that B's ability to rely on § 818 III BGB will be markedly more restricted where he has acquired the painting in pursuance of an invalid reciprocal contract: see above, Chapter III.C.3 (pp 71–77).

[44] § 822 BGB constitutes another exception to the general precedence of performance relationships (*Vorrang der Leistungsbeziehung*): cf n 23 and corresponding text, as well as n 33 above. It differs from § 816 I 2 BGB in respect of the 'at the expense of' inquiry. In § 816 I 2 BGB, C acquires possession at B's and ownership at A's expense, while in

mitted that § 822 should also be applied if B, to make space for the new painting, had given a less valuable work of art to C.[45] Here B is only partially disenriched. Again, C ought to give up what he has gratuitously obtained.[46] Of course, C's liability is in all cases restricted to his surviving enrichment. To the extent that he, too, has in good faith changed his position, A's personal claim against him is excluded (§ 818 III BGB).[47]

C. The Relatively Weak Position of Third Parties in English Law

1. Scope of the *bona fide* Purchase Rules

In the comparative analysis of two-party situations, it was argued that although there was a sense in which transfers of title effected by delivery could be described as 'abstract', English law lacked the 'gist' of the principle of abstraction *à la* BGB.[48] Proprietary restitution is (or ought to be) virtually always available after an impaired consent transfer of the kind considered here, provided only that the object in question[49] is still in existence.[50] As a result, abstraction plays no or at least no meaningful role in the protection of third party purchasers under English law. Instead, the rules on *bona fide* purchase carry all the weight. If A, under some relevant impairment of consent, conveys a painting to B, any purchaser from B

§ 822 BGB both C's ownership and his possession are acquired at B's expense. As in the context of § 816 I 2 BGB, there is a question whether § 822 BGB applies by analogy where, instead of being gratuitous, C's acquisition from B is *sine causa*: cf n 33. Most authors deny this: eg *Palandt* (n 16) § 822 [6] (Sprau); *Staudinger* (n 33) § 822 [9] (S Lorenz).

[45] Cf Bockholdt *Haftung des unentgeltlichen Erwerbers* (n 41) 113–17, 233–34; F Bockholdt, Anmerkung zum Urteil des BGH vom 10.02.2004 (case note) in JZ 2004, 796, 798. More cautious: *Reuter/Martinek* (n 41) 370. Critical, but only on the basis of a very narrow reading of § 818 III BGB which does not appear appropriate outside the context of reciprocal contracts: *Staudinger* (n 33) § 822 [6] (S Lorenz). BGH NJW 1999, 1026, 1027, left the issue open.

[46] In line with the principle underlying BGHZ 158, 63 (where the third party donee had actually received a traceable substitute asset from the immediate 'enrichee'), there is a question whether C should have a choice between surrendering to A the painting received from B or merely its value.

[47] If a gratuitous transfer by C to a fourth party, D, accounts for C's disenrichment, then D will, in turn, be liable to A under § 822 BGB: *Münchener Kommentar: vol 5* (n 32) § 822 [7] (Lieb); *Palandt* (n 16) § 822 [2] (Sprau); *Reuter/Martinek* (n 41) 362–63.

[48] See above, Chapter V.C (pp 191–202).

[49] Or its traceable substitute(s): cf below, Chapter VIII.B.1 (esp pp 289–94).

[50] See above, Chapter IV.D (pp 125–59, esp pp 151–53).

(like C) acquires a title which is good as against A only if he comes within one of the recognized 'exceptions' to the basic principle that *nemo dat quod non habet*.[51]

In contradistinction to German law, there is no general rule that a purchaser who, in good faith, acquires an object from a person not entitled to dispose of it, thereby becomes its 'owner', unless the object in question was lost or stolen. For one, English law affords proprietary protection only to purchasers *for value*.[52] Secondly, and more importantly, it has not generalized the rules on *bona fide* purchase except in relation to money used as currency, bills of exchange and similar negotiable instruments.[53] As Bramwell B pointed out in *Higgons v Burton*,[54] the common law never arrived at the proposition "that whenever a party was intrusted with goods for any purpose, even as a mere warehouseman, he might dispose of them".[55] Such a principle would, in Bramwell B's view, have been "very dangerous to trade".[56] It is therefore necessary to determine in each case whether the circumstances of C's purchase from B were such that he takes free from A's right or other interest *in rem*. Often – but not invariably – one of the *nemo dat* 'exceptions' will apply. We need to distinguish between cases where C acquires the painting before A purports to exercise his (legal or equitable) power *in rem*, and those where he acquires it only after A has avoided the conveyance to B (either at law or in equity).[57]

---

[51] See above, Chapter II.D.4 (at pp 51–52). In English law, it is better to view (most or all of) the *bona fide* purchase rules not as *nemo dat* 'exceptions', but as instances of situations in which a relevant (legal or equitable) interest is extinguished.

[52] Cf already text to n 35 above. On the meaning of the word 'purchaser' see n 2. In order to be a purchaser for value, the purchaser must actually have provided the consideration in question, ie rendered performance. A mere promise to perform is not enough: cf *Story v Lord Windsor* (1743) 2 Atk 630, 26 ER 776; *Hardingham v Nicholls* (1745) 3 Atk 304, 26 ER 977.

[53] Cf *Miller v Race* (1758) 1 Burr 452, 97 ER 398; *Peacock v Rhodes* (1781) 2 Doug 633, 99 ER 402; *Wookey v Pole* (1820) 4 Barn & Ald 1, 106 ER 839; Bills of Exchange Act 1882, s 29.

[54] (1857) 26 LJ Exch 342.

[55] Ibid 344. His Lordship added that "[i]t might or it might not be reasonable that an act of parliament should pass, providing, by analogy to the law of bankruptcy, or to reputed ownership, or by an extension of the principles of the Factors Act, that whenever one person intrusted another with property under such circumstances as to allow him to appear as the owner, such person so intrusted should have the power of disposing of the property. But that is a different question. The Courts of law have no legislative power".

[56] Ibid. Note the interesting divergence between Bramwell B's perception and that of German law, where the broad principle of *bona fide* purchase is generally thought to *facilitate* trade.

[57] Cases where no title passed to B in the first place, eg because A was deceived into mistaking B for another individual, will be referred to where they provide a useful point of contrast or comparison. By and large, C's position in such a case is similar to that of a

a) *Bona fide* Purchase before Exercise of Power *in rem*

A transferor who has not managed to secure for himself proprietary restitution *in specie* by 'pulling back' title to the object transferred when a third party purchaser for value acquires it, is in a relatively weak position. Section 23 of the Sale of Goods Act 1979 provides:

> "When the seller of goods [here B] has a voidable title to them, but his title has not been avoided [by A] at the time of the sale, the buyer [here C] acquires a good title to the goods, provided he buys them in good faith and without notice of the seller's [ie B's] defect of title."

If therefore C, not knowing and without notice of the circumstances under which B obtained the painting from A, buys it from B and pays the agreed purchase price, he takes B's title free from any power *in rem* which A may have had in respect of it. Put differently: C's ability to rely on the *bona fide* purchase defence contained in section 23 'kills off' A's power *in rem*.

Like its predecessor in the Sale of Goods Act 1893,[58] the provision is essentially a codification of the old common law rule protecting *bona fide* purchasers for value without notice against certain defects in the proprietary interest they acquire.[59] So long as A's conveyance to B was effective to pass title and B still retains this title when he makes the transfer to the innocent buyer C, the latter need not subsequently concern himself with the relationship between A and B. This is why it is often said to be crucial whether a contract of sale between the transferor A and the transferee B is 'void' or merely 'voidable'.[60] It should be noted that the common law rule on *bona fide* purchase, which sometimes appears in the confusing guise of the so-called 'third party rights bar to rescission',[61] is of wider application than section 23. It protects all purchasers for value, not just 'buyers'. If C

---

purchaser who acquires B's title to the painting after A has revested his own (former) title by exercising a common law power *in rem*: cf below, section C.1.b of the present chapter (esp text to nn 71–75 on pp 230–31).

[58] Sale of Goods Act 1893, s 23.

[59] Pre-1893 cases: eg *White v Garden* (1851) 10 CB 919, 138 ER 364; *Kingsford v Merry* (1856) 11 Exch Rep 577, 156 ER 960, rev'd on other grounds (1856) 1 Hurl & N 503, 156 ER 1299; cf also *Babcock v Lawson* (1880) 5 QBD 284 (CA) 286 (Bamwell LJ).

[60] Contrast *Cundy v Lindsay* (1878) 3 App Cas 459 (HL); *Ingram v Little* [1961] 1 QB 31 (CA); with *King's Norton Metal Co Ltd v Edridge, Merrett, & Co Ltd* (1897) 14 TLR 98 (CA); *Phillips v Brooks Ltd* [1919] 2 KB 243 (KBD); *Lewis v Averay* [1972] 1 QB 198 (CA). In the most recent precedent on the issue, *Shogun Finance Ltd v Hudson* [2003] UKHL 62, [2004] 1 AC 919, the reason why it mattered whether the contract between the rogue and the claimant finance company was 'void' or 'voidable' was slightly different. It was a contract of hire purchase, which – if merely 'voidable' – would have enabled a *bona fide* purchaser from the rogue to rely on the *nemo dat* exception in section 27 of the Hire Purchase Act 1964. The Sale of Goods Act 1979, s 23, was not at stake.

[61] See below, Chapter VII (pp 259–74).

receives the painting from B in exchange for his bicycle (or even as a pledge to secure a debt), he also takes the relevant property right free from A's power *in rem*.[62]

While common law powers *in rem* to revest title thus give way to *bona fide* purchase of any proprietary interest recognized by the common law, equitable powers *in rem* are more fragile still.[63] If A was not defrauded or coerced by duress into making the transfer to B, but was acting under the impression of some material non-fraudulent misrepresentation, undue influence or – outside the contractual context – a spontaneous mistake, he can avoid the conveyance in equity only.[64] His ability to turn B into a trustee of the painting is a 'mere equity'. As such, it can be defeated even by purchasers of equitable interests.[65] If B were, for valuable consideration, to declare a trust of the painting in C's favour before A has exercised his power *in rem*, or – in practice much more importantly – if B grants C an equitable charge to secure a debt,[66] C's vested equitable interest is not subject to A's power.[67]

Section 23 of the Sale of Goods Act 1979 and the corresponding *bona fide* purchase rules at common law and in equity may serve as another

---

[62] Cf *Kingsford v Merry* (n 59); *Whitehorn Bros v Davison* [1911] 1 KB 463 (CA); *Phillips v Brooks Ltd* (n 60). Note that a delivery by way of pledge does not involve an outright transfer of title to the pledgee, but merely results in the creation of a 'special property': cf eg *Babcock v Lawson* (n 59). It is therefore submitted that, in the case of a pledge by B to C, A's power *in rem* should not be extinguished by *bona fide* purchase, but – upon its exercise – A's revested right *in rem* (title) should instead remain subject to C's rights as *bona fide* pledgee. In *Kingsford v Merry* (1856) 11 Exch Rep 577, 579; 156 ER 960, 961, Pollock CB indeed stated that the claimant transferors were "not in a condition to maintain an action against the defendant [third party pledgee], in which they insist upon a right to the possession of the [goods], *until they have paid or tendered to him his demand in respect of the advance* to [the transferee]" (emphasis added).

[63] Query whether section 23 of the Sale of Goods Act 1979 is intended to encompass such cases or whether it is confined to the common law.

[64] See above, Chapter IV.D.2–3 (pp 130–53).

[65] *Phillips v Phillips* (1861) 4 De G F & J 208, 218; 45 ER 1164, 1167 (Lord Westbury LC); *Cave v Cave* (1880) 15 ChD 639 (ChD) 646–49 (Fry J). Critical of the principle for which these cases have come to stand: D O'Sullivan, "The Rule in *Phillips v. Phillips*" (2002) 118 LQR 296.

[66] One of the reasons why Lord Browne-Wilkinson in *Westdeutsche Landesbank Girozentrale v Islington London BC* [1996] AC 669 (HL) was worried about affording mistaken payers an *immediately vested* equitable interest was that the payer would thereby obtain priority over creditors who subsequently advance a loan to the recipient which is secured by an equitable charge over his assets (at 704). On the *power model* of proprietary restitution endorsed here, such equitable chargees would not be bound by the transferor's equitable power *in rem*.

[67] In practice, this means that C's equitable rights rank above A's to the extent that the two can co-exist.

illustration of English law's inclination to conceive of proprietary interests (re)vesting only prospectively upon rescission.[68] In German law, it makes no difference to the operation of §§ 932 ff BGB whether A rescinds the real agreement before or after B's transfer to C. In both cases, B is treated as a non-owner. English law, by contrast, differentiates sharply between the situation where A has avoided the conveyance to B before C acquires the painting and where he purports to exercise his power *in rem* only afterwards. We will see that vested property rights are harder to destroy than mere powers *in rem*. For the time being, it suffices to notice that the English law on *bona fide* purchase, like the English law of wrongs, does not appear to accord retroactive effect to A's revocation of his consent to the transfer.[69]

b) *Bona fide* Purchase after Exercise of Power *in rem*

Where A exercises his power *in rem* before the painting reaches C's hands, C's position is markedly weaker. Although *bona fide* purchase remains possible in certain situations, vested rights *in rem* are less susceptible to the defence than mere powers (unless the chattels in question are notes, coins, or the like)[70]. We must again distinguish the position at common law from that in equity.

Car & Universal Finance Co Ltd v Caldwell[71] best illustrates the basic common law position. Caldwell had sold and delivered his Jaguar car to a man calling himself Norris. He accepted a cheque in payment which was later dishonoured. As soon as he became aware of the fraud, Caldwell informed the police and the Automobile Association and asked for their help with finding the vehicle. This had happened before the Finance Company, an innocent purchaser for value, had obtained the car further down a chain of transactions (via an intermediary who had notice of the fraud). In interpleader proceedings, the Court of Appeal held that although Caldwell had been unable to communicate his intention to rescind to Norris, the fact that he had done everything he could to regain possession of the Jaguar was

---

[68] Cf above, Chapter IV.D.4.c (at pp 157–58) and Chapter V.D.1 (at pp 203–4).

[69] It would be tempting to say that English law simply does not allow A to revoke his consent at all after a *bona fide* purchaser has intervened (and that there is therefore no issue of retroactivity). However, we will see later on, when considering the nature of the so-called 'third party rights bar to rescission' and the transferor's claims to traceable substitute assets, that this is not necessarily the case: cf Chapter VII.D (esp text to nn 49–50 on p 269) and Chapter VIII.B.1.b (pp 289–94). Moreover, the pledge example (cf n 62 above) shows that A is only debarred from exercising his power in respect of the original object in so far as his revested right would be incompatible with C's interest.

[70] See above, n 53 corresponding text.

[71] [1965] 1 QB 525 (QBD), aff'd [1965] 1 QB 525 (CA).

sufficient to effect rescission. Title to the car had consequently revested in Caldwell before the Finance Company bought it. Section 23 of the Sale of Goods Act 1893 did not operate. Applying the *nemo dat* principle, Caldwell's revested title was stronger than that acquired by the Finance Company. In our example, the starting point is therefore that *bona fide* purchase by C is not possible where A has exercised a common law power *in rem* before the painting is conveyed by B to C.

However, an immediate *caveat* is warranted. It derives from the decision in *Newtons of Wembley Ltd v Williams*,[72] handed down soon after *Car & Universal Finance Co Ltd v Caldwell*.[73] The possibility of rescission without communication as recognized in *Caldwell*, while advantageous to victims of fraud, is correspondingly disadvantageous to innocent third party purchasers from the rogue.[74] So long as A was required to find B before he could rescind the sale, C's chances of acquiring title to the painting before avoidance were good. Rogues are in the habit of disappearing quickly. *Bona fide* purchase under section 23 of the Sale of Goods Act 1893 was usually possible. After *Caldwell*, the practical relevance of the provision (and its 1979 successor) is much reduced. The conveyance to B will often have been avoided by the time the painting reaches C's hands. *Prima facie*, C is then in the same position as if title had never passed from A to B at all (eg because of A's mistake about B's identity).[75] This prompted both Davies LJ at first instance and the Court of Appeal in *Newtons of Wembley Ltd v Williams* to find another way of protecting innocent third party purchasers such as C. The facts of the case were remarkably similar to those in *Caldwell*. The claimant car dealers had sold a motorcar to a man named Andrews and allowed him to take it away. Andrews' cheque bounced, and the claimants immediately took all available steps to disaffirm the contract. Andrews subsequently sold the car on Warren Street market to a good faith purchaser for value without notice, who in turn sold it to the defendant. The claimants' action for detinue and conversion failed. Although title to the car had, in accordance with the *Caldwell* principle, revested in the claimants before Andrews disposed of the vehicle,[76] the particular circumstances of the intermediary's purchase on Warren Street enabled the defendant to rely on the *nemo dat* exception contained in

[72] [1964] 1 WLR 1028 (QBD), aff'd [1965] 1 QB 560 (CA).

[73] See above, n 71 and corresponding text.

[74] This is one reason why J O'Sullivan, "Rescission as a Self-Help Remedy: A Critical Analysis" (2000) 59 CLJ 509, 531–33, disapproves of rescission as a self-help remedy.

[75] As in *Cundy v Lindsay* (n 60) and *Ingram v Little* (n 60).

[76] There was a question whether a retention of title clause in the contract of sale had prevented property from passing to Andrews in the first place, but it was thought not to matter: [1964] 1 WLR 1028, 1035 (Davies LJ); [1965] 1 QB 560, 571–72 (Sellers LJ).

section 9 of the Factors Act 1889. This provision, which has a counterpart in section 25(1) of the Sale of Goods Act 1979, envisages the possibility of *bona fide* purchase from a buyer who is in possession of the goods with the consent of his seller. It reads:[77]

> "Where a person having bought or agreed to buy goods [here B] obtains, with the consent of the seller [here A], possession of the goods ..., the delivery or transfer by that person ... of the goods ... under any sale, pledge, or other disposition thereof, to any person [here C] receiving the same in good faith and without notice of any lien or other right of the original seller in respect of the goods, has the same effect as if the person making the delivery or transfer were a mercantile agent in possession of the goods ... with the consent of the owner."

When enacted, the section was primarily intended to protect purchasers from buyers let into possession of the goods before they had acquired the seller's title to them (eg because of a retention of title clause)[78] or while the unpaid seller's lien persisted despite a temporary release of the goods.[79] Through the extensive interpretation adopted in *Newtons of Wembley*, it now also covers situations in which a seller has initially parted with both possession and any proprietary interest in the goods, but where he has since rescinded the contract of sale and thereby revested title in himself.[80] *Newtons of Wembley v Williams* thus mitigates the harsh consequences of the *Caldwell* decision as far as third parties are concerned. However, it does not eradicate them completely. The rules about *bona fide* purchase from buyers in possession are more limited than the principle underlying section 23 of the Sale of Goods Act 1979. For one, they do not apply

---

[77] The provision is quoted as enacted in the Sale of Goods Act 1979. Before the coming into force of this Act, it was contained in the Sale of Goods Act 1893, s 25(2). In *National Employers' Mutual General Insurance Association Ltd v Jones* [1990] 1 AC 24 (HL), the House of Lords made clear that, where this *bona fide* purchase provision operates, it serves to defeat only the original seller's title, and not – as the wording suggests – any superior right to possession (such as that of the 'true owner' from whom the object in question has been stolen).

[78] If there was a retention of title clause in *Newtons of Wembley v Williams* (cf n 76 above), then rescission of the contract by the claimant sellers had – at any rate – brought to an end the possibility of Andrews obtaining title by fulfilling the condition.

[79] Cf M Bridge, *Personal Property Law* (3rd edn OUP, Oxford 2002) 132–33; AG Guest (gen ed), *Benjamin's Sale of Goods* (7th edn Sweet & Maxwell, London 2006) [7–071] (Guest).

[80] Unfortunately their Lordships failed adequately to deal with the question whether, after rescission, the transferee (Andrews) could still be regarded as a "person having bought or agreed to buy goods". They were content to point out that the subsequent withdrawal of the principal's (here: 'seller's') consent was irrelevant under section 2(2) of the Factors Act 1889: [1964] 1 WLR 1028, 1033–34 (Davies LJ); [1965] 1 QB 560, 573–74 (Sellers LJ). However, as a matter of statutory construction, section 2 can only apply if all the requirements of section 9 are met.

where A's relationship with B is not one of sale. If A has transferred title to the painting to B pusuant to a contract of barter or by way of gift and later avoids the conveyance at common law (typically for B's fraud), a subsequent good faith purchase for value without notice by C would not seem to fall under section 9 of the Factors Act 1889 or section 25(1) of the Sale of Goods Act 1979. Second, as a result of their convoluted wording and the reference to a fictional mercantile agency, the operation of these provisions depends on whether the "buyer is doing something which would constitute acting in the ordinary course of business if he were a mercantile agent".[81] In *Newtons of Wembley*, the rogue's sale of the car on Warren Street market fulfilled this requirement,[82] but a sale on private premises, for example, would not have done. Third, the statutory provisions only apply where the *bona fide* purchaser acquires the goods directly from the 'buyer' and not from some intermediary. This explains why the Finance Company in *Caldwell* lost, while Mr Williams won his case against the claimants. The trial judge in *Newtons of Wembley* distinguished *Caldwell* on the basis that, in *Caldwell*, the first purchaser from the rogue had notice of the fraud, while the first purchaser in *Newtons* did not.[83] In our example, where C is a direct purchaser from B, we are therefore left with the curious common law position that C takes title to the painting free from A's revested better right to possession if and only if the contract between A and B was one of sale *and* C acquires title in circumstances which are consistent with the ordinary course of business in mercantile agency.

Turning to equity, the position is more straightforward. Where a trust has arisen as a consequence of A exercising an equitable power *in rem* to avoid the transfer to B (eg because the transfer was induced by B's undue influence), A's equitable interest will be defeated by any third party purchaser for value who, in good faith and without notice of A's rights, acquires a *legal* interest in the painting from B. C therefore qualifies as a *bona fide* purchaser ('equity's darling') if he buys the painting from B or exchanges it for his bicycle, but not where he is granted merely an equitable interest (eg in the form of an equitable charge).[84] 'Where the equities are equal, the first in time prevails'.[85]

---

[81] [1965] 1 QB 560, 579 (Pearson LJ).

[82] [1964] 1 WLR 1028, 1034 (Davies LJ); [1965] 1 QB 560, 575 (Sellers LJ), 580 (Pearson LJ). Warren Street was regarded as a well-established street market for second-hand cars.

[83] [1964] 1 WLR 1028, 1033.

[84] The distinction between the different categories of purchasers for value is well-illustrated by *Cave v Cave* (1880) 15 ChD 639 (ChD), where the equitable interest of trust beneficiaries was defeated by a legal mortgagee, but not by equitable mortgagees.

[85] As Lord Westbury LC explained in *Phillips v Phillips* (1861) 4 De G F & J 208, 215; 45 ER 1164, 1166: "[G]rantees and incumbrancers claiming in equity take and are

2. Third Party Liability where the *bona fide* Purchase Rules do Not Operate

a) Assertion of Property Rights by the Transferor and Connected Wrongs-Based Liability

If C is not a *bona fide* purchaser,[86] he takes title to the painting subject to A's proprietary interest.[87] The way in which A asserts that proprietary interest depends on its exact nature: whether it is a vested property right or a mere power *in rem*, and whether it is legal or equitable.

Vested rights *in rem* are asserted in the ordinary way. At common law, a purchaser who acquires B's title in circumstances where A's revested (superior) right to immediate possession is not extinguished commits the tort of conversion by receiving the painting and treating it as his own. A can claim damages from C or, if C is still in possession of the painting, ask the court to exercise its discretion to order delivery up.[88] To the extent that C, not knowing of A's superior title, has expended money on improving the painting (eg by having it professionally restored), any resulting increase in value is taken into account. It reduces the amount of damages payable to A or, where A seeks specific recovery, serves to establish a counter-claim by C based on A's unjust enrichment at his expense.[89] Moving to equity, the

---

ranked according to the dates of their securities; and the maxim applies 'Qui prior est tempore potior est jure.' The first grantee is *potior* – that is, *potentior*. He has a better and superior – because a prior – equity".

[86] On the basis of what was said immediately above, in section C.1 of the present chapter, there are several reasons why C may not qualify as a *bona fide* purchaser. First, where A has not yet avoided the conveyance to B (or where he has avoided it in equity only), C's *bona fide* purchase defence will fail if C knew of A's rights, had notice of them, or did not provide valuable consideration in exchange for the painting. Second, where A has exercised a common law power *in rem*, C may – like the Finance Company in *Caldwell* – be unable to rely on the Sale of Goods Act 1979, s 25, or on the corresponding provision in the Factors Act 1889, s 9 (cf n 71 and text to n 83 above). Third, except in money cases, there is no *bona fide* purchase defence where A's transaction with B was completely void, eg for A's identity mistake as in *Cundy v Lindsay* and *Ingram v Little* (cf nn 57, 60). This is because the above-mentioned rules about dispositions made by 'buyers in possession' would never seem to apply in such a situation.

[87] Cases where C acquires (or purports to acquire) a proprietary interest other than title, eg the 'special property' of a pledgee or an equitable interest, will not be specifically considered: see n 1 above.

[88] Torts (Interference with Goods) Act 1977, s 3.

[89] Torts (Interference with Goods) Act 1977, ss 3(7), 6(1); *Greenwood v Bennett* [1973] QB 195 (CA). The court's order for delivery up will be made conditional on the satisfaction of that counter-claim. On the problem of quantification cf R Stevens, "Three Enrichment Iusses" in A Burrows and A Rodger (eds), *Mapping the Law: Essays in Memory of Peter Birks* (OUP, Oxford 2006) 49, 50–54. For a comparison of English and

position is roughly parallel. Where C acquires B's title to the painting subject to a trust in A's favour, A can force C to 'execute' the trust under the principle in *Saunders v Vautier*.[90] C will have to transfer his title to A (typically by delivery), and this will revest in A a right to immediate and exclusive possession which can subsequently be defended against all interference through a claim in conversion. In the trust scenario, there is a question whether C, by the mere fact of acquiring the painting, has already become liable to A for the equitable wrong of 'knowing receipt'.[91] In contrast to conversion, knowing receipt is – as the name indicates – not a strict liability wrong.[92] However, the level of fault required is still unclear. Suggestions range from dishonesty[93] via negligence[94] to the vague standard of 'unconscionability'[95]. It is submitted that we need to distinguish *two* possible types of wrongs-based liability. Both are potentially in play in so-called 'knowing receipt' cases. First, C's conduct may give rise to a form of secondary liability for breach of trust,[96] but it can only do so where B

German law in respect of claims to reimbursement of a possessor's expenditure see esp D Verse, "Improvements and Enrichment: A Comparative Analysis" [1998] RLR 85.

[90] (1841) 4 Beav 115, 49 ER 282; aff'd (1841) Cr & Ph 240, 41 ER 482.

[91] We are here concerned only with the *wrong* of 'knowing receipt', not with a (possibly) competing receipt-based liability in unjust enrichment for which liability would be strict: see below, section C.2.b. of the present chapter (esp at pp 238–40).

[92] Some authors suggest that it should be: eg W Swadling, "Some Lessons from the Law of Torts" in P Birks (ed), *The Frontiers of Liability* (OUP, Oxford 1994) vol 1, 41, esp 42–47. The argument against regarding knowing receipt as a strict liability wrong is that equity – unlike the common law – allows for the direct 'vindication' of property rights and does not therefore need to have recourse to the law of wrongs as far as their bare assertion is concerned.

[93] *Re Montagu's Settlement Trusts* [1987] Ch 264 (ChD), esp 285, where Sir Robert Megarry VC referred to categories (i) to (iii) of the so-called *Baden Delvaux* scale: cf *Baden v Société Générale pour Favoriser le Développement du Commerce et de l'Industrie en France SA* [1993] 1 WLR 509 (ChD). This includes (i) actual knowledge, (ii) wilfully shutting one's eyes to the obvious, and (iii) a wilful and reckless failure to make such inquiries as a reasonable and honest man would make.

[94] Cf *Belmont Finance Corp v Williams Furniture Ltd (No 2)* [1980] 1 All ER 393 (CA).

[95] *Bank of Credit and Commerce International (Overseas) Ltd v Akindele* [2001] Ch 427 (CA). Cf also S Thomas, "'Goodbye' Knowing Receipt. 'Hello' Unconscientious Receipt" (2001) 21 OJLS 239.

[96] This is the view advocated by D Nicholls, "Knowing Receipt: The Need for a New Landmark" in WR Cornish and others (eds), *Restitution Past, Present and Future: Essays in Honour of Gareth Jones* (Hart, Oxford 1998) 231, 243–44, who describes the wrong as "dishonest participation in a breach of trust". The approach was later adopted by P Birks, "Receipt" in P Birks and A Pretto (eds), *Breach of Trust* (Hart, Oxford 2002) 213, 225–28, who refers to the "wrong of misappropriation".

actually commits a 'breach of trust' by disposing of the painting,[97] and it should depend on C's dishonesty and/or knowledge of all the relevant facts.[98] Second, having acquired title to the painting subject to A's equitable interest, C may be liable to A if he subsequently puts it out of his power to comply with A's *Saunders v Vautier* demand.[99] For want of a better name, we can describe this liability as a primary liability for 'breach of (constructive) trust',[100] but it is probably not a strict liability. The case of *Re Montagu's Settlement Trusts*[101] indicates that all depends on the 'constructive trustee' being aware of his position.[102] C would therefore

---

[97] It is unclear whether there is technically a 'breach of trust' where A exercises an equitable power *in rem* and B subsequently puts it out of his capacity to comply with A's request under *Saunders v Vautier* (n 90). It was suggested in Chapter IV.D.4.c (at pp 157–58, esp in n 320) that there would be a lacuna in the law if non-consensual 'bare trustees' could never be personally liable in such a case. For want of a better name, the wrong may be described as a 'breach of trust'. The only question is whether the wrong is better conceived of as fault-based or strict, ie whether the equitable wrong requires the 'bare trustee' to be aware of holding title on trust for another and whether it requires him to act culpably. In our case, B will *ex hypothesi* have the relevant knowledge (as a result of A's communication), and his disposal to C will be deliberate. The necessary primary liability for 'breach of trust' should thus always be established.

[98] A high fault threshold is also envisaged by Nicholls in *Restitution Past, Present and Future* (n 96) and by Birks in *Breach of Trust* (n 96). The reason for this is evident if one considers that the recipient's secondary liability for participation in a breach of trust will line up with (or slot into) the equitable wrong conventionally thought of as 'knowing' or 'dishonest assistance' in a breach of trust: cf *Royal Brunei Airlines Sdn Bhd v Tan* [1995] 2 AC 378 (PC), *Twinsectra Ltd v Yardley* [2002] UKHL 12, [2002] 2 AC 164. As Nicholls in *Restitution Past, Present and Future* (n 96) 243, points out: "Dishonest receipt and dishonest assistance are two instances of similarly wrongful conduct: dishonest participation by third parties in a breach of trust. In both cases liability is triggered by the same degree of fault: dishonesty".

[99] This is essentially how P Jaffey, "The Nature of Knowing Receipt" (2001) 15 TruLI 151, understands liability for knowing receipt. On the beneficiary's rights under *Saunders v Vautier* (n 90) see above, text to n 90.

[100] Jaffey (2001) 15 TruLI (n 99) 153, describes the wrong as a "breach of the duty of preservation".

[101] [1987] Ch 264 (ChD).

[102] Sir Robert Megarry VC explained (esp ibid 270–73, 276–78, 285) that it was one thing to require volunteers and purchasers with notice of an existing equitable interest to surrender what remains of the trust property (or its traceable proceeds), but that it was quite another to hold the recipient "liable for what he has disposed of in all innocence, believing that it was truly his" (ibid 271) merely because he does not qualify as 'equity's darling'. Note that, throughout his judgment, his Lordship uses the term 'constructive trust' in a different sense from the one employed here, focusing on the personal – as opposed to the proprietary – relationship between 'trustee' and 'beneficiary'. On the different meanings of the 'constructive trust' terminology see Jaffey (2001) 15 TruLI (n 99) 158.

again have at least to know of A's equitable interest before incurring this second type of wrongs-based liability.[103]

Should A not yet have exercised his power *in rem* to avoid the transfer to B when the painting reaches C's hands, then he will need to do so before he can assert any rights vis-à-vis C.[104] The elements of the tort of conversion are not established unless A can demonstrate that he has a better right to possession of the painting than C. Similarly, only a beneficiary under a fully vested trust can call for the transfer of legal title to himself under *Saunders v Vautier*. A 'mere equity' is insufficient for this purpose. There remains a question about the relevance of C's disenrichment in these circumstances. Does the fact that C is no longer enriched when A purports to exercise his power provide him with a defence? Clearly, A's power *in rem* is destroyed where the object to which it relates perishes leaving no traceable substitute. But what if C is an innocent donee from B who, in reliance on his receipt of the painting, takes his wife out to an expensive celebratory dinner? Can he set up this change of position and insist that the exercise of A's power *in rem* is conditional on his being reimbursed for the cost of the dinner? English law provides no answer to this question.[105] Looking at the matter from a purely proprietary angle, there appears to be no good reason for allowing a disenrichment defence to defeat powers *in rem* any more than vested rights *in rem*. Anybody who does not qualify as a *bona fide* purchaser bears the risks associated with the existence of superior proprietary interests. On the other hand, we saw in the two-party relationship between A and B that good faith changes of position by B could affect the exercise of a power *in rem* generated by B's unjust enrichment even though they had no relevance as far as A's vested rights *in rem* were concerned.[106] It is submitted that the answer to our problem lies in the nature and proper classification of the relationship between A and C. If the underlying *reason* why A's power 'survives' the transfer of title from B to C is C's unjust enrichment at A's expense, then the disenrichment defence should in principle be available to C, but not otherwise.[107]

---

[103] Even if, therefore, C is not liable for participating in B's 'breach of trust' (eg because he was an innocent volunteer), he may nevertheless be liable for his own 'breach of trust' where he has subsequently learnt of A's equitable interest. There is a further question whether C needs to have acted culpably when putting it out of his power to convey the painting to A: cf n 97 above (where the issue is discussed in relation to B).

[104] It is submitted that A should have to communicate his intention of exercising the power *in rem* to C (and not merely to B).

[105] B McFarlane, *The Structure of Property Law* (Hart, Oxford 2008) 334, suggests that the defence operates in C's favour, without – however – explaining why exactly.

[106] See above, Chapter IV.D.4.b (esp at p 156).

[107] From a comparative point of view, the issue can be highlighted as follows. If English law enabled C to invoke the defence, this would be tantamount to German law

We will again touch on this question below, when looking at the possibility of A 'leapfrogging' B in order to establish a purely personal claim in unjust enrichment against C.[108]

b) Personal Receipt-Based Liability in Unjust Enrichment

Before doing so, we must briefly consider the converse issue: does C's receipt of the painting in circumstances where he is not a *bona fide* purchaser expose him to a personal liability in unjust enrichment which can be characterized as a *product* of A's surviving proprietary interest?[109] Is a person who acquires title to a chattel subject to another's proprietary interest (whether that interest be a better legal title, a beneficial interest under a trust, or a legal or equitable power *in rem*) by virtue of this fact alone unjustly enriched at that other's expense? If so, then the change of position defence could certainly be invoked to reduce or even defeat the proprietary interest holder's *personal* claim to restitution.

It is impossible within the confines of this book to deal exhaustively with all the arguments advanced for and against a receipt-based liability in unjust enrichment.[110] What will, however, be attempted is an outline of the main theoretical issues underpinning the debate within our present framework. Conceptually, the existence of a personal receipt-based claim against third parties like C depends on two components: the recognition of an unjust factor called 'ignorance' or an equivalent concept such as 'infringement of rights', and the proper relationship between proprietary interests and personal restitutionary claims. The problem is essentially parallel to that considered for two-party cases in Chapter IV.[111] Let us briefly recall the different views identified there and apply them to the present three-party scenario. The 'exclusionary view', which goes hand in hand with the

allowing third parties who are affected by an act of rescission to claim their reliance losses from the rescinding party under § 122 BGB. However, as German law stands, only the actual recipient of the declaration of intention (in our case B) has the benefit of the claim under § 122 BGB: cf n 38 above.

[108] See section C.3 of the present chapter (pp 243–49).

[109] It should be noted that a positive answer would have no implications for the question about the availability of the disenrichment defence against the exercise of A's power *in rem* (cf text to n 107 above). The issue there is whether the existence of the power *depends* on C's unjust enrichment at A's expense, while we are here asking whether – granted the existence of a right or power *in rem* – this proprietary interest *entails* a personal claim in unjust enrichment.

[110] For an overview of the debate see eg Birks in *Breach of Trust* (n 96) 228–39; A Burrows, *The Law of Restitution* (Butterworths, London 2002) 186–206; L Smith, "Unjust Enrichment, Property, and the Structure of Trusts" (2000) 116 LQR 412 (in respect of 'title-based claims').

[111] See above, Chapter IV.C (pp 119–25).

rejection of 'ignorance' as an unjust factor, altogether denies the possibility of receipt-based personal claims.[112] It holds that where A's proprietary interest (of whatever kind) survives the conveyance of the painting from B to C, C is not enriched, or at any rate not at A's expense.[113] At the other end of the spectrum, those who believe in the possibility of so-called 'alternative analysis' consider a personal claim in unjust enrichment to be available whenever A is ignorant of (or powerless to prevent) the transfer from B to C.[114] Take the example of a vested interest.[115] If, as in *Car & Universal Finance Co Ltd v Caldwell*,[116] A has 'pulled back' his former title before C receives the painting from B, he can either just point to C's factual benefit (actually 'having' the painting), or will at any rate be able to 'waive' his better right to possession for the purpose of establishing that C is unjustly enriched at his expense.[117] Where C acquires B's title subject to an equitable interest in A's favour, so the argument runs, a similar claim should exist.[118] Unlike the wrongs-based liability for 'knowing receipt',[119] C's receipt-based liability in unjust enrichment would be strict.[120] According to what was above labelled the 'intermediate view', alternative analysis

---

112 Cf above, Chapter IV.C.1 (pp 121–22).

113 W Swadling, "Ignorance and Unjust Enrichment: The Problem of Title" (2008) 28 OJLS 627, 628 fn 4, makes clear that his objection to the concurrence of vested property rights and personal claims to restitution for unjust enrichment is not confined to the common law (C receiving an object from B to which A has a better title), but applies equally in equity (C receiving an object from B which is subject to an equitable interest in A's favour). For Swadling, all unjust enrichments have to be participatory enrichments and have to involve a transfer of rights.

114 Cf above, Chapter IV.C.2 (pp 122–24).

115 We will see below (text after n 123) that the argument from 'alternative analysis' is easier to sustain for vested interests than for powers *in rem*.

116 [1965] 1 QB 525 (CA). Cf text after n 71 above.

117 There is a debate amongst proponents of 'alternative analysis' whether a normative concession of the 'elective relinquishment' kind is required and appropriate, or whether enrichment is a purely factual concept: see text to nn 112–115 on p 123.

118 An important driving force behind this argument is the 'fusionist' ideal according to which law and equity should be streamlined as far as possible: cf eg P Birks, "Misdirected Funds: Restitution from the Recipient" [1989] LMCLQ 296, 309–10; Burrows *Restitution* (n 110) 202; Nicholls in *Restitution Past, Present and Future* (n 96) 236–43, esp 238. Critical: Smith (2000) 116 LQR (n 110) 434–36, supported by Thomas (2001) 21 OJLS (n 95) 249–51. It seems that the best way of 'constructing' an unjust enrichment claim based on A's equitable interest would be to say that A can 'waive' or choose not to rely on his equitable interest for the purposes of establishing that C (whose title is now freed from its previous encumbrance) has been enriched at his, A's, expense.

119 See above, text to nn 91–103.

120 *Ministry of Health v Simpson (Re Diplock's Estate)* [1951] AC 251 (HL), affirming [1948] Ch 465 (CA), is usually cited as authority for such a strict liability claim in equity. Critical: Smith (2000) 116 LQR (n 110) 437–44.

is not possible.[121] If A has revested in himself title to the painting or an equitable interest under a trust, he has to assert these rights *in rem* in the way already outlined.[122] A personal claim in unjust enrichment will on this approach only be available where A's revested property right is subsequently destroyed leaving C's assets swollen.[123]

It will not have escaped the attention of the reader that the account of the last two views is incomplete as it stands. The case where it is a power *in rem* of A's (rather than a vested property right) which survives the conveyance from B to C has not been considered so far. Authors who are happy with a co-existence of proprietary interests and personal unjust enrichment claims generally regard any kind of 'proprietary link' (including powers *in rem*) sufficient to establish C's enrichment at A's expense.[124] On the 'intermediate' approach, it could similarly be argued that a personal claim against C is not only warranted where a vested property right of A's is subsequently destroyed, but also where A refrains – or is otherwise precluded – from exercising his power *in rem*. Yet can the 'proprietary link' constituted by an unexercised power *in rem* really justify A's personal claim against C?[125] How is 'alternative analysis' supposed to work if the claimant has no vested right *in rem* to 'waive'? Or why is C's (factual)[126] enrichment at A's, rather than B's expense, despite the fact that A's power remains inchoate?[127] In short: can a receipt-based unjust enrichment claim actually be parasitic upon a mere power?

---

[121] Cf above, Chapter IV.C.3 (pp 124–25).

[122] By a claim in conversion or by 'executing' the trust: see above, text to nn 88–90.

[123] Eg by accession/specification or an instance of *bona fide* purchase. In the latter case, A may – as will be seen in Chapter VIII below – have a power *in rem* in respect of traceable substitute assets, but he would, on the 'intermediate view', be entirely free to refrain from exercising this power.

[124] Cf eg P Birks, " 'At the Expense of the Claimant': Direct and Indirect Enrichment in English Law" in D Johnston and R Zimmermann (eds), *Unjustified Enrichment: Key Issues in Comparative Perspective* (CUP, Cambridge 2002) 493, 514–16; Burrows *Restitution* (n 110) 191; J Edelman and E Bant, *Unjust Enrichment in Australia* (OUP, Sydney 2006) 135. The 'proprietary link' between the parties, it is said, imports the requisite relationship of enrichment creditor and debtor.

[125] In a different context (that of rights to traceable substitute assets), this problem is seen and discussed by L Smith, *The Law of Tracing* (OUP, Oxford 1997) 326, esp fn 133 and corresponding text.

[126] On the purely factual approach to the enrichment inquiry, which does not rely on the possibility of 'elective relinquishment', see n 117 above.

[127] In the two-party scenario, there was no problem about B's enrichment being at A's expense where A chose not to exercise – or was prevented from exercising – his power *in rem*. This was because the participatory nature of the enrichment, coupled with the relevant unjust factor (mistake, duress, undue influence), was sufficient to establish the requisite creditor/debtor relationship: cf text to nn 4–7 on pp 101–2.

The answers to these questions depend partly – it is submitted – on the correct interpretation of *Lipkin Gorman (a firm) v Karpnale Ltd.*[128] In that case, a man named Cass, who was a partner in the claimant firm of solicitors, had withdrawn funds from the firm's client account and used the proceeds to gamble at the defendant casino (the 'Playboy Club'). The claimants' action for money had and received was successful in so far as the defendant club had not changed its position by paying out on Cass' winning bets. Although Lord Templeman, who gave one of the two leading speeches, consistently spoke of Cass as a "thief" who had handed "stolen money" to the Playboy Club,[129] it was clear on earlier Privy Council authority that since Cass was an authorized signatory on the client account, he had acquired title to the money when the bank paid it over to him.[130] Lord Goff, giving the other leading speech, said that the cash was the traceable substitute of the claimants' original chose in action (the debt owed to them by the bank) and that the claimants would have been able to assert a proprietary interest in it had they chosen to do so.[131] We are not here concerned with the principles of tracing,[132] but should notice that the claimants appear to have had something akin to a common law power *in rem* in respect of the money in Cass' hands.[133] Gambling contracts were null and void at the time of the decision,[134] and so their Lordships unanimously held that the Playboy Club did not qualify as a *bona fide* purchaser when it exchanged the cash for casino chips.[135] On the facts of the case, the claimants did not purport to exercise their power *in rem* (nor could they have done so after the money had become untraceably mixed with the casino's general funds),[136] but merely sought to recover the value of Cass'

---

[128] [1991] 2 AC 548 (HL).

[129] Ibid 559–63. Note that Cass seems indeed to have been convicted of theft (ibid 669), but under the Theft Act 1968 this is not necessarily inconsistent with his obtaining title to the money: see eg *R v Hinks* [2001] 2 AC 241 (HL).

[130] [1991] 2 AC 548, 573. Cf *Union Bank of Australia Ltd v McClintock* [1922] 1 AC 240 (PC); *Commercial Banking Co of Sydney Ltd v Mann* [1961] AC 1 (PC).

[131] [1991] 2 AC 548, 573–74.

[132] On the nature of a claimant's proprietary interest in traceable substitutes see below, Chapter VIII.B.1.a.ii (pp 282–86).

[133] The point seems to have been conceded by counsel for the Club: [1991] 2 AC 548, 555. McFarlane *Structure of Property Law* (n 105) 293–98, argues that the claimant firm actually had a vested equitable interest ('persistent right') in the money Cass used for gambling.

[134] Gaming Act 1845, s 18. The legal position changed with the Gambling Act 2005.

[135] [1991] 2 AC 548, 560–65 (Lord Templeman), 577 (Lord Goff).

[136] Lord Goff stated (ibid 572) that "at common law, property in money, like other fungibles, is lost as such when it is mixed with other money". If this is correct, then it must *a fortiori* be true of a legal power *in rem* relating to the money. Since, however, there are some doubts about the legal effect of granular mixing (see above, n 210 on pp 140–41),

various payments to the Playboy Club. The fact that this personal claim was allowed – albeit subject to the Club's changes of position – and the great emphasis placed by the House of Lords on the solicitors' proprietary entitlement to the money withdrawn by Cass is widely taken to indicate that the existence of a mere power *in rem* at the moment of receipt justifies treating the recipient as unjustly enriched at the power-holder's expense.[137]

In order to explain *Lipkin Gorman* as a case in which the unjust enrichment claim was *parasitic* upon the firm's (unexercised) power, we have to go down one of two paths. We must either regard the 'interference' with or 'infringement' of mere powers as a relevant unjust factor, or – what amounts to the same thing – we must accept a purely hypothetical exercise of powers *in rem* with retroactive effect for the purposes of the law of unjust enrichment. This needs fleshing out. It will be recalled that powers *in rem* can only be exercised prospectively as far as the law of wrongs is concerned.[138] It is thus not an actionable breach of duty for B or C to interfere with a property right that has not yet revested in A.[139] Yet the question of retroactivity may have to be decided differently for different purposes. If the 'proprietary link' analysis of *Lipkin Gorman* is correct, then the reason why the Playboy Club was unjustly enriched at the claimant firm's expense was because the latter were notionally able to exercise their power *in rem* with retroactive effect, leaving the Playboy Club enriched when it received the money from Cass, or at the very latest when the money became untraceably mixed with its general funds.[140] Without recourse to such a hypothetical and retroactive exercise of the claimant firm's power, the only way to explain the Club's unjust enrichment on a 'proprietary link' analysis is to say that powers *in rem* are in themselves sufficiently wealth-allocating

the most we can say is that the *proceeds* of the money paid over by Cass could no longer be traced. Note counsel's concession that no mixing had occurred while the money was still in Cass' hands: cf [1991] 2 AC 548, 572–73, 574.

[137] Cf the references cited in n 124 above, as well as A Tettenborn, "Lawful Receipt – A Justifying Factor?" [1997] RLR 1, 5. G Virgo, *The Principles of the Law of Restitution* (2nd edn OUP, Oxford 2006) 570–71, 645–46, explains *Lipkin Gorman* as a case where the action for money had and received 'vindicated' the claimant firm's proprietary interest (rather than as one based on the casino's unjust enrichment).

[138] See above, Chapter IV.D.4.c (at pp 157–58).

[139] Nor is the infringement of a mere power *in rem* wrongful.

[140] The 'intermediate view' probably has to insist on this second point in time. It requires vested rights *in rem* to be asserted in the normal way while they exist and does not allow for 'elective relinquishment' (cf Chapter IV.C.3 above, esp p 124). Neither can it therefore accept the possibility of a purely hypothetical 'elective relinquishment' for the purposes of establishing that the casino was already enriched when Cass paid over the money which was (hypothetically and retroactively) the firm's.

to warrant a restitutionary response when they are infringed or destroyed.[141] No actionable wrongdoing would be required.[142]

3. Leapfrogging the Transferee?

Peter Birks, despite acknowledging the possibility of a 'proprietary link' analysis of *Lipkin Gorman v Karpnale Ltd*,[143] eventually argued that the case should better be regarded as one of 'leapfrogging'.[144] His change of mind was prompted by the difficulty of explaining the source of the claimant firm's supposed common law power *in rem*.[145] Moreover, even where there is a power, we have seen that the argument from 'alternative analysis' is not entirely easy to sustain in respect of an inchoate right.[146] This leads us to a more general question about the English law of restitution. Is there a principle similar to that in § 822 BGB which allows a mistaken transferor in certain circumstances to 'leapfrog' the immediate enrichee and recover from a remote recipient? Birks thought that a direct claim was in principle available whenever the defendant's receipt was causally connected with the mistaken transfer, provided only that the transferor was not trying to leapfrog out of an initially valid contract, and perhaps subject to

---

[141] It is interesting to note that Birks in *Unjustified Enrichment: Key Issues* (n 124) 517–18, expressly considers the parallel between *Lipkin Gorman* (n 128) and the special *Eingriffskondiktion* which justified the claim in BGHZ 55, 176 (*Jungbullenfall*), discussed in n 27 above (on p 221). However, he leaves open whether English law actually needs a stark distinction between performance-based and other enrichment claims: Birks in *Unjustified Enrichment: Key Issues* (n 124) 496.

[142] In *Lipkin Gorman* itself, Lord Goff was at pains to emphasize that the casino was not a 'wrongdoer': [1991] 2 AC 548, esp 574, 578, 580.

[143] Cf Birks in *Unjustified Enrichment: Key Issues* (n 124) 514–16; P Birks, *Unjust Enrichment* (2nd edn OUP, Oxford 2005) 86–87.

[144] Birks in *Unjustified Enrichment: Key Issues* (n 124) 518–19; Birks *Unjust Enrichment* (n 143) 95–96.

[145] Cf Birks in *Unjustified Enrichment: Key Issues* (n 124) 519: "[T]o explain the firm's power to revest the money which traceably went into the coffers of the casino, it is necessary to know that it had a proprietary interest in the money at the moment at which the gambler received it. And that is not said".

[146] See above, text to nn 126–127. It was suggested here (cf text after n 137) that a personal claim which is 'parasitic' upon the power *in rem* can only be justified by either (1) allowing a purely hypothetical and retroactive exercise of the power for the purposes of the law of unjust enrichment, or (2) regarding the power as sufficiently wealth-allocating to warrant an unjust enrichment claim where it is infringed or otherwise interfered with. Smith *Tracing* (n 125) 325–26, solves the problem by explaining *Lipkin Gorman* as a case in which the claimant firm had a *vested* legal interest in the money paid over by Cass, albeit one "less than full common law ownership". On the nature of rights to traceable substitute assets see below, Chapter VIII.B.1.a.ii (pp 282–86).

the further restriction that he exhaust his remedies against the immediate enrichee first.[147]

There are several reasons why it is important to know whether a personal claim in unjust enrichment can be established without the existence of a 'proprietary link'. The first is the chicken-and-egg problem hinted at above. Assuming that C is not a *bona fide* purchaser of the painting, is any personal unjust enrichment claim which A may have against C a result of the 'proprietary link'?[148] Or is there a logically prior relationship of unjust enrichment between the parties which is established independently of any 'proprietary link' and which may in fact account for the survival of A's power in the first place?[149] If the latter, then C should in principle be able to set up the disenrichment defence when A purports to exercise a (legal or equitable) power *in rem* in respect of the title which C has acquired from B.[150] In other words, the Playboy Club in *Lipkin Gorman* could then have relied on the change of position defence even if the solicitors had sought to exercise their power *in rem* before the money paid over by Cass had become untraceably mixed with the casino's general funds (eg while it was still identifiable in the safe). The second reason why the issue of leapfrogging needs to be addressed is connected with the proper scope of proprietary restitution in two-party cases. We saw in Chapter IV that there is some doubt over whether a conveyance made under the impression of a spontaneous mistake warrants proprietary restitution at all.[151] If – contrary to the view taken in this book– the courts were to hold that no equitable power *in rem* exists where, for example, A pays money to B in the mistaken belief that it is owing, then the question of A 'leapfrogging' B to establish an unjust enrichment claim against remote recipients like C will

---

[147] Cf Birks in *Unjustified Enrichment: Key Issues* (n 124) 520–24; Birks *Unjust Enrichment* (n 143) 89–98. Similar: A Burrows (ed), *English Private Law* (2nd edn OUP, Oxford 2007) [18.32]–[18.39] (C Mitchell). In his contribution to *Unjustified Enrichment: Key Issues* (n 124) 522, Birks suggested that his criterion of 'exhaustion' would make leapfrogging in English law broader than § 822 BGB (mistakenly referred to as § 816 I 2 BGB). Yet note that § 822 BGB, too, is arguably not restricted to cases of the immediate enrichee's disenrichment, but can also apply in his insolvency: cf n 41 above.

[148] See above, section C.2.b of the present chapter (esp text after n 123 on p 240).

[149] This is not to suggest that unjust enrichment principles can account for the entire law of *bona fide* purchase. Where A's title survives the transfer to B and then that to C (eg in an identity mistake case), any unjust enrichment claim which A may have against C can only be *parasitic* upon the title retained by A. It does not explain the retention.

[150] See above, text to nn 104–108. In a case where A's vested title survives the transfer from B to C (cf n 149), it is clear that the disenrichment defence does not avail C. Neither the innocent third party purchasers in *Cundy v Lindsay* (n 60) nor the one in *Ingram v Little* (n 60) were able to deduct from their damages liability in conversion the amount which they had paid as purchase price to the respective rogues.

[151] See above, Chapter IV.D.3.c.iii (pp 151–53).

acquire great practical relevance, especially where B's liability is extinguished as a result of his change of position.

In order to explore the issue of 'leapfrogging' without the uncertainties imported by a 'proprietary link' between A and C, it is convenient to vary our example slightly. Assume that A had mistakenly made a gift of a painting worth £ 1,000 to B.[152] Overjoyed by the receipt, B gives £ 50 to his nephew C, a present which he would not otherwise have made.[153] Given that A's recovery from B will, in value terms, be confined to the amount of B's surviving enrichment (here £ 950),[154] can he claim the remaining £ 50 from C, assuming that C has not yet changed his position in any way? While § 822 BGB can provide an affirmative answer for the analogous scenario in German law,[155] many Common lawyers reject such a claim.[156] A restitutionary 'privity principle', so one strand of the argument runs, prevents A leapfrogging B where C has lawfully received a chattel from B which was B's "unencumbered property".[157] C's enrichment was then at B's rather than A's expense.[158] Another objection frequently invoked is that leapfrogging can entail a danger of short-circuiting the contractual relationships between the parties.[159]

---

[152] The example is chosen for the sake of convenience. In line with what was said above about mistaken gifts (cf Chapter IV.B.3, pp 113–19), it assumes that any causative mistake can in principle warrant restitution of a gratuitous transfer in English law. For an alternative example see n 153 immediately below.

[153] An alternative example, which avoids the problem of restitution for mistaken gifts in the relationship between A and B (cf n 152 immediately above) is a variation of that given by Tettenborn [1997] RLR (n 137) 1: A mistakenly overpays his creditor B by £ 1,000. B, who is pleasantly surprised with his next bank statement and entirely unaware that anything is wrong, proceeds to give £ 50 from another account to his son C.

[154] On the supposition that proprietary restitution is available even in spontaneous mistake cases (cf text to n 151 above), A has a choice between bringing a personal claim for B's abstractly surviving enrichment (£ 1,000 minus £ 50) or paying B £ 50 so as to be able to exercise his equitable power *in rem*: see below, text to n 161. If proprietary restitution were not so available, A would be restricted to the personal claim.

[155] In German law, a mistaken gift can – of course – only be recovered if the mistake is one which allows for rescission of the 'gift contract' (eg a mistake as to an essential quality of the painting). A simple motivational mistake is not enough. Yet § 822 BGB would certainly apply in the mistaken payment case mentioned in n 153 (provided only that B's disenrichment is referable to the receipt as such and is thus relevant under § 818 III BGB). On § 822 BGB generally see above, text to nn 40–47.

[156] Eg Burrows *Restitution* (n 110) 31–34, 41; *Edelman & Bant* (n 124) 138–41; Tettenborn [1997] RLR (n 137); Virgo *Principles* (n 137) 105–7.

[157] Tettenborn [1997] RLR (n 137) esp 1–4. Agreeing: Virgo *Principles* (n 137) 106–7.

[158] Cf eg Burrows *Restitution* (n 110) 32–33; *Edelman & Bant* (n 124) 141.

[159] Recall the precedence of performance relationships in German law (so-called *Vorrang der Leistungsbeziehung*): cf n 23 and corresponding text. JP Dawson, *Unjust Enrichment: A Comparative Analysis* (Little Bown & Co, Boston 1951) 126–27, draws on

However, where – as in our example – there is no risk of undermining any bargains, it may well be appropriate to dispense with the requirement that the defendant's enrichment must derive directly from the claimant. Conceptually, a claim by A (as the mistaken donor of the painting)[160] against C (as the recipient of the £ 50 from B) is justifiable as follows. Whether A asserts a personal claim to B's abstractly surviving enrichment (£ 950) or reimburses B for the change of position before exercising his equitable power *in rem* and vesting in himself a restitutionary equitable interest,[161] he bears the immediate cost of B's disenrichment (£ 50). Yet the very fact that B can rely on the change of position defence as against A shows that his own gift to C was based on a false premise, namely that his receipt of the painting would be permanent. In a sense, B therefore remains enriched at A's expense. If he could recover £ 50 from C without accounting to A, the entire transaction would leave him with a windfall profit.[162] Technically, this outcome can be avoided by forcing B to assign his restitutionary claim against C to A when invoking the change of position defence.[163] Allowing A to recover directly from C is a shortcut route to the same end.[164] Conceived of in this way, there can be no objection to leap-

---

the German distinction between direct and indirect enrichments to put forward a similar 'privity principle' for the Common law. Since, however, he was fully aware that § 822 BGB constituted a recognized 'exception' to the general *Vorrang der Leistungsbeziehung*, the extent to which his view actually ousts leapfrogging should not be overstated: cf JP Dawson, "Indirect Enrichment" in E von Caemmerer, S Mentschikoff and K Zweigert (eds), *Ius Privatum Gentium: Festschrift für Max Rheinstein zum 70. Geburtstag am 5. Juli 1969* (Mohr Siebeck, Tübingen 1969) vol 2, 789, 795–96, 816–17.

[160] Or the mistaken payer: cf the example given in n 153 above. Note that the alternative (mistaken payment) example does not wholly avoid the problem of restitution for spontaneously mistaken gifts: see comment in n 162 below.

[161] The latter option exists only if the transferor's spontaneous mistake can generate a power *in rem*: cf above, n 154 and text to n 151.

[162] Two *caveats* are warranted here. First, depending on our view of restitution for mistaken gifts (cf n 152 above), B may not actually have a claim in unjust enrichment against C. Secondly and more fundamentally, we are in danger of encountering a vicious circle if spontaneous mistakes do count. This is because – once we accept that the change of position defence applies – B could be regarded as not having been mistaken at all. He made the gift to C in the belief that he had £ 1,000 to spare. He would not have made the gift had he known of his restitutionary liability to A. But this restitutionary liability is excluded to the extent that B is disenriched. So where is his mistake...?

[163] This construction is similar to the German theory of 'twofold *condictio*' (*Lehre von der Doppelkondiktion*), which is applied by those who reject the equation of acquisitions *sine causa* with gratuitous acquisitions in the context of §§ 816 I 2, 822 BGB: cf nn 33 and 44 above.

[164] This construction resembles (but is not necessarily identical to) the German theory of 'simple *condictio*' (*Lehre von der Einheitskondiktion*) which equates acquisitions *sine causa* with gratuitous acquisitions in the context of §§ 816 I 2, 822 BGB: cf nn 33 and 44

frogging. C is not exposed to the risk of double liability.[165] If B relies on the change of position defence, A can proceed directly against C.[166] If not, B retains his personal and proprietary rights to restitution for C's unjust enrichment, which is then truly at his (rather than at A's) expense.

Let us return to our core example. If, instead of conveying £ 50 to C, B had simply made a gift of the painting he had gratuitously acquired from A, the same reasoning applies. A's personal unjust enrichment claim against C does not need to be justified by reference to any unexercised power *in rem*. It is simply the ability to recover what was – in reliance on A's gift – transferred by B to a remoter recipient C. It might be objected that this is not genuine 'leapfrogging' at all, but merely a form of subrogation.[167] A test case for genuine leapfrogging would be whether a similar claim exists where C is a purchaser for value (eg the buyer of the painting) who knows of B's restitutionary liability and for this reason does not qualify as a *bona fide* purchaser.[168] Here C has a valid contract with B.[169] Were A allowed a personal claim against C in these circumstances (irrespective of any power),[170] he would be leapfrogging into the bargain between B and C. Whether we are prepared to go so far will ultimately be determined by our view of the *bona fide* purchase defence. If it is merely a way in which English property law, in the interest of commercial certainty, destroys or

---

above. The objection generally raised against this theory is that a direct claim cuts C off from any defences which would have been specifically available against B and which could also have been invoked against A on the assignment construction (cf § 404 BGB, the equivalent of the English rule that an assignee takes 'subject to equities').

165 This concern is voiced by Burrows *Restitution* (n 110) 32.

166 In this case, A ought arguably to be able to assert not only a personal unjust enrichment claim against C, but also any restitutionary power *in rem* B may have in respect of the £ 50 or its traceable proceeds.

167 The subrogation argument can be understood as an application of the German theory of *Doppelkondiktion* (cf n 163 and corresponding text) coupled with an assignment by operation of law (*cessio legis*). It has the advantage of preserving C's defences against B: cf comment in n 164 above.

168 Another test case would be where B knows of his restitutionary liability towards A when making the gift to C, but where – despite B's inability to rely on his disenrichment – A cannot recover from B, eg because B is insolvent. Birks' criterion of 'exhaustion' would be satisfied in this situation: cf above, n 147 and corresponding text.

169 The argument from subrogation (cf n 167 and text to nn 163–164) does not work where B does not have any claim against C which can be 'assigned' to A by operation of law. It would therefore also have to fail in our original examples (cf nn 152–153 and corresponding text) if either (1) English law did not allow restitution for spontaneously mistaken gifts, or if (2) B could not properly be regarded as 'mistaken' when making the gift of £ 50 to C (cf n 162 above).

170 We are not here concerned with a personal unjust enrichment claim which is *parasitic* upon A's power *in rem*, but with a 'pure' leapfrogging claim.

defeats pre-existing property rights and other proprietary interests,[171] then the fact that C is not a *bona fide* purchaser has no bearing on A's ability or inability to leapfrog B. If, on the other hand, the *bona fide* purchase defence is in some way related to the change of position defence,[172] then it would not only extend to both personal claims and property rights alike,[173] but might in fact serve to determine the outer boundaries of leapfrogging. The basic principle would then be that the transferor cannot leapfrog *out of* a valid contract, but that he can leapfrog *into* a valid contract unless the third party qualifies as a *bona fide* purchaser. In *Lipkin Gorman v Karpnale Ltd*,[174] Lord Goff explained the relationship between the two defences thus:

> "The defence of change of position is akin to the defence of bona fide purchase; but we cannot simply say that bona fide purchase is a species of change of position. This is because change of position will only avail a defendant to the extent that his position has been changed; whereas, where bona fide purchase is invoked, no inquiry is made (in most cases) into the adequacy of the consideration".[175]

The observation that *bona fide* purchase principles do not inquire into the adequacy of the consideration is a crucial one. But it does not rule out the possibility of regarding *bona fide* purchase as a type of change of position defence in a leapfrogging (unjust enrichment) case.[176] It would merely be a

[171] This is the view of eg P Key, "Bona Fide Purchase as a Defence in the Law of Restitution" [1994] LMCLQ 421; W Swadling, "Restitution and *Bona Fide* Purchase" in W Swadling (ed), *The Limits of Restitutionary Claims: A Comparative Analysis* (UKNCCL, London 1997) 79, esp 92–104. Cf now also R Grantham and C Rickett, "A Normative Account of Defences to Restitutionary Liability" (2008) 67 CLJ 92, 112–16.

[172] Cf P Millett, "Tracing the Proceeds of Fraud" (1991) 107 LQR 71, 82: "[I]t may come to be recognised that the defence of bona fide purchaser for value is simply the paradigm change of position defence, and that the true rule, embracing both volunteers and those who have given consideration, is that equity will not permit a defendant to set up a title to property in which the plaintiff has a beneficial interest unless he has given value or otherwise changed his position to his detriment without notice, actual or constructive, of the plaintiff's interest".

[173] Most authors who regard *bona fide* purchase as a defence to claims in unjust enrichment see it as distinct from the change of position defence: cf eg K Barker, "After Change of Position: Good Faith Exchange in the Modern Law of Restitution" in P Birks (ed), *Laundering and Tracing* (Clarendon Press, Oxford 1995) 191; repeated in K Barker, "Bona Fide Purchase as a Defence to Unjust Enrichment Claims: A Concise Restatement" [1999] RLR 75; Burrows *Restitution* (n 110) 585–91. More restrictive: Virgo *Principles* (n 137) 714, who argues that – in contrast to the general change of position defence – "the *bona fide* purchase defence is a specific defence which only applies where the [personal] restitutionary claim is founded on the vindication of property rights".

[174] [1991] 2 AC 548 (HL).

[175] Ibid 580–81.

[176] To say that *bona fide* purchase principles may determine the outer boundaries of 'leapfrogging' claims and in this respect constitute a variant change of position defence

change of position defence with two special features. They can be formulated as follows. Firstly, the purchaser's change of position is necessarily conclusive where the exchange relationship is governed by a valid contract.[177] Secondly, the disqualification threshold is 'notice', not knowledge or dishonesty. If C has notice of A's rights in respect of the painting (the power *in rem*), then any purchase price he may have paid to B should not count as a relevant change of position.[178]

On this understanding of leapfrogging and *bona fide* purchase, it is possible to regard the survival of A's power *in rem* at the moment of conveyance from B to C as a *product* of C's unjust enrichment at A's expense (rather than vice versa). And only on this understanding can a third party purchaser who is not protected by the *bona fide* purchase rules ever be allowed to set up the change of position defence when faced with the exercise of the transferor's power *in rem*. In our earlier example,[179] the innocent donee C would be able to recoup the cost of the dinner from A.

---

does not mean that all instances of *bona fide* purchase can be accounted for in this way. The *bona fide* purchase rules which apply to vested property rights (cf above, text to nn 53–55 on p 227, and section C.1.b of the present chapter at pp 230–33) show very little resemblance to a change of position defence. This leads Birks *Unjust Enrichment* (n 143) 240–45, to adopt a narrow view of *bona fide* purchase. He confines its function to the realm of formulating *nemo dat* exceptions (cf n 171 and corresponding text) and describes its relevance in the law of unjust enrichment as based on the need to prevent 'stultification'. His conclusion is indeed practically inescapable as far as vested (legal) interests are concerned. If C acquires the painting from B subject to A's better right to possession, the fact that he may have paid market price for it is neither here nor there. However, unless one believes in the possibility of 'alternative analysis', vested interest cases lie outside the remit of the law of unjust enrichment in any event. Proponents of the 'exclusionary' and the 'intermediate' view would not accept that C is unjustly enriched at A's expense by the receipt of A's painting from B (cf text to nn 111–123 on pp 238–40). In power cases of the type we are considering here, this is different. The *bona fide* purchase rules which apply to powers *in rem* need not be conceptually distinct from the special change of position which occurs when a remote enrichee gives value in exchange for (title to or another vested legal interest in) the object to which the power relates.

177 The absence of a valid contract in *Lipkin Gorman v Karpnale Ltd* (n 174) meant that the casino had to rely on the ordinary *pro-tanto* change of position defence: cf text to nn 134–135 above.

178 Only in very exceptional cases will C be in a position similar to that of the casino in *Lipkin Gorman v Karpnale Ltd* (n 174), where he has no notice of A's rights but at the same time provides valuable consideration without qualifying as a *bona fide* purchaser.

179 See above, section C.2.a of the present chapter (at p 237).

D. Comparative Observations on the Position of Third Party Purchasers

1. Abstraction and *bona fide* Purchase

The foregoing analysis has shown that the position of a third party purchaser, C, from the transferee, B, vis-à-vis the transferor, A, depends primarily on the existence and operation within the legal system of a principle of abstraction and on the extent to which the possibility of *bona fide* purchase is recognized. Broadly speaking, the proprietary protection thus afforded to third party purchasers could be said to be too broad in German law and, by comparison, too narrow in English law.

a) *Mala fide* Purchasers from the Enrichee in German Law

We have seen that the German BGB incorporates both layers of proprietary protection. Because most types of defects in A's consent, though indirectly relevant to establishing a personal restitutionary claim against B, do not entitle A to avoid his conveyance of the painting, there is little danger of C acquiring it from a 'non-owner'. And even where rescission of the real agreement is, exceptionally, possible (as eg in the case of fraud), the general principle of *bona fide* purchase contained in §§ 932 ff BGB ensures that C, unless he is in bad faith, will nevertheless usually become owner of the painting. Yet the proprietary protection of third party purchasers was not always as pronounced as it is today, and there are strong reasons for thinking that it may in fact be going too far.

Historically, the current legal position is the product of two almost contemporaneous developments. First, the 'discovery' by Friedrich Carl von Savigny of the principle of abstraction in 1840,[180] and its subsequent endorsement in the BGB.[181] The element of 'transactional security' (*Verkehrsschutz*) entailed by abstraction was and remains an important teleological factor in its general acceptance and application.[182] The second,

---

[180] FC von Savigny, *System des heutigen römischen Rechts: vol 3* (Veit & Co, Berlin 1840) esp 312–13, 354–58. On the (hitherto underrated) influence of Gustav Hugo on Savigny's thinking see HH Jakobs, "Gibt es den dinglichen Vertrag?" ZSS (RA) 119 (2002) 269, 280–294.

[181] Cf *Motive* (n 3) vol 3, 6–9, 332–36. A brief overview of the legislative history is contained in Stadler *Gestaltungsfreiheit* (n 3) 52–55.

[182] Cf already R von Jhering, *Geist des römischen Rechts auf den verschiedenen Stufen seiner Entwicklung: vol 3/1* (4th edn Breitkopf & Härtel, Leipzig 1888) 178–241, esp 210–15; and still Stadler *Gestaltungsfreiheit* (n 3). It has been doubted whether Savigny's concern was actually teleological: Jakobs ZSS (RA) 119 (n 180) 295–300, esp 298–99. Although Savigny stated in *System: vol 3* (n 180) 354–55: "[E]ine aus Irrthum entsprun-

parallel development is that which led to the inclusion in the BGB of §§ 932 ff. Under the *ius commune*, as in classical Roman law, the *nemo dat* principle prevailed.[183] But from the late 18th century onwards, several European states revived the Germanic legal tradition[184] and began to incorporate rules on *bona fide* purchase into their codifications of private law, either restricted to specific situations or as a principle of general application.[185] Without apparently adverting to the potential for a functional overlap with Savigny's principle of abstraction, the fathers of the BGB decided to follow suit.[186] Critics of the principle of abstraction have since variously pointed out that the introduction of broad *bona fide* purchase rules obviated any need for abstraction.[187] They highlight in particu-

---

gene Tradition ist vollgültig. In dieser regelmäßigen Unwirksamkeit des Irrthums liegt sogar die einzige Rettung des Verkehrs gegen gränzenlose Unsicherheit und Willkühr" ("A *traditio* founded on a mistake is fully valid. Indeed, it is the general irrelevance of mistakes which provides the only rescue of commerce from unlimited insecurity and arbitrariness"), he was there referring only to the general non-recognition of motivational mistakes rather than to a specific justification for the principle of abstraction. This is rightly pointed out by Jakobs ZSS (RA) 119 (n 180) 299. Yet the passage has nevertheless come to be interpreted in the latter sense: eg W Felgentraeger, *Friedrich Carl v. Savignys Einfluß auf die Übereignungslehre* (Deichert, Leipzig 1927) 40 fn 2: "Eine solche rechtspolitische Begründung ist bei Savigny selten, noch dazu in dieser leidenschaftlichen Form". ("This kind of reasoning in terms of legal policy is rare for Savigny, especially in such passionate form"). Contrast: D Haag Molkenteller, *Die These vom dinglichen Vertrag* (Lang, Frankfurt/Main 1991) 107–8.

183 Cf Digest 50.17.54 (Ulpian): "*Nemo plus iuris ad alium transferre potest, quam ipse haberet*". ("No-one can transfer to another greater rights than he himself has").

184 The maxims "*Hand wahre Hand*" and "*Wo Du Deinen Glauben gelassen hast, mußt Du ihn suchen*" ("go and look for your confidence where you have reposed it") express the idea that the owner who entrusts his goods to another must bear the consequences of his trust being disappointed. Note that some of the *bona fide* purchase provisions referred to in n 185 immediately below went beyond the entrustment principle.

185 Cf eg Prussia's *Allgemeines Landrecht*: Part I, Title 15, §§ 42 ff ALR (enacted 1794); France: Art 2279 Code Civil (enacted 1804); Austria: §§ 367, 368 ABGB (enacted 1812); summary and further references in *Motive* (n 3) vol 3, 341–43. For details on the history of *bona fide* purchase (which is, in fact, much more complex than the present rough sketch might suggest) see eg H Coing, *Europäisches Privatrecht: vol 2* (Beck, München 1989) 389–403; K Lux, "Die Entwicklung des Gutglaubensschutzes im 19. und 20. Jahrhundert mit besonderer Berücksichtigung des Wechselrechts" ZHR 1939, Beiheft 16, esp 3–43; D Olzen, "Zur Geschichte des gutgläubigen Erwerbs" Jura 1990, 505; HJ Wieling, *Sachenrecht: vol 1: Sachen, Besitz und Rechte an beweglichen Sachen* (2nd edn Springer, Berlin 2006) 359–65.

186 Cf *Motive* (n 3) vol 3, 341–50 (but note the reference at 334 to the French causal transfer system and its relationship with Art 2279 CC). On the legislative history see esp Wieling *Sachenrecht: vol 1* (n 186) 365–70.

187 Eg P Heck, *Das abstrakte dingliche Rechtsgeschäft* (Mohr Siebeck, Tübingen 1937) 20–25; G Kegel, "Verpflichtung und Verfügung: Sollen Verfügungen abstrakt oder

lar the inappropriateness of affording protection to a *mala fide* purchaser from the enrichee.[188] If the transfer from A to B is not itself voidable, but if C is aware of B's (potential) restitutionary liability to A, so the argument runs, he ought not to be 'immune' to claims by A merely as a result of the operation of the principle of abstraction. Of course, C will not be safe in all cases. Where he has acquired ownership of the painting gratuitously, he may be liable to surrender it to A under § 822 BGB. It is even possible that a delictual claim for compensation under § 826 BGB will lie against him if he has dishonestly colluded with B and thus intentionally and *contra bonos mores* inflicted a loss upon A.[189] Yet this does not change the fact that an ordinary *mala fide* purchaser for value will be protected by the law as it stands, and it is indeed hard to deny that the combination of abstraction and *bona fide* purchase within the BGB leads to a measure of overkill.[190]

---

kausal sein?" in W Flume and others (eds), *Internationales Recht und Wirtschaftsordnung: Festschrift für FA Mann* (Beck, München 1977) 57, 79–81; H Lange, "Rechtsgrundabhängigkeit der Verfügung im Boden- und Fahrnisrecht" AcP 146 (1941) 28, 30, 37–41; H Lange, "Rechtswirklichkeit und Abstraktion" AcP 148 (1943) 188, 226; E May, *Die Möglichkeit der Beseitigung des Abstraktionsprinzips bei den Verfügungsgeschäften des Fahrnisrechts* (Möller, Rendsburg 1952) 35–36, 57; R Neuner, "Abstrakte und kausale Übereignung beweglicher Sachen" RheinZ 14 (1926) 9, 29; J Streier, *Eigentumsübergang und Kausalgeschäft* (Ludolph & Co, Bochum 1938) 32. J von Staudinger (Begr), *J von Staudingers Kommentar zum Bürgerlichen Gesetzbuch: §§ 925–984* (Neubearbeitung 2004: Sellier de Gruyter, Berlin 2004) Vorbemerkung zu §§ 929–932 [16]–[18] (Wiegand), favours retaining abstraction, but pleads for a less strict application.

188 Cf esp Kegel in *Festschrift Mann* (n 187) 80–81; Lange AcP 146 (n 187) 40; May *Möglichkeit der Beseitigung des Abstraktionsprinzips* (n 187) 37. Similar already E Strohal, "Rechtsübertragung und Kausalgeschäft im Hinblick auf den Entwurf eines bürgerlichen Gesetzbuches für das Deutsche Reich" JherJB 27 (1889) 335, 407–8.

189 Cf Stadler *Gestaltungsfreiheit* (n 3) 379–80; E von Caemmerer "Rechtsvergleichung und Reform der Fahrnisübereignung" RabelsZ 12 (1938/39) 675, 712–13, reprinted in HG Leser (ed), *Ernst von Caemmerer: Gesammelte Schriften, vol 1: Rechtsvergleichung und Schuldrecht* (Mohr Siebeck, Tübingen 1968) 146, 185–86. Kegel in *Festschrift Mann* (n 187) 68, 81, suggests that A's personal claim against B (a relative right) should be recognized as protected by § 823 I BGB (which normally encompasses only absolute rights and interests).

190 This is even conceded by Stadler *Gestaltungsfreiheit* (n 3) 372, who defends the basic effect of abstraction: "Entscheidend ist das Interesse der Allgemeinheit an der Leichtigkeit das Waren- und Handelsverkehrs. Ob es nun allerdings angeht, das Verkehrsinteresse in so hohem Maße über den Kausalschutz des ursprünglichen Eigentümers zu stellen, daß auch ein unredlicher Zweiterwerber geschützt wird, ist ein berechtigter Einwand". ("The public interest in the ease of trade and commerce is decisive. Whether, however, it is appropriate to accord commercial interests such high priority over the 'causal' protection of the original owner that even a *mala fide* third party purchaser is protected, is a valid objection"). Contrast: HC Grigoleit, "Abstraktion und Willensmängel: Die Anfechtbarkeit des Verfügungsgeschäfts" AcP 199 (1999) 379, 384–85.

The question is what could and should be done to remedy the situation. One option would be simply to 'abolish' abstraction. But, as noted in the previous chapter, it is usually better to adopt a less radical solution, leaving the legal system as a whole intact.[191] We must remind ourselves that abstraction is not primarily, or at any rate not merely, a policy-based concept.[192] Indeed, given the background of German contract and property law, the principle of abstraction is – as Horst Heinrich Jakobs has put it – "no more than the product of precise thinking".[193] Instead of doing away with abstraction, we ought to find a way of extending A's personal restitutionary claim to reach not only the immediate transferee B, but also the *mala fide* purchaser C.[194] It is submitted that what is called for is a provision similar to § 822 BGB. C should not only be personally liable to A where his receipt is gratuitous, but also where, though a purchaser for value, he is aware of B's (potential)[195] obligation to surrender the painting to A.[196]

We have seen that under § 822 BGB C's personal liability to A depends on the exclusion of A's restitutionary claim against B (cf §§ 812 I alt 1,

---

[191] See above, Chapter V.D.3. (esp at pp 207–8, 210).

[192] Though policy considerations were an important factor in the legislative endorsement of the principle of abstraction (cf esp *Motive* (n 3) vol 3, 7), they were not at the forefront of Savigny's mind: see n 182 above. W Flume, *Allgemeiner Teil des Bürgerlichen Rechts, vol 2: Das Rechtsgeschäft* (3rd edn Springer, Berlin 1979) 176, sees the legislator as influenced by both policy and doctrinal or systematic considerations: "So sehr die Meinung der Verfasser des BGB durch doktrinäre und systematische Erwägungen bestimmt war, so stehen doch auch diese Erwägungen unter der Intention der sachgerechten Lösung". ("However much the opinion of the compilers of the BGB may have been determined by doctrinal and systematic considerations, these considerations were nevertheless subject to the aim of [finding] an appropriate solution [in policy terms]").

[193] Jakobs ZSS (RA) 119 (n 180) 300 ("nichts als das Produkt genauen Denkens"). Compare and contrast Flume *Rechtsgeschäft* (n 192) 176: "Das Abstraktionsprinzip ist weder apriorisch 'richtig', noch 'unrichtig' ". ("The principle of abstraction is neither *a priori* 'correct' nor 'incorrect' "). Jakobs ZSS (RA) 119 (n 180) 300, concedes that the principle of abstraction is a "logical necessity" *only* on the assumption of the particular notion of 'obligation' upon which Hugo's and Savigny's thinking was premised.

[194] Such an extension (or a similar one) is also envisaged by Jakobs ZSS (RA) 119 (n 180) 322–23.

[195] Cf § 142 II BGB.

[196] There is a question whether, for the purposes of a direct liability towards A (*Durchgriffshaftung*), *mala fides* on C's part should only be found where C has positive knowledge of B's position, or whether – as in § 932 II BGB – his grossly negligent ignorance should suffice. The more restrictive approach would appear to be preferable. Differently to the *bona fide* purchase scenario, is it here not C who has to overcome B's lack of ownership, but A who has to overcome the objection that B *was* the owner when effecting the conveyance to C.

818 I, II BGB) by virtue of the disenrichment defence (§ 818 III BGB).[197] There are two different ways of implementing a similar enrichment claim against *mala fide* purchasers for value from B. The more radical solution is to make C's liability depend not on the extinction of B's enrichment liability as such, but merely on the exclusion of A's claim to restitution *in specie* (cf § 812 I 1 alt 1 BGB). In order to prevent double recovery, A would have to choose between demanding re-conveyance of the painting from C and suing B for restitution of the (surviving)[198] value of B's enrichment.[199] A lesser inroad to the maxim that claims in unjustified enrichment have to respect the precedence of performance relationships (*Vorrang der Leistungsbeziehung*)[200] could be achieved by insisting that A fully exhaust his remedies against B before pursuing C.[201] Since relevant cases (in which C knows of B's restitutionary liability,[202] while B himself does not, and where – additionally – B's disenrichment plea is successful[203]) will be extremely rare in practice,[204] this second solution corrects

[197] See above, section B.2.b.ii of the present chapter (pp 225–26). On the question whether § 822 BGB also applies in B's insolvency cf n 41 on p 225.

[198] Even where B's conveyance to C is not gratuitous, B may – exceptionally – be able to rely on the disenrichment defence in § 818 III BGB (eg if he was the supposed legatee under a void testament who did not know of his restitutionary liability and, having sold the painting to C, spent the proceeds on a luxury holiday).

[199] The former option may, of course, entail difficulties in unravelling the transaction between B and C, but it is submitted that the solution should as closely as possible mirror cases where C fails to obtain ownership under §§ 932 ff BGB because he is *mala fide*. No problem arises as far as sales warranties in B's bargain with C are concerned. Although exposure to A's claim amounts to a defect of title in respect of the painting (§ 435 BGB), C's rights against B are excluded if he knew about the 'defect' when entering the contract (§ 442 I 1 BGB). On the question of C's grossly negligent ignorance: see § 442 I 2 BGB, but cf comment in n 196 above.

[200] Cf above, n 23 and corresponding text.

[201] On the repercussions for the relationship between B and C see n 199 above (exclusion of sales warranties). Where B acted in good faith, it is clear that C must be denied any claim for recovery of the purchase price. This is to prevent § 818 III BGB (which relieves B of his restitutionary liability towards A: cf n 203 below) from being undermined, as would be the case if B were made to bear the cost of his own disenrichment indirectly through exposure to liability vis-à-vis C.

[202] A requirement of positive knowledge is preferable to the standard of 'bad faith' as set out in § 932 II BGB: cf n 196 above.

[203] In accordance with the so-called 'modified two-claims theory', B may not be able to rely on § 818 III BGB if his disenrichment is referable to his own conduct rather than the enriching receipt: see above, Chapter III.C.3.c (pp 75–77). Where B is a purchaser for value under a supposed reciprocal contract with A, it will therefore be harder for him to invoke § 818 III BGB than where he is a gratuitous recipient (as in the legatee example given in n 198 above).

[204] If the case of B's insolvency were equated with that of B's disenrichment (cf n 41 above for the claim under § 822 BGB), the practical relevance of allowing the proposed

the abstractionist overkill without unduly undermining the normal restitutionary pattern of the basic three-party framework.

b) Reforming the English Law on *bona fide* Purchase

While German law offers too much protection to third party purchasers, English law arguably offers too little. Since it lacks the 'gist' of abstraction,[205] one would expect English law to embrace a broad principle of *bona fide* purchase.[206] This is indeed the position as far as equitable rights and interests are concerned,[207] and it is also true of common law powers *in rem* to revest title.[208] However, with the exception of cases concerning money and bills of exchange,[209] there remains a lacuna at common law in relation to situations in which title has revested in the original transferor (here A) by the time the chattel in question (here the painting) reaches the hands of a *bona fide* purchaser for value without notice (here C).[210] Although the expansive interpretation of the provisions dealing with purchases from 'buyers in possession' (ie Sale of Goods Act 1979, s 25(1), and Factors Act 1889, s 9) has to some degree bridged the gap, it requires courts to stretch the meaning of the relevant statutes and leaves us with a number of unprincipled and undesirable distinctions.[211]

Suggestions for reforming the law on *bona fide* purchase are floated from time to time, but have as yet not borne fruit. Two different approaches are conceivable. The first is to tinker with individual rules. In 1966, for example, the Law Reform Committee recommended that sale contracts void for the vendor's identity mistake should be regarded as only 'voidable' as far as third party purchasers were concerned, and that rescission should always have to be communicated to the other party (thus reversing the *Caldwell* ruling).[212] The second proposal is more far-reaching

---

direct claim by A against the *mala fide* purchaser C would be much increased. At the same time, however, the exhaustion requirement could be maintained.

205 See above, Chapter V.C.2 (pp 198–202).

206 We are here concerned with *bona fide* purchase in the traditional sense, namely as an 'exception' to the *nemo dat* principle: cf above, n 171 and corresponding text.

207 Cf *Phillips v Phillips* (n 65); *Cave v Cave* (n 65); and see also text to nn 63–67, 83–84 above.

208 Cf Sale of Goods Act 1979, s 23, and text to nn 58–62 above.

209 Cf above, n 53 and corresponding text.

210 The lacuna is exacerbated by the so-called *Caldwell* principle: cf above, n 71 and corresponding text.

211 Cf above, text to nn 72–83.

212 Law Reform Committee, *Twelfth Report: Transfer of Title to Chattels* (Cmnd 2958, 1966) esp [15], [16]. The Committee also recommended that the old section 25(2) of the Sale of Goods Act 1893 (now section 25 of the Sale of Goods Act 1979) should not require the buyer in possession of goods after sale to have acted as if he were a mer-

and fundamental. Aubrey Diamond, reporting in 1989, advocated a general 'entrustment' principle, very similar to that underlying §§ 932 ff BGB.[213] This would solve the problems created by the distinction between 'void' and 'voidable' contracts as well as the *Caldwell* principle in three-party situations without in any way affecting the well-established categories and rules applicable in 'pure' two-party cases.

Unfortunately, reform is not high up on the political agenda. Although the Law Commission recently again planned to review the entire area,[214] this project has since been put on ice.[215] It is nevertheless to be hoped that legislative intervention will in due course solve the problem. Whether a general principle of *bona fide* purchase based on the 'entrustment' of goods by one person to another would encroach too much on the sanctity of property rights or be too perilous to trade (as Bramwell B thought in *Higgons v Burton*),[216] depends, of course, on wider considerations than those canvassed here.[217] Yet the difficulties of treating contracts as 'void' for some and as 'voidable' for other purposes, coupled with the undesirability of operating different rules depending on whether the third party's acquisition occurs before or after the original transferor's 'rescission',[218] are certainly factors militating in favour of a broad sweep.

---

cantile agent when disposing of them (ibid [23]) and that a buyer whose voidable title has *already* been avoided by the seller should no longer be regarded as a 'buyer in possession' for the purposes of this provision (ibid [24]).

[213] AL Diamond, *A Review of Security Interests in Property* (HMSO, London 1989) 76–78.

[214] Law Commission, *Ninth Programme of Law Reform* (Law Com No 293, 2005) [3.51]–[3.57].

[215] Law Commission, *Tenth Programme of Law Reform* (Law Com No 331, 2008) [4.2]–[4.4]. The project has not been abandoned entirely, but is due to be reconsidered for the next programme if by then "the climate has become more conducive to tackling this long-standing problem" (ibid [4.4]).

[216] See above, nn 54–56 and corresponding text.

[217] It would, for example, also open up the possibility of *bona fide* purchase from a bailee (eg a borrower) to whom title was never intended to, and never did, pass.

[218] On the Law Reform Committee's proposals (cf above, n 212 and corresponding text), contracts entered into as a result of a fraudulently induced identity mistake would be treated as 'void' *inter partes* but – pending 'rescission' – as 'voidable' vis-à-vis third parties. After 'rescission' (by communication with the other contracting party), different rules would apply. The Committee did not envisage section 23 of the Sale of Goods legislation continuing to operate after rescission, as the Report (n 212) makes clear at para [16]. Since the Committee also wished to reverse the effect of the decision in *Newtons of Wembley v Williams* (n 72), a subsequent third party purchaser could no longer rely on section 25 of the Sale of Goods Act 1979. And even if this latter suggestion were not implemented, so that *bona fide* purchase remained possible despite rescission, the discrepancies between *bona fide* purchase under section 23 and section 25 of the Sale of Goods Act 1979 would be hard to eradicate completely.

2. The Weakness of Gratuitous Acquisitions

One theme which has come to the surface in various parts of this chapter is the weakness of gratuitous acquisitions in both English and German law. In English law, this weakness is most evident on the proprietary level. Where *bona fide* purchase is possible at all, it has to be a *bona fide* purchase *for value*. A third party such as C cannot defeat any proprietary interest which the original transferor has in respect of the object concerned (whether a mere power *in rem* or a revested legal or equitable right *in rem*) unless he provides value in exchange for its receipt.[219] In German law, by contrast, the weakness of gratuitous acquisitions lies exclusively at the personal level. Even donees can be *bona fide* purchasers where they are not already protected by the principle of abstraction. However, ownership obtained gratuitously may have to be given up under § 816 I 2 or § 822 BGB. To this extent, the law of obligations reverses resource allocations made by the law of property.

Clearly, English law has less need for personal restitutionary claims of the type contained in §§ 816 I 2, 822 BGB than the German Civil Code. In view of the extensive availability of proprietary restitution and the requirement that a *bona fide* purchaser give value in order to defeat pre-existing proprietary rights and interests, few donees will be immune from claims by the original transferor. If C receives title to the painting from B gratuitously, he inevitably acquires it subject to A's (legal or equitable) right or power *in rem*. Yet he seems to escape liability towards A[220] if B, rather than conveying the painting, makes a disenriching gift of £ 50 to him. The argument here has been that English law should allow A to leapfrog B in this situation in order to recover C's enrichment.[221] Such a personal claim would bear similarities to § 822 BGB. If introduced, it would ensure that the weakness of a gratuitous acquisition is reflected on the personal level where the transactional set-up precludes its recognition at the proprietary level.

---

[219] It will be recalled that this requires more than just providing 'consideration' in the sense of a counter-promise. The counter-promise needs actually to have been performed: cf *Story v Lord Windsor* (n 52); *Hardingham v Nicholls* (n 52). Critical: Barker [1999] RLR (n 173) 83.

[220] C's liability *towards B* depends on whether English law allows for restitution of (spontaneously) mistaken gifts, and additionally on whether B can be regarded as in fact mistaken: cf n 169 above.

[221] Above, section C.3 of the present chapter (esp text to nn 152–166 on pp 245–47).

E. Summary

The summary of this chapter can be brief. Much of it is already contained in the comparative observations set out above. In German law, the combined effect of the principle of abstraction and §§ 932 ff BGB results in too much third party protection. To an extent, this is counteracted by the personal restitutionary liability imposed on volunteers in § 816 I 2 and § 822 BGB. However, *mala fide* purchasers for value are only liable to the original transferor if the latter happens to be able to avoid his initial conveyance. By introducing a personal claim against third party recipients who have obtained ownership from a transferee-enrichee under § 929 BGB in the knowledge of his (potential) restitutionary liability, the perceived defect could be remedied without sacrificing abstraction as a whole.

In English law, the brunt of distinguishing between those third parties who are shielded from claims by the original transferor and those who are not is borne by the rules on *bona fide* purchase. These are designed to exclude from protection not only *mala fide* recipients and those with notice of the original transferee's lack of (full) entitlement, but also innocent volunteers. A person who does not qualify as *bona fide* purchaser for value acquires title subject to the original transferor's rights or interests *in rem* and may even be exposed to a receipt-based personal liability in unjust enrichment. Considering the great practical importance of the various *nemo dat* exceptions, it is unfortunate that there should remain gaps between them. The courts having already stretched certain statutory provisions beyond their intended limits, legislative reform is now called for. A generalized principle of *bona fide* purchase for value without notice could eradicate the anomalies besetting the current case law while leaving its cornerstones intact. If such a generalized principle of *bona fide* purchase (mainly relevant after a revesting of title) were flanked by the possibility of 'leapfrogging' the immediate transferee in appropriate circumstances (mainly relevant while any enrichment-generated power *in rem* of the original transferor's remains unexercised), a consistent regime at the proprietary level would be coherently supplanted by a matching pattern of personal restitutionary liability.

Chapter VII

The English Third Party Rights Bar to Rescission

A. Introduction

The present chapter is, in a sense, the odd one out. It addresses a specific problem of English law which cannot arise under the BGB. Given that the argument is of no relevance to German law and builds on the pattern of rights and liabilities as expounded in previous chapters, it will be relatively short. The aim is to dispel the notion that third party rights *in rem* can and should ever act as a bar to rescission of contract in English law.[1] Unlike impossibility of *restitutio in integrum*, the so-called 'third party rights bar to rescission' has hitherto not attracted much academic attention and is widely – but, it will be seen, incorrectly – accepted as the necessary corollary of the protection afforded to *bona fide* purchasers.[2]

---

[1] See already B Häcker, "Rescission and Third Party Rights" [2006] RLR 21. The argument proceeds from the orthodox understanding of the bar and concerns only the intervention of third party *property* rights. Different considerations may apply where the acquisition of *personal* rights is concerned: see n 64 on p 273 below.

[2] Cf eg H Beale (ed), *Chitty on Contracts* (29th edn Sweet & Maxwell, London 2004) [6–126]; G Jones (ed), R Goff and G Jones: *The Law of Restitution* (7th edn Sweet & Maxwell, London 2007) [9–029]; AG Guest (gen ed), *Benjamin's Sale of Goods* (7th edn Sweet & Maxwell, London 2006) [12–008] (Reynolds); E McKendrick (ed), *Sale of Goods* (LLP, London 2000) [7–068]; E Peel, *Treitel: The Law of Contract* (12th edn Sweet & Maxwell, London 2007) [9–104]. Notable exceptions (adverting to the problem either specifically or in passing): K Barker, "After Change of Position: Good Faith Exchange in the Modern Law of Restitution" in P Birks (ed), *Laundering and Tracing* (Clarendon Press, Oxford 1995) 191, 203; P Birks, *Unjust Enrichment* (2nd edn OUP, Oxford 2005) 173–76; M Bryan, "Rescission, Restitution and Contractual Ordering: The Role of Plaintiff Election" in A Robertson (ed), *The Law of Obligations:Connections and Boundaries* (UCL, London 2004) 59, 69; M Chen-Wishart, "Unjust Factors and the Restitutionary Response'" (2000) 20 OJLS 557, 566–67; D Friedmann, "Valid, Voidable, Qualified, and Non-Existing Obligations: An Alternative Perspective on the Law of Restitution" in A Burrows (ed), *Essays on the Law of Restitution* (Clarendon Press, Oxford 1991) 247, 268; NY Nahan, "Rescission: A Case for Rejecting the Classical Model?" (1997) 27 UWALR 66, 73–76; G Virgo, *The Principles of the Law of Restitution* (2nd edn Oxford, OUP 2006) 33–34; S Worthington, "The Proprietary Consequences of Rescission" [2002] RLR 28, 64–66. Now also D O'Sullivan, S Elliott and R Zakrzewski, *The Law of Rescission* (OUP, Oxford 2008) [20.01]–[20.27], who accept the gist of my paper in [2006] RLR (n 1), albeit that their account of it is somewhat misleading.

After briefly outlining the background to the third party rights bar (section B), its effects will be illustrated by contrasting a scenario where it does not operate with one where it does (section C). A closer look at the distortions created by the bar in the relationship between the contracting parties shows that its existence is neither practically desirable nor conceptually necessary (section D). English law would be better off without it.

B. Background

The third party rights bar to rescission is rooted in the fact that English law recognizes contracts of sale as a means of conveyance.[3] It will be recalled that a contract for the sale of specific goods is capable of passing title to the goods sold and, unless the parties manifest a different intention, usually does so as soon as it is concluded.[4] A sale of the painting by our transferor A to the transferee B thus vests title in B even before delivery. The flip-side of this is – it will further be recalled – that the conveyance is automatically avoided if A later rescinds the contract with B, eg for misrepresentation. Full legal title to the painting revests in A if rescission occurs at common law, while a trust comes into existence if it occurs in equity.[5] A's act of rescission thus wipes away the bargain into which the parties have entered, and at the same time effects, without more, one-sided proprietary restitution *in specie*.[6]

---

[3] It is sometimes suggested that the bar operates more widely than this and applies to all transfers of personal property *pursuant to* a contract. This assumption seems to rest on the view that conveyances under English law are generally 'causal' rather than 'abstract'. The argument in the present book is that they are not: see above, Chapter V.C (pp 191–202). Moreover, even if English law did operate a wholly causal transfer system, it is questionable whether this alone could justify the (supposed) third party rights bar, which depends primarily on the absence of a 'principle of separation': cf below, n 9 and corresponding text. Nevertheless, *if and to the extent that* a causal approach were adopted and did in fact support a broader application of the third party rights bar, the argument made here in respect of sale cases should be understood to extend – *mutatis mutandis* – beyond the sale context to all such transfers.

[4] Sale of Goods Act 1979, ss 17, 18 rule 1. The same may be true of contracts of barter and perhaps other agreements supported by consideration. If so, the present argument applies to these as well. On the scope of the *solo consensu* rule see above, Chapter IV.D.3.a (at pp 135–36).

[5] See above, Chapter IV.D.2 (esp pp 130–32).

[6] Some authors put forward a two-sided model of proprietary restitution: eg R Goode, *Commercial Law* (3rd edn LexisNexis, London 2004) 109; Worthington [2002] RLR (n 2) esp 37. This is premised on a 'causal' theory of conveyances (cf n 3 above), but see n 182 and corresponding text on p 201.

The problem with which the third party rights bar is concerned arises when a third party purchaser such as C acquires a proprietary interest in the painting from B before A purports to exercise his right to rescind. We have seen that English law sometimes prefers C's interest in the security of his receipt to A's interest in avoiding the transfer. Broadly speaking, C qualifies as a *bona fide* purchaser if he obtains B's title to the painting in good faith, for value, and without notice of A's legal or equitable power *in rem*.[7] In such a situation, so the logic of the third party rights bar apparently runs, any revesting of title in A (whether at law or in equity) must be prevented. And because rescission of contract and revesting of title go hand in hand, rescission must be barred where a *bona fide* purchaser has intervened. No rescission – no revesting; no revesting – no rescission. This is the essence of the third party rights bar.[8]

From the foregoing, the reason why the third party rights bar to rescission cannot feature in German law will have become obvious. It is premised on the possibility of transferring property rights by contractual agreement alone, such as exists in the English law of sale. In a system where the principles of separation and abstraction reign supreme, the problem with which the bar is concerned simply does not arise. Only if obligatory agreement and conveyance are contained in a single legal transaction (or are otherwise inextricably tied up with one another)[9] can the irreversibility of the latter have any conceivable bearing on the avoidance of the former.

---

[7] See above, Chapter VI.C.1.a (pp 228–30).

[8] If one accepted a 'theory of double effect' for English law (cf text to nn 170–172 on p 134), then the third party rights bar would become obsolete without more. B's voidable title would then rest on *both* the contract of sale *and* A's act of delivery, so that the former could be rescinded without any adverse proprietary consequences for C.

[9] If, contrary to the view taken in this book, English law were to adhere to a wholly causal transfer system (cf nn 3 and 6 above), a question would arise as to the necessity of barring the transferor's rescission *of contract* whenever an innocent third party purchaser's title is derived from the transferee. One might then reason that since the transferee's title vis-à-vis the transferor depended – *ex hypothesi* – on the validity of the contract, the third party would virtually always be prejudiced if rescission were allowed. However, such a conclusion is not inevitable (though it may well reflect the way the issue was historically thought about). Where contract and conveyance are *separate transactions*, as in all delivery cases, the current *bona fide* purchase rules make it relatively easy to decouple the validity of C's title from the validity of A's contract with B. The possibility of *bona fide* purchase from a person with 'voidable title' (cf Sale of Goods Act 1979, s 23) means that a subsequent rescission of A's need no longer affect C. Only the conveyancing effect of A's delivery to B will have become irreversible. Preventing A from revoking his consent to the (notionally separate) contractual transaction would not seem to be a necessary corollary. However that may be, it is unlikely that a definitive historical answer can be provided on the basis of the existing law. The only practically relevant scenario in which it is certain that the *solo consensu* principle does not apply (cf n 4 above) is the case of money, and here a general *bona fide* purchase defence is

C. The Third Party Rights Bar in Operation

1. Rescission before *bona fide* Purchase

Let us begin by considering the scenario where rescission occurs before the intervention of a *bona fide* purchaser. A rescinds his sale of the painting to B before B conveys or purports to convey the work of art on to C. C may or may not qualify as a subsequent *bona fide* purchaser who takes free from A's revested legal title or equitable interest.[10] Having dealt with C's position in the previous chapter,[11] we are now primarily interested in A's relationship with B. It is convenient to distinguish between different categories of claim.

First, B's conduct at the stage of contracting may have been wrongful and entitle A to the payment of damages.[12] Such 'inducement wrongs' mirror the unjust factor on which A's rescission was based. It will be recalled that the tort of deceit is committed whenever one party fraudulently induces another to enter into a contract and that many instances of duress overlap with some form of tortious behaviour (eg wrongful interference with goods, trespass to the person, intimidation).[13] Non-fraudulent misrepresentations will be actionable in the tort of negligence under *Hedley Byrne & Co Ltd v Heller & Partners Ltd*[14] if the defendant can be shown to have breached a duty of care towards the defendant, and they give rise to a damages claim under section 2(1) of the Misrepresentation Act 1967 whenever the defendant is unable to exculpate himself by showing that he had reasonable grounds to believe the facts represented to be true.[15] Although undue influence does not – or not yet – constitute an actionable

---

provided by *Miller v Race* (1758) 1 Burr 452, 97 ER 398. From the perspective of a devoted causalist, this alone might explain why the third party rights bar never had to be invoked where money was paid in pursuance of a voidable contract (that it was never used in money cases is an interesting fact to which Nahan (1997) 27 UWALR (n 2) 74, who is herself not a causalist, has drawn attention as part of her criticism of the bar).

[10] If A's rescission occurred at common law and title has revested in him, C may be able to rely on the *bona fide* purchase provisions relating to dispositions by 'buyers in possession': Sale of Goods Act 1979, s 25(1); Factors Act 1889, s 9. If in equity, C would have to qualify as 'equity's darling'.

[11] See above, esp Chapter VI.C.1.b (pp 230–33).

[12] We are here looking only at a loss-based measure of damages, ie compensation. Gain-based ('restitutionary' or 'disgorgement') damages are touched on in Chapter VIII.B.2 below (pp 294–96).

[13] See above, Chapter IV.E.1 (p 160).

[14] [1964] AC 465 (HL).

[15] See above, Chapter IV.E.2 (p 161).

wrong as such, it may under aggravating circumstances amount to a recognized species of equitable wrongdoing, eg a breach of fiduciary duty.[16]

Second, claims against B could arise from his unauthorized disposition of the painting to C ('disposition wrongs'). Since A has rescinded the contract of sale with B and has thereby exercised his power *in rem*, he has a (re)vested proprietary interest in the painting at the moment of B's conveyance to C. The exact nature of his interest depends on whether rescission occurred at law or in equity.[17] If the former, then B commits the tort of conversion by treating the painting as his own and by transferring or purporting to transfer good title to C.[18] If the latter, B may be liable for breach of trust by disposing of a chattel which, as a result of A's communication, he knows is subject to an equitable interest in A's favour.[19]

Finally, we must consider the possibility of unjust enrichment claims. Of course, A had already successfully effected proprietary restitution *in specie* by exercising his right to rescind the contract. For proponents of the 'exclusionary view', a personal right to restitution for unjust enrichment is incompatible with retaining or regaining a proprietary interest in the subject-matter of the impaired consent transfer.[20] However, those who accept the possibility of 'alternative analysis' should have no problem with granting restitution in value terms where the object cannot be specifically recovered despite the initially revested right *in rem*,[21] while those who adhere to the 'intermediate view' ought to allow value restitution where A's revested right is subsequently destroyed by C's *bona fide* purchase.[22]

Before leaving the analysis of A's claims against B where rescission occurs prior to *bona fide* purchase, it is worth pointing out that, subject to

---

[16] See above, Chapter IV.E.3 (p 162). In equity, monetary remedies are conventionally described not as 'damages', but as a 'liability to account'.

[17] See above, text to n 5.

[18] See above, Chapter IV.D.4.c (at pp 156–57).

[19] Unfortunately there is uncertainty over the extent to which remedies available against express trustees are also available against 'constructive' trustees in B's position. It was suggested earlier that an equitable wrong is committed by B if he knowingly puts it out of his power to comply with A's demand for re-conveyance under *Saunders v Vautier* (1841) 4 Beav 115, 49 ER 282; aff'd (1841) Cr & Ph 240, 41 ER 482: see above, Chapter IV.D.4.c (at pp 157–58, esp n 320).

[20] Cf above, Chapter IV.C.1 (pp 121–22). William Swadling, a prominent proponent of the 'exclusionary view', denies the existence of proprietary restitution and would always confine the transferor to a personal remedy: see Chapter IV.D.2 (at pp 133–34).

[21] Cf above, Chapter IV.C.2 (pp 122–24). Birks *Unjust Enrichment* (n 2) 171–79, for example, favours the universal availability of a personal claim, irrespective of any competing property right.

[22] Cf above, Chapter IV.C.3 (pp 124–25). The change of position defence will not be available in this situation to reduce the amount of B's personal liability since he will almost inevitably have acted in bad faith.

the rule against double recovery, A will also be able to assert a proprietary right to substitute assets received by B in exchange for the painting, such as the purchase price paid by C. Details about the principles of so-called 'tracing' and 'claiming' are left to the next chapter.[23] It is enough here to note that, unlike all personal claims, a proprietary interest in traceable substitute assets would afford A 'priority' in the case of B's insolvency.[24]

2. Purported Rescission after *bona fide* Purchase

The picture changes dramatically when we turn to the situation in which the third party rights bar to rescission operates. A purports to rescind his contract with B only after a *bona fide* purchaser, C, has intervened.[25] If the orthodoxy holds good, then it is now too late. A's contract with B can no longer be avoided because C has acquired a proprietary interest in the painting which was the subject-matter of the sale.

In the relationship between A and C, the third party rights bar to rescission appears merely as a facet of the *bona fide* purchase defence. It replicates the principle also laid down in section 23 of the Sale of Goods Act 1979, namely that an innocent purchaser for value without notice takes a transferee's title free from the transferor's unexercised power *in rem* to revest it. Yet in the relationship between the transferor A and the transferee B (with which we are here primarily concerned), the third party rights bar goes far beyond this. Taken seriously, it prevents A setting aside his bargain with B wholesale. This has repercussions for the taxonomy of claims between them.

Let us look at wrongs-based claims first. We distinguished above between wrongs committed at the stage of contracting ('inducement wrongs') and those committed by disposing of the painting to C ('disposition wrongs').[26] While the category of 'inducement wrongs' is unaffected by the subsequent loss of A's right to rescind the contract, the category of 'disposition wrongs' depends on A having exercised that right and thus the concomitant power *in rem*. Liability in conversion is premised on B having interfered with A's better right to possession. An unexercised legal power

[23] See below, Chapter VIII.B.1 (esp pp 276–89).

[24] More precisely: the substitute would not form part of B's estate and would therefore not be available for distribution amongst B's general creditors.

[25] Cf above, Chapter VI.C.1.a (pp 228–30). C will usually have acquired B's right to immediate possession (legal title) in good faith, for valuable consideration and without notice of A's power *in rem*. Where, however, A's power *in rem* was equitable, it is sufficient for C to have acquired a vested equitable interest (eg an equitable charge over the painting securing a loan to B).

[26] See above, text to nn 12–19.

in rem does not entail any such right.[27] As far as the common law is concerned, A's title has passed to B, albeit voidably, and it is now too late to avoid it. On the equity side of things, the picture is similar. Unless and until an equitable power *in rem* is exercised, the transferee does not hold the asset transferred on trust for the transferor and cannot therefore on any view be liable for breach of trust.[28]

What about a personal claim to restitution for unjust enrichment? There is no problem about identifying (induced) mistake, duress or undue influence as relevant unjust factors. However, so long as a valid contract governs the parties' relationship, it precludes any suggestion that B is unjustly enriched at A's expense by having received the painting or by disposing of it. Put differently: the contract of sale, while it exists, 'trumps' the unjust factor and justifies the allocation of wealth to B.[29] This is the crux of the matter. A is debarred from seeking a re-allocation of that wealth so long as the contract subsists, and he is permanently debarred from rescinding the contract by the existence of third party rights. He may be lucky. If he can find a reason to *terminate* – rather than *rescind* – the contract, restitution for unjust enrichment again becomes available. Take the example of fraud. B's fraudulent conduct may have consisted in paying with a cheque which he knew would be dishonoured. A has then not received what he bargained for. He is entitled to terminate the contract for B's repudiatory breach and can found an unjust enrichment claim on (total) failure of consideration.[30] But this strategy will not be successful where B has fully complied with his obligations under the contract. Representations made by one party to another are not always incorporated as terms.[31] Assume that B had fraudulently led A to believe that the picture was worth far less than its actual value and then paid the agreed price.[32] No breach having occurred, termination of the contract is not possible, and reliance

---

[27] See above, Chapter IV.D.4.c (at p 157).

[28] See above, Chapter IV.D.4.c (at p 158).

[29] Cf above, Chapter IV.B.2.a (pp 105–6).

[30] Of course, A could instead sue B for the purchase price (action for the agreed sum), but he may prefer to bring a claim in unjust enrichment if the bargain turns out to have been a bad one. The only question then is whether the contract, though terminated, does or should impose a cap on the value of A's personal restitutionary claim.

[31] Even where they are incorporated into the contract, termination will only be possible for breach of a 'condition' or for a sufficiently serious breach of a so-called 'innominate term'. Breach of a mere 'warranty' is not enough.

[32] Note that a false statement about the value or market price of the painting will not without more amount to a misrepresentation, especially in the context of arm's length bargaining: cf the observations in *Connolly Ltd v Bellway Homes Ltd* [2007] EWHC 895 (ChD) [126]–[131] (Stephen Smith QC).

on the unjust factor of (induced) mistake is, as we have seen, ruled out by the third party rights bar.

Taken together, the result appears to be that A has no claims whatsoever where B neither committed an 'inducement wrong' nor a repudiatory breach of contract. Various attempts have been made to bridge the liability loopholes thus entailed by the third party rights bar to rescission. Several are directed at specific unjust factors, one is more general. Unsurprisingly, the specific recommendations are geared towards non-fraudulent misrepresentations and undue influence.[33] It is argued that a court can and should award 'damages' *in lieu* of rescission under section 2(2) of the Misrepresentation Act 1967 where the victim of an 'innocent'[34] misrepresentation has lost his or her right to rescind the contract and compensation under section 2(1) is not due.[35] For cases of undue influence, we could – it is further proposed – simply draw an analogy with section 2(2).[36] Alternatively, it is suggested that 'equitable compensation' be made payable whenever rescission for undue influence is impossible,[37] or that courts should have the power to order similar 'equitable relief' in such circumstances.[38] The more general approach is to understand the 'voidability' of a contract as being in and of itself a sufficient ground for a (personal) claim to restitution, even after the right to rescind has been destroyed.[39]

---

[33] 'Unsurprisingly' because there will be an 'inducement wrong' to fall back on in cases of fraud and most forms of duress, while this will less often be the case where non-fraudulent misrepresentations and undue influence are at issue.

[34] The provision applies to all types of non-fraudulent misrepresentations, but – given the transferee's negligence liability under the principle in *Hedley Byrne v Heller* (n 14) and under section 2(1) of the Misrepresentation Act 1967 – the suggestion is primarily aimed at 'innocent' misrepresentations in the narrower sense. Section 2(2) reads: "Where a person has entered into a contract after a misrepresentation has been made to him otherwise than fraudulently, and he would be entitled, by reason of the misrepresentation, to rescind the contract, then ... the court ... may declare the contract subsisting and award damages in lieu of rescission...".

[35] P Birks, "Unjust Factors and Wrongs: Pecuniary Rescission for Undue Influence" [1997] RLR 72, 75–77; *Treitel on Contract* (n 2) [9–053].

[36] Birks [1997] RLR (n 35) 78.

[37] T Akkouh, "Equitable Compensation where Rescission is Impossible" (2002) 16 TruLI 151; L Ho, "Undue Influence and Equitable Compensation" in P Birks and F Rose (eds), *Restitution and Equity, vol 1: Resulting Trusts and Equitable Compensation* (Mansfield Press, London 2000) 193, esp 193–99. These suggestions were partially inspired by May J's decision in *Mahoney v Purnell* [1996] 3 All ER 61 (QBD).

[38] Cf *Hartigan v International Society for Krishna Consciousness Inc* [2002] NSWSC 810, esp [98], where the subject-matter of a gift procured by the donee's undue influence had been sold and could no longer be returned *in specie* (the case concerned realty).

[39] Birks *Unjust Enrichment* (n 2) 125–27, 175–76. This argument is premised on Birks' new 'absence of basis' approach to unjust enrichment: "The voidability of the

While attractive from the policy point of view, all of these proposed solutions are fraught with difficulties on closer examination. Despite the willingness of Jacob J in *Thomas Witter Ltd v TBP Industries Ltd*[40] to accede to the argument about section 2(2) of the Misrepresentation Act 1967 operating where rescission is barred,[41] this reading stretches the wording of the provision beyond its clear limits.[42] Section 2(2) only applies where the representee "would be entitled, by reason of the misrepresentation, to rescind the contract", which is precisely not the case in our scenario. Accordingly, the interpretation has since been rejected in *Government of Zanzibar v British Aerospace (Lancaster House) Ltd*[43] and in *Floods of Queensferry Ltd v Shand Construction Ltd (No 3)*[44]. In view of its narrow statutory confines, section 2(2) does not lend itself to analogous application in the context of undue influence. Nor can 'equitable compensation' for undue influence be awarded without more. That would require us to abandon the traditional requirement of a fiduciary relationship (or equivalent) existing between the parties as a precondition for recovery,[45] and perhaps even to regard all cases of undue influence as instances of wrongdoing.[46] The less restrictive language of 'equitable relief', on the other hand, gives no yardstick for the proper measure of recovery and misleadingly suggests that it should be left to the courts' discretion.[47] Overall,

---

contract sufficiently destroys the basis of the transfer even when, as events turn out, one response, namely the power to rescind and revest, is barred" (ibid 176).

[40] [1996] 2 All ER 573 (ChD).

[41] Ibid 590–91.

[42] The limitation of the statute is accepted (with reluctance) by H Beale, "Points on Misrepresentation" (1995) 111 LQR 385, 386–88. Cf also J Cartwright, *Misrepresentation, Mistake and Non-Disclosure* (2nd edn Sweet & Maxwell, London 2007) [4.64]; *Treitel on Contact* (n 2) [9–093].

[43] [2000] 1 WLR 2333 (QBD Comm) 2343–44 (Jack QC). Agreeing: *Pankhania v Hackney London BC* [2002] EWHC 2441 (ChD) [76] (Tedd QC).

[44] [2000] BLR 81 (QBD TCC) 91–93 (Lloyd QC).

[45] Cf Akkouh (2002) 16 TruLI (n 37) 157–59. While it may be possible to regard the relationship between a 'bare' constructive trustee and his beneficiary as being in some sense 'fiduciary' (cf above, n 19 and corresponding text), it is much harder to say the same for the relationship between a transferee and a transferor with an unexercised equitable power *in rem*.

[46] See the discussions by Akkouh (2002) 16 TruLI (n 37) 160–63; Ho in *Resulting Trusts and Equitable Compensation* (n 37) 196–207; V Vann, "Equitable Compensation when Rescission is Impossible: A Response" (2003) 17 TruLI 66, 68–71.

[47] In *Hartigan v International Society for Krishna Consciousness* (n 38) [98], Bryson J stated that "[i]n granting equitable relief the court has power to mould the relief granted to the circumstances of the particular case and what justice requires after making the detailed examination of the particular circumstances which the exercise of this power calls for". Interestingly, on the facts of *Hartigan*, the proper measure of relief was thought to be the amount realized by the transferee-donee's sale of the land to a third

attempts to tackle cases of non-fraudulent misrepresentation and undue influence specifically have not been successful, but have arguably helped to perpetuate the unsatisfactory state of affairs. More promising is the elegant general solution of regarding 'voidability' of a contract as alone sufficient to generate a personal claim in unjust enrichment. However, it has the drawback of effectively pre-empting A's decision whether or not to let the bargain stand. A voidable contract cannot simply be equated with a void contract. Conceptually, it remains valid until avoided. If fully-fledged unjust enrichment claims are to be made generally available to a transferor in A's position, they must be preceded by an act of rescission which sets aside the contract at least in relation to the transferee. How this can be achieved is the concern of the next section.

D. Abolition of the Third Party Rights Bar

1. Desirability of Abolition

The comparison between cases in which a contract of sale has been rescinded before *bona fide* purchase occurs and those where, subsequent to a *bona fide* purchase, its rescission is barred by third party rights, has highlighted the problems generated by the so-called third party rights bar. In – allegedly – protecting the third party (C) from the proprietary effects of the transferor-seller's (A's) rescission, it deprives the latter of claims against the transferee-buyer (B) which would otherwise be available. And while the existence of 'inducement wrongs' and the possibility of termination for breach will sometimes make up for the loss of A's right to rescind, he is left without any remedy if B, being an innocent misrepresentor who can show 'reasonable grounds' for his belief in accordance with section 2(1) of the Misrepresentation Act 1967 or a non-fiduciary who inadvertently and blamelessly exerted undue influence, complies with all the contractual terms. In short: the third party rights bar to rescission distorts the taxonomy of remedies between A and B.

To restore balance to the parties' relationship, we would have to find a way of allowing A to avoid his contract with B without at the same time prejudicing C. As far as conceptually possible, A's position where *bona fide* purchase precedes rescission should be assimilated to that where rescission precedes *bona fide* purchase. It is clear that complete assimilation is not feasible in English law. B could not be made liable for one of the 'disposition wrongs' even if A were allowed to rescind *inter partes*. A sub-

party. Bryan in *Law of Obligations: Connections and Boundaries* (n 2) 69, therefore concludes that the order was in substance one for 'personal restitution'.

sequent act of rescission could not change the fact that B's conveyance of the painting to C constituted neither an interference with any better right to possession nor a breach of trust.[48] Yet rescission would remove the obstacle standing in the way of unjust enrichment claims. A could then rely on the relevant unjust factor (induced mistake, duress, undue influence) to seek restitution for B's enrichment at his expense.

The remainder of this section will focus on the availability of personal restitutionary claims against the transferee-buyer in the form of a monetary remedy. However, it is worth bearing in mind that the abolition of the third party rights bar to rescission could also open the door to a different type of proprietary restitution. Although the transferor may no longer be able to assert a proprietary interest in the original asset, it is nevertheless conceivable that he could assert such a proprietary interest in its traceable substitute(s).[49] This depends primarily on the broader question whether powers *in rem* can constitute a sufficient 'proprietary base' for the purposes of the tracing and claiming exercise, which will be discussed in Chapter VIII.[50] Suffice it for the time being to draw the reader's attention to the possibility and to note that, as far as our present scenario goes, the removal of the third party rights bar to rescission would be the essential first step.

2. Third Party Rights and *restitutio in integrum*

One aspect of the third party rights bar to rescission which has hitherto received too little attention is its relationship with the requirement of *restitutio in integrum*.[51] It will be recalled that rescission of a contract was

---

[48] For the purposes of the law of wrongs, rescission only ever operates prospectively: see above, Chapter IV.D.4.c (at pp 157–58).

[49] P Birks, *An Introduction to the Law of Restitution* (Clarendon Press, Oxford 1985, paperback edn 1989) 172–73, denies the possibility of claiming traceable substitutes precisely because of the third party rights bar: "[T]he right to rescind is lost when a third party acquires the *res* for value is [sic] good faith. It follows from this that no restitutionary right *in rem* can be maintained in respect of the identifiable exchange product of a sale or barter of the *res* ... [I]f the misrepresentor exchanges the *res* for £ 100, any attempt to assert a right *in rem* to the £ 100 must be based upon a rescission of the original contract between misrepresentor and misrepresentee, for the misrepresentor's title remains good until it is avoided. But, since the third party's title to the *res* depends on the misrepresentor's, it is impossible to establish a claim *in rem* to the £ 100 without at the same time disturbing the third party".

[50] See below, Chapter VIII.B.1.b (pp 289–94).

[51] Authors who (expressly or impliedly) advert to the relationship and see a connection are: Akkouh (2002) 16 TruLI (n 37) 151; Birks *Unjust Enrichment* (n 2) 173–76; Chen-Wishart (2000) 20 OJLS (n 2) 566–67; Nahan (1997) 27 UWALR (n 2) 72–79; Worthington [2002] RLR (n 2) 64–66. Contrast: O'Sullivan et al *Law of Rescission* (n 2) [20.03], who regard the two bars as "fundamentally distinct".

traditionally thought to be barred whenever the parties could not be restored to their exact pre-contractual positions.[52] The widely accepted modern approach is to dissolve the requirement of *restitutio in integrum* into a broader principle about the mutuality of restitution in the contractual context.[53] Where it is not possible to return an asset *in specie*, restitution can be effected by valuing the performance received and ordering payment of the appropriate amount ('pecuniary rescission').

Although impossibility of *restitutio in integrum* usually becomes relevant where the rescinding party is unable to return to the defendant what he has received under the contract, the ambit of the rule is in fact wider. As a starting point, it seeks to ensure that both parties receive back what they parted with.[54] Looked at from this angle, the obvious thing to do is to apply the foregoing conclusions to the third party rights bar. The case in which B has conveyed the painting acquired from A to a *bona fide* purchaser, C, before A purorts to rescind the contract of sale is, after all, but one example in which precise restitution *in specie* is no longer possible. By imposing on B an obligation to disgorge the value of his enrichment (ie the market price of the painting minus – where appropriate – any part of the purchase price already paid to A),[55] we are simply substituting a personal claim for what would otherwise be a proprietary interest. Instead of relating to a specific asset, A's restitutionary claim now focuses on the amount by which his performance has increased B's wealth in the abstract.

---

[52] See above, Chapter IV.B.2.c (at pp 109–10).

[53] See above, Chapter IV.B.2.c (at pp 110–13). *Restitutio in integrum* then merges into a requirement of counter-restitution: eg Birks *Introduction* (n 49) 415–24; A Burrows, *The Law of Restitution* (2nd edn Butterworths, London 2002) 176–79, 538–42; *Goff & Jones* (n 2) [9–23]–[9–28]; Virgo *Principles* (n 2) 31–33.

[54] Cf eg *Spence v Crawford* [1939] 3 All ER 271 (HL) 289 (Lord Wright): "The *rule is stated as requiring the restoration of both parties to the status quo ante*, but it is generally the defendant who complains that restitution is impossible. The plaintiff who seeks to set aside the contract will generally be reasonable in the standard of restitution which he requires. [...] In the vast majority of cases of the transfer of property, it is a purchaser who is seeking to reduce the contract, on the terms, on the one hand, of restoring what he has purchased, and, on the other hand, of being repaid the purchase price with all proper allowances and accounts. The present case is peculiar in that it is a vendor who seeks rescission. Nevertheless, the principles must be the same" (emphasis added). The criticism voiced by O'Sullivan et al *Law of Rescission* (n 2) [20.03] fn 6, regarding my reference to *Spence v Crawford* (above) in Häcker [2006] RLR (n 1) 35 fn 96, is misdirected. The authors seem to have overlooked that I am explicitly referring only to the passage from Lord Wright's speech quoted above. The footnote immediately after the one to which they object makes clear that Lord Thankerton took a different view. See also the discussion below, text to nn 57–59.

[55] The extent to which B is able to rely on the general change of position defence, eg as far as reliance expenditure is concerned, is another question: cf n 59 on pp 112–13 and corresponding text.

Far from being unusual, the mechanism of pecuniary rescission actually brings the regime of mutual restitution following rescission of contract into line with the value-oriented general law of unjust enrichment.[56]

Support for the view that the defendant-buyer's inability to make *restitutio in integrum* does not provide him with a defence against a claimant-seller's rescission can be gleaned from *Spence v Crawford*.[57] The defendant had fraudulently induced the claimant to sell him shares in a company by misrepresenting the company's financial position. When the claimant later sought to rescind the contract, the defendant argued that mutual *restitutio in integrum* had become impossible. Upholding the claimant's appeal, Lord Thankerton said: "[I]n my opinion, the defender who, as purchaser, has been guilty of fraudulent misrepresentation is not entitled in bar of restitution to found on dealings with the subject purchased, which he has been enabled by his fraud to carry out".[58] Unfortunately, his Lordship (expressly) left open the question whether the same would be true if the misrepresentation had been made non-fraudulently.[59]

3. Feasibility of Abolition

It may be objected that the argument advanced above fails to take account of one crucial difference between the 'ordinary' *restitutio in integrum* requirement and the third party rights bar to rescission. The former is not conceptually dependent on contractual rescission having any immediate proprietary effect. Restoration of the parties to the *status quo ante* can be achieved in different ways. In money cases, for example, repayment of an equivalent sum has always satisfied the requirement. Where title to a non-fungible has passed by delivery, a re-conveyance of the chattel suffices for exact *restitutio in integrum*.[60] Deterioration of the object in question can be remedied by repair or (nowadays) financial adjustments. The reason why it

[56] On the primacy of value restitution in English law see above, Chapter II.C.2.a (esp p 32) and Chapter IV.B.1 (at p 104).

[57] [1939] 3 All ER 271 (HL). *Spence v Crawford* was a Scottish case, but the relevant principles were thought to be the same as in England.

[58] Ibid 281. His Lordship was also keen to note "that the condition of relief is the restoration of the defender to his pre-contract position, and that no stress is placed on whether the pursuer is so restored" (ibid 279).

[59] Ibid 281–82.

[60] In such a case (perhaps barter), a defrauded transferor will also be able to effect proprietary restitution *in specie* unilaterally, by exercising a common law power *in rem* which is notionally separate from the underlying contract. How much space there is in English law for the transfer of movables by delivery ultimately depends on the scope of the *solo consensu* rule: cf n 4 above. Assuming that it does not apply to barter, A will have to reverse B's performance by re-conveying the object he has received from B.

has become possible to reinterpret *restitutio in integrum* as necessitating, in appropriate cases, only a personal claim to restitution of the value transferred is because our notion of 'restoration' has become less specific over time. This is otherwise in the scenario in which third party rights are at issue.[61] The third party rights bar is intimately tied up with the specific proprietary consequences of rescinding a contract of sale. We have seen that its very ratio is the perceived need to protect the *bona fide* purchaser (C) against a revesting of title or the creation of an equitable interest in the seller.[62] If pecuniary rescission is to be allowed in such circumstances, we must find a way of severing the *in rem* aspect of the sale contract from its *in personam* effects.

Once the challenge presented by the third party rights bar to rescission is framed in these terms, the solution comes within reach. Contracts are primarily bargains to which their parties will normally be held. Rights (or powers) to rescind are escape routes out of such bargains. A bargain may oblige one or both parties to effect a transfer of title. The transfer itself is called a conveyance. For contracts of sale, English law has chosen to combine both the bargain and the conveyancing aspect in the same agreement. Subject to the parties' contrary intention, an unconditional contract for the sale of specific goods effects (part of) the seller's performance by passing his title to the buyer as soon as the contract is concluded.[63] Bargain and conveyance, though notionally distinct, are to be found in the same transaction. As a corollary, the rescission of a contract of sale will normally reverse the transaction on both counts. It destroys the parties' bargain and at the same time effects one-sided proprietary restitution *in specie*. Where a *bona fide* purchaser has intervened, the latter is no longer possible. The *in rem* aspect of rescission falls away. However, the fact that rescission cannot fulfil all its usual functions does not necessitate its wholesale prevention. Provided that third party rights are not disturbed, there can be no objection to the seller's rescission of his *bargain* with the buyer.

---

[61] The problem of third party rights can sometimes also affect the *restitutio in integrum* bar directly. If, for example, A buys an object from B, which he sells on to Y before attempting to rescind the sale contract for B's fraud, then the question arises how A's rescission of the contract can be divorced from a revesting of title in B. Unless one accepts the theory of 'double effect' (cf n 172 on p 134), both aspects would seem to go hand-in-hand, and there is a danger of disturbing Y's rights. Conceptually, the problem can only be overcome by decoupling the bargain aspect of contracting from its conveyancing effect: cf text after n 62.

[62] See above, section B of the present chapter (pp 260–61).

[63] Once title has passed, the seller is still under a duty to deliver the goods to the buyer (or to let him take possession), usually upon payment of the purchase price: Sale of Goods Act 1979, ss 27–29.

Historically, the third party rights bar to rescission probably started out as a primitive version of the *bona fide* purchase defence. Every case in which it has been applied concerned a dispute between the seller and a third party.[64] Judicial pronouncements on the matter are therefore mere *obiter dicta*.[65] With the emancipation and refinement of the rules on *bona fide* purchase, the third party rights bar has lost any justification it may have had. The enactment of section 23 of the Sale of Goods Act 1893 (now section 23 of the Sale of Goods Act 1979) puts the free-standing quality of *bona fide* purchase beyond doubt.[66] It is telling that the provision makes no

[64] *White v Garden* (1851) 10 CB 919, 138 ER 364, is the leading case. Cf also *Kingsford v Merry* (1856) 11 Exch Rep 577, 156 ER 960, rev'd on other grounds (1856) 1 Hurl & N 503, 156 ER 1299; *King's Norton Metal Co Ltd v Edridge, Merrett, & Co Ltd* (1897) 14 TLR 98 (CA); *Whitehorn Bros v Davison* [1911] 1 KB 463 (CA); *Phillips v Brooks Ltd* [1919] 2 KB 243 (KBD); *Lewis v Averay* [1972] 1 QB 198 (CA). There is no clear authority to the contrary. In *Huyton SA v Distribuidora Internacional de Productos Agricolas SA* [2003] EWCA Civ 1104, [2004] 1 All ER (Comm) 402, esp [4]–[5], where the dispute was between the original parties, the Court of Appeal suggested that the intervention of third party rights might be a reason for exercising the discretion under section 2(2) of the Misrepresentation Act 1967 to declare their contract subsisting (without, however, regarding the issue as decisive and without adverting to the problem outlined in the text to nn 40–44 above). *Society of Lloyd's v Leighs* [1997] CLC 1398 (CA) is also only an apparent exception. The defendants had been fraudulently induced to become Lloyd's names. Their purported retroactive rescission failed on the basis that it would have been incompatible with Lloyd's business. The syndicate's managing agents had already entered into contracts with third parties on behalf of the names and *restitutio in integrum* was impossible: cf ibid 1403–5. This scenario differs from that here under consideration in relation to the types of rights acquired by the third parties. In *Lloyd's v Leighs*, these were rights *in personam* against the rescinding party (acquired by virtue of the managing agents' authority to contract) as opposed to rights *in rem* in a chattel (acquired by virtue of the *bona fide* purchase rules). In the *Lloyd's* case, rescission may indeed not have been possible without prejudicing third parties, at least if the effect of rescission were to have divested the agents' authority retroactively. Note that German law exceptionally allows rescission only *ex nunc* in the case of executed employment contracts or company relationships (despite § 142 I BGB): eg BAGE 5, 159; BGHZ 13, 320. Similar cases in English company law are: *Oakes v Turquand* (1867) LR 2 HL 325 (HL); *Tennet v City of Glasgow Bank (In Liquidation)* (1879) 4 App Cas 615 (HL); *Re Scottish Petroleum Co* (1883) 23 ChD 413 (CA). The interests of third parties were not affected in *Adam v Newbigging* (1888) 13 App Cas 308 (HL): cf esp ibid 323.

[65] Most of the cases following *White v Garden* (n 64) to not even mention the third party rights bar as such. Contrast *Clough v London and North Western Rly Co* (1871) LR 7 Ex 26 (Exch Ch), and *Cundy v Lindsay* (1878) 3 App Cas 459 (HL) 464 (Lord Cairns), where *bona fide* purchase was actually described in terms of rescission being barred, but where the bar did not operate on the facts.

[66] Even to the extent that the old common law principles of *bona fide* purchase still apply beside section 23, eg where C is not a purchaser of legal title, but – as in *Kingsford v Merry* (n 64), *Whitehorn Bros v Davison* (n 64) or *Phillips v Brooks* (n 64) – a pledgee from B, they do not necessitate the existence of any 'third party rights bar to rescission'.

mention of the alleged bar. All section 23 is concerned to do is to ensure that certain third parties acquire title unencumbered by the transferor's unexercised power *in rem*. Given that innocent purchasers for value without notice need no longer rely on the crude 'third party rights bar to rescission', we would be well-advised to rid ourselves of the doctrine and its problematic connotations. If this seems too radical a step, we should at least move it from our textbooks on contract law to our textbooks on property law.

E. Summary

Like impossibility of precise *restitutio in integrum*, the existence of third party rights *in rem* should never be a ground for denying rescission of a contract for the sale of goods (or, indeed, any contract). It is possible to allow a transferor-seller to set aside his bargain with the transferee-buyer without prejudicing intervening *bona fide* purchasers. The so-called third party rights bar to rescission adds nothing to the rules on *bona fide* purchase, yet it seriously distorts the taxonomy of remedies in the contracting parties' relationship (by making the extent of the seller's rights against the buyer turn on the wholly unrelated issue of third party protection). The abolition of the third party rights bar would not only pave the way for 'pecuniary rescission', ie a personal restitutionary claim measured by the value of the buyer's enrichment, but may even open the door to new forms of proprietary restitution. The discrepancy between cases of rescission before and after *bona fide* purchase is reduced to an absolute minimum. Questions of third party protection are kept out of the relationship between seller and buyer.

In fact, a revesting of title ought to be possible in the case of a pledge, subject only to A being bound by C's 'special property': see above, n 62 on p 229.

Chapter VIII

Claiming Substitute Assets from the Transferee (and Third Parties)

A. Introduction

This last substantive chapter completes our survey of the three-party scenario. Having considered the position of third party purchasers of the original asset as against the transferor (in Chapter VI), and having argued for the abolition of the so-called 'third party rights bar to rescission' in the relationship between transferor and transferee under English law (in Chapter VII), it is now time to turn to the circumstances in which the transferor, A, can demand surrender of substitute assets which the transferee, B, has received from the third party, C. Often C will have provided value in consideration of obtaining the painting from B, usually – but not necessarily – in the form of a money payment. We are here concerned with the question of when and how A can assert claims in respect of such substitute assets (or their substitutes in turn).[1] This will primarily be of interest where the value of the substitute is greater than the value of the original asset, but it may also be of some relevance in the transferee's insolvency.

Unlike all the previous comparative chapters, this one begins with a discussion of the English law on the subject (section B). The principles of tracing and claiming, coupled with the availability of personal wrongs-based claims to the disgorgement of profits, provide a more comprehensive framework for rights to substitute assets than that offered by the BGB. German law knows no generally applicable principle of 'real subrogation' equivalent to the rules of tracing and claiming, but does allow personal claims to substitute assets in some situations (section C). From a comparative angle, the discrepancies between English and German law may never-

---

[1] For the purposes of this chapter, it will be inevitable to consider (or at least bear in mind) examples in which four and more parties are involved, eg cases where B obtains a traceable substitute of the painting from C and then passes the substitute on to D. The reference to 'third parties' in the chapter title must be understood to encompass any individual other than transferor and transferee. However, our main point of departure and central case will be that in which B effects one or several substitutions and still retains the identifiable proceeds of these transactions.

theless not be as great as they appear at first sight, particularly in the insolvency context (section D).

B. Tracing and Disgorgement Damages in English Law

1. Proprietary Interests in Substitute Assets

Before embarking on a discussion of tracing in English law, some terminological clarifications are apposite. First and foremost, 'tracing' (in the legal sense) must be distinguished from 'following'.[2] Following describes the process of locating a physical thing in space. In our example, A will be able to follow the picture he transferred to B into C's hands. Tracing, on the other hand, refers to the process of locating value amongst the assets of a substitutor. If A can identify an exchange product of the painting remaining in B's hands (eg the purchase price paid by C), he has successfully traced its value.[3] Following thus focuses on the original thing, while tracing is concerned with identifying a new thing acquired by a former holder of the original thing, where the new thing 'represents' the value inherent in the original.[4]

The second important distinction is between 'tracing' and 'claiming'.[5] Like following, tracing is a process which is neutral as to rights. The fact that A can locate the painting in C's possession, or a substitute representing its value in B's, does not tell us anything about A's rights in respect of either of these things. We have already seen that, although A may be able to follow the painting into C's hands, the latter takes it free from any claims by A if he qualifies as a *bona fide* purchaser for value without notice.[6] The same applies in the tracing context. As Lord Steyn observed in *Foskett v McKeown*[7]: "[T]racing is a process of identifying assets: it be-

---

[2] Cf eg L Smith, *The Law of Tracing* (Clarendon Press, Oxford 1997) 6–10; *Foskett v McKeown* [2001] 1 AC 102 (HL) 127 (Lord Millett).

[3] The object of the verb 'to trace' is 'value'. We trace value, not things or rights: Smith *Tracing* (n 2) 119. Cf also the title of V Behr, *Wertverfolgung: Rechtsvergleichende Überlegungen zur Abgrenzung kollidierender Gläubigerinteressen* (Metzner, Frankfurt/ Main 1986), where two whole chapters are devoted to 'economic surrogates' (chs 10–11: at 287–412).

[4] Smith *Tracing* (n 2) 8: "Following ... is always concerned with the *original thing*, and it can bring into the picture a *new person*. [...] Tracing ... always brings into the picture a *new thing*, acquired by the *original holder*" (emphasis in the original).

[5] Cf eg P Birks, "Overview: Tracing, Claiming and Defences" in P Birks (ed), *Laundering and Tracing* (Clarendon Press, Oxford 1995) 289, 290–95; Smith *Tracing* (n 2) 10–14; *Foskett v McKeown* (n 2) 128 (Lord Millett).

[6] See above, Chapter VI.C.1 (pp 226–33).

[7] [2001] 1 AC 102 (HL).

longs to the realm of evidence. It tells us nothing about legal or equitable rights to the assets traced".[8] In order to lay his hands on a substitute asset received by B, A has to establish that he is entitled to it. How this can be done is the concern of the rules on claiming. Generally speaking, A will be able to assert a proprietary interest in the substitute asset if he had a proprietary interest in the original asset,[9] the so-called 'proprietary base'.[10] In our scenario the question arises whether powers *in rem* can serve as a proprietary base in the same way as vested rights *in rem*. We will turn to this particular issue after a general examination of the principles of tracing and claiming and the problems to which they give rise.

a) The Principles of Tracing and Claiming

The principles of tracing and claiming are best illustrated by reference to the simple case in which the person seeking to show an entitlement to a particular substitute asset starts out with a vested property right. We are considering the situation in which our transferor A has either never lost title to the painting (eg because he was labouring under an operative mistake as to B's identity when purporting to make the transfer),[11] or where he has exercised a legal or equitable power *in rem* and thereby revested in

[8] Ibid 113. Cf also the statement by Lord Millett (ibid 128): "Tracing is ... neither a claim nor a remedy. It is merely the process by which a claimant demonstrates what has happened to his property, identifies its proceeds and the persons who have handled or received them, and justifies his claim that the proceeds can properly be regarded as representing his property. Tracing is ... distinct from claiming. It identifies the traceable proceeds of the claimant's property. It enables the claimant to substitute the traceable proceeds for the original asset as the subject matter of his claim. But it does not affect or establish his claim".

[9] Claiming traceable substitutes on the purely personal level is not normally an issue. Due to the maxim that 'equity regards as done that which ought to be done', a personal claim to a specific object always goes hand in hand with an equitable interest in respect of it. Section 3(1) of the Minors' Contracts Act 1987 ("or any property representing it") appears to contain a rare example of a non-proprietary right to traceable substitutes, depending entirely on an appropriate court order. Note, however, that (certain) personal claims may serve as 'proprietary bases' for the purposes of establishing a proprietary interest in substitute assets: see n 10 immediately below.

[10] The term is coined by P Birks, *An Introduction to the Law of Restitution* (Clarendon Press, Oxford 1985, paperback edn 1989) 378–85; Birks in *Laundering and Tracing* (n 5) 311–25; Smith *Tracing* (n 2) 299–303. Smith (ibid 363–65) points out that even personal rights, in particular claims against banks (credit on bank accounts), can sometimes serve as a 'proprietary base' where 'tracing in transit' is at issue (on which see ibid 243–61).

[11] As eg in *Cundy v Lindsay* (1878) 3 App Cas 459 (HL) and *Ingram v Little* [1961] 1 QB 31 (CA). Note that B will have to be aware of A's identity mistake to render the contract void: see above, Chapter V.B.1.b.i (at pp 176–77). The identity mistake will then also prevent a valid conveyance by delivery.

himself title or an equitable interest under a trust before the first unauthorized substitution occurs.[12] Three issues have a bearing on A's ability to claim a particular substitute asset from B. First, the (alleged) discrepancies in this area between the rules operating at common law and in equity. Second, the debate about the exact nature of a claimant's proprietary interest in a traceable substitute. Third, the conceptual question about the source or basis of such a proprietary interest. We will consider each aspect in turn.

(i) Discrepancies between the common law and equity

It has traditionally been thought that the equitable principles of tracing differ from those applied by the common law. Equity is said to be more generous to claimants as far as tracing through mixed funds is concerned, while it is supposedly more restrictive than the common law in requiring a pre-existing fiduciary relationship between the claimant and the substitutor as the first holder of the original asset.

The case of *Taylor v Plumer*[13] is usually cited as the first common law authority on tracing and is taken to stand for the proposition that the common law cannot trace through mixed funds.[14] Although the case was – as has been convincingly demonstrated – actually decided on equitable principles,[15] its subsequent reception must at any rate be taken to have established that a person with title to an object can assert a common law right to its exchange product,[16] provided only that at no stage of the tracing

[12] The scenario is essentially the one considered in Chapter VII.C.1 (pp 262–64) and, from C's perspective, in Chapter VI.C.1.b (pp 230–33) above.

[13] (1815) 3 Maul & Sel 562, 105 ER 721.

[14] Cf *Banque Belge pour l'Etranger v Hambrouck* [1921] 1 KB 321 (CA) 327–28 (Bankes LJ); *Agip (Africa) Ltd Jackson* [1990] Ch 265 (ChD) 285–86 (Millett J), [1991] Ch 547 (CA) 563–66 (Fox LJ); *Bank Tejarat v Hong Kong and Shanghai Banking Corp (CI) Ltd* [1995] 1 Lloyd's Rep 239 (QBD Comm) 245 (Tuckey J).

[15] S Khurshid and P Matthews, "Tracing Confusion" (1979) 95 LQR 78, esp 79–83; L Smith, "Tracing in *Taylor v Plumer*: Equity in the Court of King's Bench" [1995] LMCLQ 240; Smith *Tracing* (n 2) 168. *Taylor v Plumer* does not therefore support the proposition for which it has come to stand.

[16] D Fox, "Common Law Claims to Substitute Assets" [1999] RLR 55, 60: "[I]t appears that *Taylor v Plumer* and the equitable principles it drew upon have been transplanted into the common law. As a result it is now regarded as an instance of a common law rule allowing the legal owner of an original asset to claim title to its product". Cf also the observations to the same effect by Millett LJ in *Trustee of the Property of FC Jones & Sons (a firm) v Jones* [1997] Ch 159 (CA) 169. The proposition that the common law allows the 'owner' of the original asset to assert a legal interest in the substitute has variously been questioned on the basis that the substitutor cannot simply be 'expropriated': cf Smith *Tracing* (n 2) 322–31. The third party will, after all, have made the conveyance to the substitutor, and not to the original 'owner': B McFarlane, *The Structure of*

process "the means of ascertainment fail, which is the case when the subject is turned into money, and mixed and confounded in a general mass of the same description".[17] If A has managed to revest title to the painting in himself (eg for B's fraud), but then B sells it to C for £ 500 and deposits the money in his general bank account, A can no longer identify the substitute asset.[18] A common law claim to the purchase price is therefore precluded.[19] Equity, by contrast, has developed a set of rules and principles which allow it to overcome the evidential impasses generated by mixed funds. If A has exercised an equitable power *in rem* and has thus become the beneficiary under a trust, the tracing exercise need not stop when B pays the money into his bank account. Subject to the hurdle that the 'lowest intermediate balance' always acts as a cap,[20] the basic position is that current accounts as well as other active bank accounts follow the so-called 'first in, first out' rule,[21] while all other mixed funds (eg a deposit of

---

Property Law (Hart, Oxford 2008) 323. Smith *Tracing* (n 2) 332–39, tentatively concludes that the original 'owner' has a limited "common law proprietary right less than ownership" (ibid 337). McFarlane *Structure of Property Law* (above) 323–31, argues in favour of a vested equitable interest ('persistent right') where the substitutor is aware of all the relevant facts. The nature of a claimant's interest in traceable substitute assets is discussed further below, in section B.1.a.ii of the present chapter (pp 282–86).

[17] *Taylor v Plumer* (1815) 3 Maul & Sel 562, 575; 105 ER 721, 726 (Lord Ellenborough CJ). The 'mixed fund' restriction on common law tracing is generally – albeit often reluctantly – accepted a constituting the current law: eg A Burrows, *The Law of Restitution* (2nd edn Butterworths, London 2002) 84–85; G Virgo, *The Principles of the Law of Restitution* (2nd edn OUP, Oxford 2006) 626–28.

[18] This assumes that there was other money in the account prior to the deposit, ie that the account was in credit. It explains why there are very few cases where tracing has been possible at common law despite the involvement of active bank accounts: *Banque Belge v Hambrouck* (n 14) and *Jones v Jones* (n 16) are rare exceptions. In *Lipkin Gorman (a firm) v Karpnale Ltd* [1991] 2 AC 548 (HL), it was conceded that the gambling solicitor (Cass) had not mixed the money withdrawn from the claimant firm's client account with his own before paying it over to the defendant casino.

[19] Query whether a person who starts out with legal title to an object can trace and claim in equity where tracing at common law fails. It is submitted that this should be possible, provided only that the supposed requirement of a 'fiduciary relationship' is jettisoned: cf text to nn 26–33 below. Similar: G Jones (ed), R Goff and G Jones, *The Law of Restitution* (7th edn Sweet & Maxwell, London 2007) [2–033]; Smith *Tracing* (n 2) 343–47.

[20] *James Roscoe (Bolton) Ltd v Winder* [1915] 1 Ch 62 (ChD); *Bishopsgate Investment Management Ltd (In Liquidation) v Homan* [1995] Ch 211 (CA).

[21] *Clayton's Case* (1816) 1 Mer 572, 35 ER 781. Smith *Tracing* (n 2) 185–94, argues that this is not really a rule of tracing, but a presumption as to intention in the appropriation of payments. Similar: *Ministry of Health v Simpson (Re Diplock's Estate)* [1948] Ch 465 (CA) 553–54 (Dr Barnardo's Homes). Cf also the criticism of the rule and its impracticability in *Barlow Clowes International Ltd (In Liquidation) v Vaughan* [1992] 4

stock or the credit on a savings account) are distributed *pari passu* amongst all contributors.[22] However, both the 'first in, first out' rule and the *pari passu* principle are trumped by a general presumption against wrongdoers.[23] Where a person is aware of holding an asset on trust (as, in our example, B necessarily will be after A has communicated his intention to exercise the power), the evidential difficulty created by his mixing the money held on trust with his own will be resolved against him.[24] Assuming, for example, that, soon after paying the £ 500 proceeds from the sale of the painting into his account, B had withdrawn the same sum and used it to purchase a bicycle before squandering the remainder of his funds, A could assert an equitable interest in that bicycle.[25]

While tracing through mixtures may thus be easier in equity than at law, it has been said that the equitable tracing rules can only be invoked where a 'fiduciary relationship' exists between the original parties.[26] If this were indeed the case, then it would not be possible for a person with legal title to take advantage of equity's favourable identification rules in order to

---

All ER 22 (CA); *Commerzbank AG v IMB Morgan plc* [2004] EWHC 2771 (ChD), [2005] 2 All ER (Comm) 564, [42]–[50] (Lawrence Collins J).

[22] *Sinclair v Brougham* [1914] AC 398 (HL), overruled on other grounds by *Westdeutsche Landesbank Girozentrale v Islington London BC* [1996] AC 669 (HL); cf also *Re Diplock* (n 21) 524, 539, 554–56 (Royal Sailors Orphan Girls' School and Home).

[23] *Re Hallett's Estate* (1880) 13 ChD 696 (CA); *Re Oatway* [1903] 2 Ch 356 (ChD); *Re Tilley's Will Trusts* [1967] Ch 1179 (ChD). Note that this presumption does not relate to the wrongdoer's intention, but to the location of the relevant value. A genuine presumption of intention would have to be rebuttable by evidence to the contrary. Cf also Smith *Tracing* (n 2) 85 (making the point for the case of physical mixtures), 202–3.

[24] See P Birks, "On Taking Seriously the Difference between Tracing and Claiming" (1997) 11 TruLI 2, 5; Smith *Tracing* (n 2) 194–208, esp 197–98; *Re Tilley's Will Trusts* (n 23) 1183 (Ungoed-Thomas J). Cf also *Lupton v White* (1808) 15 Ves Jun 432, 439–440; 33 ER 817, 820 (Lord Eldon LC), where the presumption against wrongdoers was treated as a general principle of the law. It was suggested above that a person who is aware of holding an asset on trust for another commits an equitable wrong (which – for want of a better name – we can call 'breach of trust') if he puts it out of his power to comply with the beneficiary's request under *Saunders v Vautier* (1841) 4 Beav 115, 49 ER 282; aff'd (1841) Cr & Ph 240, 41 ER 482: cf n 320 on pp 157–58.

[25] The general presumption against wrongdoers can, of course, give rise to problems. It entails not only a 'punishment' of the wrongdoer, but has potential repercussions for third parties. This is because "the mixture of value [by the wrongdoer] gives every [innocent] contributor a liberty to choose in which subsequent division of the mixture his contribution ended up": Smith *Tracing* (n 2) 205. If, in our example, B had made a gift of the bicycle to D, D is saddled with the uncertainty of whether or not A will subsequently 'choose' to regard the bicycle as the traceable product of the painting (which will – in turn – depend on what B does with the balance remaining in the account).

[26] *Agip (Africa) Ltd v Jackson* [1991] Ch 547 (CA) 566 (Fox LJ); *Boscawen v Bajwa* [1996] 1 WLR 328 (CA) 335 (Millett LJ). Cf also *Sinclair v Brougham* (n 22), as interpreted in *Re Diplock* (n 21) esp 540 (Lord Greene MR).

establish at least an equitable interest in traceable substitute assets.[27] A would, merely because he has exercised a legal power *in rem*, be in a worse position than if he had only had an equitable power *in rem*.[28] Unsurprisingly, the supposed requirement of a fiduciary relationship has come under heavy attack,[29] and judges are frequently willing to circumvent it.[30]

Historically, the discrepancies between tracing at common law and in equity are only explicable by reference to the separate development of these two branches of law. The Court of Chancery was (apparently) more willing to bridge evidential impasses, but its jurisdiction depended on the claimant seeking equitable relief. Viewed in this light, the abovementioned restriction on tracing in equity can be called into question.[31] *Tracing* as such would appear never in fact to have turned on a pre-existing fiduciary relationship. The crucial jurisdiction-triggering factor was instead the claimant's assertion of an equitable rather than a legal property right in a given substitute asset.[32] And while the discovery of a fiduciary relationship will often be incidental to establishing a 'proprietary base' for the purposes of *claiming* (eg proof that the original asset was held on trust), it is neither a necessary nor a sufficient condition of success.[33] Provided, therefore, that our claimant A seeks no more than an equitable interest in the proceeds of B's sale to C, he should be able to avail himself of equity's assistance by relying on any 'proprietary base', whether legal or equitable.

---

[27] Cf above, comment in n 19.

[28] It is not entirely clear whether the mere fact that a person (B) holds his legal title on trust for another (A) in and of itself gives rise to a fiduciary relationship. It is submitted that the trustee would at least have to be aware of his position as a 'trustee' (and even then it is doubtful whether his limited duties are of a character which can properly be described as 'fiduciary'): cf comment in n 24 above.

[29] Birks in *Laundering and Tracing* (n 5) 297; Burrows *Restitution* (n 17) 93–94; *Goff & Jones* (n 19) [2–031]–[2–033]; P Millett, "Restitution and Constructive Trusts" (1998) 114 LQR 399, 416–17; Smith *Tracing* (n 2) 120–30; Virgo *Principles* (n 17) 628–30.

[30] See the express statement to this effect in *Bristol and West Building Society v Mothew* [1998] Ch 1 (CA) 23 (Millett LJ). Cf also *Campden Hill Ltd v Chakrani* [2005] EWHC 911 (ChD) [74], where Hart J recognized that a sufficient fiduciary relationship could arise from the (mere) "division of the legal and beneficial ownership". In *Westdeutsche Landesbank Girozentrale v Islington London BC* [1996] AC 669 (HL) 716, Lord Browne-Wilkinson suggested that even a victim of theft was able to trace the value of the stolen item in equity, and for this purpose his Lordship invented a 'constructive trust'.

[31] Cf Smith *Tracing* (n 2) 120–30. Note that Smith also denies that there are any special common law restrictions on the tracing process: ibid 162–74. For him, there is only one set of (evidentiary) tracing rules, and these cater for mixed funds: esp ibid 278–79.

[32] Ibid 122: "If the plaintiff asserts that she holds equitable property rights in some new asset, then that is a claim which only a court of equity can evaluate; and that is the source of the court's hearing jurisdiction".

[33] Ibid 340–47.

In relation to mixed funds, on the other hand, the divergences between tracing at common law and in equity seem too engrained in the case law to be simply ignored. Yet there are compelling reasons why these divergences should be eradicated at the next opportunity. After the procedural merger effected by the Judicature Acts 1873–75,[34] two different sets of rules relating to the identification of substitute assets cannot be justified.[35] Numerous judges have expressed their discontent at the current state of affairs, both in judicial *dicta* and extra-judicially.[36] When the rules of tracing are finally harmonized, it is likely that the generous equitable rules, with their greater ability to cope with mixed funds, will prevail over the strict common law principles.[37]

(ii) Nature of proprietary interest in substitutes

Assuming that a substitute asset can be identified and claimed, a question arises about the nature of the claimant's proprietary interest in it. If, after A has avoided his conveyance of the painting to B (at common law or in equity), the latter exchanges it for C's bicycle, does A have an immediately vested (legal or equitable) property right in the bicycle, or merely a (legal or equitable) power *in rem*? Three different approaches have been suggested. At one end of the spectrum, reliance is placed on the decision in *Cave v Cave*[38] to advance the view that the claimant acquires an immediately vested right *in rem* in a traceable substitute of the original asset.[39] At the

[34] Supreme Court of Judicature Acts 1873 and 1875.

[35] P Birks, "The Necessity of a Unitary Law of Tracing" in R Cranston (ed), *Making Commercial Law: Essays in Honour of Roy Goode* (Clarendon Press, Oxford 1997) 241; Burrows *Restitution* (n 17) 82, 93–94; Virgo *Principles* (n 17) 635. Smith *Tracing* (n 2) 133–279, already treats the tracing rules as one unitary set: cf also n 31 above.

[36] *Bristol and West BS v Mothew* (n 30) 23 (Millett LJ); *Foskett v McKeown* (n 7) 113 (Lord Steyn), 128–29 (Lord Millett); NH Andrews and J Beatson, "Common Law Tracing: Spring Board or Swan Song" (1997) 113 LQR 21, 25–26; Millett (1998) 114 LQR (n 29) 409; R Walker, "Tracing after Foskett v McKeown" [2000] RLR 573.

[37] In *Bristol and West BS v Mothew* (n 30) 23, Millett LJ said: "Until the equitable tracing rules are made available in support of the ordinary common law claim for money had and received some problems will remain incapable of sensible resolution." For those authors who believe that rights to traceable substitute assets are only ever equitable (or 'persistent') rights, the issue of assimilation does not arise: cf eg McFarlane *Structure of Property Law* (n 16) 323–31.

[38] (1880) 15 ChD 639 (ChD). In *Taylor v Plumer* (1815) 3 Maul & Sel 562, 575; 105 ER 721, 726, Lord Ellenborough CJ said that "the product of or substitute for the original thing still follows the nature of the thing itself".

[39] Smith *Tracing* (n 2) 322–26, 332–39, 358–61. Note that, for Smith, the claimant's immediately vested legal right to substitute assets does not amount to full 'ownership': see below, text to n 57.

other end, the Irish case of *Re ffrench's Estate*[40] and the House of Lords decision in *Lipkin Gorman (a firm) v Karpnale Ltd*[41] are cited in support of the proposition that the claimant has a mere power *in rem*, which he has to assert before obtaining a vested property right.[42] Finally, the intermediate position is that a claimant who starts out with a vested right *in rem* in the original object has no more than a power *in rem* in relation to the substitute so long as his property right in the original subsists, but that he acquires a vested interest in the substitute as soon as the property right in the original is destroyed.[43] In our example, this would mean that – depending on whether the power *in rem* A previously exercised in respect of the painting was legal or equitable – he would automatically acquire title[44] to or an equitable interest in the bicycle if C qualifies as a *bona fide* purchaser for value without notice,[45] but that he would otherwise obtain only a power *in rem* in relation to the bicycle.[46]

---

[40] (1887) 21 LR (Ir) 283 (CA) 312 (Lord Porter MR).

[41] [1991] 2 AC 548. For the facts cf text to nn 128–133 on p 241 above.

[42] P Birks, "Mixing and Tracing' (1992) 45 CLP 69, 89–95; Birks in *Laundering and Tracing* (n 5) 307–11. Similar: Fox [1999] RLR (n 16) 70, who writes that "[i]t seems likely that the plaintiff's title in the substitute does not vest as soon as the defendant receives it in exchange for the original asset. At that stage all he gets is a suspended right of election to abandon his original interest and to assert instead an interest in the substitute. It remains the defendant's property until the plaintiff elects to exercise this right". Fox does, however, go on to suggest that the claimant's subsequent election will lead to a retroactive vesting of title upon which a claim in conversion can be based, subject only to the *bona fide* purchase and change of position defences: ibid 70–72.

[43] This seems to be the underlying view preferred by Virgo *Principles* (n 17) 623: "[O]nce the original asset cannot be identified, the interest which was in that asset is extinguished and is automatically replaced by a proprietary interest in the substitute. Where, however, the original asset and the substitute can both be identified the claimant can elect to claim either the original asset or its substitute".

[44] The title transferred by C to B would, without more, vest in A. The difficulties of explaining how this is possible (given that C intended to – and did – pass title to B) leads McFarlane *Structure of Property Law* (n 16) 323, to conclude that A can only ever have an equitable interest (or 'persistent right') in respect of the substitute, and Smith *Tracing* (n 2) 322–39, to suggest that A's vested legal interest in the substitute has to be something less than full 'ownership'. On Smith's view cf text to n 57 below.

[45] On the rules of *bona fide* purchase operating in this situation see above, Chapter VI.C.1.b (pp 230–33).

[46] This power *in rem* could not be exercised without at the same time relinquishing the still subsisting property right in the original asset. As Virgo *Principles* (n 17) 623, goes on to explain immediately after the passage cited in n 43 above: "If [the claimant] chooses to pursue the substitute this should operate as a mechanism to extinguish the proprietary interest in the original asset and to transfer it to the substitute, unless the substitute has been obtained by a *bona fide* purchaser for value. [...] By assuming that the claimant has a power to shift the proprietary interest from the original property to its

The difficulty faced by any legal system which accepts that a person can have some sort of proprietary interest in a substitute asset while at the same time retaining his old property right in the original asset is that the person may end up with concurrent proprietary interests in several assets. This has become known as the problem of 'geometric multiplication'.[47] It is particularly pertinent in English law, where no general principle of *bona fide* purchase exists at common law.[48] Take again the case in which A exercises a common law power *in rem* and thus revests title to the painting in himself. B, who will often be a rogue, nevertheless proceeds to exchange the painting for C's bicycle in circumstances where C is not a *bona fide* purchaser[49] and subsequently sells the bicycle to an innocent fourth party D. He spends the purchase price on a piece of jewellery which he gives to his wife E. Leaving aside the extremely tricky question of how A's interest in any of the substitutes competes with possible proprietary restitutionary interests of the parties making the various conveyances to B,[50] the main issue for us to consider is A's ability to follow and claim each asset. None of the three approaches mentioned above can entirely evade the pitfalls of 'geometric multiplication', but the extent of the problem differs. Powers *in rem* are more susceptible to destruction by *bona fide* purchase than vested rights *in rem*.[51] On a full proprietary model,[52] A would appear to end up with a vested interest in the painting, the bicycle and the jewellery.[53] Of course, he cannot claim all three objects and has to

---

substitute and that this can only occur once the power of election has been exercised, it follows that the claimant is only able to bring one proprietary claim at a time".

[47] Cf eg Birks *Introduction* (n 10) 394; Smith *Tracing* (n 2) 322.

[48] See above, Chapter II.D.4 (at p 51) and Chapter VI.C.1 (at pp 227, 230–33).

[49] This may be because C has notice of A's rights, or simply because he does not fulfil all the conditions of *bona fide* purchase under the Sale of Goods Act 1979, s 25(1). On the latter provision see above, Chapter VI.C.1.b (text to nn 77–81 on pp 232–33).

[50] If, for example, B fraudulently induced C to agree to the barter (by representing himself to be the 'owner' of the painting), C will have a common law power *in rem* to revest title to the bicycle in himself. In this case, it is submitted, C's power must trump any interest of A's since A cannot acquire greater rights in respect of the substitute than the substitutor B himself obtains.

[51] See above, Chapter VI.C.1.a (pp 228–30).

[52] The discussion which follows is mainly for exposition purposes. It will be seen that Smith *Tracing* (n 2) does not ultimately subscribe to all the consequences flowing from such a model: text to n 57 below.

[53] We must assume that any interest A may have had in relation to the cash B received from D (as purchase price for the bicycle) will have been destroyed by the jeweller's *bona fide* purchase under the principle in *Miller v Race* (1758) 1 Burr 452, 97 ER 398. As regards the bicycle, the following aspect needs to be borne in mind. If C had a common law power *in rem* which was superior to A's interest in the bicycle (cf n 50 above), then this power may well have been 'killed off' by D's subsequent purchase of the bicycle: Sale of Goods Act 1979, s 23 (but note that the relevant 'voidable title'

elect between them.[54] However, until he does, all persons handling one of the objects run the risk of making themselves liable in the tort of conversion. On both of the other models, by contrast, A would – at least while retaining title to the painting – only acquire an easily defeasible power *in rem* in respect of its traceable substitutes.[55] He would therefore lose any right to the bicycle as soon as it is purchased by innocent D, and could merely choose between claiming the painting from C and claiming the jewellery from E. Given that powers *in rem* do not confer on their holder a right to immediate possession, neither B nor E could commit conversion of the jewellery until A has communicated to them his intention of exercising the power.[56] Lionel Smith, the strongest proponent of the full proprietary model, sees these objections. He concedes that at common law the claimant's interest is

> "a property right, less than ownership, which does not carry with it a right to immediate possession; hence it will not generate liability in conversion. [...] [T]his limited proprietary right should probably be a fragile one, lost if the subject matter passes to a bona fide purchaser for value without notice".[57]

However, this looks very much like a power *in rem*. It is hard to see what kind of vested legal right *in rem* could have the characteristics which Smith describes.[58] For present purposes, it is submitted that the power

---

would actually appear to be in A's, not B's hands!). If this were so, then the question arises whether this would automatically also extinguish A's (*ex hypothesi* vested) interest in the bicycle. It is submitted that the answer should be 'no'. A's interest is inferior to C's (in the sense of being subject to the power) only in so far as A cannot acquire greater rights than B had. However, there is no reason by A should be affected by D acquiring B's title free from C's power. To defeat A, D has to establish a *bona fide* purchase defence which is operative vis-à-vis A.

[54] Smith *Tracing* (n 2) 380–83. The claimant may, where appropriate, also elect to assert a purely personal claim, eg against B for conversion of the painting: cf ibid 378–79.

[55] The power model (text to nn 40–42 above) and the intermediate view (text to nn 43–46 above) do not differ in a case where, as in the present scenario, the first substitution involves no *bona fide* purchase of the original asset.

[56] It will be recalled that, as far as the law of wrongs is concerned, a power can only be exercised prospectively: see above, Chapter IV.D.4.c. (at pp 157–58). Moreover, it is submitted that where the person immediately affected is ignorant of the existence of the power, its exercise should have to be communicated to that person: cf above, n 104 on p 237. If, in our case, A wanted to assert a proprietary interest in the jewellery, he would have to inform D of his intention (which might, in turn, allow her to set up the change of position defence: cf above, p 237 in Chapter VI.C.2.a).

[57] Smith *Tracing* (n 2) 337.

[58] Smith's suggestion of a limited common law right *in rem* rests on two main considerations. On the one hand, he rejects the idea of 'expropriating' the substitutor: cf n 16 above. The claimant should therefore obtain full legal title by virtue of the substitution. On the other hand, Smith also rejects the power model of rights to traceable substitutes on the basis that the prospective exercise of a common law power could not have

model best accommodates the problems generated by 'geometric multiplication'. This is most evident at common law, but it is equally true on the equity side of things.[59]

(iii) Source of proprietary interest in substitutes

What is the source of A's proprietary interest in traceable substitutes of the painting? Although this question may look only theoretical, it could acquire practical relevance in relation to the availability of defences against A's claim to such substitutes. On one view, strongly endorsed by the House of Lords in *Foskett v McKeown*,[60] claiming substitute assets is all about vindicating pre-existing property rights.[61] Critics of this approach point out that 'property', while signifying a type of right, is not an event capable of giving rise to new rights.[62] Some other explanation has to be found for the claimant's interest in traceable substitutes of his original asset. On this alternative view, the most plausible candidate is the law of unjust enrichment.[63] The right or power *in rem* afforded to the claimant is then an in-

---

accounted for the Playboy Club's liability in *Lipkin Gorman v Karpnale Ltd* (n 41): cf Smith *Tracing* (n 2) 325–26. Explaining *Lipkin Gorman* as a case in which the claimant firm's action for money had and received was *parasitic* upon their (unexercised) power is indeed problematic. Possible solutions are discussed in Chapter VI.C.2.b (at pp 241–43).

[59] In equity, too, a power *in rem* is more susceptible to *bona fide* purchase than a vested interest: cf *Phillips v Phillips* (1861) 4 De G F & J 208, 45 ER 1164; *Cave v Cave* (1880) 15 ChD 639 (ChD).

[60] [2001] 1 AC 102 (HL), esp 127 (Lord Millett).

[61] Eg R Grantham and C Rickett "Tracing and Property Rights: The Categorical Truth" (2000) 63 MLR 905; R Grantham and C Rickett, "Property Rights as a Legally Significant Event" (2003) 62 CLJ 717, 744–48; P Millett, "*Jones v Jones*: Property or Unjust Enrichment?" in A Burrows and A Rodger (eds), *Mapping the Law: Essays in Memory of Peter Birks* (OUP, Oxford 2006) 265; Virgo *Principles* (n 17) 11–17.

[62] Eg P Birks, "Property and Unjust Enrichment: Categorical Truths" [1997] NZ L Rev 623, 659–62; P Birks, *Unjust Enrichment* (2nd edn OUP, Oxford 2005) 34–36; A Burrows, "Proprietary Restitution: Unmasking Unjust Enrichment" (2001) 117 LQR 412; A Burrows, "The Relationship between Unjust Enrichment and Property: Some Unresolved Issues" in S Degeling and J Edelman (eds), *Unjust Enrichment in Commercial Law* (Thomson Reuters, Sydney 2008) 333, 338–52, esp 342; C Rotherham, *Proprietary Remedies in Context* (Hart, Oxford 2002) 108–10. Virgo *Principles* (n 17) 572, concedes that "Birks was obviously right to state that the 'vindication of property rights' is not an 'event'", but then goes on to explain: "It is a principle which is simply not framed in those terms. But the principle could be rebranded into an event if it is necessary to do so. For example, the event could be that the defendant has interfered with the claimant's property rights in some way. There are a number of responses to that event, including compensation, but the most important involves the award of restitutionary remedies, either personal or proprietary".

[63] See the references cited in n 62 immediately above. Cf also Smith *Tracing* (n 2) 300–1, but note that he is now very critical with regard to cases where the claimant's

stance of 'proprietary restitution' for unjust enrichment, with the tracing rules – it has been said – answering the question when a defendant's receipt of title to a chattel is at the claimant's expense.[64]

It is impossible within the confines of this book to rehearse all the arguments featuring in the ongoing debate and to propose a definitive solution.[65] May it suffice to note the potential repercussions of the debate for A's claim to the traceable substitutes of his painting. Let us assume that, after A had avoided the original transfer, B sold the painting to C and invested the proceeds in profitable shares, or that he gave the proceeds to his wife D (an innocent volunteer) who subsequently made the lucrative investment. There is no doubt that English law will in principle allow A to claim these shares, even though they have risen in value.[66] However, the extent to which B and/or D can invoke the disenrichment defence will

original property right survives the substitution: L Smith, "Tracing" in A Burrows and A Rodger (eds), *Mapping the Law: Essays in Memory of Peter Birks* (OUP, Oxford 2006) 119, 131–34. The argument that rights contingent upon tracing are a form of 'proprietary restitution for wrongs' has never been convincingly made, but much depends on whether or not 'restitution for wrongs' is properly regarded as a part of the law of unjust enrichment: cf n 51 on p 29 and n 55 on p 30. Interestingly, Virgo *Principles* (n 17) 572, actually envisages the 'interference with property rights' as a possible causative event: cf the passage set out in n 62 above. Not dissimilar: L Smith, "Unjust Enrichment, Property, and the Structure of Trusts" (2000) 116 LQR 412, 424–25, who observes that "one could analyse the defendant's enrichment as title-based: it arises through an interference ... with the plaintiff's original asset", while at the same time insisting that 'title-based claims' are conceptually distinct from 'restitution for wrongs'.

64 Burrows *Restitution* (n 17) 79; Burrows (2001) 117 LQR (n 62) 415–17. Burrows in *Unjust Enrichment in Commercial Law* (n 62) 339–40, clarifies: "[I]t is not being suggested that tracing alone satisfies the 'at the expense of' element of the unjust enrichment enquiry. Rather, it is tracing plus 'title' that establishes what Birks calls the 'proprietary connection'". But see also Smith in *Mapping the Law* (n 63) 135–37, who draws attention to the fact that the adoption of an abstract conception of wealth for the purposes of the law of unjust enrichment sits uneasily with the insistence on 'transactional links' (rather than 'causal links') within the law of tracing: "The traditional tracing rules are transactional: they look for exchange transactions or their functional equivalent. This reflects the particular, and not the abstract, conception of wealth. Peter's [ie Peter Birks'] arguments about the dominance of the abstract conception imply that the tracing rules should not be transactional, but causal" (ibid 136). The issue is remotely related to that of 'leapfrogging' (which also depends on a purely causal link), discussed in Chapter VI.C.3 (pp 243–49) above.

65 One has the slight suspicion that the protagonists are somewhat at cross-purposes, one group (cf n 61) focusing on the preconditions of establishing a proprietary interest in a given substitute asset, namely a proprietary interest in the original (the 'proprietary base), the other (cf n 62) on the conceptual justification for the process by which the 'transmission' of rights from one asset to another occurs.

66 Cf *Trustee of the Property of FC Jones & Sons (a firm) v Jones* [1997] Ch 159 (CA).

partly depend on the nature and characterization of A's interest. If A's property right in the painting is, as *Foskett v McKeown* suggests, simply 'transmitted'[67] to the shares, then it is hard to see how either B or D could ever set up any change of position against A's claim to the shares.[68] The fact that the lucky investor may have expended money celebrating his or her good fortune is neither here nor there. If, on the other hand, A's proprietary interest in the shares (whatever form it takes) is a proprietary response to B's and/or D's unjust enrichment at A's expense, then the disenrichment defence is an obvious possibility.[69] Of course, not every defendant will be able to invoke it. In our example, B will inevitably be aware of A's revested property right in the painting,[70] and so cannot claim to have acted in reliance on his entitlement to the shares as its traceable substitute. He bears the cost of the celebration on any view. But it is different in the alternative scenario, in which D made the lucrative investment. Being an innocent recipient of the proceeds from the sale of the painting, D would be able to invoke the defence.[71] The success of A's claim would depend on his reimbursing her for the expenditure.[72] It might even be possible to extend this reasoning and say that any skill and effort

---

67 [2001] 1 AC 102 (HL) 127 (Lord Millett).

68 Lord Millett has indicated that change of position may be a defence to a "property based personal claim" (ie a receipt-based unjust enrichment claim: cf Chapter VI.C.2.b on pp 238–43 above): P Millett, "Proprietary Restitution" in S Degeling and J Edelman (eds), *Equity in Commercial Law* (Thomson LBC, Sydney 2005) 309, 319, 325. However, he insists that the defence is not available "where the claimant seeks a proprietary remedy": ibid 325.

69 Cf Burrows in *Unjust Enrichment in Commercial Law* (n 62) 352–57; Smith *Tracing* (n 2) 383–85. It is easier to apply the disenrichment or change of position defence in the context of powers *in rem* than in the context of vested rights *in rem*, which may be another argument for preferring the power model of rights to traceable substitute assets. If the claimant has a power, its exercise can simply be made conditional on his reimbursing the defendant for any relevant disenrichment (eg expenditure for a celebratory meal): cf Chapter IV.D.4.b (at p 156) above.

70 This is either because A will have communicated to B his intention to exercise the power *in rem* or – where B is a fraudster who deliberately absconds – due to the application of the doctrine established in *Car & Universal Finance Co Ltd v Caldwell* [1965] 1 QB 525 (CA).

71 We are here concerned with the case where A is trying to assert a proprietary interest in respect of the shares. Whether D could also have invoked the disenrichment defence if, before the shares had been purchased, A had attempted to exercise a power *in rem* (or to assert another proprietary interest) in respect of the money which D received from B depends on whether the 'survival' of A's proprietary interest in the money was a *product* of D's unjust enrichment at A's expense: cf the discussion in Chapter VI.C.2–3 (at pp 237, 247–49).

72 On the operation of the defence see n 69 above.

of D's which went into securing the profit should count as a change of position[73] and be recognized accordingly.[74]

Since our primary concern in this chapter is with A's claims to substitute assets still held by the immediate transferee B, it is enough for present purposes to highlight the potential for applying the disenrichment defence in the context of claims to traceable substitutes. As between A and B, the issue can only arise where B is unaware of A's rights in respect of the painting, as he may be if he disposes of it before A communicates to him his intention to avoid the conveyance (eg for B's innocent misrepresentation or inadvertently exerted undue influence). To this scenario we must now turn.

b) The 'Proprietary Base': Vested Rights and Powers *in rem*

Where A's transfer to B is avoided before B's transaction with C occurs, the proprietary base upon which A's claim to traceable substitute assets is founded is his revested legal title or an equitable interest in the painting. Where, however, A has not yet exercised his legal or equitable power *in rem* at the moment of the substitution, the question arises whether the power can in and of itself constitute a sufficient proprietary base for tracing and claiming. This question will be particularly pertinent where title to the painting has meanwhile passed into the hands of a *bona fide* purchaser for value (such as C if he buys it in good faith),[75] so that A's original power *in rem* is destroyed.

Given that a power *in rem* is undoubtedly proprietary, one may well ask why it should not be able to function as a proprietary base.[76] Yet it is often said that the principles of tracing and claiming operate in the context of 'unauthorized substitutions', which could lead to the inference that they

---

[73] It would, of course, not necessarily be a 'disenrichment' in the financial sense. The alternatives are either (1) to deny reimbursement or (2) to afford D an independent claim for counter-restitution to take account of her contribution.

[74] Lord Millett has suggested that, in *Jones v Jones* (n 66), an allowance might have been made for Mrs Jones' skill and effort if such an allowance had been claimed: Millett in *Mapping the Law* (n 61) 269. However, given that his Lordship rejects the applicability of the disenrichment defence to proprietary claims (cf n 68 above), this must be conceptualized as based on a notional counter-claim, similar to the allowance made in *Greenwood v Bennett* [1973] QB 195 (CA) and that envisaged by the Torts (Interference with Goods) Act 1977, s 6.

[75] From C's perspective, this is a case of the type discussed in Chapter VI.C.1.a (pp 228–30). It was argued in Chapter VII that *bona fide* purchase by C need not and should not bar rescission of the contractual bargain in the relationship between A and B.

[76] Cf D O'Sullivan, S Elliott and R Zakrzewski, *The Law of Rescission* (OUP, Oxford 2008) [16.40]: "An unexercised claim to recover property on rescission has so many proprietary features that it should be capable of being traced".

have no role to play where powers are concerned. Powers as such do not, after all, confer upon their holder any entitlement to grant or withhold consent to a substitution of the asset to which they relate,[77] and their exercise has – for many purposes – only prospective effect.[78] Some authors are therefore critical of what they regard as an unwarranted extension of the claimant's remedies. It has, for example, been suggested that a common law claim to traceable substitute assets is available only so long as the claimant still retains his original (vested) property right.[79] If this were correct, then A's ability to assert a right to substitute assets in B's hands would be severely curtailed and depend on fortuitous factors such as the exact time at which he avoids his conveyance to B and the precise circumstances of C's acquisition. On the equity side, doubts have similarly been expressed about the suitability of using an unexercised power *in rem* as a proprietary base.[80] The argument that only vested equitable interests can support a right to traceable substitutes would indeed be plausible if one saw this right as premised on the special duty of a trustee to account to his beneficiary (which may itself depend on the trustee's knowledge of his position).[81]

[77] A common law power *in rem* entails no right to immediate possession; an equitable power – unlike a vested equitable interest under a trust – does not enable its holder to give any 'instructions' to the person with legal title. Even without A's consent, B is therefore able to validly transfer to C the title he obtained from A, albeit that this title remains subject to A's power *in rem* where C does not qualify as a *bona fide* purchaser.

[78] Cf the discussion in Chapter IV.D.4.c (at pp 157–58), Chapter V.D.1 (at pp 203–4) and Chapter VI.C.1.a (at pp 229–30) above. Contrast, however, Chapter VI.C.2.b. (at p 242) and see below, text to nn 87–89.

[79] Khurshid/Matthews (1979) 95 LQR (n 15) 98: "[T]he right to trace at law lasts only so long as property subsists in the original owner at law". This is because, unless the substitutor is an agent acting within his authority (in which case title to the exchange product vests in the original owner by virtue of the agent's appropriation), "the only way of establishing [a right to immediate possession of the substitute] ... is by resorting to the doctrine of ratification": ibid 88.

[80] McFarlane *Structure of Property Law* (n 16) 327 fn 166: "[T]he principle [in *Foskett v McKeown* (n 7)] does *not* seem to apply where B initially has only a *power* to acquire a persistent right [ie a power to create a trust]. So if: (i) B pays two £ 50 notes to A by mistake; and (ii) A is unaware of that mistake and uses the money to buy a bike; then (iii) B does *not* have a power to acquire a persistent right against A's Ownership of the bike" (emphasis in the original).

[81] No duty to account can arise without the existence of a trust. Even where there is a trust, it is likely that a personal duty to account does not arise in the absence of the trustee's awareness that he is holding title to a specific asset for the benefit of another: cf end of n 24 above. For McFarlane *Structure of Property Law* (n 16) esp 305–7, 308–12, 315–16, 319–22, knowledge and trusteeship usually go hand in hand. Note, however, that McFarlane does not expressly invoke the trustee's duty to account in order to justify

Against such restrictions, it is submitted that powers *in rem* can constitute a proprietary base just as much as vested rights *in rem* can.[82] A should be free to exercise his legal or equitable power *in rem* in relation to traceable substitute assets of the painting where he is no longer able to (or no longer wants to) exercise it in relation to the painting itself. Arguments from both principle and precedent point towards this conclusion.

Let us begin by looking at the theoretical justification. If the power model of rights to traceable substitutes is correct,[83] then the conclusion follows almost as a matter of logical inevitability. We know that a person's ability to trace and claim does not stop at the first substitution. Where A starts with a vested property right in the painting, he will have a mere power *in rem* in respect of the first substitute asset, which will – in turn – constitute the proprietary base for A's claim to the second substitute, etc.[84] And even if the power model were proved to be incorrect, this would not mean that powers *in rem* could not stand at the beginning of the exercise. Whatever the conceptual reasons for granting a person rights to substitute assets, they apply irrespective of whether that person's original right was a vested interest or a power. On the view of tracing advocated by the House of Lords in *Foskett v McKeown*,[85] A's power *in rem* is – as a matter of property law – simply 'transferred' from the painting to its exchange product.[86] On the approach which sees a claimant's right to traceable sub-

---

claims to traceable substitutes (though the duty to account is probably part and parcel of what he describes as the "core Trust duty").

82 Smith *Tracing* (n 2) 365–67, does not regard a "proprietary base by avoidance" as problematic. The possibility is also accepted by O'Sullivan et al *Law of Rescission* (n 76) [16.10]–[16.11] (common law), [16.40] (equity), and in passing by Fox [1999] RLR (n 16) 69–70, as well as by D Friedmann, "Valid, Voidable, Qualified, and Non-Existing Obligations: An Alternative Perspective on the Law of Restitution" in A Burrows (ed), *Essays on the Law of Restitution* (Clarendon Press, Oxford 1991) 247, 268. Contra, but apparently only on the basis of the supposed 'third party rights bar to rescission': Birks *Introduction* (n 10) 172–73 (cf n 49 on p 269). The concern is misconceived: see above, Chapter VII. S Worthington, "The Proprietary Consequences of Rescission" [2002] RLR 28, 59–60, toys with the idea of "an extension of the tracing rules" to allow for the preservation of a "mere equity" (by which she denotes both legal and equitable powers *in rem*) as regards substitute assets. The argument here is that no extension is necessary.

83 See above, section B.1.a.ii of the present chapter (pp 282–86).

84 It cannot be objected that the real proprietary base is constituted by A's vested right in the painting, since that right may well be lost by the time the second substitution occurs. For the contrary view of Khurshid/Matthews (1979) 95 LQR (n 15) see above, n 79 and corresponding text.

85 [2001] 1 AC 102 (HL). See above, text to nn 60–61.

86 Lord Millett said (ibid 128): "[The claimant] will normally be able to maintain the same claim to the substituted asset as he could have maintained to the original asset". This statement is borne out by his decisions in some of the cases mentioned on p 293 below (cf text to n 97 as well as nn 100, 101).

stitutes as an instance of 'proprietary restitution' for unjust enrichment,[87] the explanation is slightly more tricky. It requires us to go back to our discussion in Chapter VI, where it was suggested that powers *in rem* may be sufficiently wealth-allocating to justify an unjust enrichment claim based on their infringement, or – what amounts to the same thing – that they can be exercised retroactively and purely hypothetically for the purposes of the law of unjust enrichment.[88] If this is correct, then B's receipt of title to the substitute asset, though derived from C, can be seen as unjustly enriching him at A's expense in two situations. First, where A's power *in rem* to effect proprietary restitution *in specie* is destroyed by *bona fide* purchase on C's part. Second, where A voluntarily relinquishes his original power *in rem* vis-à-vis C in order to claim the painting's exchange product from B.[89]

Turning to precedent, a number of cases have (advertently or inadvertently) recognized the possibility of a power *in rem* functioning as proprietary base.[90] At common law, *Banque Belge pour L'Etranger v Hambrouck*[91] stands out. It will be recalled that a rogue named Hambrouck had defrauded the claimant bank into parting with substantial sums of money and given a part of the traceable proceeds of this scheme to his mistress, Mlle Spanoghe. The Court of Appeal allowed the claimants to recover the amount left over in Mlle Spanoghe's bank account in interpleader proceedings.[92] What is remarkable about the decision is that two of the three judges expressly premised their conclusion on the assumption that Banque Belge

---

[87] See above, text to nn 62–64.

[88] See above, Chapter VI.C.2.b (at pp 242–43), where an attempt was made to explain *Lipkin Gorman v Karpnale Ltd* (n 41) as a case in which the firm's unjust enrichment claim against the Playboy Club was *parasitic* upon a common law power *in rem* affecting the money paid over by Cass.

[89] If one understands A as having retroactively and hypothetically exercised his original power *in rem*, then this amounts to a 'ratification' (for unjust enrichment purposes) of B's conveyance to C. From C's perspective, it has the same effect as *bona fide* purchase. It is true that the concept of 'elective relinquishment' is contentious: see Smith in *Mapping the Law* (n 63) 120–24, 131–34, and cf the 'exclusionary' or the 'intermediate view' of the relationship between property rights and unjust enrichment claims discussed in Chapter IV.C.1 and IV.C.3 above (pp 121–22, 124–25). However, the well-established case law on tracing and claiming in the context of vested property rights suggests that relinquishment may be less problematic in three-party 'substitution' cases than in two-party 'transfer' cases: cf also Smith in *Mapping the Law* (n 63) 134.

[90] In view of the supposed 'third party rights bar to rescission' (cf Chapter VII above), we should not be surprised to find that all the relevant cases concern money, where the bar never actually applied. In money cases, *bona fide* purchase occurs by virtue of the rule in *Miller v Race* (n 53), not under section 23 of the Sale of Goods Act 1979 or the equivalent common law rules.

[91] [1921] 1 KB 321 (CA). Cf also *Small v Attwood* (1831) You 407, 533–38; 159 ER 1051, 1102–4.

[92] See above, text to nn 234–236 on pp 144–45.

had lost title to the money in question when it was paid over to Hambrouck's bank. Hambrouck was said to have obtained a 'voidable title' to the proceeds of his fraud.[93] The claimants therefore started with nothing more than a legal power *in rem*.[94] This power was not destroyed when Hambrouck made payments to Mlle Spanoghe (who was a volunteer) and could subsequently be exercised in relation to the chose in action constituted by Mlle Spanoghe's claim against her bank. Banque Belge's action was brought at common law and probably succeeded only because the proceeds of Hambrouck's fraud had at no stage become mixed with other money.[95] Usually, even victims of fraud will have to have recourse to equity to circumvent the supposed impossibility of tracing through mixed funds at common law.[96] The cases using powers *in rem* as proprietary bases are consequently much more numerous on the equity side. When Millett J – as he then was – suggested in *El Ajou v Dollar Land Holdings plc* that rescission in equity vested a beneficial interest in a defrauded transferor "at least to the extent necessary to support an equitable tracing claim",[97] he was not worried by the fact that the claimant might no longer be able to recover the original asset transferred.[98] The need to identify a traceable substitute typically arises precisely because the original asset can no longer be followed or claimed. This was also recognized in *Daly v Sydney Stock Exchange Ltd*,[99] *Lonrho plc v Al-Fayed (No 2)*,[100] *Bristol and West Building Society v Mothew*,[101] *Bank Tejarat v Hong Kong and Shanghai Banking Corp (CI) Ltd*,[102] and *Shalson v Russo (Tracing Claims)*.[103] All support the

---

[93] [1921] 1 KB 321, 325 (Bankes LJ), 332 (Atkin LJ). Only Scrutton LJ thought that Hambrouck had no title as against Banque Belge: ibid 329.

[94] Although the case was effectively treated by all three judges as if there had been a direct payment by Banque Belge to Hambrouck, it is more accurate to say that Banque Belge's initial power *in rem* was already a product of the law of tracing: cf also ibid 332 (Atkin LJ).

[95] The majority in *Banque Belge* said that they were applying common law tracing rules: [1921] 1 KB 321, 328 (Bankes LJ), 333–34 (Atkin LJ). Scrutton LJ preferred to trace in equity: ibid 330.

[96] See above, text to nn 210–213 on pp 140–41 and section B.1.a.i of the present chapter (esp text to nn 13–19 on pp 278–79).

[97] [1993] 3 All ER 717 (ChD) 734, rev'd on other grounds [1994] 2 All ER 685 (CA).

[98] McFarlane *Structure of Property Law* (n 16) 327 fn 166, explains the case as one in which the defrauded claimant had a vested equitable interest even prior to rescission. But cf *Shalson v Russo (Tracing Claims)* [2003] EWHC 1637 (ChD), [2005] Ch 281, [108] (Rimer J).

[99] (1986) 160 CLR 371 (HCA) 388 (Brennan J).

[100] [1992] 1 WLR 1 (ChD) 13 (Millett J).

[101] [1998] Ch 1 (CA) 22–23 (Millett LJ).

[102] [1995] 1 Lloyd's Rep 239 (QBD Comm) 248 (Tuckey J).

[103] [2003] EWHC 1637 (ChD), [2005] Ch 281, [121]–[127] (Rimer J).

proposition that mere powers *in rem* are a sufficient proprietary base on which to found a claim to traceable substitute assets.

Summing up: whether or not A has exercised his power *in rem* to avoid the conveyance of the painting to B at the point in time when B transfers it to C, and whether or not C qualifies as a *bona fide* purchaser, A can assert a proprietary interest in any traceable substitute still held by B. He has to do no more than communicate to B his intention of claiming the substitute asset in question. B's ability to rely on the disenrichment defence depends not only on his state of mind at the time of the substitution, but also on which justification for the 'transmission' of property rights from one asset to another ultimately wins the day.

2. Personal Claims to Disgorgement of Profits

Although the transferor, A, will often be able to establish a proprietary interest in a particular substitute asset, this is not the only way in which he can get at profits made by the transferee, B, in dealing with the object conveyed under a defect of consent. Certain wrongs-based claims allow the victim to choose between the normal loss-based compensatory measure of damages and a gain-based measure ('restitution for wrongs').[104] In so far as the latter extends to the disgorgement of profits over and above the amount by which B is *directly* enriched at A's expense, the award is best described as 'disgorgement damages'.[105] Although such damages will not accord the transferor priority in the transferee's insolvency, and although they do not confer on him any entitlement to a specific object, a personal claim to profits may nevertheless be attractive to A where B is solvent and A unable or unwilling to complete the tracing exercise.

---

[104] The possibility of opting for a gain-based measure of damages is generally referred to as 'waiver of tort'. However, as explained by the House of Lords in *United Australia Ltd v Barclays Bank Ltd* [1941] AC 1, choosing this option does not amount to a ratification of the defendant's wrongful conduct by the claimant. It was pointed out above (in n 55 on p 30) that some authors argue in favour of regarding 'restitution for wrongs' as a part of the law of unjust enrichment: J Beatson, "The Nature of Waiver of Tort" in J Beatson, *The Use and Abuse of Unjust Enrichment: Essays on the Law of Restitution* (Clarendon Press, Oxford 1991) 206; D Friedmann, "Restitution for Wrongs: The Basis of Liability" in WR Cornish and others (eds), *Restitution Past, Present and Future: Essays in Honour of Gareth Jones* (Hart, Oxford 1998) 133; T Krebs, "The Fallacy of 'Restitution for Wrongs'" in A Burrows and A Rodger (eds), *Mapping the Law: Essays in Memory of Peter Birks* (OUP, Oxford 2006) 379.

[105] The term is coined by J Edelman, *Gain-Based Damages: Contract, Tort, Equity and Intellectual Property* (Hart, Oxford 2002) 65–111, who contrasts 'disgorgement damages' with 'restitutionary damages' proper. Cf also J Edelman, "Gain-Based Damages and Compensation" in A Burrows and A Rodger (eds), *Mapping the Law: Essays in Memory of Peter Birks* (OUP, Oxford 2006) 141, 147–52.

Not every wrong will allow the claimant to claim disgorgement damages. Reverting to our distinction between wrongs committed by B in the course of inducing A's conveyance of the painting and wrongs consisting of the disposition to C, we must remember that the latter are only at issue where A has exercised his legal or equitable power *in rem* before B's disposition occurs.[106] It is not entirely clear which, if any, 'inducement wrongs' are capable of yielding disgorgement damages. Deceit is probably the safest candidate,[107] intentional trespass may be another.[108] In *Rookes v Barnard*,[109] a case involving the tort of intimidation, Lord Devlin suggested that so-called 'exemplary damages' should be available whenever "the defendant's conduct has been calculated by him to make a profit for himself which may well exceed the compensation payable to the plaintiff".[110] He said that "[e]xemplary damages can properly be awarded whenever it is necessary to teach a wrongdoer that tort does not pay".[111] This is one reason which leads James Edelman to argue that disgorgement damages, being "less objectionable" than exemplary damages, should always be available to strip a cynical and wilful wrongdoer of his profits.[112] If he is right, then this suggests that A may be able to claim disgorgement damages whenever B has committed an intentional tort at the inducement stage.[113] This will encompass fraud and some forms of duress. At the disposition stage, the existing law is more straightforward. Provided that B's

---

106 See above, Chapter VII.C (at pp 263, 264–65).

107 Cf *Hill v Perrott* (1810) 3 Taunt 274, 128 ER 109; *Abbotts v Barry* (1820) 2 Brod & Bing 369, 129 ER 1009; *Murad v Al-Saraj* [2004] EWHC 1235 (ChD) [342]–[347] (Etherton J), aff'd on other grounds [2005] EWCA Civ 959. But contrast: *Halifax Building Society v Thomas* [1996] Ch 217 (CA) esp 226–28 (Peter Gibson LJ).

108 Cf *Oughton v Seppings* (1830) 1 Barn & Ad 241, 109 ER 776 (trespass to goods).

109 [1964] AC 1129 (HL).

110 Ibid 1226.

111 Ibid 1227. As this statement indicates, exemplary damages are an exceptional remedy whose purpose it is to punish the defendant for his wrongdoing and to deter other potential defendants from behaving in a similar way.

112 Edelman *Gain-Based Damages* (n 105) 143–45.

113 The only argument against allowing such a claim to A might be that B's profit from the transaction with C is too remote or lies outside the scope of the duty breached by B (eg the duty not to make a fraudulent misrepresentation): cf Edelman *Gain-Based Damages* (n 105) 108–11. However, we know that in the case of a loss-based damages claim, the remoteness rules normally work against fraudulent defendants: *Doyle v Olby (Ironmongers) Ltd* [1969] 2 QB 158 (CA); *Smith New Court Securities Ltd v Scrimgeour Vickers (Asset Management) Ltd* [1997] AC 254 (HL). There is something to be said for applying the same generosity to gain-based damages and for stripping fraudsters of all consequential gains. It does not matter for present purposes whether this is achieved by an appropriately broad definition of the scope of the duty or by virtue of special remoteness (here: remoteness of profit) rules governing intentional and cynical wrongdoing.

conduct amounts to the tort of conversion (at common law)[114] or to a breach of trust (in equity),[115] he will be liable to pay gain-based damages.

C. Limited Personal Rights to Substitutes under German Law

In order to establish the extent to which our transferor A can claim substitute assets from the transferee B under German law, it is necessary to distinguish again cases in which A has retroactively avoided his conveyance of the painting to B (eg for fraud or duress in accordance with § 123 BGB) from cases in which he started with no more than a personal claim to a re-transfer of ownership under a *condictio indebiti*.[116] We will look at the former scenario in the first part of this section, and at the latter in the second part. Broadly speaking, a personal claim to substitutes is thought to be available where A was owner of the painting when B made the substitution, but not (without more) where he had only a right *in personam ad rem acquirendam*.

1. Claims to Substitute Assets after Avoidance of Real Agreement

a) No General Principle of 'Real Subrogation'

Like English law, German law sometimes allows the owner of an object that has been disposed of without authorization to assert a proprietary interest in its traceable substitute asset(s). The process by which the owner's property right is 'transferred' from one asset to another is usually described as 'real subrogation' (*dingliche Surrogation*).[117] Yet the mechan-

---

[114] Cf *Lamine v Dorrell* (1701) 2 Ld Raym 1216, 92 ER 303; *United Australia Ltd v Barclays Bank Ltd* [1941] AC 1 (HL); *Chesworth v Farrar* [1967] 1 QB 407 (QBD) esp 417 (Edmund Davies J). In our example, B will necessarily be an intentional converter. Note that there is a question whether disgorgement damages are or should also be available for innocent conversion: cf Edelman *Gain-Based Damages* (n 105) 139–40.

[115] In equity, gain-based damages are properly described as an 'account of profits': cf eg *Boardman v Phipps* [1967] 2 AC 46 (HL) (breach of fiduciary duty). It is not entirely clear whether a 'bare trustee' in B's position, who disposes of an object which he knows to be subject to A's equitable interest, commits a breach of trust, but it was suggested above (in n 320 on pp 157–58) that there would be a lacuna in the law without such an equitable wrong.

[116] Cf above, Chapter III.B–D (esp at pp 58–63, 64–65, 77–78).

[117] The BGB refers to it as 'immediate substitution' (*unmittelbare Ersetzung*). For an overview see M Wolf, "Prinzipien und Anwendungsbereich der dinglichen Surrogation" JuS 1975, 643, 710; JuS 1976, 32, 104; D Coester-Waltjen, "Die dingliche Surrogation" Jura 1996, 24. Detailed: R Beyer, *Die Surrogation bei Vermögen im Bürgerlichen Gesetzbuche* (Elwert, Marburg 1905); D Strauch, *Mehrheitlicher Rechtsersatz: Ein Bei-*

ism does not operate nearly as widely as it does in English law. Real subrogation is the exception, not the norm. Its main field of application lies in the realm of family law and the law of succession, where it typically ring-fences certain separate funds (such as a deceased's estate or the jointly owned property of spouses).[118] The scenario here under consideration does not concern this type of case. Hence, even if A avoids his conveyance of the painting, he will not be able to vindicate any substitute asset which B has acquired from C. Real subrogation does not feature in our example.

b) Personal Claims under § 687 II 1 BGB and § 816 I 1 BGB

Despite the lack of a general principle of real subrogation, German law nevertheless enables a transferor in A's position to assert at least a personal claim to substitute assets obtained by B. A has a right *in personam ad rem* rather than a right *in rem*. There are two potential bases for such a claim: § 687 II 1 BGB and § 816 I 1 BGB.

(i) 'False' negotiorum gestio*: § 687 II BGB*

The first provision to consider is § 687 II BGB, which deals with a situation of 'false' *negotiorum gestio* (*unechte Geschäftsführung*) and only applies where B's disposal of the painting was *mala fide*. If B sells and conveys the painting to C after A has exercised his right to avoid the original transfer or – if before – knowing that A could rescind the real agreement in question (cf § 142 II BGB), B is deliberately treating A's affairs as if they were his own. Deciding whether and when to dispose of an asset is no-one's business but the owner's. Under these circumstances, A is entitled to assert against B all the rights he would have been able to assert had B acted honestly in the course of a genuine *negotiorum gestio* (§ 687 II 1 BGB).[119] They include, *inter alia*, the right to make the intervener

---

trag zur 'dinglichen Surrogation' im Privatrecht (Gieseking, Bielefeld 1972). The idea of 'immediate substitution' bears a striking resemblance to the justification given in *Foskett v McKeown* (n 60) for a claimant's rights to traceable substitutes: cf text to n 61 and to n 67 above.

118 Instances of real subrogation are to be found, *inter alia*, in §§ 1370, 1473, 2019, 2041, 2111 BGB. Note that § 1370 BGB is currently under review and likely to be abolished in the near future.

119 Cf RGZ 138, 45, 48–49. There is a question about the relationship between § 687 II BGB and §§ 987 ff BGB in such a case. Does the fact that A chooses to proceed under § 687 II BGB automatically exclude recourse to the rules applying between the owner of an object and its illegitimate possessor for other purposes? Some authors think that this would be appropriate: K Rebmann, FJ Säcker and R Rixecker (eds), *Münchener Kommentar zum Bürgerlichen Gesetzbuch, vol 4: §§ 611–704* (4th edn Beck, München 2005) Vor § 677 [18] (Seiler); J von Staudinger (Begr), *J von Staudingers Kommentar*

account for and surrender anything he has obtained from his management of the principal's affairs (§§ 681 2, 667 BGB).[120] Provided that B acted in bad faith, he is therefore liable as if he were a necessitous intervener to give up to A whatever he may have received from C in exchange for the painting.[121] This includes, in particular, an account of profits.[122]

(ii) Scope of recovery under § 816 I 1 BGB

The second – and in practice much more relevant – provision on which a claim to a substitute asset may be based is § 816 I 1 BGB. In contrast to § 687 II BGB, the defendant's state of mind is irrelevant under § 816 I 1 BGB. Commonly classified as a special type of *Eingriffskondiktion*,[123] the section reads:

---

zum Bürgerlichen Gesetzbuch: §§ 657–704 (Neubearbeitung 2006: Sellier de Gruyter, Berlin 2006) § 687 [59] (Bergmann). The Federal Supreme Court, however, has not ruled out a free competition of claims: BGHZ 39, 186, 188.

[120] There is an interesting parallel here with the reasoning in *Lamine v Dorrell* (n 114), a 'restitution for wrongs' case, where Powell J observed: "It is clear that the plaintiff might have maintained detinue or trover for the debentures; but when the act that is done is in its nature tortious, it is hard to turn that into a contract, and against the reason of assumpsits [note: 'assumpsit' was a form of action enforcing an obligation (debt) voluntarily undertaken by the defendant]. But the plaintiff may dispense with the wrong, *and suppose the sale made by his consent, and bring an action for the money they were sold for, as money received to his use*" (emphasis added).

[121] To prevent circularity of claims, § 687 II 2 BGB must be read restrictively. It governs only the extent to which the 'false' *negotiorum gestor* can recover his expenditure (namely reimbursement in accordance with the principles of unjustified enrichment): cf RGZ 138, 45, 50; *Münchener Kommentar: vol 4* (n 119) § 687 [15] (Seiler). Were this otherwise, then the principal (A) would, under § 684 1 BGB, immediately have to surrender the substitute asset itself back to the *gestor* (B).

[122] The scenario was expressly envisaged by the historical legislator: A Achilles, H Gebhard and P Spahn (eds), *Protokolle der Kommission für die zweite Lesung des Entwurfs des Bürgerlichen Gesetzbuchs: vol 2* (Guttentag, Berlin 1898) 742–43. Note that B will be able to counter-claim for any expenditure he may have incurred in order to secure the profit: see n 121 immediately above.

[123] Cf eg BGH NJW 1970, 2059; O Palandt (Begr), *Bürgerliches Gesetzbuch* (67th edn Beck, München 2008) § 816 [1] (Sprau); J von Staudinger (Begr), *J von Staudingers Kommentar zum Bürgerlichen Gesetzbuch: §§ 812–822* (Neubearbeitung 2007: Sellier de Gruyter, Berlin 2007) § 816 [2] (S Lorenz). This classification is not uncontentious: cf esp K Rebmann, FJ Säcker and R Rixecker (eds), *Münchener Kommentar zum Bürgerlichen Gesetzbuch, vol 5: §§ 705–853* (4th edn Beck, München 2004) § 816 [12] (Lieb). In depends in part on one's understanding of the proper relationship between § 816 I 1 and § 816 I 2 BGB. For an overview of the debate see eg *Münchener Kommentar: vol 5* (above) § 816 [1]–[12] (Lieb); D Reuter and M Martinek, *Ungerechtfertigte Bereicherung* (Mohr Siebeck, Tübingen 1983) 282–91.

"If an unauthorized person disposes of an object in such a way that the disposition is effective vis-à-vis the person entitled, he is obliged to surrender to the person entitled what he has obtained by virtue of the disposition."

Given that the avoidance of a conveyance has retroactive effect in German law (cf § 142 I BGB), B is 'unauthorized' when making the transfer to C irrespective of whether A has already exercised his right to rescind the real agreement at the moment of the disposition. The disposition is effective vis-à-vis A (as the 'person entitled') if C acquires ownership as a *bona fide* purchaser under §§ 932 ff BGB or – where the *bona fide* purchase provisions do not apply – if A subsequently ratifies B's conveyance to C (§§ 185, 184 I BGB).[124] It is now well-settled that, despite its retroactivity, ratification does not amount to an authorization of the disposing party's conduct.[125]

The most contentious question relating to § 816 I 1 BGB concerns the extent of the defendant's liability. On the currently prevailing view, the claimant has a personal right to any asset obtained in exchange for the object which he formerly owned, even if the value of such asset(s) exceeds the value of the original object.[126] If B had sold A's painting to C at a profit, A could demand disgorgement of the full purchase price.[127] On the opposing view, the claim of the 'person entitled' is strictly capped by the

[124] RGZ 106, 44; BGHZ 56, 131; BGHZ 107, 340; *Münchener Kommentar: vol 5* (n 123) § 816 [25] (Lieb); *Palandt* (n 123) § 816 [9] (Sprau); *Staudinger* (n 123) § 816 [9] (S Lorenz).

[125] BGH NJW 1960, 860, 860 (passage not contained in the official report BGHZ 32, 53); *Reuter/Martinek* (n 123) 299–301. For English law cf *United Australia Ltd v Barclays Bank Ltd* (n 104); Fox [1999] RLR (n 16) 65–69.

[126] RGZ 88, 351, 359–60; BGHZ 29, 157; BGH WM 1975, 1179, 1180–81; BGHZ 112, 288, 295; BGH NJW 1997, 190, 191; J Esser and HL Weyers, *Schuldrecht: vol 2/2* (8th edn Müller, Heidelberg 2000) 84–85; K Larenz and CW Canaris, *Lehrbuch des Schuldrechts: vol 2/2* (13th edn Beck, München 1994) 267–70, who are, however, cautious with respect to authorization cases; U Loewenheim, *Bereicherungsrecht* (2nd edn Beck, München 1997) 106–8; E Lopau, *Surrogationsansprüche und Bereicherungsrecht* (Duncker & Humblot, Berlin 1971) 14–23; *Münchener Kommentar: vol 5* (n 123) § 816 [30] (Lieb); *Palandt* (n 123) § 816 [23]–[24] (Sprau); *Reuter/Martinek* (n 123) 321–25. Similar, if more value-oriented: HH Jakobs, *Eingriffserwerb und Vermögensverschiebung in der Lehre von der ungerechtfertigten Bereicherung* (Röhrscheid, Bonn 1964) 17–66, esp 54–60, who makes an exception for cases where an innocent substitutor would have made the same profit using one of his own assets. Also arguing for a disgorgement of profits, but with a different justification: HG Koppensteiner and E Kramer, *Ungerechtfertigte Bereicherung* (2nd edn de Gruyter, Berlin 1988) 122–25, who want to apply a 'deobjectivized' § 818 II BGB (cf n 133 below).

[127] On the question as to whether an allowance can be made for B's contribution see n 140 below.

value of the original object.[128] In our example, A's right to restitution would be confined to the market price of the painting.

Part of the difficulty stems from the unfortunate wording of § 816 I 1 BGB. After effecting the conveyance of the painting to C, B is obliged to surrender to A "what he has obtained by virtue of the disposition". The BGB legislator intended this to refer to the counter-performance received by the party making the unauthorized disposition (here B) from the third party purchaser (here C),[129] which accords with the dominant interpretation of the provision.[130] However, it has been pointed out that, as a consequence of the principles of separation and abstraction, the counter-performance cannot properly be regarded as having been obtained "by virtue of the disposition".[131] B's conveyance of the painting to C merely discharges B's contractual obligation to bestow ownership upon C. His enrichment thus consists of being freed from a liability.[132] Since that is an enrichment which cannot be surrendered *in specie*, so this reasoning suggests, A's claim against B extends to the monetary equivalent of the discharge (cf § 818 II BGB) and therefore only to the market value of the painting.[133]

---

[128] E von Caemmerer, "Bereicherungsausgleich bei Verpfändung fremder Sachen" in *Festschrift für Hans Lewald* (Helbing & Lichtenhahn, Basel 1953) 443, 446–48, reprinted in HG Leser (ed), *Ernst von Caemmerer: Gesammelte Schriften, vol 1: Rechtsvergleichung und Schuldrecht* (Mohr Siebeck, Tübingen 1968) 279, 282–85; E von Caemmerer, "Bereicherung und unerlaubte Handlung" in H Dölle, M Rheinstein and K Zweigert (eds), *Festschrift für Ernst Rabel* (Mohr Siebeck, Tübingen 1954) vol 1, 333, 356–60, reprinted in HG Leser (ed), *Ernst von Caemmerer: Gesammelte Schriften, vol 1: Rechtsvergleichung und Schuldrecht* (Mohr Siebeck, Tübingen 1968) 209, 232–36; K Larenz, "Zur Bedeutung des 'Wertersatzes' im Bereicherungsrecht" in HC Ficker and others (eds), *Festschrift für Ernst von Caemmerer zum 70. Geburtstag* (Mohr Siebeck, Tübingen 1978) 209, 218–19, 228–29; P Schlechtriem, *Schuldrecht: Besonderer Teil* (6th edn Mohr Siebeck, Tübingen 2003) [804]; T Soergel (Begr), *Bürgerliches Gesetzbuch, vol 5/1: §§ 705–822* (12th edn Kohlhammer, Stuttgart 2007) § 816 [29] (Mühl/Hadding).

[129] Cf *Motive zu dem Entwurfe eines Bürgerlichen Gesetzbuches für das Deutsche Reich* (2nd edn Guttentag, Berlin 1896) vol 3, 224 (the formulation as such leaves open whether the understanding should be object- or value-oriented). For an overview of the legislative background see *Staudinger* (n 123) § 816 [1] (S Lorenz).

[130] See above, n 126 and corresponding text.

[131] D Medicus, *Bürgerliches Recht* (21st edn Heymanns, Köln 2007) [723]; *Koppensteiner/Kramer* (n 126) 125; H Reeb, *Grundprobleme des Bereicherungsrechts* (Beck, München 1975) 76.

[132] Medicus *Bürgerliches Recht* (n 131) [723]. Cf already A von Tuhr, *Der Allgemeine Teil des Deutschen Bürgerlichen Rechts: vol 2/2* (Duncker & Humblot, Berlin 1918) 144–45, esp fn 49. Critical of this argument despite agreeing with the result reached by Medicus: *Soergel: vol 5/1* (n 128) § 816 [29] (Mühl/Hadding). Reeb *Grundprobleme* (n 131) 76, also regards the wording of § 816 I 1 BGB as ultimately not decisive.

[133] Cf Medicus *Bürgerliches Recht* (n 131) [723]. Critical of a purely 'objective' determination of value for the purposes of § 818 II BGB: HG Koppensteiner, "Probleme

Another argument for confining A's claim in this way is the perceived need to bring the remedial regime of § 816 I 1 BGB into line with that of the general *Eingriffskondiktion* in § 812 I 1 alt 2 BGB.[134] Moreover, the subjective requirement of knowledge contained in § 687 II BGB – it is maintained – supports the inference, by way of *argumentum e contrario*, that a person who innocently or negligently disposes of an object belonging to another should not be liable to disgorge profits.[135] There is thus something to be said for regarding B's profits from the sale to C as irrelevant under § 816 I 1 BGB (unless they are a reflection of a generally rising market price) and only allowing A to claim the proceeds, via §§ 687 II 1, 681 2, 667 BGB, where B acted *mala fide* (in the sense of knowingly).

Yet a number of weighty arguments also point the other way. Mention has already been made of the fact that the fathers of the BGB intended the substitute itself to be surrendered.[136] They modelled § 816 I 1 BGB, *inter alia*, on a provision of the Prussian *Allgemeines Landrecht* which was to the same effect.[137] It is practically beyond doubt that, where the unauthor-

---

des bereicherungsrechtlichen Wertersatzes" NJW 1971, 588, 1769, esp 1769–75 (arguing for a 'concrete and individual' valuation); *Koppensteiner/Kramer* (n 126) 155–74; Reeb *Grundprobleme* (n 131) 77–78, 96–101. These authors want to solve the problem of § 816 I 1 BGB by requiring the substitutor to disgorge his profits under § 818 II BGB.

134 Esp von Caemmerer in *Festschrift Lewald* (n 128) 446, reprinted in *Gesammelte Schriften: vol 1* (n 128) 282–83. Cf also the parallel provision of § 951 I 1 BGB, catering for accession, specification, etc. Note that where money belonging to A becomes indistinguishably mixed with money belonging to B, this will either lead to co-ownership of the resulting fund (§§ 948, 947 I BGB), or – if A's contribution is negligibly small – may entail accession (§§ 948, 947 II). Only in the latter case does § 951 I 1 BGB have to be invoked. Many details are contentious: cf eg the discussion in K Rebmann, FJ Säcker and R Rixecker (eds), *Münchener Kommentar zum Bürgerlichen Gesetzbuch, vol 6: §§ 854–1296* (4th edn Beck, München 2004) § 948 [7] (Füller).

135 Von Caemmerer in *Festschrift Rabel* (n 128) 359–60, reprinted in *Gesammelte Schriften: vol 1* (n 128) 235–36; Schlechtriem *Schuldrecht BT* (n 128) [804].

136 See above, n 129 and corresponding text.

137 *Motive* (n 129) vol 3, 224, referring to Part I, Title 15, § 28 ALR. The ALR provision applied where an innocent purchaser of a thing belonging to another had himself innocently disposed of it. He was then obliged to surrender to the owner the 'profit' made from the disposition ("*den bey der Veräußerung gezogenen Vortheil zu verabfolgen*"), but only if the owner could not otherwise obtain adequate 'compensation' (presumably through finding/claiming the original object). 'Profit' was understood to encompass the entire counter-performance: *Reuter/Martinek* (n 123) 318, referring to F Förster and ME Eccius, *Preußisches Privatrecht* (7th edn Reimer, Berlin 1896) vol 3, 303. This edition was not accessible to me. The previous edition of *Förster/Eccius* (6th edn Reimer, Berlin 1892) vol 3, 296, does indeed contain a statement of the sort, though it must be assumed that both the Prussian ALR and the BGB legislator had in mind the 'normal' case in which the substitutor obtains the actual market value of the object when he sells it on: cf *Staudinger* (n 123) § 816 [1] (S Lorenz). Note that *Förster/Eccius* (6th edn) vol 3, 296, further suggest that an innocent substitutor was able to deduct from his liability the pur-

ized disposition is made at an undervalue, the claimant cannot recover more under § 816 I 1 BGB than what the defendant actually obtained.[138] Thus, if B sells A's painting to C for less than its market price, A bears the loss. As a corollary, it seems appropriate that the financial gain made from a disposition above market value should also be allocated to A,[139] at least to the extent that the profit is not attributable to any special skill and effort on B's part.[140] Conceptually, the inclusion of profits can be justified by reference to the so-called doctrine of the 'attributive content' of ownership (*Lehre vom Zuweisungsgehalt des Eigentums*).[141] According to this doctrine, the right to exploit the earning opportunities inherent in an object is

---

chase price he paid for the object. This must be understood as a repercussion of the so-called '*Lösungsrecht*' in Part I, Title 15, §§ 25, 26 ALR (by which an innocent purchaser for value who did not qualify as a *bona fide* purchaser under I, 15, §§ 42 ff ALR had to surrender the original object only if the owner compensated him accordingly).

[138] *Koppensteiner/Kramer* (n 126) 121; *Münchener Kommentar: vol 5* (n 123) § 816 [33] (Lieb); *Staudinger* (n 123) § 816 [23] (S Lorenz). Disagreeing: *Reuter/Martinek* (n 123) 325–27. Note that the claimant may, in appropriate circumstances, be able to claim full compensatory damages under §§ 989, 990 BGB: see above, Chapter III.D.2.b (at pp 82–83).

[139] Cf Loewenheim *Bereicherungsrecht* (n 126) 109; *Koppensteiner/Kramer* (n 126) 123; Reeb *Grundprobleme* (n 131) 100; D Rothoeft, Review of Jakobs *Eingriffserwerb* [n 126] in AcP 166 (1966) 146, 150. Note that *Koppensteiner/Kramer* and Reeb *Grundprobleme* approach § 816 I 1 BGB from the angle of a 'de-objectivized' § 818 II BGB: cf n 133 above.

[140] An allowance for B's contribution is made by Esser/Weyers *Schuldrecht 2/2* (n 126) 85; C Kellmann, *Grundsätze der Gewinnhaftung* (Duncker & Humblot, Berlin 1969) 140–41; W Wilburg, *Die Lehre von der ungerechtfertigten Bereicherung nach österreichischem und deutschem Recht* (Leuschner & Lubensky, Graz 1934) 128–33. More differentiated: Jakobs *Eingriffserwerb* (n 126) 57–60, 123–27. Cf also the discussion by *Reuter/Martinek* (n 123) 319–20. Critical: *Koppensteiner/Kramer* (n 126) 123–24, who apply only the disenrichment defence in § 818 III BGB.

[141] The doctrine was developed by Wilburg *Lehre von der ungerechtfertigten Bereicherung* (n 140) 27–51, and von Caemmerer in *Festschrift Rabel* (n 128) 352–60, reprinted in *Gesammelte Schriften: vol 1* (n 128) 228–36. Note, however, that von Caemmerer himself actually rejects a claim to surrogates under § 816 I 1 BGB: *Festschrift Rabel* (above) 356–60. Critical of the doctrine of 'attributive content': Jakobs *Eingriffserwerb* (n 126) 23–41, who instead adheres to the so-called *Rechtswidrigkeitslehre* developed by F Schulz, "System der Rechte auf den Eingriffserwerb" AcP 105 (1909) 1. As Jakobs' work shows, application of the *Rechtswidrigkeitslehre* also requires a disgorgement of profits: Jakobs *Eingriffserwerb* (n 126) 41–66. It is not possible within the confines of this book to discuss the two rival theories. Suffice it to draw the reader's attention to the brief overview in *Münchener Kommentar: vol 5* (n 123) § 812 [240]–[246] (Lieb), and to point out that any comparative assessment of the *Rechtswidrigkeitslehre* would have to get to grips with the tricky question of the proper relationship between 'restitution for unjust enrichment' and 'restitution for wrongs' in English law: cf nn 51, 55 on pp 29–30, and see esp Krebs in *Mapping the Law* (n 104).

solely attributed to the owner. It includes the option of realizing the economic value of the object through, for example, sale or exchange, and it encompasses in particular the possibility of making a profit.[142] When B disposes of the painting without A's consent, he not only interferes with A's entitlement to the painting as a physical object (which has a certain market value), but also appropriates to himself its inherent earning potential. B should therefore be required to disgorge not merely the painting's objective value (equivalent to the *commodum ex re*), but – in principle at least – whatever he has received in exchange (*commodum ex negotiatione cum re*), in our case the entire proceeds of sale. Viewed in this light, the discrepancy between the claim under § 816 I 1 BGB and the general *Eingriffskondiktion* in § 812 I 1 alt 2 BGB becomes explicable. While under the latter the defendant's enrichment tends to consist of an increase of his wealth (conceived of as an abstract fund),[143] the former provision can be understood as entailing a claim to specific substitute assets following a loss of ownership (*Eigentumsfolgeanspruch*).[144] Though not an instance of 'real subrogation', it is nevertheless informed by the idea of subrogation.[145]

---

[142] Cf BGHZ 29, 157, 160: "[D]as Recht, die Sache gewinnbringend zu verwerten, entspringt den dem Eigentümer zustehenden Befugnissen". ("The right to dispose of the object at a profit has its source in the powers allocated to the owner"). Cf § 903 BGB, the legislative expression of the idea of ownership as an all-embracing *ius utendi, fruendi, abutendi* (a right to use, to make a profit, and to exploit in any way).

[143] Notwithstanding the theoretical specificity of the primary claim under §§ 812 I 1 alt 2 BGB, 818 I BGB, there will typically be no particular asset to surrender, eg where fungibles have been consumed. In any event, it is worth noting already at this point that there is a question about the extent to which *commoda ex negotiatione* are encompassed by § 818 I BGB: cf discussion below, in section C.2.a of the present chapter (pp 305–8).

[144] Cf Larenz/Canaris *Schuldrecht 2/2* (n 126) 268: "Vindikationsersatzfunktion" ("function of a substitute *vindicatio*"). Note that these authors would be happy to restrict the claimant to recovery of the objective value of the object under § 818 II BGB where his position as owner depended on what they describe as an entirely 'fortuitous' consequence of abstraction: ibid fn 12. They do not, however, regard our scenario, in which the transferor's consent is sufficiently impaired to render the conveyance void or voidable, as 'fortuitous' in this sense: cf ibid 341–43.

[145] Most forcefully endorsing the subrogation theory: Loewenheim *Bereicherungsrecht* (n 126) 107–8; Lopau *Surrogationsansprüche und Bereicherungsrecht* (n 126) 14–23; *Reuter/Martinek* (n 123) 321–25. Critical: Jakobs *Eingriffserwerb* (n 126) 55–57. It is, of course, true that 'subrogation' is not a general principle of the law which can in and of itself justify the claimant's right to any substitute. This is already evident from the fact that the 'substitution' of a right *in personam* for a right *in rem* conforms to the idea of subrogation only in a very imperfect sense: cf Schulz AcP 105 (n 141) 445. However, the notion of 'subrogation' does reflect the underlying idea that a particular asset in the defendant's estate was acquired by means of the unauthorized 'realization' of the earning potential inherent in a right which the legal system had allocated to the owner. The comprehensive protection of that right requires the defendant to be stripped (by means of the

If one bears in mind that, unlike a person who knowingly treats another's business as his own, a *bona fide* defendant of a claim under § 816 I 1 BGB will be able to deduct any disenriching expenditure incurred in connection with the disposition (§ 818 III BGB),[146] the inconsistencies between the broad reading of this provision and § 687 II BGB are more apparent than real.[147]

Overall, the dominant interpretation of § 816 I 1 BGB, which allows A to claim the full purchase price of the painting, including profits, seems preferable both from the historical and the conceptual point of view. A's claim is, in the first instance, a right *in personam ad rem*, ie a personal claim to a specific substitute, irrespective of the substitute's value.[148] Only where the substitute cannot be surrendered *in specie* is B's obligation turned into one for restitution in pecuniary terms (§ 818 II BGB).[149] In the

law of unjustified enrichment) of the asset which constitutes the immediate product of this 'realization' and which in this sense actually 'represents' the original asset.

[146] BGHZ 100, 95, 101, is not inconsistent with a broad interpretation of § 818 III BGB in the context of § 816 I 1 BGB. It was concerned with expenditure on the original object while the claimant still retained ownership of it (which expenditure was not causally connected with the subsequent disposition and could only be recovered under the conditions set out in §§ 994, 996 BGB). On the question of an allowance for B's skill and effort see the references in n 140 above. In accordance with the idea that B ought to be stripped (only) of what he has acquired by 'realizing' the earning potential inherent in A's painting (cf n 145 and text to n 142 above), the 'proceeds' of his own contribution to a profitable sale must indeed be allocated to him rather than A.

[147] Cf *Koppensteiner/Kramer* (n 126) 123; *Reuter/Martinek* (n 123) 324, 539. A 'false' *negotiorum gestor* has a counter-claim against the owner who seeks disgorgement of profits under § 687 II BGB only to the extent that his expenditure actually *augmented* the profit (as would, for example, be the case where B had the painting restored before selling it at a correspondingly higher price): cf n 121 above.

[148] In view of the fact that the claimant may not have any use for the substitute asset if it is not money, some authors afford him the option of bringing a claim based on the value of the defendant's enrichment instead: Lopau *Surrogationsansprüche und Bereicherungsrecht* (n 126) 72–84; *Reuter/Martinek* (n 123) 327–28. Contra or more restrictive: O Jauernig (ed), *Bürgerliches Gesetzbuch: Kommentar* (12th edn Beck, München 2007) § 816 [12] (Stadler); Larenz/Canaris *Schuldrecht 2/2* (n 126) 270; *Münchener Kommentar: vol 5* (n 123) § 816 [32] (Lieb).

[149] It will be recalled that some authors regard a value-based claim under § 818 II BGB as the primary remedy, but argue that it encompasses the defendant's profits: cf n 133 above. They reject the orthodox view that the value of an enrichment has to be determined 'objectively'. However, even if one accepts the 'objective' interpretation of § 818 II BGB, then – on the two-step approach adopted here – the value of B's enrichment should still be determined by reference to the market value of the *substitute asset* instead of by the market value of the original: cf also *Münchener Kommentar: vol 5* (n 123) § 816 [34] (Lieb).

case of money, it will usually[150] not matter to A whether he receives the specific notes and coins paid by C to B or the equivalent amount.

2. Claims to Substitute Assets where Real Agreement is Not Avoided

Let us now consider the scenario where A cannot avoid the real agreement with B. Instead of disposing of an object belonging to another, B disposes of something belonging to himself. All he deprives A of is the latter's personal right under § 812 I 1 alt 1 BGB (*condictio indebiti*) to have what was transferred without a valid legal basis or *causa* given back.[151] Assume that B exchanged the painting for C's bicycle, and assume further that the bicycle is worth € 150, while the painting had a market value of only € 100. A's right to a re-conveyance of the painting having been destroyed, the question arises what he can claim in its place. Subject to what will be said below about the special position of *mala fide* enrichees,[152] this depends primarily on the proper interpretation of § 818 I and II BGB.

a) Application of § 818 I and II BGB

Under § 818 I BGB, the enrichee's obligation to make restitution encompasses secondary benefits as well as anything which he acquires "on the basis of an obtained right or as compensation for the destruction, damage or deprivation of the object obtained". § 818 I BGB clearly covers some substitute assets. If the painting had been destroyed, B would, for example, be under an obligation to surrender an insurance payout or the damages received from the person responsible for the destruction (so-called *commoda ex re*).[153] Substitutes obtained through bargaining (*rechtsgeschäftliche Surrogate* or *commoda ex negotiatione*), on the other hand, are generally thought to be excluded from the ambit of the provision.[154]

---

[150] On the position in the defendant's insolvency see below, section D.2 of the present chapter (esp at pp 315–16).

[151] The special issues and problems arising where A and B are parties to a non-existent or rescinded (executed) reciprocal contract (keyword: *Saldotheorie* versus two-claims theory) will not be addressed again in this chapter. For an overview and discussion see above, Chapter III.C.3 (pp 71–77).

[152] See section C.2.b of the present chapter (pp 308–9).

[153] Cf *Jauernig* (n 148) § 818 [10] (Stadler); *Münchener Kommentar: vol 5* (n 123) § 818 [29] (Lieb); *Palandt* (n 123) § 818 [15] (Sprau); *Staudinger* (n 123) § 818 [19] (S Lorenz). Similarly, if A had given B a lottery ticket to which B was not entitled, any winnings would have been acquired by B "on the basis of an obtained right".

[154] RGZ 86, 343, 347; RGZ 101, 389, 391; RGZ 133, 283, 287; BGHZ 24, 106, 110–11; BGHZ 75, 203, 206; BGHZ 158, 63, 67; *Jauernig* (n 148) § 818 [11] (Stadler); Loewenheim *Bereicherungsrecht* (n 126) 136–37; *Palandt* (n 123) § 818 [14] (Sprau); *Reuter/Martinek* (n 123) 550–52; *Staudinger* (n 123) § 818 [17] (S Lorenz); HP Wester-

This was the express intention of the historical legislator,[155] and it is borne out by the discrepancies between the wording of § 818 I BGB and § 816 I 1 BGB.[156] As German law stands, A cannot demand surrender of the bicycle instead of the painting under §§ 812 I 1 alt 1, 818 I BGB. He is confined to a claim for the value of B's enrichment under § 818 II BGB, conventionally measured by reference to the objective value of what the transferee has obtained through the *indebite* transfer.[157] In our example, B would therefore have to pay to A the sum of € 100, constituting the market price of the painting.[158]

As an interesting addendum from a comparative point of view, and for the sake of completeness, mention must be made of two approaches which do accommodate (and indeed require) the disgorgement of B's enrichment from the profitable substitution. On the first view, § 818 I BGB should be understood to encompass *commoda ex negotiatione* despite its restrictive wording and the legislative background.[159] Reliance is placed on § 285 BGB, which is seen as parallel to § 818 I BGB.[160] The provision concerns the case in which performance of an (eg contractual) obligation to transfer a specific asset becomes impossible. Although the debtor is thereby freed

---

mann (ed), *Erman: Bürgerliches Gesetzbuch* (12th edn Schmidt, Köln 2008) vol 2, § 818 [14] (Westermann/Buck-Heeb).

[155] See *Protokolle: vol 2* (n 122) 709.

[156] In other provisions employing the same wording as § 818 I BGB, the legislator has systematically added the words "or by virtue of a legal transaction" to indicate that *commoda ex negotiatione* were intended to be encompassed: cf eg §§ 1473 I, 2041, 2111 I, 2374 BGB.

[157] Cf RGZ 86, 343, 347; RGZ 101, 389, 391; BGHZ 75, 203, 206; BGHZ 82, 299, 307–8; BGHZ 112, 288, 294–95; BGHZ 132, 198, 207; BGHZ 168, 220, 239; *Jauernig* (n 148) § 818 [14] (Stadler); *Palandt* (n 123) § 818 [18] (Sprau); *Staudinger* (n 123) § 818 [26]–[27] (S Lorenz).

[158] Minus – where appropriate – the amount of any disenrichment: § 818 III BGB. Note that where a substitute asset has been gratuitously transferred to a third party, its recipient will be liable under § 822 BGB to make *value restitution* (a consequence of the prevailing interpretations of § 818 I BGB on the one and § 822 BGB on the other hand), but with the option of surrendering the substitute instead: cg BGHZ 158, 63.

[159] Esser/Weyers *Schuldrecht 2/2* (n 126) 101; F Hartmann, *Der Anspruch auf das stellvertretende commodum* (Mohr Siebeck, Tübingen 2007) 279–85; H Lange, "Zur Umstellung der Bereicherung" NJW 1951, 685, 687; Schulz AcP 105 (n 141) 339–43. Similar, but restricted to the *Eingriffskondiktion* (and thus not for our case of a *condictio indebiti*): *Münchener Kommentar: vol 5* (n 123) § 818 [31] (Lieb). Also similar, but conceding that a claim to *commoda ex negotiatione* cannot be based on § 818 I BGB as it stands: HA Fischer, "Bereicherung und Schaden" in *Festschrift für Ernst Zitelmann* (Duncker & Humblot, München 1913) 32–37.

[160] Lange NJW 1951 (n 159) 687; Schulz AcP 105 (n 141) 342. Critical of this analogy: *Erman* (n 154) vol 2, § 818 [14] (Westermann/Buck-Heeb); Koppensteiner NJW 1971 (n 133) 1172. Note that, prior to 2002, § 285 BGB was contained in § 281 BGB.

from his primary liability (§ 275 BGB), § 285 BGB imposes on him a duty to surrender to the creditor any relevant substitute. It is today widely accepted that § 285 BGB applies to all kinds of substitutes, including *commoda ex negotiatione*.[161] Viewed in this light, the exclusion of bargained-for exchange products from § 818 I BGB does indeed appear anachronistic. A broader strand of the argument accordingly sees §§ 285, 816 I 1 BGB and § 818 I BGB as all founded upon the same principle against unjustified enrichments.[162] Whether A's right is an absolute or a relative one, ie whether he actually owns the painting or has only a personal claim to have it conveyed, the mechanisms for the protection of that right should be the same. In each case, B has to be stripped of what he would not have acquired but for his interference with A's right (albeit that this interference may have been perfectly innocent) and what thus constitutes an enrichment illegitimately obtained at A's expense.[163]

The second approach accepts that the *commodum ex negotiatione* itself is not encompassed by § 818 I BGB, but maintains that it is nevertheless appropriate to require a disgorgement of profits. Horst Heinrich Jakobs has argued that the draftsmen of the BGB wanted only to ensure that the substitute would not be forced on the claimant against his will, but did not at

[161] BGHZ 46, 260, 264; BGH NJW 1983, 929, 930; BGH NJW-RR 2005, 241, 242; *Jauernig* (n 148) § 285 [7]–[8] (Stadler); *Palandt* (n 123) § 285 [7] (Heinrichs); FJ Säkker and R Rixecker (eds), *Münchener Kommentar zum Bürgerlichen Gesetzbuch, vol 2: §§ 241–432* (5th edn Beck, München 2007) § 285 [22]–[23] (Emmerich); J von Staudinger (Begr), *J von Staudingers Kommentar zum Bürgerlichen Gesetzbuch: §§ 255–304* (Neubearbeitung 2004: Sellier de Gruyter, Berlin 2004) § 285 [38] (Löwisch). For a powerful recent defence of this view see Hartmann *Anspruch auf das stellvertretende commodum* (n 159) esp 269–89. Historically, the matter was more contentious. The assumption that the former § 281 BGB (now § 285 BGB) did not encompass the *commodum ex negotiatione* was widespread: cf the overview and discussion by G Römer, "Ist § 281 BGB auf das durch Rechtsgeschäft erlangte Entgelt anwendbar?" AcP 119 (1921) 293, esp 294–300. It has been suggested that the more restrictive approach accorded with the intention of the BGB legislator: HH Jakobs, *lucrum ex negotiatione* (Mohr Siebeck, Tübingen 1993) 105–9; P Schlechtriem and M Schmidt-Kessel, *Schuldrecht: Allgemeiner Teil* (6th edn Mohr Siebeck, Tübingen 2005) [492]. More cautious: Hartmann *Anspruch auf das stellvertretende commodum* (n 159) 276–78.

[162] Cf Hartmann *Anspruch auf das stellvertretende commodum* (n 159) 269–302, esp 278–89; Schulz AcP 105 (n 141) 336–43, who invokes § 2019 BGB as an additional parallel.

[163] Hartmann *Anspruch auf das stellvertretende commodum* (n 159) esp 245–60, 281–89, speaks of a "*widerrechtliche Vermögensherrschaft*" ("wrongful asset control"), though he is careful to point out that the 'wrongfulness' is not so much determined by the defendant's *conduct* as by the mere *fact* that his 'asset control' prevents (or prevented) the realization of the claimant's right: ibid 14–16. Note the qualifications Hartmann makes for cases where the profit cannot be ascribed to the claimant's right (alone): ibid 296–99. On Schulz' *Rechtswidrigkeitslehre* see n 141 above.

the same time wish to leave the substitutor with a windfall.[164] A similar conclusion is reached by proponents of a subjective interpretation of § 818 II BGB, for whom the 'concrete and individual' valuation of the defendant's enrichment can take account of lucrative substitutions.[165] Were this approach to prevail, then it would to some extent make up for the legislative exclusion of the *commodum ex negotiatione* from the ambit of § 818 I BGB. In our example, A would be able to claim € 150, and not merely € 100.[166]

b) Personal Claim to Substitutes via §§ 819 I, 818 IV, 285 BGB

Before concluding that the transferor A can never demand substitute assets as such where he is unable to avoid his real agreement with B, we must briefly advert to the possibility of establishing a claim to substitutes via §§ 819 I, 818 IV, 285 BGB. It will be recalled that the liability of an enrichee who is or becomes aware of the lack of legal basis or *causa* for his receipt[167] is determined in accordance with the 'general provisions' of the BGB.[168] There is a dispute over whether § 285 BGB (already mentioned)[169] qualifies as one of these provisions.[170] If it does, as the case law strongly suggests,[171] and if one accepts the broad reach of § 285 BGB,[172] then its application entails an obligation on the part of the *mala fide* enrichee to

---

[164] Jakobs *lucrum ex negotiatione* (n 161) 110–19. He regards most judicial pronouncements on the exclusion of profits from §§ 812, 818 BGB (cf n 157 above) as *obiter*: ibid 119–29.

[165] Cf Koppensteiner NJW 1971 (n 133) 1771–72; *Koppensteiner/Kramer* (n 126) 127, 158–59. More differentiated: Reeb *Grundprobleme* (n 131) 101–5.

[166] Again subject to any relevant disenrichment (cf n 158 above): § 818 III BGB.

[167] Knowledge of the ground for rescission of the obligatory contract is also sufficient: cf § 142 II BGB.

[168] See above, Chapter II.C.2.b (at p 34) and Chapter III.C.2.b (esp at pp 68–69).

[169] See above, text to n 160–161.

[170] For an overview of the debate see eg R Frank, "Anwendbarkeit des § 281 BGB auf den verschärft haftenden Bereicherungsschuldner" JuS 1981, 102, esp 105; *Reuter/ Martinek* (n 123) 631–42. Note that, prior to 2002, § 285 was contained in § 281 BGB.

[171] BGHZ 75, 203, esp 206–9. The Federal Supreme Court there reasoned that an owner who knowingly disposes of an asset obtained *sine causa* should not be in a better position than a possessor who knowingly disposes of an asset belonging to another (and who is liable to surrender the *commodum ex negotiatione* under §§ 687 II 1, 681 2, 667 BGB: cf section C.1.b.i of the present chapter, on pp 297–98). Critical of this argument: *Reuter/Martinek* (n 123) 636. Agreeing with the conclusion of the BGH: Larenz/Canaris *Schuldrecht 2/2* (n 126) 315; Frank JuS 1981 (n 170) 105. Cf also the discussion by W Schubert, Anmerkung zum Urteil des BGH vom 11.10.1979 (case note) in JZ 1980, 199, 200, who regards the Federal Supreme Court's solution as "methodologically viable" ("*[m]ethodologisch ... gangbar*") if historically inaccurate.

[172] See above, n 161 and corresponding text.

surrender *in specie* any substitute received in exchange for the original asset, provided only that he was already in bad faith when effecting the substitution.[173] As a result, there exists on the predominant view a bright dividing line in German law between *bona fide* and *mala fide* enrichees as far as their liability to surrender *commoda ex negotiatione* is concerned.

D. Comparative Observations on Claims to Substitute Assets

1. Personal and Proprietary Rights to Substitutes

Within both English and German law, the various debates about the extent to which substitute assets in the form of *commoda ex negotiatione* can be claimed by the original transferor expose a tension between two divergent principles. Let us identify these up-front. On the one hand, there is a concern to protect the person entitled to a specific asset, A, as comprehensively as possible against the infringement of that entitlement by another, B. This concern exists irrespective of the infringer's state of mind. However, A's entitlement is generally regarded as worthy of full (profit-stripping) protection only if it amounts to a right or interest *in rem*. In German law, for example, § 816 I 1 BGB forces even innocent possessors to surrender *commoda ex negotiatione*, while § 818 I BGB does not impose the same liability on *bona fide* enrichees.[174] The second approach comes at the issue from a different angle. It couches claims to *commoda ex negotiatione* in terms very reminiscent of a special personal duty to account. This requires either a fiduciary-like relationship between the parties or at least B's awareness of A's rights in respect of the original asset. For German law, we see it reflected most clearly in the *mala fide* possessor's liability as a 'false' *negotiorum gestor* (§ 687 II BGB),[175] but it is also

[173] Those authors who argue that § 818 I BGB should encompass the *commodum ex negotiatione* (cf n 159 above) tend to regard recourse to §§ 819 I, 818 IV, 285 BGB as superfluous: Esser/Weyers *Schuldrecht 2/2* (n 126) 120; Hartmann *Anspruch auf das stellvertretende commodum* (n 159) 299–301, who goes on to argue for an application of § 687 II BGB irrespective of whether or not ownership has passed (ibid 301–2); *Münchener Kommentar: vol 5* (n 123) § 818 [157] (Lieb).

[174] See above, section C.1.b.ii and C.2.a of the present chapter (pp 298–305, 305–8). Those who would wish to see *commoda ex negotiatione* encompassed by § 818 I BGB are essentially arguing for an equation of personal (relative) with proprietary (absolute) entitlements: cf text to nn 159–163 above.

[175] See above, section C.1.b.i of the present chapter (pp 297–98). Those who argue in favour of liability under § 816 I 1 BGB being capped by the value of the original asset believe that it is inappropriate to make *bona fide* possessors account in a similar way as *mala fide* possessors: cf text to n 135 above.

evident from the *mala fide* enrichee's liability under §§ 819 I, 818 IV, 285 BGB.[176] As far as English law is concerned, the second ('duty to account') approach is what might sustain an argument that A should not be able to claim the traceable proceeds of the substitution effected by B if this occurred before A had exercised his power *in rem* and/or B became aware of A's rights.[177] Neither system completely resolves the tensions between the different conceptual bases for B's liability, but both show a distinct inclination to the first ('infringement') approach where the claimant starts out with a right which is classified as 'proprietary'.[178]

A convenient anchor point for our comparative discussion is therefore the observation that claims to bargained-for substitute assets typically arise where the claimant had a proprietary interest in the original asset. In English law, rights to traceable exchange products are established by pointing to a 'proprietary base' at the beginning of the tracing exercise. It has been argued that powers *in rem* can serve as proprietary bases no less than vested rights *in rem*, even if their exercise has normally only prospective effect.[179] Under the German BGB, by contrast, where a real agreement is avoided retroactively if it can be avoided at all, the focus is on the claimant's ownership prior to the unauthorized disposition (cf § 816 I 1 BGB). Given that the scope of proprietary relief in cases of impaired consent transfers appears to be much broader in English than in German law,[180] it is unsurprising that claims to substitute assets should also be more widely available in the former. For both legal systems, the prime instance in which a claimant may wish to assert a right to an exchange product now in the defendant's hands is where his proprietary interest in the original asset has been lost through *bona fide* purchase. Yet neither system insists on this. If a third party purchaser for value does not qualify as a *bona fide* purchaser (eg because he knew of his contract partner's lack of entitlement), the claimant has a choice between following the original asset (into the hands of the third party) and asserting a right to its traceable substitute (now in the hands of the substitutor). To avoid double recovery, the latter

---

176 See above, section C.2.b of the present chapter (pp 308–9, esp n 171).

177 See above, nn 79–81 and corresponding text. Note that Khurshid/Matthews (1979) 95 LQR (n 15), for whom tracing and claiming at common law is only possible while the claimant's original property right survives, expressly draw on the principles of agency law to justify their view: cf the passage set out in n 79.

178 L Smith, "Unravelling Proprietary Restitution" (2004) 40 Can Bus LJ 317, 329–30, neatly sets out the distinctions between the two approaches in respect of trust law and concludes (at 330) that "[t]he fact that the rules about traceable proceeds are applied to innocent defendants ... shows that they have effectively hardened into rules responding to interferences with other people's property".

179 See above, section B.1.b of the present chapter (pp 289–94).

180 See above, Chapter V.D.1 (at pp 202–3).

course of conduct involves abandoning the proprietary interest in the original asset by a mechanism best described as 'ratification without authorization'.[181]

Despite the structural similarities between § 816 I 1 BGB on the one hand, and the process of tracing and claiming under English law on the other, they differ in an important respect: the nature of the claimant's right to a substitute asset. In English law, the claimant has a proprietary interest in it. On the view advanced here, it is always a power *in rem*.[182] The power may be legal or equitable,[183] depending on the nature of the claimant's proprietary base.[184] While the BGB also recognizes a principle of 'real subrogation' in some instances, it does not extend this to unauthorized substitutions generally.[185] Instead, § 816 I 1 BGB is the default provision, and it affords the claimant only a personal right to the exchange product of the original object. However, being a specifically enforceable claim to a particular asset (in other words, a right *in personam ad rem*), its assertion roughly mirrors the effects of asserting a property right in English law. It will be recalled that the beneficiary under a trust, if of full age and competent, can call for transfer of title to himself under the rule in *Saunders v Vautier*,[186] and that, where a claim in conversion is brought, the court has a discretion to order specific delivery under section 3 of the Torts (Interference with Goods) Act 1977.[187] Just as proprietary restitution of the original asset shares some features of the *condictio indebiti*,[188] so the principles of tracing and claiming to an extent align with the *Eingriffskondiktion* in § 816 I 1 BGB.

Leaving the insolvency context aside for the time being,[189] one of the main aims of identifying and claiming substitute assets instead of merely demanding restitution of the value transferred to (or 'appropriated' by) the defendant is to reap the benefits of a particularly lucrative substitution. Although concerns are regularly voiced about the insufficient recognition of the defendant's skill and effort as factors contributing towards the

---

181 See above, n 125 and corresponding text.

182 See above, section B.1.a.ii of the present chapter (pp 282–86).

183 For McFarlane *Structure of Property Law* (n 16), who denies that the common law recognizes proprietary entitlements to traceable substitute assets, common law powers *in rem* are essentially the same as vested equitable interests: ibid 150–52, 224, 299–303.

184 Note that if a person who starts out with legal title has resort to the equitable tracing rules, eg in order to follow value through a mixed fund (cf n 19 and text to nn 26–33 above), he will also end up with an equitable power *in rem*.

185 See above, section C.1.a of the present chapter (pp 296–97).

186 (1841) 4 Beav 115, 49 ER 282; aff'd (1841) Cr & Ph 240, 41 ER 482.

187 See above, Chapter IV.D.4.a (pp 154–55).

188 Cf above, Chapter V.D.1 (at pp 202–3).

189 See below, section D.2 of the present chapter (pp 314–19).

profit, both legal systems in principle acknowledge the claimant's right to participate in the economic gain. In England, the cases of *Trustee of the Property of FC Jones & Sons (a firm) v Jones*[190] and *Foskett v McKeown*[191] stand out as clearest examples of this. Under German law, the unfortunate wording of § 816 I 1 BGB has bolstered the argument that the claimant's personal right against the person effecting the unauthorized substitution ought to be capped by the value of the original asset,[192] but there are good historical and conceptual reasons for thinking otherwise.[193] Part of the reason why English law has not hitherto had to confront squarely the issue of windfall profits is probably that the claimant's proprietary interests in substitute assets are not traditionally thought of as based on the defendant's unjust enrichment. If, as *Foskett v McKeown* suggests,[194] they are simply manifestations of how 'property' behaves, then the transmission of rights from one object to another needs no justification. If, on the other hand, the interests in question are properly regarded as proprietary responses to unjust enrichment,[195] then a right to more valuable substitutes can only be sustained by those committed to a non-subtractive view of enrichment law.[196] The relevance of classification does not end here. As far as German law is concerned, the claim to *commoda ex negotiatione* under § 816 I 1 BGB is unequivocally located within the law of unjustified enrichment. In consequence, the defendant's disenrichment will – in appropriate circumstances – reduce the extent of his liability (cf § 818 III BGB).[197] We have seen that the same is not necessarily true of English law.[198] Besides the intricate technicalities of setting up a defence premised on the valuation of the defendant's wealth in the abstract against the claimant's proprietary interest in a specific chattel,[199] the change of position defence can only be meaningfully applied to powers *in rem* relating to traceable substitutes if these powers are in fact generated by unjust enrichment.

Looking at the bigger picture, we find that, with regard to substitute assets, English law is much more generous than German law to claimants

[190] [1997] Ch 159 (CA). On a possible allowance which might have been made for Mrs Jones' skill and effort see n 74 above.

[191] [2001] 1 AC 102 (HL).

[192] See above, text to nn 131–133.

[193] See above, text to nn 136–147.

[194] See above, text to nn 60–61.

[195] See above, text to nn 62–64.

[196] Cf also Smith in *Mapping the Law* (n 63) 124–26, 138–39.

[197] For substitutes other than money, this is achieved by a 'simultaneous exchange' (*Leistung Zug-um-Zug*) of the substitute and compensation for the defendant's disenrichment: cf BGH NJW 1980, 1789, 1790.

[198] See above, text to nn 67–74.

[199] Cf above, Chapter IV.D.4.b (at p 156).

in the position of our transferor A. One factor which has already been mentioned is the wider availability of proprietary restitution after impaired consent transfers. Under the BGB, very few transferors will be able to avoid the real agreement as well as their obligatory contract with B. But even where the conveyance is set aside, § 816 I 1 BGB is not nearly as far-reaching as the English principles of tracing and claiming. For one, § 816 I 1 BGB stops at the first substitution. Given the narrow interpretation of § 818 I BGB,[200] the claimant does not normally have the possibility of claiming substitutes of the substitute. His personal claim to a specific asset evaporates as soon as the defendant disposes of the first substitute, at least if the defendant acts in good faith.[201] In English law, by contrast, where tracing and claiming amount to a form of 'real subrogation', there is no theoretical limit to the number of relevant substitutions. The claimant's proprietary interest in one substitute asset serves to establish[202] his power *in rem* in respect of the next. Moreover, equity's ability to overcome evidential impasses ensures that the tracing process will not be defeated easily by the difficulties of identifying substitutes in the context of mixed funds.[203] Finally, the English approach allows the claimant to follow substitute assets into the hands of third parties and, unless the third party is a *bona fide* purchaser for value without notice, to claim them. Because § 816 I 1 BGB establishes a mere right *in personam* against the person making the unauthorized disposition (in our case the transferee B), German law is much more restrictive on this count. In accordance with § 822 BGB, third party recipients of the first substitute asset are only liable to surrender it if they received ownership gratuitously, and only to the extent that the claimant's personal right against the defendant is, as a result, excluded.[204] Hence, where B has – in good faith – exchanged A's painting for C's bicycle and then made a present of the bicycle to D, § 822 BGB imposes a duty on D to convey the bicycle to A because B is now disenriched (§ 818 III BGB). Where, however, D is a purchaser for value, the fact that he may have been

---

[200] See above, section C.2.a of the present chapter (esp text to nn 154–157).

[201] A claim to subsequent substitutes against *mala fide* defendants may arise under §§ 687 II 1, 681 2, 667, 285 BGB (cf above, n 161 and corresponding text) and/or under §§ 816 I 1, 819 I, 818 IV, 285 BGB: cf above, section C.1.b and C.2.b of the present chapter (pp 297–305, 308–9). There is a question whether § 285 BGB is applicable to claims which are themselves based on § 285 BGB. If so, the provision would enable the claimant to assert rights to a potentially endless chain of substitutes.

[202] Whether by direct 'transmission' or via the law of unjust enrichment: see above, section B.1.a.iii of the present chapter (pp 286–89).

[203] On mixed funds in German law see n 134 above (physical mixtures) and n 210 below (bank accounts).

[204] § 822 BGB undoubtedly applies in the context of § 816 I 1 BGB: RGZ 98, 131, 136. On the operation of § 822 BGB see above, Chapter VI.B.2.b.ii (pp 225–26).

aware of B's obligation to surrender the bicycle to A is irrelevant under the current German law. It was argued above that, subject to the rule against double recovery, A's personal claim against B should also be exigible against the *mala fide* purchaser in this situation.[205] The argument applies in the context of § 816 I 1 BGB (*Eingriffskondiktion* establishing claim to substitute asset after unauthorized substitution) as much as in the context of § 812 I 1 alt 1 BGB (*Leistungskondiktion* establishing claim to original asset after *indebite* transfer). Although the claimant's rights to substitute assets would still be less extensive in German than under English law, they would at least survive as against *mala fide* purchasers from the defendant owner.

2. Segregation of Substitute Assets in Insolvency

Normally, one of the characteristic distinctions between having a property right relating to a thing (right *in rem*) and having a personal right to demand a transfer of that thing (right *in personam ad rem acquirendam*) is that the former, but not the latter, privileges the claimant right-holder in the defendant's insolvency. What belongs to another person does not form part of the insolvent's estate. A mere obligation to convey a specific asset, by contrast, has no effect on the estate, and unless the claimant can assert special priority over the defendant's general creditors, he ranks *pari passu* and joins the queue for the quota. When comparing the German and English positions on the transferor's rights against the transferee with regard to the original asset, we saw this borne out. It was observed that while the wide availability of proprietary restitution in English law afforded the transferor a significant measure of protection in the transferee's insolvency, transferors under the BGB were only 'privileged' if they managed to rescind the real agreement.[206] Unlike the *vindicatio* (§ 985 BGB), which is backed by a right of segregation in insolvency (*Aussonderungsrecht*: § 47 InsO), the *condictio indebiti* (§ 812 I 1 alt 1 BGB) was deliberately denied any form of preference by the BGB legislator.[207]

---

[205] See above, Chapter VI.D.1.a (at pp 253–55). Two versions of a direct claim by A against the *mala fide* purchaser D were floated there. On the first, D would always be liable to A, irrespective of whether or not B can rely on § 818 III BGB (ie irrespective of B's *bona* or *mala fides*). On the second, more restrictive version, D's liability to A would depend on the latter exhausting his remedies against B first. No direct claim by A against D would normally exist if B was aware of his liability to A under § 816 I 1 BGB when entering into the transaction with D. An exception might only be envisaged for cases where B has meanwhile become insolvent and A fails fully to realize his rights against B (on which question cf section D.2 of the present chapter, esp text to nn 222–224 below).

[206] See above, Chapter V.D.3 (at pp 206–7).

[207] Cf *Protokolle: vol 2* (n 122) 721–24.

One might expect that the *Eingriffskondiktion* in § 816 I 1 BGB, being no more than a right *in personam ad rem*, would be treated in very much the same way as the *Leistungskondiktion* in § 812 I 1 alt 1 BGB, and that therefore rights to substitute assets would generally receive less protection in German than in English law. Yet this is not the case. Entitled 'segregation of substitutes' (*Ersatzaussonderung*), § 48 InsO provides:

"If the debtor, prior to the commencement of the insolvency proceedings, or after their commencement the administrator, has, without authorization, disposed of an object which was subject to a right of segregation, then the person entitled to segregation may demand assignment of the right to the counter-performance to the extent that the latter is still outstanding. He can claim the counter-performance from the [insolvent's] estate to the extent that it still remains identifiable within the estate."

This provision, which has come to be understood as premised on – rather than generating – a personal right to the substitute asset,[208] ensures that a person who had or would have had a right to segregate a particular object from the insolvent's estate (cf § 47 InsO) is not disadvantaged by the fact that the object has since been disposed of by the insolvent or his administrative receiver.[209] In short: where the original asset did not form part of the estate, its substitute should not do so either. If the substitute has not yet reached the defendant's estate, the claimant can demand assignment of the defendant's contractual right to counter-performance. If the counter-performance has already been rendered, then – provided it is still identifiable – it will be segregated from the estate.[210] Like its slightly more

---

[208] RGZ 115, 262, 264; RGZ 138, 89, 92; E Jaeger, *Kommentar zur Konkursordnung, vol 1: §§ 1–46* (6th/7th edn de Gruyter, Berlin 1931) § 46 [3]; HG Ganter, "Zweifelsfragen bei der Ersatzaussonderung und der Ersatzabsonderung" NZI 2005, 1, esp 2–3; P Gottwald (ed), *Insolvenzrechts-Handbuch* (3rd edn Beck, München 2006) [41.2] (Gottwald); U Gundlach, *Der Ersatzaussonderungsberechtigte* (Lang, Frankfurt/Main 1994) 37–41; HP Kirchhof, HJ Lwowski and R Stürner (eds), *Münchener Kommentar zur Insolvenzordnung, vol 1: §§ 1–102* (2nd edn Beck, München 2007) § 48 [7] (Ganter); S Smid (ed), *Insolvenzordnung: Kommentar* (2nd edn Kohlhammer, Stuttgart 2002) § 48 [9]–[12] (Gundlach). Cf also R Böhm, *Surrogation trotz Unwirksamkeit einer Verfügung?* (Doctoral Thesis, Hamburg 1973) 55–59. Contrast: H Hess, *Insolvenzrecht: Großkommentar, vol 1: §§ 1–112 InsO* (Müller, Heidelberg 2007) § 48 [3] (Hess), who refers to the claimant's *original* right being supported by means of a "*haftungsrechtliche Surrogation*" ("subrogation for liability purposes") without adverting to the requirement of a personal claim to the substitute. Insufficiently clear: B Kübler and H Prütting (eds), *Kommentar zur Insolvenzordnung, vol 1: §§ 1–128* (last update April 2008: RWS, Köln 1998–2008) § 48 [4] (Prütting).

[209] Cf eg *Münchener Kommentar InsO: vol 1* (n 208) § 48 [3]–[4] (Ganter).

[210] Interestingly from a comparative point of view, the Federal Supreme Court now applies a kind of 'lowest intermediate balance rule' (so-called '*Bodensatztheorie*') to identify the traceable proceeds of an unauthorized disposition where money has been

restrictive predecessor in § 46 KO (in force until 1998),[211] § 48 InsO has its main field of application in the context of § 816 I 1 BGB.[212] Returning to our example, assume again that B exchanges A's painting for C's bicycle and then becomes insolvent. § 48 InsO allows A to assert his claim to the bicycle (§ 816 I 1 BGB) irrespective of B's insolvency. In practice, he is no worse off in German than under English law. To this extent, the possibility of segregating substitute assets via § 48 InsO obliterates the distinction between a personal claim to and a property right in *commoda ex negotiatione*.

Two particular questions arising in the context of § 48 InsO have a bearing on the scenario here under consideration. One is whether the provision applies where the unauthorized disposition, though not effective without more, is subsequently ratified by the claimant. In other words, does C have to be a *bona fide* purchaser (§§ 932 ff BGB), or is it sufficient that A's claim against B (unter § 816 I 1 BGB) is based on retroactive ratification (§§ 185, 184 I BGB)? It has been suggested that B's disposition should not count as 'unauthorized' in the latter case.[213] This looks plau-

---

paid into a current account, ie a mixed fund: BGHZ 141, 116. On the English position see above, n 20 and corresponding text.

211 Under § 46 KO, it was not possible to segregate the substitute itself if it had been conveyed to the insolvent before the commencement of insolvency proceedings. Where performance had not yet been rendered, the claimant could demand assignment of the contractual right to performance. Critical of the expansion effected by § 48 InsO: A Dieckmann, "Zur Reform des Ersatzaussonderungsrechts" in W Gerhardt and others (eds), *Festschrift für Wolfram Henckel zum 70. Geburtstag am 21. April 1995* (de Gruyter, Berlin 1995) 95, 101–14; L Häsemeyer, *Insolvenzrecht* (4th edn Heymanns, Köln 2007) [11.19]–[11.20].

212 It is not entirely clear whether § 48 InsO also applies where substitutes are claimed under §§ 687 II 1, 681 2, 667, (285) BGB. The normal claim by a mandator against his mandatee (§ 667 BGB) does not attract the privileges of 'segregation' unless it coincides with a *Treuhand* relationship: *Münchener Kommentar InsO: vol 1* (n 208) § 47 [355] (Ganter). Such a *Treuhand* relationship is commonly thought to exist in respect of goods which the mandator has entrusted to the mandatee for the purposes of the mandate (claim under § 667 alt 1 BGB), but tends to be denied as far as the mandatee's obligation to surrender *other* objects acquired in connection with the mandate (claim under § 667 alt 2 BGB) is concerned: *Münchener Kommentar InsO: vol 1* (n 208) § 47 [355] (Ganter). The reason why a mandator cannot usually segregate substitute assets must be because he has authorized the original disposition (as 'owner' and/or *Treuhand* 'beneficiary'). In our case, however, the claimant's decision to assert his rights under § 687 II 1 BGB need not necessarily amount to a genuine 'ratification' of the defendant's conduct any more than in the context of § 816 I 1 BGB. Viewed in this light, § 48 InsO should probably indeed be applicable to claims based on §§ 687 II 1, 681 2, 667, (285) BGB.

213 Jaeger *Kommentar KO: vol 1* (n 208) § 46 [3]; E Jaeger, *Lehrbuch des Deutschen Konkursrechts* (8th edn de Gruyter, Berlin 1932) 108 fn 27. Similar: Häsemeyer *Insolvenzrecht* (n 211) [11.22]. Insufficiently clear: *Münchener Kommentar InsO: vol 1* (n 208)

sible if one considers that A has deliberately chosen to demand the substitute asset instead of following and claiming the original from the third party C. However, the prevailing view is that segregation of substitutes is possible despite ratification.[214] A's act of ratifying B's transfer to C does not, after all, amount to an endorsement of B's conduct (it is a 'ratification without authorization').[215] § 48 InsO would therefore seem to apply to all counter-performances and claims to counter-performance, provided that the defendant's disposition is effective either through *bona fide* purchase or ratification.[216]

The second issue we need to address concerns the question of so-called 'chain segregation of substitutes' (*Kettenersatzaussonderung*). Imagine that B, after exchanging A's painting for C's bicycle, sells the bicycle for € 100 and later uses the money to buy a valuable book. Can A now rely on § 48 InsO to argue that the book does not form part of B's estate? It is widely suggested or simply assumed that this should be possible.[217] Attempts to

---

§ 48 [27] (Ganter), but contrast [43] (Ganter); *Kübler/Prütting: vol 1* (n 208) § 48 [14] (Prütting), but contrast [13] (Prütting). This question is closely connected to – but not necessarily co-extensive with – the question whether a claim under § 816 I 1 BGB can be established through retroactive ratification of the unauthorized disposition: see above, n 124 and corresponding text. On the predominant understanding of § 48 InsO (cf text to n 208 above), a positive answer to the second question would be a necessary, but not a sufficient, condition for holding that § 48 InsO also applies in the ratification context.

[214] Böhm *Surrogation* (n 208) 66–69; Dieckmann in *Festschrift Henckel* (n 211) 115–16; W Henckel, "Grenzen der Vermögenshaftung" JuS 1985, 836, 840; U Gundlach, "Notwendigkeit einer wirksamen Veräußerung für die Ersatzaussonderung" KTS 1997, 211, 216–17. Contra: Häsemeyer *Insolvenzrecht* (n 211) [11.22]. Note that where A chooses to (or if he were forced to) bring a *vindicatio* against C in respect of the original asset, any consequential claim of C's against B (eg for repayment of the purchase price) would – bar exceptional circumstances – rank *pari passu* with the claims of B's general creditors. Ratification by A therefore effectively diminishes the estate.

[215] See above, text to n 125.

[216] Although the necessity for a valid conveyance has been disputed, there is no good reason why the claimant should not be made to choose between claiming the original asset from the third party recipient and ratifying the conveyance in order to claim its substitute: cf Böhm *Surrogation* (n 208) 66–69; Gundlach KTS 1997 (n 214) esp 215–18. Indeed, on the predominant view of § 48 InsO as dependent on the existence of some other private law claim (see above, n 208 and corresponding text), the effectiveness of the conveyance is a *conditio sine qua non*: cf also comment in n 213.

[217] Ganter NZI 2005 (n 208) 6–7; W Gerhardt, "Der Surrogationsgedanke im Konkursrecht – dargestellt an der Ersatzaussonderung" KTS 1990, 1, 3; *Kübler/Prütting: vol 1* (n 208) § 48 [6] (Prütting); U Gundlach, V Frenzel and A Schirrmeister, "Nochmals – die sogenannte zweite Ersatzaussonderung" KTS 2003, 69; *Münchener Kommentar InsO: vol 1* (n 208) § 48 [74]–[77] (Ganter). Dealing with the issue only for substitutions by the administrator after commencement of insolvency proceedings (under the regime of the old § 46 KO): Gundlach *Der Ersatzaussonderungsberechtigte* (n 208) 111–19, esp 116–17; U Gundlach, "Die sogenannte 'Zweite Ersatzaussonderung'" KTS 1997, 453,

justify the conclusion usually focus on the functional similarity between § 47 InsO and § 48 InsO as well as on the deserving position of the claimant when compared with the defendant's other creditors.[218] However, at least in the ordinary case of § 816 I 1 BGB, it is hard to see how such a 'chain segregation' could work conceptually.[219] Given that § 48 InsO merely re-enforces an existing claim and does not itself generate a right to substitutes,[220] A would have to show that B was under an obligation to surrender the book to him (rather than just an amount of money). Yet we have already seen that § 816 I 1 BGB stops at first substitutions and that § 818 I BGB – in the next instance – does not yield a claim to the *commodum ex negotiatione*.[221] With the possible exception of cases in which B acted *mala fide*,[222] A cannot demand surrender of the third substitute (book) any

---

esp 456–59. Against the possibility of 'chain segregation': Dieckmann in *Festschrift Henckel* (n 211) 103–5; Häsemeyer *Insolvenzrecht* (n 211) [11.24]; I Scherer, "Zulässigkeit einer 'zweiten Ersatzaussonderung'?" KTS 2002, 197.

218 Cf esp Gerhardt KTS 1990 (n 217) 2–3, 10–11; Gundlach KTS 1997 (n 217) 457–58; Henckel JuS 1985 (n 214) 840–41.

219 On the case in which B acted *mala fide* see n 222 below.

220 See above, n 208 and corresponding text.

221 See above, text to n 200. The problem created by the fact that the second substitution leads to a value-based claim under §§ 816 I 1, 818 II BGB is seen by some of the authors who favour chain segregation. In the first edition of HP Kirchhof, HJ Lwowski and R Stürner (eds), *Münchener Kommentar zur Insolvenzordnung, vol 1: §§ 1–102* (Beck, München 2001) § 48 [75], Ganter wanted to solve it by repeated recourse to § 816 I 1 BGB. However, he now concedes that § 816 I 1 BGB is inapplicable and seeks to invoke § 285 BGB instead: *Münchener Kommentar InsO: vol 1* (n 208) § 48 [75a]. Gundlach *Der Ersatzaussonderungsberechtigte* (n 208) 118–19, concludes that, as a result of the exclusion of the *commodum ex negotiatione* from § 818 I BGB, segregation of the second substitute may be impossible after all, but the relevant passage no longer features in Gundlach KTS 1997 (n 217). The most recent publication, Gundlach/Frenzel/Schirrmeister KTS 2003 (n 217) 72–74, also places reliance on § 285 BGB. Note, however, that the application of § 285 BGB requires the substitution to have been effected *mala fide*: cf above, n 201, and immediately below, n 222 and corresponding text.

222 A claim to second and perhaps further substitutes would seem to be available under §§ 816 I 1, 819 I, 818 IV, 285 BGB (where B was *mala fide* at the time of effecting the second substitution) or under §§ 687 II 1, 681 2, 667, 285 BGB (where B was already *mala fide* when disposing of the original asset): see n 201 above. There is, however, some uncertainty about the applicability of § 48 InsO to claims based on § 285 BGB: Dieckmann in *Festschrift Henckel* (n 211) 103–5, for example, doubts whether a *mala fide* defendant's liability under §§ 816 I 1, 819 I, 818 IV, 285 BGB can be used to justify 'chain segregation'. First, he asks whether § 285 (the old § 281 BGB) is at all applicable to claims which are themselves a product of § 285 BGB: ibid fn 32. Second, he disputes that § 285 BGB operates in the context of § 816 I 1 BGB: ibid fn 32. Finally, he points out that even if it were possible to construct a 'chain of substitutions' in the case of *mala fide* enrichees, a personal right to *commoda ex negotiatione* under § 285 BGB is not generally regarded as entitling the claimant to segregation under § 46 KO (now § 48 InsO):

more than he could have demanded surrender of the second substitute (€ 100: the specific notes and coins obtained from the sale of the bicycle), since both of these constitute the exchange products of assets belonging to B at the time of the relevant disposition.[223] While the acceptance of 'chain segregation' appears to open the door to a more extensive application of tracing and claiming in German law, it should not tempt us into granting to the claimant rights exceeding those he would otherwise have, merely because the defendant happens to be insolvent.[224]

E. Summary

In summary, claims to substitute assets are more widely available after impaired consent transfers under English than in German law. This is due to two main factors: the divergent extent of proprietary relief with regard to the original asset on the one hand, and the acceptance of a general principle of 'real subrogation' in English but not in German law on the other.

---

ibid 104–5. Similarly against the application of § 48 InsO to claims based on § 285 BGB: Scherer KTS 2002 (n 217) 204–5. Contrast: Ganter NZI 2005 (n 208) 5–6; Gundlach/Frenzel/Schirrmeister KTS 2003 (n 217) 73–76; *Münchener Kommentar InsO: vol 1* (n 208) § 48 [8], [8b] (Ganter). The latter authors see no reason why segregation of substitutes should not extend to cases where a privileged personal claim (such as one under § 816 I 1 BGB, § 48 InsO) is affected by the defendant's disposition. This brings § 285 BGB into the remit of § 48 InsO, and 'chain segregation' becomes a possibility. Its ultimate reach, however, depends on the proper interpretation of § 285 BGB: cf discussion in n 223 immediately below.

[223] If – as seems appropriate – one accepts the possibility in principle of 'chain segregation' for cases in which B acted *mala fide* and in which A is therefore entitled to claim the substitute's substitute from his estate via §§ 285 BGB, 48 InsO (cf n 222 above), there is still a question about how far § 285 BGB actually extends: cf n 201 above. Depending on whether the provision is applicable to claims themselves based on § 285 BGB (denied by Dieckmann in *Festschrift Henckel:* cf n 222), A's right of segregation will extend either only to the second substitute (€ 100 cash) or even beyond this, namely to the third (book) and any further substitutes.

[224] A broader view of § 48 InsO could be defended only if one saw the provision as operating independently of an ordinary civil claim to the substitute: cf n 208 and corresponding text. Such an estate-oriented interpretation seems to inform the views of Gerhardt KTS 1990 (n 217) esp 3, and Henckel JuS 1985 (n 214) 840–41. Similar concerns are evident in the work of Behr *Wertverfolgung* (n 3) esp 287–92, 336–38, 348–52, 389–98, 405, 605–6, 609–11, 613–15, who seeks ways of better accommodating 'tracing and claiming' in German law. Behr does, however, take full account of the restrictions inherent in the old § 46 KO (some of which have since been lifted: cf n 211 above), and accepts in particular that the provision allowing for 'segregation of substitutes' does not create new liabilities where none existed outside insolvency: cf Behr *Wertverfolgung* (n 3) 290–91, 349, 611.

Although personal wrongs-based claims to disgorgement of profits are of some importance in English law, attention focuses mainly on the transferor's proprietary interests in substitutes established via the principles of tracing and claiming. It has been argued that while we may not normally think of powers *in rem* as sufficient 'proprietary bases', they ought to be so recognized and have long been implicitly accepted as such in the case law. The greatest challenges on the road ahead now lie in assimilating and – ideally – harmonizing the tracing rules at law and in equity, and in authoritatively determining the conceptual foundation for proprietary interests in traceable substitute assets.

In German law, the exclusion of *commoda ex negotiatione* from § 818 I BGB puts ordinary enrichment creditors in a relatively weak position as regards substitutions effected by the transferee. This is partly counterbalanced by recourse to § 285 BGB for the purposes of stripping at least *mala fide* enrichees of their profits. The nearest functional equivalent to the broad English principles of tracing and claiming is constituted by the *Eingriffskondiktion* in § 816 I 1 BGB. It accords the transferor who has successfully avoided his conveyance of the original asset a personal claim to the (first) exchange product where an unauthorized substitution has occurred. Most significantly from a comparative perspective, the claim under § 816 I 1 BGB does not depend on *bona fide* purchase, arises independently of the substitutor's state of mind, is not capped by the value of the original asset, and is protected even in the defendant's insolvency. The difference to English law lies in the fact that second and further substitutes can (usually) only be demanded from the original substitutor, and only if that original substitutor acted in bad faith when effecting the relevant substitution(s).

Part Four:

Summing Up

Chapter IX

Conclusion

This book has sought to provide a comparative structural analysis of the English and German law governing impaired consent transfers of movable property, focusing in particular on the mechanisms of their unwinding in both two- and three-party situations. Given the complex interaction between different rules and principles within each legal system and the concomitant need for a relatively broad scope of inquiry, it has not been possible to provide more than a bird's-eye view of the landscape. As Frederick H Lawson famously remarked, "[i]n a sense, a comparative lawyer is bound to be superficial; he would soon lose himself in the sands of scholarship".[1] It is to be hoped that, despite its inevitable 'superficiality', the present study has nevertheless been successful at exposing the processes by which German and English lawyers arrive at certain solutions to certain sets of facts. Once we recognize that legal rules and principles do not exist in isolation, and once we understand the context of their operation, the 'black box' constituted by each legal system as a *system* sheds its veil and surrenders its mysteries.[2]

In view of the many levels at which comparisons and contrasts between the English and German law on impaired consent transfers are possible and illuminating (and we have only been able to touch upon the most pertinent aspects), it seems appropriate by way of conclusion to draw the strings together and to highlight some of the main themes. What follows is neither a comprehensive overview of the book, nor even a systematic summary of each chapter, but instead a collection of motifs which have in various places emerged from the discussion.

When looking at the kinds of impairments of consent relevant in the contractual/bargaining context, we saw that English law adopts a wholly 'procedural' or 'process-oriented' approach to rescission of contract, while German law contains a mix of 'process-oriented' (§ 123 BGB) and 'content-oriented' or 'substantive' grounds for avoidance (§ 119 BGB). This leads both legal systems to largely parallel results in cases of fraud or duress, but entails a patchy picture for other impairments of consent. A

[1] FH Lawson, "The Field of Comparative Law" (1949) 61 Jurid Rev 16.

[2] On the 'black box' metaphor see above, Chapter I.A (text to n 7 on p 5).

substantial overlap between rescission for non-fraudulent misrepresentation in English law and mistakes recognized by § 119 BGB exists only in the case of errors about an essential quality of the person or object to which the contract relates (cf § 119 II BGB). Mistakes about the terms of an agreement (cf § 119 I BGB), if induced by the other party, do not entail a right to rescind, but are usually addressed as a logically prior matter of interpretation. As far as 'motivational mistakes' induced by negligent misrepresentation are concerned, the German rules on liability for *culpa in contrahendo* to an extent bridge the 'lacuna' which exists between § 123 I alt 1 BGB and § 119 BGB (albeit that the gap would arguably be better filled by an analogous application of § 123 BGB). Beyond this, 'undue influence', an equitable ground for rescission in English law, will sometimes amount to an immoral exploitation of a person's emotional attachment or other dependency and thus render the transaction in question void under § 138 BGB.

The relationship between contract and conveyance is more clearly defined in German than in English law. Under the BGB, contract and conveyance are distinct legal transactions (principle of separation). The validity of the latter does not depend on the existence or validity of the former (principle of abstraction). Except in cases where the conveyance is expressly made conditional upon the effectiveness of the obligatory contract, or where both transactions suffer from the same defect (typically in cases of fraud and duress), the transfer of ownership is irrevocable. If it has to be reversed, the parties' relationship is governed not by the rules applying between the owner of an object and its illegitimate possessor (§§ 985 ff BGB), but by the law on unjustified enrichment (§§ 812 ff BGB). The transferor has a personal claim to re-conveyance of the object transferred (a right *in personam ad rem acquirendam*). In English law, contracts of sale are capable of acting as vehicles of conveyance, but a delivery is required in all (or most)[3] other cases. To that extent, English law also adheres to a principle of separation. As far as abstraction is concerned, it was argued that the effectiveness of a conveyance by delivery does not depend on the existence or validity of any underlying contract or other legal basis, and that this applies in equity just as much as at common law. Even where a right to restitution arises at the moment of transfer without the need for a prior rescission of contract, as eg in the case of a gift induced by the transferee's misrepresentation, the transferor does not have a fully vested interest under a trust, but a mere (legal or equitable) power *in rem*. It was further argued that, despite the 'abstract' nature of conveyances by delivery in English law, much of the gist of abstraction is lost as a result of English

[3] It is unclear whether – and, if so, how far – the *solo consensu* rule extends beyond sale to barter and other agreements supported by valuable consideration.

law's process-oriented approach to rescission and avoidance of agreements generally. Identity of defect is not the exception (as under the German BGB), but the norm. Moreover, if – as was suggested here – proprietary restitution in the form of a power extends to appropriate cases of spontaneous mistake, eg where the transferor was acting under a self-induced liability mistake, one could be forgiven for believing English personal property law to be wholly 'causal', at least in equity. The transferor is virtually always left with a choice between asserting a personal claim to the value of the transferee's enrichment and asserting a proprietary interest in the object conveyed (after exercising his power *in rem*). However, in contradistinction to German law, it was noted that the exercise of the power *in rem* seems, for certain purposes, to have only prospective effect under English law. This prevents innocent parties from becoming strictly liable to the transferor in the law of wrongs for acts which were entirely legitimate when carried out.

In the relationship between transferor and transferee, the wider availability of proprietary relief in English law has two main effects. The first concerns the transferor's position in the transferee's insolvency. While the fathers of the BGB consciously declined the opportunity to afford preferential treatment to ordinary enrichment creditors (thereby exacerbating the incongruities between the bulk of transfers unwound according to §§ 812 ff BGB and the exceptional cases governed by §§ 985 ff BGB), English law – though still in a state of flux – is capable of granting most transferors protection. It was argued that if such preferential treatment seems unwarranted from a policy point of view, English law should not tamper with the conceptual underpinnings of proprietary restitution, but adjust its insolvency regime (eg by extending the old doctrine of 'reputed ownership'). The second aspect is connected with the first. We have seen that both legal systems allow the transferor to claim traceable substitute assets from the transferee where he can point to a proprietary interest in the original object. Under the BGB, this shows up in the discrepancy between (the conventional understandings of) § 818 I BGB and § 816 I 1 BGB. An enrichment creditor is confined to recovering the value of the original asset, while the owner of an object disposed of by its illegitimate possessor has a right to demand surrender of the substitute itself, including any profit this entails. If the scope of proprietary restitution is indeed much broader in English than in German law, and if, additionally, the so-called 'third party rights bar to rescission' is recognized as in no way relevant to the relationship between the original contracting parties, then English law will necessarily arrive at a much more comprehensive coverage against the risk of alienation than German law. The point is reinforced when we consider that tracing and claiming in English law amount to a process of 'real subrogation', enabling the transferor to follow the value of the original asset through any number of substitutions. By contrast, even though a claim under § 816 I 1 BGB – where available – is supplanted by the possibility of segregating substitute assets in the transferee's insolvency (§ 48 InsO), it is nevertheless merely a right *in personam ad rem*. As such, the possibility of segregating further substitutes depends on the existence of a further claim *in personam ad rem* (which cannot be founded on § 818 I BGB, but may be derived from § 285 BGB vis-à-vis *mala fide* substitutors).

As against third parties who have purchased the original asset (or one of its traceable substitutes), the transferor's position is determined by several factors. A claim with respect to an object acquired by the third party from the transferee will lie if the transferor has a proprietary interest in it, or if – despite not having a proprietary interest – the legal system exceptionally allows him to 'leapfrog' the transferee and to bring a direct personal claim in unjust enrichment against the third party. In consequence of the principle of abstraction, flanked by a general defence of *bona fide* purchase (§§ 932 ff BGB), German law is very restrictive about recovery from third parties on the proprietary level. The transferor will only be able to bring a *vindicatio* for the original object if the real agreement he struck with the transferee was for some reason void or voidable *and* if the third party was in bad faith when acquiring the object from the transferee. Substitute assets received by the third party can never be vindicated. The hurdles in English law are much lower. Given that it lacks the gist of abstraction and does not have a general principle of *bona fide* purchase, the third party obtains a title which is good as against the transferor only in two situations. First, in the case where the transferor had an equitable interest in or an unexercised power relating to the asset in question (whether that be the original chattel or a traceable substitute), if the third party purchaser acted in good faith without notice of the transferor's rights and provided valuable consideration. Second, in the case where the transferor had a vested right to immediate possession of the object (especially after exercising a legal power *in rem*), if the transaction between transferee and third party happens to fall under the *nemo dat* exception contained in section 25(1) of the Sale of Goods Act 1979 as interpreted in *Newtons of Wembley Ltd v Williams*.[4] It was suggested that, in the light of the haphazard application of section 25(1), the Law Commission should consider generalizing the defence when it next reviews the law on *bona fide* purchase.

At the personal level, German law to some extent compensates for the effects of abstraction and the broad scope of *bona fide* purchase in three-party cases. If the third party has received the object in question gratui-

[4] [1964] 1 WLR 1028 (QBD), aff'd [1965] 1 QB 560 (CA). The case was actually argued and decided on the basis of the parallel provision in the Factors Act 1889, s 9.

tously, the transferor may be able to claim it back. § 816 I 2 BGB applies where the third party acquired ownership of the object by virtue of the rules on *bona fide* purchase (which in German law do not depend on the provision of consideration), while § 822 BGB operates where the transferee was actually the owner of the object conveyed to the third party, eg as a result of the principle of abstraction.[5] It was argued here that the BGB should provide a personal claim similar to § 822 BGB for cases where the third party is a *mala fide* purchaser of an object to which the transferor has a personal right (under § 812 I 1 alt 1 BGB or under § 816 I 1 BGB).

Due to the wider availability of relief at the proprietary level in English law, the possibility of 'leapfrogging' the transferee in order to establish a personal claim against third parties is of less relevance than in German law. Unless the third party qualifies as a *bona fide* purchaser for value, a 'proprietary link' will enable the transferor to assert a right in respect of the third party's 'enrichment'. Where the enrichment survives *in specie* or at least traceably, the existence of a proprietary interest is simply a function of the principles of following, tracing and claiming. So far as the third party's abstractly surviving enrichment is concerned, the transferor will have an appropriate personal claim.[6] It was suggested here that this personal claim need not (necessarily) be a product of and parasitic upon the 'proprietary link' between the parties, but that it could also constitute a hitherto unrecognized example of 'leapfrogging'. Even in the absence of a 'proprietary link', leapfrogging should be allowed whenever there is no danger of undermining the pattern of contractual relationships between the parties. We may – in the end – find that the survival of a transferor's power *in rem* as against any person who does not qualify as *bona fide* purchaser is little more than an instance of proprietary restitution from remote enrichees.

Finally, a word on different types of transactions. The doctrine of consideration accounts for a bright dividing line between bargains and non-bargain agreements in English law. German law, with its broader notion of 'contract', differentiates less sharply between the two, but nevertheless contains certain reflections of the distinction. In the realm of executed reciprocal contracts, we find special adjustments to the normal regime of the law on unjust(ified) enrichment in both jurisdictions. Under English law, the impossibility of exact *restitutio in integrum* was long regarded as a bar to rescission, but this 'bar' is now best interpreted as imposing a

[5] With regard to substitute assets, it is the lack of a general principle of 'real subrogation' which accounts for the fact that the unauthorized disposer obtains ownership of the substitute asset, which he can then pass on to any third party purchaser.

[6] The only question is whether a claimant can have both a vested property right *and* a fully-fledged personal claim based on unjust enrichment *at the same time*.

requirement of counter-restitution. German lawyers, on the other hand, have grappled with the problem through the introduction of the so-called *Saldotheorie* or – in modification of the traditional two-claims theory – via a restrictive approach towards the disenrichment clause in § 818 III BGB. In both legal systems, gratuitous transactions are in some respects 'weaker' than transactions for value. This is most evident in relation to third parties. English law premises the defence of *bona fide* purchase on the provision of valuable consideration, while German law often allows the transferor a personal claim against donees from the transferee (§§ 816 I 2, 822 BGB). The weakness of gratuitous acquisitions is less marked in two-party situations. It was argued here that, after the adoption of a causative mistake test by the landmark case of *Barclays Bank Ltd v WJ Simms Son & Cooke (Southern) Ltd*,[7] English law should allow recovery for all mistaken gifts, whether the mistake was induced or spontaneous, and whether or not it was 'fundamental'. German law is hitherto precluded by §§ 119 ff BGB from adopting a similarly generous approach. Restitution for *inter vivos* gifts made under the impression of a motivational mistake could only follow if a provision similar to that in § 2078 II BGB (governing rescission of testamentary gifts) were introduced into §§ 516 ff BGB.

"In law context is everything", Lord Steyn remarked in *R v Secretary of State for the Home Department, ex p Daly*.[8] His Lordship was considering the intensity of judicial review in administrative cases, but his observation applies equally to the comparative study of private law. The concern here has been with the legal context within which the general principles and specific rules of the English and German law of contract, property and unjust(ified) enrichment operate. Many of the issues raised would merit books to themselves. If the present one can help set the structural framework for further research, its aim will have been achieved.

[7] [1980] QB 677 (QBD Comm).

[8] [2001] UKHL 26, [2001] 2 AC 532, [28].

Appendix:

Translation of German Statutory Provisions[1]

Bürgerliches Gesetzbuch (BGB)[2]

Book I: General Part

Things and Animals [§§ 90–103]

§ 90 Concept of Thing
Under this statute, only corporeal objects count as things.

§ 99 Fruits
(1) The fruits of a thing [→ § 90] are its produce as well as any other yield which is reaped in accordance with the designated purpose of the thing.
(2) The fruits of a right are those proceeds which the right affords in accordance with its designated purpose...
(3) The proceeds which a thing or a right affords in consequence of a legal relationship also count as [its] fruits.

§ 100 Secondary Benefits
Secondary benefits are the fruits of a thing or of a right as well as the benefits which are afforded by the use of the thing or of the right.

Declaration of Intention [§§ 116–144]

§ 119 Voidability for Mistake
(1) A person who, when making a declaration of intention, was mistaken about its content, or did not intend to make a declaration with such content at all, can avoid the declaration, if it is to be assumed that he would not have made it in knowledge of all the relevant facts and on a rational appreciation of the case.
(2) A mistake about such characteristics of a person or a thing which are commonly regarded as essential is also deemed to be a mistake about the content of the declaration.

---

[1] The translation is my own. Additions in square brackets are explantory only and do not appear in the original German text.

[2] Headings are inserted for the convenience of the reader, without any attempt to reflect the various different 'levels' into which the five books of the BGB are arranged (sections, titles, subtitles, and chapters).

§ 120 Voidability for Miscommunication
A declaration of intention which has been incorrectly communicated by the person or institution used for the communication can be avoided under the same condition as § 119 stipulates for a declaration of intention made by mistake.

§ 121 Time Limit for Avoidance
(1) In the cases of §§ 119, 120, the avoidance [of the declaration of intention] must take place without culpable delay (immediately) after the person entitled to avoid [it] has acquired knowledge of the ground for avoidance. [...]
(2) Avoidance is excluded if ten years have passed since the declaration of intention was made.

§ 122 Rescinding Party's Liability to Compensate
(1) If a declaration of intention ... has been avoided on the basis of §§ 119, 120, then, if the declaration was one addressed to another party, the person making it must compensate the other ... for any loss suffered as a result of relying on the validity of the declaration, but not beyond the amount of the interest which the other ... has in the validity of the declaration [ie the expectation/performance interest].
(2) The liability to compensate does not arise if the party suffering the loss knew of the ... ground for avoidance or would have known of it but for his negligence (ought to have known).

§ 123 Voidability for Fraudulent Misrepresentation or Duress
(1) A person who has been induced to make a declaration of intention by means of a fraudulent misrepresentation or unlawfully through duress can avoid that declaration.
(2) If the fraudulent misrepresentation was made by a third party, a declaration addressed to another can only be avoided if that other knew or ought to have known [→ § 122 II] of the deception. [...]

§ 124 Time Limit for Avoidance
(1) The avoidance of a declaration of intention which is voidable under § 123 can only take place within one year.
(2) In the case of fraudulent misrepresentation, the limitation period begins to run from the moment when the person entitled to avoid [the declaration of intention] discovers the deception; in the case of duress it begins to run when the state of compulsion ends. [...]
(3) Avoidance is excluded if ten years have passed since the declaration of intention was made.

§ 133 Interpretation of a Declaration of Intention
In interpreting a declaration of intention, the true intention is to be ascertained rather than adhering to the literal meaning of the expression.

§ 134 Statutory Prohibition
A legal transaction which violates a statutory prohibition is void unless the contrary appears from the [relevant] statute.

§ 138 Immoral Legal Transaction, Usury
(1) A legal transaction which contravenes [the standard of] good morals is void.
(2) In particular, any legal transaction is void by which a person, through exploiting another's predicament, inexperience, lack of judgement or considerable weakness of will,

causes economic benefits to be promised or granted to himself or [to] a third party in return for a performance, if these economic benefits are conspicuously disproportionate to the [value of the] performance.

§ 139 Partial Invalidity
If a part of a legal transaction is void, then the entire transaction is void unless it is to be assumed that it would have been entered into even without the void part.

§ 142 Effect of Avoidance
(1) If a voidable legal transaction is avoided, it is to be regarded as void *ab initio*.
(2) A person who knew or ought to have known [→ § 122 II] of the voidability is, when avoidance occurs, [to be] treated as if he had known or as if he ought to have known [→ § 122 II] of its invalidity.

§ 143 Declaration of Avoidance
(1) Avoidance occurs by way of declaration to the opposing party.
(2) In the case of a contract, the opposing party is the other party [to the contract] ...
(3) [...]
(4) [...]

§ 144 Affirmation of Voidable Legal Transaction
(1) Avoidance is excluded if the voidable legal transaction is affirmed by the party entitled to avoid it.
(2) [...]

Contract [§§ 145–157]

§ 154 Evident Lack of Agreement
(1) So long as the parties have not reached agreement concerning all aspects ... upon which an agreement is to be reached, even if only according to the declaration of one party, the contract is – in case of doubt – not concluded. [...]
(2) [...]

§ 155 Hidden Lack of Agreement
If the parties to a contract regard it as concluded, but have not in fact reached agreement on an aspect upon which an agreement was to be reached, then that [part] which has been agreed is regarded as valid, provided that it is to be assumed that the contract would have been concluded even in the absence of a provision about the aspect in question.

§ 157 Interpretation of Contracts
Contracts are to be interpreted in accordance with the requirements of good faith and taking account of common usage.

Condition and Time Stipulation [§§ 158–163]

§ 158 Condition Precedent and Subsequent
(1) If a legal transaction is entered into subject to a condition precedent, then the effect which has been made dependent on the condition sets in when the condition is fulfilled.
(2) If a legal transaction has been entered into subject to a condition subsequent, then its effect ceases when the condition is fulfilled; at this point in time the legal *status quo ante* is restored.

Agency and Authority [§§ 164–181]

§ 177 Conclusion of Contract by Unauthorized Agent
(1) If a person, without authorization, concludes a contract in the name of another, then the effectiveness of the contract for and against the principal depends on his ratification.
(2) [...]

§ 179 Liability of the Unauthorized Agent
(1) A person who has concluded a contract as agent [for another] is, unless he proves his authority, obliged – at the other [contracting] party's option – to render performance or to compensate the other [contracting] party for his loss if the principal refuses to ratify the contract.
(2) [...]
(3) [...]

Authorization and Ratification [§§ 182–185]

§ 184 Retroactivity of Ratification
(1) Unless otherwise provided, subsequent assent (ratification) operates retroactively from the moment the legal transaction was entered into.
(2) [...]

§ 185 Disposition by an Unauthorized Person
(1) A disposition by an unauthorized person concerning an object is valid if it is authorized by the person entitled [to dispose of the object].
(2) The disposition becomes valid if it is ratified by the person entitled... [...]

Book II: The Law of Obligations

Obligation to Perform [§§ 241–292]

§ 241 Duties Arising from Obligatory Relationship
(1) By virtue of [an] obligatory relationship, the creditor is entitled to demand a performance from the debtor. The performance may also consist in refraining from an act.
(2) The obligatory relationship may, according to its content, oblige each party to have regard to the other party's rights and interests.

§ 249 Means and Scope of Compensation
(1) A person who is under an obligation to provide compensation is bound to restore the state of affairs which would obtain if the circumstance giving rise to the obligation to compensate had not occurred.
(2) If compensation is to be provided for injury to a person or damage to a thing, the creditor may, instead of [demanding] restoration *in specie*, demand the amount of money necessary to effect restoration. [...]

§ 250 Monetary Compensation after Setting of Time Limit
The creditor can set for the person obliged to compensate him a reasonable time limit within which to effect the restoration and declare that he will thereafter refuse to accept restoration *in specie*. After expiry of the time limit, the creditor may demand monetary compensation...

§ 251 Monetary Compensation without Setting of Time Limit
(1) To the extent that restoration *in specie* is impossible or insufficient to [fully] compensate the creditor, the person obliged to provide compensation must indemnify the creditor with money.
(2) [...]

§ 252 Loss of Profit
The loss for which compensation has to be provided also encompasses loss of profit. [...]

§ 254 Contributory Fault
(1) If the victim's fault has contributed to the occurrence of the loss [or damage], the obligation to provide compensation as well as the scope of compensation depends on the circumstances, in particular on the extent to which the loss [or damage] has been predominantly caused by one or the other party.
(2) [...]

§ 273 Right of Retention
(1) If a debtor has a claim against the creditor which is due and which derives from the same legal relationship as that upon which his [own] obligation is based, then, unless otherwise provided by the obligatory relationship, he may refuse to perform his obligation until the performance due to him is rendered [by the other party] (right of retention).
(2) [...]
(3) [...]

§ 275 Exclusion of Obligation to Perform
(1) The claim to performance is excluded to the extent that performance is impossible...
(2) [...]
(3) [...]
(4) [...]

§ 276 Responsibility of the Debtor
(1) The debtor is responsible for intention and negligence, unless a stricter or milder standard of liability is specified... [...]
(2) A person acts negligently if he fails to observe the standard of care generally regarded as necessary [~ reasonable care].
(3) [...]

§ 278 Responsibility of the Debtor for Third Parties
A debtor is answerable for fault on the part of ... persons whom he engages to perform his obligation to the same extent as for his own fault. [...]

§ 280 Compensation for Breach of Duty
(1) If the debtor breaches a duty arising from the obligatory relationship, the creditor can demand compensation for the loss [or damage] arising therefrom. This does not apply if the debtor is not responsible [→ § 276] for the breach of duty.
(2) [...]
(3) [...]

§ 285 Surrender of Substitute Assets
(1) If, as a result of the circumstance which frees him from his obligation to perform under § 275 ..., the debtor obtains a substitute asset or a claim to compensation for the object which was the subject-matter of the [original] obligation, then the creditor can demand the surrender of the substitute asset obtained or assignment of the claim to compensation.
(2) [...]

§ 286 Delay [*mora*] by Debtor
(1) If the debtor does not perform despite being given notice by the creditor after performance becomes due, that notice puts him into delay. [...]
(2) [...]
(3) [...]
(4) The debtor does not come into delay as long as performance fails to occur as a result of a circumstance for which he is not responsible.

§ 287 Responsibility during Delay
The debtor is responsible for every kind of negligence during the period of delay. With regard to the performance [itself], he is liable even for accident, unless the loss [or damage] would also have occurred if performance had been rendered on time.

§ 292 Liability in Case of Duty to Surrender
(1) If the debtor is under an obligation to surrender a particular object, then the creditor's claim to compensation for deterioration, loss, or other impossibility of effecting the surrender is, from the moment at which an action becomes pending, determined according to the provisions which apply to the relationship between the owner and the [illegitimate] possessor [of an object] after a *vindicatio* becomes pending, unless it appears from the obligatory relationship or the debtor's delay [→ § 287 2] that the creditor is to be treated [even] more favourably.
(2) The same applies to the creditor's claim to surrender of or reimbursement for secondary benefits as well as to the creditor's claim to be indemnified for expenditure on the object.

Creation, Content and Termination of Contractual Relationships [§§ 311–319]

§ 311 Obligatory Relationships Arising from Legal Transactions and Similar Situations
(1) Unless otherwise provided by statute, a contract between the parties is required in order to create an obligatory relationship by means of a legal transaction as well as to change the content of an obligatory relationship.
(2) An obligatory relationship with duties under § 241 sub-s 2 [§ 241 II] also arises from
1. the entry into contractual negotiations,
2. preparations for contracting [ie pre-contractual contact] in the course of which one party, having regard to a potential contractual relationship, affords to the other the opportunity of exerting influence over his rights and interests or entrusts these to the other, or
3. similar business contacts.
(3) [...]

§ 313 Disruption of the Transactional Foundation

(1) If circumstances upon which the contract was founded have materially changed after the conclusion of the contract and if the parties, had they foreseen this change of circumstances, would not have concluded the contract at all or would have done so on different terms, then an adjustment of the contract can be demanded to the extent that, having regard to all the circumstances of the specific case and in particular to the contractual or statutory risk allocation, adherence to the unaltered contract cannot reasonably be expected of one party.

(2) If essential assumptions upon which the contract has been founded later turn out to be incorrect, this is equivalent to a [material] change of circumstances.

(3) If an adjustment of the contract is impossible, or if it cannot reasonably be expected of one party, the disadvantaged party may terminate the contract. [...]

Reciprocal Contract [§§ 320–327]

§ 321 Defence of Uncertainty

(1) A person who is under an obligation to render advance performance under a reciprocal contract may refuse to render his performance if, after the contract has been concluded, it becomes apparent that his [own] claim to the other party's performance is jeopardized by the other party's inability to perform. The right to refuse performance disappears when counter-performance is rendered or if security is provided for it.

(2) [...]

Termination of Contract [§§ 346–354]

§ 346 Effects of Termination

(1) If one party to a contract has contractually reserved for himself the right to terminate it, or if that party has a statutory right to terminate, then, in the case of termination, any performances received must be restored and any secondary benefits [which have already been reaped] surrendered.

(2) [...]

(3) [...]

(4) [...]

Assignment [§§ 398–413]

§ 404 Debtor's Defences

The debtor [of an assigned claim] may raise [all] the defences against the new creditor [ie the assignee] which were available against the previous creditor [ie the assignor] at the time of the assignment.

Sale and Barter [§§ 433–480]

§ 433 Typical Duties under Contract of Sale

(1) By the contract of sale, the seller of a thing comes under an obligation to deliver the thing to the buyer and to transfer ownership of the thing to him. [...]

(2) The buyer is obliged to pay the agreed purchase price to the seller and to take delivery of the thing sold.

§ 435 Defect of Title
The thing [bought] is free from defects of title if third parties cannot assert against the buyer any rights in respect of the thing, or if they can only assert the rights which have been accepted [by the buyer] under the contract of sale. [...]

§ 442 Buyer's Knowledge [of Defects]
(1) The buyer's claims in respect of a defect [of the thing bought] are excluded if he knows of the defect at the time when the contract is concluded. If the buyer is ignorant of the defect as a result of [his own] gross negligence, then the buyer can assert claims in respect of this defect only if the seller fraudulently concealed the defect or if he gave a warranty for the quality of the thing.
(2) [...]

§ 480 Barter
The provisions relating to sale [also] apply, *mutatis mutandis*, to barter.

Loan Contract [§§ 488–498]

§ 488 Typical Duties under a Loan Contract
(1) By the loan contract, the lender comes under an obligation to make available to the borrower the agreed amount of money. The borrower is obliged to pay the interest he owes and to repay the loan made available to him when it is due.
(2) [...]
(3) [...]

Gift [§§ 516–534]

§ 516 Concept of Gift
(1) The conferral of a benefit, by means of which one party enriches another out of his own assets, is a gift if both parties are agreed that the conferral shall be gratuitous.
(2) [...]

§ 518 Form of Promise to Make a Gift
(1) A contract by which a performance is promised as a gift requires notarial attestation of the promise in order to be valid. [...]
(2) The lack of form is healed if the promised performance is [actually] effected.

§ 528 Claim to Restitution based on Donor's Impoverishment
(1) To the extent that, after the gift has been executed, the donor is incapable of adequately maintaining himself ..., he can claim surrender of the gift from the donee in accordance with the provisions about the surrender of an unjustified enrichment. [...]
(2) [...]

§ 530 Revocation of Gift
(1) A gift can be revoked if the donee becomes culpable of gross ingratitude through committing a serious misdemeanour against the donor or [against] a close relative of the donor's.
(2) [...]

§ 531 Declaration of Revocation
(1) The revocation is effected by declaration to the donee.
(2) If the gift has been revoked, the surrender of the subject-matter of the gift can be demanded in accordance with the provisions about the surrender of an unjustified enrichment.

Mandate [§§ 662–674]

§ 667 Duty to Surrender
The mandatee is under an obligation to surrender to the mandator everything which he receives for the purposes of carrying out the mandate as well as anything he obtains from his management of the mandator's affairs.

§ 670 Reimbursement of Expenditure
If the mandatee incurs expenditure for the purposes of carrying out the mandate which he may reasonably regard as necessary under the circumstances, then the mandator is under an obligation to reimburse him.

***Negotiorum gestio* [§§ 677–687]**

§ 677 Duties of the Intervener
A person who manages another's affair without a mandate or other entitlement to do so as against the other party, must manage the affair in such manner as the interest of the principal requires, having regard to the [principal's] actual or presumed wishes.

§ 679 Disregard of the Principal's Opposing Wishes
The principal's wishes, when [actually or hypothetically] opposed to the *negotiorum gestio*, are irrelevant, if a duty of the principal's the fulfilment of which lies in the public interest ... would not be discharged in time without the intervention.

§ 681 Ancillary Duties of the Intervener
The intervener is under an obligation to notify the principal as soon as is expedient of the fact that he has undertaken the *negotiorum gestio* and ... to wait for the latter's decision. For the rest, the provisions of §§ 666 to 668 concerning the mandatee are also applicable, *mutatis mutandis*, to the intervener.

§ 683 Reimbursement of Expenditure
If the *negotiorum gestio* is undertaken in accordance with the interest and the actual or presumed wishes of the principal, the intervener can demand to be reimbursed for his expenditure like a mandatee [→ § 670]. In the cases of § 679, the intervener has this claim even if [his] undertaking of the *negotiorum gestio* is contrary to the principal's wishes.

§ 684 Surrender of Enrichment
If the requirements of § 683 are not met, the principal is under a duty to surrender to the intervener everything which he acquires by virtue of the *negotiorum gestio* according to the provisions about the surrender of an unjustified enrichment. If the principal ratifies the management of his affair, then the intervener has the claim set out in § 683.

§ 687 False *negotiorum gestio*
(1) The provisions of §§ 677 to 686 do not apply if somebody manages another's affair believing it to be his own.
(2) If somebody treats another's affair as his own knowing that he is not entitled to do so, then the principal can assert the claims arising from §§ 677, 678, 681, 682. If he does assert them, then he comes under an obligation towards the intervener in accordance with § 684, 1st sentence.

Unjustified Enrichment [§§ 812–822]

§ 812 Claim for Surrender
(1) A person who, without legal cause, obtains something by way of another person's performance or in some other way at another's expense, is obliged to surrender to that person what he has so obtained. The same obligation exists if the legal cause subsequently lapses or if the result which a performance was intended to bring about ... does not eventuate.
(2) [...]

§ 814 Knowledge of Lack of Obligation
What has been bestowed on another by way of performance in order to discharge a liability cannot be reclaimed if the person making the performance knew that he was not obliged to make it, or if the performance was [rendered] in accordance with a moral duty or the demands of common decency.

§ 816 Disposition by an Unauthorized Person
(1) If an unauthorized person disposes of an object in such a way that the disposition is effective vis-à-vis the person entitled, he is obliged to surrender to the person entitled what he has obtained by virtue of the disposition. If the disposition is made gratuitously, the same obligation applies to the person who obtains an immediate legal advantage through the disposition.
(2) [...]

§ 817 Violation of Statute or Morality
If the purpose of a performance was so defined that the recipient has, by his acceptance of it, violated a statutory prohibition or [the standard of] good morals, the recipient is obliged to surrender what he has so obtained. The claim for surrender is excluded if the person making the performance is guilty of the same contravention [of the statutory prohibition or the standard of good morals], unless the performance consisted in the undertaking of an obligation; [but] a performance rendered in order to discharge such an obligation cannot be reclaimed.

§ 818 Scope of the Enrichment Claim
(1) The obligation to surrender extends to secondary benefits as well as to anything which the recipient acquires on the basis of an obtained right or as compensation for the destruction, damage or deprivation of the object obtained.
(2) If a surrender is impossible on account of the nature of what has been obtained or if the recipient is for another reason not in a position to surrender what he has obtained, he has to make restitution of its value.
(3) The obligation to surrender or to make value restitution is excluded to the extent that the recipient is no longer enriched.

(4) From the moment when an action becomes pending [against him], the recipient is liable under the general provisions.

§ 819 Stricter Liability in the Case of Knowledge and Violation of Statute or Morality
(1) If the recipient knows about the lack of legal cause at the time of receipt, or if he learns of it later, he is obliged to make restitution from the moment of receipt or supervening knowledge as if an action for surrender had become pending against him from that time [→ § 818 IV].
(2) If the recipient, by accepting the performance, violates a statutory prohibition or [the standard of] good morals, he is under the same obligation from the moment of receipt.

§ 820 Stricter Liability where Attainment of Desired Result is Uncertain
(1) If the performance was intended to bring about a particular result, the occurrence of which was considered uncertain under the terms of the legal transaction, and if this result fails to be attained, the recipient is obliged to make restitution as if an action for surrender had become pending at the time of receipt. The same applies where the performance was rendered with a view to a legal cause whose lapse was envisaged as possible under the terms of the legal transaction, if the legal cause [actually] lapses.
(2) [...]

§ 822 Duties of Third Parties to Surrender
If the recipient gratuitously bestows what he has obtained upon a third party, then, to the extent that the recipient's liability to make restitution is in consequence excluded, the third party is obliged to surrender what he has received as if he had, without legal cause, received it from the creditor.

Delict [§§ 823–853]

§ 823 Duty to Compensate
(1) A person who, intentionally or negligently, unlawfully injures another's life, body, health, liberty, property, or other right is obliged to compensate the other for the loss [or damage] resulting therefrom.
(2) The same obligation applies to a person who contravenes a statute intended for the protection of another. If, according to the provisions of this statute, a contravention does not depend on fault, the liability to compensate arises only if the contravention was culpable.

§ 826 Deliberate Infliction of Loss *contra bonos mores*
A person who deliberately causes loss [or damage] to another in a manner which contravenes [the standard of] good morals is obliged to compensate the other for the loss [or damage].

§ 831 Liability for Employees
(1) A person who employs another to perform a [particular] task is obliged to provide compensation for the loss [or damage] which the other unlawfully inflicts on a third party in the execution of this task. The obligation to compensate does not arise if the principal has exercised all due care in selecting the person employed to perform the task and, to the extent that he has to provide apparatus and equipment or [that he] has to supervise the

execution of the task, in making the provision or supervision, or if the loss [or damage] would also have occurred despite the exercise of all due care.
(2) [...]

§ 848 Strict Liability in Case of Wrongful Deprivation of a Thing
A person who is under an obligation to return a thing of which he has, through the commission of a delict, wrongfully deprived another, is responsible even for its accidental destruction, other fortuitous impossibility of surrender or accidental deterioration, unless the destruction, impossibility of surrender or deterioration would also have occurred without the deprivation.

Book III: The Law of Property

Possession [§§ 854–872]

§ 854 Acquisition of Possession
(1) Possession of a thing is acquired by obtaining factual control over the thing.
(2) Agreement between the previous possessor and the acquirer [of possession] is sufficient for the acquisition [of possession] if the acquirer is capable of exercising control over the thing.

§ 858 Unlawful Interference with Possession
(1) A person who deprives a possessor of his possession without the latter's consent, or who [otherwise] disturbs the latter's possession, acts unlawfully, unless the deprivation or disturbance is permitted by statute (unlawful interference with possession).
(2) Possession acquired by unlawful interference is wrongful. [...]

§ 861 Claim on Account of Deprivation of Possession
(1) If the possessor is deprived of his possession by an unlawful interference with it [→ § 858 I alt 1], he can demand the restoration of possession from anyone whose possession is wrongful [→ § 858 II] as against him.
(2) [...]

§ 862 Claim on Account of Disturbance of Possession
(1) If the possessor's possession is disturbed by an unlawful interference with it [→ § 858 I alt 2], he can demand elimination of the disturbance... If further disturbances are to be expected, the possessor may seek an injunction restraining them.
(2) [...]

Content of Ownership [§§ 903–924]

§ 903 Powers of the Owner
The owner of a thing may, to the extent that this does not violate the law or rights of third parties, deal with the thing as he pleases and exclude others from any interference. [...]

Transfer of Ownership of Movables [§§ 929–936]

§ 929 Agreement and Delivery
The transfer of ownership of a movable thing requires that the owner deliver the thing to the purchaser and that both parties are agreed that ownership shall pass. If the purchaser

is [already] in possession of the thing, agreement about the transfer of ownership is sufficient.

§ 930 *Constitutum possessorium*
If the owner is in possession of the thing, then an agreement between him and the purchaser creating a legal relationship by virtue of which the purchaser acquires indirect possession may replace the delivery.

§ 931 Assignment of Claim for Surrender
If a third party is in possession of the thing, the assignment by the owner to the purchaser of his claim for surrender of the thing may replace the delivery.

§ 932 *Bona fide* Purchase from Person not Entitled
(1) By virtue of a transfer under § 929 the purchaser becomes owner even if the thing does not belong to the transferor, unless he is not in good faith [→ § 932 II] at the moment when he would, according to these provisions, acquire ownership. However, in the case of § 929, 2nd sentence, this applies only if the purchaser had obtained possession from the transferor.
(2) The purchaser is not in good faith if he is either aware, or, as a result of gross negligence, unaware, that the thing does not belong to the transferor.

§ 933 *Bona fide* Purchase in Case of *constitutum possessorium*
If a thing transferred in accordance with § 930 does not belong to the transferor, then the purchaser becomes owner when the thing is delivered to him by the transferor, unless he is not in good faith at this point in time.

§ 934 *Bona fide* Purchase in Case of Assignment of Claim for Surrender
If a thing transferred in accordance with § 931 does not belong to the transferor, then the purchaser becomes owner [either], if the transferor is its indirect possessor, as soon as the claim [for surrender against the immediate possessor] is assigned, [or] otherwise as soon as he actually obtains possession from the third party, unless he is not in good faith at the moment of the assignment or acquisition of possession.

§ 935 No *bona fide* Purchase of Lost or Stolen Things
(1) No acquisition of ownership under §§ 932 to 934 occurs if the thing was stolen, lost or otherwise separated from its owner without his consent. [...]
(2) These provisions do not apply to money, bearer instruments as well as to things which are transferred at public auction.

Accession, Mixture and Specification [§§ 946–952]

§ 946 Accession to a Plot of Land
If a movable thing becomes attached to a plot of land in such a way that it becomes an integral part of the plot of land, then the ownership of the land encompasses this thing.

§ 947 Accession to Movables
(1) If movable things are attached to one another in such a way that they become integral parts of a single thing, then the former owners become owners in common of this thing; [...]

(2) If one of the [constituent] things is to be regarded as the principal thing, its owner acquires the sole ownership.

§ 948 Mixture
(1) If movable things are inseparably mixed or mingled with one another, the provision of § 947 is to be applied *mutatis mutandis*.
(2) It is equivalent to inseparability if the separation of the mixed or mingled things would be disproportionately expensive.

§ 950 Specification
(1) A person who manufactures a new movable thing through the specification or transformation of one or more materials acquires ownership of the new thing, unless the value of the [relevant] specification or transformation is significantly less than the value of the material. [...]
(2) When ownership of the new thing is acquired, [all] rights pertaining to the material cease.

§ 951 Reparation for Loss of Rights
(1) A person who suffers the loss of a right as a result of the provisions in §§ 946 to 950, can demand reparation in money from the person who benefits from the re-allocation of rights in accordance with the provisions about the surrender of an unjustified enrichment. Restoration of the *status quo ante* cannot be claimed.
(2) The provisions about the obligation to provide compensation for delicts and the provisions about recovery of expenditure on the thing ... remain unaffected. [...]

Claims Derived from Ownership [§§ 985–1007]

§ 985 Claim for Surrender [*rei vindicatio*]
The owner of a thing can demand its surrender from the possessor.

§ 986 The Possessor's Defences
(1) The possessor may refuse surrender of the thing if he ... is entitled to possession as against the owner. [...]
(2) [...]

§ 987 Secondary Benefits after Action Becomes Pending
(1) The possessor is obliged to surrender to the owner any secondary benefits which he reaps after the [*vindicatio*] action becomes pending.
(2) If, after the action becomes pending, the possessor does not reap secondary benefits which he might have reaped according to the rules of good husbandry, he is under an obligation to compensate the owner to the extent that he is at fault.

§ 988 Secondary Benefits of the Gratuitous Possessor
If a possessor who possesses a thing as his own, or pursuant to a right of use to which he is in fact not entitled, has acquired possession gratuitously, he is under an obligation to surrender to the owner any secondary benefits which he reaps before the action becomes pending in accordance with the provisions about the surrender of an unjustified enrichment.

§ 989 Compensation after Action Becomes Pending
From the moment when an action becomes pending, the possessor is responsible to the owner for any loss [or damage] which occurs because the thing deteriorates, perishes or can for another reason not be surrendered as a result of his own fault.

§ 990 Liability of the [*mala fide*] Possessor in the Case of Knowledge
(1) If the possessor was not on good faith [→ § 932 II] when he acquired possession, he is liable to the owner in accordance with §§ 987, 989 from the moment of the acquisition. If the possessor subsequently learns that he is not entitled to possession, he becomes liable in the same way from the moment when he obtains such knowledge.
(2) Any additional liability of the possessor on account of delay remains unaffected.

§ 992 Liability of the Delictual Possessor
If the possessor has obtained possession by virtue of a wrongful interference with possession [→ § 858 I alt 1] or through a criminal offence, he is liable to the owner according to the provisions on compensation for delicts.

§ 993 Liability of the *bona fide* Possessor
(1) If the requirements set out in §§ 987 to 992 are not met, the possessor must surrender in accordance with the provisions about the surrender of an unjustified enrichment any fruits that he has reaped to the extent that they are not, according to the rules of good husbandry, to be regarded as [ordinary] yield of the thing; apart from this, he is neither obliged to surrender secondary benefits nor to provide compensation.
(2) [...]

§ 994 Necessary Expenditure on the Thing
(1) The possessor can claim reimbursement from the owner for any necessary expenditure on the thing. The regular maintenance costs are, however, not to be reimbursed for the period during which he gets to keep the secondary benefits.
(2) If the possessor incurs necessary expenditure after the moment at which the action becomes pending or after the liability described in § 990 has set in, the owner's obligation to reimburse [him] is governed by the provisions on *negotiorum gestio*.

§ 996 Useful Expenditure on the Thing
For other than necessary expenditure [on the thing], the possessor can claim reimbursement only to the extent that it was incurred prior to the moment at which the action became pending and before the liability described in § 990 has set in, and only to the extent that the value of the thing is still enhanced by it at the point in time when the owner recovers the thing.

§ 1000 Possessor's Right of Retention
The possessor can refuse to surrender the thing until his claim for reimbursement of expenditure has been satisfied. He is not entitled to this right of retention if he has obtained the thing by means of a delict which was intentionally committed.

§ 1001 Action for Reimbursement of Expenditure on the Thing
The possessor may only bring an action for reimbursement of expenditure if the owner recovers the thing or ratifies the expenditure on it. Until ratification, the owner may liberate himself from the [possessor's] claim by returning the recovered thing. [...]

§ 1004 Claim for Removal [of Interferences] and [their] Prevention
(1) If [a person's] ownership is interfered with in other ways than through a deprivation or withholding of possession, the owner can demand removal of the interference from the person responsible for it. If further interferences are to be expected, the owner may seek an injunction restraining them.
(2) [...]

§ 1006 Presumption of Ownership in Favour of Possessor
(1) It is presumed in favour of the possessor of a movable thing that he is the owner of the thing. This presumption, however, does not apply as against a previous possessor from whom the thing has been stolen, who has lost it, or [who has] otherwise become separated from it involuntarily, unless [the action is] concerned with money or berarer instruments.
(2) It is presumed in favour of a previous possessor that he was the owner of the thing while it was in his possession.
(3) [...]

§ 1007 Claims of the Previous Possessor
(1) A person who has had a movable thing in his possession can demand surrender of the thing from its [current] possessor if the latter was not in good faith [→ § 932 II] when he acquired possession.
(2) If the thing was stolen from its previous possessor, if it was lost or otherwise separated from him without his consent, then he can demand its surrender even from a *bona fide* possessor, unless the latter is the owner of the thing or [unless] the thing had been separated from him without his consent prior to the time at which the previous possessor was in possession. This provision does not apply to money and bearer instruments.
(3) [...]

Book IV: Family Law

Matrimonial Property Law [§§ 1363–1563]

§ 1370 Replacement of Household Goods
Household goods which are acquired in place of [household] goods that no longer exist or have become worthless fall into the ownership of the spouse to whom the goods which no longer exist or which have become worthless belonged.

§ 1473 Immediate Substitution [in the case of a marriage with communal property]
(1) Whatever is acquired on the basis of rights forming part of the communal matrimonial property, or [what is acquired] as compensation for the destruction, damage or deprivation of an object forming part of the communal matrimonial property, or [what is acquired] through a legal transaction pertaining to the communal matrimonial property, [also] becomes communal matrimonial property.
(2) [...]

Book V: The Law of Succession

Order of Succession [§§ 1922–1941]

§ 1939 Legacy
A testator may, in a will, bestow an economic benefit upon another without naming that person as his heir (legacy).

Claim to Inheritance [§§ 2018–2031]

§ 2018 The Inheritance Possessor's Duty to Surrender
The heir is entitled to demand from anybody who has obtained something from the inheritance in pursuance of an only supposed right to the inheritance (inheritance possessor) surrender of what has been [so] obtained.

§ 2019 Immediate Substitution
(1) Whatever the inheritance possessor has acquired by means of assets forming part of the inheritance also counts as having been obtained from the inheritance.
(2) [...]

Several Heirs [§§ 2032–2063]

§ 2041 Immediate Substitution
Whatever is acquired on the basis of a right forming part of the estate, or [what is acquired] as compensation for the destruction, damage or deprivation of an object comprised within the estate, or [what is acquired] through a legal transaction pertaining to the estate, [also] forms part of the estate. [...]

General Principles Relating to Wills [§§ 2064–2086]

§ 2078 Avoidance for Mistake or Duress
(1) A last will [testament] can be avoided in so far as the testator was mistaken about the content of his declaration, or did not intend to make a declaration with such content at all, if it is to be assumed that he would not have made it in knowledge of all the relevant facts.
(2) The same applies in so far as the testator was induced to make the disposition by the erroneous assumption of a particular circumstance, or by the [frustrated] expectation of its materialization or non-materialization, or unlawfully through duress.
(3) The provision of § 122 does not apply.

Institution of Reversionary Heir [§§ 2100–2146]

§ 2111 Immediate Substitution
(1) Whatever the preliminary heir acquires on the basis of a right forming part of the inheritance, or [what he acquires] as compensation for the destruction, damage or deprivation of an object comprised within the inheritance, or [what he acquires] through a legal transaction by means of assets forming part of the inheritance, [also] forms part of the inheritance, unless he is entitled to the acquisition as a secondary benefit. [...]
(2) [...]

Legacy [§§ 2147–2191]

§ 2147 Person Charged with the Legacy
A legacy may be imposed on the heir or on a legatee. In so far as the testator has not directed otherwise, the heir is charged with the legacy.

§ 2174 Claim to Legacy
The legacy entails a right of the legatee to demand performance of the object [which forms the subject-matter] of the legacy from the person charged [with the legacy].

Purchase of Inheritance [§§ 2371–2385]

§ 2374 Duty to Surrender
The seller is obliged to surrender to the buyer the assets which formed part of the inheritance at the time of the sale, including that which, prior to the sale, he obtained on the basis of a right forming part of the inheritance, or [what he obtained] as compensation for the destruction, damage or deprivation of an object comprised within the inheritance, or [what he obtained] through a legal transaction which pertained to the inheritance.

Insolvenzordnung (InsO)

§ 47 Segregation
A person who is entitled to assert, on the basis of a proprietary or personal right, that an object does not form part of the insolvent's estate is not a creditor in insolvency proceedings. His claim to segregation of the object is governed by the legal provisions applying outside the insolvency proceedings.

§ 48 Segregation of Substitutes
If the debtor, prior to the commencement of the insolvency proceedings, or after their commencement the administrator, has, without authorization, disposed of an object which was subject to a right of segregation [→ § 47], then the person entitled to segregation may demand assignment of the right to the counter-performance to the extent that the latter is still outstanding. He can claim the counter-performance from the [insolvent's] estate to the extent that it still remains identifiable within the estate.

Konkursordnung (KO)[3]

§ 46 [Segregation of Substitutes]
If the debtor, prior to the commencement of bankruptcy proceedings, or after their commencement the administrator, has [without authorization] disposed of objects which were subject to a right of segregation, then the person entitled to segregation is entitled to demand assignment of the right to the counter-performance to the extent that the latter is still outstanding. He can claim the counter-performance from the [insolvent's] estate to the extent that [the counter-performance] was added to the estate after the commencement of bankruptcy proceedings.

---

[3] In force until the end of 1998; thereafter replaced by InsO (above).

Strafgesetzbuch (StGB)

§ 240 Coercion
(1) A person who, through the use of force or threat with a noticeable harm, unlawfully coerces another human being to commit, acquiesce in, or omit an act, is punishable with imprisonment of up to three years or with a fine.
(2) The deed is unlawful if the use of force or the threat of harm [applied] in order to achieve the desired objective is to be regarded as reprehensible.
(3) [...]
(4) [...]

§ 253 Blackmail [Extortion]
(1) A person who, through the use of force or threat with a noticeable harm, unlawfully coerces another human being to commit, acquiesce in, or omit an act, and in this way causes economic detriment to the coerced or to another person, in order illegitimately to enrich himself or a third party, is punishable with imprisonment of up to five years or with a fine.
(2) The deed is unlawful if the use of force or the threat of harm [applied] in order to achieve the desired objective must be regarded as reprehensible.
(3) [...]
(4) [...]

§ 259 Dealing in Stolen Goods
(1) A person who buys a thing which another has stolen or has otherwise obtained by means of an unlawful [criminal] deed directed against other people's assets, or who otherwise acquires [such a thing] for himself or for a third party, or who disposes or helps dispose of it, in order to enrich himself or a third party, is punishable with imprisonment of up to five years or with a fine.
(2) [...]
(3) [...]

§ 263 Fraud
(1) A person who, with the intent of securing an unlawful economic benefit for himself or for a third party, causes economic loss to another through pretending the existence of false facts or distorting or suppressing true facts and thereby inducing or maintaining a mistake [on the part of the victim], is punishable with imprisonment of up to five years or with a fine.
(2) [...]
(3) [...]
(4) [...]
(5) [...]
(6) [...]
(7) [...]

Bibliography

Achilles, Alexander / Gebhard, Hermann / Spahn, Peter (eds), *Protokolle der Kommission für die zweite Lesung des Entwurfs des Bürgerlichen Gesetzbuchs: vol 2* (Guttentag, Berlin 1898); *vol 3* (Guttentag, Berlin 1899).
Akkouh, Tim, "Equitable Compensation where Rescission is Impossible" (2002) 16 TruLI 151.
Andrews, Neil H / Beatson, Jack, "Common Law Tracing: Springboard or Swan Song" (1997) 113 LQR 21.
Anson's Law of Contract → see Beatson, Jack.
Assfalg, Dieter, *Die Behandlung von Treugut im Konkurse des Treuhänders: Rechtsvergleichende Studie zur Grenzbereinigung zwischen Schuld- und Treuhandverhältnis* (de Gruyter, Berlin 1960).
Atiyah, Patrick Selim "Economic Duress and the 'Overborne Will'" (1982) 98 LQR 197.
Atiyah's Law of Contract → see Smith, Stephen A.
Atiyah, Patrick Selim / Adams, John N / MacQueen, Hector, *The Sale of Goods* (11th edn Pearson Longman 2005).
Baker, John Hamilton, "The History of Quasi-Contract in English Law" in WR Cornish et al (eds), *Restitution Past, Present and Future: Essays in Honour of Gareth Jones* (Hart, Oxford 1998) 37.
–, *An Introduction to English Legal History* (4th edn Butterworths, London 2002).
Baloch, Tariq, "The Unjust Enrichment Pyramid" (2007) 123 LQR 636.
Bant, Elise, "*Restitutio in Integrum* and the Change of Position Defence: Lessons from Rescission" [2007] RLR 13.
–, *The Change of Position Defence* (Hart, Oxford 2009) (forthcoming).
Barker, Kit, "After Change of Position: Good Faith Exchange in the Modern Law of Restitution" in P Birks (ed), *Laundering and Tracing* (Clarendon Press, Oxford 1995) 191.
–, "Bona Fide Purchase as a Defence to Unjust Enrichment Claims: A Concise Restatement" [1999] RLR 75.
Battersby, Graham, "Acquiring Title by Theft" (2002) 65 MLR 603.
Battersby, Graham / Preston, AD, "The Concepts of 'Property', 'Title' and 'Owner' Used in the Sale of Goods Act 1893" (1972) 35 MLR 268.
Beale, Hugh, "Points on Misrepresentation" (1995) 111 LQR 385.
Beale, Hugh (gen ed), *Chitty on Contracts* (29th edn Sweet & Maxwell, London 2004).
Beatson, Jack, "The Nature of Waiver of Tort" in J Beatson, *The Use and Abuse of Unjust Enrichment: Essays on the Law of Restitution* (Clarendon Press, Oxford 1991) 206.
–, *Anson's Law of Contract* (28th edn OUP, Oxford 2002).
Behr, Volker, *Wertverfolgung: Rechtsvergleichende Überlegungen zur Abgrenzung kollidierender Gläubigerinteressen* (Metzner, Frankfurt/Main 1986).

Bell, Andrew, *Modern Law of Personal Property in England and Ireland* (Butterworths, London 1989).

Benjamin's Sale of Goods → see Guest, Anthony Gordon (gen ed).

Beyer, Reinhard, *Die Surrogation bei Vermögen im Bürgerlichen Gesetzbuche* (Elwert, Marburg 1905).

Beyerle, Franz, "Der dingliche Vertrag" in *Festschrift für Gustav Boehmer: Dem Siebziger von Freunden und Kollegen dargebracht* (Röhrscheid, Bonn 1954) 164.

Bigwood, Rick, "Undue Influence: 'Impaired Consent' or 'Wicked Exploitation'?" (1996) 16 OJLS 503.

Birks, Peter, *An Introduction to the Law of Restitution* (Clarendon Press, Oxford 1985, paperback edn 1989).

–, "Misdirected Funds: Restitution from the Recipient" [1989] LMCLQ 296.

–, "Mixing and Tracing" (1992) 45 CLP 69.

–, "Restitution and Resulting Trusts" in S Goldstein (ed), *Equity and Contemporary Legal Developments* (Hebrew University, Jerusalem 1992) 335, reprinted in P Birks and F Rose (eds), *Restitution and Equity, vol 1: Resulting Trusts and Equitable Compensation* (Mansfield Press, London 2000) 265.

–, "Establishing a Proprietary Base" [1995] RLR 83.

–, "Overview: Tracing, Claiming and Defences" in P Birks (ed), *Laundering and Tracing* (Clarendon Press, Oxford 1995) 289.

–, "Definition and Division: A Meditation on *Institutes* 3.13" in P Birks (ed), *The Classification of Obligations* (Clarendon Press, Oxford 1997) 1.

–, "On Taking Seriously the Difference between Tracing and Claiming" (1997) 11 TruLI 2.

–, "Property and Unjust Enrichment: Categorical Truths" [1997] NZ L Rev 623.

–, "The Necessity of a Unitary Law of Tracing" in R Cranston (ed), *Making Commercial Law: Essays in Honour of Roy Goode* (Clarendon Press, Oxford 1997) 241.

–, "Unjust Factors and Wrongs: Pecuniary Rescission for Undue Influence" [1997] RLR 72.

–, "Misnomer" in WR Cornish and others (eds), *Restitution Past, Present and Future: Essays in Honour of Gareth Jones* (Hart, Oxford 1998) 1.

–, "Mixtures" in N Palmer and E McKendrick (eds), *Interests in Goods* (2nd edn LLP, London 1998) 227.

–, "Rights, Wrongs, and Remedies" (2000) 20 OJLS 1.

– (ed), *English Private Law* (OUP, Oxford 2000).

–, " 'At the Expense of the Claimant': Direct and Indirect Enrichment in English Law" in D Johnston and R Zimmermann (eds), *Unjustified Enrichment: Key Issues in Comparative Perspective* (CUP, Cambridge 2002) 493.

–, "Comparative Unjust Enrichment" in P Birks and A Pretto (eds), *Themes in Comparative Law: In Honour of Bernard Rudden* (OUP, Oxford 2002) 137.

–, "Receipt" in P Birks and A Pretto (eds), *Breach of Trust* (Hart, Oxford 2002) 213.

–, "Undue Influence as Wrongful Exploitation" (2004) 120 LQR 34.

–, "Change of Position: The Two Central Questions" (2004) 120 LQR 373.

–, *Unjust Enrichment* (2nd edn OUP, Oxford 2005).

Birks, Peter / Chin, Nyuk Yin, "On the Nature of Undue Influence" in J Beatson and D Friedman (eds), *Good Faith and Fault in Contract Law* (Clarendon Press, Oxford 1995) 57.

Blackstone, William, *Commentaries on the Laws of England: vols 1–4* (Clarendon Press, Oxford 1765–69), reprinted in facsimile by the University of Chicago Press (Chicago 1979).

Bockholdt, Frank, *Die Haftung des unentgeltlichen Erwerbers gemäß § 822 BGB* (Lang, Frankfurt/Main 2004).
–, Anmerkung zum Urteil des BGH vom 10.02.2004 (case note) in JZ 2004, 796.
Böhm, Rainer, *Surrogation trotz Unwirksamkeit einer Verfügung? Zum Anwendungsbereich der §§ 816, 2019 (2111, 2041) BGB sowie des § 46 KO* (Doctoral Thesis, Hamburg 1973).
Bracton → see Woodbine, George (ed).
Bridge, Michael, *Personal Property Law* (3rd edn OUP, Oxford 2002).
Bryan, Michael, "Rescission, Restitution and Contractual Ordering: The Role of Plaintiff Election" in A Robertson (ed), *The Law of Obligations: Connections and Boundaries* (UCL, London 2004) 59.
Büdenbender, Ulrich, "Die Berücksichtigung der Gegenleistung bei der Rückabwicklung gegenseitiger Verträge" AcP 200 (2000) 627.
Burrows, Andrew, "Quadrating Restitution and Unjust Enrichment: A Matter of Principle?" [2000] RLR 257.
–, "Proprietary Restitution: Unmasking Unjust Enrichment" (2001) 117 LQR 412.
–, *The Law of Restitution* (2nd edn Butterworths, London 2002).
–, "Change of Position: The View from England" (2003) 36 Loy LA L Rev 803.
–, "Clouding the Issues on Change of Position" (2004) 63 CLJ 276.
–, "Absence of Basis: The New Birksian Scheme" in A Burrows and A Rodger (eds), *Mapping the Law: Essays in Memory of Peter Birks* (OUP, Oxford 2006) 33.
– (ed), *English Private Law* (2nd edn OUP, Oxford 2007).
–, "The Relationship between Unjust Enrichment and Property: Some Unresolved Issues" in S Degeling and J Edelman (eds), *Unjust Enrichment in Commercial Law* (Thomson Reuters, Sydney 2008) 333.
Burrows, Andrew / Barker, Kit / Krebs, Thomas / et al, "The New Birksian Approach to Unjust Enrichment" [2004] RLR 260.
Burrows, Andrew / Rodger, Alan (eds), *Mapping the Law: Essays in Memory of Peter Birks* (OUP, Oxford 2006).
Caemmerer, Ernst von, "Rechtsvergleichung und Reform der Fahrnisübereignung" RabelsZ 12 (1938/39) 675, reprinted in HG Leser (ed), *Ernst von Caemmerer: Gesammelte Schriften, vol 1: Rechtsvergleichung und Schuldrecht* (Mohr Siebeck, Tübingen 1968) 146.
–, "Bereicherungsausgleich bei Verpfändung fremder Sachen" in *Festschrift für Hans Lewald* (Helbing & Lichtenhahn, Basel 1953) 443, reprinted in HG Leser (ed), *Ernst von Caemmerer: Gesammelte Schriften, vol 1: Rechtsvergleichung und Schuldrecht* (Mohr Siebeck, Tübingen 1968) 279.
–, "Bereicherung und unerlaubte Handlung" in H Dölle, M Rheinstein and K Zweigert (eds), *Festschrift für Ernst Rabel* (Mohr Siebeck, Tübingen 1954) vol 1, 333; reprinted in HG Leser (ed), *Ernst von Caemmerer: Gesammelte Schriften, vol 1: Rechtsvergleichung und Schuldrecht* (Mohr Siebeck, Tübingen 1968) 209.
–, "Leistungsrückgewähr bei gutgläubigem Erwerb" in *Festschrift für Gustav Boehmer: dem Siebziger von Freunden und Kollegen dargebracht* (Röhrscheid, Bonn 1954) 145, reprinted in HG Leser (ed), *Ernst von Caemmerer: Gesammelte Schriften, vol 1: Rechtsvergleichung und Schuldrecht* (Mohr Siebeck, Tübingen 1968) 295.
–, "Grundprobleme des Bereicherungsrechts" in HG Leser (ed), *Ernst von Caemmerer: Gesammelte Schriften, vol 1: Rechtsvergleichung und Schuldrecht* (Mohr Siebeck, Tübingen 1968) 370.
–, "'Mortuus Redhibetur': Bemerkungen zu den Urteilen BGHZ 53, 144 und 57, 137" in G Paulus, U Diederichsen and CW Canaris (eds), *Festschrift für Karl Larenz zum*

70. Geburtstag (Beck, München 1973) 621, reprinted in HG Leser (ed), *Ernst von Caemmerer: Gesammelte Schriften, vol 3: 1968–1982* (Mohr Siebeck, Tübingen 1983) 167.

Calnan, Richard, "Imposing Proprietary Rights" [2004] RLR 1.

Canaris, Claus-Wilhelm, *Die Vertrauenshaftung im deutschen Privatrecht* (Beck, München 1971).

–, "Die Verdinglichung obligatorischer Rechte" in HH Jakobs and others (eds), *Festschrift für Werner Flume zum 70. Geburtstag* (Schmidt, Köln 1978) vol 1, 371.

–, "Die Gegenleistungskondiktion" in B Pfister and M Will (eds), *Festschrift für Werner Lorenz zum siebzigsten Geburtstag* (Mohr Siebeck, Tübingen 1991) 19.

–, "Der Vorrang außerbereicherungsrechtlicher, insbesondere dinglicher Wertungen gegenüber der Saldotheorie und dem Subsidiaritätsdogma" JZ 1992, 1114.

Canton, EM Clare, "Sale of Goods and Barter" (1976) 39 MLR 589.

Capper, David, "Undue Influence and Unconscionability: A Rationalisation" (1998) 114 LQR 479.

Cartwright, John, *Misrepresentation, Mistake and Non-Disclosure* (2nd edn Sweet & Maxwell, London 2007).

Chambers, Robert, *Resulting Trusts* (Clarendon Press, Oxford 1997).

–, "Resulting Trusts and Equitable Compensation" (2001) 15 TruLI 2.

–, "Resulting Trusts in Canada" (2002) 16 TruLI 104 and 138, reprinted from (2000) 38 Alberta L Rev 378.

–, "Resulting Trusts" in A Burrows and A Rodger (eds), *Mapping the Law: Essays in Memory of Peter Birks* (OUP, Oxford 2006) 247.

–, *An Introduction to Property Law in Australia* (2nd edn Thomson LBC, Sydney 2008).

Chambers, Robert / Penner, James, "Ignorance" in S Degeling and J Edelman (eds), *Unjust Enrichment in Commercial Law* (Thomson Reuters, Sydney 2008) 253.

Chen-Wishart, Mindy, "Unjust Factors and the Restitutionary Response" (2000) 20 OJLS 557.

Cheshire, Fifoot & Furmston → see Furmston, Michael.

Chitty on Contracts → see Beale, Hugh (gen ed).

Clerk & Lindsell on Torts → see Dugdale, Anthony (gen ed).

Coester-Waltjen, Dagmar, "Die dingliche Surrogation" Jura 1996, 24.

Coing, Helmut, *Europäisches Privatrecht: vol 1* (Beck, München 1985); *vol 2* (Beck, München 1989).

Crossley Vaines on Personal Property → see Tyler, Edward Lawson Griffin.

Dannemann, Gerhard, "Comparative Law: Study of Similarities or Differences?" in M Reimann and R Zimmermann (eds), *The Oxford Handbook of Comparative Law* (OUP, Oxford 2006) 383.

–, "Unjust Enrichment as Absence of Basis: Can English Law Cope?" in A Burrows and A Rodger (eds), *Mapping the Law: Essays in Memory of Peter Birks* (OUP, Oxford 2006) 363.

Dawson, John Philip, *Unjust Enrichment: A Comparative Analysis* (Little Brown and Co, Boston 1951).

–, "Indirect Enrichment" in E von Caemmerer, S Mentschikoff and K Zweigert (eds), *Ius Privatum Gentium: Festschrift für Max Rheinstein zum 70. Geburtstag am 5. Juli 1969* (Mohr Siebeck, Tübingen 1969) vol 2, 789.

Diamond, Aubrey L, *A Review of Security Interests in Property* (HMSO, London 1989).

Dieckmann, Albrecht, "Zur Reform des Ersatzaussonderungsrechts" in W Gerhardt and others (eds), *Festschrift für Wolfram Henckel zum 70. Geburtstag am 21. April 1995* (de Gruyter, Berlin 1995) 95.

Diesselhorst, Malte, *Die Natur der Sache als außergesetzliche Rechtsquelle verfolgt an der Rechtsprechung zur Saldotheorie* (Mohr Siebeck, Tübingen 1968).
Domat, Jean, *Les Loix Civiles dans leur Ordre Naturel, le Droit Public, et Legum Delectus* (nouvelle édition Durand, Paris 1777, revue par M de Héricourt).
Drobnig, Ulrich, "Transfer of Property" in A Hartkamp and others (eds), *Towards a European Civil Code* (3rd edn Kluwer Law International, New York 2004) 725.
Dugdale, Anthony / Jones, Michael (gen eds), *Clerk & Lindsell on Torts* (19th edn Sweet & Maxwell, London 2006).
Edelman, James, *Gain-Based Damages: Contract, Tort, Equity and Intellectual Property* (Hart, Oxford 2002).
–, "Gain-Based Damages and Compensation" in A Burrows and A Rodger (eds), *Mapping the Law: Essays in Memory of Peter Birks* (OUP, Oxford 2006) 141.
–, "The Meaning of 'Unjust' in the English Law of Unjust Enrichment" (2006) 14 ERPL 309.
Edelman, James / Bant, Elise, *Unjust Enrichment in Australia* (OUP, Sydney 2006).
Eisenhardt, Ulrich, "Die Einheitlichkeit des Rechtsgeschäfts und die Überwindung des Abstraktionsprinzips" JZ 1991, 271.
Emmerich, Volker, *Das Verhältnis der Nebenfolgen der Vindikation zu anderen Ansprüchen* (Doctoral Thesis, Universität des Saarlandes 1966).
English Private Law (1st edn) → see Birks, Peter (ed).
English Private Law (2nd edn) → see Burrows, Andrew (ed).
Entwurf (BGB-E I): *Entwurf eines bürgerlichen Gesetzbuches für das Deutsche Reich: Erste Lesung* (Guttentag, Berlin 1888).
Erman → see Westermann, Harm Peter (ed).
Esser, Josef / Weyers, Hans-Leo, *Schuldrecht: vol 2/2* (8th edn Müller, Heidelberg 2000).
Felgentraeger, Wilhelm, *Friedrich Carl v. Savignys Einfluß auf die Übereignungslehre* (Deichert, Leipzig 1927).
Fischer, Hans Albrecht, "Bereicherung und Schaden" in *Festschrift für Ernst Zitelmann: Zu seinem 60. Geburtstage überreicht von Verehrern und Schülern* (Duncker & Humblot, München 1913).
–, "Fiktionen und Bilder in der Rechtswissenschaft" AcP 117 (1919) 143.
Fleischer, Holger, "Konkurrenzprobleme um die culpa in contrahendo: Fahrlässige Irreführung versus arglistige Täuschung" AcP 200 (2000) 91.
Flessner, Axel, *Wegfall der Bereicherung: Rechtsvergleichung und Kritik* (de Gruyter & Mohr Siebeck, Berlin & Tübingen 1970).
Flume, Werner, *Eigenschaftsirrtum und Kauf* (Regensberg, Münster 1948).
–, "Der Wegfall der Bereicherung in der Entwicklung vom römischen zum geltenden Recht" in Rechts- und Staatswissenschaftliche Fakultät Göttingen (ed), *Festschrift für Hans Niedermeyer zum 70. Geburtstag* (Schwartz & Co, Göttingen 1953) 103.
–, *Allgemeiner Teil des Bürgerlichen Rechts, vol 2: Das Rechtsgeschäft* (3rd edn Springer, Berlin 1979).
–, "Die Saldotheorie und die Rechtsfigur der ungerechtfertigten Bereicherung" AcP 194 (1994) 427.
–, "Aufwendungen und Erträge bei der Abwicklung nichtiger gegenseitiger Verträge als Problematik der Rechtsfigur der ungerechtfertigten Bereicherung" in W Schön (ed), *Gedächtnisschrift für Brigitte Knobbe-Keuk* (Schmidt, Köln 1997) 111.
Förster, Franz / Eccius, Max Ernst, *Preußisches Privatrecht* (6th edn Reimer, Berlin 1892).
Fox, David, "Common Law Claims to Substituted Assets" [1999] RLR 55.
–, "Relativity of Title at Law and in Equity" (2006) 65 CLJ 330.

Frank, Rainer, "Anwendbarkeit des § 281 BGB auf den verschärft haftenden Bereicherungsschuldner" JuS 1981, 102.

Frankenberg, Günter, "Critical Comparisons: Re-thinking Comparative Law" (1985) 26 Harv Int LJ 411.

Friedmann, Daniel, "Valid, Voidable, Qualified, and Non-Existing Obligations: An Alternative Perspective on the Law of Restitution" in A Burrows (ed), *Essays on the Law of Restitution* (Clarendon Press, Oxford 1991) 247.

–, "Restitution for Wrongs: The Basis of Liability" in WR Cornish and others (eds), *Restitution Past, Present and Future: Essays in Honour of Gareth Jones* (Hart, Oxford 1998) 133.

–, "The Objective Principle and Mistake and Involuntariness in Contract and Restitution" (2003) 119 LQR 68.

–, "Reversible Transfers – The Two Categories" [2003] RLR 1.

Furmston, Michael, *Cheshire, Fifoot & Furmston's Law of Contract* (15th edn OUP, Oxford 2007).

Ganter, Hans Gerhard, "Zweifelsfragen bei der Ersatzaussonderung und Ersatzabsonderung" NZI 2005, 1.

Gerhardt, Walter, "Der Surrogationsgedanke im Konkursrecht – dargestellt an der Ersatzaussonderung" KTS 1990, 1.

Goff, Robert / Jones, Gareth, *The Law of Restitution* (Sweet & Maxwell, London 1966).

Goff & Jones → see Jones, Gareth (ed).

Goode, Roy, "Proprietary Restitutionary Claims" in WR Cornish and others (eds), *Restitution Past, Present and Future: Essays in Honour of Gareth Jones* (Hart, Oxford 1998) 63.

–, *Commercial Law* (3rd edn LexisNexis, London 2004).

–, *Principles of Corporate Insolvency Law* (2nd edn Sweet & Maxwell, London 2005).

Goodhart, Arthur Lehman, "Mistake as to Identity in the Law of Contract" (1941) 57 LQR 228.

Gottwald, Peter (ed), *Insolvenzrechts-Handbuch* (3rd edn Beck, München 2006).

Grantham, Ross / Rickett, Charles, "Restitution, Property and Ignorance – A Reply to Mr Swadling" [1996] LMCLQ 463.

–, "Restitution, Property and Mistaken Payments" [1997] RLR 83.

–, "Property and Unjust Enrichment: Categorical Truths or Unnecessary Complexity?" [1997] NZ L Rev 668.

–, "Tracing and Property Rights: The Categorical Truth" (2000) 63 MLR 905.

–, "Property Rights as a Legally Significant Event" (2003) 62 CLJ 717.

–, "A Normative Account of Defences to Restitutionary Liability" (2008) 67 CLJ 92.

Graziadei, Michele, "The Functionalist Heritage" in P Legrand and R Munday (eds), *Comparative Legal Studies: Traditions and Transitions* (CUP, Cambridge 2003) 100.

Grigoleit, Hans Christoph, *Vorvertragliche Informationshaftung: Vorsatzdogma, Rechtsfolgen, Schranken* (Beck, München 1997).

–, "Abstraktion und Willensmängel: Die Anfechtbarkeit des Verfügungsgeschäfts" AcP 199 (1999) 379.

–, "Neuere Tendenzen zur schadensrechtlichen Vertragsaufhebung" NJW 1999, 900.

–, "Reformperspektiven der vorvertraglichen Informationshaftung" in R Schulze and H Schulte-Nölke (eds), *Die Schuldrechtsreform vor dem Hintergrund des Gemeinschaftsrechts* (Mohr Siebeck, Tübingen 2001) 269.

Grundmann, Stefan, "Zur Anfechtbarkeit des Verfügungsgeschäfts" JA 1985, 80.

–, "The Evolution of Trust and Treuhand in the 20th Century" in R Helmholz and R Zimmermann (eds), *Itinera Fiduciae: Trust and Treuhand in Historical Perspective* (Duncker & Humblot, Berlin 1998) 469.
Guest, Anthony Gordon (gen ed), *Benjamin's Sale of Goods* (7th edn Sweet & Maxwell, London 2006).
Gundlach, Ulf, *Der Ersatzaussonderungsberechtigte* (Lang, Frankfurt/Main 1994).
–, "Notwendigkeit einer wirksamen Veräußerung für die Ersatzaussonderung" KTS 1997, 211.
–, "Die sogenannte 'Zweite Ersatzaussonderung'" KTS 1997, 453.
Gundlach, Ulf / Frenzel, Volkhard / Schirrmeister, André, "Nochmals – die sogenannte zweite Ersatzaussonderung" KTS 2003, 69.
Haag Molkenteller, Dieter, *Die These vom dinglichen Vertrag: zur formalen Struktur der Eigentumsübertragung nach § 929 Satz 1 BGB* (Lang, Frankfurt/Main 1991).
Häcker, Birke, "Rescission and Third Party Rights" [2006] RLR 21.
–, "Rescission of Contract and Revesting of Title: A Reply to Mr Swadling" [2006] RLR 106.
–, "Still at the Crossroads" (2007) 123 LQR 177.
–, "Mistakes in the Execution of Documents: Recent Cases on Rectification and Related Doctrines" (2008) 19 KLJ 293.
Hackney, Jeffrey, *Understanding Equity and Trusts* (Fontana, London 1987).
Hager, Günter, "Grundfälle zur Systematik des Eigentümer-Besitzer-Verhältnisses und der bereicherungsrechtlichen Kondiktionen" JuS 1987, 877.
Harder, Manfred, "Die historische Entwicklung der Anfechtbarkeit von Willenserklärungen" AcP 173 (1973) 209.
Hartmann, Felix, *Der Anspruch auf das stellvertretende commodum* (Mohr Siebeck, Tübingen 2007).
Häsemeyer, Ludwig, *Insolvenzrecht* (4th edn Heymanns, Köln 2007).
Hayton, David, "Ascertainability in Transfer and Tracing of Title" [1994] LMCLQ 449.
Heck, Philipp, *Das abstrakte dingliche Rechtsgeschäft* (Mohr Siebeck, Tübingen 1937).
Hellwege, Phillip, *Die Rückabwicklung gegenseitiger Verträge als einheitliches Problem: Deutsches, englisches und schottisches Recht in historisch-vergleichender Perspektive* (Mohr Siebeck, Tübingen 2004).
–, "Unwinding Mutual Contracts: *Restitutio in Integrum* v. the Defence of Change of Position" in D Johnston and R Zimmermann (eds), *Unjustified Enrichment: Key Issues in Comparative Perspective* (CUP, Cambridge 2002) 243.
Helmholz, Richard / Zimmermann, Reinhard (eds), *Itinera Fiduciae: Trust and Treuhand in Historical Perspective* (Duncker & Humblot, Berlin 1998).
Henckel, Wolfram, "Grenzen der Vermögenshaftung" JuS 1985, 836.
Hess, Harald, *Insolvenzrecht: Großkommentar in drei Bänden, vol 1: §§ 1–102 InsO* (Müller, Heidelberg 2007).
Higgins, Michael, "The Transfer of Property under Illegal Transactions" (1962) 25 MLR 149.
Hill, Jonathan, "The Role of the Donee's Consent in the Law of Gift" (2001) 117 LQR 127.
Hilliard, Jonathan, "Gibbon v Mitchell Reconsidered: Mistakes as to Effects and Mistakes as to Consequences" [2004] PCB 357 (part 1), [2005] PCB 31 (part 2).
Historisch-kritischer Kommentar → see Schmoeckel, Mathias (ed).
Ho, Lusina, "Undue Influence and Equitable Compensation" in P Birks and F Rose (eds), *Restitution and Equity, vol 1: Resulting Trusts and Equitable Compensation* (Mansfield Press, London 2000) 193.

Hoecke, Mark van, "Deep Level Comparative Law" in M van Hoecke (ed), *Epistemology and Methodology of Comparative Law* (Hart, Oxford 2004) 165.
Holdsworth, William, *A History of English Law: vol 3* (4th edn Methuen & Co, London 1935).
Hooley, Richard, "Damages and the Misrepresentation Act 1967" (1991) 107 LQR 547.
Horst, Elsbeth, *Die Beschränkung der Bereicherungshaftung* (Doctoral Thesis, Köln 1961).
Howarth, William, "The Meaning of Objectivity in Contract" (1984) 100 LQR 265.
–, "A Note on the Objective of Objectivity in Contract" (1987) 103 LQR 527.
Hubernagel, Gerhard, "Doppelwirkungen und Konkurrenzen" AcP 137 (1933) 205.
Husa, Jaakko, "Farewell to Functionalism or Methodological Tolerance?" RabelsZ 67 (2003) 419.
Husserl, Gerhart, *Recht und Welt* (Klostermann, Frankfurt/Main 1964).
Hyland, Richard, "Comparative Law" in D Patterson (ed), *A Companion to Philosophy of Law and Legal Theory* (Blackwell, Oxford 1996) 184.
Jacobi, Leonard, "Die fehlerhaften Rechtsgeschäfte: Ein Beitrag zur Begriffslehre des deutschen bürgerlichen Rechts" AcP 86 (1896) 51.
Jaeger, Ernst, *Kommentar zur Konkursordnung, vol 1: §§ 1–46* (6th/7th edn de Guyter, Berlin 1931).
–, *Lehrbuch des Deutschen Konkursrechts* (8th edn de Gruyter, Berlin 1932).
Jaffey, Peter, "The Nature of Knowing Receipt" (2001) 15 TruLI 151.
Jakobs, Horst Heinrich, *Eingriffserwerb und Vermögensverschiebung in der Lehre von der ungerechtfertigten Bereicherung* (Röhrscheid, Bonn 1964).
–, *lucrum ex negotiatione*: *Kondiktionsrechtliche Gewinnhaftung in geschichtlicher Sicht* (Mohr Siebeck, Tübingen 1993).
–, "Gibt es den dinglichen Vertrag? Ein Epitheton zu 'Wissenschaft und Gesetzgebung' (1983)" ZSS (RA) 119 (2002) 269.
Jauernig, Othmar, "Trennungsprinzip und Abstraktionsprinzip" JuS 1994, 721.
— (ed), *Bürgerliches Gesetzbuch: Kommentar* (12th edn Beck, München 2007).
Jhering, Rudolph von, "Culpa in contrahendo oder Schadensersatz bei nichtigen oder nicht zur Perfection gelangten Verträgen" JherJB 4 (1861) 1.
–, *Geist des römischen Rechts auf den verschiedenen Stufen seiner Entwicklung: vol 3/1* (4th edn Breitkopf & Härtel, Leipzig 1888).
Jones, Gareth, Comment on *Chase Manhattan Bank v Israel-British Bank* (1980) 39 CLJ 275.
–, "Some Thoughts on Change of Position" in A Burrows and A Rodger (eds), *Mapping the Law: Essays in Memory of Peter Birks* (OUP, Oxford 2006) 65.
– (ed), R Goff and G Jones, *The Law of Restitution* (7th edn Sweet & Maxwell, London 2007).
Kahn-Freund, Otto, "Comparative Law as an Academic Subject" (1966) 82 LQR 40.
Kaiser, Dagmar, *Die Rückabwicklung gegenseitiger Verträge wegen Nicht- und Schlechterfüllung nach BGB: Rücktritts-, Bereicherungs- und Schadensersatzrecht* (Mohr Siebeck, Tübingen 2000).
Kaufmann, Willy, "Wirkt die Anfechtung des Kausalgeschäfts wegen Willensmangels auch auf die dingliche Einigung?" JW 33 (1904) 349.
Kegel, Gerhard, "Verpflichtung und Verfügung: Sollen Verfügungen abstrakt oder kausal sein?" in W Flume and others (eds), *Internationales Recht und Wirtschaftsordnung: Festschrift für FA Mann* (Beck, München 1977) 57.
Kellmann, Christof, *Grundsätze der Gewinnhaftung: Rechtsvergleichender Beitrag zum Recht der ungerechtfertigten Bereicherung* (Duncker & Humblot, Berlin 1969).

Kelsen, Hans, *Reine Rechtslehre: Einleitung in die rechtswissenschaftliche Problematik* (Deuticke, Leipzig 1934).

–, *Reine Rechtslehre. Mit einem Anhang: Das Problem der Gerechtigkeit* (2nd edn Deuticke, Wien 1960).

Kersley, Robert Henry, *Goodeve's Modern Law of Personal Property* (9th edn Sweet & Maxwell, London 1949).

Kersting, Wilhelm Christian, *Probleme der sog. Doppelwirkungen im Recht* (Doctoral Thesis, Hamburg 1964).

Key, Paul, "Bona Fide Purchase as a Defence in the Law of Restitution" [1994] LMCLQ 421.

Khurshid, Salman / Matthews, Paul, "Tracing Confusion" (1979) 95 LQR 78.

Kipp, Theodor, "Über Doppelwirkungen im Recht, insbesondere über die Konkurrenz von Nichtigkeit und Anfechtbarkeit" in *Festschrift der Berliner Juristischen Fakultät für Ferdinand von Martitz zum fünfzigjährigen Doktorjubiläum* (Liebmann, Berlin 1911) 211.

Kirchhof, Hans-Peter / Lwowksi, Hans-Jürgen / Stürner, Rolf (eds), *Münchener Kommentar zur Insolvenzordnung, vol 1: §§ 1–102* (Beck, München 2001) and (2nd edn Beck, München 2007).

Knight, Max (tr), H Kelsen, *Pure Theory of Law: Translation from the second (revised and enlarged) German edition* (University of California Press, Berkeley 1967).

Knütel, Rolf, "§ 822 BGB und die Schwächen unentgeltlichen Erwerbs" NJW 1989, 2504.

Köbl, Ursula, *Das Eigentümer-Besitzer-Verhältnis im Anspruchssystem des BGB: Zugleich ein Beitrag zur Konkurrenzlehre* (Duncker & Humblot, Berlin 1971).

Kohler, Jürgen, *Die gestörte Rückabwicklung gescheiterter Austauschverträge* (Heymanns, Köln 1989).

–, "Erforderliche und klare Worte zum Entreicherungseinwand" NJW 1992, 3145.

Koppensteiner, Hans-Georg, "Probleme des bereicherungsrechtlichen Wertersatzes" NJW 1971, 588, 1169.

Koppensteiner, Hans-Georg / Kramer, Ernst, *Ungerechtfertigte Bereicherung* (2nd edn de Gruyter, Berlin 1988).

Kornblum, Udo, "Das Geschenk der Defraudantin" JuS 1970, 437.

Kötz, Hein, *Trust und Treuhand: Eine rechtsvergleichende Darstellung des anglo-amerikanischen Trust und funktionsverwandter Institute des deutschen Rechts* (Vandenhoeck & Ruprecht, Göttingen 1963).

–, "Abschied von der Rechtskreislehre?" ZEuP 1998, 493.

Krebs, Thomas, *Restitution at the Crossroads: A Comparative Study* (Cavendish, London 2001).

–, "In Defence of Unjust Factors" in D Johnston and R Zimmermann (eds), *Unjustified Enrichment: Key Issues in Comparative Perspective* (CUP, Cambridge 2002) 76.

–, "Eingriffskondiktion und Restitution for Wrongs im englischen Recht" in R Zimmermann (ed), *Grundstrukturen eines europäischen Bereicherungsrechts* (Mohr Siebeck, Tübingen 2005) 141.

–, "The Fallacy of 'Restitution for Wrongs' " in A Burrows and A Rodger (eds), *Mapping the Law: Essays in Memory of Peter Birks* (OUP, Oxford 2006) 379.

Krüger, Wolfgang, "Vertragsrückabwicklung im Wege des Schadensersatzes" in R Bork, T Hoeren and P Pohlmann (eds), *Recht und Risiko: Festschrift für Helmut Kollhosser zum 70. Geburtstag* (VVW, Karlsruhe 2004) vol 2, 329.

Kübler, Bruno / Prütting, Hanns (eds), *Kommentar zur Insolvenzordnung, vol 1: §§ 1–128* (last update April 2008: RWS, Köln 1998–2008).

Lange, Heinrich, "Rechtsgrundabhängigkeit der Verfügung im Boden- und Fahrnisrecht" AcP 146 (1941) 28.
–, "Rechtswirklichkeit und Abstraktion" AcP 148 (1943) 188.
–, "Zur Umstellung der Bereicherung" NJW 1951, 685.
Lange, Hermann, "Verzugshaftung des Bereicherungsschuldners und des Besitzers" JZ 1964, 640.
Larenz, Karl, "Zur Bedeutung des 'Wertersatzes' im Bereicherungsrecht" in HC Ficker and others (eds), *Festschrift für Ernst von Caemmerer zum 70. Geburtstag* (Mohr Siebeck, Tübingen 1978) 209.
–, *Allgemeiner Teil des deutschen Bürgerlichen Rechts* (7th edn Beck, München 1989).
–, *Methodenlehre der Rechtswissenschaft* (6th edn Springer, Berlin 1991).
Larenz, Karl / Canaris, Claus-Wilhelm, *Lehrbuch des Schuldrechts: vol 2/2* (13th edn Beck, München 1994).
Larenz, Karl / Wolf, Manfred, *Allgemeiner Teil des Bürgerlichen Rechts* (9th edn Beck, München 2004).
Law Commission, *Ninth Programme of Law Reform* (Law Com No 293, 2005).
–, *Tenth Programme of Law Reform* (Law Com No 311, 2008).
Law Reform Committee, *Twelfth Report: Transfer of Title to Chattels* (Cmnd 2958, 1966).
–, *Eighteenth Report: Conversion and Detinue* (Cmnd 4774, 1971).
Lawson, Frederick H, "The Field of Comparative Law" (1949) 61 Jurid Rev 16.
Lawson, Frederick H / Rudden, Bernard, *The Law of Property* (3rd edn OUP, Oxford 2002).
Legrand, Pierre, "The Same and the Different" in P Legrand and R Munday (eds), *Comparative Legal Studies: Traditions and Transitions* (CUP, Cambridge 2003) 240.
Lenel, Otto, "Der Irrtum über wesentliche Eigenschaften" JherJB 44 (1902) 1.
Leser, Hans Georg, *Von der Saldotheorie zum faktischen Synallagma: Ein Beitrag zur Lehre vom Wegfall der Bereicherung* (Doctoral Thesis, Freiburg/Breisgau 1956).
Lieb, Manfred, "Vertragsaufhebung oder Geldersatz? Überlegungen über die Rechtsfolgen von culpa in contrahendo" in *Festschrift der Rechtswissenschaftlichen Fakultät zur 600-Jahr-Feier der Universität zu Köln* (Heymanns, Köln 1988) 251.
–, "Culpa in contrahendo und rechtsgeschäftliche Entscheidungsfreiheit" in V Beuthien, M Fuchs and others (eds), *Festschrift für Dieter Medicus: Zum 70. Geburtstag* (Heymanns, Köln 1999) 337.
Lightman, Gavin / Moss, Gabriel / and others, *The Law of Administrators and Receivers of Companies* (Sweet & Maxwell, London 2007).
Lindacher, Walter, "Rechte des vorleistungspflichtigen Verkäufers bei anfänglicher Kreditunwürdigkeit des Käufers" MDR 1977, 797.
Lippmann, Leo, "Studien zu § 119 Abs. 2 BGB" AcP 102 (1907) 283.
Lobinger, Thomas, *Rechtsgeschäftliche Verpflichtung und autonome Bindung: Zu den Entstehungsgründen vermögensaufstockender Leistungspflichten im bürgerlichen Recht* (Mohr Siebeck, Tübingen 1999).
Lopau, Eberhard, *Surrogationsansprüche und Bereicherungsrecht* (Duncker & Humblot, Berlin 1971).
Lorenz, Stephan, *Der Schutz vor dem unerwünschten Vertrag: Eine Untersuchung von Möglichkeiten und Grenzen der Abschlußkontrolle im geltenden Recht* (Beck, München 1997).
Lux, Karl, "Die Entwicklung des Gutglaubensschutzes im 19. und 20. Jahrhundert mit besonderer Berücksichtigung des Wechselrechts" ZHR 1939, Beiheft 16.

Macmillan, Catherine, "Rogues, Swindlers and Cheats: The Development of Mistake of Identity in English Contract Law" (2005) 64 CLJ 711.
Mankowski, Peter, *Beseitigungsrechte: Anfechtung, Widerruf und verwandte Institute* (Mohr Siebeck, Tübingen 2003).
Markesinis, Basil / Unberath, Hannes / Johnston, Angus, *The German Law of Contract: A Comparative Treatise* (2nd edn Hart, Oxford 2006).
Martens, Sebastian, *Durch Dritte verursachte Willensmängel* (Mohr Siebeck, Tübingen 2007).
Mattei, Ugo, *Basic Principles of Property Law: A Comparative Legal and Economic Introduction* (Greenwood, London 2000).
Matthews, Paul, "The Comparative Importance of the Rule in *Saunders v Vautier*" (2006) 122 LQR 266.
May, Erich, *Die Möglichkeit der Beseitigung des Abstraktionsprinzips bei den Verfügungsgeschäften des Fahrnisrechts* (Möller, Rendsburg 1952).
McFarlane, Ben, *The Structure of Property Law* (Hart, Oxford 2008).
McInnes, Mitchell, "Restitution, Unjust Enrichment and the Perfect Quadration Thesis" [1999] RLR 118.
–, "Interceptive Subtraction, Unjust Enrichment and Wrongs – A Reply to Professor Birks" (2003) 62 CLJ 697.
–, "Taxonomic Lessons for the Supreme Court of Canada" in C Rickett and R Grantham (eds), *Structure and Justification in Private Law* (Hart, Oxford 2008) 77.
McKendrick, Ewan, *Sale of Goods* (LLP, London 2000).
–, "Taxonomy: Does It Matter?" in D Johnston and R Zimmermann (eds), *Unjustified Enrichment: Key Issues in Comparative Perspective* (CUP, Cambridge 2002) 627.
McLauchlan, David, "The 'Drastic' Remedy of Rectification for Unilateral Mistake" (2008) 124 LQR 608.
Medicus, Dieter, "Die verschärfte Haftung des Bereicherungsschuldners" JuS 1993, 705.
–, *Bürgerliches Recht: Eine nach Anspruchsgrundlagen geordnete Darstellung zur Examensvorbereitung* (21st edn Heymanns, Köln 2007).
Meier, Sonja, *Irrtum und Zweckverfehlung: Die Rolle der unjust-Gründe bei rechtsgrundlosen Leistungen im englischen Recht* (Mohr Siebeck, Tübingen 1999).
–, "Unjust Factors and Legal Grounds" in D Johnston and R Zimmermann (eds), *Unjustified Enrichment: Key Issues in Comparative Perspective* (CUP, Cambridge 2002) 37.
Michaels, Ralf, "The Functional Method of Comparative Law" in M Reimann and R Zimmermann (eds), *The Oxford Handbook of Comparative Law* (OUP, Oxford 2006) 339.
Millett, Peter, "Tracing the Proceeds of Fraud" (1991) 107 LQR 71.
–, "Restitution and Constructive Trusts" (1998) 114 LQR 399.
–, "Proprietary Restitution" in S Degeling and J Edelman (eds), *Equity in Commercial Law* (Thomson LBC, Sydney 2005) 309.
–, "*Jones v Jones*: Property or Unjust Enrichment?" in A Burrows and A Rodger (eds), *Mapping the Law: Essays in Memory of Peter Birks* (OUP, Oxford 2006) 265.
Milsom, Stroud Francis Charles, *Historical Foundations of the Common Law* (2nd edn Butterworths, London 1981).
Motive zu dem Entwurfe eines Bürgerlichen Gesetzbuches für das Deutsche Reich (2nd edn Guttentag, Berlin 1896).
Münchener Kommentar → see Rebmann, Kurt (ed).
Münchener Kommentar InsO → see Kirchhof, Hans-Peter (ed).

Nahan, Nyuk Yin, "Rescission: A Case for Rejecting the Classical Model?" (1997) 27 UWALR 66.
Neuner, Robert, "Abstrakte und kausale Übereignung beweglicher Sachen" RheinZ 14 (1926) 9.
Nicholls, Donald, "Knowing Receipt: The Need for a New Landmark" in WR Cornish and others (eds), *Restitution Past, Present and Future: Essays in Honour of Gareth Jones* (Hart, Oxford 1998) 231.
O'Sullivan, Dominic, "The Rule in *Phillips v. Phillips*" (2002) 118 LQR 296.
O'Sullivan, Dominic / Elliott, Steven / Zakrzewski, Rafal, *The Law of Rescission* (OUP, Oxford 2008).
O'Sullivan, Janet, "Rescission as a Self-Help Remedy: A Critical Analysis" (2000) 59 CLJ 509.
Oakley, Anthony J, "Proprietary Claims and their Priority in Insolvency" (1995) 54 CLJ 377.
Oellers, Bernd, "Doppelwirkungen im Recht?" AcP 169 (1969) 67.
Oertmann, Paul, "Bereicherungsansprüche bei nichtigen Geschäften" DJZ 20 (1915) 1063.
Olzen, Dirk, "Zur Geschichte des gutgläubigen Erwerbs" Jura 1990, 505.
Palandt, Otto (Begr), *Bürgerliches Gesetzbuch* (67th edn Beck, München 2008).
Peel, Edwin, *Treitel: The Law of Contract* (12th edn Sweet & Maxwell, London 2007).
Peter, Karl, "Die Möglichkeit mehrerer Gründe derselben Rechtsfolge und mehrerer gleicher Rechtsfolgen" AcP 132 (1930) 1.
Pettit, Philip Henry, *Equity and the Law of Trusts* (10th edn OUP, Oxford 2006).
Pinger, Winfried, *Funktion und dogmatische Einordnung des Eigentümer-Besitzer-Verhältnisses* (Beck, München 1973).
Pollock, Frederick, *Principles of Contract at Law and in Equity* (Stevens & Sons, London 1876).
Pollock, Frederick / Wright, Robert Samuel, *An Essay on Possession in the Common Law* (Clarendon Press, Oxford 1888).
Protokolle → see Achilles, Alexander (ed).
Rabel, Ernst, "Aufgabe und Notwendigkeit der Rechtsvergleichung" RheinZ 13 (1924) 279, reprinted in HG Leser (ed), *Ernst Rabel: Gesammelte Aufsätze, vol 3: Arbeiten zur Rechtsvergleichung und zur Rechtsvereinheitlichung 1919–1954* (Mohr Siebeck, Tübingen 1967) 1.
–, "Rechtsvergleichung und internationale Rechtsprechung" RabelsZ 1 (1927) 5.
–, "Die Fachgebiete des Kaiser-Wilhelm-Instituts für ausländisches und internationales Privatrecht (gegründet 1926) 1900–1935" in M Planck (ed), *25 Jahre Kaiser-Wilhelm-Gesellschaft zur Förderung der Wissenschaften, vol 3: Die Geisteswissenschaften* (Springer, Berlin 1937) 77, reprinted in HG Leser (ed), *Ernst Rabel: Gesammelte Aufsätze, vol 3: Arbeiten zur Rechtsvergleichung und zur Rechtsvereinheitlichung 1919–1954* (Mohr Siebeck, Tübingen 1967) 180.
Rebmann, Kurt / Säcker, Franz Jürgen / Rixecker, Roland (eds), *Münchener Kommentar zum Bürgerlichen Gesetzbuch, vol 1/1: §§ 1–240* (5th edn Beck, München 2006, ed by FJ Säcker and R Rixecker); *vol 2: §§ 241–432* (5th edn Beck, München 2007, ed by FJ Säcker and R Rixecker); *vol 4: §§ 611–704* (4th edn Beck, München 2005); *vol 5: §§ 705–853* (4th edn Beck, München 2004); *vol 6: §§ 854–1296* (4th edn Beck, München 2004); *vol 9: §§ 1922–2385* (4th edn Beck, München 2004).
Reeb, Hartmut, *Grundprobleme des Bereicherungsrechts* (Beck, München 1975).
Rengier, Bernhard, "Wegfall der Bereicherung" AcP 177 (1977) 418.

Reuter, Dieter / Martinek, Michael, *Ungerechtfertigte Bereicherung* (Mohr Siebek, Tübingen 1983).
Rheinstein, Max, "Teaching Comparative Law" (1937–38) 5 U Chi L Rev 615.
Römer, Gerhard, "Ist § 281 BGB auf das durch Rechtsgeschäft erlangte Entgelt anwendbar?" AcP 119 (1921) 293.
Rotherham, Craig, *Proprietary Remedies in Context: A Study in the Judicial Redistribution of Property Rights* (Hart, Oxford 2002).
Rothoeft, Dietrich, "Vermögensverlust und Bereicherungsausgleich" AcP 163 (1963) 215.
–, Review of HH Jakobs, *Eingriffserwerb und Vermögensverschiebung* (Röhrscheid, Bonn 1964) in AcP 166 (1966) 246.
Sacco, Rodolfo, "Legal Formants: A Dynamic Approach to Comparative Law" (1991) 39 Am J Comp L 1.
Säcker, Franz Jürgen (ed), *Münchener Kommentar* → see Rebmann, Kurt (ed).
Savigny, Friedrich Carl von, *System des heutigen römischen Rechts: vol 3* (Veit & Co, Berlin 1840).
Scherer, Inge, "Zulässigkeit einer 'zweiten Ersatzaussonderung'?" KTS 2002, 197.
Schlechtriem, Peter, *Schuldrecht: Besonderer Teil* (6th edn Mohr Siebeck, Tübingen 2003).
Schlechtriem, Peter / Schmidt-Kessel, Martin, *Schuldrecht: Allgemeiner Teil* (6th edn Mohr Siebeck, Tübingen 2005).
Schloßmann, Siegmund, *Der Irrtum über wesentliche Eigenschaften der Person und der Sache nach dem Bürgerlichen Gesetzbuch: Zugleich ein Beitrag zur Theorie der Gesetzesauslegung* (Fischer, Jena 1903).
Schmidt-Rimpler, Walter, "Eigenschaftsirrtum und Erklärungsirrtum" in HC Nipperdey (ed), *Das deutsche Privatrecht in der Mitte des 20. Jahrhunderts:Festschrift für Heinrich Lehmann zum 80. Geburtstag* (de Gruyter, Berlin 1956) vol 1, 213.
Schmitthoff, M, "The Science of Comparative Law" (1939–41) 7 CLJ 94.
Schmoeckel, Mathias / Rückert, Joachim / Zimmermann, Reinhard (eds), *Historisch-kritischer Kommentar zum BGB, vol 1: §§ 1–240* (Mohr Siebeck, Tübingen 2003).
Schneider, K, "Zur Bestimmung des Umfangs der Bereicherung nach Erfüllung eines nichtigen Vertrages" JherJB 61 (1912) 179.
Schubert, Werner, Anmerkung zum Urteil des BGH vom 11.10.1979 (case note) in JZ 1980, 199.
Schulz, Fritz, "System der Rechte auf den Eingriffserwerb" AcP 105 (1909) 1.
–, *Classical Roman Law* (Clarendon Press, Oxford 1951).
Schwarz, Günter Christian / Wandt, Manfred, *Gesetzliche Schuldverhältnisse: Deliktsrecht, Schadensrecht, Bereicherungsrecht, GoA* (2nd edn Vahlen, München 2006).
Scott, Austin Wakeman, "The Nature of the Rights of the *Cestui Que Trust*" (1917) 17 Colum L Rev 269.
Scott, Helen, "Restitution of Extra-Contractual Transfers: Limits of the Absence of Legal Ground Analysis" [2006] RLR 93.
Seah, Weeliem, "Mispredictions, Mistakes and the Law of Unjust Enrichment" [2007] RLR 93.
Sheehan, Duncan, "What is a Mistake?" (2000) 20 LS 538.
Siber, Heinrich, "Eigentumsanspruch und schuldrechtliche Herausgabeansprüche vom Standpunkte der Rechtsneuordnung" JherJB 89 (1941) 1.
Siebert, Wolfgang, *Das rechtsgeschäftliche Treuhandverhältnis: Ein dogmatischer und rechtsvergleichender Beitrag zum allgemeinen Treuhandproblem* (Elwert, Marburg 1933).

Singer, Reinhard, *Selbstbestimmung und Verkehrsschutz im Recht der Willenserklärungen* (Beck, München 1995).

Smid, Stefan, *Insolvenzordnung (InsO) mit Insolvenzrechtlicher Vergütungsverordnung (InsVV): Kommentar* (2nd edn Kohlhammer, Stuttgart 2002).

Smith, Lionel, "Tracing in *Taylor v Plumer*: Equity in the Court of King's Bench" [1995] LMCLQ 240.

–, *The Law of Tracing* (Clarendon Press, Oxford 1997).

–, "Unjust Enrichment, Property, and the Structure of Trusts" (2000) 116 LQR 412.

–, "Unravelling Proprietary Restitution" (2004) 40 Can Bus LJ 317.

–, "Tracing" in A Burrows and A Rodger (eds), *Mapping the Law: Essays in Memory of Peter Birks* (OUP, Oxford 2006) 119.

Smith, Stephen A, *Atiyah's Introduction to the Law of Contract* (6th edn Clarendon Press, Oxford 2005).

Soergel, Hans Theodor (Begr), *Bürgerliches Gesetzbuch mit Einführungsgesetzen und Nebengesetzen, vol 5/1: §§ 705–822* (12th edn Kohlhammer, Stuttgart 2007); *vol 14: §§ 854–984* (13th edn Kohlhammer, Stuttgart 2002).

Stadler, Astrid, *Gestaltungsfreiheit und Verkehrsschutz durch Abstraktion: eine rechtsvergleichende Studie zur abstrakten und kausalen Gestaltung rechtsgeschäftlicher Zuwendungen anhand des deutschen, schweizerischen, österreichischen, französischen und US-amerikanischen Rechts* (Mohr Siebeck, Tübingen 1996).

Staudinger, Julius von (Begr), *J von Staudingers Kommentar zum Bürgerlichen Gesetzbuch mit Einführungsgesetzen und Nebengesetzen: §§ 90–133* (Neubearbeitung 2004: Sellier de Gruyter, Berlin 2004); *§§ 255–304* (Neubearbeitung 2004: Sellier de Gruyter, Berlin 2004); *§§ 311–312f* (Neubearbeitung 2005: Sellier de Gruyter, Berlin 2005); *§§ 657–704* (Neubearbeitung 2006: Sellier de Gruyter, Berlin 2006); *§§ 779–811* (Neubearbeitung 2002: Sellier de Gruyter, Berlin 2002); *§§ 812–822* (Neubearbeitung 2007: Sellier de Gruyter, Berlin 2007) and (Neubearbeitung 1999: Sellier de Gryuter, Berlin 1999); *§§ 826–829* (Neubearbeitung 2003: Sellier de Gruyter, Berlin 2003); *§§ 840–853* (Neubearbeitung 2007: Sellier de Gruyter, Berlin 2007); *§§ 854–882* (Neubearbeitung 2007: Sellier de Gruyter, Berlin 2007); *§§ 925–984* (Neubearbeitung 2004: Sellier de Gruyter, Berlin 2004); *§§ 985–1011* (Neubearbeitung 2006: Sellier de Gruyter, Berlin 2006); *§§ 2064–2196* (Neubearbeitung 2003: Sellier de Gruyter, Berlin 2003).

Stevens, Robert, "Three Enrichment Issues" in A Burrows and A Rodger (eds), *Mapping the Law: Essays in Memory of Peter Birks* (OUP, Oxford 2006) 49.

–, "Objectivity, Mistake and the Parol Evidence Rule" in A Burrows and E Peel (eds), *Contract Terms* (OUP, Oxford 2007) 101.

–, *Torts and Rights* (OUP, Oxford 2007).

–, "Is there a Law of Unjust Enrichment?" in S Degeling and J Edelman (eds), *Unjust Enrichment in Commercial Law* (Thomson Reuters, Sydney 2008) 11.

Stoll, Hans, "Zur Legitimität und normativen Relevanz rechtsvergleichender Argumente im Zivilrecht" in H Koziol and P Rummel (eds), *Im Dienste der Gerechtigkeit: Festschrift für Franz Bydlinski* (Springer, Wien 2002) 429.

Strauch, Dieter, *Mehrheitlicher Rechtsersatz: Ein Beitrag zur 'dinglichen Surrogation' im Privatrecht* (Gieseking, Bielefeld 1972).

Streier, Joseph, *Eigentumsübergang und Kausalgeschäft* (Ludolph & Co, Bochum 1938).

Strohal, Emil, "Rechtsübertragung und Kausalgeschäft im Hinblick auf den Entwurf eines bürgerlichen Gesetzbuches für das Deutsche Reich" JherJB 27 (1889) 335.

Swadling, William, "Some Lessons from the Law of Torts" in P Birks (ed), *The Frontiers of Liability* (OUP, Oxford 1994) vol 1, 41.

–, "A Claim in Restitution?" [1996] LMCLQ 63.
–, "A New Role for Resulting Trusts?" (1996) 16 LS 110.
–, "Property and Unjust Enrichment" in JW Harris (ed), *Property Problems: From Genes to Pension Funds* (Kluwer, London 1997) 130.
–, "Restitution and *Bona Fide* Purchase" in W Swadling (ed), *The Limits of Restitutionary Claims: A Comparative Analysis* (UKNCCL, London 1997) 79.
–, "Rescission, Property, and the Common Law" (2005) 121 LQR 123.
–, "The Vendor-Purchaser Constructive Trust" in S Degeling and J Edelman (eds), *Equity in Commercial Law* (Thomson LBC, Sydney 2005) 463.
–, "Unjust Delivery" in A Burrows and A Rodger (eds), *Mapping the Law: Essays in Memory of Peter Birks* (OUP, Oxford 2006) 277.
–, "Explaining Resulting Trusts" (2008) 124 LQR 72.
–, "Policy Arguments for Proprietary Restitution" in S Degeling and J Edelman (eds), *Unjust Enrichment in Commmercial Law* (Thomson Reuters, Sydney 2008) 359.
–, "Ignorance and Unjust Enrichment: The Problem of Title" (2008) 28 OJLS 627.
Tang, Hang Wu, "Proprietary Relief without Rescission" (2004) 63 CLJ 30.
–, "Restitution for Mistaken Gifts" (2004) 20 JCL 1.
Tettenborn, Andrew, "Remedies for the Recovery of Money Paid by Mistake" (1980) 39 CLJ 272.
–, "Lawful Receipt – A Justifying Factor?" [1997] RLR 1.
–, "Misnomer – A Response to Professor Birks" in WR Cornish and others (eds), *Restitution Past, Present and Future: Essays in Honour of Gareth Jones* (Hart, Oxford 1998) 31.
–, *The Law of Restitution in England and Ireland* (3rd edn Cavendish, London 2002).
Thomas, Susan, "'Goodbye' Knowing Receipt. 'Hello' Unconscientious Receipt" (2001) 21 OJLS 239.
Tiedtke, Klaus, "Der Wegfall des Bereicherungsanspruchs nach Rechtshängigkeit des Rückgewähranspruchs: Eine Besprechung des BGH-Urteils vom 26.10.1978" DB 1979, 1261.
Treitel on Contract → see Peel, Edwin.
Trupp, Andreas, "Die Bedeutung des § 133 BGB für die Auslegung von Willenserklärungen" NJW 1990, 1346.
Tu, Changfeng, *Abstrakte Verfügungen und kausale Verpflichtungen? Über die Bedeutungslosigkeit der Einordnung eines Rechtsgeschäftes als Verfügungs- oder Verpflichtungsgeschäft für die Frage nach seiner Abstraktion oder Kausalität* (Nomos, Baden-Baden 2007).
Tuhr, Andreas von, "Zur Lehre von der ungerechtfertigten Bereicherung" in *Aus Römischem und Bürgerlichem Recht: Ernst Immanuel Bekker zum 16. August 1907* (Hof-Buchdruckerei, Weimar 1907) 291.
–, *Der Allgemeine Teil des Deutschen Bürgerlichen Rechts: vol 2/1* (Duncker & Humblot, Berlin 1914); *vol 2/2* (Duncker & Humblot, Berlin 1918).
Tyler, Edward Lawson Griffin / Palmer, Norman, *Crossley Vaines on Personal Property* (5th edn Butterworths, London 1973).
Vann, Vicky, "Equitable Compensation where Rescission is Impossible: A Response" (2003) 17 TruLI 66.
Verse, Dirk, "Improvements and Enrichment: A Comparative Analysis" [1998] RLR 85.
–, *Verwendungen im Eigentümer-Besitzer-Verhältnis: Eine kritische Betrachtung aus historisch-rechtsvergleichender Sicht* (Mohr Siebeck, Tübingen 1999).
Virgo, Graham, *The Principles of the Law of Restitution* (2nd edn OUP, Oxford 2006).

Vliet, Lars van, *Transfer of Movables in German, French, English and Dutch Law* (Ars Aequi Libri, Nijmegen 2000).
–, "The Transfer of Moveables in Scotland and England" (2008) 12 Edin L Rev 173.
Vorster, JP, "A Comment on the Meaning of Objectivity in Contract" (1987) 103 LQR 274.
Walker, Robert, "Tracing after Foskett v McKeown" [2000] RLR 573.
Walters, DWM, "The Nature of the Trust Beneficiary's Interest" (1967) 45 Can Bar Rev 219.
Waltjen, Dagmar, "Das Eigentümer-Besitzer-Verhältnis und Ansprüche aus ungerechtfertigter Bereicherung" AcP 175 (1975) 109.
Watts, Peter, "Mistaken Payments and the Law of Restitution" [1993] LMCLQ 145.
–, "A Philanthropist Recovers His Gift" (1996) 2 NZBLQ 5.
–, "Birks and Proprietary Claims, with Special Reference to Misrepresentation and to Ultra Vires Contracts" in C Rickett and R Grantham (eds), *Structure and Justification in Private Law: Essays for Peter Birks* (Hart, Oxford 2008) 361.
Weir, Tony, "The Common Law System" in R David (gen ed), *International Encyclopedia of Comparative Law, vol 2: The Legal Systems of the World, ch 2: Structure and Divisions of the Law* (Mohr Siebeck, Tübingen 1974) 77.
–, "Taking for Granted – The Ramifications of *nemo dat*" (1996) 49 CLP 325.
– (tr), K Zweigert and H Kötz, *An Introduction to Comparative Law* (3rd edn OUP, Oxford 1998).
Wendehorst, Christiane, *Anspruch und Ausgleich: Theorie einer Vorteils- und Nachteilsausgleichung im Zivilrecht* (Mohr Siebeck, Tübingen 1999).
Westermann, Harm Peter (ed), *Erman: Bürgerliches Gesetzbuch* (12th edn Schmidt, Köln 2008).
Wieling, Hans Josef, "Die Nutzungen des gutgläubigen Besitzers, insbesondere in fehlgeschlagenen Vertragsverhältnissen" AcP 169 (1969) 137.
–, *Sachenrecht, vol 1: Sachen, Besitz und Rechte an beweglichen Sachen* (2nd edn Springer, Berlin 2006).
Wilburg, Walter, *Die Lehre von der ungerechtfertigten Bereicherung nach österreichischem und deutschem Recht* (Leuschner & Lubensky, Graz 1934).
Williams, Glanville, "Mistake as to Party in the Law of Contract" (1945) 23 Can Bar Rev 271, 380.
–, "Mistake in the Law of Theft" (1977) 36 CLJ 62.
Wolf, Manfred, "Die Verwendungsersatzansprüche des Besitzers im Anspruchssystem" AcP 166 (1966) 188.
–, "Prinzipien und Anwendungsbereich der dinglichen Surrogation" JuS 1975, 643, 710; JuS 1976, 32, 104.
Wolff, Josef, *Trust, Fiducia und fiduziarische Treuhand: Historisch-rechtsvergleichende Untersuchung mit einer Darstellung des Trust in Schottland sowie des römischen und österreichischen Fideikommiss* (Lang, Frankfurt/Main 2005).
Woodbine, George (ed) / Thorne, Samuel (tr), *De Legibus et Consuetudinibus Angliae: Bracton on the Laws and Customs of England* (Harvard University Press, Cambridge/Mass 1968–77).
Worthington, Sarah, "The Proprietary Consequences of Rescission" [2002] RLR 28.
Zimmermann, Reinhard, "Sittenwidrigkeit und Abstraktion" JR 1985, 48.
–, *The Law of Obligations: Roman Foundations of the Civilian Tradition* (Clarendon Press, Oxford 1996).
Zimmermann, Reinhard / du Plessis, Jaques, "Basic Features of the German Law of Unjustified Enrichment" [1994] RLR 14.

Zitelmann, Ernst, *Irrtum und Rechtsgeschäft: Eine psychologisch-juristische Untersuchung* (Duncker & Humblot, Leipzig 1879).
Zülch, Carsten, "*Bona fide* Purchase, Property and Restitution: *Lipkin Gorman v Karpnale* in German Law" in W Swadling (ed), *The Limits of Restitutionary Claims: A Comparative Analysis* (UKNCCL, London 1997) 106.
Zweigert & Kötz → see Weir, Tony (tr).

Table of Cases

England and other Common Law Jurisdictions

Germany

Decisions of the Imperial Supreme Court (Reichsgericht)

Decisions of the Federal Supreme Court (Bundesgerichtshof)

Decisions by other courts

Table of Statutes

Germany

England

Other

Index

9 781849 465656

Lightning Source UK Ltd.
Milton Keynes UK
UKHW020612120320
360219UK00009B/332